CHINA

中國

中華

中华人民共和国

Something of the history of a country can be known from the name which its people give it when they establish an identity of their own and separate themselves from the aliens, the barbarians who surround them. Thus, the Chinese people called their land *Zhong-Guo*, otherwise the central (*zhong*) territory (*guo*). Let us look for a moment at the first line of ideograms on the left. The first sign represents *Zhong* and the etymology here is simple: a quadrangle bisected by a line gives the idea of centrality. The word *Guo* (the second sign on the top line) is much more complex from the etymological or ideographic point of view. Within a rectangular enclosure representing the boundary line, we find the symbol of the spear – the armed force which guarantees security – and underneath, a quadrangle which has been interpreted by some as a "face" or "mouths." We therefore understand *Guo* to be a territory, whose bounds are set by the extent of a people or race (the mouths), the existence of which is secured by a spear. Did the Chinese give their country this name because they were surrounded by barbarians? Or, as is more likely, was it that during the feudal period,

the term came into use because of the central position of the Imperial rule over the surrounding lands. Later, when a stable union of these lands in the form of an empire had been achieved, the Chinese renamed their land *Zhong-Hua* (seen represented in the second line of ideograms on the left). This means central flower (*Hua*). The word "flower" frequently represents culture and civilization: in Chinese, as in other languages, civilization flourishes, is flowering, is in full bloom. Thus, "to go to China" was *lai hua* – to find civilization, to change from a barbarian into civilized man, to flourish by being cultivated. *Hua*, the flower, civilization (and China was indeed the flower of the known world) is an ancient word redolent with meaning and still remains in use today. *Zhonghua Ren Min Gonghe kuo* (the third line of ideograms) is the third and last name given to China, or, more precisely, to the People's Republic of China, as it is now called. Literally translated, it means central flower (or civilization) of a living people (or of a people aspiring towards life) in the land of universal harmony.

中国

CHINA

Keith Buchanan

Charles P. FitzGerald

Colin A. Ronan

Crown Publishers, Inc. New York

Oil painting by Jin Zheyuan.
A bridge between two mountains,
a railroad passing between them:
here we see modern China set in a
traditional landscape of grandeur
and permanence.

China

Text
Keith Buchanan
Charles P. FitzGerald
Colin A. Ronan

Foreword
Joseph Needham

Double-page spreads
Renata Pisu

*Captions, double-page spreads
and endmatter*
translated from the Italian by
Susan Powell

Editorial director
  Lorenzo Camusso
Editor-in-chief
  Mariella De Battisti
Editors
  Paola Lovato
  Marisa Melis
  Donatella Volpi
Art editors
  Enrico Segré
  Roberto Maresca
Production controller
  Piero Ling
Editorial advisor
  Renata Pisu

First published in the United
States by Crown Publishers,
Inc., One Park Avenue, New
York, New York 10016

Published simultaneously in
Canada by General
Publishing Company Limited

Library of Congress
Cataloging in Publication
Data
Buchanan, Keith
  China
  Translation of: Cina, il
passato e il presente.
  Bibliography: pp. 511–13
  Includes index.
  1. China—Civilization.
I. FitzGerald, C.P.
(Charles Patrick), 1902–
II. Ronan, Colin A.
III. Title.
DS721.B9313   951
81–2275
ISBN 0–517–54494–6
AACR2

10 9 8 7 6 5 4 3 2 1
First Edition

Printed and bound
in Italy by
Arnoldo Mondadori
Editore. Verona

CONTENTS

READER'S NOTE

Chinese script is not phonetic but ideographic. This means that any object, action or even abstract idea is represented by a graphic sign which gives few clues, if any, as to pronunciation, and these not in any systematic fashion. In order to transcribe the sounds of Chinese, it is therefore necessary to use a system of transliteration. In this book, we have used the Pinyin system (literally, it means to spell out or scan) which has been in use in the People's Republic since 1979 in all books published for foreign markets. It is also used in schools and by printers as a phonetic alternative or auxiliary of ideographic script. In fact, Chinese scholars of linguistics do not exclude the possibility of ideographic script being gradually replaced by alphabetic script using the Pinyin system.

Until now, the method of transcription most widely used by Western scholars was the Wade-Giles system which derived its name from those of the two Sinologists who conceived it. In this, the consonants have the same sound values as in English but the vowels represent purer sounds, more like the vowel sounds of Italian. In Pinyin, however, entirely new phonetic sounds are represented by letters of the Latin alphabet. For instance, *c*, *q*, *zh*, *x*, *d*, *t* and *o* have the following sounds in English: *c* = hard *z* (pronounced as in swor*ds*manship); *q* = ch (as in *ch*in); *zh* = a sound between ch and t; *x* = sh; *d* = t; *t* = a sound of an explosive t; *o* = u or oo (as in f*oo*l). This explains how the names which are written in the Wade-Giles transcription as Mao Tse-tung and Chou En-lai become in Pinyin Mao Zedong and Zhou Enlai. In Pinyin, moreover, trisyllabic Chinese names are written without the hyphen for the given name. Mao and Zhou for example are surnames, for in Chinese, the surname always precedes the first name. Just occasionally, we have used the Wade-Giles transcription in order not to confuse the reader accustomed to the traditional spelling.

CHINA

China is no longer a world remote from us. Nowadays, the writer on China must not only seek to explain the complex reality of this enormous land; he also has the task of attempting to trace the path she is likely to follow in the future. The book is divided into six parts, presenting a composite picture of this vast country in a way which is not only basically informative but stimulating and interesting. The first part ("Inside China") consists of a selection of photographs illustrating characteristic aspects of present-day China. If these show some of the differences which exist between China and the West, they also provide glimpses of our common humanity and help to increase our understanding of a country which, after all, contains one-quarter of the world's population. Three other parts constitute an appreciable body of Western scholarship in the field of Sinology:

each represents the approach of a particular discipline and thus they are complementary yet diverse. The first, "Land and People" by Keith Buchanan, describes how the Chinese people, in the course of a long dialogue with their environment, have evolved the forms and conditions of everyday living. It ends with an analysis of those influences which, even in the modern age, are still holding them back. The next part, "History and Civilization" by C. P. FitzGerald, introduces the dimension of historical time. The author describes the flow of the centuries, in the course of which China has built up a great inheritance of cultural wealth including some of the richest artistic treasures the world has ever seen. Professor FitzGerald brings the story up to date with an account of the decades during which modern China was born. The third part, "Science and Technology" by C. A. Ronan, treats of a subject which is generally left out of any treatise on aspects of Chinese culture: the changing modes of scientific thought and

the way in which the historical progress of technology in China has combined with knowledge from the rest of the world. These three sections include 17 double-page spreads edited by Renata Pisu – visual guides to a further understanding of such subjects as the notion of ideogrammatic script, the characteristic forms of the bronzes and the trade routes between China and the West, along which goods such as silk – and also ideas – used to move. Lastly there is "The Eye of the West," a collection of Western photographs and engravings of China dating from the time of the Enlightenment and the "colonial" period.

These are in no sense intended as an essay in escapism, a nostalgic glancing back at past glories. As is well known, there have been black pages in the history of relations between China and the West. It is not our intention to pass judgment, but rather to hope that pictures such as these may make us think again: the famed objectivity of the camera can sometimes descend into cruelty and injustice, leaving a bitter taste in the mouth. China may have had more than her fair share of this; it is all the more important therefore to welcome her renaissance as a strong and lively nation with joy and hope. The book ends with a bibliography, a chronological list of events and notes on major Chinese writers, artists and men of science.

This is the oldest map of China known to us. It was found during excavation of the tomb of Ma Wang Dui.

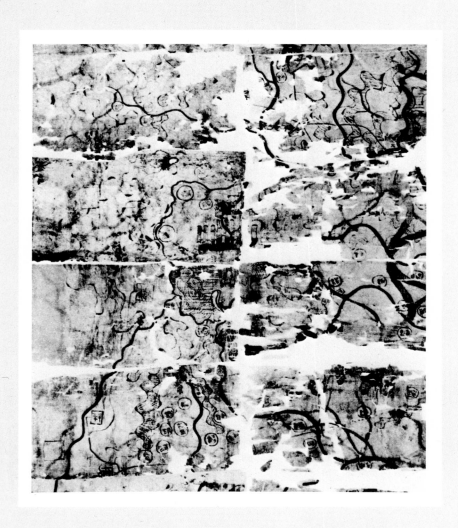

THE DIALOGUE BETWEEN EAST AND WEST

by JOSEPH NEEDHAM

It is a great pleasure for me to be asked to write a foreword introducing this book on China, in which such distinguished men as Keith Buchanan, Patrick FitzGerald and Colin Ronan have combined to explain and elucidate Chinese civilization for the benefit of Western readers. Since the primary aim of this work is to remove as many as possible of the misconceptions which always abound in the minds of Westerners about the Chinese and their culture, it occurred to me that one of the best ways in which I could introduce the book would be to think aloud about the misunderstandings of China by the West.

First of all, we were not quite sure where it was. The names were also confusing because there were several. The Greeks and Romans referred to China as the land of the Seres because that was the name for silk, which after 110 B.C. they imported in considerable amounts; but here, in the West, as the first of our misunderstandings, it was thought to be the product of a plant, the "vegetable lamb of Tartary" (not an animal), and it took literally centuries before this mistake was cleared up. Then China was also called *Sina* in the Latin tongue, a word used by the Indians too; and this undoubtedly derived from the first dynasty which unified China, namely the Qin (3rd century B.C.).

In the Middle Ages there were two other quite different names, known for example to Marco Polo, namely Cathay for the north, and Manzi for the south. The former undoubtedly took its origin from the name of a nomadic people, the Kitan Tartars, who conquered part of North China in the 10th century A.D. and founded the Liao dynasty. The other name, Manzi, was undoubtedly derived from the indigenous tribespeople in the south, called Manzi by the Chinese; and since Marco Polo was there at the beginning of the (Mongolian) Yuan dynasty, and served the Great Khan, one can see that the term Manzi was his pronunciation of a somewhat pejorative name used by the northerners for the southerners.

Among the many misunderstandings of Europeans about China, there is a rather amusing one connected with the Great Wall. In the so-called *Alexander Romance*, it was said that Alexander the Great had built a great wall of iron across the north of Eastern Asia in order to hold back the wild, violent tribes of Gog and Magog. However, it was eventually quite clear to everyone who had really built the Great Wall. Rather than having been made (as we find also in Arabic legend) to keep out the Eastern tribespeople, the truth had been exactly the opposite: it had been built by the Chinese from the 5th century B.C. onwards to keep out the nomadic peoples of the northwest; and it also succeeded in keeping the Chinese peasant-farmers in.

Another curious misunderstanding of the nature of China in

The Yellow river (3·6 × 1·8m), designed by He Shan and Li Hong-Yin and painted by He Shan. This work forms part of the imposing series of frescoes and paintings which adorn the hall of the new international airport in Peking.

the Middle Ages was connected with the legend of Prester John. According to many mediaeval stories, from about A.D. 1150 onwards, the country of East Asia was ruled by a Christian priest-king. The grain of truth, however, was the fact that many Uighurs (an important central Asian people), including some of their rulers, had been converted to Christianity by the Nestorian missionaries. But the fact was that no kingdom of Prester John existed at all, and it is now thought that the Christian kings of Ethiopia also had a hand in giving rise to the legend.

With Marco Polo in the 13th century A.D., we meet with a very sympathetic figure. "Il Milione," as he was called, because of his attempts to make Westerners understand that there were literally millions of boats and ships upon the canals and rivers of China, as well as thousands of bridges in the city of Hangzhou alone, was in fact not far wrong on such matters. It was quite true that the wealth and populousness of China, towards the end of the Song and the beginning of the Yuan, were something almost inconceivable in Europe; but even Marco Polo saw only a portion of the truth. He was pressed into the service of the Great Khan because the Mongols were desperate to get any kind of foreigners, Arabs or Europeans, who would staff their civil service, since they did not trust the scholar-gentry of their conquered people, the Chinese, to do so. But although a member of the bureaucracy himself, Marco never really understood it, and gave very little emphasis in his account to the fundamental fact that China was for more than two thousand years an essentially bureaucratic feudalism, utterly different therefore from the military aristocratic feudalism of Europe.

When the early Portuguese got to China from about 1520 onwards, more misunderstandings arose. For example, when they first penetrated into Chinese temples they took the statues of Taoist gods and Buddhist bodhisattvas as Christian saints; and it was some time before this misapprehension was put right. But the Portuguese had considerable success in expounding Chinese life and customs to the West. For example, in connection with public security and imprisonment, they were loud in their praise of the Chinese magistrates who, they said, would go to almost any lengths to avoid condemning a man or woman to death; and this contrasted strikingly, they thought, with what happened in Europe.

In 1584 the great Jesuit mission entered China, and then began a couple of centuries of intercourse at an intellectual level hardly to be surpassed by any other example one could name. Many of the Jesuits were of the highest intellectual attainments, and they were able to bring a version of the newly developing modern science that was arising in what we call the Scientific Revolution. Their theory of conversion was that they should appeal to the best scholars and the most powerful court officials first of all, after which the influence of Christian thought would filter down to the masses. But there was a fundamental paradox about all their activities. On the one hand they wanted to represent the Chinese to Europeans as the most highly cultured people imaginable, in order to acquire maximum financial support for their mission. On the other hand, they represented to the Chinese that Christendom alone could have produced

modern science, at the same time extolling European philosophy because it had grown up in a Christian environment.

Finally the Jesuit mission was dynamited by the so-called "Rites Controversy." The Dominicans and Franciscans, who had also come in some numbers into the country, regarded the approach of the Jesuits as fundamentally wrong, and they themselves went about courting the displeasure of the magistrates and preaching to the mass of the people. They had no better success, but they managed to get the whole Jesuit mission condemned by Rome, and there followed for a time the suppression of the entire Jesuit order, so their mission came temporarily to an end.

Even the Jesuits themselves, however, were taken in for quite a long time by a failure to realize that Chinese and Western astronomy had been built upon two entirely different principles. Chinese astronomy had always been fundamentally equatorial, while Western or Greek astronomy had been ecliptic. The field of observation was exactly the same, but the Chinese and the Greeks had emphasized different aspects of it.

A parallel misunderstanding occurred with regard to the basic conception of Chinese philosophy, especially the Neo-Confucianism of the Song, when, after Leibniz, Europeans began to get to know about it. The Neo-Confucians built the whole universe out of two elementary conceptions, *li* and *qi*. It was no doubt natural that these should be quickly aligned with the Aristotelian form (*eidos*) and matter (*hulē*) – but this turned out to be quite inadmissible. *Li* has to be regarded as the principle of organization and pattern at all levels of existence in the universe, while *qi* is what today we might call matter-energy.

After the earlier part of the Jesuit mission in China came the school of the *Physiocrates* in France. The Physiocrats wished to emphasize the importance of agriculture for the nation, as opposed to trade and commerce, and they believed that China had always been ruled by a "benevolent despotism," no matter which dynasty had been in power. Actually this was another misunderstanding, because in China the autocrat had never been able to be truly autocratic – what mattered much more was the line which the bureaucracy took. The real nature of the bureaucratic form of society was not seen until the time of François Bernier, physician to the Grand Mogul, in the 17th century. Bernier was perhaps the first to wonder whether the absence of the "meum and tuum" principle as applied to landed property was a good thing or not. He realized that there was essentially no aristocracy in China, and that high rank and office depended on the results of the Imperial examinations.

When one turns to the details of scientific and technological matters, one finds there also many intriguing misunderstandings. For example, it has been established that there was a tradition of mechanical timekeeping and clockwork-making six hundred years earlier in China than in Europe. No mass industrial production of clocks developed, however; the Chinese put all their ingenuity into public timepieces. Now it is a remarkable fact that these Chinese hydromechanical clocks, from A.D. 700 onwards, required the winding up of the water or mercury at the end of each day into tanks above, so that it could flow down at constant rate into the scoops on the periphery of a driving wheel, the rotation of which was arrested by an escapement mechanism. Somebody, some time or other, seeing this from the outside, thought that magnetism must be involved, with the result that both in Indian and European speculation from the 13th century onwards, it was believed that if one could find out how to do it, one could slow down a wheel to keep time with the diurnal revolution of the heavens by the aid of magnets.

Another amusing misunderstanding concerned the development of gunpowder. It has long been an *idée reçue* in the West that the Chinese invented gunpowder, but used it only for fireworks until the late date when it was applied to war weapons.

But in fact the first mention of the gunpowder mixture (saltpetre, sulphur and charcoal) occurs in the middle of the 9th century A.D., and it is then first found in warlike use in 919. It looks now as if all the stages, from the first development of the formula to the appearance of the true metal-barrel gun and cannon, were passed through in China by 1290, before Europeans knew anything about the applications of gunpowder at all (first mention 1267, first appearance of cannon 1327).

Let us now consider what has been perhaps the greatest misunderstanding of all, namely that the Chinese had no science nor technology. Over the years many Westerners have been prepared to accept the Chinese nation as entirely composed of scholar-officials, poets and peasant-farmers. There has been little or no realization of the important part played by scientific men and technologists in China before the Scientific Revolution. That occurred only in Europe indeed, but for 14 previous centuries the Chinese had been much more effective than Europeans in acquiring knowledge of nature and applying it.

The modern Chinese philosopher, Fêng Yu-lan, once said that the Chinese sage had no desire to understand or control nature, because it was himself that he wished to be able to control. As someone has well said, this is only the half of a half-truth. Otherwise it would have been impossible that many volumes on the history of science, technology and medicine in Chinese culture should have been written. It must be said that we owe to the Anglo-Saxon Protestant missionaries of the 19th century most of the pioneering work in opening up this aspect of China.

Lastly, it is surely a misunderstanding to suppose that China contributed nothing to the Scientific Revolution. Of course Euclidean deductive geometry (which the Chinese did not have) was one root, and Ptolemaic planetary theory (also foreign to them) was another; but the third was magnetical science, and all the foundations of that had been laid in China before Europeans knew anything about it at all. It has indeed been said that the Chinese were worrying about the declination before the Europeans even knew of the polarity. And yet the growth of modern science could never have happened without the field theory, the ideas of magnetic attraction and repulsion, action at a distance, and all the electrical cornucopia that flowed from magnetic phenomena.

So let us welcome warmly this book as the cure of many misunderstandings. *Pereat separatio et fiat lux*!

Detail of a picture painted on porcelain, *The Song of the Forest*, which decorates the walls of Peking airport. This work, which measures 20 × 3·4m, is made up of more than three thousand porcelain tiles which were painted and fired by craftsmen from Jingdezhen, in the province of Jiangxi, after a design by the painter Zhu Danian.

Heaven is eternal,
the Earth everlasting.

INSIDE CHINA

Pages 20–21
Sampans and branches of cherry tree in flower over the banks of Lake Taihu, in the province of Jiangsu. Is this a true image of China? Perhaps. Just because it is so conventional, because it represents everyone's idea of what China should be, it has been chosen as the first in this photographic sequence. The fact that it is conventional does not make it any the less

true, for China is a land of sampans and flowering cherry blossom as well as of steelworks and the Red Flag, of historical monuments and paddy-fields and of peasants bound to the earth by hard work. It is the aim of these photographs to evoke this complexity: it is hoped that they will provide momentary insights into a world which has many faces.

Page 26
The "Pine tree of the Sleeping Dragon" on Mount Huangshan. The Chinese say that on this mountain "pine trees grow on every rock and every pine tree bears some bizarre shape." Mount Huangshan, in the province of Anhui, is also famous for its high peaks (of which the highest is 1800 meters) and for the pointed and polished rocks worn by the elements into human and animal shapes.

Page 28
Peasant dwellings in the province of Hunan, which has always been the country's major rice-producing area. An old proverb says, "If the harvest is good in Hunan, no-one will starve."

Page 29
Harvest time in a commune in Central China. Agricultural mechanization is one of the main objectives of the "program for modernization."

Pages 28–29
One of the paddy-fields of Hunan. It is harvest time and the crop is being cut with sickles. In Hunan the main rice-growing areas are the plain of Dongting and the basin of the Yangtze. Since 1961, the policy of the

Chinese government has been to import 5,000,000,000 kilos of wheat every year and to export rice instead of using it for home consumption. This is because rice has twice the value of wheat on the international market.

Page 26
From the "Pine tree of the Sleeping Dragon" to the roofs of the Imperial Palace in Peking. This work of human hands seems almost to echo the architecture of nature, imitating its harmonious assymetry.

Page 24
Ximing Hill, near Xikou, in the province of Zhejiang (Central China) and one of its most important agricultural zones. Although this is one of the smallest provinces, it is noted for the beauty of its capital, Hangzhou, which stands on the banks of the famous Western Lake.

Page 25
Girls resting with their Red Flags in Tian-an-men Square in Peking after a parade. The generation of young people now in their twenties is the one which has been most influenced by the various conflicting ideological campaigns and sudden changes in hierarchy which have taken place in the last few years. Nowadays, in China, as in the West, the integration of the younger generation into the productive life of the community can pose problems.

Page 27
The "Temple of Heaven" in Peking, the most splendid example of Imperial Chinese architecture, built in three sections in the 15th century.

Page 30
The steelworks at Anshan in the province of Manchuria and the most important metal-working complex in China. The process of industrialization has gone forward by leaps and bounds (if with occasional lapses) in the last 30 years.

Page 31
A "neighbourhood" or "street workshop." The integration of small scale labour-intensive production with large scale factory production in the larger towns has meant that more use can be made of manual workers, particularly women, without recourse to large investment.

Page 32
The "Pavilion of the Jade Screen" on Mount Huangshan. This is one of the best-known sights in China. It appears in this picture emerging from a sea of clouds with the "Peak of the White Goose" rising up in the background. At the main entrance, stand "the Pine tree of Welcome" and the "Pine tree of Leave-taking."

Pages 34–35
A view of the countryside surrounding the town of Guilin, in the province of Guangxi. This region is floored by limestone (see map

on page 69) and is in an advanced stage of dissection so that the original limestone survives only in the steep-sided isolated hills typical of karstic landscapes.

Page 40
The desert of Takla Makan, in the Autonomous Region of Xinjiang. It has an area of 330,000 square kilometers with sand-dunes which are often as high as 200 meters and shaped by the wind into pyramids.

Page 41
A frontier patrol in Xinjiang. This enormous territory, which is bordered by Mongolia, U.S.S.R., Afghanistan, Pakistan, India and Tibet, covers 1,600,000 square kilometers.

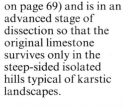

Page 33
Nets spread out on the banks of the river Tanshui, in the province of Guangxi. Freshwater fishing is very important in China and there are more than 500 excellent varieties of river fish and shellfish commonly used in Chinese cooking.

Page 36
Landscape in Shaanxi, in North China, typical of the manmade landscapes of the Loess Plateau.

Page 37
The transportation of bamboo canes on the Lijiang river. Bamboo, like the lotus flower and the chrysanthemum, is a most evocative symbol of China.

Pages 40–41
A celebration in an encampment of nomads in Inner Mongolia, an Autonomous Region of the People's Republic, like Tibet

and Xinjiang. It has an area of 1,800,000 square kilometers and a population of 1,200,000, composed for the most part of nomadic herdsmen.

Page 33
Fishing with cormorants. These fish-catching birds are used by fishermen in China to help them in their work. The birds' throats are ringed to stop them swallowing their catch.

Page 38
A herd of wild horses on the steppes of the Inner Mongolian Autonomous Region in the extreme north of China photographed in summer which is the rainy season.

Page 39
Shaoxing, one of the most beautiful towns in the province of Zhejiang, was likened by Western visitors in the 18th century to Venice, by virtue of its network of canals.

Page 42
An elementary school in Tianjin. Statistics tell us a Chinese baby is born every second. It is therefore no surprise that the population increase is around thirty million a year. China is in the vanguard of preschool education, compared with even developed societies.

Page 43
Acrobats in the Shanghai Circus. Chinese circuses are quite different from their Western counterparts. They are above all wonderful spectacles, in which acrobats, jugglers, mimics, magicians and conjurers show their skills.

23

善建者不拔

What Tao plants
cannot be plucked.

LAND AND PEOPLE

by KEITH BUCHANAN

THE REALITY OF CHINA

Opposite: one of the many canals of Suzhou, in the Yangtze delta. These internal waterways often have houses, shops and markets backing on to them. They are a direct link between town and country and form an important system of transportation for commercial traffic.

Above: cultivated terraces on the slopes of the Taihang mountains in the province of Shaanxi. Terracing in this area was especially important because of the nature of the soil (loess), which is subject to subsidence and erosion.

Pages 46–47
From a watercolour by a contemporary painter. This picture contains many of the most characteristic aspects of the Chinese countryside: expanses of cultivated fields, steep, forested hillsides and busy river traffic.

For long the Western vision of China was flawed by ignorance. The country was known to be vast and believed to be, like the rest of Asia, monotonous, lacking in diversity, and hot. The Chinese people were clearly very different from the peoples of Europe – they were "strange" or, later, "exotic," and believed to be racially and culturally uniform, imprisoned within a timeless and unchanging pattern of existence, passive victims of what Montesquieu called "the first of all empires," that of climate.

The reality of China is, as we shall see, much more complex than is conveyed by these early stereotypes.

Few nations have as diverse an environment as China. The spread of Chinese power over the centuries welded together an area as big as Europe. It was an area which extended from 55°N to 17°N, the distance from Moscow to the southern tip of Arabia; from almost 200 meters below sea level in the oases of Central Asia to over 8000 meters in the high peaks of the Himalayas; from the sandy deserts of the Northwest or the cold forests of Manchuria to the tropical rain forests of Hunan. No uniformity, then, but a rich diversity of environments, each offering particular challenges, or opportunities, to the human groups occupying them.

And an equally great diversity among these human groups. A diversity of race, for while most Chinese are Mongoloid, the peoples of China's Northwest are related to the Alpine branch of the white race, and many of the hill peoples of the tropical zone are brown-skinned and related to the Mediterranean peoples of Southern Asia and Europe. A diversity of languages: Sino-Tibetan, Austro-Asiatic, Altaic or Indo-European, written in a variety of scripts: Chinese ideographs, Arabic or Cyrillic scripts; moreover, some groups were scriptless until recently. A diversity of religious faiths. A great diversity of ways of life, ranging from intensive rice cultivation to nomadic herding and migratory slash-and-burn agriculture.

The geography of China (and much of its history) can best be understood in terms of the interaction between these diverse peoples and the very different physical environments they came to occupy. And in this interaction culture plays a critical role in each group's relation to its environment; the degree to which it can confront the challenge of that environment, the extent to which it transforms it, these are governed by its cultural level. And thus, while the pastoral peoples of Western China and the tribal peoples of the South adapted passively to their environment, the Han Chinese early developed an agricultural system whose sophisticated techniques of irrigation, terracing and levelling made possible those far-reaching and *purposive* changes which transformed the plains and the low hills of Eastern China into the supreme example of a manmade landscape. Moreover, as the last 30 years have demonstrated, when a society's culture, technology and political organization change, the ways in which that society uses and transforms its landscapes become more complex and diversified.

In the pages which follow we shall explore this richness and this diversity and in doing so, we shall draw out yet another theme, that of the duality which characterizes the physical and human geography of China. It is a duality which assumes many forms: the duality of lowland and upland; of humid East and arid West; of tropical and subtropical South and temperate and subarctic North; of intensive garden-style cultivation and extensive livestock rearing; of crowded landscapes and empty landscapes; above all, the duality of Han and minority peoples. And while recent changes, such as the narrowing of the gulf between Han and minority peoples or the reduction of the differentials between city and countryside, have attenuated some of the contrasts, the theme of duality remains as important in the geography as it is in the philosophy of China.

THE OCCUPATION OF THE CHINESE LAND

China is not only one of the most closely-settled, intensely humanized parts of the earth's surface, it is also one of the most anciently settled.

Some 300 generations have passed since the first hesitant beginnings of the transformation of the Chinese land by scattered peasant communities in the Yellow River valley. It is an immense span of time and as the years passed these peasant families multiplied and the number of mouths to be fed began to exceed the food-producing capacity of this peasant economy. New generations had perforce to move out to seek new land. And, being farmers practicing an intensive garden-style type of cropping based on cereals and vegetables, they selected some areas and rejected or by-passed others. They sought land which would lend itself to intensive use: the alluvial lowlands, the loessial highlands, the gentle and easily-terraced slopes. The hills they left empty or in the occupation of more primitive tribal peoples.

Flood and drought which led to famine, the attacks of the barbarian peoples from the northwest steppe-lands, these accelerated the millennial-old drift of these early Chinese. It was a drift generally southwards – as the peasant saying went, "Better a thousand miles south than one brick's width north" – towards the lake-studded lands of the middle and the lower Yangtze and the Red Basin of Sichuan.

Then, as these lands were peopled, the tide of migrants flowed into the alluvial lowlands which girdle the southeast coast, into the valleys whose alluvium-covered floors probe deep into the uplands of South China, ultimately reaching the tropical forest environment of China's southern periphery.

A slow, steady, and purposive advance, which two millennia ago took land-hungry peasants to the very limits of the œcumene of Inner or Agricultural China. And the centuries since have seen no major change in the pattern then established, a pattern of closely-knit peasant communities occupying selectively the patches of "good earth." New technologies, above all new crops,

A portrait of Chen Tsong, emperor of the Song dynasty. At the beginning of the 11th century, Chen Tsong introduced a new variety of fast-ripening rice into Southern China. This was a turning point in the history and development of China. As well as providing two or three harvests a year, this new variety of rice needed less irrigation. It could therefore be grown on higher ground and on slopes, thus extending the area of cultivable land.

Opposite: a paddy-field in Central China. Rice production is concentrated in the warmer more humid regions, that is, in the central south of so-called "Agricultural China," an area where ecological conditions were most favourable to the development of agriculture.

made possible a more intensive utilization and a denser settlement of the lowlands, even some encroachment onto the margins of the uplands of Central and South China. Population pressure was responsible for limited settlement in the oases of the dry Northwest and, in this century, for a massive migration into the cold, forested lowlands of the Northeast. But these episodes were exceptions and we may say that the dominant theme of the last two millennia has been the consolidation of the Han occupation of Inner China, a consolidation which involved a far-reaching transformation of the physical environment and, as the tribal peoples of Central and South China were displaced or absorbed, the creation of a new human geography of China.

The dominating duality within modern China, the contrast between the closely-settled, intensively-farmed and dominantly Han East and the thinly-settled, agriculturally-marginal West, with its dominantly non-Han population – thus dates back to a very early period in China's history.

THE BEGINNINGS

Thus did
Men of old
Who left us this land
To have and to hold.   *The Book of Songs*

The earliest stages of this Han occupation of Eurasia's eastern fringe are lost in the mists of time, in the uncertainty which still envelops much of the prehistory of the East Asian mainland. The Han people, as William Watson observes, "has occupied the valley of the Yellow River from time immemorial.... The manner and time of the colonisation of the great Central Plain of North China, supposing such a thing were ever a definable historical event, is beyond knowledge and conjecture alike." So ancient is the association of the Han folk with their yellow-earth cradle area that they have been termed "the Children of the Yellow Earth" and the intimacy of this bond between man and land is captured by Robert Payne; the Chinese, he says, are a people "whose dust was so intermingled in the soil that they perhaps alone of all nations do not feel themselves strangers to the land."

The story goes back at least half a million years, to the time of the pre-*sapiens* type known as Peking Man. These peoples were Paleolithic in culture, possessing rudimentary tool-making skills; genetically they belonged to the group *Sinanthropus* (or, as it is nowadays termed, *Homo erectus pekinensis*). For hundreds of thousands of years there appears to have been a remarkable stability of race type and indeed some of the distinctive anatomical features of the population (e.g. dental characteristics) were carried over into the modern populations of the region. Towards the end of the Paleolithic, the archaeological record in this north Chinese region yields remains belonging to modern man, *homo sapiens*; this was possibly 20,000 to 30,000 years ago and by this date the ancestors of the Han people were sufficiently developed to practice the deliberate burial of the dead and to carry on trade over considerable distances.

Opposite, above: the pressure on land. Wherever an area can be levelled, it is brought into cultivation and the agricultural area extended, if possible, by hewing fields out of the mountain slopes. Below: loess-land landscape. Large unirrigated fields on the plateau surface, smaller fields, dyked and irrigated, along the valley floor.

Above: ancient farming tools found in the course of excavation in Northern China. On the left, a pick; on the right, a weeding implement.

The succeeding Mesolithic period was milder and warmer and the basis of life was provided by hunting, fishing and gathering. Rather similar climatic conditions prevailed during the early Neolithic and it is from this period, when the habitability of North China was probably at its maximum, that the beginnings of settled agriculture can be dated. The Yellow River delta was too wet and marshy to attract man at this period but to the west, close to the junction of the Wei and Yellow Rivers, the transition from food-gathering to food production is illustrated by the archaeological finds at Shayuan. And with the beginning of crop production began the clearing of the vegetation cover of the northern loess-lands and the large-scale transformation by man of China's natural environment.

By about 2500 B.C. the North China cradle area (page 57) appears to have supported a dense village-dwelling population with hundreds, even thousands, of villages. These farming communities possessed an already complex civilization: their basic cereal was millet, supplemented later by rice and wheat; they possessed domesticated sheep and cattle as well as dogs and pigs; they practiced highly-developed techniques of pottery-making. Above all, with the transition from swidden (shifting) agriculture which was made possible by the use of irrigation, settlement became permanent, production increased and, as the storage of grain surpluses became possible, the gradients of wealth within society began to rise.

The Han cradle area

This Han cradle area had a very distinctive geographic character. It lay in the middle basin of the Yellow River, in an area of loess or loess-derived alluvial soils. In early historic times it would have had an attractive landscape with fertile and easily-worked soils and possibly an open woodland cover. The "islands" of harder rock projecting through the loess mantle were more densely forested and provided wood and water. Its climate five millennia ago was probably not greatly different from that of today, though possibly slightly wetter. Very clearly, it was an area which had many attractions for early man – a fertile and easily-worked soil, stone, timber and water close at hand and, above all, the advantage of contact, via the "corridor" of Gansu and the oases beyond, with Central Asia and the Middle East.

This was of major importance, for however favoured the region's climate and soils, it seems to have lacked many of the basic food plants and domestic animals. Without these, a high civilization could scarcely have developed. But it appears that at a very early date plants and animals, and technologies, were being carried eastwards along the great trans-Asian routeway which was subsequently to be known as the Silk Road (see pages 82–83). Thus wheat and millet are Middle Eastern cultigens, and the sheep and cow were almost certainly domesticated in the Middle East and became part of the early Chinese culture-complex.

Such culture contact has always been an important factor in the rise of high civilizations and the Han civilization was clearly no exception. For the area in which it developed was not only

Boys at work in a maize field. The production of this cereal and others (wheat, barley and sorghum) is concentrated in the northern margins of "Agricultural China." The dry climate and the variable rainfall make irrigation necessary to ensure high and steady yields.

Opposite: yoked oxen on a tile from the Han period. Ever since ancient times, agriculture has played a highly important part in Chinese culture. Proof of this is the position held by peasants in the social hierarchy, second only to men of letters.

strategically located with regard to the trans-Asian routes. It lay also at the overlap of four major cultures, and elements from each of these were integrated into the nascent Han civilization. From the "proto-Tungus" peoples of the Northeast were derived a matriarchal organization of society, the elements of a shamanistic religion, and the use of pit-dwellings. From the "proto-Tai" groups of the Southeast came the use of bamboo, iron and lacquer work; dragon-myths and ancestor-worship; the domestication of the water buffalo and terraced rice cultivation. The two streams fused in the Bronze Age civilization of the Shang which integrated elements from two other neighbouring cultures: the "proto-Turkic" culture of the Northwest, and the "proto-Tibetan" culture to the West. From the first of these were derived the use of mound burials and the worship of heavenly bodies; from the second the practice of cremation and polyandry.

Thus, from the earliest stages Han civilization has integrated elements from many sources. The recent assimilation (and transmutation) of the doctrine of Marxism-Leninism demonstrates that this capacity for synthesis is still a major feature of Han civilization.

The occupation of the Chinese land involved three main processes: first, the development of a distinctive and coherent society based on a distinct agricultural system in the yellow-earth cradle area; secondly, the discontinuous but increasingly effective assertion of Han control over the nomad peoples of the dry Northwest and over the oases of Central Asia; thirdly, the southwards extension of Han settlement and Han political control into the subtropical and tropical lands beyond the Yangtze, lands held by mainly Tai tribal peoples. To these ancient processes may be added the population shifts of more recent times: the agricultural colonization of the cold lands of the Northeast and the diffusion of Chinese settlers into the Nanyang, the lands of Southeast Asia and of the Southern Ocean. And in all these processes we can see at work that interplay between man and environment which continues to be a major theme in China's geography.

For, as Owen Lattimore has pointed out, the Yellow River cradle area, while favoured by easy-working soils, was subject to a high measure of rainfall variability. This could be offset by simple irrigation techniques which used the network of small streams draining into the Yellow River. And having adopted irrigation-based cultivation Chinese agriculture, and Chinese society, were, in Lattimore's words, "predestined to a certain evolutionary bias." The individual family might cope with the rudimentary irrigation and cultivation of its own small plot but "beyond that, the control of soil and water in combination lay only within the reach of groups of people, helping each other to dig larger channels and perhaps to build embankments that would keep flood water out of the bottom lands."

Progress in agriculture then, as in China today, "made collective action unavoidable." It also necessitated the coordination and unification of water control over wider and wider areas and was a potent influence making for political unification; by the 7th century B.C. the hundreds of tiny city-states (many river-basin units) had been reduced to a dozen. And given the availability of large bodies of forced labour, it became possible to begin the large-scale terracing and irrigation which eventually transformed China into a land of intensive cultivation. And, as the population grew and expansion became necessary, these techniques of water control and labour mobilization made possible the large-scale flood control works which were necessary for the settlement and agricultural development of the alluvial but flood-prone lowlands of the North China Plain to the east. Once this technological breakthrough was achieved, "both the land and its tribes could be brought within the scope of the expanding Chinese culture and made Chinese."

The expansion of "China" is thus largely the history of the expansion of a specialized agricultural economy whose technological roots go back to the first elaboration of a "hydraulic civilization" in the valleys of the yellow-earth country more than four millennia ago. Because of the "evolutionary bias" to which Lattimore refers, it was an economy which became increasingly uniform, showing an unusual homogeneity from the steppe margins of the Northwest to the tropical forests of the South. Its objectives have been well described by Lattimore: "In the North, as in the South, the determining consideration is the farming of the best land, the concentration of the most people on the most productive land, and multiple cropping in order to keep the land and the people busy." And the preoccupation with "farming the best land" (especially that suited for irrigation) dictated the direction and character of Han Chinese expansion and settlement, for, seeking such land, migrants by-passed the uplands, leaving them empty or in the occupation of tribal peoples, following selectively the patches of good earth offered by river valleys, lake basins, or fringing coastal lowlands.

By the Han period, Han Chinese settlers had occupied much of that humid eastern area we know as Agricultural China and a measure of Chinese political control had been established. Since then, the centuries have witnessed a gradual process of "filling in," a process of adjustment to the potentialities of the land, a process too of reappraisal and readjustment made possible by the introduction of new crops and new technologies.

Towards the Western Regions

As population built up in the Han core region the land became increasingly crowded and subdivided; as Pao Zhao put it: "After five centuries or three dynasties, the land was divided like a melon, or shared like beans." Eventually the point was reached when migration became essential and hopeful settlers moved out to seek new land and new lives on the western and southern margins of the cradle area. The problems encountered were very different in these two areas.

Would-be settlers migrating towards the Northwest moved towards a "margin of differentiation and limitation." The attempts of the migrants to extend intensive irrigated agriculture soon encountered diminishing returns as the irrigable areas became smaller and more patchy and rainfall scantier and less

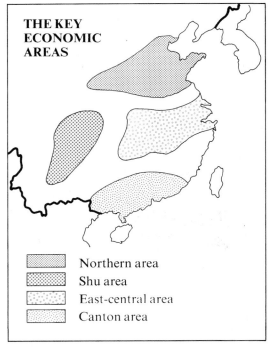

THE KEY ECONOMIC AREAS

Northern area

Shu area

East-central area

Canton area

We use the phrase "Key Economic Areas" to denote those regions where agricultural productivity and ease of transport permitted the accumulation of the grain surplus on which political and economic power ultimately rested. The loess and loess-derived alluvium of North China represents the primary center. Later centers developed in Sichuan (the Shu region), the middle and lower Yangtze and the valleys and coastal plains of the South.

Opposite: illustrating the gradual migration of the original Han population towards the south of the country and the effects of this on the major ethnic groups in the South. This series of displacements was spread over millennia; it resulted in the occupation by settled agriculturists of the Han stock of the river valleys and coastal lowlands of Central and South China. The Mon and Tai tribal peoples who originally occupied most of South and Central China were forced to migrate either southwards or into the upland areas unattractive to the Han cultivator. In the inset, we see the situation as it was around 2500 B.C. before this Han expansion. The original center of Han civilization was in the basin of the Yellow River. Most of central southern China was populated by the Tai and Mon peoples, many related to the peoples of Southeast Asia today.

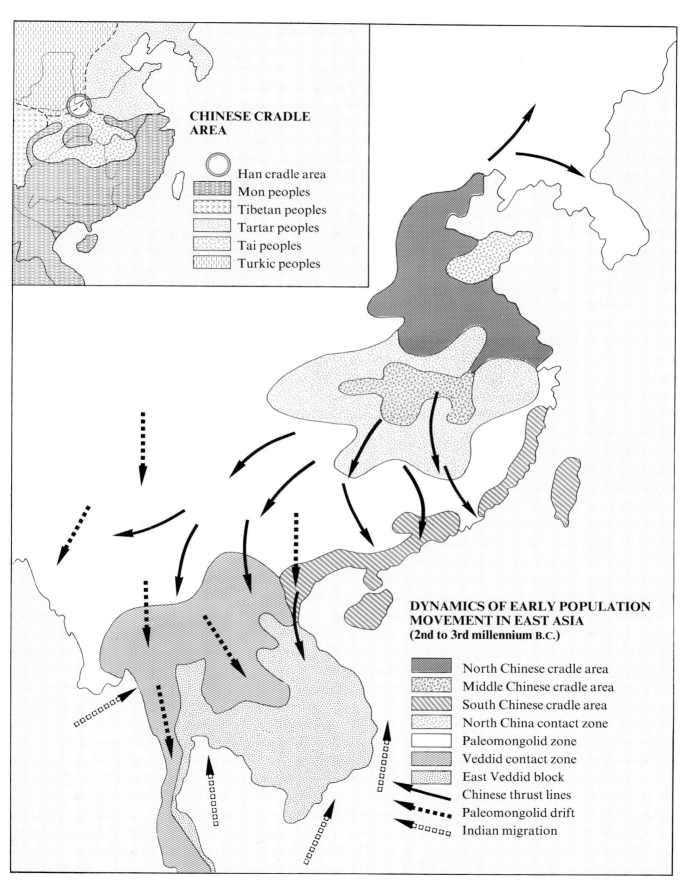

CHINESE CRADLE AREA

- ◎ Han cradle area
- Mon peoples
- Tibetan peoples
- Tartar peoples
- Tai peoples
- Turkic peoples

DYNAMICS OF EARLY POPULATION MOVEMENT IN EAST ASIA
(2nd to 3rd millennium B.C.**)**

- North Chinese cradle area
- Middle Chinese cradle area
- South Chinese cradle area
- North China contact zone
- Paleomongolid zone
- Veddid contact zone
- East Veddid block
- Chinese thrust lines
- Paleomongolid drift
- Indian migration

certain. The limits of agricultural expansion towards the Northwest seem to have been reached by the 3rd or 4th century B.C. Then a process of differentiation began as less developed groups, originally of Han stock, were progressively extruded from those areas suited to the intensive cropping which had become the basis of Han life. They moved out, into an environment unsuited for farming but suited to pastoralism and, having evaluated the potential of those subhumid lands, they began to develop an independent and alternative way of life, that of pastoral nomadism.

There thus emerged an alien world, dominated by nomadic-herding people and one contrasting in virtually every respect with the garden-cultivating, earthbound world of peasant China. And political and economic factors added to the almost dramatic sharpness of this contrast. For the intensive irrigated agriculture of the Han demanded a plentiful supply of cheap labour and diversification, and the development of a secondary economy would have had the effect of reducing such a supply. Consequently, as Lattimore stresses, "Political tradition had from the very beginning to be hostile to any diversification of the basic agricultural economy, and to treat as recalcitrants any marginal communities whose local interest would otherwise have prompted them to ... make themselves independent by eliminating idle time and engaging in the maximum number of different kinds of activity."

This process took place along the whole of the northwest of Inner China and in the "sub-oases" of Gansu and Ningxia. The "frontier problem," whether the mobile society of the steppe or the earthbound society of the Han was to prevail, had emerged. The Great Wall was an attempt to establish a clearly-defined and defensible frontier, a barrier which would protect the vulnerable northwest flanks of China. It was, however, of only limited value and, in an attempt to integrate these Western Regions into the Chinese state, China was drawn ever deeper into the steppes and deserts of the West. Armed force, deployed against an elusive and mobile enemy, was costly and inconclusive; a shrewd trading policy, which aimed at giving the rulers of the western oases an interest in an affiliation with China, was more successful. But effective Chinese control was discontinuous – for Kashgar (Kashi) it has been estimated at 425 years out of some two millennia – and it is only in the more recent period of Chinese history that the political and economic integration of the Far West has become a reality.

Towards the South
The main thrust of Han expansion was, however, towards the South, towards the lands which lay beyond the east-west trending ridges of the Qinling-Dabashan.

Here the subhumid environment gave place to a humid tropical environment. Temperatures and rainfall are high most of the year and the growing season long. The natural vegetation is luxuriant; it includes bamboo, citrus fruits, palms and broad-leaved evergreen trees. A tropical fauna, including elephants, monkeys, rhinoceros and water buffalo replaced the northern grassland fauna. And even though the amount of lowland alluvial soils was limited, this was more than offset by the possibility which the climate afforded of taking several harvests a year. It was a region of very great potentialities, a "margin of indefinite expansion," and much of the last two millennia has been concerned with the realization of these potentialities and with the absorption of those southern lands into the expanding culture of the Han people.

This Han occupation was a slow and at times difficult process. The world of the South, with its landscapes, "stern, sober and correct," to the Chinese accustomed to the ordered and harmonious landscapes of the North, was an abnormal world. It was a hostile world, with a strange climate, a strange vegetation and strange diseases, yet it was a more fertile world, warm and luxuriant and therefore attractive; in the words of Sima Qian, the great Han historian, "Since the land is so rich in edible products, there is no fear of famine, and therefore the people are content to live from day to day ... in the regions south of the Yangtze and Huai rivers no one ever freezes or starves to death."

The Han colonist, however, faced not merely the problem of adjusting to a new environment; he faced also the problems posed by the existence in the region of a sizeable tribal population. The majority of these tribal peoples were Tai for, prior to the Han expansion, China south of the Yangtze was a dominantly Tai land. They were clearly set apart from the Han people by their speech, their customs, and their colour and, in the initial stages, labelled with the adjectives all colonizing groups apply to those they overrun or displace: they were "cruel" and "treacherous," "barbarous" and "infidels." For centuries they resisted the Chinese advance but were slowly, inexorably, either wiped out, assimilated (the syncretic character of Han culture was an important factor explaining the speed and the thoroughness of this assimilation) or simply pushed back into the forested uplands by settlers interested solely in the easily cultivable valleys and plains. It is this process that explains the complex pattern of Han and minority peoples in South China today, the Zhuang of the Guangxi-Zhuang Autonomous Region representing the largest remaining group of the Tai-speaking aboriginals of Jiangnan (i.e. the lands south of the Yangtze).

By the late Han period the sinicization of the area was well advanced. The Chinese, says Edward Schafer, "moved into the rich valleys of the south in 'pools,' dense aggregates of hopeful humanity," and this southward stream of migration was swollen by refugees from the barbarian invasions of North China during the Middle Ages, by the catastrophic impact of flood and famine in the northern plains and by peasants seeking to escape the double burden of heavy taxation and increasingly onerous tenancy. This southward thrust of the Han people can be illustrated in very general terms by the population estimates for North and South at various periods (see table).

And the southward displacement of the economic center of the country is demonstrated by the fact that by the Tang dynasty nine-tenths of the tax revenues came from the lands south of the Yangtze, from the area of Jiangnan.

Opposite: an old painting showing a water buffalo harnessed to an irrigation wheel. Irrigation was essential for the development of intensive agriculture and has therefore always been a priority in the Chinese economy. The first large-scale systems were in use in the 5th century B.C.

The system for pumping water from the soil shown in the photograph above is very similar to that used in ancient times. A donkey works a kind of screw. This method (along with other more modern systems) is still used in the Chinese countryside today. Approximately two-thirds of the cultivated land in China is still irrigated by artificial means.

The filling-in of the countryside

In the earliest part of the historical period the landscape was little modified. Shang China for example had a population of possibly four to five millions; this would mean a density of 20–30 people per square mile, about the density of the better settled parts of Europe in mediaeval times. Wild beasts were abundant, many of the animals being those whose habitat was forest or marsh such as deer and boar, elephant and rhinoceros.

Succeeding centuries saw the gradual build-up of population and the increasing transformation of the Han œcumene. By the end of the Zhou period, in the 3rd century B.C., the population had reached 50 million and the landscapes of the lowlands were beginning to take on a rectangular pattern: pathways and field boundaries ran E–W and N–S and the walled cities were gridded in layout. But much land was farmed under the slash-and-burn system: cultivated land alternated with old fields under second-growth woodland or with areas of untouched marsh or woodland. Population densities within the cradle area probably reached 200–300 per square mile; once it rose much above this level, the motive force was provided for those outward drifts of land-hungry colonists we have described earlier.

The early centuries of our epoch were marked by growing intensification of farming; terraced rice cultivation had probably come to North China as early as the 1st century B.C. and improved tools and a wider range of crops enhanced agricultural productivity. But, as has been the case for so much of China's history, the individual peasant family, however hard its members worked, remained vulnerable to flood and drought. Indeed, as Yi-fu Tuan comments, "It was taken for granted that in every generation there were years of famine and years of plenty." Flooding and a change in the course of the Yellow River brought disaster to millions in the 1st century A.D. and drove untold numbers to migrate east towards Shandong or south towards the Yangtze and the lands beyond. And after the end of the Han dynasty the ravages of nomad tribes in North China and almost three and a half centuries of civil strife gave added impetus to these movements.

But by the early Middle Ages the environment of Inner China was becoming increasingly transformed by man. The demand for charcoal in a wide variety of industries: salt production, brickmaking, the manufacture of liquor and of iron, led to an increasing destruction of the accessible forest land. The demands of shipbuilding and the construction industry added to the deforestation as did even the making of Chinese ink which called for pure soot; as Edward Schafer observes, "Even before T'ang times, the ancient pines of Shantung had been reduced to carbon, and now the busy brushes of the vast T'ang bureaucracy were rapidly bringing baldness to the Taihang mountains between Shanxi and Hopeh."

The pressure on the upland areas was paralleled by an increasing pressure on the lowlands which manifested itself in the extensive draining of marshes, ponds and lakes. This was partly made possible by the development of more complex pumping and draining machinery. In certain areas, such as the Yangtze delta, the program of draining was encouraged by

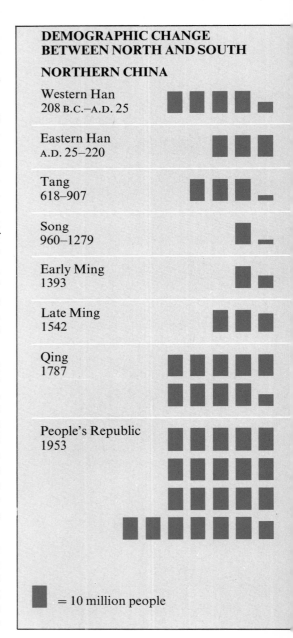

DEMOGRAPHIC CHANGE BETWEEN NORTH AND SOUTH

NORTHERN CHINA

Western Han
208 B.C.–A.D. 25

Eastern Han
A.D. 25–220

Tang
618–907

Song
960–1279

Early Ming
1393

Late Ming
1542

Qing
1787

People's Republic
1953

■ = 10 million people

The balance of population between the North and South of China has undergone a complete reversal through the centuries. The colonists who went in search of new lands to cultivate during the Tang period were later followed by others escaping from flood, disease and famine or invasions by barbarians. The more favourable agricultural conditions and the introduction of new strains of rice during the Middle Ages resulted in a major increase in population in the lands south of the Yangtze.

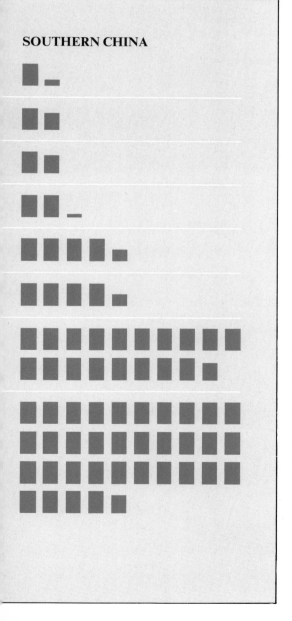

SOUTHERN CHINA

government in order to attract refugee settlement; settlers were given free seed and rents were remitted. But in many areas the process of drainage and reclamation was on a scale sufficient to disturb the economic and ecological balance by withdrawing from use areas which were important as sources of supplementary foodstuffs or which helped to regulate the drainage and irrigation systems on the smaller holdings. The process was described by an official in the 12th century who commented, "Not a single year passed without the powerful clans and families following one after another in the occupation of large areas of lake-bottom land. Thus the people were deprived more and more of the benefits of reservoirs and lakes, and marshes have all become land during the last thirty years." And the disturbance of the water balance which this program of draining involved was sufficiently great to worry another official at the same period about the situation in Zhejiang: "Tracts of reclaimed land cover hundreds of thousands of *mu* in Zhejiang. Tanks, ponds, reservoirs, streams and creeks are all turned into farms. No trace of any storage for surplus water can be found and no water to relieve drought is available. If not strictly prohibited, the situation will become worse and years of good harvest can hardly be expected."

The increasing pressure of increasing numbers of human beings on the upland and lowland environments of Inner China is reflected in the Chinese attitudes to nature from the Han dynasty onwards. During Han times, the natural environment, and especially the forested wilderness south of the Yangtze, was too much of a threat, too alien, to possess charm. By the Tang dynasty the self-confidence man acquired from his colonization of the South and from his modification of the lowland environments had given him a much greater awareness of the beauty and the fragility of nature. Nature had become, as Edward Schafer points out, less threatening than threatened.

A MILLENNIUM OF CHANGE

During the last millennium man has continued his appraisal of the potentialities of the area we know as Agricultural China. He has adjusted his land-use practices increasingly finely to the details of the physical environment and has profoundly changed the vegetation pattern, the soil structures, even the relief and drainage patterns of the areas he chose for settlement. Increasingly sophisticated techniques of cultivation and of drainage and irrigation permitted a continuous build-up of population in the lowlands and the introduction of new varieties of crops and of new crops made possible both by the fuller utilization of the existing cultivated area and the expansion of cultivation into areas once considered marginal for settled agriculture. Both these sets of developments added greatly to the food supply and laid the basis for a continuing, if irregular, increase in population.

These crops, which can be regarded as "biological auxiliaries" which enabled the peasant to make more effective use of the Chinese living-space, fell into three groups: the northern "dry-land" crops; the rapid-maturing rices; and the new crops of American origin.

The northern dry-land crops included wheat, barley and the sorghums. The cultivation of these was extended southwards, partly by Imperial decree and partly as a result of the great southward migrations of population. They were especially useful in areas liable to heavy flooding, for they could be sown after the floods retreated and they made possible the agricultural utilization and the colonization of many formerly marginal areas in Central and South China.

The rapid-maturing rices were introduced from the Indo-Chinese peninsula (whence their name *Champa* rices, referring to the kingdom of the Chams) at the beginning of the 11th century. The traditional strains of rice demanded 180 days from sowing to harvesting and so a second crop was difficult to obtain. These new rices, reputed to mature in 100 days, made possible the double-cropping which is a distinctive feature of South China and provided a crop which ensured a steady supply of food throughout the year. And requiring less water than the older rices they could be grown on higher and sloping land which had formerly been unsuited to rice. The subsequent development of rices which would mature in an even shorter period and which could be harvested in late autumn or winter made possible the extension of settlement into a wide range of formerly marginal environments. The impact of these new rices was revolutionary; it has been summed up by Ping-ti Ho. Says Ho: "Within two centuries of the introduction of Champa rice the landscape of the eastern half of China's rice area had already been substantially changed. By the 13th century much of the hilly land of the lower Yangtze region and Fujian, where water resources, climatic and soil conditions were sufficiently suitable for the cultivation of early-ripening rice, had been turned into terraced paddies. The early-ripening rice not only ensured the success of the double-crop system but also prolonged the economic hegemony of the Yangtze area."

It appears that over the past millennium the rice area, and the

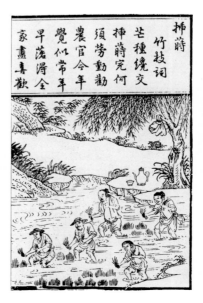

food output, may have doubled. Consequently the food situation and the potential for continued population growth (page 133) were more favourable in China than in Europe which went through its agricultural revolution in the 18th century.

In terms of landscape these first two groups of new crops led to a growing differentiation between the uplands, which continued to be thinly settled or left to tribal peoples practicing shifting cultivation, and the intensively utilized lowlands. This contrast was attenuated by the introduction of the third group of crops, the so-called "American crops." These included maize, sweet potatoes, Irish potatoes and peanuts. They became of major importance in the 18th and 19th centuries, at a time when the impact of the "rice revolution" was diminishing, and they either complemented, or, because of their higher yields, competed with, the traditional dry-land crops. Most important of all, they made it possible for the Chinese, historically a folk of the plains and the valleys, to use dry uplands and sandy areas too light for rice and other traditional crops. The uplands of the Yangtze region and North China were largely unoccupied at the beginning of the 18th century, but during the next two centuries they were occupied by agricultural colonists who converted their forested slopes into maize and sweet potato farms.

These American crops and the traditional dry-land crops thus played an important role in the fuller utilization of the Chinese land; such crops were, as Ho has underlined, "the peasant's main weapon in his struggle with new land." Their expansion added to the country's total food output and because they could be grown in the marginal areas of the North they. helped to redress somewhat the strong southward shift of the demographic and economic center of the country which had resulted from the extension in the South of the rapid-maturing rices. But their cultivation inevitably involved the ruthless destruction of the forest cover and the exploitation of soils which were of low fertility, fragile and easily erodible. As yields fell the farmer abandoned his fields and moved on and cleared new land. There thus developed a cyclical pattern of upland colonization,

A series of drawings from the Ming period which show the different stages in the cultivation of rice, from sowing the seed, through the processes of transplanting and harvesting to threshing. The series, which ends with a picture of a harvest feast in a farmer's house, was used to illustrate a book from the 16th century. The drawings accompany some rhythmic verse which exalts manual work in the fields and the merits of and satisfaction gained by those who dedicate themselves sufficiently to it.

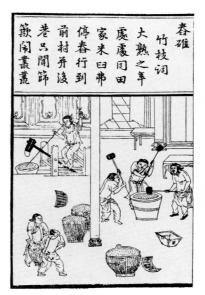
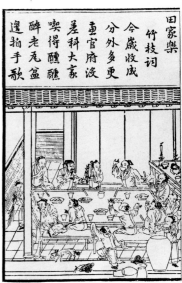

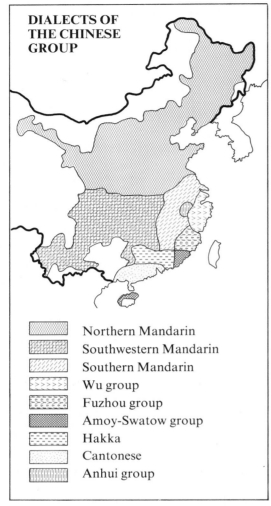

DIALECTS OF THE CHINESE GROUP

Northern Mandarin
Southwestern Mandarin
Southern Mandarin
Wu group
Fuzhou group
Amoy-Swatow group
Hakka
Cantonese
Anhui group

The area occupied by peoples of Han origin is both complex and interesting from a linguistic point of view. The linguistic unity of the North contrasts strikingly with the diversity of the South where there is a range of Chinese dialects as well as pockets of non-Chinese speech. The grammatical differences between the various Chinese dialects are almost entirely to do with the disposition of vowels and variety of idioms. There are also some phonetic differences, which arise from different interpretations of written words which, however, retain the same form throughout the country.

followed by the build-up of population, increasing deforestation, overcultivation, erosion and finally abandonment. The ravaged vegetation and eroded soils of so much of upland China are a legacy of this exploitative upland economy; so too is the silting of the rivers and increasingly frequent flooding of the intensively-cropped areas in the lowlands.

The 19th century

By the middle of the 19th century the processes of agricultural colonization described above had resulted in the occupation of most of the cultivable land of Agricultural China. By that date "the Chinese people, with the technological means then at their disposal, had probably approached a maximum in land utilization in China Proper" (Ping-ti Ho). During the early 19th century the slow increase in pressure of population, building up within a stagnant and by now backward economy, led to increasing social unrest. This culminated in the Tai Ping rebellion, probably the greatest civil war in history. The appalling slaughter in this and other rebellions reduced the population in the provinces affected (the population of the Yangtze provinces fell by 36 millions between 1850 and 1953) and gave a short respite during which migration brought about a new balance between population and resources. But the respite was localized and temporary and for much of the next century Chinese society was to exist poised on the knife edge of starvation and tragically vulnerable to the "catastrophic deterrents" of flood and drought.

By the early 1940s China, in the opinion of many experts, was "overpopulated." Observers spoke of "the unbearable pressures on the land," of the impossibility of feeding China's half a billion inhabitants, of the "inevitability of extensive famines." Yet by 1978 the Chinese land was feeding, and feeding well, close on one billion people. Population had grown by almost two-thirds in the 25 years between 1953 and 1978; this is twice as much as the growth over the century 1850–1953. We have stressed earlier the importance of bearing in mind a society's cultural level if we wish to understand that society's relationship to its environment and its capacity to transform that environment. China provides a dramatic illustration of this, and of Carl Sauer's axiom that "natural resources are cultural appraisals." And the problems of "overpopulation" which China faced in the 19th century and which grew steadily worse in the first half of this century were not due to lack of natural resources. Certainly the potentially cultivable area was limited but even this limited area was not all under cultivation and what was under cultivation produced less than could have been produced with the then existing techniques.

To understand this we have to bear in mind the importance of social and institutional factors. In many areas the arable land and other resources (such as work-animals) were monopolized by a small and rapacious landlord group (page 127). The individual peasant family was helpless in the face of this group and natural disasters such as famine simply drove the peasant deeper into its clutches. Land pressure could have been reduced by diversification, by opening up new sectors of the economy (as

Eastern and agricultural China is solidly Han; the Northern grasslands Mongol; the Northwest desert region occupied by Turkic groups such as the Kazakhs and Uighurs and the high plateau of the Southwest is Tibetan. Note the complex area of mixed population in the broken mountain and valley country of tropical China which is made up of a mosaic of racial pockets: there are groups of Han, Tibetan, Tai, Miao, Yi, Hani and Mon-Khmer.

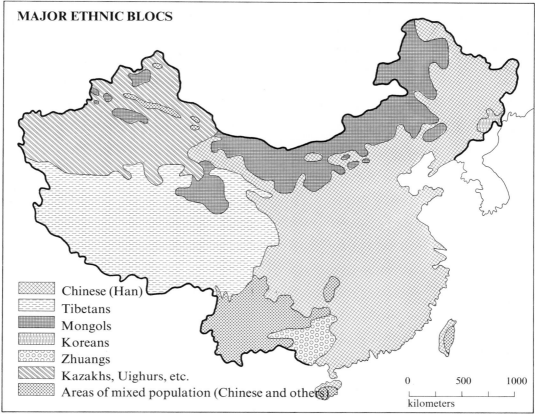

MAJOR ETHNIC BLOCS

Chinese (Han)
Tibetans
Mongols
Koreans
Zhuangs
Kazakhs, Uighurs, etc.
Areas of mixed population (Chinese and others)

0   500   1000
kilometers

From the left (above): a group of the Li people from southern China; a Kazakh mother with her baby. Below: a Tibetan girl and a Mongol woman. One of the articles of the constitution declares the People's Republic to be a multinational state, respecting the rights of all nationalities and guaranteeing to all the use of their own language and the preservation of national customs.

has been done since 1949). But various institutional factors: the greater profitability of monopoly trade, the diversion of wealth to noneconomic uses, and the influence of an increasingly outmoded educational system, impeded such change. And political conditions, including peculation, official extravagance, and the increasing tax burden on the peasantry, disrupted life and led to deteriorating living levels for the masses.

It was left to the present regime to tackle the causes of population pressure and peasant poverty by removing these social and institutional barriers to increased productivity and by modernizing and diversifying China's rural economy.

Mid-20th century patterns

Ever since that distant period when their ancestors began to move out from the Yellow River cradle area and confront the challenge of new soils and new climates, the peasants of China have been adjusting their land-use and settlement patterns increasingly finely to the intricacies of the Chinese environment. The population map of the mid-20th century (page 133) shows the results of these millennia of advance and retreat, experimentation and consolidation.

The basic feature is the contrast between Inner or Agricultural China and Outer China, and, within the former, the contrast between lowland and upland.

Nine-tenths of the population are concentrated into one-sixth of the area of the country. Densities within this peasant œcumene exceed 250 per square kilometer (1953) or approximately 500 per square kilometer of cultivated land. To better appreciate these densities they should be compared with agricultural densities in other parts of the globe; thus a Chinese village of 500–600 people may find a living on an area equal to that of an American family farm supporting five to six people.

In 1953 three-quarters of China's population were concentrated into four major regions. First, the North China plain. Here the loess and loess-derived alluvial soils support a "dense mat of people," representing almost one-quarter of China's population. Densities rise locally to over 400 per square kilometer and even in the rocky massif of Shandong in the East they exceed 200. Secondly, the middle and lower valley of the Yangtze; this region contains one-fifth of China's population and densities rise to over 700 per square kilometer in the delta region (or over 2000 per square kilometer of cropped land). Thirdly, the Red Basin of Sichuan; this is a region of dense population and rural population densities reach the very high figure of 660 per square kilometer. Finally, South China; here the high density areas form a series of scattered "islands" along the alluvial floors of the valleys, in interior lowlands and in the delta region of Canton. As elsewhere in China there is a sharp contrast between densities in lowlands and uplands; in the Pearl River delta densities exceed 400 per square kilometer but in the fringing uplands they are below 50.

With the exception of the great flow of migrants towards Manchuria in the 1920s and 1930s, the pattern described above and shown in map on page 127 has been remarkably stable over recent centuries. Only natural or manmade calamities – drought and flood, civil war or banditry – brought about major changes and these were often temporary. This stability of pattern is due to many causes, partly to the fact that the level alluvial lowlands or loessial flats are juxtaposed with areas of difficult relief, poor soils, or adverse climate, areas unsuited to intensive agriculture. Partly it is due to cultural and social factors: the attachment to family or village, the veneration of the ancestors, the difficulties of language – all of which impeded migration. And partly stability has been imposed by poverty, for an impoverished peasant family dare not venture out into the unknown, to break in land of doubtful agricultural value. Except when forced out by war or famine the peasant clung to the known landscape he and his ancestors had created.

And, on a broader scale, the historical continuity between these high-density areas of the mid-20th century and what Chi Chao-ting has termed the "Key Economic Areas" of Chinese history (page 56), the areas where agricultural productivity and ease of transport permitted the accumulation of the grain surplus on which military and political power ultimately rested, underlines the remarkable stability of the major features of China's social geography. Even the remarkable changes of the last 30 years have done little to diminish the control which, for so much of China's history, a highly developed and specialized agricultural system has exerted on the distribution of population in the country.

Opposite: pig-breeding in a commune. The raising of pigs and poultry is common throughout China. Generally, the best breeders are kept in the commune while the rest are assigned to individual families who either fatten them up for their own consumption or for sale in local markets where it has been permitted to sell pigs and poultry since 1964.

Ducklings in a hatchery near Peking. As soon as they reach maturity, they will be sent to the kitchens of the numerous restaurants in the city. Peking Duck, one of the best known dishes in Chinese cooking, requires hours of preparation: after an elaborate process for tenderizing the carcass, it has to be hung by the neck in the oven, half-filled with water and blown up with air under the skin. Thus the meat remains moist while the skin becomes golden and crackling.

THE DIVERSITY OF THE PEOPLES OF CHINA

"China has a large territory, abundant material resources and numerous population. Of these three the Hans possess one, namely, they are many in number; minority peoples possess two, namely, they have vast territories and rich resources."

Mao Zedong

As a result of the processes of historical development sketched in the preceding chapter and elsewhere in this volume, China is a multinational state. This ethnic diversity was emphasized by the old flag of the Republic; its five bars represented the five major groups: Chinese (or Han), Manchu, Mongol, Mohammedan and Tibetan. The non-Chinese groups make up only six percent of the population but their absolute numbers are large, some 35–40 millions in 1953, and they occupy two-thirds of the area of China. The quotation from Mao Zedong cited above emphasizes the duality which dominates the human geography of China, the contrast between the densely peopled, dominantly Han, lands of the East and the thinly peopled minority regions of the West. And it adds a further dimension by stressing that the Western Regions, for long backward and semicolonial, have a rich resource endowment, a wealth of minerals, energy resources and agro-pastoral potentialities. The full inventory of these potentialities is still incomplete but their realization is already changing the ways of life and levels of living of the minority peoples, adding also to the well-being of their fellow-citizens in the rest of China.

The Han people

We have already sketched in the main stages in the occupation and agricultural development of China by the Han or Chinese group. The group today occupies a compact area which coincides broadly with Inner or Agricultural China. Towards the northwest, Han farmers have long been established in the "sub-oasis zone" of Gansu, along the line of the old Silk Road, but the Han occupation of the Manchurian lowland in the northeast has taken place during this century. To the southwest, Han farmers penetrated deep along the alluvium of the river valleys flowing eastward from the Tibetan uplands; they occupied also the alluvial floors of the old lake basins such as that of Kunming in Yunnan. But the upland areas were left in the occupation of non-Chinese tribal peoples so that the map (page 65) shows a complex interpenetration of Han and minority peoples.

The Han group is not homogeneous linguistically and is subdivided into eight major groups. These, and their distribution, are shown on page 64.

The theme of duality again asserts itself, for there is a striking contrast between the plains and plateaux of North China on the one hand and the more broken uplands of South China on the other. The Han area of the North is, as will be seen from the map (page 64), linguistically homogeneous; it is a solid area of Northern Mandarin speech. The South, by contrast, shows a great diversity of Chinese dialects as well as large pockets of non-Chinese speech.

The three groups of Mandarin dialects: Northern Mandarin, Southern Mandarin and Southwestern Mandarin, are as close to one another as, say, the languages of various English-speaking nations or, possibly, the dialects of Italy. The other groups of dialects bear much the same relationship to Mandarin as Dutch or Low German to English. Generally speaking, educated people whose home language is a non-Mandarin dialect will acquire sufficient Mandarin to obviate linguistic difficulties. And the use by all Chinese-speakers of a uniform system of ideographs is an important unifying factor.

The minority peoples

The extension of Han influence and power over the centuries took two main forms: in the grasslands and deserts of the West and Northwest conditions were unfavourable to intensive agriculture; Han settlement was on a small scale and the Chinese contented themselves with establishing political control over the non-Chinese peoples of these regions. In the subtropical and tropical South, by contrast, there was massive Chinese settlement in the valleys and lowlands and this resulted in large-scale displacement of the pre-Chinese inhabitants, a displacement sometimes "lateral," i.e. to the south and southwest, sometimes "vertical," i.e. towards the upper slopes of the valleys and the mountain masses. The broad distribution of minority peoples today reflects these historic processes (see map on page 65).

The whole of northern China, from Xinjiang in the west to the uplands of Manchuria in the east, is occupied by peoples

A picture of the north face of Everest (8848 meters) with the Rongbu glacier. The Himalayan chain, of which Everest is a part, forms the southern boundary of China. It is backed by the high plain of Qinghai-Tibet. The chain is 2400 kilometers long and consists of between 200 and 300 peaks. It is the largest and the highest mountain range in the world. It has many summits rising to over 6000 meters and nine which are over 8000 meters. Apart from one group formed by comparatively recent movement of the Earth's surface, this range belongs to the tertiary era.

This map shows, in simplified form, the main types of rock found in China.
1. Alluvial deposits;
2. Loess; 3. Desert sands and gravel;
4. Sedimentary marine rocks (from the Paleolithic era);
5. Younger sedimentary rocks (from the Mesolithic era);
6. Major karst region;
7. Compacted metamorphic and sedimentary rocks;
8. Igneous and metamorphic rock;
9. Igneous and metamorphic rock (associated with 5 in Fujian). Geological data for Western China is as yet too uncertain for inclusion in this map.

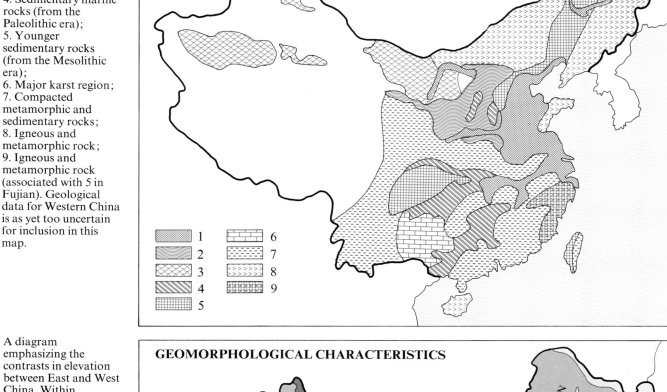

SURFACE GEOLOGY

1		6	
2		7	
3		8	
4		9	
5			

A diagram emphasizing the contrasts in elevation between East and West China. Within Agricultural China, we can see the contrast between the coastal plains and the plateaux of the North and the rolling hill country to the south of the Yangtze. There is an even sharper contrast between the compact plateau of Tibet and the great basins and girdling mountain chains of the North.

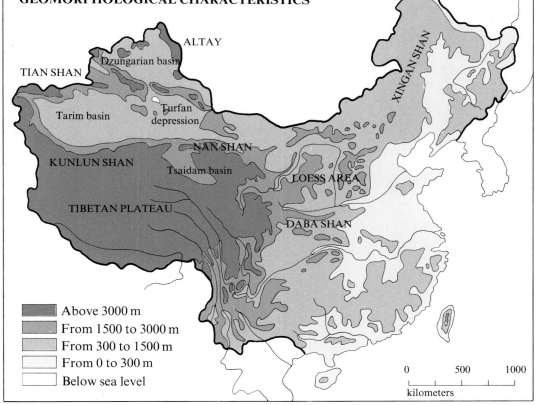

GEOMORPHOLOGICAL CHARACTERISTICS

ALTAY
TIAN SHAN
Dzungarian basin
Turfan depression
Tarim basin
XINGAN SHAN
NAN SHAN
KUNLUN SHAN
Tsaidam basin
LOESS AREA
TIBETAN PLATEAU
DABA SHAN

- Above 3000 m
- From 1500 to 3000 m
- From 300 to 1500 m
- From 0 to 300 m
- Below sea level

0   500   1000
kilometers

belonging to the Altaic group; these include Turkic, Mongol and Tungus elements. They occupy their historic homelands but were incorporated in the Chinese state as early as the Han dynasty, though effective political control has been discontinuous.

The great block of upland country in the west of the country, comprising Tibet and Qinghai, is the historic homeland of the Tibetan people. Though nominally under Chinese suzerainty at an early date, effective integration into the Chinese state has only recently begun.

The broken country of Southwest China, including much of the plateau of Yunnan and the valleys of the great rivers which drain southwards from it, is occupied by a great variety of tribal peoples speaking languages of either the Sino-Tibetan or Austro-Asiatic families. Such peoples, as we have seen, formerly occupied much of subtropical China but were displaced southwards by the expansion of the Han people. Parts of this region show a well-marked ethnic zonation: the hot and humid valleys of rivers such as the Lancang or the Mekong are occupied by Mon-Khmer and Tai peoples; the high plateaux by Tibetans and the uplands by groups such as the Yi or Hani. Han settlers filtered in from the northeast and occupy intermediate levels.

As noted earlier, these groups differ from the Han people, and from one another, racially as well as culturally. The Turkic-speaking groups of Gansu and Xinjiang for example are basically Caucasoids, belonging to the Alpine branch of the white race. Caucasoid features are also evident among many of the southwestern minority peoples who appear to have originated from mixing between Mongoloids and wavy-haired, narrow-headed Caucasoids related on the one hand to the Mediterranean peoples of Europe and on the other to the peoples of Indonesia.

The diversity of languages is very great as can be seen from the table below:

THE MINORITY LANGUAGES OF CHINA

Family	Group	Branch	Area
Altaic	Turkic	Uighur, Uzbek, Kazakh & Kirghiz	Xinjiang & Gansu
	Mongol	Kalmuck Buryat	Inner Mongolia & Xinjiang
	Tungusic	Tungus	Inner Mongolia, Xinjiang, Lower Sungari
Sino-Tibetan	Tai-Zhuang	Zhuang, Tai	Southwest China
	Miao-Yao	Li, Miao, Yao	West & Southwest China
	Tibeto-Burman	Tibetan, Yi, Kachin	West & Southwest China
Austro-Asiatic	Mon-Khmer	Kawa, Palaung, Pu	Western Yunnan
Indo-European	Iranian	Tadjik	Southwest Xinjiang

A small vineyard in a commune in Northern China. In China, grapes are mostly eaten as fruit and are scarcely ever made into wine. Alcohol is made mostly from cereals such as rice and kaoliang. The diversity of climates in Agricultural China has meant that an enormous variety of fruits can be grown. As yet, however, fruit is not grown on a large scale, partly because of the cost of setting up plants for the treatment of fresh fruit and partly because of the lack of distribution outlets. For these reasons, most fruit is destined for local consumption. Of late years, there has been a considerable development of the fruit preserving industry.

Languages belonging to four of the world's major linguistic families are thus spoken by China's minority peoples. By far the most dominant is the Sino-Tibetan family (to which the Han speakers also belong): languages of this family are spoken by 75 percent of the population of national minorities. Some 24 percent speak Altaic languages, one percent Austro-Asiatic languages and about 0·1 percent of the non-Chinese speaking population speaks languages of the Indo-European family.

Languages of the Sino-Tibetan family are spoken by most of the minority peoples of the Southwest. This family includes the Tai-Zhuang group, some ten million strong (Zhuang 6·6 million, Tai 0·6 million); the Miao-Yao group totalling over three million (Miao 2·5 million, Yao 0·64 million); and the Tibeto-Burman group totalling 7·5 million (Yi 3·2 million, Tibetan 2·8 million, Kachin 0·11 million). The formerly much wider range of these groups is indicated by isolated islands, or "outliers," of Tibeto-Burman groups in northern Hunan and of Miao-Yao groups in the Jiangxi and Zhejiang hill country.

The heavily dissected upland country of the far Southwest, a typical "refuge zone," is also the home of the Mon-Khmer peoples; these too had a much wider distribution before being pushed south into the remote tropical valleys of the Yunnan-Burma border region.

Of these various languages Tibetan has a script of Indian origin. Most of the other languages either lacked a script or possessed scripts which are little suited to present-day needs. The traditional scripts of the Zhuang and Yi peoples were thus imitations of Chinese ideographs and known only to the initiated few; for others, such as Miao or Kawa, Christian missionaries devised phonetic scripts but these were not widely used and are unsatisfactory. Under these conditions the creation of new scripts for these minority peoples was an essential prerequisite to any advance, whether educational, political or social.

The Far West and the northern grasslands are the homeland of peoples who belong to the Ural-Altaic family. They include the Turkic (4·3 million), Mongol (1·5 million) and Tungus groups. Each group comprised a number of languages. Thus the Turkic group includes Uighur (3·6 million), Kazakh (0·47 million), Kirghiz (0·08 million), and Uzbek (0·01 million). In contrast to the minority peoples of the Southwest, these western and northern groups have long possessed their own scripts. Most of these are derived from the Koranic or Arabic script, though since 1955 the Mongols have used the Cyrillic script.

The religious diversity is great. The most important and the most widespread religion among the minority peoples is Islam, the faith of ten million people belonging to ten different national groups; these include most of the peoples of China's far Northwest such as the Uighurs, the Kazakhs and the Tadjiks. The Tibetans and Mongols are Lamaists. Other minority groups are Buddhists, Taoists, ancestor-worshippers or polytheists whose beliefs and practices include survivals of totemism and magic. There is also a small number of Christian converts.

Finally, there is great social and economic diversity. The Moslem peoples of China's Far West such as the Kazakhs, the

Right: illustrating the "Four Quarters" of China. Note the broad contrast between the rolling hills and plains of Eastern China and the high plateaux and basins of Western China. There is a great contrast between the plains of North China and the hill country of the South and between the Tibet-Qinghai Plateau and the mountains to the North.

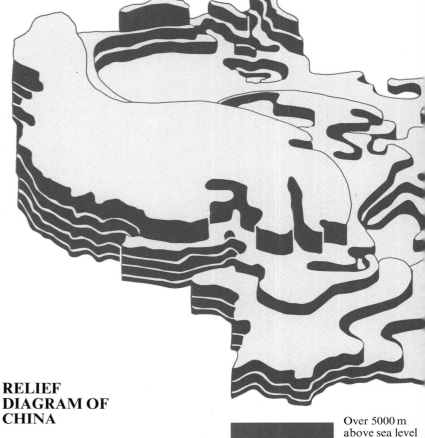

RELIEF DIAGRAM OF CHINA

	Over 5000 m above sea level
	From 3000–500
	From 2000–300
	From 1000–200
	From 500–100

In the drawings on these pages, we see the geological structure of the country depicted by artists in the course of the centuries. Above, the permian basalt rocks of Mount Emei in western Sichuan. Right: the topography of Guanxi; here, particularly around the city of Guilin, erosion of the underlying limestone has created what is perhaps the most striking example of karst landscape in the world.

Mount Guangwu, in the province of Henan (literally "south of the river," the Yellow River, that is). The western part of this province is formed of a region of hills and mountains in which many great tributaries of the Yellow River have their source. The eastern part is a huge alluvial plain. Because of their size, many rivers are used as boundaries or demarcations of territory.

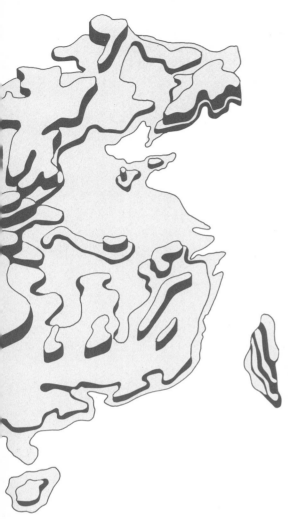

Left and below: two examples of the work of water as an erosive force in the mountainous East. In the first, we can see the rounded boulders left by fluvial erosion, and in the second, a platform of marine denudation with wave-cut arches.

A U-shaped glacial valley in the north of the province of Sichuan, with stratified rocks dipping to the right. Sichuan, which is to the west of the great northern plain of China and of the hilly South seems almost like another country which has been rather hastily tacked on to the other two regions. It is an extraordinarily fertile land and very densely populated. The western part of the province is, on average, some 3000 meters above sea level: narrow, deep valleys cut into a plateau which slopes gently down from the northwest to the southeast.

Uighurs or the Kirghiz are either oasis-cultivators or nomads who, until recently, lived in a feudal type of society which had changed little since the Moslem empires of the Middle Ages. The Mongols and a proportion of the Tibetans are pastoral nomads; the latter, in 1949, lived in one of the few surviving theocracies and were dominated by a small serf-owning class totalling possibly 50,000. The minority peoples of the uplands of the Southwest are, like related peoples in Southeast Asia, mainly primitive farmers practicing a shifting agriculture supplemented by hunting and food-gathering.

A. Palat, the Czech Sinologist, has given us a classification of the minority peoples based on social organization; his classification is as follows: 1. Nationalities with a rather developed system of feudal landlordship, sometimes penetrated by capitalist elements. Examples of groups falling into this category are the Huis, Zhuangs, Manchus, Uighurs and most of the Mongols. 2. Nationalities with a prevailing system of feudal serfdom. The Tibetans in 1949 fell into this category. 3. Nationalities where slavery still existed as a system. This category included some of the Southwest tribal peoples, notably the Yi. 4. Nationalities living in primitive communes or in various stages of transition between primitive communism and class society. This category included some of the tribal peoples of China's tropical zone and some of the groups along China's northern frontier.

There was thus a diversity of social structures which nonetheless had one thing in common: the underdevelopment of human and material resources which spelled poverty for the great mass of the people. And the new communist regime which came to power in 1949 perceived clearly that only by a drastic remodelling of society could the burden of poverty be lifted and a full utilization of the environmental and human resources of these minority regions be made possible.

Perhaps even more important has been the achievement of the present regime in wiping out the suspicion and fear and memories of exploitation from which many of the minority groups suffered. The old policies of assimilation and "divide and rule" have been rejected and the human diversity of China is recognized by a tiered system of administrative units. The present regime's policy towards the nation's minority groups is transforming the political, social and economic geography of the nation; it has created, perhaps for the first time in history, a real and living unity between the many peoples of China.

THE DIVERSITY OF THE CHINESE EARTH

The four quarters of China

To understand the structural pattern of the Chinese land we must refer briefly to the major tectonic elements distinguished by geologists; the most useful account is that of Li Si-guang (J. S. Lee). According to Li two major elements can be distinguished: a series of NE—SW trending fold zones and a series of generally

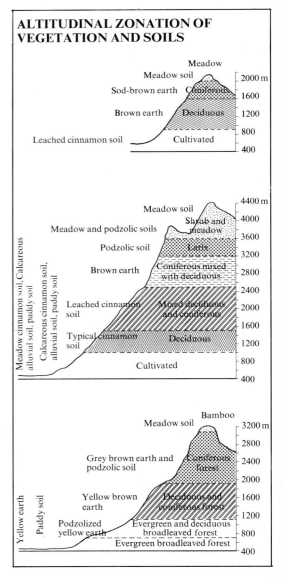

ALTITUDINAL ZONATION OF VEGETATION AND SOILS

This diagram shows the altitudinal variation of soil and vegetation types in three areas of Agricultural China. Top: a section of the northern hill country (between Liaoning and Hebei); in the center a section of a mountainous region of Central China (Daba Shan, Shaanxi); and below, Emei in Sichuan.

CLIMATIC REGIONS

The subdivision of China into climatic regions shows very clearly the wide extent of arid and cold climates.
1. Tropical climates;
2. Arid climates (Steppe); 3. Arid climates (Desert);
4. Mesothermal climate with rain all year round, mild winters, hot summers;
5. Mesothermal climate with summer maximum of rain, mild winters, hot summers;
6. Mesothermal climate with summer maximum of rain, cool summers;
7. Microthermal climate with cold winters, hot summers, summer maximum of rain;
8. Microthermal climate with cold winters, cool summers, very dry winters; 9. Tundra climates.

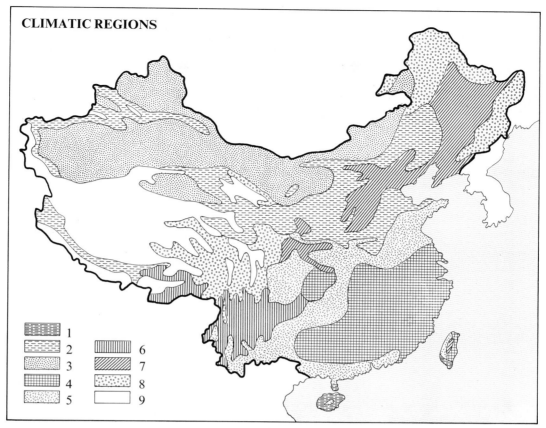

1. Coniferous forest-podzol region;
2. Mixed coniferous and broadleaved forests – podzol and brown forest soils;
3. Deciduous broadleaved forest – brown forest and cinnamon soils; 4. Mixed deciduous and evergreen broadleaved forests – yellow podzolic and yellow cinnamon soils; 5. Evergreen broadleaved forest – yellow and red podzolic soils; 6. Tropical monsoonal rain forest – yellow lateritic soils;
7. Forest steppe – chernozem and dry cinnamon soils;
8. Steppe – chestnut soils; 9. Mountains of Northwest China;
10. Semidesert and desert – sierozem and desert soils; 11. Plateaux of Eastern Tibet;
12. Tibetan plateau.

VEGETATION-SOIL REGIONS

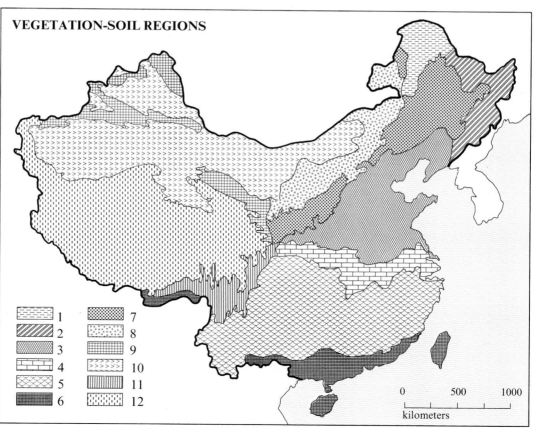

E–W trending folds; these two sets of elements give a "latticed," compartmentalized, structure to the country.

The first element, the fold zones, consists of a series of great upfolds and downfolds: the downfold represented by the Pacific Deep; the upfold which runs through Japan, the Liezhou Islands and Taiwan; the downfold of the Straits of Taiwan and the Korea Straits; the great upfold represented by the mountains of the South China coast, extending northwards to the mountains of Korea; and the upfold which runs from the Sikhota Alin of eastern Manchuria through the Liaotung Peninsula into Shandong.

To the west this last zone is flanked by the great downfold or trough which Li calls the "Neocathaysian geosyncline." This is a zone of accumulation of younger sediments and it is here that most of the key areas of Chinese history are to be found: the Great Plain, the central and lower valley of the Yangtze, and the Manchurian lowland. The disposition of the uplands, however, is such as to isolate most of this zone from the coast and indeed, as Joseph Needham has emphasized, this down-warped zone has contact with the sea at two points only: in the province of Hebei in the North and in the Yangtze delta area.

This downfold is bordered on the west by two "steps" which lead up to the high plateau of Tibet. These, according to Li, form part of a great upfold which begins in the north with the Great Xingan range, is continued by the Taihang Shan and the Gorge Mountains of the Yangtze, then by the eastern Guizhou Plateau and the Yaoshan of Guangxi. The highest step is formed by the margins of the Tibetan Plateau with the Daxue Shan running along the west of Yunnan, the Daliang Shan along the upper Yangtze and the Nan Shan to the northwest. These ranges all present their steepest face outwards to the east and to the north.

Cutting across these longitudinal zones are the latitudinal fold zones. Three such zones can be distinguished, framing the basins of Shaanxi and Sichuan, the Guizhou Plateau and what Needham terms "the southern marine amphitheatres," namely, Canton. The most northerly is the Yin Shan running E–W above the great northerly bend of the Yellow River and dividing Mongolia from the self-contained world of Guanzhong. The biggest of these E–W folds is that of the Tsin-ling, which continues the line of the Kun Lun mountains and which separates the Guanzhong area from the Red Basin to the south. The southernmost zone is much shattered; it is represented by the Nan Ling which separates the trough of the Neocathaysian geosyncline from the marine-oriented Canton lowland.

This pattern of intersecting longitudinal and latitudinal folds gives a gridded, compartmentalized build to much of China. We have a series of "core areas," of alluvial plains, coastal lowlands or interior basins, cut off from one another and from the sea by high and broken upland country. Four-fifths of China lies above the 500-meter contour and the height of many of the mountain chains leads to a marked zonation of vegetation and soil types (pages 69, 72–73, 75) and to wide expanses of thin vegetation and poor and shallow mountain soils, thus accentuating the compartmentalization of the country. To these difficulties we must add those arising from hydrographical factors. The deep

Above: a painting executed by the peasant artists of Huxian showing the members of a commune, men, women and children, engaged in a massive terracing project.

Opposite: an expanse of cultivated fields, in the vicinity of Canton, divided up by canals for irrigation. Although only 15 percent of the land of China is potentially cultivable, in 1971 the government announced that the country was completely self-sufficient in basic foods.

THE POETRY OF LANDSCAPE

From the earliest times, the countryside of China has been regarded as the proper place for poetic communion with nature. When the officials and men of letters spent time in their country houses, their favourite pastime was not hunting or horse-racing, but writing poetry. This is typical of a society which has always valued the "civil" above the "military," the exercise of the mind above that of the body. A love of nature, which was almost Romantic and which has only appeared in the West in the last three centuries, has always been a characteristic of the Chinese mentality, to the point where it is possible to glean very precise information about the physical aspects of the countryside from poetry. For many the word "China" conjures up a vision of a land of intensively cultivated alluvial lowlands, interrupted by the occasional spectacular holy mountain, and of meticulously terraced hills, the whole framed on the east by the sea and on the west by the Great Wall. In fact, such landscapes, while supporting the great majority of China's people, occupy no more than a quarter of the total area of the country.

For the poets the heart of China was Eastern China, more especially the level landscapes of the loess country and of the lowlands to the east. Its landscape was evoked by the 5th century poet Pao Zhao: "The immense plain / Runs south to the foamy waves of the sea / And north to the purple passes of the Great Wall. . . ."

It was an intensely humanized area. In it "Canals are cut through the valleys / And rivers and roads / Lead to every corner." This was the known landscape, "stern, sober and correct," contrasting sharply with the "strange

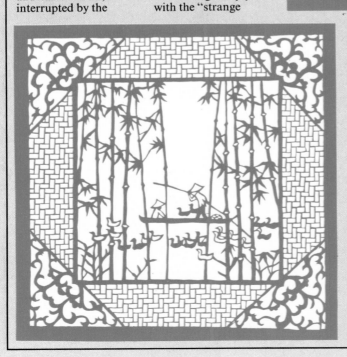

savage country"
beyond the Great Wall
and the Jade Gate.
Tsen Shen, writing in
the middle of the 8th
century, captures the
harshness of these
Western regions, in his
poem *The White Snow*:
"The North wind
sweeps across the
land, / Twisting and
tearing at the whitening
grass. / From the
barbarian sky fall the
first snowflakes of
August. . . ."
An altogether different
world is that of tropical
and subtropical China
which stretches south
from the cradle area of
the Han people. Today,
the extreme south is
part of the Republic of
China and its
countryside has found
new poets and artists to
sing its praises.
This Chinese sensitivity
to nature is illustrated
by these delicate paper-
cuts, an art form that is
one of the "poorest"
and oldest in the
history of Chinese
popular art, further
evidence of the refined
sensibility of the people
and their great
attachment to their
land.

down-cutting of many of the rivers in their upper reaches (e.g. Southwest China) makes them major barriers; it also results in a low base level for tributary streams and thus predisposes wide areas to soil erosion. Elsewhere, in the lower reaches of the rivers, where their momentum slackens, deposition of eroded materials builds up the river beds above the level of the flood plain so that the draining-off of surplus water is a major problem. And in the West huge areas are without any drainage to the sea, consisting of arid basins set within a frame of high, often snowcapped, mountains.

Needham has underlined the contrast with the much more favourable, because accessible, structure of Europe and draws attention to the immense difficulties of unifying, then holding together, a country so sundered by its physical conditions. And indeed the thorough and pervasive Sinicization of so much of China in the face of these difficulties was an achievement with few parallels anywhere in the world; it was carried through by what Teilhard de Chardin has termed, "an enormous mass of concentrated peasant."

Perpetual summer to perpetual winter
The great latitudinal and longitudinal extent of China, together with the great diversity of topographical conditions, is responsible for a wide variety of climatic conditions ranging from the perpetual frost climates of the Tibet-Qinghai plateau to the lands of perpetual summer such as the tropical valleys of the South. These directly influence the farming pattern through the limitations they may place on the length of the growing season (because of insufficient heat or insufficient moisture or a combination of both). Moreover, they exercise an important indirect influence on farming since they play a major role in the evolution of the soil/vegetation complex. And the variability and extremes of the climatic elements are an important challenge to the Chinese in their attempts to create a stable and high-yielding agriculture on which a modern economy can be based.

The basic contrast in climate is between the humid and subhumid East (the region Chinese geographers term the Eastern Monsoon Sector) and the arid or subarid West. But climatically, no less than topographically, each of these major regions itself can be subdivided: the East into the temperate and cold regions of the Northeast, sere and yellow in winter, and the perpetually green subtropical and tropical regions of Central and South China; the West into the cold winter-hot summer deserts of the Northwest and the cold high plateau of Tibet-Qinghai. Each of these four regions occupies approximately one-quarter of China.

Temperature contrasts are especially great in winter when cold air pours out of Inner Asia (the Mongolian steppes have a

A picture of the Yangtze, the longest river in China and the third longest in the world (5800 kilometers). In this part of Sichuan, the waters of the river have been brought under control by dams and reservoirs in a massive irrigation system, making possible the intensification and stabilization of crops over a wide area of the province.

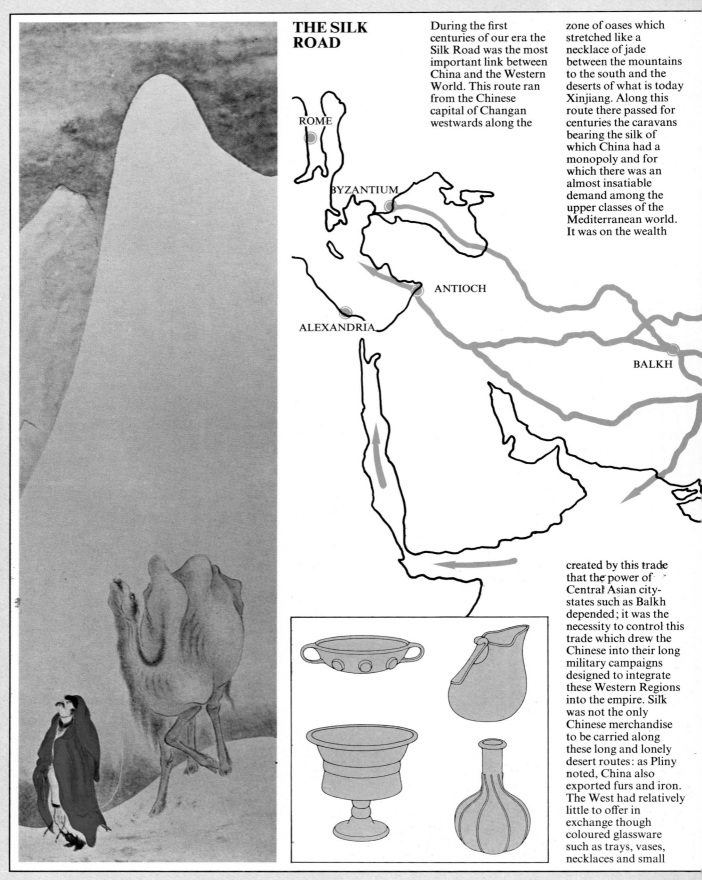

THE SILK ROAD

During the first centuries of our era the Silk Road was the most important link between China and the Western World. This route ran from the Chinese capital of Changan westwards along the zone of oases which stretched like a necklace of jade between the mountains to the south and the deserts of what is today Xinjiang. Along this route there passed for centuries the caravans bearing the silk of which China had a monopoly and for which there was an almost insatiable demand among the upper classes of the Mediterranean world. It was on the wealth created by this trade that the power of Central Asian city-states such as Balkh depended; it was the necessity to control this trade which drew the Chinese into their long military campaigns designed to integrate these Western Regions into the empire. Silk was not the only Chinese merchandise to be carried along these long and lonely desert routes: as Pliny noted, China also exported furs and iron. The West had relatively little to offer in exchange though coloured glassware such as trays, vases, necklaces and small

ROME

BYZANTIUM

ANTIOCH

ALEXANDRIA

BALKH

82

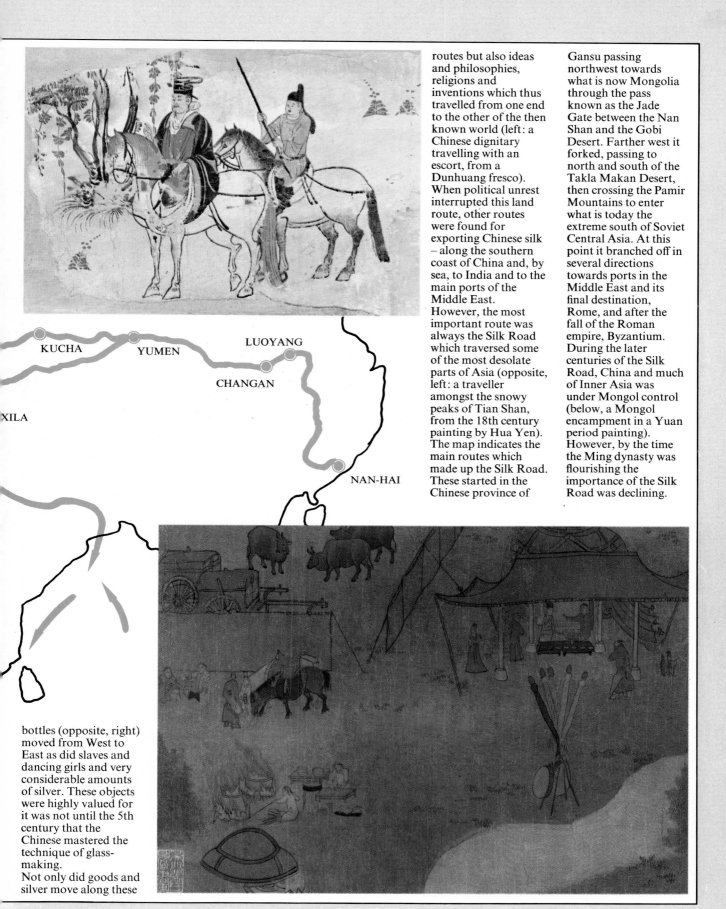

routes but also ideas and philosophies, religions and inventions which thus travelled from one end to the other of the then known world (left: a Chinese dignitary travelling with an escort, from a Dunhuang fresco). When political unrest interrupted this land route, other routes were found for exporting Chinese silk – along the southern coast of China and, by sea, to India and to the main ports of the Middle East. However, the most important route was always the Silk Road which traversed some of the most desolate parts of Asia (opposite, left: a traveller amongst the snowy peaks of Tian Shan, from the 18th century painting by Hua Yen). The map indicates the main routes which made up the Silk Road. These started in the Chinese province of Gansu passing northwest towards what is now Mongolia through the pass known as the Jade Gate between the Nan Shan and the Gobi Desert. Farther west it forked, passing to north and south of the Takla Makan Desert, then crossing the Pamir Mountains to enter what is today the extreme south of Soviet Central Asia. At this point it branched off in several directions towards ports in the Middle East and its final destination, Rome, and after the fall of the Roman empire, Byzantium. During the later centuries of the Silk Road, China and much of Inner Asia was under Mongol control (below, a Mongol encampment in a Yuan period painting). However, by the time the Ming dynasty was flourishing the importance of the Silk Road was declining.

KUCHA   YUMEN

LUOYANG

CHANGAN

XILA

NAN-HAI

bottles (opposite, right) moved from West to East as did slaves and dancing girls and very considerable amounts of silver. These objects were highly valued for it was not until the 5th century that the Chinese mastered the technique of glass-making.
Not only did goods and silver move along these

mean January temperature lower than −20°C) leading to a marked southward deflection of the isotherms. As a result, Peking, which is closer to the Equator than Naples, may experience winter freezing of the soil to depths of up to 50 centimeters. South China is, however, in part protected by the E–W ridges of the Qinling – Daba Shan from this outpouring of cold air and enjoys mild winters with mean January temperatures ranging from 4°C in the Yangtze valley to 20°C in Hunan. Summer temperature differences are much less; much of South and Central China has mean temperatures of 30°C in July but even north of the Great Wall mean temperatures for July are as high as 20°C.

The length of the frost-free period, which is so critically important to the farmer, reflects these contrasts. In the steppe lands north of the Great Wall it is scarcely more than three and a half months. At Peking it is somewhat over six months and the extreme south is virtually frost-free. So too is the heart of the Red Basin, sheltered in winter by mountains to the west and north and enjoying the "greenhouse effect" of a heavy cloud cover (the number of hours of sunshine in a year is only half the total in the Peking area); its year-round greenness contrasts sharply with the seasonal colour changes in the landscape below the Gorges.

Most of China's rainfall is derived from the summer monsoon winds drawn inland towards the low pressure zone of Central Asia; it therefore diminishes from south to north and with increasing distance from the sea. Subtropical China receives between 1500 and 2000 millimeters of rain yearly, the lower Yangtze between 1000 and 1250 millimeters and much of the North China Plain less than 500 millimeters. Towards the interior rainfall totals drop sharply, for the longitudinal zones of mountains intercept the rain-bearing winds blowing towards the interior; the area northwest of the Great Wall and in the rain shadow of the Xingan Mountains receives less than 50 millimeters of rain yearly and the mountain-girt basins of the Far West less than 20 millimeters.

Over one half of the area of China is either arid or semiarid. Only in favoured areas of this vast zone is dry farming or intensive irrigated cropping possible; the remainder of the area is suited only to extensive livestock production.

Drought and flood

So far we have been discussing climate in terms of averages, data for temperature or rainfall averaged out over periods of years. But to be realistic we have to stress that man does not live in this rather hypothetical set of average conditions but in a climate which varies greatly, and disastrously, from year to year. And for centuries the Chinese farmer, living so close to the soil, living too on a crop area derisory by European standards, has been tragically vulnerable to such variability.

In the more humid areas he has had to confront the menace of flood, due to the typhoons of late summer or to swollen rivers fed by heavy rains falling on steep and deforested hillsides. In the subhumid and semiarid areas – almost two-fifths of the country – drought has been the major menace, the greatest killer. For as

A shady corner of the Imperial Gardens in Peking which are now open to the public and thronged with crowds on public holidays.

Opposite: the Bund, the main street of Shanghai, which follows the left bank of the Yellow River. With an estimated population of around 12,000,000, Shanghai is the largest city in China and indeed in the whole of Asia. For more than 50 years a stronghold of foreign profiteers, since 1949 it has undergone a radical transformation and is now completely integrated in the social and economic structure of China.

A family walking in a street in Peking. The norm in China today is the two-offspring family, the children born two or three years apart. In towns, couples with only a single child are more common than in the country where the tradition of large families still survives. One of the measures taken to encourage population control was a campaign to discourage early marriage: today the average marrying age is 25 and single people and childless couples are extremely rare.

Opposite, above: a view of Tian-an-men Square, in Peking, the world's largest. In the foreground are the five marble bridges leading to the Gate of Heavenly Peace (Tian-an-men), gateway to the Forbidden City. In the background, the imposing edifice which houses the Assembly of the People. The square, which covers over 40 hectares, is the geographical, political and cultural center of Peking and the venue for the vast popular demonstrations of the last three decades. Below: another view of Peking: a quiet, tree-lined street by the waterside.

in so many parts of the world, as rainfall totals diminish, the variability tends to rise so that while the high rainfall areas have a variability of some 15 percent, where the annual totals drop below 500 millimeters the variability rises to over 30 percent. And these fluctuations tend to be particularly marked in June, the most critical month for the farmer; thus over a period of 55 years, Peking had a total of 21 in which the June rainfall was less than 50 millimeters and in five of these rainfall was below 10 millimeters. These are the fluctuations which caused the murderous drought-famines of the past. The data for the incidence of flood and drought in East China since the 17th century has been assembled by Co-ching Chu:

East China: Recorded Floods & Droughts						
Province	Floods			Droughts		
	17th century	18th century	19th century	17th century	18th century	19th century
Shandong	14	20	35	11	8	30
Jiangxi	28	37	41	11	5	24
Anhui	15	31	42	9	5	22
Zhejiang	13	16	27	20	8	15
Fujian	n.a.	n.a.	17	6	5	2

Climate cannot be changed but the disastrous impact of such variations can be attenuated by afforestation which controls run-off, shelter-belt plantings which create a favourable micro-climate, or water storage and irrigation which permit cropping even in years of low rainfall. But the individual peasant was unable to carry out any of these measures on his own. One of the most important results of the restructuring of Chinese rural society has been to overcome this helplessness and to make possible the completion of ambitious schemes of afforestation and water control which have wiped out the age-old vulnerability of the peasant in China's climatically marginal areas.

From ice-desert to tropical forest: soil-vegetation assemblages
The influences of topography, geology and climate are expressed in the soil-vegetation assemblages of China (pages 74–75). In areas such as the North China Plain these have been greatly modified by man but over wide areas the original soil-vegetation climax gives a broad indication of agricultural potentialities.

Since the character of the soil mantle is profoundly influenced by the character of the vegetation cover and since both reflect the influence of other elements of the environment, the soil- and plant-assemblages of China can conveniently be considered together. The same four-fold pattern we noted in the case of climate is repeated: a Western Region of deserts and grasslands, which can be subdivided into the high alpine-tundra region of Tibet-Qinghai; and the desert soils and cold desert vegetation of the Northwest mountain-and-basin region; and an Eastern Monsoonal Region which consists of coniferous or broadleaved deciduous forests, with podzol and brown forest soils, north of the Yangtze; and of evergreen broadleaved forests growing on red and yellow lateritic soils to the south. Each of these regions contains approximately one-quarter of the area of China.

In the northeastern quadrant of China, the western upland margins of the Manchurian lowland carry a coniferous forest vegetation; soils are leached and podzolic, with permafrost soils at higher elevations and the whole region is agriculturally marginal. But on the climatically less harsh eastern margins the dominant vegetation consists of mixed coniferous and deciduous forests growing on soils which vary from thin leached podzols on the hills to more fertile brown forest and alluvial soils at lower levels. The most fertile of these are important agriculturally, though the main arable region of Manchuria coincides with the forest-steppe zone, a zone of black earth or cinnamon-coloured soils, which occupies most of the lowland zone.

Southwards the climate is milder, with a growing season of 150–240 days. In Southern Manchuria and Shandong, this is the zone of deciduous forest and brown forest or cinnamon soils and it seems likely that the Great Plain of North China originally carried a vegetation-soil assemblage of this type. Today most of the plain is under a man-maintained "climax" vegetation of grain crops, soy beans and vegetables, but forest remnants around old temples and historical evidence provide a clue to the original plant cover and this gives a guide to tree species most likely to be of use in the protective and shelter-belt plantings which are key elements in the present program of agricultural development.

Beyond the transition zone of the Yangtze valley, a zone of mixed deciduous and evergreen forests, where the Han Chinese gained their first experience of the subtropical and tropical world, the southern quadrant of China is dominated by a great block of broadleaved evergreen forest; this originally extended over some 1·75 million square kilometers and was characterized by a great diversity of species but much has been cleared and it is now either cropland or open secondary forest and grassland. The upland soils are mainly red and yellow earths, fragile and with a low nutrient status, and this, together with the broken topography and climatic conditions which favour rapid tree growth, explains the emphasis on forestry development; by 1970 some 85 percent of China's commercial afforestation was concentrated in the lands to the south of the Yangtze. And in the extreme South this broadleaved evergreen forest gives place to tropical monsoon forest growing on red lateritic soils. This zone of a quarter of a million square kilometers, overlapping the Tropic of Cancer, is warm and moist and this is reflected both in the luxuriance of the vegetation, with a great profusion of lianas, climbing palms and epiphytes, and in the poverty of the soils whose humus is rapidly destroyed by the high temperatures and whose nutrients are removed by high rainfall. But the hot humid climate also makes possible multiple cropping, so much of the area has been cleared and the forest replaced by an artificial climax vegetation of crops. These include tree crops such as mulberry, lichee and citrus and, in recent years, rubber, cacao and coffee. And timber trees such as eucalyptus or poplar show phenomenal rates of growth in this tropical environment.

There is a striking contrast between these environments of the

Opposite: pictures of Peking life. Above, from the left: a modern underground station, a shop selling electrical goods, and a library.

Below: one of the city's many restaurants. A group of friends tries the "Mongolian stockpot," a Pekinese speciality. The copper stoves contain boiling water in which pieces of vegetables and slices of meat are cooked, then dipped in a variety of sauces.

Eastern Monsoon Sector and the harsh and agriculturally marginal environments of Western China.

Most of the southwestern quadrant of China, the Tibetan-Qinghai region, lies between 4000 and 5300 meters above sea level. Rainfall may be as little as 100 millimeters, winter temperatures as low as $-16°C$ and only on the southeastern margins do summer temperatures reach $10°C$. Cropping potentialities are confined to the Lhasa valley which has a five-months growing season while the humid eastern borderlands of the plateau are clothed in dense coniferous forests (representing China's biggest reserves of softwood outside Manchuria). The main plateau block (which has an area of 1·75 million square kilometers) is fringed by forest on its warmer margins but the plateau surface itself has a thin salt-tolerant scrub or grass vegetation growing on alpine meadow or desert soils. It has only a very sparse nomadic population and such agricultural and pastoral settlement as there is is largely confined to the southeast margins towards the Cangbu valley.

The northwestern quadrant of China, extending from the Kunlun Mountains towards the Altay Mountains and the Sino-Soviet boundary, comprises almost two million square kilometers. With the exception of the mountain ranges, which break the region into a series of basins, the area has less than ten millimeters of rainfall, with severely cold winters (January mean varies from $-6°C$ to $-20°C$) but hot summers ($24°C$ to $26°C$, reaching $33°C$ in the Hami and Turfan depression). Soils are mainly unstable desert sands and sand and dust storms may occur at any season. The vegetation of such sands is grass or scrub, sparse in distribution and salt-and-drought-tolerant. But along the fringes of the sand plains the junction of basin floor and fringing mountains is masked by fluvioglacial gravels, well watered and supporting a relatively luxuriant deciduous vegetation and important areas of intensive oasis-style cultivation. The mountains are characterized by a pronounced altitudinal zonation of vegetation and soils, ranging from the steppe vegetation and chestnut soils at their feet, through coniferous forest with grey leached soils to high-level alpine meadows. This juxtaposition of contrasting environmental zones provides the setting for a transhumant economy which uses the high-level grazings during the brief summer period.

In earlier pages we have emphasized the immensely long history of man in China and his gradual but cumulative modification of the Chinese environment. The evidence of both history and soil profiles demonstrates that Old China was a land of forests; these, however, have been destroyed over extensive areas and even the shrub and grass vegetation which replaced them has been grubbed for use as fuel. By 1949 less than one-tenth of the country was forested, major reserves were confined to inaccessible and thinly-peopled areas, and in the densely-settled provinces of the East and the developing provinces of the Northwest, forest occupied less than 0·5 percent of the land area. This deforestation, by reducing the water retaining capacity of the land, accelerated erosion, encouraged flooding and was an important cause of rural impoverishment.

The soil pattern and the hydrological processes have likewise

A peasant takes his vegetables to market by bicycle. The communes reserve a small percentage of land for cultivation by individual families, where they can grow vegetables and rear livestock.

Opposite: there are many street markets in the cities where the peasants from the communes can sell the produce from their private plots of land.

been transformed by the activities of countless millions of peasants, extending back in some regions over four millennia. One of the most obvious manifestations of this is to be seen in the zones of high fertility which surround all the great cities of China. This is the result of the continuous transfer of nutrients from often distant hinterlands which supply the cities with food; the organic and nutrient content of this food, in the form of human excreta, is eventually returned to the soils of the peri-urban area and these show a very high humus, nitrogen and base content which makes possible high and stable yields. The use of night soil diminishes sharply with increasing distance from the city so these are surrounded by concentric zones of diminishing fertility and decreasing lushness.

Man's activity results in other and equally important changes in soil conditions. The major rivers remove from their upper reaches great quantities of soil and this is transported and redistributed over the alluvial lowlands to the east. Part at least of this load is further redistributed by the canal systems which, over the centuries, man has built up in the plains. And the digging and the cleaning of the canals further transforms the soil pattern; the earth and mud are piled on the fields, creating what are, in effect, artificial meadow soils which may add a depth of 50–100 centimeters to the original soil profile. And the deliberate working into the soil of sand or, as in Sichuan, shales with a high mineral content, similarly creates a specific "cultural layer" whose thickness may vary from 20 to 50 centimeters.

We have seen how the adoption of irrigation gave an "evolutionary bias" to Chinese society at a very early date; it similarly played a decisive role in the shaping of the Chinese land. For irrigation demands level surfaces over which the water can be distributed and this involved the conversion of even gentle slopes into "micro-plains" separated by vertical terrace walls and on these terrace surfaces distinctive "meadow-bog soils," ideal for rice cultivation, are developed. Such terrace systems are most strikingly developed in Sichuan, the loess regions of the Northwest and the South China hill country.

And finally, in the lowland areas irrigation has a two-fold role: to maintain high ground-water levels in the dry season and drain off excess water in the wet season. Ground-water levels – and conditions of soil formation – are thus largely man-controlled in much of China. The best example is the Grand Canal which is not only a waterway but also plays a major role in regulating the water regime over the eastern section of the Great Plain.

Plagues, pests and parasites: the biological environment
So far we have been concerned with the visible physical environment of human life in China. But we cannot ignore, because it is for the most part unseen, the biological environment as represented by the great complex of diseases and parasites which take such a toll in human suffering and death and which are of primary importance in understanding the problems of poverty and backwardness.

Max Sorre, in his map of major disease realms, distinguishes China as a subdivision of his Pacific Region. It is a region

One of the large covered markets of Peking. Until a few years ago, these had all the features of the oriental bazaar, with stalls and kiosks spread all over the place in picturesque disorder. One of the best-known was the "Market of Eastern Peace."

Besides being one of the commercial centers of the capital, it was also a favourite meeting place. During the cultural revolution, these markets were "restructured" to make them more efficient, the stalls strictly arranged according to type of merchandise. The provision of food to the markets is guaranteed by the communes located in the vicinity.

characterized by cholera and plague, by malaria, kala-azar and leprosy and by a variety of parasitic worms. The literary evidence alone suggests that many of these diseases have a long history in China.

There are three main insect-transmitted diseases whose distribution is governed by the ecological preferences of their vectors. Malaria, a mosquito-transmitted disease, is a typical disease of tropical and subtropical China. For breeding, the mosquito prefers the water of upland streams and avoids the saline or muddy waters of the delta lands or the rice fields. Part of the aversion of the Han people to the upland regions is undoubtedly to be explained in terms of this disease; as late as the 1930s some two-thirds of the population of Central China were affected by it. Kala-azar, which brings about spleen and liver changes and growing emaciation, is transmitted by the bite of an infected sandfly. It is as northern in its distribution as malaria is southern and in 1949 it was endemic in 12 provinces north of the Yangtze. And typhus, a lice-borne disease, could become epidemic in winter when cold led to the close crowding of people in squalid housing.

Parasitic worm infections, long a major cause of peasant ill-health, were encouraged by the moist soils and open channels of the irrigation system and by the universal use of human excreta to maintain fertility. Similarly, the moist environment of irrigated farming was essential to the survival of the freshwater snail which served as an intermediate host in the infection cycle of schistosomiasis. Surveys in the early 1950s showed that some ten million people suffered from this disease and that possibly 100 million were at risk. And hookworm, again a disease of the warmer humid areas, affected between 50 and 100 million people. The ravages of this "unseen environment" in pre-1949 China can scarcely be overemphasized. And yet there was no inevitability about this pattern – the past 30 years have shown that, given technical knowledge, a favourable socioeconomic organization and the necessary drugs or prophylactics, the biological environment can be transformed as dramatically as the physical.

THE SHAPING OF MODERN CHINA

The population of the People's Republic of China is stated to have reached 975 million in 1978; this is an increase of almost 400 million on the total recorded in the 1953 census.

More striking, it is over twice the population of the country in those prewar days when politicians and other experts were concluding that the Chinese population problem was insoluble. The then United States Secretary of State, Dean Acheson, in a letter to President Truman, spoke of the "unbearable pressure on the land"; he added, "The first problem every Chinese Government has had to face is that of feeding the population. So far none has succeeded."

That the Chinese have succeeded in proving wrong such prophets of gloom, that they have been able to feed adequately, to clothe and to provide an increasing range of services for their

An impressive view of the Yellow River (5,464 kilometers), the second longest in China after the Yangtze. This great river passes through regions of easily eroded soils, the silt from which in the course of time has raised the level of the riverbed, forcing the river to find other courses. Over the centuries, this has led to disastrous flooding. The construction of dams and dykes has removed this danger and harnessed the huge potential of the river for the production of hydroelectric power.

Opposite: the island of Orfana on the Yangtze with its monastery; in the foreground, fishing boats. The Yangtze, like all the rivers of Southeast China, has a regular flow and is navigable along most of its course. In its upper reaches, its waters are used to provide electricity. In the fertile basin of the Yangtze, which covers about 19 percent of Chinese territory, nearly 300 million people work and live.

immense population – this must rank as one of the most important developments of our time. Comparison with other Third World nations, many of which have become increasingly dependent on food imports, underlines the magnitude of the achievement.

And second only to the eradication of hunger in importance has been the diversification of the whole economy; lack of diversity was a major cause of poverty in Old China and, though the late 19th and early 20th centuries saw some degree of industrialization in the Treaty Ports of the east coast, industry's share in the combined output of industry and agriculture was no more than one-third in 1949. By 1979 it had risen to almost three-quarters of a greatly expanded national output and China had made a decisive transition from a dominantly agrarian nation to a nation with an increasingly sophisticated mixed economy.

These remarkable achievements must be a central theme in any discussion of the geography of modern China.

For what we have to do is to provide an understanding of a process of economic and social development and of landscape change which in terms of its scale and its speed is without any parallel in human history. It is, moreover, an ongoing process; the changes to date are, the Chinese stress, but "one step in a thousand-league march," and this means that simple description is not enough, for any descriptive account becomes rapidly dated. What we have to attempt is to interweave description with an analysis of the processes of change which have transformed the landscape, no less than the social and political structures of the country.

And at this point the contrast between the landscapes of China and the landscapes of our Western world must be stressed. The latter, the landscapes with which we are most familiar, have been shaped by the play of the free-enterprise system. The landscapes of China, by contrast, and this includes the patterns of both agriculture and industry, are increasingly planned landscapes, moulded in a distinctive way and in the light of certain clear-cut ideas on "the good life" which are very different from our Western concepts. Under these conditions, if we are to understand the geography of China today, we must have a clear awareness of the "point of departure" of Chinese society in 1949, and we must understand and concern ourselves even more with the direction and purpose of development and with its ultimate objectives. And this direction and purpose have their roots in the Sinicized form of Marxism developed by Mao Zedong and his successors, a doctrine which, it is claimed, furnishes the broad lines of a solution to many of China's problems and which has as a major goal the eradication of poverty through the building of a socialist society.

Development: the Chinese way

In 1949 China was a classic example of an underdeveloped country. Its economy was ramshackle and undiversified, unable to provide an adequate level of living for more than a favoured few. The majority lived briefly and lived precariously – ill-fed, ill-clothed, ill-housed, disease-ridden and illiterate.

CONTROL OF THE WATERS

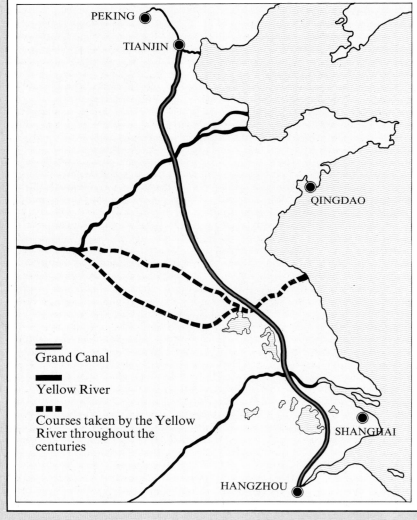

Schemes for water storage and river-control have always figured large in the history of China. Such schemes have had both an agrarian (dykes and irrigation canals) and a non-agrarian importance (aqueducts and navigation canals). It has induced some scholars (Wittfogel for example) to define Chinese society as "hydraulic" or "agro-bureaucratic," with a tendency to require the subordination of all individual and private interests in order that the State may have absolute power to set in motion the organization and planning of great water control schemes. It is noteworthy that, in Chinese mythology, supreme importance is attached to the control of the waters, notably so in the case of the first emperor of the Xia dynasty, Yu the Great (shown opposite, above) who, even before his coronation, had become famous for winning control over the waters after the Great Flood which, according to Chinese tradition, lasted from 2085 to 2072 B.C. In historical time, directions regarding water control (and other related works such as canals, bridges, barges and ferries) are contained in statute books and written orders, as evidence of the control which the State exercised in this matter. With the accession of the Tang dynasty, water legislation became more precise and, as well as serving as a model for other countries (Japan, Korea and Burma), provided a basis for much of the subsequent control organization. In order to administer effectively all the activities associated with water, there was a department responsible "for rivers, trenches, pools and lakes of the Empire" which kept records of all rivers, springs, tributaries and bridges. As well, there was a Directorate of Waterways which was responsible for water transport and fishing and which divided responsibility for irrigation and water conservation with the Department of Rivers. Irrigation of the cropland and especially the paddy-fields (engraving on opposite page (above)) has always been a major problem in China; traditional methods of irrigation were crude but effective. Two such methods can be seen in the engravings on the lower half of the opposite page. One of the peculiar features of Chinese law, which may be seen in the water legislation, was the concept of the personal responsibility of the individual administrator in the public service. These officials were personally responsible not only in cases of negligence or wrong-doing, but also in the event of damage or loss through natural causes. The offence of causing a flood was considered a very grave one. In 29 B.C., after the dam on the Yellow River burst, the Grand Secretary of the Department of Rivers committed suicide. In the map on the left, we see the route of the Grand Canal and the modifications in the course of the Yellow River throughout the centuries.

PEKING

TIANJIN

QINGDAO

SHANGHAI

HANGZHOU

Grand Canal

Yellow River

Courses taken by the Yellow River throughout the centuries

閑午風視
與滾北笈
挪擲不停
亂行我教
勞民莫忍

高轉筒車

踏車

And like all countries facing such problems of poverty and underdevelopment China had three options open to it: it could follow the Western pattern of free-enterprise development; it could follow the Soviet model of development or, alternatively, it could pioneer a "Third Way," drawing on the experience of other countries but modifying these models in the light of conditions specific to China.

The Chinese rejected both the Western and Soviet models. This they did partly for historical reasons, partly because such models offered no solution to the problems of a peasant country almost entirely lacking in infrastructure and characterized by a very high density of population. And in the formulation of an alternative development strategy they were greatly influenced by historical factors, by the very ancient Chinese tradition of State participation in economic life, as well as by the more recent experience accumulated in the guerrilla base-regions during the long years of civil war and the war which preceded the communist victory.

Over the last 30 years they have shown that an alternative strategy to that of the two great power blocks is not only possible but that such a strategy can be so devised as to provide a solution to many of the problems which appear insuperable to most nations of the Third World. And while the Chinese model cannot be taken as a blueprint for the successful development of other societies (the Chinese themselves are the first to insist on the highly specific character of their strategy), the originality of their approach to social and economic development, to the problems of the agricultural sector and the techniques of industrialization, to the whole question of how educational and welfare systems may be devised so that they serve as agents of liberation rather than tools of manipulation – the originality of their approach in these issues does contain lessons for the peoples of both the developed and underdeveloped countries.

The parameters of the Chinese experiment may be summarized thus:

– the need to develop agriculture in order to wipe out famine and to create the necessary food surplus on which diversification of the economy ultimately depends;

– the recognition that society will continue to be a peasant society and that development of the peasant sector depends on the vulgarization of new and improved techniques, contingent on real changes in land tenure; on the creation of new forms of rural organization and the encadrement and education of the peasant so that new ideas may be swiftly diffused;

– the need for structural change so as to mobilize the full human potential of the masses. This means the replacement of élites by new community institutions; the development of community-controlled welfare and education systems; the integration of all groups (especially those who have long been marginalized because of race, sex or social class) into the development process;

– the recognition of the primacy of the employment problem. This means the rejection of urban-based, capital-intensive models; the careful integration with agriculture of small and medium-scale industry (industries producing or servicing

River transport in a drawing of the Song dynasty. Two long oars, one at the prow, the other at the stern, are used to steer and move the boat.

Below: a modern barge. Waterways have always played a highly important role in the social and economic development of China. Traffic is heavy on the navigable stretches of river and the countless canals.

agricultural machinery; industries processing agricultural raw materials; or industries whose labour needs can be integrated with the seasonal labour needs of agriculture);

– a strong emphasis on self-reliance, manifested by dependence on national or local markets, rather than on overseas markets, and on the creation of balanced communities which offer full scope to individual potential and whose level of well-being is sufficiently high to make mass exodus to the bright lights of the city unecessary;

– the recognition that, once the appropriation of rural surplus by local or outside groups has been arrested, this surplus should be channeled into the public sector to create the maximum diffusion of well-being. Since the wealth of the community is measured not by the abundance of goods each individual can lay his hands on but by the abundance of goods accessible to the community as a whole, such a policy is completely compatible with a policy of individual austerity;

– the recognition that development is a political process, inspired by a particular vision of man and society; that it can be carried through only by the masses themselves. Mao observed, "The knowledge which enables us to grasp the laws of the world must be redirected to the practice of changing the world," and this is especially true of the process of development. The sort of mass participation involved demands careful and dedicated political education at the grass-roots level. It is largely in the failure to recognize this that the explanation for the faltering progress – or the stagnation – of so many developing societies must be sought.

Let us now look at the "point of departure" of this immense experiment.

Point of departure

By the 19th century, as we have seen, the effect of the agricultural revolutions of the earlier period, revolutions based less on changes in technology than on the introduction of new crops, had been cancelled out by population growth. Industrialization which, by diversifying the economy, would have increased the carrying-capacity of the Chinese earth was impeded by institutional factors and by the country's semicolonial status. The result was increasing population pressure leading to growing impoverishment, social and political instability and, ultimately, to declining rates of population growth. Much of Chinese society existed on the brink of starvation; and so delicate was the balance, that drought or flood could precipitate famines which killed millions of people. China became the prime example of "overpopulation," the classic "land of famine."

The collapse of the Manchu empire and the establishment of the Republic in 1911 changed nothing, for the sickness of society was too deep-rooted. The countryside was ravaged by warlords, its economy warped and plundered by outside interests based on the Treaty Ports and by their local collaborators, the comprador group. By the 1930s administrative incompetence, the ravages of war (including the civil war), the strangling hold of the landlord group on the peasant masses and of Chinese capitalists and outside interests on the truncated economy of the

coast cities, all these combined to plunge the Chinese people, almost one-quarter of humanity, into a nightmare existence of hunger and impoverishment. These were the days when the streets of great cities such as Shanghai were littered with the victims of cold and starvation, when the peasant survived by eating grass and roots and by selling the children he could not feed. The point reached for the great majority was the level of mere survival, a subhuman level below anything ever experienced in the West, even in the darkest and hungriest days of the Great Depression.

We can learn something of the quality of life in those days – and understand better the communist success in 1949 – from the novels of writers such as Pearl Buck (*The Good Earth*) or Evan King (*Children of the Black-Haired People*). The poets of China capture for us the horrors of life in the great and impersonal cities of the coast, specially Shanghai, which for Tsung K'o-chia represented "The Zero Degree of Life," a "society where man eats man." But the most vivid accounts are those of older peasants who somehow survived these bitter years, accounts recorded by Jan Myrdal in his remarkable volume *Report from a Chinese Village*. The beginning of Fu Hai-tsao's account of his life for example:

> "We came to Yenan from Hangshan when I was five. That was during the great famine of 1920. We had been thrown out. My father brought the family with him here. Father starved to death the next year. We went about begging in 1929. We had nothing to eat. Father went to Chaochuan to gather firewood and beg food, but he didn't get any. He was carrying elm leaves and firewood when he fell by the roadside.... He was lying on his face and was dead. The elm leaves and the firewood were still there beside him. No one had touched a thing. The elm leaves were for us to eat. He wasn't ill; he had just starved to death.... That is my earliest memory; of always being hungry, and of father lying there dead in the road."

These stories, multiplied by the tens of millions, give us some understanding of what it was like to live in Old China, of the living which was a kind of dying.... They underline the marginal quality of life for the rural masses, of life balanced always on the knife edge of starvation; they focus attention on the poverty which was the product of an undiversified and highly seasonal agricultural system with its inevitable underemployment or unemployment; they emphasize the power of the landlord group which, through its control of much of the country's arable land, possessed the power of life and death over the peasant. Above all, such fragments of autobiography illustrate the vulnerability of the individual peasant family confronted by natural disasters such as drought or flood. And unless we understand this marginal and precarious quality of existence we will find ourselves unable to understand the transformation of the rural scene since 1949, above all the complete restructuring of rural society which has taken place and the preoccupation of the new society with peasant welfare and peasant security.

The physical and social roots of poverty

In an earlier section we have described the elements in the physical environment which gave birth to such an attitude. Because of elevation or difficult topography or poor soils, possibly not more than one-fifth of the country is suited to intensive cropping. Climate factors have in the past been a major cause of poverty: over one-half of the country is arid or semi-arid and much of the moister eastern half of China is plagued by a high year-to-year variability in rainfall totals.

Famine caused by drought has been a major cause of poverty and until the most recent period of Chinese history has periodically wiped out millions of people. Alexander Hosie has shown that, over the thousand years between 630 and 1620, 610 were drought years in one province or another and 203 of these were years of serious famine. Such droughts are especially typical in the North China Plain and on the Loess Plateau where rainfall totals, even in an average year, are low and where there is a high year-to-year variability. In Central and South China excess of rain may be as damaging as shortage farther north, such excess leads to widespread flooding and loss of crops and of human life especially in those areas where the great rivers flow in dyked courses high above level and densely settled alluvial lowlands. The menace has been increased in recent centuries by deforestation of the hills which led to more rapid runoff and to erosion which provided the silt which built up the beds of rivers such as the Yangtze and Yellow River high above the levels of the surrounding lowlands.

And more localized natural calamities: earthquakes in the loess region of the Northwest and tropical cyclones in the coastal regions of the Southeast, even when they did not directly cause famine, certainly aggravated famine due to other causes.

Biological factors add to poverty; these include animal and insect pests and the diseases peculiar to subtropical and tropical regions and those which are both a cause and a result of poverty. Locusts ravage crops and cause famine on the subhumid fringe of Northwest China.

But the impact of all these natural factors was, in Old China, aggravated by social conditions. As Josué de Castro remarks, "The so-called natural causes [of famine] are only the immediate factors, and are themselves the result of social causes in the background, of factors inherant in the structure of the Chinese economy." In other words, if the social environment had not been so favourable to the spread of calamity, the impact of flood or drought or disease would have been far more limited. And the major social factor which magnified the effects of catastrophes was the landholding system. Holdings were small and production levels low, yet in many areas the landlords took between one-third and one-half of the crop as rent; it was thus impossible for the individual peasant family to accumulate those reserves of grain which would have cushioned its members against the impact of drought or flood.

Social structure, overpopulation and hunger

The relationship between the landholding system and the problems of "overpopulation" and hunger can be illustrated by

Opposite: barges adapted for transporting cotton. The rivers are constantly being improved for navigation, either by operations which control the flow of the waters or by the construction of flood gates.

Above: transportation of timber by river. The rafts are borne along by the current, a section of tree-trunk serving as a rudder.

conditions in a small community in northern Jiangsu; the data, taken from the investigations of René Dumont, are summarized below:

Class	Number of Families	Arable Land (ha)	Number of Buffaloes
Landlords	12	441	—
Rich Peasants	45	24	45
Middle Peasants	11	6·4	26
Poor Peasants & Wage Earners[1]	845	—	3
TOTAL	913	471	74

1. Including 314 middle peasant families, possessing farming equipment and sometimes draught animals, but without land.

The number of people supported by the community's 471 hectares of arable land was 3936; they lived in ten small villages within an area two by two and a half kilometers square. The "nutritional density," the density per unit-area of cropland, was 837 per square kilometer; 93 percent of the land was, however, in the hands of a dozen landlords and the great majority of the peasants existed by farming tiny pieces of rented land. Rents were exorbitant: 43 percent of a normal year's harvest, which meant almost 5000 quintals of the total production of 12,250 quintals; even if the crops were ruined by flood, rents were still due. And in spite of heavy population pressure and hunger, 40 hectares remained uncultivated because the rents demanded were beyond the capacity of the peasants to pay.

The poverty of the peasant meant that his equipment was poor, manuring was inadequate and cultivation ineffective; the rich peasant achieved yields of 38 quintals to the hectare while the poorer peasant on a contiguous plot attained only 21 quintals.

This single community showed, in sharp focus, the two basic agrarian issues which, in the last generation, the Chinese people have had to tackle: first, the isolation and the helplessness of the individual peasant family; secondly, the monopolization of the land and of other productive resources by a corrupt and rapacious landlord group.

Land reform: transition to a cooperative agriculture

The success of the communist movement in China was due in large measure to the understanding of the agrarian situation shown by the communist leaders and especially Mao Zedong. They realized that the poor peasant group, the great mass of the landless and most severely exploited, represented the critical group; in Mao's words, "Without the poor peasants there would be no revolution. To deny their role is to deny the revolution." They realized too the need for involving the middle peasants in the struggle to build a new society; from this emerged the policy of "resolutely relying on the poor peasant and firmly uniting with the middle peasants." And the correctness of this analysis, which derived from long years of experience of handling peasant problems acquired in the communist base region in Shanxi-Shaanxi, was demonstrated in 1949 when peasant armies broke

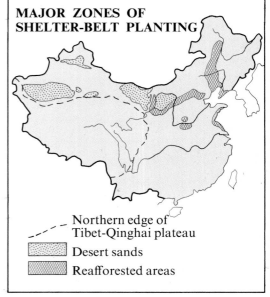

MAJOR ZONES OF SHELTER-BELT PLANTING

— · — Northern edge of Tibet-Qinghai plateau

▨ Desert sands

▨ Reafforested areas

These plantings are designed to protect the agricultural lands of the margins of Eastern China from the winds sweeping out of Central Asia and to stabilize some of the major areas of desert sands. Smaller schemes are designed to protect the coast zone and the more erosion-susceptible areas of the margins of the loess country.

Opposite: illustrating the major water conservancy schemes and the most important hydraulic engineering plants built in the last few years. These, linked with smaller commune-constructed projects, have now given the Chinese a high degree of control over flood and drought, two great scourges of pre-revolutionary China.

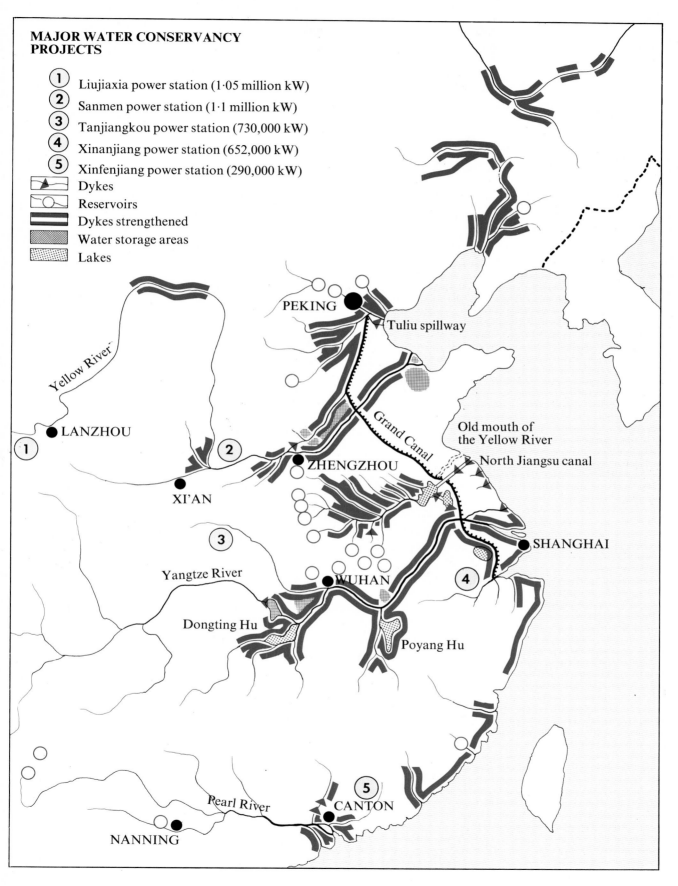

MAJOR WATER CONSERVANCY PROJECTS

1. Liujiaxia power station (1·05 million kW)
2. Sanmen power station (1·1 million kW)
3. Tanjiangkou power station (730,000 kW)
4. Xinanjiang power station (652,000 kW)
5. Xinfenjiang power station (290,000 kW)

Dykes

Reservoirs

Dykes strengthened

Water storage areas

Lakes

Yellow River

LANZHOU

XI'AN

ZHENGZHOU

Grand Canal

PEKING

Tuliu spillway

Old mouth of the Yellow River

North Jiangsu canal

SHANGHAI

Yangtze River

WUHAN

Dongting Hu

Poyang Hu

Pearl River

CANTON

NANNING

the power of the Guomindang and established in Peking the first communist government in Asia.

The first major structural change carried out by the new government was a complete transformation of the landholding system; this was applied to all areas except the Shanxi-Shaanxi border region (where the communist administration had carried out land reform in the late 1920s) and the areas inhabited by national minorities. The landlord group was dispossessed, in many cases physically eliminated, and the land passed to the tiller. This was achieved not by simple legislation but by teaching the peasants what their new rights were and arousing them to demand these rights. Such a process of involving the peasants themselves in the process of land reform was an important form of political education.

It soon became clear that a program of "The land to the tiller" was but the first stage in a long process of experimentation, advance, and consolidation. For while the abolition of landlordism improved the lot of the poorer peasants who now kept the grain formerly appropriated by the landowners, they still could not greatly increase output; some had land and no equipment to work it, some had work-animals and not enough land to employ the animals fully, yet others still had plots too small to be worked efficiently. The development of mutual aid teams, of the lower-stage cooperatives, then of the advanced cooperatives, can be regarded as attempts to overcome these contradictions and others which emerged as production, and earnings, began to increase and as the infrastructure of agriculture such as drainage and irrigation schemes became more complex. By 1957 the "advanced cooperatives" had become the norm and China's 500 million peasants were organized into some 740,000 advanced cooperatives, each consisting of some five original cooperatives and between 150 and 175 households.

These changes in agricultural organization illustrate what has been a distinctive feature of Chinese development since 1949, that is the "chain-reaction" quality of institutional and environmental change. For social change, and especially land reform, made possible the shaping of a new environment but, at the same time, the very processes of remodelling the environment stimulated further institutional change; as one Chinese writer expressed it, "As man transformed nature, their own way of thinking was transformed too." And with the development of the advanced cooperatives a whole series of new contradictions made further institutional change inevitable. There were contradictions between cooperatives in the implementation of major schemes of water conservation and irrigation; contradictions within the cooperatives themselves between the unit for accounting and the unit for production; contradictions too between the economic unit and the administrative unit. These were largely solved by the creation of the People's Communes.

By late 1958 the 740,000 cooperatives had been merged into 26,000 communes. The average commune thus consisted of almost 30 advanced cooperatives and had a population of some 20,000. Its area was usually coextensive with that of the country or *xiang* so that the contradiction between the administrative

Workers engaged in drilling a well. A painting by peasant artists from Huxian.

Opposite: students from Peking University mobilized in building an earth dyke in the vicinity of the Summer Palace. The mobilization of the masses and the call for voluntary work has been, especially during the early years of the People's Republic, a factor of not inconsiderable importance for the economy of the country, particularly since China has a long way to go before achieving the technological level of Western industrial societies.

unit and the economic unit was eliminated and the administration of county and commune could be merged. More important was the fact that these bigger units, with greater resources of capital and manpower and often taking in a whole river basin or catchment area, were able to confront far more effectively than the smaller cooperative those schemes of water conservation, irrigation and afforestation which were clearly the next tasks which the peasant masses had to undertake if they wished to create a solid base for rural development.

The economic and social role of the People's Commune

One of the most important functions of the commune has been its role as a means of mobilizing the enormous latent productivity represented by the unemployed and underemployed masses of rural China. The huge population of China, conventionally regarded as a burden, has become "an enormous source of capital accumulation [devoting] part of its labour . . . to the increase of the productive potential of the country."

As long ago as 1954 René Dumont had recognized the critical importance of achieving such a mobilization if the Asian nations were to emerge from underdevelopment and poverty. Applied to such things as irrigation, drainage and flood control such labour investment would raise the levels of food production and thus the productivity of the labour force; the old vicious circle in which malnutrition led to low productivity and this in turn intensified malnutrition would be broken.

Yet because much of this labour potential consisted of seasonally underemployed or unemployed workers it could not readily be "invested" in capital formation without institutional change. The cooperatives, and above all the communes, made possible the beginning of a rational use of labour. Farm work could be attended to by fewer workers, working full time and with some specialization; the labour of the remainder was made available, if only seasonally, for long-term improvements such as irrigation, terracing, afforestation or the creation of rural industries, all of which represented increases in the productive potential of the countryside. By 1958 underemployment and unemployment had been virtually wiped out and electrification and mechanization were being pursued as solutions to the growing labour shortage.

For in addition to providing the framework within which the cadres and peasant masses can apply improved farming techniques and lay the foundations of a widely dispersed rural industry, the commune is also a social unit, organizing welfare and education services. Its network of hospitals and clinics makes possible a frontal attack on disease, inculcates basic elements of hygiene, and initiates a "medical revolution" whose major manifestations are the sharply declining child mortality rates, the longer expectation of life and the gradual elimination of that dragging burden of ill-health which was a major cause of poverty in Old China. Its schools ensure the combination of modern science and traditional peasant wisdom, of theory and practical work which is one of China's most original contributions to the elimination of rural underdevelopment. Its machine shops and construction teams make possible a high

The members of a commune undergoing instruction by a government technician on methods of improving and increasing the harvest. The education of the commune workers in modern farming techniques is seen as one of the most important aspects of agrarian development, particularly now that increasing mechanization is bringing vast change in the lives of the peasants.

Below: a painting on cloth showing the land farmed by the Hua tung commune. Due to the system of irrigation in use, this has been one of the most progressive communes in recent years. In the painting, the irrigation canals can be clearly seen.

degree of self-reliance and provide a channel through which the techniques of modern industry can be disseminated deep into the countryside. And, last but not least, its provision of basic services such as electricity and water supply and its communal laundries and grain mills release tens of millions of women from the backbreaking chores of peasant life so that they can participate with their menfolk in productive work in field or factory. No longer downtrodden victims of a marginal society, women now participate on a basis of equality in the building of the new society.

The "three bitter years" following 1958, when drought and flood ravaged many parts of China, put the new system to the most exacting of tests. It emerged successful. And when drought again struck North China in 1972–74 it was a major tribute to the system that there was no significant drop in agricultural production. And because it confronted these catastrophic years with success, because its organization made possible the rational deployment of the country's resources in a vast campaign of well-digging, irrigation and drainage, and the implementation where necessary of relief measures, the commune system emerged strengthened and more effective. Strengthened because the peasant masses saw that, given the appropriate form of organization, they could confront – and surmount – a sequence of natural calamities which would have meant starvation and death for millions in the old days. More effective, because, since the system was never regarded as final or static, the Chinese have not hesitated from time to time to introduce modifications designed to correct any weaknesses in the light of their experience over the years.

Major modifications were introduced at the beginning of the sixties and took three forms: first, the reduction in size of the commune in some areas; secondly, structural changes within the commune; and thirdly, the introduction of a small individual sector.

The reduction in size was made because it became evident, after two or three years' experience, that many of the original communes were too large for successful operation; such communes were therefore subdivided into more workable units so that by the middle of the 1960s, they totalled approximately 78,000. The trend towards smaller units was most marked in the "regions of difficulty" such as the uplands; in more favoured environments the commune remains a large unit (thus the average population of commune in Guangdong is over 30,000, as against the national average of 7000–8000).

The structural changes were designed to overcome the difficulties encountered in organizing intensive and specialized agricultural production on the very large scale of a commune. The changes involved considerable decentralization within a tiered structure of which the component units were the commune, the production brigade and the production team, the latter comprising "the workers of 20 or 30 neighbourhood families."

The third modification was the incorporation of a small individual sector into the commune's economy. This individual sector represents some 3–7 percent of the total cultivated area of the commune. The individual parcels are usually devoted to the production of vegetables for the family, though grain may be produced as well as vines or fruit trees, and much of the livestock production (pigs, but especially poultry) is produced by the individual sector. Surplus production is disposed of at regular markets where price levels depend on the conditions of supply and demand.

The economy of the commune: balance sheet for 18 communes (1966)
The table below illustrates the contrasting income levels and patterns of distribution of income for a group of communes which, we believe, are representative of the wide range of agricultural environments in Eastern China.

ECONOMIC BALANCE SHEET OF SELECTED COMMUNES
% of Total Revenue

	Total Revenue (yuan)	Taxes	Production Expenses	Accumulation and Welfare	Distributed to Members	Average Wage per Worker (yuan)
PEKING AREA						
Commune 1	—	3	35	13	40	600
Commune 2	17·0 M	7	23	15	50	330–360
Commune 3	12·0 M	3	40	12	45	380
SHANXI						
Commune 4	3·5 M	7	30	12	51	246
HENAN						
Commune 5	(2·3 M)[a]	7–8	26–8	6	60	140
Commune 6	2·5 M	7	20	8	65	200[d]
Commune 7	2·26 M	3	30	6	60	122–141 (?)
SHAANXI						
Commune 8	6·0 M	5	20	9–11	65	400
Commune 9	2·6 M	7	20	7–10	63	340
Commune 10	3·0 M	7	30	8	55	280–300
JIANGSU						
Commune 11	2·22 M[b]	3·3	18	6·1	72	230–240
Commune 12	2·28 M	4	—		65	215
Commune 13	2·49 M	4·8	(21)[a]	6·6	66	256
Commune 14	6·76 M	5	20·7	6·4	68	194
SHANGHAI AREA						
Commune 15	8·16 M[b]	4	33	11	52	382[f]
GUANGDONG						
Commune 16	11·0 M[c]	(6)[a]	20	8 7	55	280
Commune 17	9·6 M	7	26	6–10	57	278[f]
Commune 18	(3·24 M)[a]	15	c.20	7–11	54	300[e]

Notes: a Estimate. b Excluding industry. c Industry contributes 45 percent of this total. d Including sideline occupations. e Sideline occupations add 20 percent. f Sideline occupations add 15 percent.

Commune workers engaged in transplanting rice. The seedlings are transplanted when they are about 15 centimeters high. Later, when they reach a height of 20 centimeters, the paddy-field is drained and watered again when the plants begin to bloom and produce seed.

There is, it is clear from the table, a great diversity of conditions as between one commune and another; nevertheless, some broad generalizations may be made. First, many of the communes are, in financial terms, very large units; five of those listed had gross incomes of over $2,500,000 and one was handling a budget of almost $6,250,000. The aggregate income of these 18 communes is close on $35,000,000. To get this figure into its Asian perspective it should be underlined that it is larger

The complex mosaic of Agricultural China contrasts with the Western Regions where utilization is conditioned by morphology and climate.
1. Cotton, Kaoliang.
2. Soya, Kaoliang.
3. Kaoliang. 4. Wheat, Oil Seeds. 5. Wheat, Cereals. 6. Cotton, Wheat. 7. Maize.
8. Maize, Millet.
9. Potatoes, Cereals.
10. Rice, Wheat.
11. Rice, Maize, Timber.
12. Rice. 13. Cotton, Rice. 14. Cotton.
15. Rice, Wheat, Silk.
16. Tea. 17. Rice, Sugar cane, Tropical Fruits. 18. Rubber, Tropical Crops.
19. Semi-farming, Livestock. 20. Desert grazing. 21. Mountain grazing. 22. Oases of West. 23. Forest.
24. Desert.
25. Boundary of Agricultural China.

China's agricultural development is concentrated on speeding up modernization and improving productivity in those areas which are environmentally privileged, that is the vast plains in the East. The last few decades have not brought major changes in the traditional spatial patterns; production is still concentrated in the humid lowlands of the East, and Outer China and the upland areas of Agricultural China are still only partially exploited (map after Stavis).

USE OF THE SOIL

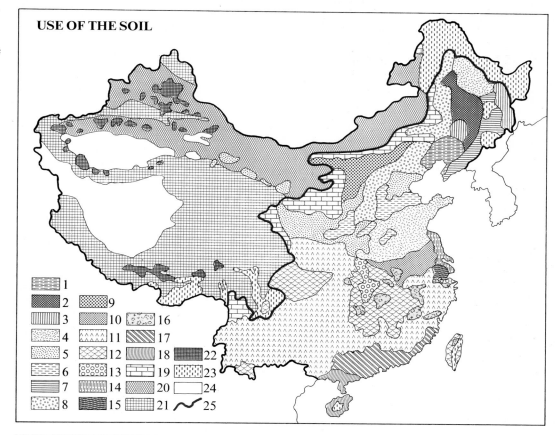

ADVANCED AGRICULTURAL REGIONS (c. 1975)

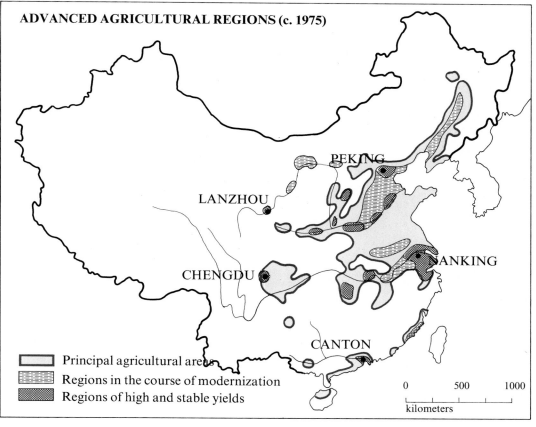

Principal agricultural areas

Regions in the course of modernization

Regions of high and stable yields

0   500   1000
kilometers

109

than the GNP of some of the smaller Asian nations. Secondly, the proportion of the commune's income distributed among its members varies from about three-quarters to, more usually, one half; the remainder is set aside to meet operating costs or to finance activities such as the construction of housing, schools, or power plants, which will contribute directly to raising the living level of the commune's members (to this extent the figures for average wages represent an understatement). Thirdly, there is a considerable range in average incomes between communes – for the group studied a ratio of some 4:1 between the highest and the lowest average wages; between the various teams on a commune the ratio was 2:1; between individuals 3:1. But perhaps the most significant feature is the continuous investment of a sizeable proportion of the commune's revenues, represented by the amounts set aside under the heading of "Accumulation and Welfare." This appears to range between 5 and 12 percent and this steady investment in the production and welfare infrastructure of the Chinese countryside is unparalleled in any other "developing" country.

In part, the contrasts between communes in various parts of China reflect environmental and historical factors, as well as such factors as the presence of exceptionally able and dedicated cadres. But in part only, for official policy has contributed to heightening the differences between various regions and communes by applying in the agricultural sector the Maoist military strategy of "concentrating forces and winning battles of annihilation." Clearly, at the present stage of development, the various inputs needed for high levels of, for example, grain production: machinery, irrigation, fertilizer, new seed varieties, cannot as yet be applied to all the cropland of the country; they have therefore been concentrated on the so-called "high and stable yield areas" (page 109).

These highly productive areas consisted originally of such ecologically favoured regions as some of the river valleys and the lake basins, together with those regions near the major cities where, over the centuries, the use of night soil and other organic wastes made it possible to build up a high level of soil fertility. Subsequently, in the late 1960s and the early 1970s, the extension of irrigation by deep tube-wells made possible the stabilization and intensification of production in the North China Plain, while major water conservancy schemes provided the infrastructure for similar stabilization and intensification along the margins of the Plain and in the valley of the Yangtze.

By 1974 the agricultural environments of China could be classified thus: traditional regions, some marginal change, 69 percent; improved regions 23 percent; high and stable yield regions 8 percent. It is in the regions of the second and third type, the "modernizing regions," that rural industrialization and economic diversification are most marked. In free-enterprise economics the processes of development tend towards the increasing concentration of economic activity – and wealth – in economically advanced regions, e.g. North Italy, the Paris Basin, S.E. England. Chinese development strategy is designed to offset this tendency and to create conditions which favour the spread of improved farming techniques and rural industrializa-

The nursery in a commune near Peking. Commune families today have their own homes but use the communal services provided. These include, besides nurseries, primary schools and hospitals, and workshops for the repair of farm implements.

The two maps illustrate aspects of the spatial pattern of the Hua Shan Peoples Commune near Canton.
Map (left) shows the breakup into production brigade areas, the close settlement in small hamlets and villages and the distribution of social services. Right: illustrating the close grid of irrigation ditches fed by recently-constructed reservoirs in the hilly areas to the north of the commune and by the diversion of river waters along the central east–west irrigation channel.
1. Pumping station; 2. Mountain area; 3. Hills; 4. Reservoirs; 5. Rivers; 6. Irrigation ditch; 7. Public road; 8. High tension wire; 9. Brigade boundary.

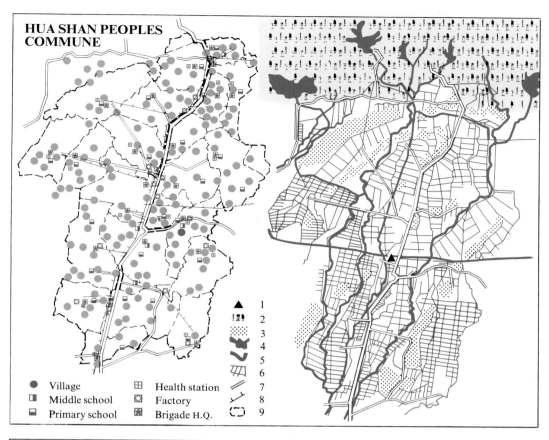

HUA SHAN PEOPLES COMMUNE

▲	1	
	2	
	3	
	4	
	5	
	6	
	7	
	8	
	9	

● Village ⊞ Health station
▯ Middle school ◇ Factory
▭ Primary school ⊞ Brigade H.Q.

The contrast between the arid and subarid West and the humid East is illustrated by comparing the density of the populations of communes. While the communes of the West have an average area of 1741 square kilometers and an average population of 1600 families, the communes of the East, in an area a twelfth of the size (155 square kilometers), contain an average population of about 2900 families.

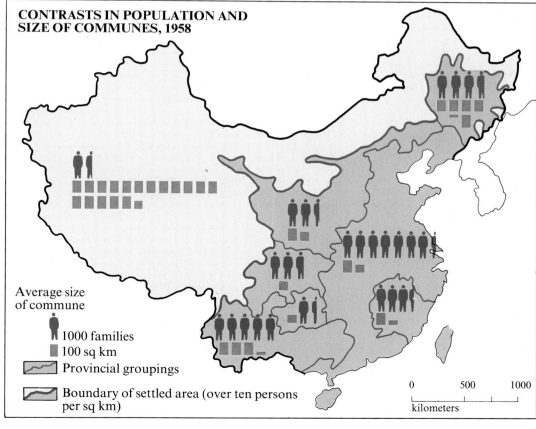

CONTRASTS IN POPULATION AND SIZE OF COMMUNES, 1958

Average size of commune

▮ 1000 families
▪ 100 sq km
Provincial groupings

Boundary of settled area (over ten persons per sq km)

0   500   1000
kilometers

111

tion from the "modernizing regions" to the more backward "traditional" regions.

The diversity of conditions can be illustrated by details for four sample units (data for 1972 unless otherwise stated). The first, a production brigade in the South China hill country, illustrates conditions in those traditional regions whose development is only now beginning to get under way. The second and third examples, from the loess country, are selected to illustrate stages in the development process; Wei-zhu commune, for which we give the 1966 details, is broadly typical of the so-called improved regions at an early stage; Maji commune represents a more advanced stage in the development process, transitional to the state of high-and-stable yields. Finally, the Long March commune, close to Shanghai, is representative of conditions when high-and-stable yields have been achieved and a combination of very intensive cropping and industrial development makes it possible to support very high population densities.

The beginnings of development: a South China example. The Lu-dung brigade farms in what was until recently a remote and backward region of South China, a region of rolling stream-gashed uplands, with a cover of bamboo forest and soils of red laterite inlaid with occasional narrow deposits of fertile alluvium. It is a region of very great beauty with a virtually year-long growing season.

Lack of roads hampered development, making the transport of essential commodities such as cement and fertilizers prohibitively expensive and cutting off the peasants from any save the most tenuous contact with the outside world. Today, a well-constructed road, planned and built by the people themselves, has opened up the valley to a wider world; the pace of life has quickened as the truck replaces the human carrier and the slow-paced cart. Everything needed to realize the agricultural potential of the area can now be brought into the valley. Today, a network of seven pumping stations, linked with a carefully planned system of contour-line canals, means that nine-tenths of the cropland can be irrigated. More water means higher crop yields, leading to an increase in the pig population which in turn ensures more manure ... and thus a continuing increase in yields. Some ten tons of organic manures (mainly pig manure) are applied per acre, and approximately 100lb of nitrogenous fertilizers so that crop yields have increased fourfold since 1950. And with increasing prosperity because of higher productivity it has become possible to acquire tractors and threshing machines, develop small-scale industry and build up the educational and health services.

The upward spiral of development, of locally-generated development, has clearly begun, yet it would be foolish to claim that all problems had been solved. Thus the brigade, like many collectives in South China, had been engaged in expanding its crop area by terracing and cultivating some of the red laterite soils of the uplands. Thousands of man-hours were devoted to terracing and levelling some of these upland areas, yet the crops on these fields suggested the slenderest of returns on the efforts expended.

Development and diversification: a loess-land commune. The Wei-zhu commune, to the south of Xi'an, combines two contrasting types of terrain: rolling loess hills which are, because of their topography, unirrigated and given over to grain, and an alluvial riverine margin under intensive and irrigated cultivation of grain and vegetables. Its population is slightly over 16,000, comprising 3000 households and a work force of 6300; this population is organized into 16 production brigades and 74 production teams. The cultivated land totals 3750 acres, or approximately a quarter of an acre per head of population; most of this land is under grain, grown either on the unirrigated hill-slopes or on the irrigated valley floor, the only other major crop being vegetables which occupy 170 acres. Large stock (cattle and horses) number 600 and there are 2000 pigs, 40 percent of which belong to the collective, the remainder being reared by the individual peasants, i.e. an average of one pig to 2·5 households.

Measured against many of the North China communes, this commune had progressed much less along the path of diversification. The sinking of over 200 wells and the creation of an elaborate network of irrigation ditches on the lower land of the commune now makes it possible to irrigate one-third of the surface. Further extension of the irrigated area depends partly on levelling and terracing and almost 400 acres have been levelled and 60 acres terraced. Electrification facilitates the program of agricultural development, such as threshing and grinding. Seven-tenths of the land is ploughed by tractor.

Industries are those which tie in closely with agriculture: six mills manufacturing bean noodles, three brickkilns, cart-making and constructional teams and a tool-repairing shop; with the exception of the latter, which employs 27 workers permanently, these industries are seasonal, employing up to 800–900 workers in the slacker winter period.

The commune runs two part-work, part-study schools, five State-provided elementary schools offering a six-year course and four offering a four-year course, and one middle school; in addition each brigade runs a night school for older members of the commune. One small hospital run by the county is located within the commune and the commune itself has a health clinic and each brigade a health center. There is also a home for the aged.

Fifty-five percent of the commune's income is divided among its members; this gives an average wage of some 300 yuan, of which 20–30 percent is in kind, in the shape of grain, fruit and vegetables.

A suburban commune in loess-land. Maji people's commune lies on the outskirts of Xi'an in Shaanxi. Its yellow-brown loess-derived soils are amongst the most productive in China, even though they are thirsty soils, needing constant water over the growing season; and their topography, often slightly rolling, meant that the implementation of irrigation schemes was difficult. There is abundant subsurface water, but at depths which defied the crude technology of the individual peasant farmer or the cooperative; there is abundant river water though the river presented major problems of control. And the use of sewage water from the nearby city of Xi'an provides both

A countryside scene near Canton. The most common beast of burden throughout Asia is the water buffalo. In China, all such animals are owned by the commune and the only livestock held by individual commune members is poultry or pigs.

moisture and plant nutrients. The most recent development has been the construction of some two miles of underground irrigation ditches.

With irrigation it becomes possible to boost the levels of manuring; some 30 tons per acre of organic manures and some 20cwt of chemical fertilizer are now applied. Higher grain yields have meant that larger numbers of livestock can be kept (the number of pigs has doubled since 1966), ensuring in turn a heavier application of nutrients to the soil: an upward spiral of development is thus decisively initiated. The loess region is traditionally one of the great breadbaskets of China but in the past it had suffered from all the problems, agricultural and nutritional, associated with single cropping of grain year after year. But by 1966 the proportion of commune area given over to grain had dropped to 70 percent and to 63 percent by 1972 and a 50 percent increase in grain yields more than offset the reduction of grain acreage. And with less land being used for grain cultivation, new cropping patterns became possible: vegetables now take up about one-fifth of the commune's crop land; cotton, important not only as a fibre but as a source of vegetable oil, one-eleventh; while orchard fruits not only help to diversify the commune diet but, with vegetables, are an important cash crop.

The old carbohydrate-based economy, one of the most impoverished in China, has been replaced by a new polyculture, high yielding, nutritionally far superior, no longer at the mercies of a marginal climate. Moreover, and this is critically important in a part of rural China where the annual population growth is still two percent per year, this polyculture offers greatly increased employment in the rural sector. René Dumont's figures, collected in the mid-fifties, had shown that in some parts of Shaanxi the peasant was employed on average 74 days a year, but by 1972 the intensification of land use meant that this vast pool of underemployment was eliminated.

Rural industries too contributed to the wiping out of seasonal unemployment, employing 200 workers full time and scores of others, seasonally.

The total income of the commune is $1,800,000 and of this 56 percent is distributed between commune members, 2 percent is set aside for the welfare schemes of the commune, and 8 percent as "public accumulation" which will serve to finance future development. Annual income per household is approximately $250, an increase of 25 percent since 1966. In addition, the individual sector, represented mainly by livestock rearing, increases the household income by one-sixth. But as elsewhere in

China, if we are to understand the real achievements of recent years we have to take into account the non-quantifiable elements represented by the extension, to these formerly marginal communities, of health and education services which have no parallel in other developing societies. The commune has a hospital, 81 clinics, ten doctors, 68 "barefoot doctors" and over 100 health workers, 16 primary schools and one middle school.

A commune in the Yangtze delta. In China, agricultural and urban life blend together more than in any other area of the world, for not only do most country areas show some measure of industrialization but agriculture penetrates deep towards the heart of China's great cities; the ten counties which make up Shanghai for example contain almost 200 communes. Some of the distinctive features of these highly-developed communes in peri-urban regions may be illustrated by a commune on the fat alluvial soils of the Yangtze delta, close to Greater Shanghai with its 12 million inhabitants. It is a commune consisting of some 2800 acres of cultivated land, supporting 25,600 people, 53,000 pigs, 170,000 poultry and 5000 sheep. Ninety-five percent of the area is irrigated, 75 percent cultivated by machinery and 95 percent of the crop area given over to vegetables. The commune markets some 90,000–100,000 tons of vegetables annually.

It has a wide range of small industries. Many of these are concerned with the working up of agricultural produce (vegetable processing and bamboo work); others with the provision of the agricultural infrastructure (maintenance and repair of tools and machinery); yet others are more specialized such as the manufacture of machine tools. Since 1965/6 the number of industrial workers has tripled, to reach 1450; the net value of their output has quadrupled. And the continuing expansion of the commune's economy as a whole is indicated by the rate of investment which is some ten percent of total income.

With economic advance has come improvement in welfare facilities. The commune had no doctor in 1966, it now has 24 while over the same period the number of health workers increased from 125 to 171 and clinics increased from two to 14. Economic development has made it possible in this, one of the most densely settled areas of Asia, to support this mass of population at a level of well-being far removed from the famine conditions of the old days. It has also made it possible for the people themselves to create a welfare and medical system which has played a major role in slowing the rate of population growth. Some four-fifths of married couples were employing contra-

A series of pictorial instructions illustrating the "Eight Point Agricultural Charter" formulated by Mao Zedong in 1958. This was aimed at the peasants and brought together some fundamental ideas for improving and intensifying agricultural production.

From the left: correct preparation of the soil; adequate fertilization; irrigation; selection of seed; close planting; plant protection; tools reform; and field management.

ceptive techniques and by 1971 the growth rate of the population had dropped to 0·8 percent (1966, two percent). This is a demonstration of the truth that effective population control is contingent on economic development and the progress of medical and welfare services.

The commune and the reshaping of the Chinese earth. For the immense mass of Chinese the most outstanding achievement of the new agricultural system is undoubtedly the eradication of hunger.

However,we must remember that the expansion of food production is but one part, albeit the most important part, of an integrated and overall plan of rural development and that achievements here have been intimately dependent on progress in other sectors. Three critically important facets of this rural reconstruction program have been the increasing mastery of water resources made possible by the levelling and terracing of the fields and by a great expansion of water storage and irrigation schemes; secondly, the large-scale afforestation and shelter-belt projects which are essential if flooding is to be reduced and soil erosion arrested and which create new resources in the countryside (page 102); thirdly the increasing control of the biological environment as a result of the campaign against human and plant diseases and pests.

Over most of China a high and dependable level of food output depends on the effectiveness of the irrigation system.

Chinese agriculture had traditionally been flat-land agriculture and during the last three decades hundreds of millions of man-hours have been devoted to extending the area of level land. Such levelling is necessary in some areas if machinery is to be used but most of the terracing and levelling is part of the program of extending irrigation and is designed to convert the landscape into a series of "micro-plains" which make possible increasingly complex and productive techniques of water control. These, it is now recognized, are without parallel in any other country.

The scale and progress of the reshaping of the landscape can be indicated briefly. The country's crop area is put at 1271 million hectares. In 1952 20 million hectares were irrigated; by 1958 and after the Great Leap Forward the irrigated area had reached 67 million hectares and by 1971 it was put at 99 million hectares. In less than 30 years the Chinese increased the area under irrigation fivefold.

Initially, the Chinese were attracted by the giant all-purpose scheme but with the consolidation of the commune system the policy of development became much more flexible, a policy of "walking on two legs" in which smaller projects devised and carried out by the communes were integrated with giant multipurpose projects undertaken by the State. The most spectacular of these major schemes is the Yellow River project which envisages the transformation of the main channel into a "water staircase" with the construction of 46 dams, a giant scheme of flood prevention, irrigation and power generation. Such a program depends for its effectiveness on the control of erosion and runoff in the whole of the upper basin of the river and it is in this context that the integration of such schemes with

The courtyard of a commune in the suburbs of Tianjin. One of the most ambitious attempts of Chinese planning has been to try to avoid the dichotomy between urban, industrial areas and the countryside. Communes have therefore been set up in or near towns while small industries established in rural communes have provided a useful source of extra income.

Opposite page, above: weighing baskets of peanuts in a commune before they are sent off to the city.
Below: a mill in a rural commune.

the commune-constructed projects has been so important and given Chinese rural society a hitherto unknown security. It has also helped eliminate unemployment and expand and diversify food output.

The second major aspect of China's rural development planning that is transforming the countryside is the afforestation program. Like the schemes for irrigation its implementation has involved massive investments of human labour and the forests created represent a new and important source of wealth.

We have described the processes which led to the deforestation of much of China and seen how, especially in upland South China, the expansion of farming was for generations carried out at the expense of the forests. By 1949 some 90 million hectares, rather less than one-tenth of the land area, were left under forest. This figure is probably an overestimate, for it included a good deal of degraded and cut-over forest land and some experts put the total forest area in 1949 at between 65 and 70 million hectares. In many densely-peopled provinces less than 0·5 percent of the area was forested and in the developing Northwest (Shanxi, Shaanxi, Gansu) the forest area was negligible. But by 1960 the forest area had been increased to 125 million hectares, and by 1971 it was given as between 200 and 210 million hectares (this total excluding low density plantings as on the hills of the North and plantings along roads or around villages). The afforestation program has aimed at an annual planting of some five to ten million hectares.

But the achievement in the field of afforestation is considerable. By the early 1970s a total of possibly 130 million hectares, almost one-seventh of the area of China, had been afforested and these plantings, seen from the air, are beginning to spread a mist of greenery over the ravaged hill country of the South and the ravine-gashed surface of the Loess Plateau. Equally striking are the shelter belts which form gridded patterns protecting the prime agricultural lands of the North China Plain. These are, however, dwarfed by the immense shelter-belt plantings on the margins of the deserts of Western China.

A third major development has been the transformation of the biological environment resulting from the elimination of many of those diseases which were major causes of rural poverty. The campaign was directed particularly against diseases such as malaria, schistosomiasis and hookworm, now virtually eliminated. Again success depended on the total mobilization of the population. The health campaign was complemented with an equally successful one against pests.

Common to all these programs (which changed the face of the Chinese countryside) was the large-scale investment of labour, and in this the organization of the commune played no small part. Indeed the implementation of the "Eight Point Charter for Agriculture" (pages 114–15), which laid down the principles on which agricultural development was to be based, demanded an intensification of labour inputs. It is true that some of the developments such as the widespread and early use of improved high-yielding seed strains brought an increase in production without additional labour. But others, such as the very heavy manuring with organic manures, the techniques of close-

Below: an open-cast coal mine in Fushun. There is a long history of mining and use of coal in China. Coal was discovered in the 3rd century B.C. and by the time of the Tang dynasty was being used as fuel. China is rich in this mineral. Coal is widely used in industry, for transport (railroads and river traffic) and in power generation.

Opposite: a modern painting of an industrial zone on the coast. Before 1949, Chinese industry, which was dependent on foreign capital, was mostly concentrated in the coastal regions. The communist government, although it has developed and made use of industrial plants inherited from the previous régime, has sought to encourage a policy of decentralization and has encouraged the development of new plants in the interior of the country.

planting and the close tending of each plant, involved a very considerable intensification of labour per unit-area. And the application of these techniques to the existing crop area meant that the population contrasts between lowlands and upland became accentuated. Moreover, this intensification took place at a time when massive diversion of labour towards industrialization was beginning. It thus led to labour shortages and demonstrated the importance of agricultural mechanization if the most effective use was to be made of available labour.

The data on the communes given earlier reveal the extent to which small-scale industry was becoming a part of the Chinese rural economy; in a sample of communes studied by the writer in 1966 the proportion of the total income derived from industry ranged from 17 percent to 45 percent. This widespread labour-intensive rural industrialization is, indeed, a distinctive aspect of the rural landscape of New China and in this respect there is a very sharp contrast with most other Third World countries whose industry has tended to be city-located and capital-intensive and where development has merely sharpened the contrast between the modernizing cities and the stagnating and impoverished countryside.

We have seen that one of the major causes of poverty in Old China was lack of economic diversification. This was recognized by the new government in 1949 by the placing of a heavy emphasis on a policy of rural industrialization. This has taken two forms: the decentralization of large industries, a feature which will be discussed later, and the widespread establishment of small-scale industries developed and managed by the commune. Such rural industries have converted what was formerly a liability and a major problem – the immense wastage of human resources created by a backward and highly seasonal agriculture – into an asset in the shape of tens of thousands of small enterprises employing millions of people in the production of goods desperately needed by the country dweller. These industries use supplies of local raw materials too small to justify the setting up of larger industrial units; by catering for the needs of the local market they cut down the burden on the transport system; above all, they convinced the peasant that industrial development does not depend on the specialist and the technician, on large-scale financial resources or State aid. They have thus played a major part in accelerating the transformation of the Chinese countryside. While the individual units may be small, their aggregate importance is considerable; as early as 1959 they accounted for one-tenth of China's industrial output.

THE NEW INDUSTRIAL MAP

Rural and urban poverty in Old China were, as in most Third World countries, closely interdependent. Agriculture, as we have seen, was characterized by a low level of productivity and, because of its lack of diversification, could provide employment in the rural sector for only part of the year. The resulting semi-employed peasantry, existing always on the knife edge of starvation and with a negligible cash income, offered no market for the products of industry, for consumer goods or, more important, for the improved agricultural equipment which have made possible the stabilization and expansion of food output. And in the cities an underemployed proletariat, existing somehow on starvation wages, offered no incentive to the expansion or diversification of food output. The problems of countryside and city could not be tackled separately and the poverty, hunger and wastage of human life common to all parts of China could be eliminated only by tackling the condition, the lack of a diversified and balanced economy, of which they were but symptoms.

We have described the sweeping social, economic and environmental changes which are creating a new and diversified rural economy. No less sweeping have been the changes in the industrial sector which have led to China's emergence as a major industrial power. And in recognizing this two-fold transformation we must avoid the tendency to think in Western terms. For the dichotomy which characterizes most Western nations, that between a rural, largely nonindustrial, sector on the one hand and an urban, largely industrial, sector on the other, has little relevance in China today.

Chinese policy since 1949 has been designed to avoid the sharp clash of urban and rural interests, the domination of the country by a handful of giant industrial cities or the economy by an urban-based technocratic élite. This policy has resulted in a landscape characterized by an interpenetration of industry and agriculture, which is very different from that of most Third World countries. This must be kept clearly in mind, for in discussing industry separately we fragment the economic and social unity between countryside and city, between agriculture and industry, whose integration has been a major objective of Chinese planning.

"Beautiful words . . . beautiful pictures"
The organization of society and then the disintegration of this society following the impact of the West were major obstacles to industrial development in Old China. Much of the country's limited production came from small-scale units employing little capital and primitive equipment; in 1912, for example, only 363 out of the 21,000 "factories" enumerated used mechanical power and 93 percent employed less than 50 workers. Foreign initiative had resulted in a limited development of modern industry but this development was confined to the coastal regions. Here the extraterritorial regime of the Treaty Ports meant comparative security at a period when the rest of China was torn by civil war. Here the foreign industrialist could combine modern production methods and easy access to raw materials with the abnormally cheap labour supply provided by the overcrowded masses of the coast towns. And such Chinese, as opposed to foreign, industrialization as took place was concentrated for the same reasons in the same areas: 43 percent of the registered companies were in Shanghai and Jiangsu, another 20 percent in the Peking-Tianjin area or Canton.

Some limited development of heavy industry had begun in the

regions of the lower Yangtze valley (Wuhan) and southern Manchuria but the output of capital goods, such as textile machinery, was negligible; only one percent of the invested capital was in the machine-building industry and most machinery replacements had to be imported. Under these conditions China could never hope to stand on her own feet as an industrial power. Some three-quarters of the industrial production before 1949 consisted of consumer goods such as textiles, foodstuffs and tobacco, but even for these products Chinese production met only a fraction of the country's needs.

The dependent character of China's economy and the semi-colonial status of the country was further emphasized by the extent to which this fringe of modern industry was foreign-owned or foreign-controlled. An estimate for 1933 put the foreign share at approximately one-third but in individual industries it was much higher: in cotton textiles it was 42 percent; in shipbuilding and repairing 58 percent; in the tobacco industry 63 percent. And the infrastructure, the communications and power systems, was similarly dominated by foreign interests.

On the eve of the Second World War then the industrial economy was retarded, geographically very highly localized, and partially dominated by outside interests. The war with Japan, the civil war which followed, reduced this ramshackle structure to rubble; by 1949 the effective capacity of the industrial economy was zero. The immensity of the task and the opportunities which this offered the new government in 1949 were summed up by Mao Zedong: Chinese society was, in his words, "a sheet of blank paper" on which the new government could inscribe "the newest and most beautiful words ... the newest and most beautiful pictures."

The bases of industrialization

One of the first tasks which confronted the People's Government when it came to power in 1949 was not only the rebuilding of the shattered industrial structure but the need to transform China from a backward agrarian country into an advanced socialist industrial nation. And the policy of rapid industrialization which was to bring about this transformation rested on three main bases; the country's resource endowment; the accumulation of funds; and the effective utilization of the country's vast labour force. And the breaking down of the isolation of much of China by the development of communications was an essential prerequisite for any such policy.

A reason commonly advanced for the backwardness of Old China was the inadequacy of those resources such as metals and fuels needed to sustain a modern industrial economy.

It is now clear that this situation did not reflect any real inadequacy of resources so much as the backwardness of China's science, especially the field sciences such as geology. This of course meant that little was known of the country's resource endowment and in the absence of such information it was tacitly assumed that China had but limited mineral resources and, more especially, that the broad range of resources needed to build a modern economy was lacking. Geological

Boxes of fish are unloaded in the port of Luda, the present-day name for the conurbation which includes Dalian (Dairen) and Lushun (the one-time Russian naval base of Port Arthur). It is situated at the southern tip of the Liaotung peninsula, in the province of Liaoning. Luda, a city of about three million inhabitants, is a busy commercial port and industrial center. Its main industries are iron-working, chemicals and petrol-chemical products.

discoveries since 1949 have demonstrated the inaccuracy of these early judgements.

From the beginning the People's Government showed that it was aware that, to quote an American analysis, "the key to China's industrial progress lies in the uncovering and efficient utilization of its mineral wealth." Consequently, the new government early set about making a systematic inventory of the country's natural resources by calling in soil scientists, geographers, geologists and similar experts to undertake a nationwide search for minerals. The work in the field of geology was particularly important. Pre-communist China had less than 200 active geologists but by the middle of the 1950s some 21,000 "geological workers," aided by 400 geologists from other socialist countries, were engaged in this nationwide geological survey. The deposits of the major metallic minerals so far revealed including iron, tin, tungsten and nickel are "so extensive that they appear to make China one of the world's chief reservoirs of raw materials." Coal deposits would appear to be among the largest in the world and oil reserves, long considered to be limited, are now known to be considerable and widely distributed in offshore waters, in the lowlands of Manchuria and North China and in the Far West.

It is this wide distribution, and not merely the range of minerals discovered or the size of some of the deposits, that was important. Survey work showed that practically every province had exploitable coal resources and many had considerable iron-ore deposits; the old belief that industrial development in the South would inevitably be blocked by shortages of coal and iron was shown to be baseless. And the country's energy base is strengthened by its natural gas production (estimated in 1979 at 60 billion cubic meters yearly) and by the hydroelectric potential of the great rivers.

The accumulation of funds

In the "orthodox" development process as illustrated by Northwest Europe the funds needed to initiate industrialization came from overseas trading, from exploitation of overseas colonies or from forced saving on the part of the workers. China had no major overseas sources of wealth and, except for the aid received from the Soviet Union during the first ten years, had therefore to depend entirely on internal resources. In the initial stages of development a temporary source of investment funds was provided by the seizure of Japanese assets and the property of the feudal and comprador groups; taxation of the private sector of the economy also made a useful but declining contribution in the first decade. Increasingly, however, China's development program has been financed by the profits of the State industrial sector, of the cooperatives and of the sector of State capitalism. Only very recently have overseas loans and limited overseas investment begun to assume some importance.

By 1955 over three-quarters of the budget receipts were coming from the State-operated sector of the economy. Meanwhile, the rehabilitation of the pre-communist industrial structure, the careful planning of production and maximum utilization of equipment made it possible to set aside increasing

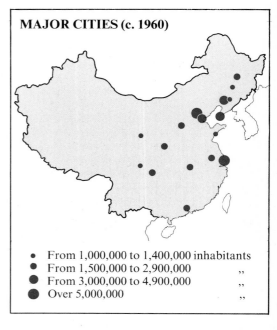

MAJOR CITIES (c. 1960)

- From 1,000,000 to 1,400,000 inhabitants
- From 1,500,000 to 2,900,000 ,,
- From 3,000,000 to 4,900,000 ,,
- Over 5,000,000 ,,

In 1960, more than 40 million people, a third of the urban population of China, were concentrated in cities with more than one million inhabitants. Even at that time, Peking and Shanghai numbered more than five million each. In three other cities (Tianjin, Luda and Shenyang), the population was above three million. Recent data suggest that city populations are increasing at a rate greater than that of China as a whole.

Opposite: a fish market in Peking. Fish is very popular in China. Vast fish ponds exist along the coast and rivers. Many communes engage in fish breeding, thus assuring regular supplies to the large cities.

sums for investment. By the time of the Second Five Year Plan (1958–62) the increasing role played by new large-scale industrial enterprises and by the gradually rising level of technical competence in the work force created the conditions for a sustained advance on the industrial front. Living levels improved, but official policy ensured that personal consumption received low priority and that a very high proportion of the national income was invested in laying the basis for future industrial development. This proportion has rarely been less than one-quarter and in the last decade has exceeded one-third of the national income. Such a rate is two to three times that of most developed societies and far exceeds the level attained in any other developing nation. This policy of abstinence from consumption – or forced savings – has been possible only because the austerity imposed has been a shared austerity, participated in by all from the top levels of government to the members of the smallest commune. It is this quality of self-reliance in economic development which most clearly distinguished China from other emerging countries such as India; only in the most recent period has there been an apparent departure from this line.

In industry as in agriculture much of the progress achieved during the last 30 years has been the result of the policy of "turning labour into capital," of using very large investments of unskilled or semiskilled labour in lieu of scarce capital and skills to achieve a high rate of growth. This policy was well established by the time of the First Five Year Plan and was central to the strategy of the Great Leap Forward in 1958; in that one year 15·5 million people moved into industry, and this obviously does not include the estimated 60 million who participated in varying degree in the campaign to produce more iron and steel.

Meanwhile, developments in the 1950s, and especially in 1958, revealed how swiftly in a developing economy such as that of China an apparent labour "surplus" could be mopped up. By the end of the 1950s labour shortages in various sectors demonstrated clearly that, if development were to be consolidated, there was a major need to improve the productivity of the labour force by a nationwide program of technical education. Such a program laid the foundations for subsequent development for, in a country such as China, where, until the late 1950s, virtually the entire labour force was illiterate and ignorant of any technical skills, a rising level of competence may increase production as effectively as an increase in the labour force. Moreover, experiments such as the iron and steel campaign of 1958 demonstrated that the improvement of quality was as important as the expansion of production and that better quality could be achieved only with an educated and trained labour force.

Transport and the integration of the Chinese economy
The mobilization of resources and the planned and integrated development of the Chinese economy had long been impeded by an inadequate transport system. In this respect China resembled most Third World nations: her economy, especially as regards mining and industry, consisted of a series of isolated "islands" of

Opposite: a group of small children in a commune school. After nursery school (which they attend from three to seven years old) Chinese children must attend a primary school until they are 13. Teaching in such schools is concerned above all with mathematics and learning to read and write Chinese, a language which has between three and four thousand characters. In the last years of primary school other subjects are introduced: history, geography and the elements of a foreign language.

Above: peasants returning from work in the fields. Between 50 percent and 60 percent of the total income of the commune goes on workers' salaries, the amount paid depending on the work done. This wage may be augmented by income earned from sale of the produce grown on the private plot assigned to each family. In general, these plots do not exceed 7 percent of the commune area and their size varies between 60 and 200 square meters, depending on the density of population.

development, often oriented towards an overseas market, and set in a stagnant sea of subsistence production. Under such conditions the resources of the interior were inaccessible and it was impossible to create either a national economy or any real unity between the many peoples of China.

China's railroad system had been partly developed by outside interests with the aim of facilitating the commercial penetration of the closely-settled East. It was a fragmented system, focused on the Treaty Ports, and little related to the needs of China. Vast areas were without any access to rail transport and, indeed, the whole of Southwest and Northwest China had a total of only 800 kilometers of railroads. On coming to power in 1949 the People's Government embarked on a program of track re-laying and double-tracking in the East, pushed ahead with the creation of a series of desperately-needed N–S links and the extension of the rail network into the hitherto inaccessible regions of the West and Southwest. Four-fifths of the construction work in these early years was in these "less developed" regions. Much of the new track crossed previously unsurveyed deserts and high mountains.

Some of the roads constructed since 1949 are similarly major achievements in the face of difficult terrain; examples are the Tibet-Qinghai and Tibet-Xinjiang roads which cross mountain terrain at heights of over 4000 meters. However, the greatest emphasis in the road-building program has been on the creation of a dense net of all-weather roads designed to integrate the rural areas into the national transport system; by 1964 every *xian* in the country had been linked up and by the early 1970s some 98 percent of all communes in Agricultural China were linked to the national grid. Most of these local roads were planned and built by the communes, thus reducing the burden on the national budget. And with this expansion of the road system there was a simultaneous expansion of truck production so that by 1971 each province had at least one truck factory of its own.

The third element in the transport infrastructure is represented by the waterways. Eight major rivers have been opened to heavy steamer traffic and the Grand Canal has been modernized to provide a major north-south waterway designed to link five rivers: the Hai He, the Yellow River, the Huai River, the Yangtze and the Qiantang, and provide an integrated waterway system covering almost half of China. The commune-built water conservancy and drainage schemes provide a dense network of local waterways linking together the communes and cities. The development of the waterways has made it possible to move an increasing proportion of industrial raw materials, building materials, and grain by water and thus relieve pressure on the railroads. The priority accorded to the construction of river boats and boat engines and the mass-construction of concrete barges (an important industry on many communes) have added greatly to the efficiency of this sector of transport.

Finally, the development of a relatively dense air-transport network has played an important role in the economic, and especially industrial, development of Outer China. More than any other factor the plane has integrated these resource-rich but formerly inaccessible regions into the Chinese economy and today technicians, blueprints, and delicate precision equipment can be rushed to the developing mining and industrial areas of the West in hours rather than the weeks that would have been necessary in the old days.

Designing the new industrial map

The initial target of Chinese planners in 1949 was to attain, by 1952, the 1943 level of industrial production; in reality, the level achieved in 1952 was almost one-quarter above the 1943 level. From this point the development of the economy was regulated by a series of Five Year Plans. An important aspect of Chinese development planning has been its flexibility.

Until the Great Leap Forward of 1958 the development pattern followed closely the Soviet model. A central plan laid down growth rates for the various sectors; consumption levels were held down to make possible high rates of investment, with the emphasis on industry, especially heavy industry. In this early phase almost nine-tenths of industrial investment went to the producer goods industry, slightly over one-tenth to consumer goods; this was designed to give an annual rate of growth for the two sectors of 17·8 percent and 12·4 percent respectively. Output expanded sharply. Between 1949 and 1959 the aggregate output of agriculture and industry increased five-fold and the gross output value of industry increased twelve-fold. By 1959 industry accounted for two-thirds of the gross output value of agriculture and industry (compared with one-third in 1949) and over one-half of the industrial output consisted of producer goods such as machines for manufacturing all types of industrial products.

This early period also saw the beginnings of progress towards the planners' third aim: the attempt to correct the imbalance in the geographical distribution of industry by developing the interior regions. In 1949, as we have seen, China had two relatively small and weak industrial bases. The first was the heavy industrial base of Southern Manchuria; developed by the Japanese in the 1930s, it had been largely dismantled by the Soviet forces in 1945/46 to prevent it falling into Guomindang hands. The second, represented by the coastal cities where industry, light industry for the most part, had been developed by foreign or foreign-allied capital, lay in ruins, a situation brought about by hostilities and civil war. The First Five Year Plan concentrated on the reorganization and expansion of these industrial bases (a policy assisted by Soviet technical aid and equipment) and their industries played an important role in the accumulation of funds for the construction of new industrial bases in the interior. Two-thirds of the new major industrial enterprises established during this period were constructed in the interior and here output increased almost twice as rapidly as in the coastal cities.

This policy of industrial dispersal was motivated by several considerations: the need to minimize pressure on the transport system by locating new projects near energy and raw material sources and close to the major centers of consumption; the need to achieve a better balance between agriculture and industry in each major economic region; the strategic need to avoid the exposed and vulnerable coastal regions; and the belief that

This diagram refers to a community in Northern Jiangsu but is typical of much of China prior to the Land Reform promulgated by the government of the People's Republic. The means of production, cultivable land and farm animals, were in the hands of a minority of landowners and rich peasants. The redistribution of land was one of the major objectives of the communist government.

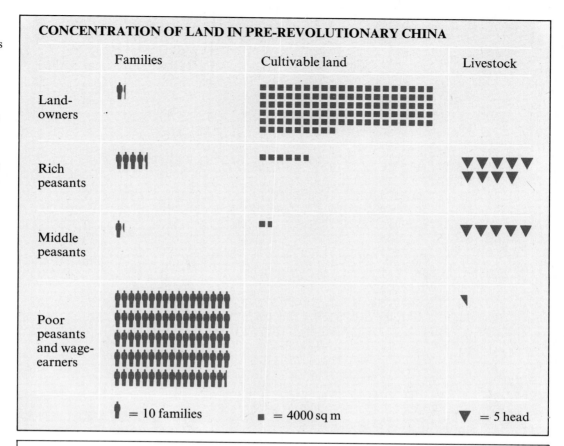

The present distribution of the population is the result of centuries of adaptation to natural surroundings and reflects fairly accurately the food-crop potential of land in China. The greatest concentration of population is in the plains of Northern and Central China, in the Sichuan basin and in the scattered plains and valleys of the South.

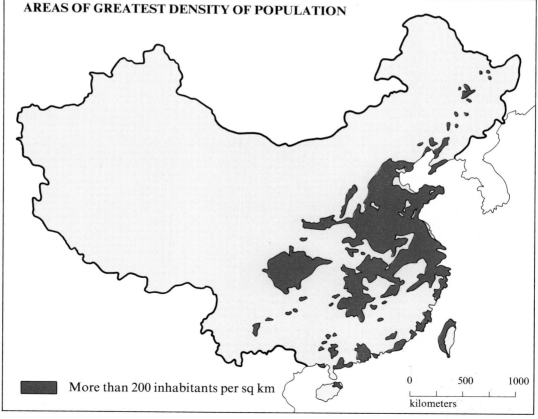

dispersed industrialization could help to reduce the economic differentials between the urban and rural sectors of the population and between the Han majority and the non-Han minority groups. Perhaps the success achieved was less than the planners had hoped for and certainly as late as 1960 seven-tenths of China's modern industrial capacity remained concentrated in the East, North and Northeastern Regions. This was probably inevitable, given the emphasis in the First Plan on large-scale modern industry, but with the Great Leap Forward and the new emphasis on "native-style industry" and the maximum degree of economic decentralization, the techniques of industrialization began to penetrate into the remotest corners of the Chinese land.

Towards a Chinese development model
At the beginning of this essay we stressed that the capacity for synthesis – and transmutation – has been a distinguishing feature of Han civilization from very early times. The years since 1949 have shown that this is still true. For the Chinese, having embraced the doctrines of Marxism-Leninism and having begun to apply them in their development planning, did not rest content with servilely copying them; rather did they transmute them into a form more relevant to the realities of their country.

Economic development policies, and with these the landscape patterns of China, illustrate this process. Initially, Chinese planners were very strongly influenced by Soviet development ideas; the call was to "learn from the Soviet model." The overwhelming emphasis on heavy industry, organized in large units and employing capital-intensive techniques of production, reflected Soviet influence; it inevitably led to a high degree of concentration in a limited number of large cities (a majority of the above-norm projects was, in fact, concentrated in 18 cities). However, the very real dangers latent in such a policy were soon recognized by the Chinese, for such a policy of creating a series of giant enterprises would have but limited impact on a country the size of China; its cultural impact would be small and the great mass of the population would remain cut off from the industrialization and mechanization which are the basis of modern life. Only by decentralization could the maximum diffusion of the new technologies throughout the countryside be achieved, and the creation of a "new class," a new technocracy, be avoided. A limited number of modern capital-intensive enterprises would do little to solve China's critical employment problem, something never experienced by Soviet planners.

Moreover, there was a growing realization that the Soviet Union, in 1917, enjoyed advantages which were lacking in China in 1949. The transport infrastructure was more highly developed; the pool of skilled and semiskilled labour was, proportionately, much larger than that of China; capital was less scarce; and finally, Russian pre-1917 industrial development was more advanced than was the case in China in 1949 and the degree of war and civil war destruction less. In sum, China's "point of departure" was from a much lower level than that of the USSR. To these differences must be added the contrast in scale of the two experiments, which rendered unworkable the type of centralized planning which had been possible in a

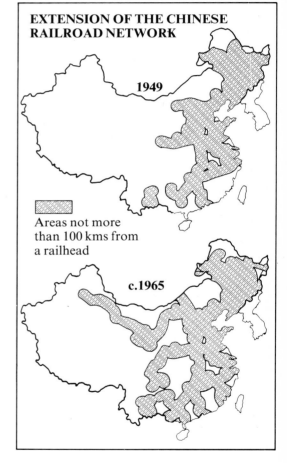

EXTENSION OF THE CHINESE RAILROAD NETWORK

1949

Areas not more than 100 kms from a railhead

c.1965

country with a population one-quarter that of China in 1949.

1958, the year of the Great Leap Forward, saw the beginnings of the attempt to create a specifically Chinese development model. The most original and far-reaching move, one which more than any other helped give the Chinese countryside a character different from the countrysides of other Third World nations, was the abandonment of rigid centralization in the industrial sector and the creation of a second sector characterized by smaller, labour-intensive units widely dispersed throughout the length and breadth of the countryside. Chinese industry was henceforth to "walk on two legs," integrating the most modern, technically-sophisticated and capital-intensive units with small labour-intensive units using less sophisticated technologies of production.

This policy of "walking on two legs" is one of the biggest contributions made by the Chinese to solving the problems posed by poverty, underemployment and economic backwardness. It mobilized local savings capital to a degree central government could never have hoped to achieve; it led, through its emphasis on labour-intensive forms of production, to the utilization of the tens of millions of unemployed and underemployed; it made possible the use of deposits of raw materials which were too small to justify the creation of a major enterprise; it provided vitally important supplies of consumer goods which the modern State sector was in no position to supply; finally it broke the "mystique" surrounding industrialization and demonstrated to the peasant masses that they themselves could initiate the process of industrialization without the aid of outside experts or capital. And in doing these things, it enabled the State to concentrate its limited resources of capital and technical skills on the development of heavy industry, especially the manufacture of capital goods.

A very large proportion of this "native-style" industry was initiated and operated at the commune level, and by the end of 1958 it was claimed that this commune-based industry was accounting for one-tenth of China's total industrial output. But with continuing expansion of the State sector the need for yet further decentralization became apparent and the management (but not the ownership) of almost 80 percent of the industrial enterprises (accounting for 40 percent of capacity) was transferred to the provinces.

Thus, by 1959–60, when the ideological rift with the Soviet Union became public, China was in the process of discarding some of the essential features of the Soviet development model and was creating a new model closely tailored to the specific needs of the Chinese people.

"Walking on two legs": power and steel

One of the distinctive features of the Chinese countryside today is the great proliferation of small-scale hydroelectric generating plants, built by the communes themselves with local materials and commune labour, and providing the electricity on which the modernization of the rural economy and the development of industry depend.

Their advantages are many. They require only a small head of

Wood engraving of the Luda diesel locomotive factory. As the maps (opposite) show, prior to the proclamation of the People's Republic, the railroad network served only the Northeast of China and the most densely inhabited parts of the Eastern plain. The extension of the system was one of the first objectives of development planning and vast areas of the Northwest, the Center and the Southwest, which had previously been extremely isolated, were integrated into the existing network.

water, minimal investment and no very specialized skills in their construction, and they can be built rapidly. While it is recognized that such plants do not provide a final solution to the power problem, they supply the electricity that is urgently needed and they do so cheaply. Even more important is their educational role, for in their construction and operation the peasant acquires experience which will prove of major value as the communes move on to the creation of larger and more complex plants; their building thus helps to speed up the technological transformation of the countryside. Meanwhile, parallel to, and integrated with, this pattern of small-scale projects, the State has been pushing ahead with a series of giant hydroelectric plants.

The iron and steel industry illustrates this same pattern of development. The rate of advance has been rapid: from 1·3 million tons of steel in 1952 to 32 million tons in 1978, and this has been achieved on the one hand by the creation of large-scale integrated iron and steel complexes of the modern type and on the other by the development of medium-sized units and small-scale "native-style" blast furnaces capable of utilizing ore and fuel resources too small to justify the establishment of a major industry.

Thus the existing iron and steel plants at Wuhan and Anshan were extended and modernized in a new complex set up at Baotou in Inner Mongolia. By the end of 1958 smaller plants, with a capacity of between 100,000 and one million tons, had been constructed in Sichuan, Hebei, Shandong, Anhui, Hunan, Hubei and Zhejiang. In the communes and the cities some two million "native-style" furnaces had been built by local people; altogether, 60 million Chinese were participating in the mass campaign to produce iron and steel. In terms of production and quality the campaign was dubbed a costly failure by the West. Certainly output was low (4·2 million tons of pig iron and 3·2 million tons of steel) and the quality poor. But the campaign cannot be dismissed out of hand for it helped to close the gap between steel production and rural needs more rapidly and cheaply than having to extend modern plants; it reduced the burden on the transport system, and it also meant that higher quality steel produced in modern plants could be earmarked for projects where it really mattered. Most important of all, the campaign paved the way for the transition, in succeeding years, to large, more modern, furnaces and, like the myriad small-scale hydroelectric projects, it had an important educational function: by their participation in it, tens of millions of Chinese took the first step from a preindustrial to an industrial society.

As late as 1964 some 1400 small iron and steel works, with capacities of from 1200 to 10,000 tons per annum, continued to operate in the commune sector; another 200 larger plants had been transferred from the commune to the State sector. However, most of the "peasant-style" blast furnaces were abandoned in 1960 though the iron and steel industry still continued to "walk on two legs," the one represented by the giant modern complex such as Baotou, the other by small, widely-dispersed, blast furnaces. These latter may develop in size and degree of mechanization into medium-sized works of

200,000–800,000 tons capacity or, where conditions are suitable, into bigger integrated steel works of 800,000 to one million tons capacity.

These development policies brought about a high rate of industrial growth on a very broad front. Heavy investment in the economy (rarely falling below 25 percent of the national income and reaching 36 percent in 1978), together with the skilful integration of large-scale, medium-sized, and small industrial plants, has led to very rapid growth in the industrial sector. Between 1952 and 1978 coal production increased ten-fold, electricity output thirty-six-fold, pig iron production eighteen-fold and steel production twenty-four-hold; the output of cotton cloth tripled. The contrast between the rate of increase in the output of heavy industry and consumer goods as typified by cotton cloth is significant; it results from a planning policy which has consistently directed investment to the heavy industrial sector at the expense of consumer goods. Since 1952 heavy industry has benefitted by eight times the amount of investment in light industry, and between 1966 and 1970 the ratio was as high as 14 to one.

The second aspect of industrial advance which is so impressive has been the increasingly wide range of products turned out by Chinese industry; it ranges from antibiotics to locomotives, trucks and merchant ships, from complex electronic equipment to aircraft, from synthetic textile fibres to traditional Chinese textiles such as silks and brocades.

Interrelationship of agriculture and light and heavy industry

We have so far discussed the "dualistic" approach, the policy of "walking on two legs," solely in relationship to industry. But to see this policy working to maximum effect, we have to study its wider application to the economy as a whole. For just as a judicious balancing and integration of large and small units, the capital-intensive and the labour-intensive, is necessary for optimum progress in any industry so too must agriculture and industry be harmoniously balanced for the healthy development of the economy as a whole.

The earliest phase of development, with its clearly-defined order of priorities, heavy industry, light industry, agriculture, in that order, ignored this. After the tumultuous episode of the Greap Leap Forward it became evident that concentration on the development of industry, especially heavy industry, led to an imbalance in the economy and that the peasantry, the group which above all had made the 1949 revolution possible, was benefitting to only a limited degree from the country's economic progress. Moreover, the abnormal climatic conditions of the early 1960s drove home the necessity for further consolidation of the agricultural sector as a prerequisite for sustained economic advance.

And so a reorientation of economic policies, or a "readjustment," as the Chinese prefer to call it, was initiated with the slogan, "Agriculture as the base of the national economy with industry as the leading factor." Agriculture was reemphasized, as was the simultaneous development of those industrial sectors closely related to agriculture such as the production of fertilizers

Opposite: two aspects of a modern residential area of Peking. The furnishings in the photograph below are unusually comfortable and the television set, kept in a glass case and admired by all, is an unwonted luxury.

Above: lesson time in a Peking school. Most Chinese children leave primary school at 13 and start work immediately, but their studies are unlikely to be completely at an end. Secondary school continues until 19 and it is then possible to go on to higher education at a university (of which there are about 40 in the whole of China), polytechnic or a vocational college.

and agricultural machinery. From 1962 the State allocated increasing supplies of raw materials to factories supplying the needs of agriculture and increased its investment in the agricultural sector. It was this consolidation of the agricultural base of the economy, one in which the commune played a critical role, that made possible the real "economic takeoff" of China.

The achievements in the agricultural sector have thus been considerable but in the last year or so it has been increasingly stressed that for a long time agriculture has been allocated less than one-tenth of the total national expenditure and that this allocation has to be increased if the supply of food to the growing urban population, and of raw materials from the communes to the factories, is to be maintained. And, if the supply of consumer goods needed to boost living levels and offer an incentive to increased production in the agricultural sector is to be ensured, higher levels of investment in light industry are essential.

This continuing "readjustment" expresses itself in the 1979 budget which increased investment in agriculture from 10·7 percent of the total investment to 14 percent; raised investment in light industry from 5·4 percent to 5·8 percent of the total and cut back investment in heavy industry from 54·7 percent of the State budget to 46·8 percent. In this we can see a recognition of the validity of Mao's emphasis on the critical role played by agriculture and light industry in the accumulation of capital for heavy industry; we can see also the continuing flexibility of Chinese planning. And these latest priorities, and the new and growing concern with the importance of consumption needs, once the initial industrial "takeoff" has got under way, may be regarded as an index to the growing maturity of the Chinese economy.

Some considerations, subjective and otherwise, of progress
If changes in Chinese urban life and landscape strike the foreign visitor as less impressive than those effected in rural areas, it may be because most visitors to China are from the developed cities of the Western World. Only gradually does one come to realize the scale of the rehousing effort which has shifted millions from the squalor and overcrowding of the slums to the spacious if austere blocks of multistorey housing which are typical of every Chinese city. But occasionally the extent of the change is dramatically demonstrated, as in Shanghai where, juxtaposed with a new housing estate, a small huddle of squatter shacks has been preserved, a museum piece which serves as a constant reminder of the point of departure – and the progress – of modern Shanghai. Multilane roads, bus services, parks and open spaces, piped water and systems of waste and sewage disposal, these we regard as commonplace, yet we have only to wander away from the main thoroughfares of most Third World cities to appreciate the immensity, perhaps the uniqueness, of the Chinese achievement. Added to which the planned industrial development of China's cities and the highly-developed system of welfare services (operated by the local community) give a security and stability which contrasts sharply with the unemployment and desperate insecurity which are endemic to most Third World cities.

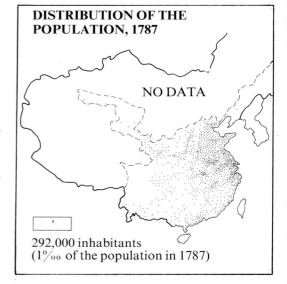

DISTRIBUTION OF THE POPULATION, 1787

NO DATA

292,000 inhabitants
(1‰ of the population in 1787)

The difference between the situation in 1787 (opposite page) and in 1953 (right) shows how the distribution of the population has changed during this period. There has been a build-up of population in Central and Southwestern China and a relative decline in the semiarid regions of the Northwest.

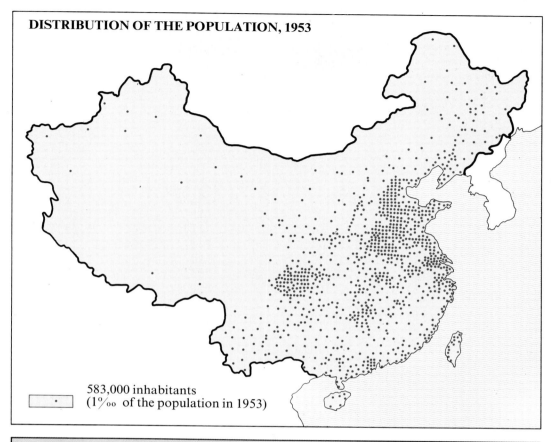

DISTRIBUTION OF THE POPULATION, 1953

583,000 inhabitants
(1‰ of the population in 1953)

For about 50 generations, the population of China remained static. Then, during the Qing period, this stable situation underwent a rapid change and the population started to increase. The most recent evidence suggests that this tendency is likely to continue up to the end of the present century. By 1978, the population of China had risen to 975,000,000. Growth is at present around 10,000,000 per annum and it therefore seems likely that one billion people live in China today.

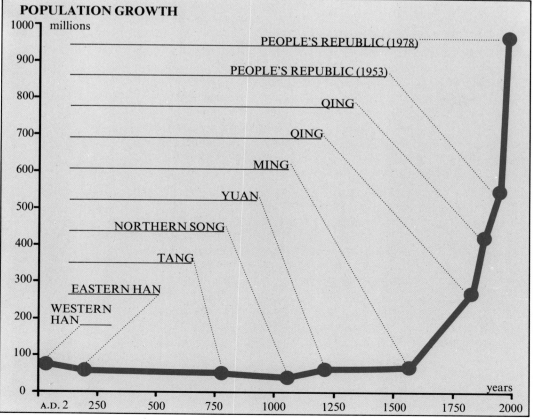

POPULATION GROWTH

1000 millions

PEOPLE'S REPUBLIC (1978)
PEOPLE'S REPUBLIC (1953)
QING
QING
MING
YUAN
NORTHERN SONG
TANG
EASTERN HAN
WESTERN HAN

years

A.D. 2   250   500   750   1000   1250   1500   1750   2000

INDICES OF DEVELOPMENT	1952	1978
Population (incl. Taiwan)	602 millions	975 millions
Food grains (million tons)	154·5	304·7
Cotton (million tons)	1·3	5·8
Sugar cane (million tons)	7·1	18.9
Pigs (millions)	89·8	301·3
Sheep and goats (millions)	61·8	169·9
Large animals (millions)	56·6	93·9
Coal (million tons)	63·5	618·0
Crude oil (million tons)	0·3	104·0
Electricity (000 million KWh)	7·3	256·5
Pig iron (million tons)	1·9	34·8
Steel (million tons)	1·3	31·8
Machine tools (000 units)	13·7	183·0
Trucks (000 units)	7·5(1957)	149·1
Cement (million tons)	2·9	65·2
Cotton textiles (000 million m²)	3·3	10·3

Yet while we may attempt to convey a subjective impression of China after a quarter of a century of the People's Government, it is less easy to set the achievements into some sort of statistical context which would permit comparison with other societies. This is partly because, until quite recently, much of the economy and economic planning was less concerned with maximizing production than with promoting equality. It is also partly that it is not always clear whether official data include the commune or local sector production or refer simply to the output of the State sector. But perhaps the most important factor of all is that much of the capital construction is undervalued since little or no account is taken of the value of labour input by the communes.

The most convincing estimate of China's Gross National Product, an estimate in which allowance is made for this "systematic undervaluation of the Chinese physical effort," is that of Curtis Ullerich for the period 1970/71. He suggests a total of US$180,000 million (at 1952 prices) as a rough measure of the Chinese GNP. Agriculture's output he estimates at $30 billion, that of industry at $90 billion, while the output of the tertiary sector is put at 25 percent of the combined material product of agriculture and industry, i.e. $30 billion. To compensate for the undervaluation of the material product in financial terms and for price deflation he suggests a "corrective" amounting to 20 percent of the value of the output of the three sectors, i.e. $30 billion. For comparison, he cites the GNP of Britain which in 1970 (and thus swollen by inflation) was US$119·6 billion; the 1970 GNP of the USA was, for comparison, US$723 billion, that of the USSR about US$520 billion. Such an estimate would mean that a decade ago the Chinese per capita GNP was of the order of US$250; this represents a five-fold increase over the 1950 figure.

Finally, we should stress the ongoing process of change. We have described how, after 1949, the Chinese embarked on a thorough appraisal of the Chinese earth, a reappraisal which

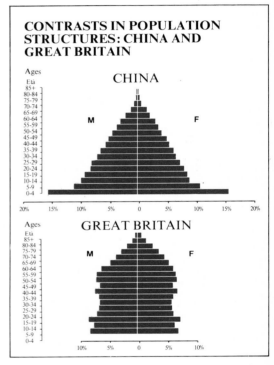

CONTRASTS IN POPULATION STRUCTURES: CHINA AND GREAT BRITAIN

CHINA

GREAT BRITAIN

This diagram shows the contrast between China and an industrial Western country in terms of the age composition of its population.

China's broad-based pyramid with over one-third of the population aged less than 15 years (as compared with less than a quarter in Great Britain) is typical of countries with a rapidly-expanding population.

Opposite: it happens to be Peking but the scene could be duplicated in any Chinese city. There are estimated to be about three million bicycles in the capital. Together with the tricycle (often made in small workshops), the bicycle is the most common means of private transport. China produces more cycles than any other country in the world – eight million machines a year – still not enough to meet popular demand. A system of preference in the purchasing of a bicycle favours those with real need. Bicycle repair shops are a feature of every Chinese town (200 in Peking alone).

brought to light ever new resources and potentials. That reevaluation is continuing. And along with this the Chinese are in the process of discovering their own latent potential, and in this the Maoist concept of education, with its emphasis on the interplay between theory and practice, education and production, has been of fundamental importance.

THE FUTURE

The long-term aims of Chinese development, spelled out by Zhou Enlai in 1975 and taken up by the new leadership in 1976, are to attain for the country a place among the world's major economies; in production terms this involves catching up with the USA by the year 2000. The basis for future expansion is there. Chinese agriculture produces one-fifth of the world's grain and over one-third of the world's pigs. The targets for grain production are 375 million tons by 1980 and between 400 and 450 million tons by 1985. To achieve such an expansion (which would leave China with a sizeable export surplus) there is to be heavy emphasis on mechanization (70 percent of the crop area will, it is claimed, be mechanized by 1980) and an increased application of fertilizers. These are ambitious, possibly over-ambitious, targets; even if, as Deng Xiaoping claims, the supply of fertilizers available in 1980 will be sufficient to increase grain production by 50 million tons, the provision of mechanized equipment on the scale envisaged would account for more than half the total steel output and require twice as much energy as now produced. And the social dimensions of massive rural mechanization, the problem of how the scores of millions displaced by machines will be found employment in the countryside, appears to have received only limited attention.

On the industrial front the aim is the establishment by 1980 of an independent and "relatively complete" economic system. This means making good existing gaps in the industrial system, chiefly in the machinery, electronics and communications sectors, and the replacement of imports of automobiles, fertilizers and certain types of steel by home production. During the Fifth Plan (1981–1985) the aim is to attain levels of industrial productivity close to those of the West; the target for steel production in 1985 is 57 million tons and coal production is to be pushed to 900 million tons in 1987, and 1800 million tons by the end of the century.

The events of the most recent period suggest that, to achieve these goals, the Chinese leadership envisages considerable shifts away from the pattern of self-reliant and integrated development which China so successfully pioneered under the leadership of Mao Zedong. These shifts are becoming evident at both the international and national levels.

Internationally, the old pattern of self-contained and self-reliant development is being replaced by an increasing integration into the international (and multinational) economy. Mixed ventures, involving foreign and Chinese capital, are developing in the fields of mining, manufacturing and tourism.

Increasing purchases of foreign equipment and technology place a heavy burden on China's balance of payments and necessitate a continuous expansion of exports and an increasing recourse to foreign credits. Particularly significant have been the recent decisions to establish "special districts" for development of export-oriented production by enterprises with foreign participation at Shenzhen on the border with Hong Kong and at Zhuhai on the Macao border.

No less important have been the internal manifestations of the new economic strategy. While the first 25 years of the People's Government were characterized by a deliberate policy of "spreading" development and encouraging the maximum degree of self-sufficiency at the level of the province, the hsien or the commune, today's policies are leading to growing centralization and specialization, to the emergence of growing inequalities in the countryside.

The implied reduction in the economic power of the commune and the production brigade and in the control of the peasant over the technology employed in the countryside seems to represent a major break with Mao's themes of decentralization and the creation of a polyvalent socialist man. In industry also the emphasis on decentralization and integration appears to be giving place to centralization and specialization. In the automobile and agricultural machinery industries for example the emphasis on each province producing all its own needs is being replaced by specialization by province and interprovincial cooperatives. These changes are accompanied by changes in the organization of work: managerial and technical staff regaining most of the power they lost during the 1960s, material incentives replacing the "moral incentives" of Maoist days and provision being made for a much wider range of salaries.

Today the Chinese leadership appears to be initiating one of the most dramatic policy shifts since 1949. To attain the ambitious economic goals set for the country many of the policies which lifted the Chinese people out of poverty and powerlessness, are being abandoned. For China, the new policies, including the use of foreign credits and the mass importation of foreign technology, represent a new and untried path. The dangers of technological dependence were spelled out for an earlier generation of Chinese by Mao Zedong who said, "For a country to remain indefinitely in a state of underdevelopment it is sufficient for the foreigner to place permanently at its disposal a ready-made technology." The truth of this has been demonstrated in many Third World countries.

It remains to be seen whether China, having successfully confronted the problems of hunger and exploitation which still cripple most Third World countries, can with equal success confront the problems, the massive problems, posed by the large-scale importation of technology, the increasing use of foreign credit, and the drastic internal restructuring the new policies involve. What is certain is that the scale of change in the next 30 years will be as sweeping as that in the 30 years since the People's Government came to power and that the transformation of the Chinese countryside is, as the Chinese put it, "but the first step in a ten thousand league march."

A street in Peking, in the quarter of the Bridge of Heaven (Tian-Qiao), one of the most popular and lively parts of the city, given over to restaurants, theaters and cinemas.

In the last few years, the government has tried by various means, including the compulsory evacuation of young people to the country, to create new settlements in an attempt to halt urban population growth and lessen the strain on employment and housing. City life, however, with its many attractions, continues to cast its spell. How to promote the industrialization of the country without putting agriculture at risk is a difficult and much debated question in China today.

Never mind if the people
are not intimidated
by your authority.

民不畏威則大威至

HISTORY AND CIVILIZATION
by CHARLES P. FITZGERALD

遠
煙如
乾隆廿八年
竹冬

PREHISTORY AND THE CHINESE CLASSICAL AGE

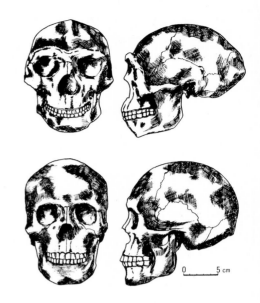

There are two versions of early Chinese history, the traditional, and that provided by modern archaeology and scholarship. The Chinese people never endowed themselves with a myth in which gods framed their origin and planned their destiny: they chose instead to create a legendary history which merges into the fully and genuinely historical record without apparent break. Sages, not gods, taught men to rise from the condition of brute beasts, to turn to hunting, then to the cultivation of the soil, building houses and towns, organizing a state. The progress is represented as taking many generations and several centuries. Nevertheless it is not true history, even if as a theory of man's development it has much in common with modern thought. Archaeology, which in China has only developed in the past 70 years, has revealed a different tale. Peking Man, discovered at a cave near that city in the second decade of this century, shows that man inhabited North China more than 100,000 years ago, had the use of fire, and in the view of some scientists, had already certain characteristics of bone structure which continue in the present people of China. The Chinese in fact have always inhabited China.

A very long gap still exists between these first evidences and the Neolithic age, which in China is dated from about 5000 B.C. The painted pottery of high quality recovered from the tombs of that age is plentiful and widespread in many sites covering most of North China. There appear to have been at least two cultures, and it is not certain whether one is older than the other, or that they were roughly contemporary. Yangshao, named from a site, seems to have prevailed in the western part of the great North China Plain; Longshan, also the name of a site, in the eastern part and in particular in the province of Shandong. In the case of the Longshan site this place is an earthen-walled enclosure, which developed into a city, and then into the capital of a small state, which is known to later history. At Longshan the evolution of the ceramic art continues into the Bronze Age. Neolithic China knew several domestic animals and the soil was cultivated for the production of millet and probably vegetables. The bone structure of the skeletons recovered in tombs is virtually identical with that of the present inhabitants of the neighbouring countryside.

Traditional history records that at the end of the era of the Sage monarchs, who did not practice hereditary succession, but chose the worthiest man as king, Yu the Great, the tamer of rivers and founder of irrigation, was succeeded by his own son, thus founding the first Chinese dynasty, the Xia, which reigned for 439 years, under 17 kings. This is not an impossible chronology, but in fact no archaelogical evidence of the Xia dynasty has been found. It may have existed, for there is other evidence of the general reliability of Chinese tradition. According to that tradition the Xia were finally overthrown and

The skull of Peking Man (*Pithecanthropus pekinensis*) seen (above) from the front and in profile. Below is a contemporary skull. The discovery of Peking Man in a cave near the city of Peking, in the second decade of this century, provided evidence that the inhabitants of China more than 100,000 years ago knew the use of fire. Moreover, according to some authorities, there are some characteristics of bone structure which are still present in the race of modern Chinese.

Pages 140–141
Bamboo in the snow, painted in ink on paper by Zheng Xie, 1753. Princeton University Art Museum.

Opposite: a painted vase from 2500–2000 B.C. Neolithic period of Yangshao, Gansu. Height 19 cms. About 3000–2000 B.C., northern China produced a flourishing pottery-making industry, particularly in the provinces of Gansu, Shaanxi, southern Shanxi and Henan. Especially beautiful were the vases made for domestic use or as funeral urns. The clay is very finely worked and the usual form of a vase consists of a small base, swelling to a fairly bulbous middle, then narrowing again at the neck. Handles were sometimes added. Form and decoration vary and take their names from the districts in which the vases were produced. The spiralling decoration on this vase shows that it is a product of the Ban shan culture, a characteristic of which is the unity of form and decoration. This vase, with its design of spirals ornamented by small toothlike edgings, was perhaps utilized as a funeral urn.

succeeded by the Shang in 1766 B.C. All dates are rendered in their equivalents in the Western calendar.

The circumstances of their fall so closely resemble the much more authentic record of the fall of the Shang themselves that it is difficult to discredit the idea that it was a projection back into the past of a story well known to later historians. But up to modern times there was equally no certain archaeological evidence for the Shang dynasty. Now we know that the Shang dynasty of 30 kings practiced fraternal succession. However, modern, particularly Western scholars, dismissed the dynasty as a myth. The discovery of royal tombs and a city deeply buried in the silt of subsequent floods at Anyang, in the province of Hebei, in 1928, altered all these ideas. Anyang was the penultimate capital of the Shang kingdom. Among the finds were the oracle bones, the shin bones of oxen and also tortoise shells, which were used for divination by applying the point of a red-hot rod to the bone and reading the meaning of the cracks so produced. Inscriptions in the early form of the Chinese script accompanied the divination cracks and stated the occasion, and the questions asked of the oracle by the king – in fact, the names of 28 kings were found in oracular inscriptions on this site.

The names of the past kings of the Shang dynasty were thus found, and fitted, with two miscopyings: the traditional list of Shang kings as recorded in history. But the compilers of the traditional history lived in the 1st century B.C. and the Shang oracle bones had been then buried for much more than 1000 years, and were to remain buried for another millennium. So traditional history depended on sources available in the 1st century B.C., now otherwise lost, but evidently independent of the buried records, and handed down for over 1000 years. After this discovery the traditional history has been treated with more circumspection. The Anyang site yielded much more information on the art, social customs and religion of the ancient Chinese. The Shang were superb workers in bronze. They not only cast very large pieces, weighing more than a ton, but they decorated them, large and small alike, with intricate and beautiful designs, the symbolism of which is not yet fully understood. The earliest example of the dragon appears on them, and many other continuing motifs of later Chinese art. The Shang cast their bronzes in moulds, and not by the lost wax process, known in the ancient Middle East. Large pieces were formed in two or sometimes several moulds, and when cast, welded together and the joins filed down so that no join is easily visible. The skill of this craft is comparable to the finest metal work of any age or country.

Scholars still are unsure whether the casting of bronze was an independent invention of the Shang, or introduced from Western Asia where it was historically much older. Routes between China and the fertile lands of Mesopotamia or Egypt, were extremely long and there is no direct evidence that they were used at all. If so, it would perhaps have been by the route through southern Siberia, believed to have been more temperate in climate than it is today, and the evidence is that people along this route also cast bronze at about the same time. But whether they obtained knowledge of the art from the Chinese, or

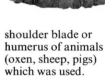

Oracle bones dating from the Neolithic period, used by soothsayers of the Shang period, which provide important evidence of the links between the Neolithic Longshan culture and the Shang dynasty. On the bone in the illustration on the right appear scratches which are obviously an early form of writing. The discovery of such oracle bones has led to a better understanding of the earliest Chinese script. The oracle bone on the left shows a number of holes, in which the point of a heated bronze spear-head was placed, and from the cracks generated by the heat, answers were forthcoming to the questions put to the oracle. Differences between small and large cracks also determined whether the answers were favourable or unfavourable. Such rituals are known as "scapulamentation" (scapula – shoulder blade) because, for the most part, it was the

shoulder blade or humerus of animals (oxen, sheep, pigs) which was used.

Opposite: two types of vases from the Neolithic period, used in rituals such as sacrificial ceremonies and funeral offerings. The vase (below), known as *kuei*, with feet which look like the udders of a nanny goat, belongs to the Neolithic Longshan period.

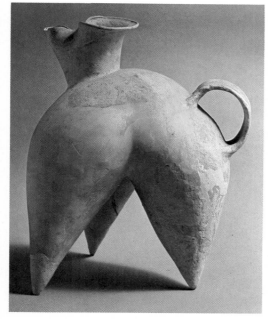

transmitted it to the Chinese, is undetermined. What is clear is that the Chinese neither used the Western Asian lost wax technique nor did they at any time in any known example employ Western Asian art motifs or forms in their bronze vessels. On balance the probability is that bronze working in Shang China was a separate invention. The transmission of a skilled technique, rather than an individual object of value, by a primitive system of communications, from tribe to tribe, seems at least rather unlikely.

An earlier Shang capital, at Zhengzhou, in Henan province, has in recent years proved that some two centuries before Anyang, the Shang were casting bronzes, but less elaborate and plainer in decoration. But at Zhengzhou there has as yet been no discovery of inscriptions and it seems possible that the first beginning of the Chinese script is therefore to be placed in the interval between the date of Zhengzhou and that at Anyang, roughly between 1400 and 1200 B.C. On the Anyang bone inscriptions the style of ideograph used is very much more complex than the modern style (which itself dates from the 2nd century B.C.). Yet it is the direct ancestor of the later forms, and legible to scholars who have specialized in it. That it is related to a simple picturegram writing is obvious. There must, it seems, have been a preceding period in which picture writing, similar to that of the Aztecs of Mexico, was used, and developed into the ideograph script. Two centuries seems much too short for this major development. The Shang style also used the cyclic system of ideographs for the chronology of years, and as this has continued in use until modern times, it was a helpful clue to the deciphering of these ancient texts. The real date and origin of the Chinese ideographic script thus remains a mystery, but the presumption is that it was during the Shang period, and probably in the latter half of that age.

Apart from the oracle bone inscriptions, divinatory in purpose, the only other Shang texts are very brief inscriptions on the bronze vessels, dedicatory in nature, "Let Sons and Grandsons cherish this precious vessel for all time." Sometimes the name of the owner, or donor is added. It is accepted that they were made for ritual use in the religious ceremonies of early ancestor worship which at that time taught that the spirits of dead forefathers actively protected their descendants and could intervene in human crises. To what extent the Shang honoured any other deities is still obscure. According to traditional history the pantheon of gods worshipped by the Zhou in the next age is assumed to have been known and honoured by the Shang. But archaeology does not yet confirm this.

During the Shang dynasty the first systematic astronomical observations were made (Chinese astronomy represents the longest history of observational science). Use of the gnomon dates from this time, as do the first observations of eclipses and nova (14th century B.C.). By 240 B.C. Halley's comet was regularly observed. Mathematics developed to the point that by the 4th century B.C. a fully developed decimal, place-value system was in use. Within the next century Pythagoras' theorem was known and a symbol for zero used. In practical mechanics the balance, steelyard, and scaling ladder were understood. In optics the principles of refraction and reflection from place and curved surfaces were also understood.

The Shang kingdom was devoted to war: oracle inscriptions often refer to the chances of victory over this or that neighbour, usually unidentifiable, as the ideographs do not give the sound of a word, and the names of these obscure neighbours have long since been lost. Prisoners of war were made slaves: but apart from this there is no real evidence of a system of slavery, much to the discomfort of Chinese Marxist historians. That the agricultural population were serfs bound to the soil is certain, as continued to be the system until much later in Chinese history; but serfdom is not slavery.

The extent and the boundaries of the Shang kingdom are not established facts. It was relatively large, comprising at least the whole of the modern provinces of Shaanxi and Henan, possibly some parts of Shandong and Shanxi and Hebei. Quite recently a site in Hubei, well to the south in the Yangtze valley, has been found and in part excavated, and appears to be unmistakably a Shang palace. If so, it is a revolutionary find, for no Shang presence so far south had been expected. Even if it is assumed to have been the capital of an outlying fief, this would be the first evidence that the Shang kingdom had dependencies at such a great distance from its own center. The area which can thus be assigned to have certainly belonged to the Shang kingdom would be equivalent to the combined areas of France, the Low Countries, West Germany and possibly also Spain. What may have been the size of the population is completely conjectural.

Apart from the bronzes, the oracle bones, and the tombs of the kings at Anyang, the archaeological records of the Shang dynasty also include carved ivories (for example mammoth tusks, imported from Siberia) and a small number of stone sculptures, highly decorated with the intricate designs, characteristic of Shang art. The traditional record of the dynasty, apart from the confirmed list of kings, is bare and scant: mention of a few wars, court intrigues and even fewer incidents of a supernatural character. The record only becomes precise and copious when it deals with the alleged evil acts of the last king, Zhouxin, who provoked his vassal, Wu, duke of Zhou to rebel. The rebellion triumphed, the Shang were destroyed and Wu, assuming the title of king, ushered in the Zhou dynasty (circa 1100 B.C.).

Traditional history assigns the conquest of the Shang by the Zhou to the year 1122 B.C. (in Western chronology). Chronology before 800 B.C. is uncertain; besides there were two differing systems in use. 1100 B.C. is the approximate date. As is often the case, the accepted version of an historical event tends to be a polished and tidied-up account, in which everything is swift, decisive and easily remembered; whereas the real facts are often awkward, untidy, indecisive, and much more inconclusive. So it was with the Zhou conquest. To the traditional historians, all was decided at the memorable battle on the plain of Mu. The Shang king was slain, his people submitted, and Wu, the new Zhou king, proceeded to divide his extensive kingdom into feudal fiefs allotted to close and not so close relatives.

The king was responsible for sacrifices to his ancestors and to

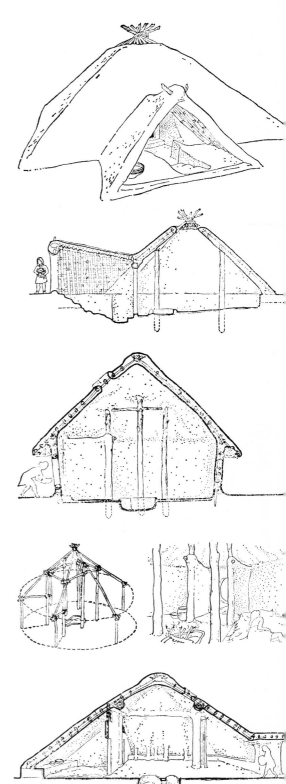

Opposite: drawings of dwellings, dating from the Neolithic period (c. 2000 B.C.), discovered near the city of Yangshao, in the province of Henan, showing in each case, the position of the hearth. The roofs of these houses were supported by wooden poles, a method which is still in use in many Chinese dwellings today. It is to the Swedish archaeologist Andersson that we owe many of the discoveries relating to Neolithic life around Yangshao.

Right above: sectional reconstruction of a house built in circular form, from the Neolithic period.
Below: remains of a Neolithic dwelling in Banpo (Shaanxi).

the gods of the soil, and for the agricultural calendar, as well as for administration. The peasantry lived a communal life in the summer fields and winter villages, tilled common land for their prince, and practiced exogamic group betrothals and marriages.

Archaeology has some changes to make in this neat solution. Firstly the conquest was not complete. Forty years later a Zhou nobleman, as evidenced by the bronze vessel on which is inscribed his honours and history, was given an additional fief in the central-southern province of Anhui as reward for his services against the Shang supporters who still held the region. Secondly, it was always admitted that the state of Song, in much the same region, was not ruled by any Zhou relative, but by the heir of the fallen Shang dynasty. He was permitted to have his own territory so that "his ancestral sacrifices should be continued," for no noble family without its own territory could offer valid sacrifices to the ancestors. In fact Song was far too strong to conquer, and became, some centuries later, one of the major powers of the Chinese feudal world. Confucius, incidentally, claimed descent from the princes of Song.

It is also clear that some of the major fiefs into which the Zhou kingdom was divided were ruled by families, local to the region, with no connection, other than later intermarriage, with the royal house of Zhou. Such was Qi in western Shandong and along the coast. And as the kingdoms farther to the south, the lower Yangtze valley, came under Chinese cultural influence, they were fitted into the established myth and their kings given fictitious pedigrees connecting them with the Zhou. The construction of the new kingdom was therefore on the model of the extended Chinese family, all branches owing respect and loyalty to the senior house, but each governing its own patrimony as the rulers willed.

The term feudal, for this system, is in part justified by the fact that nobles received fiefs in return for which they were pledged to defend and fight for the king, and that these enfiefments were recorded on ceremonial bronze vessels, with details of the ceremony which took place. The doubtful question is how far the king could or in fact did control the feudal lords. At first, no doubt, effectively; most of them were his brothers, first cousins and other close relatives. But gradually the relationship became more remote, and the high ranking dukes, descended from the brothers of King Wu, became less powerful than families with no such ties. The ancient Chinese, and their posterity, up to most recent times, practiced exogamy. No intermarriage between men and women of the same patrilineal stock was valid. This interdict later took the extreme form of forbidding marriage between men and women of the same surname.

It was therefore unlawful for the king to give his daughters in marriage to the sons of the dukes, who were his patrilineal kinsmen. Equally their daughters could not marry the king or his heir. It was thus inevitable that within a century or two at the most the family links between king and feudal lord had become weak and ineffective. A picturesque story tells of how one of the king's concubines, with whom he was infatuated, falsely summoned the feudal lords to the capital by persuading the king to order the alarm beacons to be lit, as she wanted a good laugh

Decorated ceramic vases from the Yangshao culture of Gansu, of the type used in tomb furniture known as *ma zhang*, a name taken from a locality in the valley of the river Tao. These painted funeral vases were found in four ancient cemeteries excavated by Andersson in 1923. Much clandestine exploration followed the discovery of these tombs and great numbers of amphorae were stolen and sold abroad, which accounts, in part, for the large collections in Western museums today. In form they are round and not very high, with a flattish base and a short neck, or sometimes with the flatter end at the top. The red-painted type are decorated with geometric or wavy designs. The colours used, pigments of iron and manganese, were red and black and brown applied to a polished surface. The geometric decoration is broken up into areas, a lighter colour often outlined by a dark line, toothed on the inside, denticulation, as Andersson noted, being a symbol of death.

Right: a libation vase (*hu*) in bronze from 13th or 12th century B.C., during the Shang dynasty, and today in the St. Louis Art Museum. Ritual vases made of bronze or grey ceramic, like that illustrated below, formed the largest part of tomb furniture, both in the Neolithic and Shang periods. The great variety of forms which these vessels take is evidence of the complexity of these rites, in which food and drink were offered to the gods. Relatively simple both in line and the geometric decoration of the lower part, these bronze vases often repeat Neolithic ceramic motifs. Many bronze objects were found in the excavations in Anyang, proof of the refinement and sophistication of metal-working and casting during the Shang period.

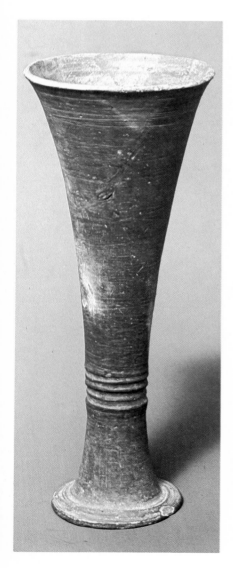

at the expense of the feudal lords. They came, but they were not amused; they had travelled hundreds of miles at, presumably, their own expense. They went home in anger, and never answered such a summons again. True, or founded on an embroidered tale of some such grievance, it confirms the evidence of the decline of royal power as the feudal lords' relationship with the royal house became remote.

It is not possible on the scanty records remaining, and the still sporadic contributions of archaeology, to measure the stages and extent of the decline of the royal power. In 841 B.C. a foolish king was deposed and a regency set up, known as the *Gung He* regency (Public Harmony), from which date Chinese history is accurately dated and recorded year by year, forming by far the longest reliable record of any human society.

Less than a century after the Gung He regency, in 722 B.C., an important event marked the real end of the Zhou royal supremacy. In that year the barbarian tribes, nomadic it would seem, whom the Chinese called Rong and Di, in alliance invaded the Zhou kingdom from the northwest, and captured and destroyed the capital city, close to the modern Xi'an. The Zhou king fled eastwards, and founded a new capital in the province of Henan, at Luoyang. From the fact that this city is two or three hundred miles east of Xi'an, the later Zhou kingdom is called Eastern Zhou. One consequence of the flight was that the king enfeoffed one of his nobles as duke of Qin, the country round the former capital, now the province of Shaanxi, with the duty of driving out the invaders. This he did, no doubt easily enough, as the nomads invaded to plunder, not to settle.

But the duke of Qin consolidated his fief in this highly defensible country, called by later Chinese, "The Land within the Passes" (*Guangjong*). The factors which had made the Zhou strong enough to overthrow the Shang, now worked to make Qin an even stronger power. The flight to Luoyang also further diminished the royal authority. In the new age little is said of the king or his acts, except when he is called upon by some dominant feudal lord to ratify his spoliation of a neighbour. The Eastern Zhou period bears an almost uncanny likeness to the Holy Roman Empire of Europe's Middle Ages. A virtually powerless overlord, deeply respected, legally essential, presides over a community of progressively more aggressive and quarrelsome feudal lords, the greater of which defy the king, and seize the lands of their small neighbours, unless these in turn ally themselves with a lord who is both powerful and the enemy or rival of their oppressor.

The period fom 722 to 481 B.C., known as the Chun Qiu age, is so named from a chronology of the state of Lu (where Confucius was born), which records the decay of the Zhou feudal system, something which Confucius deplored. For this reason the authorship of the chronicle (*Spring and Autumn*) was for centuries attributed to Confucius himself, and morals drawn from its curt phraseology and use of correct, but obsolete titles. Confucius probably knew the work and admired it, but he was not the author.

Warfare in this Spring and Autumn period was still a courteous, knightly encounter between gentlemen and nobility,

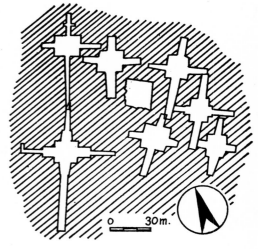

Plan of the group of huge tombs of Xi Bei Kang, near Anyang, dating from the later Shang period. There are eight tombs, one quadrangular, the other seven of cruciform design, so closely sited that in parts they overlap. The structure of such burial chambers remained unchanged until the end of the Zhou period. In three of these tombs were discovered the remains of human victims and in two others the skeletons of a man and a dog. These victims, most probably prisoners of war, some decapitated, and the remains of horses, also slain, had been placed before the royal bier and on the ramps leading from the deep central tomb to the surface. Elsewhere, human victims were found in kneeling positions, their mouths wide open. Very few objects of value remained in these sepulchers, probably as the result of repeated visits by tomb robbers. However, some beautiful bronzes in the style of the Shang period were found on the ramps giving access to these tombs. It is generally held that the quadrangular tomb in the center is false, despite other evidence.

Right top: the remains of a chariot and skeletons of horses found near Xi'an. Center right: a tomb with human remains and objects made of copper and bronze. Below right: a chariot with two skeletons of horses, found in Anyang. During the Shang period, from which these finds date, the chariot was much used in warfare, particularly for military operations which required the fast movement of troops. It was only later, particularly in 4th and 3rd centuries, B.C., that the chariot gave way to cavalry and infantry, the latter having an important role to play in the defense of the Great Wall. The construction of the Shang chariot, which was made almost entirely of wood, was quite simple. In the middle was the box, supported by a wooden frame; below were fixed the axis and shaft. The rims of the wheels were of wood, as were the slender wheel spokes, fixed with joints or held together by cord or some other perishable material. The horses were short, with large heads, and they were probably harnessed by means of a halter around the neck.

The three smaller illustrations, right, show respectively (from top to bottom): a comb, a pipe made of bone and another made of ivory. These, together with other funerary objects with a personal history, were found in a tomb in Shandong. Several important centers of Shang culture have been discovered in this region.

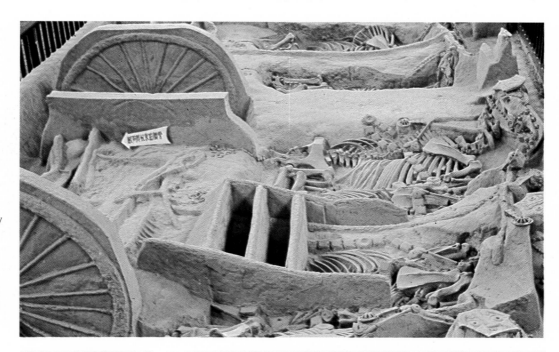

151

meticulously based on rules of chivalry which had but little to do with strategic or tactical problems. The Chinese, except in the then rare cases of nomad invasion on remote frontiers, fought only among themselves, and war was a noble game. Nobles rode in chariots, attended by one man. If the gentleman fell from, or was knocked out of, his chariot, his opponent, bowing, courteously assisted him to rise and remount: it was definitely "infra dig" to attack a gentleman who had fallen. A general who observed the rule that one should not attack a fleeing foe, and permitted the enemy to cross a river, giving them the chance to attack and defeat him in turn, replied, when chided by his officers, that, "Victory or defeat does not matter, so long as the laws of chivalry are observed." Several such examples of these rules and their consequences are given in the contemporary historical works which still survive.

There is very little mention of the common people in these records. Some of them followed their lords to battle, on foot and probably armed only with spears. All were serfs, tied to the soil. It seems probable that they engaged in group fertility rites in spring, and that formal marriage in the manner of the aristocracy was not for them. They had no surnames, while the aristocracy had clan names, which did not identify the actual family, but the noble clan to which it belonged.

One of the oldest texts in Chinese literature, the *Book of Odes*, seems to be simple peasant poetry, but scholarship has discovered that in truth it is sophisticated court imitation of simple peasant poetry, more in the manner of the pastoral vein in the European Renaissance. The art of the period also reveals this taste. The formal, massive, but magnificent bronzes of the Shang, and also of the early Zhou, are now replaced by more delicate shapes, with fine inlay of gold and silver, and elegant inscriptions in a stylized script. The eternal pattern of the development of art from classical, romantic to avant-garde, reveals itself in this age of ancient China as surely as it was to appear many centuries later in Europe.

The Spring and Autumn Period, covering the 5th and 6th centuries B.C. also marks the beginnings of Chinese philosophy and the recording of sophisticated thought. Confucius (551–479 B.C.) lived through the later part of the period, and although probably not the first teacher of a new doctrine, was certainly an early one, and became the most celebrated. ("Confucius" and "Mencius" are latinized forms of the Chinese *Kung fu zi* and *Meng zi* respectively.) He had rivals, some of them his younger contemporaries, others who arose after his death, and the variety and number of their doctrines were such that they acquired the name of the "Hundred Schools." Not so many can be identified; no more than four or so left any lasting mark.

While Confucianism was essentially concerned with man's role in society, and in training the young to fill that role with honesty, courage and loyalty to their superior ruler, the Taoists (the name is taken from *Dao* or *Tao*, meaning "The Way") preached the exact opposite. Society was a sham and a delusion; power and wealth a futility. The duty of man was to cultivate his inner understanding of the Way and to conform with the laws of

Two examples of bronze receptacles used in the elaborate ceremonies of sacrifice to the gods and ancestors. Types of vase like the one pictured above, known as *yu*, with lid and free-swinging handle, were probably used to hold wine.

Opposite: two ceremonial daggers, the blades in white jade fixed to handles of bronze encrusted with turquoise mosaic. These have been attributed to the end of the Shang dynasty (12th century B.C.).

Opposite: a vase (*ting*) used for cooking sacrificial food, from the later Shang dynasty (14th–11th century B.C.). Typical is the zoomorphic mask decoration (*tao tie*), although its significance is unclear. The most generally held view is that the *tao tie* represents the dragon, beneficent god of rain in the old Chinese mythology, who could, however, also bring flood and catastrophe. The use of a high percentage of lead in the metal lessened the danger of bubbles and flaws in casting. The precision of relief and accuracy of incision are also present in the receptacles for cereals (*tou*) on the right, and in the zoomorphic jug and the vase with lid, decorated with geometric shapes, both of which are illustrated below.

155

nature. The value of a dish is not in its shape but the empty space it contains. A wheel is useless, except for the empty hole through which the axle can be fitted. These and many such illustrations were used to emphasize the principle of *Wu Wei* (Non-action), which underlay all Taoist thinking. Perhaps because it was so directly opposed to Confucianist order, and contained the mystical element which Confucianism ignored, Taoism has continued to live on as a system of thought, and for many centuries as a kind of popular religion made up of magic and superstition.

Mo Ti (Mozi) was a near contemporary of Confucius, whose doctrines he also opposed. Mo Ti taught that universal love was the only solution to the evils of the world. Let every man love not only his family, but his neighbours and distant people, and wars would cease, oppression end, and society would be wholly transformed. But it was the factors which prevented this glorious consummation which aroused a rather unloving response in the followers of Mo Ti. Family ties, the very basis of Chinese society (as the Confucians wisely saw) were obstacles to universal love. So were royal power, feudal lordship and the structure of society. Mohism thus became associated with subversion, and developed into sects, some of which departed far from the original teaching, but retained the gift for organization which seems to have been Mo Ti's personal characteristic.

The School of the Law, which owed its origins to a mixture of Mohism and elements taken from Taoism, was in the next age to be dominant. It was harsh, logical, but inhuman. The Law (meaning the criminal Law) should be above all, and everyone should be subject to it, princes and nobles as much as commoners. Penalties were invariably harsh, horrible and usually mortal. The only purpose of the state was aggrandizement by war. Thus war and agriculture, as the means of feeding the army, were the only proper activities. All else was bad, or at best had only a very limited value, such as commerce, the buying of necessary materials for war. Art, philosophy, history, poetry and every form of aesthetic life were utterly condemned. The School of the Law, by its own writings, stands as an almost incredibly crude forerunner of the extremist Nazi doctrine. These ideas, without the thin cover of a long accepted but no longer practiced religion, emerge in all their stark simplicity, shameless and crystal clear.

When Confucius died, the age of Spring and Autumn, of feudal decline, was about to be transformed into the period called the Warring States, which lasted until the end of the Zhou period in 221 B.C. This was indeed an age of continuous and widespread warfare in which all the feudal states engaged, steadily destroying each other until the remaining, now much larger kingdoms, engaged in a final round of mutual wars, the avowed object of which was the total conquest of all China and its consolidation into one imperial state.

In the period before the unification of China and the adoption of the new title *Huang Di* (which we translate as emperor) the supreme title was *Wang*, king. No one but the by now titular head of the Zhou dynasty, virtually ruling no more than his capital city of Luoyang, could bear this title. But it was assumed

Above: wine vase (*yu*), made of bronze. The propitiatory rites called for the preparation of cooked dishes and rice wine in vessels which, while not dissimilar to the utensils in everyday use, were exclusively used for ritual purposes.

Opposite: ritual vase made of bronze in the shape of an owl. Vases cast in zoomorphic shapes (owl, tiger, rhinoceros and elephant), used to hold the sacrificial wine, were in common use during the Shang and the Zhou dynasties.

BRONZES

Of the arts of the Shang period, the one we are most familiar with is that of bronze-making, because of the great number of objects in bronze which have come to light in the course of excavations carried out in Northern China. We know of more than 2000, one-third of which bear inscriptions, forming a corpus of fascinating material for the historian. These vessels, for the most part intended for ritual use, are not easy to classify, although apart from secondary differences, most fall into one group or another. The traditional vase forms

each have a name which in some cases is the same as was used at the time of making (as we know from the inscriptions). Other names were coined during the Song dynasty when there was a strong interest in antiquity. The table below illustrates the most common types of bronze vases: on the top row are shown the ceramic prototypes (in cases where it has been

possible to discover what they were like from excavations); underneath is the bronze form which was derived from these; this is followed by the ancient sign for that particular type of vase (which in some cases is a pictorial representation of the actual shape); finally there is the modern Chinese name under which it is classified today.

If we leave out the bronzes which were for everyday use (which in

any case are comparatively few and of little artistic value), it is possible to group the ritual vessels into three types according to the uses to which they were put: vessels for cooking, serving and preserving food or wine. In the table below the first three examples are vases used for cooking. We note the unusual form of the first vase (*li*) which has a bulbous

form and stands on three hollow legs which have an extraordinary resemblance to breasts, which may have had some magical significance. More practically, the legs served to bring the food into closer contact with the flame. This is a typically Chinese form, unknown in other parts of the world. Receptacles for serving or conserving the offerings which were made to ancestors or to the gods are shown in the fourth and fifth examples, while the third is almost certainly a libation vase. All the others are for holding wine (including some used for heating the

| *li* | *ting* | *xien* | *kuei* | *yu* | *tou* | *tuei* | *pan* | *chien* | *yu* |

wine or mixing it with water) or as water pitchers or basins. The last two examples are a kind of teapot used for boiling water and a sauceboat. There are no terra-cotta prototypes for these containers, and the forms in which the bronzes exist are extremely various.

As regards the style of decoration of ancient Chinese bronzes, it is essential that we remember that each design has a symbolic significance and is therefore often deliberately far from nature. The most common motifs are zoomorphic but it is often difficult to tell exactly which animal is represented as the figures are frequently extremely stylized. There are also many purely geometric designs but, as William Willets notes, it is not possible to escape from the overpowering presence of animals, especially since the animals in the bronzes tend to be heraldic or even abstract. They are presented in contorted poses, by reason of technical limitations but nonetheless have tremendous life, even if they are "monsters." Thus, the horn of a stag turns into the heads of birds, and fishes' tails become rams' heads. The same thing applies to the so-called dragon designs. As we have already said, these patterns have a compositional freedom about them which is reminiscent of the nomadic art of the steppes: several heads may be attached to one body, or perhaps several bodies end up in a single head. The geometric base which is the foundation for all these stylizations and zoomorphic fantasies is the spiral. Not that there are no bronzes with identifiable pictures of plants or even human forms but these are the exception, not the rule. One of the decorative motifs which has given us most to think about is the *tao tie* (seen on the front of the bronze vase on the left and shown in detail in the drawing below). It consists of two animals facing each other, seen from the side view, forming the right and left sides respectively of an animal seen from the front. There are widely differing, not to say contradictory explanations of this: a monster is eating a man, but in the act of swallowing, his own body is being destroyed; or perhaps a single body is being formed from two opposed animals. Both of these explanations could be seen as allegories on the inevitable end of all human life or on the sure decline of power. Thus it seems that the prevailing idea is one of dissolution, and interestingly, in the *tao tie* of a later period, only the eyes stand out from the intricate labyrinth of spirals making up the rest of the body.

hu   *lei*   *fang*   *chih*   *ku*   *tsun*   *chia*   *chueh*   *ho*   *kuang*

by the ruler of the great Chu kingdom in the middle Yangtze valley, who was not seen as "Chinese" by the northerners, but as an alien, claiming no connection with the kings of Zhou. Yet Chu had now become an integral part of the power struggle which was to decide the fate of China.

Nothing has been said so far about the early history, or prehistory, of the southern half of China, from the Yangtze valley southwards. This is because very little is known. The kingdom of Chu, in the middle reaches of the great river, spreading southwards into the province of Hunan, with its southern capital at Changsha, was well known to the northern Chinese, and its history is recorded by them. But archaeology in the Changsha neighbourhood has revealed that underlying the imported northern culture of ideographic script, bronze casting, and literature, there had been an earlier, very different culture, quite unlike that of North China. Its art is fantastic: wooden figures with protruding tongues and flowers growing from the limbs, all of which has affinities, however strange this may be, with the Polynesian culture which flourished in the Pacific islands and New Zealand more than 2000 years later.

It poses a major problem: did the bearers of this southern Chinese culture move southeast to the coast, and then in the course of unrecorded migrations finally reach the Pacific? It is highly improbable that the migration could have been the other way round at so early a period. In Yunnan, the most southwesterly province of China, excavated tombs near the capital, Kunming, have produced bronzes which although owing their technology to China, are decorated with figures of a wholly non-Chinese character, seeming to represent a pastoral people. In some other parts of what is now South China, Paleolithic man has been excavated, and would seem to have been of a different species to Peking Man from the North. It is clear that except for Chinese-influenced Chu the peoples of the South were illiterate, and their cultures distinct. Ethnically they may well have been the ancestors of the "minority peoples" who today inhabit parts of these provinces in many different groups and communities.

Along the lower Yangtze and the southeast coast of China there arose two kingdoms, that of Wu along the river, and Yue on the coast. The people of Wu were certainly not close kin of the northern Chinese, and their language, or dialect, still influences the speech of the region, where it is often called "Shanghai dialect" but more correctly the language of Wu. The Yue people along the coast of the provinces of Jiangsu and Zhejiang are in fact the same ethnic people as the Viet of modern Vietnam, and in fact "Yue" is the Standard Chinese pronunciation of *Viet*. This people were widespread along the southern Chinese coast, and in the view of some scholars may have formed one of the components of the later Japanese people. They were seafarers, and for a short time intervened effectively in the affairs of northern and Yangtze China. The two kingdoms of Wu and Yue fought a war, immortalized in later Chinese dramatic art, in which there were complete reversals of fortune and many dramatic incidents. Modern scholars tend to think that some of these have crept into history from drama.

Four-legged *fang-ting* vases are considered to be a variation of the tripod type made by vase makers of the Longshan period. The chief decorative motifs are heads of animals (masks of oxen, bulls, stags and rams). More rarely, human faces are found, as for instance on the *ting* type of vase (above), where the mask appears on all four sides, framed by stylized spirals and broken lines. This particular vase, dating from 11th century B.C., comes from Henan, the most ancient site of bronze-making in China.

Opposite: a *fang-ting* vase embossed with geometric decoration, originating from the first dynasty of the Eastern Zhou and dated around the 10th century B.C. The four legs and the handles are modelled in zoomorphic forms of horned animals, and the upper part of the frontal decoration shows two birds facing one another.

In Northern China the internecine war between the states continued with ever greater ferocity. Gone were the restraints of feudal chivalry. Treachery, surprise, unprovoked aggression, ruthless slaughter of defeated armies marked its progress. The small states were annexed by more powerful neighbours; the aristocracy, displaced by these annexations, sold its services to the highest bidder among the remaining greater powers. The harsh regime and doctrines of the School of the Law were formed and taught by refugee noblemen from the eastern states, not by natives of rather uncultured Qin.

Among a host of scheming adventurers there were also the "wandering scholars," of whom Confucius can be counted the first, who travelled from court to court seeking the just king who would put their doctrines into practice. Alas, they never found one. From 325 B.C. all the rulers of the remaining large states had usurped the title of king. The real king of Zhou was reduced to a petty princeling holding only his capital at Luoyang. In reality the Zhou dynasty as a force of any political significance ended then, but historians have preferred to treat it as still the ruling house until the final unification of China in 221 B.C. At first it had seemed that the inevitable victory of one of the great states would resolve itself into a conflict between Qin in the Northwest and Chu in the South, since they were the most powerful. But Chu was fatally harmed by a long war with Wu, down river along the Yangtze, and Qin annexed the two remote but rich states of Ba and Shu, in the modern province of Sichuan, southwest of Qin. This gave Qin an economic power far superior to its rivals and also access to the territories of the great enemy, Chu.

So, in the end, it was Qin that triumphed. Qin was, in the eyes of the eastern Chinese, a semi-barbarous state: rough, uncultured, fierce and possibly partly of alien ethnic stock. Qin had absorbed elements of the Rong or Di, the nomadic peoples who had plagued the Zhou kings when they ruled in the West. But the eastern powers would not unite to oppose their common enemy; they still attacked each other, failed to uphold treaties of alliance, and thus exposed themselves, one by one, to invasion and destruction by Qin. The historian of the early Han dynasty, Sima Qian, graphically describes what happened. "As a silkworm devours a mulberry leaf, so Qin swallowed up the kingdoms of the Empire." It was a result profoundly unwelcome to the cultured Chinese of the eastern kingdoms. But it was also the most important turning point in Chinese history until modern times. The king of Qin was now entitled *Shi Huang Di*, First Emperor, and he hoped that his descendants would continue the sequence for "ten thousand years." Like other more modern conquerors who thought they were founding long-lasting empires, he was to be disappointed.

During his 11 years as sole monarch of the Chinese world, he endeavoured, aided by convinced ministers of the School of the Law, to transform Chinese society. Feudalism was abolished in all its forms, and thus private ownership of land became the rule. Weights and measures, even the width of cart axles were standardized. The script was made uniform in all parts of the new empire. Books, except for those on the history of Qin and

Amulet in jade in the form of a human figure, originating from the mid- or late-Eastern Zhou dynasty, dated about 9th–8th century B.C.

Opposite: bronze figure of a young Mongol holding two birds, in jade, dating from the late Zhou period, 4th to 3rd centuries B.C. During the first Zhou period, the working of jade was limited to the production of amulets, ritual objects and some few personal ornaments, produced in a stylized, unimaginative and allusive manner typical of a primitive art which rarely occupied itself with the human form, its subject matter being in the main animalistic. Jade working became widespread about the beginning of 5th century B.C., with the large-scale production of ornaments for wearing with apparel

and as decoration for arms. The craftsmen soon achieved a perfection of design and execution which has remained unsurpassed throughout all the centuries of Chinese tradition in this field.

technical subjects such as agriculture, were prohibited or publicly burned as in the famous "Burning of the Books." We would have little knowledge of early Chinese history or thought if devoted scholars, at risk of their lives, had not hidden away many books. As these scholars were mainly Confucian, they preserved the works of their own school rather than those of their rivals. Much of ancient Chinese literature survives only in fragments or quotations.

This loss is the more serious as we know, from what has survived, that this tumultuous period of the Warring States was also the great age of early Chinese philosophy and innovative thinking. Confucius himself, never much heeded in his lifetime, had before long a large following from whom came other famous thinkers. Mencius (372?–?289 B.C.) was perhaps the most influential on the formation of a coherent doctrine. Some of the later Confucians differed on fundamental points. Xun Ze held that the nature of man was basically bad, whereas Confucius and Mencius taught that it was good. Xun Ze's teaching found favour with the new School of the Law, who based their harsh theories on this doctrine. The Taoists also flourished, and it is now believed that their basic text, the *Dao De Jing* (translated under the title *The Way and Its Power* by Arthur Waley), was written by an unknown Taoist scholar in the 3rd century B.C.

There were many others, of whose teaching little now remains extant. It is also clear that the differentiation into "Schools" strictly following the teaching of one master is more the rationalization of the ancient surviving literature than a true picture of the age in which it was produced. There were masters and disciples, but there were also many independent-minded thinkers who did not gather a great host of followers, but were known, respected, or condemned by their contemporaries, and sometimes quoted, even if often in derision. It was a very active age of intellectual adventure.

There are certain characteristics which seem to Western eyes surprising or unexpected. The great debate was twofold: the real nature of man and his role in the universe, and the proper form which the state should take and the extent of its power. But the gods hardly enter into the discussion. Confucius remarked that man should first study how to behave towards his fellowmen before considering the needs of the gods. Other teachers such as Mo Ti emphasized an abstract idea, Love, Law, or moral authority. None evoked the sanction or the blessing of a god to support their teaching. Gods did indeed receive their worship. Tian (Heaven), an ancient sky god, was now seen, rather vaguely, as the supreme arbiter of the universe, but could only be directly worshipped by the overlord king. The many local deities of the rivers, mountains, and crops, were more honoured by the common people than by the educated ruling classes.

This humanistic outlook is a very deep and enduring characteristic of Chinese thought. It shows the high place which history, whether ancient and mostly legendary, or later, accurately recorded, holds in Chinese culture. History is the record of the acts of men, not the interventions of deities. There was never a powerful priesthood in ancient China (nor in later

Blade made of jade from the first Zhou dynasty (8th–7th century B.C.) decorated with dragon motifs – one of the most frequently recurring themes in Chinese art. In Chinese iconology, the dragon represents the positive *yang* principle, the bringer of rain and therefore of prosperity. The ancient Chinese regarded jade as the most precious stone and it therefore had a symbolic significance when used in religious ceremonies and propitiary rituals. The use of jade on arms signified a ritual object, not an offensive weapon.

Opposite: bronze *hu* or ceremonial vase for wine, with silver and gold inlay, from the period of the Warring States (3rd century B.C.).

A bronze from 5th century B.C. (period of the Warring States), probably a bell (height: c. 18·2 cms.), decorated both outside and within. As regards the outside decoration, which is all that is visible in this picture, the chief iconographic motif would seem to represent an animal firmly entwined with other animals and birds. On the upper part, we see talons clutching a bird with a long beak, surrounded by scrolls and other purely decorative ornamentation. Bells of this sort were used for the cult of the ancestors: it was common practice to mix the blood of a sacrificial victim (such as a sheep or a bull) with the molten metal during casting.

Opposite: painting on silk, detail from a screen showing the battle between a warrior and a dragon. Period of the Warring States (from an excavation in Changsha).

centuries either). The rites reserved for the gods and above all for the ancestral spirits were carried out by the elders of the family, or by civil officials appointed to conduct them. The very emphasis on the ancestral cult is humanist, not deist. Ancestors were not deified, they hardly needed to be, for they were far more profoundly respected than any god, and were believed, in ancient times, to be able and willing to intervene to protect their posterity. Gods, on the other hand, were impersonal, little more than forces of nature, to be placated with sacrifices or entreated for favourable weather by offerings. No morality is attributed to the gods, only power.

In the realm of politics the Chinese thinkers hotly debated which doctrine should be upheld by the state, that is by the king, but they never at any time questioned the institution of monarchy. There was no state not ruled by an absolute monarch, great or small. The question at issue was, should the king make this or that the orthodox teaching and impose it by law. The second was, how could the character of the king be formed so that he should rule with justice and moderation and avoid extravagance and luxurious debauch, cruelty and excessive ambition. Each teacher had his own views on this all-important question. Confucius put his faith in moral training, and in the course of history his faith was sometimes, to some degree, justified. The Taoists denied the problem. Let the king, like any other wise man, give his entire being to conformity with the *Dao*, the Way, and all difficulties would be solved because they would cease to be relevant. The School of the Law, seeing that kings were but men, had little hope in their instinctive wisdom or justice. They devised their rigid law to make government possible and effective, even if the reigning king was a weakling, a debauchee, or an arbitrary man of whim. What to do about the character of the king, and the corollary, the nature of the doctrine upheld by the state, formed the kernel of Chinese philosophic thinking.

The courts of the rival monarchs in the age of the Warring States were hardly places where the just king was likely to be found: the great thinkers did indeed try to find one, but without success. Mencius reproached the king of Wei for the cruelty of his actions. "But it is not I, it is my officers who do these things," replied the king. "And if you take a sword and kill a man, will you say, 'it is not I, it is the sword that did it?'" Mencius replied.

The philosophers, other than the School of the Law, had little effect on the rulers of their age, but are far better remembered by later generations. The fact that the Confucians based their teaching on the moral training of young people, i.e. on the duties of the family, was perhaps the key to their ultimate triumph over a host of rivals more popular in their day. The family system was not only the basis of Chinese society, but also of its political system. The reason why Chinese thinkers never contemplated alternatives to monarchy nor even framed a term for liberty (only "to let loose") was that the king was deemed to be the head, the father, of a great family to which all his subjects belonged, and in which each had his defined place and duty. Loyalty was the greatest virtue, sincerity and kindness followed suit.

A doctrine which related what every Chinese family knew to be the clue to happy relations and harmony in the home, to the moral imperatives of heaven itself, and duty and loyalty to the king, had an instinctive appeal. Here were no high abstractions: honour the heads of the family, obey the king, be not oppressive to inferiors, nor insolent to superiors; be just, be sincere, and above all be loyal. Every Chinese could understand that.

In China there is thus the paradox, as it often seems to the Westerner, of a people who produced a profound philosophy which considered all aspects of the human condition, but never questioned the system of absolute monarchy, nor sought the sanction of divine revelation for their thought.

The great revolution which overturned the Warring States and led to the unification of China into a centralized empire, the form of government which has remained the ideal, and for most of the succeeding centuries represented the central fact of China's history, was as far-reaching in its social as in its political consequences. The whole system of the old feudal aristocracy was swept away. Those of that class who were not slain in the final wars were forced by the conqueror to live in the vicinity of his capital, where they existed on miserable pensions. The former ruling families were, as far as they could be identified, massacred. Land ownership was made free to all, which meant in effect the rise of a landlord class, recruited from the richer official families, and the substitution of tenant status for serfdom for the peasantry.

This change of status can only have been of very marginal benefit to the peasants. Trade, and the merchants, on the other hand benefited greatly. The whole extent of the empire was now open to trade and travel; no internal frontiers, except the borders of administrative districts, remained. The Qin empire built roads to connect all regions, mainly for military reasons. The empire was now ruled by officers directly appointed by the emperor, no local lords remained, and the officials in charge were more often from Qin itself. The whole empire was subjected to the very drastic Qin code of law which was ruthlessly applied.

Therein lay the first Qin emperor's great mistake. The Chinese people, as a critic of the next century was to record, wanted only peace after more than two centuries of incessant war, vast loss of life, and constant devastation by warring armies. They would have gladly given their full loyalty to the Qin empire, if its rule had been moderate and humane. But it was not: the School of the Law ruled in Qin, and took over the new empire. The harsh laws were enforced in all their severity, taxation increased; the alien Qin officials feared and distrusted the population they were appointed to govern. Only the military power of Qin held the empire in trembling, sullen, obedience.

Such is the picture of Qin rule transmitted by the next age, but as the work of enemies of Qin, or their grandsons, it may well be biased. Indeed a recent major archaeological discovery has gone some way to confirm the fact that the Qin held their conquered subjects in fear and suspicion. The first emperor was buried not far from his capital, near to modern Xi'an. His vast tomb mound, an artificial hill, dominates the locality. In 1972, about a kilometer to the east of the tomb, the digging of a well in the

Small figure in silver, representing a Northerner, at that time considered a "foreigner," dating from 6th–5th century B.C., the period of the Warring States; found in the Henan region.

Opposite: female figure in squatting position, made of clay, found in the modern state of Shaanxi. Below left: copper weight with inscriptions. These two objects date from feudal times or, to be more exact, from the reign of the Qin during the period of the Warring States. Top right: finely-worked rhinoceros, chiselled in gold and silver, found in the province of Shaanxi and dating from 5th–3rd century B.C., during the period of the Warring States. Center right: a *hu* or vase for wine, from 5th–4th century B.C., with engravings of hunting and battle scenes. The drawing (bottom right) illustrates the details which include, top part, practice with the bow and arrow and the gathering of the leaves of the mulberry bush; center panel, bird netting, the pounding of rice and a concert with bronze bells and musical stones; bottom panel, a battle by land and sea.

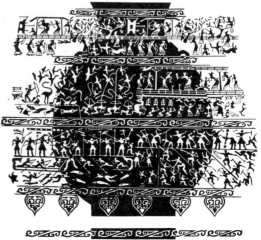

local commune, led to the discovery of a huge underground vault in which, as subsequent excavation revealed, were some 6000 life-size terra-cotta figures, in all probability those of the imperial guard. Each individual statue has a character of its own, with distinctive features. All are armed and drawn up in battle array; placed as they are to the east of the tomb and the capital, they form a spirit army ready to repel by magic powers invaders from the east. The eastern provinces were precisely the lands that Qin had conquered. The first emperor still feared revolt and revenge by his enemies when he planned his own tomb.

That he also contributed to our own time a treasury of works of art unrivalled of its kind anywhere in the world was of course no part of his intention. Tomb figures were never intended to be seen by mortal eyes following interment. But the site has largely revised the accepted view of Qin as a society dedicated to philistine values as taught by the School of the Law. Whoever made the "Spirit Army" were great artists, perhaps conquered subjects from the former kingdoms; no trace of their names would have been left, they will for ever remain unknown. The Qin empire, traditionally decried as an unmitigated tyranny, has been more kindly viewed by contemporary Chinese scholars, and Mao Zedong himself was an admirer, in some respects at least, of his great royal predecessor in revolution, Shi Huang Di.

The first emperor's fears were fully justified. He died on a journey to the east coast, undertaken to stimulate the quest for the legendary islands of the Immortals, who possessed the drug of longevity, which the emperor craved to obtain for himself. When he in fact found that other kind of immortality, his entourage concealed his death (easily done, since he lived in total seclusion, never seen by his subjects), and induced the crown prince, then on the northern frontier, to take his own life on the production of a false order from the emperor charging him with conspiracy. The ministers and chief eunuch then put the second son, a silly youth, on the throne as Er Shi Huang Di, or second emperor. The background to the plot was the known opposition of the crown prince to the harsh rule of his father, who had he come to the throne, would have dismissed the ministers who supported and upheld it.

It was a decision fatal to the Qin empire. The new ruler was a mere tool in the hands of his unscrupulous ministers. Within a year his weak rule and the hatred felt for his government provoked the very revolt that the first emperor had clearly feared.

It began as a local protest against the transportation of convicted men to labour on the construction of the Great Wall, a form of forced convict labour particularly oppressive and hated by the people. Once one revolt broke out, others followed at once in all parts of the empire, and the central authority collapsed. At first the rebels sought to enthrone obscure members of the former royal houses, but these phantom kings did not last long: they were swept aside by the real leaders, men of various origin, some from the old aristocracy, some from the peasantry, who not only proclaimed themselves kings of the regions they seized, but made war on the imperial army, as well

Objects of everyday use, decorated with lacquer, from about 3rd to 2nd century B.C. The small bowls and the box in red and black lacquer were used for toiletries, probably containing rouge, face powder and hair combs.

Opposite: lacquered wood carvings from the feudal age. At this time, lacquer decoration rose to new heights and reached a pitch of perfection

which has never been equalled in any other country. Lacquer, a resinous secretion also used for protective covering, could be applied to all kinds of material: wood, terra cotta, bronze, paper or cloth for instance. It is quite probable that artists of the Shang period already knew the use of lacquer but it was only during the 3rd and 4th centuries B.C. that this artistic medium became widely known and used.

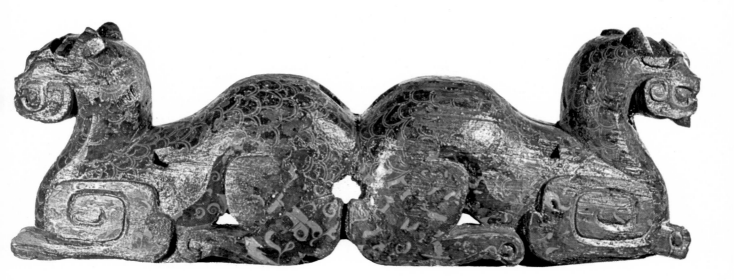

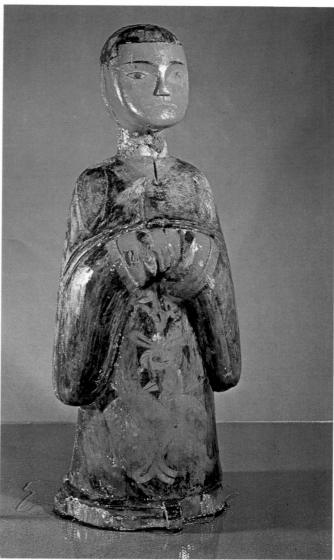

人 大 天 女 家

Present outline of the character meaning "man." In the archaic, picturegraphic form, the representation of the human body was more clearly distinguishable, if already somewhat stylized, with the addition of a dot to indicate the head.

This character is derived from the preceding one: it represents a male adult with arms stretched out. In its extended meaning, it represents the abstract concept of "large, greatness."

Another logical derivation from the picturegram meaning "man." A thick line or other sign at the top changes the meaning to "sky, Heaven."

This is the present-day form of the character for "woman." In its original picturegraphic form, the outline for woman was the same as for man. Later, however, it was refined by emphasizing the belly.

This character signifies "home, family." This abstract idea is composed of two concrete images: a pig, which was a family's precious possession, placed under the sign meaning "roof" or "enclosure."

CHINESE WRITING: SYMBOL AND LOGIC

The examples illustrated above give some idea as to the concept of Chinese script and the logic which inspired these combinations of symbols. It was a logic which allowed a progression from the concrete to the abstract and from the particular to the universal. This kind of writing does not indicate a word by means of its phonemes but rather by imparting an idea of its sense. It is therefore pointless to ask what the letters of the Chinese alphabet are: each character represents a word, an idea, in its completness. Thus, Chinese civilization may be seen to have brought picturegraphic writing, once common to so many cultures, to a height of complexity and usefulness. In the Shuowen lexicon, compiled in the 2nd century, there are listed 364 true picturegrams (some, with their evolutionary forms, are shown in the table on the left). These characters are defined as "simple symbols" along with 125 signs,

so-called "indicators" suggesting content or action (some are shown in the table in the center of the opposite page). Then come the complex symbols or "logical aggregates" which form the most interesting group from an etymological point of view, since their meaning has to be derived from an understanding of the meaning of two or more characters, of which they are composed. The Shuowen lists 1167 of these and on the table at the top of the opposite page, we give several examples. The greatest number of Chinese characters, however, belong to the group known as "phonetic aggregates." These are composed of two or more simple symbols, one of which indicates the group meaning while the others provide a generic indication as to pronunciation of the whole. The Shuowen lists 7697 characters of this type: in the table below left are some examples which show the logical progression

Meaning	Archaic form	GRADUAL EVOLUTION						Modern form
elephant								象
stag								鹿
tiger								虎
dog								狗
horse								馬
ox								牛
bird								鳥
swallow								燕
sparrow								雀
snake								蛇
tortoise								龜

IDEOGRAMS OR LOGICAL AGGREGATES

Modern form / Archaic form

The sun 日 above a line ━ (the horizon) means "dawn, the beginning of the day."

A tree 木 (with vertical trunk, branches and roots), together with another similar sign, means "forest."

Two men 从 seated on the 土 ground talking means "sitting down, to be seated."

A man 儿 in an enclosed 囗 means "prisoner, to be imprisoned."

A hand 手 which shields the eye 目 means "to look, to observe closely."

A foetus Ɛ in the womb means "to wrap, to contain."

An ear 耳 near to two others means "to plot, conspiracy."

An axe 斤 being used to make a box 匚 means "carpenter."

INDICATORS

These are signs which suggest a meaning, often of action, and can be used either by themselves or in the formation of other, more complex characters.

A sign 卜 written above a line (the horizon) ━
Meaning: up, above, to climb, superior.

A sign 卜 written below line representing horizon ━
Meaning: down, below, underneath, to descend, inferior.

Sinuous sign 勹 conventionally used to mean breathing, breath, meats an obstacle, represented by a line ━
Meaning: to breathe with difficulty, hiccup.

Breathing 勹 has overcome the obstacle 二 and is free expands. Meaning: to speak, to articulate, to demonstrate.

PHONETIC AGGREGATES

This sign is the phonetic indicator. It means "prince." It is used to form other characters with different meanings but with the same pronunciation (*zhu*) as the indicator.

This character means candle, incense stick. It is composed of the indicator with the sign for "fire," on the left.

The indicator is joined with the character meaning "man" (always in stylized form in compounds). The meaning is "to live in, to reside."

This character means "to explain, to comment." It is formed from the phonetic indicator and, on the left, the character for "word."

Meaning "to lean against." It is formed from the phonetic indicator and, on the left, the symbol for "hand" (stylized in compounds).

The meaning of this character, formed from the indicator and the picturegram for "horse," is "to stop, to pause."

of thought in the formation of these signs. It should be remembered that these written phonetic aggregates, when first introduced, had the effect of differentiating between words of the same pronunciation, spoken at that date or in whatever dialect. However, owing to the natural evolution of the spoken language, the pronunciation of many words has changed so much that today the phonetic constituent of a high percentage of characters no longer has any reference to the sound or even to the meaning of the words which helped to form them. In the written language, on the other hand, there is no possibility of confusion between the many words which sound similar, for each is represented by a different combination of signs. Why is it then that, considering the difficulty and impracticability of this form of writing, there was no move to a phonetic notation, to alphabetic script in fact? Since every Chinese word is formed of a single, unvarying syllable, an entity in itself, it was impossible to divide it up into separate phonetic components (letters of the alphabet). Nowadays, the Chinese feel strongly the need for an alphabetic script, but its adoption would depend on the widespread diffusion of *Putonghua*, the dialect of the Peking region which is considered the nearest to a national standard of reference.

In olden times, the characters were engraved with a stylus made of bamboo or metal, with which it was possible to draw lines of all shapes and of equal thickness.

Later, at the beginning of the first century A.D., the Chinese began to write with brushes dipped in ink and the characters assumed their typically painted appearance: they became flowing lines of variable thickness, either straight or delicately curved. From a calligraphic point of view (see table below) all the characters can be formed of between nine and 17 signs.

SIMPLE SIGNS

These are the basic calligraphic elements from which all the characters are formed.

as on their rivals. In this chaos the second emperor, his chief minister and great supporter of the School of the Law, and the chief eunuch, who had engineered the plot on the death of the first emperor, all perished in successive *coups d'état* and assassinations; a rebel army captured the capital, massacred what remained of the Qin royal family, and burned and looted the city.

Thus fell the Qin empire. The rival rebels then fought a long civil war to decide who should reconstruct and refound the fallen empire; but not to restore the past system of feudalism. The conflict, famous in Chinese literature and drama, was won by the founder of the Han dynasty, by birth a village headman.

Drawings showing the type of armour worn by soldiers of the first Qin emperor, Shi Huang Di. When his extremely complex tomb, spread over a hilltop, was excavated, more than 6000 life-size terra-cotta statues of warriors and royal officials were brought to light.

Opposite: kneeling warrior. The discovery of this tomb, near Xi'an, in the province of Shaanxi, in 1972, was an event of exceptional archaeological interest, not least because of the high artistic quality of the finds. Shi Huang Di assumed the title of first emperor of China in 221 B.C., having conquered and united for the first time the different Chinese kingdoms. Legend, and also written fragments, testify to the wonderful treasures which had been buried in the emperor's tomb. Almost certainly it was broken into and robbed a few months after the entombment of the emperor.

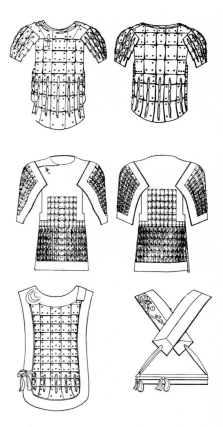

Shown here are some of the most important finds from excavations of the area surrounding the tomb of Shi Huang Di at Xi'an. Statues of horses, busts and full-length figures of soldiers, officials and courtiers, were superbly modelled in clay. The horses and soldiers, collectively given the name of "the Qin army," were in fact the imperial guard.

Opposite below, from left to right: spearheads, the trigger mechanism of a crossbow and a bronze bell.

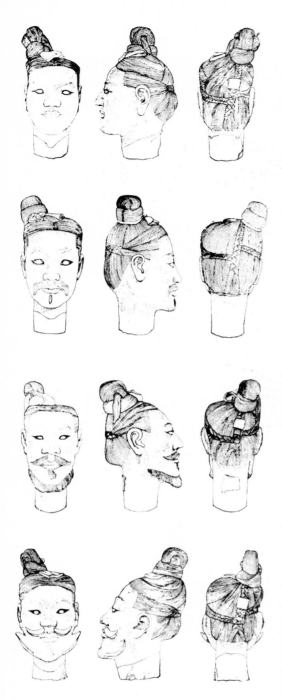

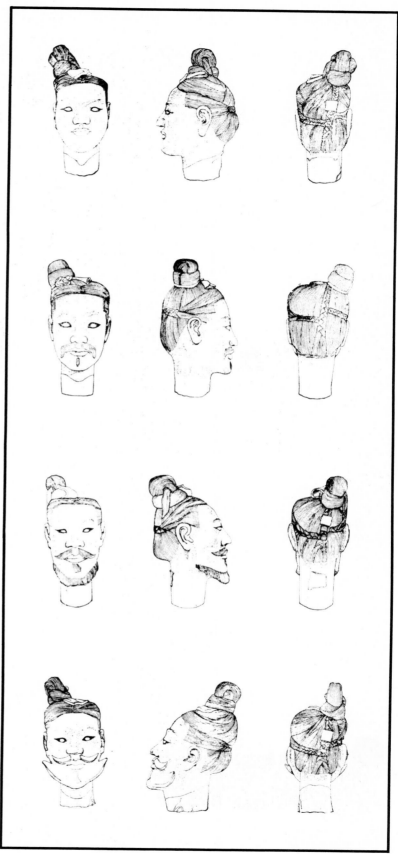

These drawings illustrate soldiers' hairstyles around the 3rd century B.C.

Opposite: a clay bust of a warrior unearthed during the excavations of the tomb of the first Qin emperor. In Chinese history, the figure of Shi Huang Di is linked with the first great revolution in 221 B.C. In that year, he took control of the country, completely destroying the feudal system of ancient China and installing in its place a centralized monarchy. According to popular tradition, his name became universally hated and despised during the building of the Great Wall, a massive project which cost the lives of over 1,000,000 men.

THE EARLY EMPIRE

Opposite: gilded, bronze statuette of a girl holding a lamp, dated around 100 B.C. On it are inscribed the words "Chang Xin" (eternal faithfulness), and it was probably a wedding gift to Tou Wan, wife of prince Liu Sheng and sister-in-law of the emperor Wu (141–87 B.C).

Above: marble figurines in an attitude of prayer (Han period), found in 1968 in the tomb of the princess Tou Wan.

Although the Qin first unified China, the event might have been shortlived had not the Han dynasty consolidated the new political system. Just as Alexander briefly unified the Middle East, it was Rome that founded the long-enduring empire. So the Han played, at a shorter interval of time, the role of Rome.

Liu Bang, founder of the Han dynasty, was by birth a village headman, and quite probably illiterate. This in itself was something unheard of in China at that period. That anyone other than a gentleman, an aristocrat, could aspire to be a ruler, let alone the supreme emperor, would a few years earlier have been unthinkable. But during the long civil war that followed the collapse of Qin, many other men of obscure origin had risen to high command. Liu Bang was simply the most able, crafty and politically skilful of many competitors. He was also, when it seemed wise, merciful; and when it appeared expedient, cruel and ruthless. Those were the conditions in which men of power then lived; and he was successful.

As it developed over four centuries, with one break of short-lasting usurpation, the Han empire followed in its organization and system of government the model of the Qin, but with policies more humane, less precipitate, and not at all anti-cultural. It is true that the founder had no knowledge of books nor respect for scholars; but a story told of him (whether true or not, it is famous) is revealing.

One day, riding forth from his palace to a hunt, the emperor was stopped by a kneeling scholar, who offered him a bundle of books, saying, "These will help Your Majesty to govern the Empire." The emperor smacked the rump of his horse, and said, "On horseback I conquered the Empire, what need have I for books?" The scholar replied, "Yes Sire, you conquered the Empire on horseback, but can you also govern it from the saddle?" The emperor is said to have been so impressed by this answer that from then on he admitted scholars to his council. But the tale epitomizes what was a fact.

The persecution of scholars, the prohibition of books, was discontinued; it was not that the emperors immediately adopted the teaching of Confucianism as an orthodoxy, but that when persecution ceased the Confucians were the strongest surviving group, and profited most from the revival of the hidden and half-lost literature of the former age. Thus they gained the dominant position in education. Taoism also flourished, and recent archaeological discoveries of great importance in Hunan province, near Changsha, have brought to light the entire library of a Han nobleman of the 2nd century B.C., which contains the Taoist classical writings and many other books on a wide variety of subjects. This in itself goes far to confirm the historical record of a great revival of literature in the early Han period.

In political matters the early Han rulers were cautious. They revived a limited feudalism, to satisfy the critics, but confined it to members of their own imperial family. Moreover the new "kings" had relatively small realms, sandwiched in between provinces ruled by directly appointed imperial governors. After a revolt in 154 B.C. by the seven chief kings of the eastern provinces had been suppressed, the then emperor ruling decreed that all the sons of the king of any feudal realm should divide his kingdom among them at his death, all having equal status. In a very few generations this law reduced the "kingdoms" to small districts without political importance. The numerous sons of a royal polygamous family always claimed their rights, and became in a short time simply members of a provincial aristocracy, bearing the imperial surname.

Another consequence of the established rule of exogamy in marriage, which no Chinese government ever questioned, was that as the emperor, except for his feudatories, all members of his family, was now the sole monarch in the Chinese world, he could not marry any girl of royal birth, because there were none. It was never considered conceivable that the emperor could marry the daughter of some chief of a nomadic tribe, or one from the mountains of the Far West. So the monarch must marry a commoner; or at best the daughter of a high official. But this was risky, the new consort family at once became the second family of the empire, and the prime target for envy, hate, and intrigue.

To defend themselves from these dangers, they tried to fill the government service with their own relatives and loyal clients, with the result that they increased the envy and jealousy of rival grandees. When the ruling emperor died his successor married into another family; these in turn acquired the prestige and rank of the consort family, and promptly massacred the members of the former one on the grounds that they were conspiring to usurp the throne, a charge which was quite probably true, for they had no other possible escape route.

This problem continued to plague the Han dynasty. For if the emperor fell in love with a pretty girl around the court, she was quite likely to belong to a family of no great power or influence. If he then made her empress, her upstart family, knowing too well what jealousies they aroused, would be all the more determined to preserve and extend their new-found power. One way was to try to betroth the heir to the throne to another girl of the same family as his mother, the empress, for the rule of exogamy was not scientifically based, it did not in any way impede marriage between close cousins provided they were not of the same patrilineal descent.

There were therefore frequent disturbances at court, but they had very little effect on the provinces; just as the assassinations of emperors in Rome made little stir in Syria or Gaul, so the fall of one consort family and the rise of another were matters for the ambitious nobles of the capital, not for the quiet routine life of distant provinces. For a very long period the greater part of China was at peace. The historian Sima Qian relates how he could, and did, travel all over the empire safely. Men held the local offices that their fathers had occupied, and often took their surnames from these positions (i.e. *Zang*, the Storekeeper).

The Han empire was not at first quite as extensive as that of

Above and opposite: model towers from the Han period. The custom of putting these small, painted clay models in tombs was fairly widespread. They provide us with inestimable evidence of Han period architecture, being miniatures of the houses, granaries, pagodas, etc., of the rich, landed proprietors.

Below: a vivid illustration of farm life, from a tile dating from the Han period.

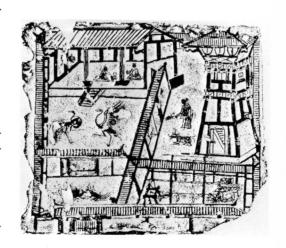

the Qin. Shi Huang Di had conquered the kingdom of Nan Yue, now the Canton region, but it revolted and regained independence at his death. But in the reign of the emperor Wu (141–87 B.C.), when the scars of the great civil wars had long been healed, the Chinese empire engaged in a long period of expansion and frontier wars, which were ultimately entirely successful. Nan Yue, to the south, was invaded and conquered; so was the Yue kingdom, in what is now the province of Fujian. North Korea, to the northeast, became a Chinese province, and constant and dramatic wars with the nomad peoples of Inner Mongolia, called Xiong Nu by the Chinese, and presumed to be the early ancestors of the Huns, ended after many years in the breakup of the Xiong Nu confederacy and the flight to the far west, beyond the Chinese horizon, of a great part of these nomads.

These wars, partly to secure the frontier, partly to gain rich lands (in the South) brought China into contact with Southeast Asia, and since what is now called North Vietnam was a province of Nan Yue, Chinese rule was imposed there also. The Korean colony was rich and, to judge by the furniture of the tombs of the ruling Chinese officials, also cultured.

The war against the northern nomads led to the opening, first by exploration, then by war, of the great caravan road across Central Asia from Northwest China to Kashgar, Persia, and down to India, and on to the frontiers of the Roman world. In the emperor Wu's reign this road was not only pioneered by one of his envoys, but used by one of his armies, sent to reduce to obedience a contumacious local king, whose state was in what is now Russian Turkestan. Chinese imperial expansion in the reign of emperor Wu was on a grand scale; Canton was permanently annexed to the empire; the suzerainty imposed on the southwest provinces of Yunnan and modern Guizhou was to lead to full conquest in later times; Korea remained a tributary after it ceased to be a province, and the same was true of Vietnam. Inner Mongolia, for long the stronghold of the persistent foes of China, was ultimately reduced and finally largely settled by Chinese. Thus the emperor Wu roughed out the extent and the borders of what in the course of time was to become the Chinese empire, and ultimately the People's Republic of our own age.

In the internal affairs of the empire, under emperor Wu, we have the historian Sima Qian's contemporary account of the economic problems which emerged in the newly-united empire, and how they were solved. Sima Qian was not a favourable critic: he had himself suffered, being accused of participation in a conspiracy, and his ill will towards the emperor is apparent. Nevertheless it is a rare example of concentration on economic issues from the pen of an ancient historian.

China, with the foundation of an unified state, had changed to a money economy, in place of the largely barter trade of earlier, smaller political units. The empire was now one, and trade could pass freely across former frontiers. The unit of common exchange was a copper coin, but silver ingots were also in use. The mint was not a government monopoly, and soon all those who found copper on their estates began to make vast fortunes by coining the metal. Inflation gripped the economy.

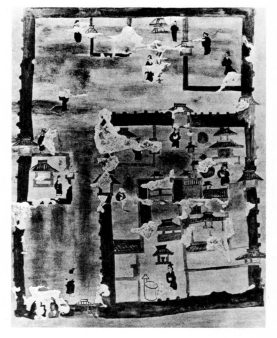

A planimetric representation of government buildings in a fresco of the Han dynasty which illustrates the secular flavour of the art of that time.

As well as hunting scenes, processions, historical and socially significant events, portraits of government officials and dignitaries were favourite subjects for artistic expression. An example is the illustration opposite showing a detail from a Han tomb fresco. The expressions of the two figures are particularly idiosyncratic.

Top and center: processions of dignitaries in their carriages.
Below: a chariot and horses in bronze (from a Han dynasty tomb, 2nd century B.C).

Opposite: bronze sculptures of horses and a carriage with a parasol, dating from the Han period. Horses and chariots were symbols of a privileged social class and are recurring themes in the decoration and furnishing of burial chambers. Artists of the Han period, both painters and sculptors, achieved the most fascinating effects in their representations of the horse, as may be seen in the bronze statues shown on these pages. They form part of a series of 126 sculptures found at Wuwei (Gansu) in the tomb of general Chang and his wife (Eastern Han dynasty, 25 B.C.–A.D. 220).

The emperor's first measures were more romantic than effective. He slew a rare white stag in his park, cut the skin into small pieces which he passed off as banknotes and which the rich were then compelled to redeem for great sums, all in the hope of mopping up the excess money in circulation. But the limited quantity of magical white deer's skin soon defeated this plan. The emperor, to the rage and contempt of the scholar officials, then turned to a member of the despised merchant class, Song Hung-yang, and made him his chief economic adviser.

Song suggested what would now seem the obvious, but at the time it was a highly revolutionary policy, namely involving the government in the economic running of the country. First, the minting of coin was made a government monopoly. That soon solved the inflation problem; but there were others. Salt and iron were essential commodities. For some centuries China had been passing from the Bronze Age into the Iron Age. Weapons of bronze were now more for ceremony than use, and iron agricultural tools had preceded the use of that metal for weapons. To control the price of iron, also forced up by monopolists who owned the mines, iron was, as we would say nowadays, "nationalized," that is made into another state monopoly. Salt, which in some inland parts of China is either mined, or has to be carried great distances from the coast, was also in the hands of grasping owners and traders. It too was made a state monopoly, and has remained so ever since.

All these changes were fiercely opposed by the conservative scholar officials. A Han text, not by Sima Qian, *Discourses on Salt and Iron*, survives with a full account of the debate which accompanied the setting up of these monopolies. The arguments of the merchant advisers are essentially practical, eschewing flights of philosophical discourse. Those of the opposing officials are not at all concerned with the practical issues, but concentrate on the Confucian views that trade is not the business of gentlemen, and still less of the emperor and his government. Exhortations to imperial virtue, admirable in themselves, were expected to cure economic ills. The emperor either had less faith in his own virtues and those of his officials, or more in the practical advice he received from his merchant advisers. He took the latter.

The last major problem was the perennial one of recurring glut and famine: while some areas of the great empire suffered droughts or floods, others enjoyed a good harvest. The scholar officials were inclined to leave nature alone and trust to their favourite remedy of curtailing court expenses and enhancing imperial virtue to overcome the problems. Emperor Wu, none too willing to cut down on court luxury, proposed another way out, the suggestion in fact coming from the ingenious Song Hung-yang. It was called the "Equalization" system, by which all provincial governors were ordered to build great granaries in which, in good years, the government bought up and stored excess grain rather than leave this activity to speculating merchants. In time of shortage, the grain from the government stores was sold at a reduced price, and if these measures proved inadequate, the surpluses stored in more favoured provinces were shipped, by the river system, to areas in distress. Not all

Above and opposite: three examples of chariots of the Han period (details of tomb-wall frescoes and relief). Light, elegant, even fragile in appearance, the two-wheeled chariot seems to have been the type most commonly used, not only by nobles and court dignitaries but also by rich merchants and landowners. These gentry showed how powerful they were in the number of their horses and escorting guards. The horses have harnesses fixed to their bodies and at the base of the neck – an innovation of the Han period.

Below: a lively representation of a battle between the Chinese and the Huns, in a print made from a relief found in a tomb in Shandong (end of 2nd century A.D.). The art of bas-relief appeared in China during the Han period, having probably been imported from the West. In the use of this new medium, Chinese artists remained completely faithful to their own thematic and stylistic traditions. Even though they were designed for funerary use, these reliefs illustrate episodes from everyday life or from the outstanding events of history. The scenes illustrated are full of life and possessed of tremendous wealth of detail.

such areas were easily reached by river, and there must have been massive overland traffic which in turn provided employment for a distressed peasantry. Some of these plans were revived in later ages, and on the whole, in spite of the organizational difficulties, they seem to have worked. Even Sima Qian admits so by implication, when he recounts how he could travel the empire and find it everywhere contented and at peace.

Emperor Wu had still to face one other unchanging problem, that of the consort families. He had himself succeeded to the throne at the age of 16, unmarried. His solution was radical and ruthless. He chose his bride, married her, and then put all her family (at least the males) to death. Thus there could be no consort family to scheme for power and try to defend itself against the envy of rivals. Those families who aspired to becoming consort families in the future were at least somewhat discouraged by this drastic prospect. But the emperor's successors did not follow this grim example. They married, permitted the ambitions of the consort family to take their accustomed course, with the predictable result.

Emperor Wu, partly perhaps by good fortune in having a great contemporary writer to record his reign (even if sometimes critical in tone), is one of the early Chinese rulers of whom most is known, and whose character can be assessed. He was able, innovative, open-minded and decisive. He agreed to the limitation of private holding of land and slaves so that there should be no undue concentration of wealth resulting from commerce and mining on a national scale. He was, obviously, also ruthless. In addition to his economic policies, which were successful, his foreign wars (in which he delegated command to his generals) were also on the whole successful and beneficial to his subjects: new lands and increased trade in the South, security from nomad raids in the North, and the opening of a window to unknown countries, of comparable civilization in the North-west. These conquests determined the frontiers of China as we think of her, and gave the Chinese the best lands in their known world. And during the next century Chinese officials would travel at least as far as the Indian Ocean, exchanging gold and silk for glass and pearls.

As to the question, all-important for the Chinese, of state orthodoxy in religion and philosophy, the emperor chose to make the Confucian doctrine supreme, according it a dominance which remained unshaken until the coming of the People's Republic. The earlier Han emperors had dabbled in Taoism, at times seeming to favour a form of the School of the

Law or, like the founder, had been basically indifferent, or unable, to indulge in such thinking.

It is very probable that the emperor's choice was dictated by practical political reasons; the Confucians had the best-preserved classical literary inheritance from the feudal past, which was now seen as an age of great philosophic development. They therefore had a near monopoly of the education of the young of the literate ruling class, now chosen by merit, not by noble descent. Taoism despised the world and took no interest in its affairs; the Confucians were devoted to the improvement of the moral quality of political and official life. Loyalty to the prince, now to the emperor, was a basic tenet of their doctrine and teaching. The School of the Law was discredited and remembered with hatred. Mo Ti's teaching had largely failed to survive the persecution under the Qin.

Practically therefore it was either a question of giving the award of orthodoxy to the Confucians, or making them enemies of the state. The results of doing the latter were all too clear from the history of the Qin. Emperor Wu avoided that peril. He appointed the Doctors of the Five Classics: the *Yi-jing* or Changes (an early divination manual); the *Shi-jing* or Odes; the *Shu-jing* or History; the *Chun Qiu* or Annals of Confucius; and the *Shi-li* or Rituals. All were studied in terms of moralistic and ritual commentaries, and a Grand College to train civil servants was eventually founded. But he himself was more interested in the strange cults, magical and mystical, which flourished on the east coast, notably in Shandong province, with their emphasis on the elixir of earthly immortality and the philosopher's stone which would turn dross into gold.

He patronized these sects; their leaders, able conjurors perhaps or at best inventive adventurers, enjoyed his favour and profited highly from it. One fashioned for the emperor a set of chessmen made of lodestone, which could be made to move on the board by themselves. This is one of the earliest, if not the first, known example of the discovery of magnetism, which later led in China to the invention of the maritime compass. Another magician, who promised to restore to life a favourite concubine, showed her in the recesses of a half-darkened room, but forbad the emperor to approach the phantom. His search for the elixir of life in the magical islands of the eastern sea, led to the despatch of several costly expeditions. Some did not return; it has been conjectured that their magician leaders thought it politic not to return, the large treasuries they controlled assuring them positions of wealth and power in the lands where they settled.

The weakness of every system of absolute autocracy is the problem of succession. Under an emperor such as Wu it works well enough; but who shall follow him, and will this successor be of adequate quality? The Chinese adhered to the law of primogeniture. Only the eldest son, by the principal wife, could be the true heir. Failing such, the emperor could remarry, or promote to the rank of empress a concubine who had a son. But this solution was always risky. Emperor Wu had quarrelled with his crown prince, accused, rightly or wrongly, of conspiracy. The young man took his own life, and when the old emperor died he was succeeded by a youth without much quality. Before long, when the new emperor's wife's family had risen to power, the old problem of the consort family reappeared.

In the 80 years that followed the death of emperor Wu no strong character occupied the throne; and towards the end of the 1st century B.C. a Wang family, established as consort family for more than two generations by the marriage of their daughters to the short-lived emperors, and the consequent regencies over minors, had acquired supreme power in the state, which they had held since 49 B.C. In A.D. 9, Wang Mang, the head of the family, swept aside all pretenses and deposed the reigning child-emperor, to usurp the throne himself, and call his regime the Xin (New) dynasty.

Wang Mang was able, and attempted some useful reforms: nationalization of land with division of large estates and manumission of slaves was repealed; a tax on slaveholding was substituted; to monopolies of salt, iron and coinage was added one on wine and other mining profits were taxed. Seven regional commissions were ordered to establish annual high, low and mean price levels for staple products, to buy surplus goods at cost, and to fix the market price by sales above the seasonal index. In order to curb usury, loans were offered free up to 90 days for funerals, and at three percent a month or ten percent a year for productive purposes. However, Wang had the misfortune to live through a major flooding of the Yellow River, which produced widespread ruin and disorder, giving his enemies, supporters of the Han, the chance to organize a rebellion. A long struggle ended with the victory of the Han claimant (scion of a fairly remote collateral branch) and the death of Wang Mang. The new Han emperor moved the capital eastwards from Changan (modern Xi'an) to Luoyang, in Henan province; hence the second half of the Han dynasty, which lasted almost exactly two centuries, is known as Eastern Han.

In all respects the Han system was once more restored. The phantom feudalism of the early Han period was now virtually extinct. The first of the new line, known by his "temple," i.e. posthumous, title of Guang Di (Brilliant Emperor), was indeed a fitting founder; sober, balanced and prudent, a skilful commander. His main object was to restore and maintain peace and he rejected all advice which suggested further wars. He made no significant innovations in the form of practice of government, but he did succeed in restoring the efficient working of the system which had operated under the Western Han, the first period of the dynasty.

The system of public examinations for careers in the civil service had not yet been devised. Officials were the protégés of great men, whose recommendation was the key to appointment. This system of "placemen," as it was known in 17th century England, was not necessarily as open to corruption as it may appear. The grandee had to vouch for his candidate's ability, literacy and reliability. A bad choice reflected on the grandee himself, and could rebound upon him. In effect it meant government by the literate, gentry class under the patronage of the most powerful and influential members of that class.

Under the Eastern Han, the policy of emperor Wu, that of

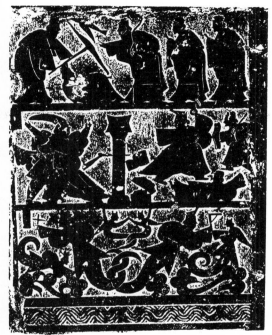

Three scenes from a funeral relief of the Wu family (2nd century B.C.), which reveal the compositional excellence of the Han sculptors. The scene at the top depicts a feudal situation: a charioteer protects his lord armed only with the canopy torn from the chariot and thus forces the attackers to admire such loyalty and strength. The central panel shows the attempted assassination of Shi Huang Di, first emperor of the Qin dynasty, by a cut-throat hired by the hereditary prince of the Yen. Only grazed by the dagger which instead becomes embedded in the pillar in the center, the king flees, calling for help (on the right) while the assassin is arrested by a guard (on the left). On the bottom panel appear Fu Xi and Nu Kua, two divinities, depicted with intertwined fishes' tails, from Taoist mythology.

expanding the influence of the empire and adding to its domains, was resumed. The route across the deserts of Turkestan to Persia and the Roman Orient now became the "Silk Road," travelled by caravans carrying this much sought-after commodity, of which the Chinese were both the inventors and sole producers, to Western Asia and the Roman empire, where it commanded a very high price. In return the Romans exported glass, which was new to the Chinese, but which they soon copied for themselves.

Along the Silk Road also travelled missionary Buddhist monks from India; and in the reign of the second Eastern Han emperor, Buddhism was formally recognized as a permitted and beneficial religion. The emperor had a dream: Buddha appeared to him and expounded the truths of the Buddhist faith. The emperor then recognized the merit of this divine revelation, and legalized its teaching. This device assured that imperial prestige would not be undermined by the spread of an unofficial religion which must have already made much headway. In reality, Buddhism was introduced by missionaries from Central Asia and later from India, probably about the time of Christ. In A.D. 65, the presence of monks and lay believers at his brother's court was favourably mentioned in a decree by the emperor Ming. Archaeology, however, has yet to unearth the site of a Buddhist monastery of Han date.

The art of Eastern Han still continued to use the motifs and themes of the earlier period of Western Han. The religious themes are concerned with the unofficial but widespread polytheistic beliefs which were gradually becoming incorporated with Taoist popular teaching. There are no recognizable Buddhist motifs. Engraved bricks and bas-reliefs, also mural painting, are the media which have survived in tombs, but which were no doubt also present in the houses of the gentry. These show the Han gentry as hoping to enjoy after death a similar hedonistic existence as they had sought in life. Hunting scenes, processions of gentlemen in chariots, light, swift vehicles, not the heavy war chariots of an earlier age, feasts and entertainments with jugglers, dancing girls and acrobats; these outnumber the scenes portraying deities and religious rites.

Also shown are historical incidents, known from written history, such as the attempt to assassinate the Qin emperor Shi Huang Di, as well as others not readily identified. The famous tombs near Changsha, where a large library was found, have counterparts on a less rewarding scale in several recently excavated Eastern Han tombs. It is not always easy if no dated inscription is found to determine whether a tomb is of Western or Eastern Han date. Han tombs have yielded pieces of wooden furniture and many representations of such objects which prove that well-to-do Chinese no longer slept on mats on the floor but on low raised beds.

On the whole Han art is predominantly secular: the influence of Confucianism, which played down religious belief, may have been a cause; it is at least clear that if Buddhism was now a tolerated religion, it had not yet had any influence on art, and very little perhaps on the thinking of the ruling gentry. How far the people were becoming converted remains obscure; their beliefs are not recorded, but it seems at least possible that the

Scenes in relief telling the story of the legendary encounter between Confucius and Laozi. Although he was considered by the Taoists to be the founder of their religion, Laozi is not generally believed to have really existed nor even less to have written the *Dao De Jing*, the sacred book of Taoism.

Opposite: spectators at a fight between animals in the royal park of Shanglin; detail from a series of five tiles forming a tympanum (Han period, 1st century A.D.).

teaching of Buddha made more appeal to the deprived and to men who had little hope of comfort in this earthly incarnation.

Han imperialism brought the rule of the empire to the farthest western region ever to come under Chinese authority: the eastern shores of the Caspian Sea, and also into the northwest of the Indian subcontinent, in what is now Northwest Pakistan and Afghanistan. There Chinese forces had intervened in the affairs of the last Greco-Macedonian kingdoms which had inherited parts of Alexander's empire in this region. Hermaeus, king of Parapamisadae, which is Eastern Afghanistan to-day, was aided by Chinese troops and paid a nominal allegiance to the Han emperor. Perhaps the discovery of a Chinese crossbow cocking-piece in bronze, now in the museum at Taxila, is a relic of this expedition. Under the Eastern Han, after the usurpation by Wang Mang had temporarily disrupted Chinese control in Central Asia, the contact was renewed in A.D. 73. Ban Zhao, an officer of the army, was sent to restore relations and gain the allegiance of the many petty kings who ruled in the oases of the Turkestan deserts.

Even the Yue-zhi, who had recently founded the Kushana kingdom in the Indian Punjab, sent tribute in A.D. 90. The northern Xiong-nu, as a result of successive defeats by the southern Xiong-nu in A.D. 85, by the Mongol Sien-pi in A.D. 87, and by the Chinese general Dou Xian in A.D. 89, in part submitted and in part migrated westwards, leaving their lands to the Sien-pi, who in A.D. 101 began raiding the frontier. To the west the Qiang Tibetans disturbed the peace of Gansu for several decades until repulsed by the Zhao Zhong in A.D. 141–144.

A man of resource and skill, Ban Zhao was remarkably successful in building up an army of auxiliaries stiffened by Chinese troops, which in 30 years' campaigning brought him to the eastern coast of the Caspian Sea. From there he sent envoys to Persia and to Rome.

The account that the Chinese envoys gave of the Roman empire, or perhaps the synthesis of several different accounts over a fairly long period of time, is preserved in the *Han History*, and shows clear signs of incorporating eyewitness records. The fact that the Chinese description of the Roman world was not from only one visit seems clear, for the republican institution of consuls is not distinguished from the later imperial rule, and there is also mention of a bridge across the Black Sea, clearly an echo of the tradition of the bridge of boats built by Xerxes across the Hellespont. The Chinese visitors did not clearly understand the nature of Roman institutions, but this fact is really a testimony to the authenticity of their account of them.

By the end of the 1st century A.D. the Eastern Han were losing their vigour. The old problem of the consort families became once more a serious threat to stability, and the measures taken

Above and opposite above: decorations from a tomb of the Han period. A series of frescoes, depicting historical scenes, decorate the bases of the tympana which mark the limits of the burial chamber. Below: a carved tympanum depicting animals fighting, surrounded by other gratuitous decoration.

194

by the reigning emperor Han Shun Di (A.D. 126–144) to counter this danger brought a worse one into existence. Eunuchs were an ancient presence in a Chinese court. But in earlier times they were little more than slaves. Han Shun Di saw that these men, wholly dependent upon his favour, without families who could grow ambitious, and incapable of posterity, were an effective counter to the power of consort families and their tendency to fill the ranks of the official civil service with their clients and relatives. The emperor began to give rank and office to able eunuchs. They were indeed able, and particularly adept at acquiring riches by bribery and selling their good offices to aspirant officials. The emperor trusted them; their services were thus invaluable to all who hoped to rise. But these services must be bought, and at a constantly higher price.

The evil grew rapidly throughout the reign of the next emperor Han Huan Di, who died in A.D. 167. He was succeeded by a boy of 12, Han Ling Di, and there was therefore a regency under the empress mother. She tried to reverse the tide of eunuch influence by giving office to members of the association of scholars, a group formed from among the civil servants to combat eunuch influence. But Han Ling Di gave his full confidence to the eunuchs, with whom he had been familiar since childhood, and they regained their influence and soon obtained much more.

In 168 they accused the association of scholars of plotting a conspiracy to dethrone the emperor (quite possibly with some foundation in fact). The association was proscribed and a wholesale purge of its members, supporters, relatives and clients got under way. In their place, eunuch-appointed officials who had paid for their posts proved to be more concerned to recoup these expenses by rapacious and oppressive treatment of the people. The eunuchs, forbidden by law to leave the palace, remained ignorant of the damage they were causing to the provincial administration, and also to the army. The emperor Ling Di was totally unaware of what was going on, and had implicit trust in his eunuchs in all matters.

This disastrous situation before long provoked a famous rebellion among the oppressed people, a movement now acclaimed as the first rising of the people of China against their rulers. The Yellow Turbans, so called from the distinctive headdress which they wore, were founded by an itinerant magician named Zhang Zhue, who had won popular renown for himself with a magical cure during an epidemic then raging in the central provinces. Inspired by this mass appeal, in 184 Zhang Zhue raised the banner of revolt, and soon had a huge following. The Han court was compelled to raise large armies to cope with the spreading rebellion. The war against the rebels dragged on for years. In the course of the struggle new, able and ambitious officers rose to high command, growing increasingly intolerant of eunuch power and influence. The Yellow Turbans were ultimately defeated, but their revolt left the dynasty weak and shaken. For the first, but far from the last, time a Chinese dynasty survived a great rebellion, by placing its fate in the hands of the generals.

The emperor Ling Di died in 189 and his passing marked a

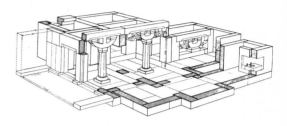

Plan of a tomb of the Eastern Han dynasty, excavated at Shandong. Below: entrance to the tomb.

Opposite: fresco with terra-cotta relief which decorated the entrance wall to a tomb of the Han period. In Chinese mythology, the ram's head motif betokens overtones of augury.

Funeral palls of the type illustrated here, made of painted silk, covered the biers in tombs of the Han period. The decorative motifs recur, with very few variants, in all the extant examples.

Opposite: objects found in the tomb of prince Liu Sheng, younger brother of the emperor Wu, and Lui Sheng's wife Tou Wan who were alive in the 2nd century B.C. The exceptionally beautiful tomb furniture found there includes several splendid works of art from the palace of Chungshan, residence of the royal couple. The numerous *hu* vases (for wine) made of bronze are enriched with inlay of gold and silver (like the two, top left) or gilded and embossed (like that top right). Center, from the left: a lantern and a silver candelabra. Bottom: the funeral covering of Tou Wan's body, similar to her husband's, Liu Sheng, which was made of small, jade rectangles linked to one another by gold thread.

fatal turning point in Han fortunes. He left no direct heir, and the empress dowager whose brother was the commander-in-chief of the recently victorious army, proffered one young prince as the proper heir, while the eunuchs supported another whom they expected to be more pliable.

The army had concentrated outside the capital, perhaps because its leader, general He, head of the consort family, expected eunuch interference when the choice of heir had to be made. At least he was quite confident of his own power and authority. Thus he went into the palace without guards to consult with his sister, the empress dowager. As he crossed the great courtyard of the throne hall the eunuchs set upon him and murdered him. It was their crowning error: on hearing that their general had been slain, the troops attacked and stormed the palace and massacred every eunuch in it. In the confusion a general of notorious brutality and violence carried off the young prince whom the eunuchs had rejected, proclaimed him emperor, and having plundered the palace and the city, set off for his own headquarters in the provinces. This was the signal for a general civil war, each commander seeking to secure the person of the wretched emperor in order to legitimize his own ambitious plans.

The civil wars continued without intermission for 32 years, ending only when the three surviving most powerful commanders divided the empire into three "kingdoms," and the most powerful, Wei, in the North forced the last Han emperor to abdicate.

Insecurity of life and property during this period contributed to the popularity of religious Taoism, a cult of mysticism and occultism which promised long life and even immortality as a reward for support, faith and monastic austerity. Its founders, Zhang Daoling who, according to legend ascended into heaven in 156 at the age of 123, and his son Zhang Heng, claimed authority from the *Dao* and philosophic Taoism, but followed the practices of alchemy, breath control, and magic inherited from charlatans who had infested the courts of Shi Huang Di

and emperor Wu. Their successors slavishly imitated Buddhism by creating a divine hierarchy, a voluminous textual canon and a monastic community.

In the period which followed the division of the empire (221–265), each of the Three Kingdoms claimed the imperial succession. Wu, in the South, had no more connection with the Han imperial house than had Wei in the North, but Shu-Han, in the West, the weakest of the three, could justify the claim that its founder was a remote collateral of the Han imperial family, and he certainly had the same surname, Liu. The short period which marked this partition of the empire is one of great romantic fame in China because the dramatic character of the fall of the Han and the contests between the successors became the subject, first of the storytellers' art, and later the inspiration of one of the great early Chinese novels *The Romance of the Three Kingdoms*, a heroic tale having some of the character of the *Morte d'Arthur*, but founded on better established historical fact. It is much better known to the Chinese reading public than the sober narrative of the dynastic history.

One event in the period of the Three Kingdoms, although it held little significance for men of the time, or interest for their posterity, was the embassy from the Roman empire which reached Nanjing (Nanking), where the court of the kingdom of Wu was situated. Chinese history records that the leader was named Chinlun, but this transcription has so far defeated all attempts to determine the Latin (or Greek?) form of the name. The Chinese also sent their own ambassador to accompany Chinlun on the return voyage, but he died at sea, and thus never reached the Roman world. The interesting thing about this embassy is that it came by sea. A contact had been made by sea route in Han times, but the Chinese court believed that the alleged ambassadors were in fact merchants, as they did not bring any products of the Roman empire, but goods bought in Southeast Asia. They did, however, tell the Chinese that the reigning Roman emperor was An Tun, that is, Marcus Aurelius Antoninus (121–180).

The Three Kingdoms came to an end in 265 with the conquest of the other two by the northern Wei, an usurper having succeeded to the throne and renamed the dynasty Jin. Under this regime the empire was once more, if only briefly, reunited. The Jin were, however, very incompetent rulers. The founder had many sons whom he appointed as governors of the provinces, and on his death they quarrelled, reducing the administration to chaos and opening the way for more dangerous enemies. After 50 years of rather disorderly rule, the Jin suffered a catastrophic defeat at the hands of nomadic invaders from the Mongolian steppe. The capital, Luoyang, was taken and destroyed, and the court fled to the South. There the Jin rallied in country unsuited to the nomad cavalry, consolidating their control of South China, the Yangtze valley and the territories to the south of it, with a new capital at Nanking.

China was now divided into two empires, that in the North where Tartar dynasties succeeded each other at short intervals, and the other in the South, where after the Jin had reigned for another century they were followed by four short-lived

Bronze candelabra of the Han period, interesting for its simple stylization of form which emphasizes the dynamics of the human body.

Opposite: this jade sculpture from the Han period offers a splendid example in formal elaboration (London, Victoria and Albert Museum).

dynasties, none of which endured much longer than 50 years. In the North some stability was established by the Wei (386–552). The Wei then split into two rival houses which lasted only about 20 years. The period is known in Chinese history as the Nan Bei, or Northern and Southern empires, and was marked by frequent warfare between the two empires, both of which claimed the whole country, and between the great rival families of both empires, who displaced each other and founded brief "dynasties" often lasting not much longer than the lifetime of the founder.

Parallels between the histories of the Han and the Roman empires: the breakup into two empires, the barbarian invasions, the conquest of one-half of the former empire, have led some Western historians to see in this series of analogous events in the West and the East, the workings of a universal law. If the phenomenon of Buddhism in China, at much the same time that Christianity triumphed in the West, is added, the parallel does indeed seem striking. But it is only superficial. In China the period of division was not a "Dark Age" in which literacy declined, and the recording of history became obscured. On the contrary, poetry which had enjoyed great favour in earlier times, now flourished as never before. The historical records continued to be kept and life in the southern capital, Nanking, was one of sophistication and luxury. Moreover, it was the North, the historic heartland of China, which suffered foreign conquest. It was then the most populous region, and deeply rooted in its Chinese culture. Consequently the invading Tartars (much less numerous) were in time absorbed into the Chinese way of life, adopting Chinese manners, customs, literature, art and forms of government, and finally also the language. No new nations like France, Spain and England in the West arose in the provinces of the fallen Han empire; no modifications of the spoken language ever came about, as happened with the Romance languages.

The South was in no sense a Chinese Byzantium; firstly it was the newer, colonial part of the Han empire, sparsely populated, with many non-Chinese peoples, who were gradually assimilated into the Chinese civilization. In this way it resembled not the eastern, but the western Roman empire. A great migration of the official and gentry class from the North had accompanied the Jin dynasty in its flight southwards. These families, with their numerous retainers, were given lands in the provinces south of the Yangtze, where they grew powerful and actively promoted the settlement of Chinese colonists and the assimilation of the natives.

After 70 years of barbarian invasions and devastation in the North, the Wei dynasty, invaders themselves, had succeeded in imposing order and stability, and had unreservedly adopted Chinese culture. There was no difference in language between North and South; the lesson of Latin and Greek did not apply. Also no real frontier existed between the two empires; in the eastern Yangtze valley for instance there was no clear border; no mountain range divided north from south; the rice-growing south shaded into the predominantly corn-growing north in a region where both crops were grown. No obstacle such as a sea impeded the movement of armies in either direction.

Wooden figure of an eunuch, wearing clothes made of silk, found together with other wood carvings near Changsha (Hunan), in the tomb of Tai, a noble lady who lived in the 1st century B.C.

Opposite: two enamelled wooden figurines, probably of ladies-in-waiting, which came from the same tomb. The dry climate of the region and the protective measures taken at the time of entombment spared the tomb from the effects of humidity and kept these figurines and other fragile things such as silks, books and lacquered objects in a remarkable state of preservation.

These physical and demographic facts made unification much easier in China than in the Western world. The real obstacle was the military weakness of unstable regimes; the so-called dynasties were in fact little more than passing dictatorships imposed by leading families, whose main preoccupation was to defend themselves from internal rivals rather than plotting the conquest of the other half of the empire. In the North, as in the South, power now rested with the great families who were not feudal lords in the ancient style, but influential landowners with a military background enabling them to raise armies, giving them an effective right to command the forces of the state.

In the North by the 5th century A.D. it was not only the aristocrats of Tartar descent who wielded this power and influence. There were Chinese aristocrats, especially in the northwestern provinces, who had come to be accepted as too strong to dislodge, and in the course of time these families, and those of Tartar origin, had extensively intermarried, so that there hardly remained any real distinction based on ethnic origin between them. This made it easy for a capable leader to reunite the North, potentially the stronger half of China, and then conquer the South. This indeed is what finally brought the period of partition to an end.

In 581 the Northern Zhou dynasty, which had reigned for a brief 32 years, was overthrown by a leading general, Yang Jian, himself of Chinese patrilineal origin, but also brother-in-law of the emperor of Northern Zhou. The new dynasty, the Sui, having first gained control of the North, had no difficulty, seven years later, in conquering the South, then governed by the weakest of the many dynasties which had risen to power. The fact that the founder of the Sui was Chinese (at least on his father's side) no doubt helped his cause.

Chinese historians have tended to treat the period of the North-South partition as an "age of confusion." In the sense that it was a period of frequent inconclusive warfare, this is true, but beneath the surface very important social changes were at work. The ideal of a united empire, the restoration of the Han system, had never been repudiated. Weak though they were, the successive dynasties all claimed to be the legitimate, unique empire, and all, more or less, preserved the Han political and administrative system. The difference now was that, under weak rulers, the grandees who nominated men for office were also the holders of high military command, and potential usurpers of the throne.

Buddhism had spread widely, under the patronage of some of the more powerful of the emperors. The splendour of the Buddhist pantheon and ritual, with its conceptions of ten heavens, ten hells, rebirth, and the salvation of the individual souls of common men, proved irresistible. Sutras were translated in terms borrowed from philosophic Taoism mostly by Indian and Central Asiatic missionaries, among whom the most prolific was Kumarajiva, circa 344–413, son of an Indian and of a princess of Kucha. Indian sectarian divergencies became reflected especially in versions of the monastic law (*vinaya*). Desire for direct intelligence of authoritative texts led at least 82 Chinese pilgrims to visit India during the period

Top: depicting a lively game of *liu bo*, an ancient Chinese pastime; taken from a relief of the Han period.
Above: the demeanour of the figures here, also *liu bo* players, is much more composed. This ceramic also comes from a tomb of the Han dynasty and is now kept in the British Museum. We do not know what the rules of *liu bo* were: from the depictions of the game which remain it seems that each player had six pieces and that the moves were determined by the throw of six sticks.

Opposite above: a group of musicians, carved in wood, which came from a Han tomb near Changsha.
Below: a performance by acrobats. This grouping, made of painted terra cotta, dates from the Western Han dynasty (2nd–1st century B.C.) and was found in a tomb at Jinan (Shandong).

200–600 (61 in the 5th century alone). Fa-xian travelled across Central Asia and returned by sea (399–414), and Song-yun followed the land route to and from Udyana and Gandhara (518–522). The most popular text of the 6th century was the *Parinirvana-sutra*, which recounts the birth, illumination, first teaching and death of the Buddha. Buddhism, however, did not dethrone Confucius, however; the sage's doctrines continued to be the basis of education of officials for office. But art was largely transformed by the new faith, and literature and philosophic thought deeply influenced by it. Monuments and works of art of these two and a half centuries clearly show Buddhist inspiration. For instance, the Northern Wei cut cave temples in the Yungang cliffs near Datong and decorated them with Buddhist sculpture in imitation of the Caves of the Thousand Buddhas at Dunhuang, then at the point of bifurcation of trade routes north and south of the Tarim basin. After 495 new caves were cut at Longmen near Luoyang. The various Buddhas, bodhisattvas, saints and militant guardians of the law reflect Indian iconography given form by Greek artisans in Gandhara, as well as Iranian influence.

The old polytheism had been largely incorporated into the rival religion, popular Taoism, devoted to the magical arts and the search for immortality. This led to a continuing and indirectly fruitful interest in the natural sciences.

To find the secret of the elixir of life, many experiments were conducted, some of which produced useful discoveries in other fields. The original Taoist ideal of withdrawal from the world was transformed into a mysticism associated with belief in immortality gained from contemplation and dedication to following the *Dao*, the Way. Legends of such immortals, living for great spans of time in the recesses of the mountains, became part of Chinese folklore.

From time to time rulers who were more Confucian in outlook often engaged in mild persecution of the Buddhists, insisting that the celibacy of monks and nuns was antisocial, and forcing them to marry. But examples of martyrdom are extremely rare. On the other hand there was very little innovation in the thinking of the Confucians; the old orthodoxy was accepted without change. The period can be seen as China's "Age of Faith," but the Buddhists did not have a monopoly of religious devotion; the Taoists were persistent critics, imitators and rivals, and the Confucians clung to their domination in literature and education.

"Three Ways to One Goal," the traditional Chinese view of the religious and philosophic contest, stems from this age; it is a view of the universe which has never been acceptable to the Western mind since the rise of Christianity, but it is inherently connected with Chinese Humanism, for the "Goal" to which man may travel by any one of the three roads is not spiritual salvation, Heaven, or any form of the future life, but a harmonious, moral, and sincere relationship with his fellow mortals here on earth. The fact that the Buddhist doctrine of reincarnation and the transmigration of souls is obviously completely at variance with the Confucian belief in the power of ancestors and the duty to revere them, as also to the Taoist ideal

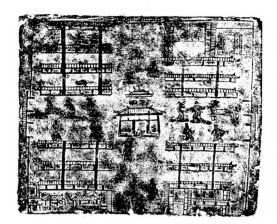

Right: painting on stone from a tomb of the Han period.
Far right: a Han relief on a funeral tile found in the Chengdu region, in Sichuan (Eastern Han dynasty, 25 B.C.–A.D. 221). On the upper panel, we see a hunting scene set in a luxuriant landscape. Hunting, which was a favourite pastime of the rich and noble in the Han period, is here linked with a scene (lower panel) of peasants working in the fields. It was during the Han period that the art of bas-relief first appeared in China, having probably emanated from Persia and Syria.
Below: a court scene, painted on a tile found during the excavations at Luoyang and now kept in the Boston Museum of Fine Arts.

of physical immortality, and that the "Three Roads" in this respect lead to quite different goals, never troubled the Chinese mind. It can only be conjectured that as in so many other aspects of thought, form was to them much less significant than content.

The fall of the Han and its sequal have been taken by orthodox Confucian Chinese historians as the model on which the fate of dynasties should be judged: the Han rose swiftly to power, flourished, grew indulgent and decadent, fell in great disorder. The power of eunuchs was the deadly evil, the ambition of consort families, the contributory cause. But this model, in historical fact, was rarely true in later times. The short

regimes of the partition period were too transitory for the cycle of rise, splendour, and decline; the consorts had equally no span of power to be important, and in a brief dynasty dominated by military aristocrats the influence of eunuchs was minimal.

Confucian-inspired history has a moral purpose, to act as a "mirror" in which contemporary rulers can see the error and the virtues of the past, avoid the one, and copy the other. Hence everything significant to this purpose must be accurately recorded; matters which do not bear upon this central preoccupation are either ignored, or relegated to relative obscurity. Religion, as opposed to Confucian ethics, is therefore not important except as a negative influence distracting a ruler from his proper duty to provide a model of Confucian rectitude. Economics is only important if it illustrates either improper imperial intervention in matters which the ruler should not meddle with, or shows the consequences of vicious extravagance and reckless expenditure.

Below: a warrior.

Opposite: a sorcerer engaged in a ritual dance. These figures, made of terra cotta, were found in tombs dating from the Han period and still bore traces of their original colouring. These tiny sculptures possess an extraordinary vitality by virtue of their life-like attitudes and flowing movement.

THE MIDDLE EMPIRE:
THE TANG AND SONG DYNASTIES

Opposite: detail of a Buddhist limestone stele, height about three meters, from the Eastern Wei dynasty, and dated A.D. 543. In the center of the upper front (which has suffered severe damage) two young people are supporting a brazier for burning incense while at the sides two hermits hold in their hands a skull and a bird respectively. In the middle section, on the right, the head of the house is shown in conversation with a throned bodhisattva, seen on the left surrounded by his followers.

Above: tile paintings, of which many were found during excavations of the Wei and Jin tombs near the city of Jiayu in the Gobi desert. These show various agricultural activities; from the top: horse breeding, ploughing and corn winnowing.

Pages 212–213
Detail from a silk scroll in colour and black ink, painted by Gu Kaizhi in the 4th century A.D. The scene shows palace courtesans in the act of having their hair arranged and face and eyes made up.

The Sui dynasty briefly reunited the whole of China, but it only lasted for 29 years. Its ruin is attributed by the Confucian historians to the megalomania and folly of the second emperor, Yang Di. He stands as the archetype of the "bad emperor," just as his successor, the second emperor of the Tang, Tai Zong, represents the "good emperor." Yang Di's great mistake was a persistent and unavailing effort to conquer the North Korean kingdom of Koryugo which occupied what is now North Korea, together with the adjoining modern Chinese province of Liaoning, or South Manchuria.

This region had been a province of the Han empire; Yang Di considered that therefore it should once more be brought under Chinese rule. He may also have thought that, as modern history has more than once shown, the ruler of North Korea is in a position to menace North China. Yang Di is not given credit for any such political acumen by the historians, who represent him as vain, ambitious and reckless. Another of his extravagances, equally condemned, was the building of the Grand Canal which links the north of China with the Yangtze, and which was later extended south of the river to the city of Hangzhou, capital of Zhejiang province. Yang Di is accused of carrying out this great work purely to indulge his own comfort when travelling from his northern capital at Luoyang to the new southern capital at Yangzhou. No credit is allowed for the very real economic benefit which the Grand Canal brought to China, even if forced labour was used to build it. Nor is it admitted that the ruler of a long-partitioned empire needed to improve communications between north and south in order to consolidate the restored united empire. Yang Di must of necessity be wrong.

Whatever the justice of some of these strictures, it is certainly true that the long war with Korea and other costly ventures led to deep unrest and finally to open revolt. Not just one, but no less than nine contestants emerged to oppose Yang Di. The wars lasted for seven years and ended in the complete triumph of the Tang dynasty, whose armies were led by the founder's second son, Li Shimin, known to history under his posthumous "temple title" of Tang Tai Zong, the Great Ancestor.

He was only 16 when he goaded his father into revolt against the Sui, on the pretext that Yang Di planned to exterminate the Li clan. They were of Chinese patrilineal descent, and had been semi-independent princes in the northwest of China, and claimed descent from a famous general of emperor Wu of the Han dynasty. The Li family were thus typical of the military aristocrats who had dominated the divided empire, and, like their rivals, the Yangs of the Sui and others also, were all related to each other and to great families such as the Dugu who were of Tartar descent. The genius of the Tang imperial family was to break the fatal chain of usurpation and rival ambitions, and set

人咸知修其容莫知飾其性性之不飾或愆禮正斧之藻之克念作聖

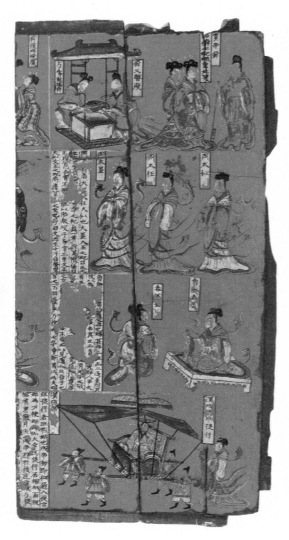

Detail of a painting on lacquer found in a tomb of the Wei period.

Opposite: the colossal statue of Buddha at Yungang, not far from the town of Datong in the province of Shanxi, the most ancient rock sanctuary of northern China. It can be dated about the middle of the 5th century A.D., during the Wei dynasty. The Buddha, with a serene smile on his face and with eyes lifted up to the heavens, is shown in the traditional pose of meditation with arms crossed and resting on the legs which are in the lotus position. More

than 40 images of the Buddha were carved on the walls of Yungang during the years 460–550. The enormous statue was originally enclosed in one of the numerous caves of which the sanctuary is formed. However, the crumbling of the cave's outer wall has exposed the statue to full view.

up a long-enduring dynasty which consolidated the united empire and made it the Chinese norm and political ideal.

Tai Zong was indeed a just and wise ruler, being that rarity, a military genius who also had a flair for politics. It is true that he could be ruthless, and that he slew his elder brother, the crown prince, in an ambush at the palace gate. (The prince was not a promising successor and had in his turn intrigued to get rid of his younger brother.)

The new emperor (his father soon abdicated after the *coup d'état*) carried out very important reforms and initiated new policies of far-reaching consequence. The army, the instrument of his own rise to power, was assigned to the northern frontier to guard against the constant incursions of the nomadic peoples of Inner Mongolia, at that period the Turks, remote ancestors of the later Ottomans. But the new army was commanded by professional generals, often of relatively humble origin, appointed by the emperor himself. The power of the great military aristocrats was subtly weakened until it disappeared completely. Such grandees now preferred to serve in civil office at court rather than command frontier armies against Turkish raiders. No forces other than the imperial guard were stationed at court.

The emperor instituted a system of paying off, or pensioning, serving soldiers with land in the frontier zone, and making them liable to call up as reservists if needed. This helped to sustain a standing army, and to keep it out of politics. It had plenty to do fighting the Turks before Chinese supremacy was finally established and the Turkish hordes split up, part moving away across the deserts to Western Asia, to become the forebears of the Ottoman Turks.

The civil service was restored as the real power in government, and a new method of recruitment, first tentatively tried by the Sui, was elaborated and gradually perfected. This was the public examination for office, the awarding of successive degrees for merit, and the slow decline and final disappearance of the patron-client system used by the Han, and abused by the short, military-dominated dynasties of the partition period.

The civil service examination, at first held only in the capital, was open to all literate candidates except, strangely enough, members of the imperial family. In Tang times the subjects for study were wide, comprising not only history, Confucian classics and poetry, but administration and government. In later centuries the form of the examination became much more exclusively literary. There can be no doubt that Tai Zong promoted this reform with the purpose of reducing the power of his own class, the military aristocrats, who were the traditional danger to any new dynasty. The mass of the gentry scholars who could now compete for civil service careers, had no great land-owning power behind them, did not exercise military command, and could be promoted, dismissed or transferred to distant provinces at the behest of the central government. The central government came to rely increasingly on such men to govern the empire. The emperor also instituted a far-reaching reform of the taxation system: he had the talent for gathering into his service men of real ability, whom he trusted, and who in turn, relied

POPULAR RELIGION

Laozi, Buddha and Confucius are here portrayed together in an illustration of the popular saying *San jiao i jiao* or "Three religions, one religion." Even though Confucianism cannot be said to be a religion, not having been an organized Church with priests, etc., like Buddhism or Taoism, it nonetheless provided many of the elements which went to form popular religion. This was in fact a syncretistic synthesis of the three "faiths" which varied from place to place. Thus it was that a kind of spontaneous, anarchic pantheon was created, in which ancient gods, spirits of the earth, the thunder and the waters, ancestors and Buddhist and Taoist saints all had a place.

Among the divinities of the Chinese Mount Olympus, all of whom are honoured with complete impartiality, is the goddess Guan Yin (shown above in an illustration from a sacred text). She was originally a male Buddhist divinity, Amithaba, but was absorbed into Chinese culture, given female characteristics and adored as the goddess of mercy and fertility. The most important domestic divinity is the god of wealth, honoured together with the god of the hearth and those of the doorway, who stand guard at every entrance (below, two famous generals deified after death).

It has been said that Chinese civilization, for all its complexity, is characterized by a lack of religious spirit such as dominates the Western idea of life and the world. The truth is that in China religion has never been detached from everyday activity and thus materialism and spirituality, the two great dialectic antagonisms of Western philosophic and religious thought, have never been seen by the Chinese as extreme or irreconcilable opposites. This does not mean to say, however, that the Chinese have no sense of what is sacred, for this is something extremely important to them even if the objects of veneration are not gods, or beings set apart from mankind. Sages, heroes, ordinary mortals can all aspire to be honoured by virtue of their ideas or their actions as benefactors of humanity.

The illustration (left) shows a sacrificial ceremony before the altars of the ancestors. These family ceremonies in which one of the youngest members of the family impersonated the ancestor who was being honoured were approved by Confucius who considered them a good discipline. He thought that these rites fulfilled the need for the expression of feeling, sublimating it into an act of courtesy. The family honoured all the divinities which thronged the Chinese pantheon as well as the souls of the prematurely dead who, not being able to descend to the Underworld, carried on their existence amongst the living in the forms of animals.

On the left, the mother goddess of the west, one of the most ancient and venerated female divinities of the Chinese pantheon who was later assimilated into the Taoist spirit hierarchy.

It has never been the Chinese way to repudiate a previous faith entirely, so that absolute conversion leading to the abjuration of the previous belief was unknown. There were, however, periods of intense religious persecution which were generally determined by political events. On the right is an image of the kingdom of the next world which, according to the Buddhist idea, consists of a complex of ten hells. However, the Chinese idea of the world as a unified and organic whole means that the concept of absolute evil is a difficult one for them to grasp.

upon him to treat them with sincerity and justice. For these reasons, perhaps mainly for these reasons, Tai Zong is *par excellence* the "good emperor" for the historians.

By contrast his real successor, the second great personality of the early Tang period, the later empress Wu, is treated by the historians as a "calamity." She was one of Tai Zong's junior concubines at the time of his death. She had already, it is alleged, probably with some truth, seduced the weak-charactered young man who was the heir to the throne (thus committing incest, at least technically). When Tai Zong died she had to retire to a Buddhist convent, like all the other widowed concubines. But when the new emperor made a formal visit to this convent she managed to beguile him once more, obtained her restoration to court, and before very long had won the new emperor's, Gao Zong, entire affection.

She got rid of her rivals, including the childless empress, by ruthless intrigue. She managed to rid herself of critics among the high aristocracy in like manner; she obtained promotion to the rank of empress, and she governed her weak and ailing husband to his dying day, and through him, the empire. When he died she quickly deposed her own son, his successor, and put another son in his purely nominal place. Soon wearying of this pretense, the emperor was made to abdicate and the empress Wu herself ascended the throne as full sovereign and sole monarch, the first and only time a woman has reigned in her own right in China. She held the throne until, in extreme old age, very sick, she was at last deposed by a *coup d'état*, and retired to die in respected comfort in her own palace.

This strange career has aroused the total condemnation of the orthodox historians. But they cannot conceal that with all her ruthless ambition, the empress Wu was a very capable ruler. She did much to promote the new civil service, using men who, by preference, came from the lower gentry rather than the high aristocracy. She appointed the generals who carried on the successful war which ended in the conquest of all of Korea. She maintained internal peace, and the army was loyal to her. So was the civil service. All this cannot be denied. Reluctantly, the historians admit and confirm it; their solace is to blacken her moral character, not difficult, and attribute to her the deaths of every prominent member of the imperial family, although the record often suggests to modern readers that natural causes were at least as probable as deliberate poisoning.

Much of what was done during her reign had the effect, not entirely intentional, of promoting important social changes. She broke the power of the military aristocracy to secure her own safety; but it was a necessary step in the evolution of Chinese society and the consolidation of the empire. She relied on men of

Statue of the Buddha with bodhisattvas at his side, from cave 432 at Dunhuang, in the province of Gansu. It dates from the Wei dynasty, about the first half of the 4th century.

Pages 220 – 221 Detail from a fresco painted on the wall of cave 120 at Dunhuang, dating from the Western Wei dynasty. An inscription has permitted accurate

dating of the frescoes in this cave, which are among the best preserved at Dunhuang, as being the year 538 to 539. The detail here shows a battle scene.

less influential families, and thereby increased the influence of the lesser gentry, and the effectiveness of the new examination system. She was an ardent Buddhist, and although her favouritism towards some monks may well have been excessive, it did indirectly stimulate the great artistic contribution which Buddhism made to Chinese culture in the Tang period.

The third great personality of the Tang dynasty, the emperor known to history as Xuan Zong, but more familiar by his popular name of Ming Huang, the "Brilliant Emperor," was her grandson, who succeeded to the throne after another successful *coup d'état*, an example first set by Tai Zong and all too readily followed by his posterity.

Ming Huang was a man who for most of his long life deserved his popular title. His reign (712–756) is the high point of the Tang dynasty and perhaps of the earlier Chinese civilization. The emperor was a strong supporter of the arts, poetry and literature, and is credited with being the patron under whom the Chinese drama first flourished. He has remained the patron-founder of the drama to this day. It was during his reign that a census, taken in 754, gave the total population of the empire as 9,069,154 families or 52,880,488 persons. It might be thought that this precision is hardly credible at the period, but an archaeological discovery of a census return for the family of a retired soldier in the far northwest of China included his wife and children.

In 755 the rebellion of An Lushan, commander-in-chief of the army on the northern frontier, brought about a catastrophe from which the Tang dynasty never fully recovered. An Lushan was of Turkish origin, a soldier of fortune who had enlisted in the Tang army and risen to high command. Traditional history claims that his revolt was inspired by a realization of the increasing weakness of the rule of the aged emperor, compounded by his infatuation with a concubine, Yang Guei Fei, who actually favoured the general.

The story of Ming Huang and Yang Guei Fei has become, in art and drama, the Chinese equivalent of Antony and Cleopatra in the West, the fatal entanglement of an able man by an ambitious beauty. The fact that Ming Huang was over 60 when he insisted on taking into his own harem the concubine of his son, then herself no longer a young girl, is ignored by art. But the story of their tragic love is enshrined in the work of the great poet Bai Juyi and in a great number of later plays based on this epic. It has become to the Chinese, just as Shakespeare's *Antony and Cleopatra* has to the Western world, more familiar and more "authentic" than the real facts. When An Lushan was approaching the defenseless capital the emperor, before fleeing, was forced by his mutinous guards to order the execution of his favourite. This is the "everlasting wrong" which inspired Bai Juyi's great epic.

The rebellion of An Lushan, himself assassinated by a rival, was suppressed after a devastating civil war in the northern provinces. The South remained at peace. The old emperor came back to ruined Changan to die, and his son and successors grappled with new and difficult problems. The great generals who had crushed the rebellion became military governors of the

A painting on lacquered wood found during excavations in the province of Shaanxi, dating from about the 6th century.

Opposite: statue of a warrior in grey pottery from the period of the Northern dynasties (Paris, Cernuschi Museum).

Pages 224 – 225
Limestone relief from the Pin-yang cave at Longmen, dating from the first half of the 6th century, Wei dynasty. The Wei emperors, who were Buddhists, initiated the construction at Longmen of a new temple to be built in a complex of caves on the model of those at Yungang. The elegant figure in the center, with a crown in the shape of a lotus flower, is the empress; the figure on the right, also crowned with a lotus flower, is perhaps a lady of high rank. The rest are courtiers.

provinces they had recovered. The court strove to prevent these fiefs from becoming hereditary, with success, but mainly by playing off one governor against his rivals. Thus there were many local, if brief, conflicts, and the power of the court and the authority of the civil service were weakened. The short lives of most of the emperors of the 9th century only added to the problem. There were frequent regencies, and if the eunuchs never acquired the dangerous influence they had enjoyed in the later period, it was more because the court had little influence over appointments in the provinces, than from want of ambition.

The 9th century was not wholly a period of decline; political power was weakened, but art, literature and culture in a more general sense thrived. Recent archaeological work near Changan has revealed the very high quality of decoration and objects of art found in the sepulchers of princes of the time of empress Wu; but although work has been started on her own tomb, its finds have yet to be fully discovered.

So far no intact imperial tomb of the earlier dynasties has been found; all were reputed to have been looted in ages long past. Tang tombs of both the first and second period of the dynasty are plentiful, and have yielded many works of art, in particular the great variety of clay figures, painted and made of pottery, which testify to the variety of wealth of the Chinese culture of the age. Apart from figures of protective spirits from the old pre-Buddhist religion, there are many figures of foreign servants, merchants, and travelling musicians, which reveal the wide contacts the Tang had with the whole of Western Asia, and even Africa and Eastern Europe. Other figures of domestic character include dancing girls, high-ranking ladies and gentlemen, and some showing girls playing polo, a custom which did not descend to later ages. These figures were expected to be magically animated to serve the spirit of the deceased in the afterlife. None of them, however high their artistic quality, were intended for the eyes of the living.

Very little, except city walls and a few brick pagodas, survives of Tang architecture: all palaces and such structures were destroyed or replaced in centuries long past. Their sites can be identified, there remain literary and contemporary descriptions, but the buildings have gone. It is above all by the literary works of the period, and in recent years, from the findings of funerary art, that Tang civilization can be assessed. The best-known names of Chinese poetry flourished in this dynasty and most of them were at the court of Ming Huang: Li Bo, Du Fu and Meng Haoran, all contemporaries; and Bai Juyi from the next generation. No other period of Chinese civilization can match this superb florescence.

Chinese society in the Tang period was more open to foreign influences and had closer contacts with foreign peoples than any previous or later age, right up to modern times. Embassies were exchanged between Changan and Constantinople. From an account of one of these we have a description of the capital of the Byzantine empire and its court dating from the late 8th century, which includes details not elsewhere recorded. Japan was the ardent imitator and borrower of Chinese civilization in the Tang

Drawings showing the evolution of the sacred figures in the sculptures at Yungang and Longmen. From the roundish figures of the earliest caves at Yungang (5th century), clothed in soft drapes, the preference at the beginning of the 6th century is for strict symmetry, with a preponderance of vertical lines.

Opposite: mirror in bronze from the Tang dynasty, with inlay of gold and mother-of-pearl. To be noted is the repetition of the phoenix, symbol of the empress, stylized in a manner typical of the time. During the Tang period, objects such as these – boxes, or more usually mirrors, were very popular. The motifs and techniques were mostly derived from Persia but the symmetry and balance between nature and art were part of the Chinese tradition.

age. The treasures of early Japanese architecture at Nara and Kyoto are in fact pure Tang-style buildings, better preserved than their models in China. The street names of Kyoto are exact copies of those of Changan, and the old name of the city of Kyoto, Heian, is a close approximation to that of Changan, meaning "Abiding Peace," and "Enduring Peace," respectively.

The Tang also had contact with Persia; the last Sassanian king of that country, driven out by the Arab Muslim conquest, took refuge in China, his son lived all his life at Changan, and his grandson was a general in the Chinese imperial guard. Later descendants no doubt merged with the Chinese gentry. The Arabs in Persia became for a short time active enemies of the Tang empire, and defeated a Chinese army on the frontiers of what is now Xinjiang, or Chinese Central Asia. Later Muslim mercenaries in the war against An Lushan are believed to have introduced the faith of Islam into North China, just as Arab merchants brought it to the South, at Canton. India was well known to the Tang, although they did not intervene militarily in the rivalries of its many kingdoms. India was the Holy Land of Buddhism, visited by pilgrims in search of relics and sacred texts. It also inspired many popular legends, which were later incorporated into Chinese fiction. The Tang certainly knew of Africa; one of the imperial tombs near Changan has a carving of an ostrich. There are extant literary references to the African peoples, and some tomb figures clearly portray negroes.

It was not until the late 9th century, in 868, that the Tang dynasty became seriously menaced by internal collapse. Its external foes were never a real danger. The northern nomads, the Turks, had been so heavily repulsed in the early period of the Tang, that they remained comparatively quiescent for more than a century. In the southwest, China had to confront the only relatively strong power which ever arose on her southern frontiers, the kingdom of Nanzhao, centered on the province of Yunnan, which had expanded into the neighbouring Chinese provinces, and for a time annexed parts of them. Nanzhao was under strong Chinese cultural influence, like Vietnam at a later date, but resolutely independent.

The Tibetans were also troublesome neighbours on the western mountain fringes of the empire. They were at that time a warlike and still largely savage people, and as yet unaffected by Buddhism. In the confusion of the rebellion of An Lushan they became a real menace, and actually raided and sacked Changan in 763. Less than a century later internal troubles removed the Tibetan kingdom as a threat to China.

The leader of the great rebellion of 868 was a failed competitor for the civil service, named Huang Chao. As a rebel he was more successful than as a scholar. The army which was stationed on the frontier between Nanzhao and the then Chinese frontier province of Annam (the exact reverse of the modern situation, where Yunnan is part of China, and Vietnam an independent state) mutinied. It had been stationed in what to northern Chinese was an unhealthy climate; it had not been paid for a long time. Huang Chao took over command and brought the army home to China, looting cities on the way, but occupying no place permanently.

Two court valets, enamelled terra-cotta figures which came from a tomb of the Tang dynasty. The numerous examples which exist show that these funerary objects must have been fairly widespread, often made in series by means of moulds.

Opposite above: detail of a fresco from the Tang dynasty which decorated the tomb of the princess Yung Tai, daughter of the emperor Zhong Tsong. She was killed in 701, when only 17 years old, by order of the empress Wu.
Below: painting on silk of the Tang dynasty showing various moments in the lives of ladies at the court.

In South China he continued this type of insurrection, apparently with no thought as yet of dethroning the dynasty. His success was facilitated by the lack of cooperation among the provincial governors, each only too anxious to see the rebels move on into the territory of his neighbour. For 13 years the rebellion raged all over South China, for so long spared the devastation of war, until the increasing disorder and weakness of the court induced Huang Chao in 880 to strike at the capital. His advance was feebly opposed; in 881 he took Changan, the court fled to Sichuan, like Ming Huang before, and the Tang dynasty, although nominally in power until 904, was in reality an anarchy of warring rebels and nominally loyal generals, all out to win sufficient following to replace the dynasty. Huang Chao was slain; so was his successor; the court returned, shorn of power, to Changan. In 904 one of the contending generals seized the city, massacred the imperial family, proclaimed himself emperor, destroyed Changan and moved his court to the east, to Kaifeng, a city of Eastern Henan, never previously a capital, but the headquarters of the usurper.

The Tang, in spite of their catastrophic end, have remained in Chinese eyes one of the greatest of the early dynasties. Their achievements in administration, art, literature, poetry and the beginnings of drama, their prestige throughout Asia, and the striking personalities they threw up, have secured them an enduring and deserved fame. Above all the Tang were the last great Chinese dynasty which was not overthrown by foreign invaders. When the Ming recovered the throne from the alien Mongols, the founder inscribed on his tomb at Nanking the injunction to his successors, "Rule like the Tang and Song"; and that injunction remained a Chinese ideal to be striven for.

The Tang had restored and consolidated the unity of the empire; and that became the political ideal which every following regime, Chinese or alien, sought to perpetuate, including the People's Republic of the present day. In this sense, and not only in the one sense, the Tang were the bridge between early and later China. Before them the united empire was an experience virtually confined to the Han dynasty; since the Tang, periods of partition have either been the direct

Terra-cotta horses (height, 28 cms.) found in the tomb of the princess Yung Tai and dated 706.

Opposite: detail of a limestone bas-relief which decorated the tomb of a Tang emperor, found during archaeological excavations in Shaanxi. The adoption of the long stirrup, evident in the relief, made the Tang cavalry one of the most feared fighting forces in the whole of Asia.

Below: one sees in the rigorous technique and forceful manner in which the animals in this painting from the Tang period are depicted, the profound realism so characteristic of the so-called Northern style, a critical rationalism which extended to all forms of art.

consequence of partial foreign conquests or intervals of confusion between strong unifying dynasties.

Another significant achievement of the Tang was the final and complete integration of the South of China into the empire, and its final colonization. Within two centuries of Tang rule, the South was to become the richest and most cultivated part of China. Men of Canton call themselves *Tang Ren*, men of Tang, while all other Chinese prefer *Han Ren*, men of Han, as the national and ethnic definition. There was only one field where the Tang achieved little: philosophy. The Confucian doctrine received little stimulus in this period, and only one great name, that of Han Yu, who was more a statesman than a thinker, is respected as a defender of Confucian doctrine.

After the Tang followed 53 years during which China was partitioned into no less than eight states, the larger ones each claiming to be "the empire." Chinese historians have awarded this fictitious title to the northern state, covering most of North China, which was ruled by five successive dynasties, the longest of which survived for 17 years, the shortest for only four. It was possible for a man to have been a young adult in the last years of the Tang, and still be not much more than 70 when the empire was once more reunited under the Song.

But while in the North the 53-year period was one of political instability and constant wars, the South enjoyed relative tranquility, and prosperity. The southern rulers, all the heirs of the military governors of provinces of the last years of the Tang, did not make war upon each other, being mostly too weak to hope for victory. In their capitals, and in particular Nanking, in the state of Nan Tang, much of the culture of the old Tang dynasty still flourished, as evidenced by the many names of painters, poets and men of literature recorded in the annals of the period.

It was here that about 950 the first assured proof of an important change in customs can be detected. The change from sitting on the floor, on mats, as in Japan up to the present day, to the use of chairs, spread in China from limited usage in the Middle Tang age to become the universal custom by the 11th century; and a well-known painting of a reception given by the prime minister of Nan Tang (one of the oldest extant pictures) shows his mansion furnished with chairs and sofas, no mats, and all his guests seated on the new style furniture. Another well-known picture from the middle of the Song period, portraying a national holiday in the capital, shows people, rich and poor alike, seated at table on chairs and benches. Many literary allusions to the change confirm the pictorial record. Outside of Europe only the Chinese adopted the chair; it would appear to have come about largely for social reasons and only very little from outside influence.

The most significant development during the so-called Five-Dynasty period was the cession of the northeastern port of Hebei province, including the city which was built on the present site of Peking, to a new power which had arisen in the southern part of what was later known as Manchuria, or today as the Three Eastern Provinces. The Kitan, a Tartar people, had driven the Turks from the northeast in late Tang times. After learning

Detail of a fresco from the tomb of Li Zhongshun showing tapering towers of a kind usually found at the entrances of imperial palaces or aristocratic residences. Li Zhongshun was the younger son of the Tang emperor Gao Zong and of the empress Wu, who died in 701 at Luoyang when he was only 19 years of age. The tomb, which was found in 1971–2, is the largest among those of medium size so far discovered.

Pages 234–235
A hunting scene from a fresco found in the tomb of prince Li Xian (654–84), second son of the emperor Gao Zong. The subjects favoured by artists of the time were those depicting palace life, ceremonies, the pastimes of the nobles and of the ladies of the court. Above all, they were absorbed by crowd scenes, depicted realistically but with an eye for the sumptuous.

CHANGAN: BLUEPRINT FOR A CAPITAL

The city of Changan (Long Peace), heart and symbol of the centralized but strict and fair rule of the Tang emperors, was at the height of its splendour in the first half of the 8th century A.D. It stood at the eastern end of the great intercontinental commercial routes which crossed Central Asia, the capital of the largest empire the world had ever known. It was founded at the end of the 7th century under the Sui who had reunited China. However, it was the Tang emperors in the next two centuries who were mostly responsible for building the city, in such magnificence and on so rational a plan

that it was taken as a model for the building of many other Chinese cities and even of the Japanese capital, Nara, founded in 710. Conceived on a scale which matched the continent it presided over, Changan at the end of the 7th century numbered about 1,000,000 inhabitants within its walls which stretched 9·7 kms. from east to west and 8·2 kms. from north to south. The huge rectangle so enclosed was divided into 108 districts, crisscrossed by 11 roads running north–south and 14 running east–west. The great poet Bai Juiyi (776–846), who lived near the eastern wall, wrote, in his *Song of Eternal Sadness*, an

account of the dramatic flight from the capital in July 756 of the emperor Xuan Zong, following a revolt led by An Lushan. Accompanying the emperor was his

favourite concubine, the beautiful Yang Guei Fei (she is shown above, mounting a horse). However, she was killed by the mutineers in the sight of the emperor and this

was considered one of the reasons for the dynasty's downfall. The death of Yang Guei Fu, a romantic heroine, and the flight of the emperor mark the end of the Golden Age of

Changan which never again knew the magnificence of its early days. This flowering of urban life was accompanied by a pronounced "secularization" of Chinese culture coincident with the decline of Buddhism. The landed nobility, no longer obliged to live on their estates or in villages, helped to create a refined style of life which thenceforward was to be the hallmark of the gentry urban culture and of the court. The detail from a painting on silk of the Ming period, illustrated below, depicts a palace scene with ladies of the court engaged in various refined pursuits. The plan (shown on the right) and the organization of Changan are examples of the strict control exercised by the state over all aspects of social life. These walled-in quarters had no communication with each other except by a single gate which led to the main street. These gates were closed at sunset and opened again at dawn in the interests of civil order. It was forbidden, except for officials of the first and second degree, to have doors giving directly on to the street. The preoccupation with civil order becomes even more apparent when one considers that another chain of walls enclosed the imperial city, seat of authority and that the imperial palace was surrounded by its own walls. This was the system in every Chinese capital.

1 Imperial Palace
2 Administrative center
3 Daming Palace
4 Markets
Surrounding residential areas

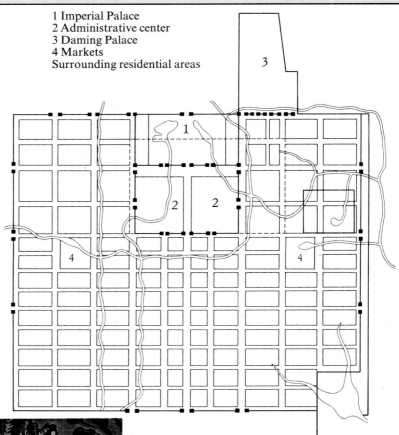

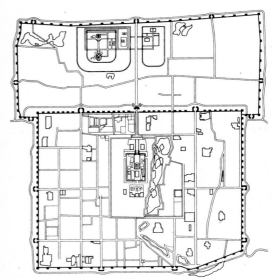

Above: urban plan of Peking, capital of China since 1421. It is interesting to note the similarity in urban planning of the two capitals, both based on a strict geometric plan. Originally, Peking was composed of four separate cities, divided from each other by walls, covering a total area of 67 square kilometers. The "Forbidden City," seat of the emperors, remains one of the finest examples of architectural splendour.

of the fall of the Tang, their chief assumed the imperial title, named his dynasty Liao, and was able to extend its authority within the Great Wall at the expense of the weak rulers of the Five Dynasties. The Liao soon adopted Chinese customs, educating their sons as Confucian gentlemen. Some fine examples of the art of the Liao remain in the temples at Datong, in northern Shanxi, one of their capitals. Another, for they still clung to a certain nomadic taste for migration, was Peking itself, which now for the first time became capital of an imperial dynasty. The Liao in northeast China could not be dislodged, not even by the early emperors of Song. Their presence within the Great Wall was to be the Achilles heel of the Song dynasty.

In 960 one of the generals of the short-lived northern dynasty called Northern Zhou, was aroused one night from sleep by his officers who placed an imperial yellow robe upon him and proclaimed him emperor. The subject of this quasi-Roman treatment (unique in Chinese history) was not just another ambitious general who had usurped the throne of a weak ruler. Zhao Kuangyin, known in history as Song Tai Zu, founder of the Song dynasty, was a man of extreme prudence, and a politician of the first order. He not only consolidated the northern kingdom, but extended his power over all the southern states, not by war, but by appealing to the universal desire for unity and peace, and by promising, and practicing, a hitherto unheard of clemency to the southern rulers who voluntarily submitted to his rule.

Having reunited the empire by consent rather than by arms, the new emperor cleverly got rid of his greatest danger, the army, and its generals, his erstwhile colleagues. He induced them to surrender their commands and largely disband their troops, in return for magnificent rewards and rich pensions. That they agreed and trusted him to keep his word is striking proof of his unusual character and the confidence he inspired. Their trust was not betrayed.

The Song dynasty, although seen by the Chinese as a period of great significance in their history, had a character markedly different from the Tang. It never controlled the whole of North China. Like the Liao territories within the Great Wall in Hebei and Shanxi, the far northwest had become the independent kingdom of Xia, ruled by a dynasty of the Tangut people, who had displaced the Turks in the northwest of Mongolia, just as the Kitans had done in the northeast. The Xia culture was only partly Chinese; it used a script of ideographs, copied from Chinese, but of a different form, and to this day remains almost entirely undecyphered, for the Xia and their culture were to be wholly destroyed by the later Mongol conquest.

If the Song were weak in the North, they also refrained from pushing their claims in the South. At the fall of the Tang, the Vietnamese had revolted and become independent of China. The Song were content to accept the role of suzerains, not direct rulers, and Vietnam was never to be a Chinese province again. Equally, Song Tai Zu refused to try to conquer the now rather weaker kingdom of Nanzhao in Yunnan province. He was not in direct contact with Korea, so that kingdom, now united, also slipped from Chinese control.

Above: noblewomen of the court walking in a garden in a fresco from the tomb of Li Xian. The portrayal of courtiers, often included in crowded group scenes, was very popular among artists of the Tang period.

When depicting the human figure, Chinese artists were more concerned to portray realistic, physical expressions rather than mere physique as one can see (opposite) from the faces of these dignitaries in a fresco from the tomb of Li Zhongshun (8th century).

THE MANDARINS

A distinctive feature of the Chinese world was the institution of the mandarinate. During the 2000 years of the Chinese empire, these government officials, who were also men of letters, formed a non-hereditary élite to which, at least in theory, anyone could aspire. They were in fact the real receptacles of power by virtue of the indispensable social functions which they performed. The system of imperial examinations for recruitment of these functionaries, introduced during the Han period then abandoned and reorganized under the Tang emperors, was based upon a study of Confucius' works: the Four Books and the Five Classics, therefore leaving out everything which was not specifically concerned with the art of government. In the doctrines of Confucius, the First Master (seen in the engraving below, teaching his disciples), the mandarins found the perfect expression of all those virtues most highly prized by them: respect, humility, docility and obedience to those of higher rank, to others older than oneself. These virtues of course were consistent with a totalitarian concept of the state and an élite whose prime consideration was to perpetuate itself. Not that it wished for this solely in order to win aristocratic privileges, or to obtain riches, which were regarded as ephemeral, but in order to pass on a monopoly of culture. Although the mandarins were authoritarian towards the other classes of society, Confucianism always advocated a democratic system within the aristocracy. They were in possession of the culture which rendered the literate person "noble," in contrast to the masses of the illiterate, and this gave them the right to rule. The defects of this system were conservatism and traditionalism and hostility towards any innovation or show of initiative. On the other hand, it had the advantages that during many periods, it could recruit most of the country's talent to the service of the state and also that it favoured a certain social mobility. Finally, it served to unite the country from a cultural point of view and to produce men of outstanding talent. However, the limitations of their programs of study tended to produce a ruling class which was not well-informed, whose culture was too narrowly based so that, in the 19th century, a period of rapid change elsewhere in the world, modernization and renewal were held back in China.

Drawing showing an examination cell and, in the illustration on the right, the examination quarter at Nanking.

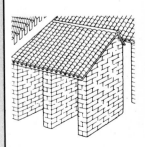

240

The mandarins were divided into nine classes, each of which had the right to wear a particular costume with the insignia of rank richly embroidered on the front and back (opposite: a mandarin in his official robes). Considering the absolute power which the imperial bureaucracy wielded over the whole of society, it is rather surprising to discover the small numbers of its representatives. During the 18th century, the number of permanent officials for whom there were posts available in the capital and in the provinces hardly exceeded 9000. There were, however, many supernumerary and unassigned officials who were, so to speak, given a job "without portfolio." Also considerable was the number of officials employed at the *yamen*, the offices of provincial government (below, the plan of a *yamen* which was really a small citadel, provided with storehouses, dwellings for staff and servants, assembly and tribunal halls and prisons). Notwithstanding the prestige which was accorded to them, the officials earned comparatively low salaries, paid out by the treasury in the capital. To this, the provincial treasury added a rather larger sum called "money for living honestly." In spite of this, the bureaucracy lived on "systematic corruption" which frequently degenerated into mere extortion. Mandarins were also required to administer justice (below, engraving of a trial in process). In general, the letter of the law was always subordinated to the ethical judgment and wisdom of the judge-administrator. During the Ming and Qing periods, three grades of examinations

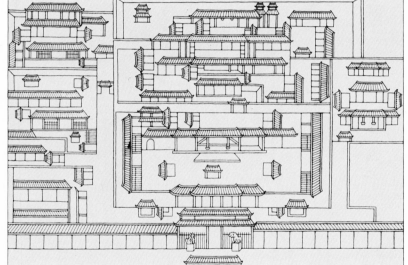

were in force: the first at district level opened the way to successive exams taken at the headquarters of the prefecture. Success in these entitled one to become part of the class of "men of letters." However, to reach the higher grades, it was necessary to take still more examinations from time to time, like the great triennial examinations which were held in the provincial capitals. Thousands of candidates spent days and days with paper and brush in the cells of the examination quarter. Success in these examinations meant that one had the right to take the third grade of examinations held in the capital, also once every three years. Generally candidates had to repeat the exams several times and the ages of the successful examinees varied between 20 and 80 (above, a print showing how good or worthy actions are rewarded).

An interest in the human form was shared by even minor craftsmen of the Tang period as shown by this clothed figure of a girl, made of wood and stone, discovered in excavations in the region of Turfan in Sinkiang.

Opposite: a typical terra-cotta statuette of the Tang period. Apart from the human form and horses, camels were among the most popular subjects for carvings and sculptures. These statuettes were reproduced in a number of colours, obtained by mixing metallic oxides.

The Song, on the whole pacific towards these neighbours, were determined to stop further encroachments, and maintained an army, for which they found difficulty in obtaining remounts, as the horse-breeding lands along the Mongolian border were now foreign and often hostile territory. Militarily the Song were weak, and also cautious. In their administration they were much more humane than any previous regime. Officials, however high, who fell into disfavour were not executed, but assigned as lowly district magistrates to remote posts, sometimes in unhealthy regions. From this exile, a turn of the political wheel could bring them back to power. The military aristocracy had now wholly disappeared; the civil service was recruited solely by public examination, and it is really from this period that the characteristic social structure of China, enduring until the communist revolution, dates.

Many historians now see the Tang as the last age of the early Chinese culture, or as some see it the Chinese Middle Ages. The true divide is probably midway through the Tang when the civil service examination began to be the major factor in recruiting the ruling élite. The Song are therefore seen as the first or early period of the modern age in China.

The growing importance of commerce, including export trade to the southeast of Asia and beyond, which had been an Arab monopoly in Tang times, can in part be credited to the use of the compass, now developed for navigation. By the 13th century the state revenue from customs and excise exceeded the land revenue for the first time; after the Song it was not to happen again for several centuries. Fine porcelain, at one time made only for the royal court, began to be manufactured on an ever-growing scale, and became a valuable export, with markets as far away as Iraq, East Africa and of course Southeast Asia. The land route, the old Silk Road, no longer under Chinese control, fell into disuse as sea routes replaced it, and the Song were the first Chinese dynasty to create a navy to protect them. There can be no doubt that the luxurious and sophisticated style of living which so impressed the Venetian Marco Polo even after the Song dynasty had fallen was still more in evidence when it controlled most of China. The population rose to 100 million, about double that of the Tang empire in 754.

The variety and extent of Song literature, better preserved than that of the earlier dynasty, is prodigious, but it is in the art of painting, so much more of which has survived, that the Song are seen to excel. Landscape was their speciality, or rather it is the genre which is most admired of their work. The essence of this art is to emphasize the grandeur of nature and the miniscule role of man within this vast frame. It is inspired by partly Taoist ideas, sophisticated, but without the magical character which popular Taoism relied upon. Dong Yuan, late 10th century, and Guo Xi, circa 1020–1090, combined mastery of continuous composition and linear technique with that of suggestion of atmosphere through gradations of ink-tone. Li Gong-lin, circa 1040–1106, excelled in vigorous contrasts of light and shade, of broad and delicate line, and in airy architectural renderings in ruled and measured style. Mi Fu, 1051–1107, used hardly any lines, building mountains and forests from graded accumu-

lations of blobs of ink. What is also very significant of Song society is that great painters, famous philosophers, historians and prominent statesmen were often one and the same person.

The major contribution of the Song to Chinese culture was the reshaping of Confucian philosophy to meet the needs of an age very different to that of Confucious himself and his great disciples. Since the advent of Buddhism there had been no real effort to meet its challenge in the fields of cosmology and philosophy. Confucian teaching had concentrated on morality and ethics. The dispute about the nature of man, whether naturally good but liable to become perverted, or basically bad and needing the control of severe discipline, had been considered closed, as those who favoured the latter view had merged with the discredited School of the Law. The Song philosophers not only reopened this question, but went on to investigate a wider field of problems. Their method was nonetheless characteristically Confucian. They did not claim, indeed they denied, that they were innovators. Their arguments were based on what they said was the true interpretation of passages in accepted Confucian classical texts, which had been ignored or forgotten in the course of time.

Zhou Dunyi (1017–73), the founder of the Song Neo-Confucian philosophy, discovered in the *Yi-jing*, one of the oldest surviving works of Chinese literature, mainly concerned with divination, a phrase containing a reference to Tai Ji, "The Supreme Ultimate." He then constructed a theory which equated Tai Ji (the ancient Tian, the original sky god) with Li, the Moral Law. These ideas and their corollary, the nature of man, were disputed, elaborated, and finally acquired the status of Confucian orthodoxy as formulated by Zhu Xi who lived in the second period of the Song dynasty (1129–1200). So far-reaching were the changes that some scholars suggest that later Confucianism should really be called the Doctrine of Zhu Xi. His teaching virtually abrogated the idea of personality in Tai Ji, the Supreme Ultimate: "There is no man in Heaven judging sin." And the view that Li, the Moral Law, is an impersonal

Bronze bell from the Liao dynasty (11th century) with engravings in relief depicting events in the history of the Kitan, a Tartar people who inhabited the eastern part of the steppes. In 916, in the confusion following the downfall of the Tang dynasty, the Kitan occupied huge tracts of northern China. "Cathay," the name by which China at one time was known in the West, is in fact a corruption of Kitan.

Opposite: the Tian-ning-ssu pagoda, in Peking, dating from the 11th or early 12th century, during the time of the Liao dynasty. This was the dynastic name assumed by the Kitan who, in 926, took possession of the area to the north-east of the province of Hebei which included Peking. In fact the construction of this pagoda, on an octagonal plan with projecting floors, is much less elaborate than many others of the same type. One thinks particularly of the beautiful pagoda of Yün-chü-ssu, built in 1117 on Mount Fang, to the southwest of Peking. The huge statues standing at the sides of the doors are fairly conventional and the other sculpture and architectonic motifs are likewise unremarkable. In style, the Tian-ning-ssu pagoda is reminiscent of others of the Song dynasty.

Huge clay statues in the temple of Tu-lo-ssu at Chi-hsien in the province of Hebei, about 100 kilometers to the east of Peking. This temple, which was built in 984, is the oldest of those which remain from the Liao dynasty. The statues are to be found in the pavilion of Avalokitesvara, which is built on three interior levels.

force came to be the dominant doctrine of later Confucianism. This was a great obstacle to the acceptance of Christianity by the Chinese educated class in later times.

Li, the Moral Law, was of universal application and there was no separation between natural phenomena and human conduct. Earthquakes, droughts and floods were just as much the consequences and reflections of human imperfections as were crimes and cruelty. The emperor, as the "Son of Heaven," a title which meant the adopted and delegated ruler of mankind, not a claim to divinity, must be held responsible for the disturbances in nature. On the nature of man there had been more contention among the Neo-Confucian philosophers. There was no support for the view that the nature of man was bad. But one group held that it was neither good nor bad, but determined by the mode of upbringing. They used the simile of water seeking the easiest outlet when confined in a rocky gorge, and were therefore called the "Whirling Water School."

Zhu Xi rejected this idea. For him, the nature of man was determined by its origin, the Moral Law, and must therefore be good, and in essence, incorruptible. Defects in human nature were due to neglect. He used similes such as the bright mirror covered with dust; if the dust is cleaned off and the surface polished, the mirror will shine as if new. A pearl in a bowl of dirty water was another favourite illustration. The pearl remains the same, once taken out of the foul water.

The great philosophic debate of the Song scholars was also part of the political life of the age. The philosophers were sometimes statesmen of great authority, and all were intimately linked with members of the official class, since all derived from the scholar-gentry who now constituted the ruling élite.

Such a man was Wang An-shi who was the driving force in the government from 1068 to his death in 1086. He inaugurated a new social and economic policy designed, as he saw it, to strengthen the Song empire in the face of the constant menace from the Liao dynasty beyond, and in part within, the Great Wall. He and his followers who formed the party of the "Innovators," were bitterly opposed by a conservative party led by Sima Guang, a great historian. Wang introduced many laws aimed at equalizing the economic rewards of Chinese society and relieving poverty and famine. Other laws encouraged the breeding of horses, since the hostile northern powers now controlled the border regions which normally provided the mounts needed for the Chinese cavalry.

The main objection to Wang's laws made by his opponents was not their regulative character, which has even brought the suggestion from some historians that Wang was an early forerunner of modern socialism, but that the reforms were clearly inspired by the example of the Han emperor Wu and his

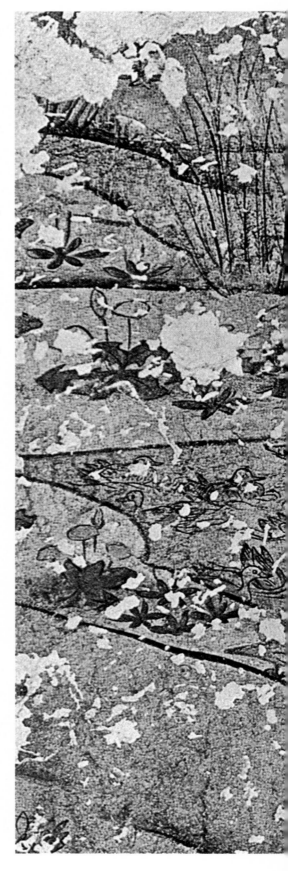

Detail from a fresco in the imperial tomb of the Liao dynasty found in excavations at Ching-Ling in Mongolia. The fresco itself forms part of a series dedicated to the seasons, this being a tribute to spring. The careful observation of nature shown in the fluid composition and the delicate colouring is evidence that this is a work of considerable stylistic maturity.

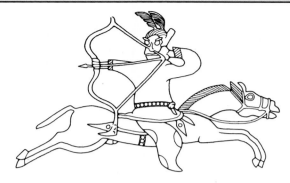

THE CHINESE AND THE BARBARIANS

This design on a tile of the late Zhou period shows a horseman in the act of loosing the "arrow of delivery," a feat performed while facing backwards and shooting at full gallop. It was the horse that made the nomad peoples to the north of China a menace to be feared, inducing a strongly defensive reaction from the Chinese in the form of the huge walls built along the northern frontier. About the same period, that is towards the end of the 6th century B.C., the Chinese started to use saddle horses in place of war chariots and their cavalry now bore

the main force of the enemy attacks. The use of saddle horses was made possible by what is now regarded as a Chinese invention – the stirrup. China was the only country of the ancient world to have satisfactorily resolved the problem of horse harness. This they did by developing the collar (to be seen on the horse on the opposite page), made of soft and solid parts so arranged as to ensure maximum control of the animal.

At the same time,

following the social and economic advances made during the Zhou period, there was a rapid development in political unification and of Chinese civilization in general which had by now acquired certain characteristics of its own. The Great Wall (in the illustration below left, the first Qin emperor is seen studying its course on a sand model) was China's answer to the need to protect her "civilized," agricultural

population from the "barbarian" herdsmen of Central Asia, Mongolia and Manchuria.

Nonetheless we may well ask ourselves why the Chinese felt the need to go to such monolithic lengths to define their northern border while leaving their southern frontiers untouched. The most convincing argument is that put forward by Lattimore who suggests that during their expansion northwards, which began around the 4th century B.C., the Chinese eventually found themselves in territory quite unsuited to their methods of irrigated cultivation; they would therefore have had to abandon the system which had made them what they were – a rural-urban people. They would have been forced to take another road, losing their cohesion as

a people and over-extending their economy. Their social institutions were already too far developed to be subjected to such change; so their answer was to put a limit on their own expansion. The physical expression of this decision was the Great Wall. The main characteristic of China's northern border is that, over the centuries, it has become one with the geographical boundaries beyond which the Chinese could not, or would not, export their "way of life."

This rigid frontier, however, has never been a barrier to invasion, as Chinese history shows, or to commercial exchange and cultural influences. By the 4th century A.D. Buddhism had taken a hold in China. It had been introduced into

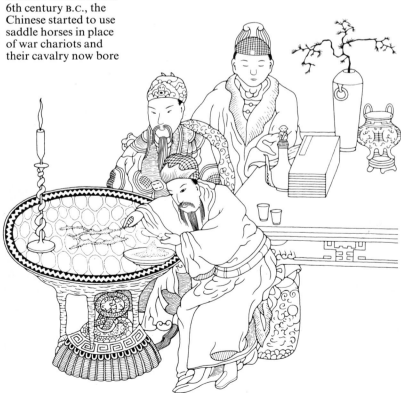

China during the 1st century A.D. and soon found adherents, particularly among people who had contact with the colonies of foreign merchants living in the cities of northern China. It had first become confused and then synthesized with Taoism; called the "religion of salvation,"

Buddhism exercised a very considerable appeal. In order to re-establish the true teaching and study of the sacred texts, many Chinese monks undertook long pilgrimages across Asia between the 4th and the 11th centuries. One of the most famous of these pilgrims was Xuanzang (pictured on

the right) who lived during the Tang period. Together with Yi Jing, a contemporary, he was one of the greatest translators of the Indian holy books. The enormous work which was done by these two had a considerable influence on Chinese thought: the speculations of the

Neo-Confucian philosophers of the Song dynasty would not have been conceivable without an understanding of Indian metaphysics, nor would the unprecedented flowering of the plastic arts (in the caves of Dunhuang, Longmen and Yungang) have taken place.

In the regions between Persia and India, the Hellenistic influence was sufficiently strong to have had an influence on Buddhist art. One of the most striking proofs of the unity of our world is, in the words of Gernet, "the distant memory of Greek sculpture which exists in certain Buddhist statues in China." Buddhism also brought a new understanding of literature to China via the northern frontier. In fact, the first Chinese romances in

the spoken language have striking similarities with Buddhist sermons from which they probably derive. And it was in order to disseminate their written works that the Buddhist monks built the first printing presses.

The situation which evolved in the course of centuries on the border between the Chinese and the "barbarians" was characterized by an exchange of goods of a particular type which may best be described as "the exchange of gifts" between the rich and privileged. (The Chinese print illustrated opposite, below right, is entitled: "The barbarians bring

their tributes." The illustration, above left, shows two "barbarians" in attitudes of reverence; above right, a caravan in progress). The

Chinese saw the passage of goods across the border in a political rather than an economic light. Some goods, such as silk, ended up in the hands

of merchants who knew the "right people" with whom to establish contacts and alliances across the frontiers. The envoys sent by the

"barbarians" reasoned in the same way. Which explains why so often they themselves actually proposed the payment of tribute to the Chinese.

251

Painting on silk from the Southern Tang dynasty (10th century) whose court was at Nanking. This is a very famous painting by Gu Hungzhong, one of the most important Chinese portrait painters, and forms part of a scroll which illustrates four similar episodes. Alarmed by rumours concerning the night life of an extremely learned man whom he wished to honour with high position, the emperor asked the artist to attend these evening parties and to paint what he saw. In the scene reproduced here, he has captured a moment of rapt attention on the part of the guests as they listen to a young girl playing the *pi-pa*, a kind of guitar. The definition of detail is particularly arresting.

confidence in merchant advisers to solve economic problems. The opponents were traditionalist, they objected to state intervention in commerce as contrary to Confucian doctrine. They had other points of difference with Wang which were purely philosophic; and they had a criticism of real substance in claiming that the administration of these reforms created a host of new officials and place seekers.

Both Wang and his enemies depended nonetheless on the support and confidence of the emperor. While he reigned, Wang could count on the friendship of the sixth sovereign of the Song dynasty, known by his temple name of Shen Zong (1068–85). When the emperor died, the regent empress dowager recalled Sima Guang to power, repealed all the new laws and reversed the entire state policy. When she herself died, emperor Zhe Zong, in turn, recalled the Innovators to power, under the leadership of an ardent disciple of Wang An-shi, Cai Jing. Cai Jing and the Innovators continued in power until the invasion by the new Jin Tartar dynasty which had conquered the Liao, and almost at once attacked and overran the whole of the northern provinces of the Song empire. The Chinese rallied in the South and set up a new capital at Hangzhou, the city which Marco Polo admired and called Quinsay. Cai Jing has been, perhaps rightly, held responsible for this disaster, and his subsequent policy of appeasing the Jin enemy earned him undying contempt as one of the great "traitors" of Chinese history (which of course was written by his enemies). Wang An-shi was tarred with the same brush, and he and all his work condemned out of hand.

There are other, more objective, ways of judging things. One aspect of the Song dynasty which sharply differentiates it from the Tang and also from the later dynasties, is that the Song were never challenged internally by any great rebellion. It is therefore reasonable to conclude that their rule, and the innovations of Wang An-shi, did not provoke the violent protest and despairing reaction which had caused great upheavals in the past. Moreover, again unlike the Tang, the Song dynasty was free from the troubles provoked by dynastic intrigue, *coups d'état*, and irregular successions to the throne. The Song emperors may not have been such colourful characters as their Tang or Han predecessors, but they were sober, diligent and well-meaning; they seem to have seriously concerned themselves with the main problems of their empire, and to have sought for solutions.

It is also clear that neither the power of consort families nor eunuch favourites was a serious issue under the Song. The structure of Chinese society, in a far more populous empire than that of the Han, had reduced the opportunities for ambitious families, and incidentally the dangers to which they might be exposed. The greatly increased power of the civil service, now entirely recruited by public examinations, was an obstacle to eunuch influence.

The last of the line of northern Song emperors, who reigned in the city now named Kaifeng, was Hui Zong (1100–26). As a ruler he must be regarded as a failure, since it was under him that foolish policy provoked the Jin invasion, which ended in the fall of Kaifeng and the emperor's captivity for the rest of his life. But

TRIGRAMS AND THE ART OF DIVINATION

The text of the *Yi-jing* or "Book of Changes" originated long before the advent of Confucianism or Taoism, of which it contains some prenotions. In the *Yi-jing*, we can trace those fundamental concepts which form the essence of Chinese thought, such as the concept of Dao (Tao), of "yin" and "yang." Dao originally meant (as it still does in everyday language) "road, way," and thus by extension, "course, the way of things," with the implied notion of the principle of movement which governs all natural processes. The alternation of life and death, of the seasons, of day and night are the result of the play of change between yin and yang. They are not seen as contrary and independent sources of energy but rather as abstract categories which express every alternation or duality. Everything which is double, antithetical or complementary, can be classified under the categories of yin and yang. Light, warmth, movement are yang, man and sky are yang; darkness, cold, stillness are yin, so is woman and earth. All things have their origin in the interaction of yin and yang.

These concepts, in the *Yi-jing*, a treatise of the art of divination which came into existence during the Zhou period, are illustrated by a system of symbols based on trigrams and hexagrams formed of continuous or broken lines which represent the forces of yin and yang. The continuous line is yang, symbol of the masculine principle and the broken line is yin, the feminine principle. From the eight basic trigrams (shown in the table below with the meanings, animals and cardinal points of the compass which they represent) are derived the 64 hexagrams. Fu Xi, who is said to have been the inventor of this divinatory system, enlarged the basis of calculation by multiplying the eight original trigrams by eight. The 64 hexagrams were obtained by doubling up each of the trigrams, first with itself, then with the other seven. There are numerous other possible systems of multiplication and the fact that there are only 64 hexagrams and not an infinite number is due to an arbitrary decision taken in compiling the *Yi-jing*. Used as a manual of divination, it can produce 4096 answers to the 64 hexagrams, enough it was evidently thought to solve any problem. It is interesting to note that hexagrams do not consist of two trigrams fused together, but of two trigrams placed

Ch'ien	Tui	Li	Chên	Sun	Kan	Kên	K'un
Sky	Stagnant water, lake	Fire, sun, beauty	Thunder	Wind, wood	Running water, rain, spring water, moon, abyss	Mountain, hill	Earth
Inexorable force, power	Pleasure, satisfaction, contentment	Luminosity, elegance	Force of attraction, vivacity	Flexibility, penetration, gentleness	Danger, difficulty	State of repose, quiet	Vastness, capacity, passivity
Horse	Goat	Pheasant	Dragon	Hen	Pig	Dog	Ox
South	Southeast	East	Northeast	Southwest	West	Northwest	North

one above the other, of which the second (on top) is said to modify the first (underneath). Present in the hexagram therefore is the concept of change, from the lower trigram to the upper, and therefore this system of divination is called "changes." The diviner interprets and relates the inner meaning of this change to the question asked.

For more than 2000 years the *Yi-jing* has been used in China for divinatory purposes: the process consists of the singling out of a number by a series of complex operations performed with yarrow sticks, then looking up the hexagram corresponding to that number in order to give the appropriate interpretation. In recent years the *Yi-jing* has enjoyed considerable popularity in the West. The Swiss psychiatrist Carl G. Jung, in the preface to Wilhelm's English translation of the text, asserted his total faith in the predictions of the *Yi-jing*, suggesting that their function is to delve into the subconscious and bring to the surface of our consciousness what is necessary in order to understand a problem and to find a solution to it. An interesting example of interpretation is the hexagram which, in 1900, was used as the flag of the Boxer rebellion. The hexagram (illustrated below) is number 29 in the *Yi-jing*. It is called "the abyss." It is formed of two water trigrams, one above, one below. The accompanying text reads: "Water on

water, grave danger. But he who crosses the abyss without losing faith and has a steady heart will win through." The Boxers interpreted this hexagram to mean: Water on water, China is flooded with foreigners but the rebels have faith and are winning respect,

therefore they will triumph. History has shown that this was a wrong deduction but it provides an interesting example of the interpretation of a hexagram and shows how much this divinatory system has entered into popular culture.

Moving to another level, it is interesting to note the refined symbolism which pervades the whole of Chinese artistic expression. The decoration of the painted porcelain plate (*famille rose*: 1723–35) on this page shows a shepherdess (yin) with three sheep (in Chinese, the word for sheep is

pronounced "yang," although the written character is not the same as is used for the masculine principle of "yang"). The whole picture with its two rams and an ewe is thick with reference: it is both symbolic and a play on words for it represents the trigram meaning "stagnant water, a lake," a broken yin line on top of two continuous yang lines. A large number of Chinese pictorial compositions suggest or refer, in a subtle and allusive manner, to the augural properties of trigrams indirectly evoked by representations of flowers, landscapes and animals.

Opposite above: the eight trigrams stand above the figure of the mythical general Zhang Taigung. The circular sequence of the eight trigrams with the symbol of Dao in the middle (the yin which contains the embryo of the yang and vice-versa) is one of the most widespread prophetic motifs in Chinese iconography.

Hui Zong is remembered also for the fact that he was not only a great patron of the arts, but was himself an artist of the first order. His collection of ancient and contemporary paintings, long since dispersed, is known from its catalogue, perhaps the first ever compiled, which survives and is a major source of knowledge of early Chinese art. His own works are still in part extant, and are among the best treasures of Song painting. There was a school of painting in his palace, over which the emperor personally presided. If Hui Zong had not been emperor his fame as a great artist would be untarnished.

After the disaster of 1126, the Song dynasty rallied in the South under a new emperor belonging to a collateral branch of the Zhao imperial family. At first the victorious Jin, crossing the Yangtze, seemed invincible. They swept down as far as Hangzhou in Zhejiang province, and it was due more to the early death of the Jin ruler that South China was saved for the Song. They did indeed find an able and devoted general, Yo Fei, who in 1131 drove the Jin back across the Yangtze. He had plans for the reconquest of the whole North, but was the object of an intrigue directed by the chief minister Cai Jing, who accused Yo Fei of planning to usurp the throne, and had him put to death. For his act of treason, Cai Jing is still execrated, and Yo Fei has become one of China's heroes. Peace with the Jin was established, with the frontier fixed along the northern watershed of the Yangtze valley, as it had been in the period of partition in the 4th and 5th centuries. For more than a century the Song reigned over the southern half of the empire, now the richer, in peace and great prosperity.

It was above all in this second, "Southern" Song age, that rapid advances were made both in the development of high-quality industry on a large scale, notably silk weaving and porcelain, and also in navigation and overseas commerce. A book written by a senior official of the customs and excise, Zhao Rugua, himself a distant collateral of the imperial family, testifies to the extent of Chinese knowledge of Western Asia and Europe, much of it probably derived from Arab merchants familiar with the Mediterranean zone. Sicily, including Mount Etna, is described, but the behaviour of volcanoes (there are no active ones in China) was misunderstood. Zhao Rugua says that after eruption the lava flows back into the crater, clearly a mistaken translation of some Arabic text or spoken account. His book also refers to Spain and states that, "if one travels by land northwards for 200 days, the days are only six hours long." The distance so calculated, at roughly the rate of 20 kilometers a day (as was the rule in China in recent years) would, with halts, give a distance of about 2000 kilometers, and would thus bring the traveller to Scandinavia, where it is in fact true that in winter, daylight can be as short as six hours.

In art, particularly landscape painting, the Southern Song period at least equals the dynasty's earlier age; and the work of its famous artists, a considerable amount of whose output has survived, is esteemed as highly. In philosophy, it was in this Southern Song century that Zhu Xi lived and taught, formulating what was to become the settled orthodox doctrine of Neo-Confucianism. He was not in fact highly honoured by the

During the Song period, painting reached new levels of achievement and was held in very high esteem. Indeed Hui Zong, the last Song emperor (1082–1135), dedicated his life to art – particularly to the art of painting, even to the exclusion of affairs of state. The two landscape on silk (opposite), representing autumn and winter respectively, can both be attributed to Hui Zong. He founded the first academy of painting in China, which he organized like a Confucian college, under his own guidance and that of other worthy artists. The

most frequently recurring subjects of these artists were stylized landscapes, flowers, animals and birds, executed with the minimum of detail, as shown below.

The imagination of the Song artists and their inventiveness in terms of form and decoration can be seen from the examples on these pages. Left: stylized *mei-ping* (vase for a branch of plum tree) with black design, typical of the Hebei region, which was much in vogue. Below left: an elegant white porcelain wine jug in a lotus-shaped bowl which would have held warm water. Below right: a *guan* vase, of which the characteristics are its spare lines and long neck; these vases were reserved for court use.

Opposite below left: another *mei-ping* vase, this time decorated with a black dragon, one of the most popular shapes at this time. Center: a brown bowl, its interior spotted by means of ferrous oxide and much imitated in Japan. Opposite right: a splendid example of a celadon vase of pale jade colour. Made of terra cotta these vases were covered with an enamel glaze containing iron oxide, the decoration being obtained by use of a sharp instrument which removed parts of the outer surface.

CERAMIC POTTERY

Prior to the Song period there had been developed in China a technique for making a type of grey ceramic pottery which had similarities with porcelain, while lacking the properties of true porcelain which is white and semi-transparent. It was during the Song period that the greatest number of shapes and designs in porcelain occurred. Of these, some owed their beauty to a happy combination of form and glazing, others to the decorative technique known as *sgraffiato* ("scratched"). This technique foreshadowed the transition from the Song to the Ming style. In the latter, decoration was by means of coloured enamel applied to the glazed surface. The Ming period was also a time when many new shapes were introduced (for example, the large dinner plate)

and porcelain replaced earthenware and pottery. Finally, under the Ming dynasty, the porcelain industry became concentrated in a single area, the northeastern part of Jiangxi, which was rich in china clay. From a craft practiced by artisans (prints of the Qing period, illustrated above, show various stages of manufacture), porcelain became a huge industry. Thus Chinese porcelain acquired the inevitable characteristics of mass production. The technical perfection achieved in the Qing period which followed meant that all sorts of decoration could be tried. However, although the pieces destined for export were sometimes characterized by excessive ornamentation, those which graced the imperial court retained their purity of design and form.

Some examples of vases from the Northern Song dynasty: the decoration is sometimes replaced by a light covering of cracked or fissured glaze.

Porcelain from the Southern Song dynasty. Here, the decorative motifs are engraved or appliquéd before glazing. Particularly interesting is the vase on the left.

Porcelain from the Ming and Qing dynasties. The *wucai* or "five colour" pieces, an example of which is the vase with fishes on the left, mark the beginning of the so-called *famille verte* type of china, first made at the end of the 17th century.

During the Qing period, the manufacture of porcelain at Jingdezhen was considerably expanded and classified according to the predominant colour of the decoration.

This octagonal pagoda, built around 1044 at Kaifeng, in the province of Henan, is a typical example of Song architecture of the period. Its name

Tie-ta (pagoda of iron) refers to the colour of the brickwork.

Opposite: detail of the ornamentation.

contemporary emperors, who favoured other doctrines and other policies, being opposed to what they deemed the hopeless expectation of recovery of the North, while Zhu Xi was an ardent advocate of reconquest.

He and his disciples remained out of favour till his death in 1200. But 27 years later, when the Song were already facing the devastating Mongol invasion, the reigning emperor rehabilitated Zhu Xi, whose views and philosophic doctrines he shared, and went on to honour the great sage of Neo-Confucianism with the posthumous title of duke, and an official eulogy claiming Zhu Xi as the rediscoverer of the true interpretation of the classical literature, lost for some 13 centuries past. This new orthodoxy was never again in question. The immediate successors of the Song, the alien and uncultured Mongols, were in no way concerned with philosophy: when the Chinese recovered control and the Ming dynasty took power, Zhu Xi and his teaching had been the accepted orthodox Confucianism for nearly 200 years.

It is often said that the Mongol conquest of China, resisted valiantly, but disastrously by the Jin in the North, was virtually uncontested in the Song southern empire. This is hardly in accord with recorded history. The Mongols had conquered the Jin in the years following 1210, but they did not invade the Song empire until 1235, 18 years after the death of the terrible Genghis Khan. It took his successors 44 years, till 1279, to destroy the last Song resistance in the far South. The Song navy was one main cause of this long resistance; and it was still on sea power, now outmatched by the new Mongol navy (manned by Chinese), that the last Song emperor relied, till in a fatal sea battle off the coast of modern Hong Kong, he went down with his fleet in 1279.

The Song dynasty remains, to this day, a somewhat controversial period in Chinese history. There are the patriots who deplore its failure to recover all the lost territory of the Tang period, and its alleged unreadiness to meet the dangers of the northern nomadic invaders. Others stress the humane quality of Song rule, the mainly respectable if not glamorous character of the successive emperors (there is no Song "bad emperor" in Confucian eyes although Shen Zong, the patron of Wang An-shi, is seen as being misled).

All agree on the high quality of art and literature, and in more modern work emphasis has been placed on the growth of mass industry, aimed largely at an export market; the progress in navigation, including the general use of the maritime compass and the establishment of a navy; and changes in the economy which for the first time in Chinese history made the revenue derived from excise and customs on commerce higher than that of the traditional land tax. It has been suggested that the Chinese economy with its quality large-scale handicraft industry was ready, in the 13th century, to "take off" into the first stage of an industrial revolution, anticipating that in England by 700 years. The reason it did not achieve this transformation was not, it is suggested, economic, but political, and was above all due to the devastation of more than half the empire by the destructive Mongol invasion.

The records of the Song period, both the official dynastic

Above: a celadon-type vase in the traditional *mei-ping* shape (height: 38 cms.) from the Southern Song dynasty. Vases of this type were used for holding a single branch of a plum tree.
Below: a *kuan* cup, made of blue porcelain, dating from the 12th century (Southern Song dynasty).

Opposite: *An imaginary journey in the region of Xiaoxiang*, painted in ink on paper and attributed to Li Lung-mien (1040–1106). All three works are now in the National Museum, Tokyo.

而後合不異豐
城之遇也乾隆
御識

history and other texts, are more ample, indeed overwhelming, than those of any earlier period; they provide information on which varying theories can be based and the character of leading personalities assessed. The similarity of Song problems to some of those in the contemporary world, the modern character, in the 11th century, of much of Song thought is a stimulus to Western interest, at present very active in the field of Song studies, in this period.

The bastioned gateway of Bian liang, present-day Kaifeng, in a drawing from the first half of the 12th century by Chang Tse-tuan, a celebrated artist who was active at the court of the Northern Song. During the period of the Five Dynasties and then again during the Northern Song dynasty (between 960 and 1126), Kaifeng was the imperial capital city. The latter period was one of intense urbanization and the cities and city dwellers became increasingly important. Situated on the Great Plain, Kaifeng was vulnerable but very important from an economic point of view, as it stood at the confluence of the Grand Canal and the Yellow River. Its court was a center of enlightened patronage and many of the foremost artists of the age benefitted.

Opposite: a splendid example of wood carving with traces of colour, from the Song dynasty and now in the Metropolitan Museum, New York. It represents the goddess Guan Yin, the Chinese derivation of the bodhisattva of compassion and mercy, always ready to come to the help of mankind. Bodhisattva, in Buddhist terminology, means one who has reached the state preceding that of Buddhahood and who lives on earth voluntarily. The expression of calm and smiling benevolence, with which she is depicted, suggesting an empathy with suffering humanity, made Guan Yin a particularly meaningful deity.

THE LATER EMPIRE: MONGOL AND MING

Above: portraits of Genghis Khan (on the left) and of his nephew (Kublai Khan), key figures in the Mongolian conquest of China. The Mongol tribes came from the far lands of Outer Mongolia and of Altay. They had remained entirely uninfluenced by Chinese civilization, their own way of life being one of violence, characterized by ruin and devastation wherever their lust for conquest took them. This mutual incompatibility, arising from the absolute disparity between the two cultures, did not stop the Mongols from

building an immense empire in China, which under Kublai assumed the chinesified name of Yuan (1271). The conquest was completed in 1279 with the overthrow of the Southern Song dynasty. The name of Kublai became known in the West from the travels of Marco Polo who lived for 17 years at the emperor's court whose cosmopolitan magnificence he described vividly in *Il Milione*.

Opposite: a porcelain statue of the goddess Guan Yin, dating from the Yuan dynasty, found near Peking.

It is usually recognized that the last three dynasties of imperial China constitute an epoch distinct from the earlier dynasties and are seen in Chinese eyes as the "modern period." This designation is becoming, with time, outmoded. Only the last of these dynasties, the Qing, or Manchu, merges with the really modern age of the 19th century. It seems more convenient therefore to divide the Chinese recent past into two parts, the Mongol and Ming dynasties, and the last imperial dynasty, the Qing.

The Mongol conquest of China began in 1210 with the invasion of North China, then under the rule of the Jin dynasty, which was a Tartar house of the Nuchen tribe. The Jin had assimilated Chinese civilization so thoroughly in the century of their rule that they had engaged in the philosophic discussions of the Song period, employed many Chinese scholars in their administration and, to the embarassment of a ruling Song emperor who did not support the views of the Neo-Confucian philosopher Zhu Xi, had on one occasion, through an embassy, enquired after the health and prosperity of the "Great Zhu Xi."

The civilization of North and South alike was essentially identical, and Chinese. The Jin proved no match for the Mongols, who had become under Genghis Khan the dominant power of the steppes. The Mongols were ruthless and, in effect, savage nomads; their rule of war was that any city which shot off as much as one arrow in its defense was subjected, on capture, to the total massacre of every man, woman and child. When they took Peking in 1210, this rule was applied. Having conquered most of the Jin empire with these methods, Genghis left the remainder of the task to his generals and set off to conquer Western Asia, using the same technique. Returning in 1224, he fell upon the northwestern semi-Chinese kingdom of Xia, and so utterly destroyed and devastated it that this region has never fully recovered. Contemporary accounts record that less than one percent of the population survived. Many of the cities have remained uninhabited ever since.

Genghis Khan died three years later, in 1227, and his successor, Ogotai, proved to be a less sanguinary ruler. He listened to the advice of his counsellor, Yelu Chu-cai, a descendent of the Kitan Liao dynasty, who, when the Jin capital, Kaifeng, was forced to surrender, and the Mongol general in command proposed to massacre every inhabitant, pointed out that dead men paid no taxes, and that the million or so skilled craftsmen among the inhabitants and refugees, would be more useful as serfs than as corpses. Kaifeng was spared. Nevertheless a great part of the provinces of North China were devastated: an enormous host of refugees, living as best they could, moved about the ruined country, while many thousands more escaped to the South. The origin of the Hakka people of South China, whose dialect has still close links with the speech of North

China, is in part due to this migration, which had a previous model in the flight before the Jin invasion in 1126. These catastrophes left long-lasting effects and undoubtedly contributed to the relative economic decline of the North.

The Song empire in the South was not invaded until 1235, and for some years the Mongols did not make the rapid progress which their invasions usually achieved. It was not until 1276 that the Southern Song capital was taken, 41 years after the invasion began. But only three years later, in 1279, the last Song emperor died when his fleet was destroyed off the coast of South China. The long resistance was due to the difficulty that the Mongol cavalry found in the damp climate of South China, where the valleys are all rice fields and the hills covered with forest or tea plantations. The Song fleet also impeded their communications along the great rivers. It was Kublai Khan, the next Mongol emperor, who struck the fatal blow by invading the South, not across the middle Yangtze, but by a western route through Sichuan and then down to Yunnan, the old kingdom of Nanzhao, which he destroyed. By that time, since the accession of Kublai in 1263, the Mongol dynasty was firmly established in China, but the vast Mongol empire in Asia and Europe was already close to splitting up.

The majority of the subjects of the Western Khans, in Persia, Iraq and Central Asia, were Muslims: the popes had endeavoured on several occasions to enlist the support of the Mongols against the Islamic foes of the Crusaders, and had entertained hopes of converting the pagan Mongols. But the Khans saw that such a change of religion would fatally alienate their own subjects. They finally decided that it would be wiser if they embraced Islam, and in 1295, they did so.

Kublai had been acknowledged as the Great Khan, but the allegiance of the Western Khans was nominal. He died in 1294; the Western Khans refused to acknowledge his successor as overlord since he was a Buddhist. The Mongol empire split into several independent states of which the Chinese empire was the largest. The reign of Kublai in China (he had moved the capital from Karakorum, in Mongolia, to Peking, which he largely rebuilt, in 1263) was marked by several attempts to extend Mongol rule farther to the south, and also to Japan. The invasion of Burma led to that country submitting to Mongol suzerainty; while in Indo-China, Vietnam and Cambodia, the combination of tropical diseases, which decimated the Mongol army, and jungle guerrilla warfare finally forced Kublai to withdraw, after accepting the rather nominal suzerainty offered by the kings of these countries. The invasion of Java, at first successful, ended in another retreat for similar reasons. Attempts to invade Japan were frustrated, first by a typhoon which destroyed the Chinese and Korean-manned Mongol fleet, and on the second occasion by the fierce resistance offered by the Japanese feudal armies to the invading forces. Kublai probably intended to renew the attack, but died before he could mount it.

Marco Polo, who worked for Kublai, as did many other Europeans and Asians, has made him the best known in the West of any Chinese ruler before modern times. Much of what Polo admired was in fact the heritage of the fallen Song dynasty.

Miniature showing Genghis Khan (literally "Emperor of the Seas") talking to a crowd in the mosque at Bukhara. It comes from an illuminated manuscript on the history of the Mongols.

Opposite above: two battle scenes showing Mongolian cavalry in action. These are Arab miniatures dating from the 13th century, clear evidence of the great interest and good relations which existed between the Arabs, lords of the trade routes across the Indian Ocean, and the Yuan dynasty. The Arabs were allowed to reside in such centers as Canton and the port of Hangzhou.

Below: terra-cotta statuettes of two actors from the Yuan period. With the accession of the Mongol Yuan dynasty, the theater, which had previously been considered a rather plebian pastime by cultivated people, became known for the quality of its texts. These were frequently written by the officials of the deposed Song dynasty who had been ousted by the Mongol administration and who were therefore constrained to use their talents in other ways in order to earn a living.

Above: detail of a delicate work by Tsou Fu-lei called *A Breath of Spring* (1306), now in the Freer Gallery of Art in Washington. This painting, executed in ink on paper, deals with one of the favourite subjects of artists of the Yuan dynasty: plum trees in

flower. Tsou Fu-lei has used the technique called *fei-bai* (literally, "flying white") which consists in passing the brush rapidly across the paper so that the hairs of the brush spread out and the resulting shape is not of a uniform thickness. It achieves

一氣為春玄必回誰
物消息付寒梅蕊珠
仙妍妙夷巧偷先東
風特地來
用圖閒元顏幽題

results which are light and transparent. A certain impressionistic immediacy is a characteristic of this form of painting and contrasts strongly with the attention to detail which is so typical of Song art.

Below: detail of a painting of the Yuan period, showing a group of horsemen watering and washing down their horses.

Polo did not read Chinese, in fact it is not certain that he spoke the language either, as Mongol was the official tongue, and his place names are always inaccurate renderings of Chinese. He is in this way typical of the large number of foreign officials whom the Mongols recruited to their service. Just as foreigners were employed to administer China, so the western parts of the original Mongol empire used Chinese. The Mongols had to rely on foreign officials since they were themselves illiterate and quite unaccustomed to the civil administration of great and civilized states.

After the separation of the Chinese and Western Asian parts of the empire, Chinese officials in the west diminished, but in China itself the employment of foreign officers continued. It is no doubt for this reason that the Mongol regime is a break in the continuity of the Confucian-trained civil service, which was only in part restored in the last period of the Mongol dynasty. The foreign officials were hated by the Chinese, especially the corrupt Central Asians and Iranians whom the court favoured. Polo, the Venetian, was, if not unique, probably a rather uncommon case; the Chinese historical records do not make mention of Europeans among the more conspicuous foreign officials. Apart from Russia, there were no European countries permanently subjected to Mongol rule.

The Mongol rulers also, after conversion to Budhhism, bestowed inordinate favour, lands and wealth, on the Tibetan Lama sect, to which the Mongol court belonged. This was not popular with Chinese of any class, and was seen as another example of favouritism to foreigners.

Under the united Song empire the census had recorded a population of around 100 million: under Kublai the figure was 58,834,711, and the Mongol dynasty in China ruled over a much wider realm. Even allowing for the wholesale massacres of Genghis Khan, it seems improbable that a generation later the population should be little more than half of what it had been at the beginning of the 12th century. It must be assumed that the rather improvised civil service of the Mongols was far less competent in conducting a census that the trained officials of the Song. Whatever the merits of Kublai himself as the restorer of unity and peace to the troubled empire, his successors have not been seen as anything but incompetent, self-indulgent and feeble. In less than 40 years after Kublai's death, a spate of seven emperors followed one after the other, some of whom were murdered in palace plots. The last Mongol to reign, Togan Timour (1333–68), is only memorable for the length of his tenure of a throne which was steadily losing all control over an empire wracked by rebellions, which continued from 1348 to the fall of the dynasty in 1368.

The Mongol dynasty, known as the Yuan to the Chinese, gave no encouragement to Chinese studies, as few of the rulers even spoke Chinese, and some of them, even in the last age, were so violently hostile to the Chinese that they still advocated wholesale massacre to deter the rebels, and passed vexatious laws to repress the rest. It is therefore hardly surprising that the Song philosophic debate was not continued, and that no one challenged the orthodoxy of Zhu Xi's interpretation. Scholars

Two illustrations taken from an early edition of the 14th-century adventure story *Shui Hu Zhuan* (*Tales of the Riverbank*) which tells of the exploits of a group of bandits, defenders of the poor and oppressed, whose chief eventually comes to an understanding with the imperial power. The content of these romances of the Ming period was often critical. If disapproved of by officialdom, they were banned but were nonetheless widely known and read.

Two Taoist genii from Tao mythology, Han-shan and Shih-de, painted on silk by Yan Hui, a painter active during the Yuan dynasty. The pair, representing two complementary ideas, were always portrayed together. Han-shan is the symbol of practical wisdom which sweeps before it the worries of the world; Shih-de represents spiritual and mystical wisdom, which explains the scroll of the "Book of Nature" which is peeping out of Shih-de's wide sleeve.

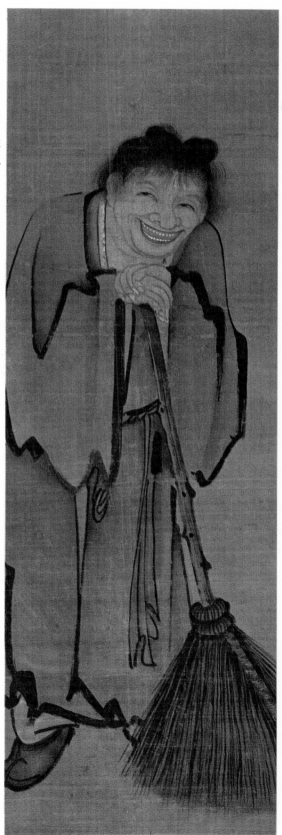

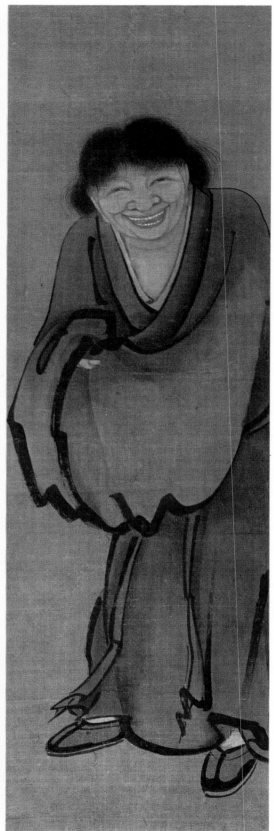

who could not gain office by the Confucian-orientated examination system, since that system no longer functioned, turned their activity to new forms of literature, and the Yuan dynasty is remembered as the first period in which the drama truly flourished.

The Yuan plays, still performed and much admired, were written of course by Chinese men of letters. The question whether they were inspired only by Chinese historical and folk sources, or owed something to foreign influence is still debated and obscure. The language and the subject matter is wholly Chinese; the conventions, as they have been inherited in later centuries, do not seem to have any convincing foreign origin (women's parts were played by boys, but so they were on the English stage in Shakespeare's time). If there was then a highly literary and well-developed drama in the west of Asia, or even in India, it has left few traces. The weight of evidence seems to be perhaps similar to the story of the chair in Song times; the idea may have owed something to slight foreign contact, the development and the characteristic form were purely Chinese.

It is known that the folklore of China had been enriched in the Song period by the popularity of storytelling, a popular amusement at markets and street corners. These tales were soon given lasting form in the provision of a précis to aid the memory of the storyteller; such précis served the novelist of the next, Ming, age and may have also been available to the dramatists of the Mongol period. Drama is in essence an art form intended for a large audience, not just for the well educated; it was so with the popular story; the connection between the two genres has not been firmly established, but it seems possible.

Song painting maintained a certain continuity under the Mongols; and new horizons opened in the manufacture of porcelain, due to new materials becoming available through trading, now carried on across the width of Asia. Thus the blue and white porcelain, which was to become so famous in the next period, made its first appearance under the Mongols. We know that the blue colouring whose basis, a cobalt ore, called "Muslim blue" by the Chinese, was known in 1352, as a dated piece proves. It came from Western Asia (hence the name) and was not always freely available in China.

In the Mongol age, as a result of their wide conquests, trade and travel between Western Asia, Europe, and China was easier and safer than ever before, and certainly more extensive. Arab travellers, from as far west as Tangier, met fellow countrymen in Canton: the Venetian Polos made more than one journey to China, as did papal envoys. This intercourse was both by sea and overland. The caravan routes of Central Asia, under Mongol control, enjoyed their last age of prosperity; the sea routes, which were not entirely in the control of the Mongols, seem to have been used more than ever before. Marco Polo returned from China by sea, disembarking at a Persian port. These were the beneficial consequences of the conquests of Genghis Khan, paid for, however, in millions of lives.

Partly because the Polos and other travellers brought back to Europe the first authentic information concerning the Chinese empire, the Mongol period has enjoyed in the West a fame

Above and opposite: blue-patterned cup, jugs and a plate from the Yuan period. During the Mongol Yuan dynasty, China became more open to influences from abroad and a notable expansion took place in the exportation of goods, especially porcelain. The porcelain industry had reached a pitch of great perfection during the Song dynasty and was now enriched by new patterns and shapes of Mongol inspiration. The provinces of Fujian and, more especially, Guangdong were major centers of porcelain production, exporting mainly to Southeast Asia and Japan. Celadon-type plates and wine jugs, with blue and white decoration, typical of the period, were produced especially for export to India and Central Asia. The plate (opposite), decorated with flowers and qi-lin (a mythical animal), was taken to Persia from China and thence to Turkey, probably as part of the war booty of an Ottoman sultan. It is now in the Topkapi Museum in Istanbul.

which, however, is not accorded by Chinese tradition. For the Chinese, the Mongols were cruel and ruthless barbarian invaders. Had a Chinese been able to visit Europe when the Huns were overrunning that continent, he could have well come to the conclusion that the remaining signs of Roman civilization were the work of these savages. The real surprise is the survival and recovery of the Chinese culture after such an assault. It was damaged and its development set back, perhaps for centuries, but it lived on. Few if any innovations can be directly credited to the Mongol rulers; those they introduced such as the employment of foreign officials, were detested by the Chinese, and abjured by later rulers.

Mongol rule had never been welcomed by the Chinese people, and after the death of Kublai it also ceased to be competent and its authority quickly declined. In 1348, just 50 years after the death of Kublai the great revolts of the Chinese against their Mongol overlords began. They were never to cease, but rather to increase steadily until the Mongols were driven from the country. It was significant that the revolts began in the South, the old Southern Song empire, and that their main strength was always drawn from this part of China. It is also noteworthy that the strength of the rebels rested upon sea power, a revival of the means and methods which the Song had used to resist the Mongol invasions. The court early lost command of the sea; the Mongol fleet in fact was manned by Chinese seamen. Thereafter for 20 years, the struggle was as much between rival Chinese contenders as against the Mongols, who clung to the great cities which they could garrison. Only in the remote province of Yunnan, which had never been part of the Song or the Tang empires, did Mongol control remain effective.

In 1356 the founder of the Ming dynasty gained a decisive advantage by capturing Nanking which he made his capital, and then proceeding to annex the holdings of the surrounding warlords. Zhu Yuanzhang, known to history as Ming Hung Wu, was by birth a poor peasant from the Huai river region, just north of the Yangtze. He was thus a southerner, in northern eyes. His parents and most of his family died in a famine; he became first a shepherd boy, and then a Buddhist monk. Soon he abandoned the cloister and became a beggar, and then a bandit. Entering the ranks of the rebels against the Mongols, he made rapid progress, finally breaking with the leader of his band and setting himself up as an independent rebel commander.

He had found his true vocation, for he did not confine himself to widespread raids for loot as his rivals tended to do, but concentrated on taking cities of strategic importance, holding them and extending the territory of a compact and orderly state. Ten years sufficed to reduce all his opponents to accepting his authority. Then, turning upon the Mongols who had been unable to offer any effective opposition, he swept north towards Peking, as leader of a Ming army numbering, according to the records, nearly a quarter of a million men. The Mongol emperor did not wait its coming; he fled to the north and abandoned China.

A few years of further campaigning in Yunnan and the Northwest eliminated Mongol rule from any part of China. The

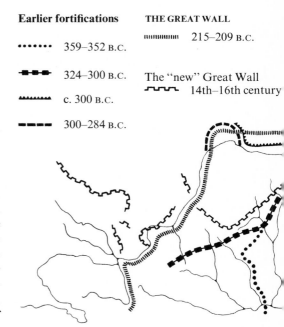

Earlier fortifications

•••••• 359–352 B.C.

■■■ 324–300 B.C.

▲▲▲▲▲ c. 300 B.C.

■ ■ ■ ■ 300–284 B.C.

THE GREAT WALL

⊔⊔⊔⊔⊔⊔ 215–209 B.C.

The "new" Great Wall
⌐⌐⌐⌐ 14th–16th century

Ming armies had advanced far to the north, burning down Karakorum, the old Mongol capital of Genghis Khan, and crossed the Yablonovyy mountains. No Chinese army had ever before, or since, penetrated so far to the north. Liaoning, in South Manchuria, was incorporated into the province of Shandong; Korea reverted to a suzerainty. But no attempt was made to conquer Xinjiang or Chinese Central Asia, over which both the Han and Tang had ruled. Hami, the first oasis on the old Silk Road, was occupied, but the Ming armies went no farther. The old caravan route had by this time fallen into disuse; long-range trade now went by sea.

The importance of sea power was fully appreciated by the early Ming rulers, and under the third emperor, Yung Lo, who had himself usurped the throne from his nephew, a series of great naval expeditions was launched to contact and explore the kingdoms of Southeast Asia. The traditional historians have attributed the motives for these costly enterprises solely to Yung Lo's anxiety lest his dethroned nephew, who had disappeared when Nanking fell, had taken refuge overseas. But this is a rather critical if not hostile view. The main motive, apart from enhancing the prestige of the throne, was simply commercial. The Ming imperial fleets had a monopoly of the more lucrative forms of foreign trade; in the guise of "tribute" they imported large quantities of valuable foreign goods, mainly raw materials, and exported to the kingdoms of the southeast as "gifts" much less valuable articles of Chinese manufacture, silk, porcelain and decorative objects. The court sold the imported goods at a good profit; the exports were provided by the taxation system, which was partly in goods as well as money.

The Ming navy was organized in a curious manner. It was entirely a court enterprise, outside the jurisdiction of both the military and the civil service. At first it had been partly financed by the sale of the huge areas in North China which, depopulated by the Mongul conquest, had been turned into vast hunting reserves by the Mongol emperors. The Ming court sold off this land and resettled it, largely with discharged soldiers, thus killing two birds with the one stone. The Tang had kept an army on the northern frontier, the Song having no secure northern borders had no need to demobilize their much smaller forces. The Ming settled many thousands of ex-soldiers in Yunnan where their descendants still form the core of the older Chinese colonization. The great hunting resources were thus used to resettle the many thousands who had helped to establish the Ming dynasty. Thus financed independently of the regular treasury, the Ming navy was commanded by men whom the emperor could regard as wholly faithful to him, the palace eunuchs. This may seem a very unlikely employment for such people, but it proved extremely successful. The navy was commanded by Zheng He, a Muslim from Yunnan, itself a province with no sea coast.

The expeditions which set out between 1405–33 were large by any standards; more than 70,000 men set sail in ships built for the purpose, the largest vessels ever constructed in China up to modern times. Their voyages took them to what is now Indonesia, the Philippines, Malaya and Thailand, across the

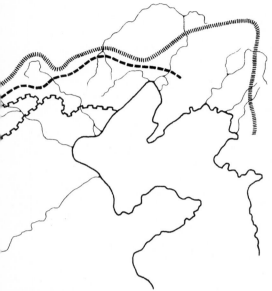

Plan of the Great Wall. The key on the left above shows where the Chinese built their first border fortifications against foreign peoples, known as "the barbarians." These defenses were constructed over a span of time from 359–284 B.C. The key on the right shows the course of the Great Wall built during the reign of the first Qin emperor and of the "new" Great Wall, constructed under the Ming dynasty.

Pages 280–281
Panoramic view of the Great Wall. This rampart, which originated as a military highway, stretches for about 6000 kilometers along the northern frontier of China. It extends eastwards as far as the sea and westwards to extreme

Gansu. The Wall was begun by the first Qin emperor who decided to link the existing bastions, dating from feudal times, with fortified walls. These were later extended and strengthened, especially under the Ming dynasty, when the capital moved to Peking, only 65 kilometers away. The Great Wall was conceived, not as a continuous line of defense, but as an early warning system of invasion: soldiers were garrisoned along its length, able to summon aid in time of need by smoke signals.

Indian Ocean to southern India, up the Persian Gulf, and round Arabia to the Red Sea. Some of the later voyages sailed down the coast of East Africa, possibly as far as Zanzibar, certainly to Somalia. From one of these voyages a live giraffe was brought back as a gift to the emperor; a painting of it still survives.

Ming naval activity has received little attention either in Chinese dynastic history or, until recent years, by Western scholars. For two reasons, Chinese Confucian historians disliked the whole episode because, firstly, it was commercial and it besmirched the honour of the emperor to be mixed up in business; secondly, it was controlled and financed by the court and thus beyond the authority of the civil service (that meant less pickings for the officials). Western scholars tended to ignore the naval expeditions because they were of short duration, and had ended before European penetration of the Indian Ocean, and thus had no bearing on the history of European expansion into Eastern Asia.

It was therefore the consequences of abandoning the naval policy of the early Ming emperors, and the decay and ultimate disappearance of their great fleets, that is more significant than what was actually achieved, however remarkable these expeditionary feats were. After the death of the third emperor, Yung Lo, there was only one more expedition, commanded by Zheng He. Yung Lo died in 1425, his son, already a very sick man, died in the same year; his grandson Xuan De reigned for only 11 years. Thus the throne passed to Yung Lo's great-grandson, less than 12 years after his own death.

This was a moment of great weakness for the dynasty, for the new emperor, Zheng Tung, was a boy of eight, so a regency was necessary, and the old Han trouble of eunuch influence reappeared. The civil service, always hostile to the navy, took the opportunity to call a halt to its overseas activity, and since the navy was now financed from the treasury, to let it run down and decay. Chinese sea power was renounced just 64 years before Vasco da Gama rounded the Cape of Good Hope and opened the era of European imperialism in Asia. Part of the navy's duty had been the suppression of piracy; once it was unable to fulfil this task, native and Japanese pirates, sometimes acting in concert, multiplied rapidly along the Chinese coast and became a serious menace to trade and communications. The later Ming court responded by clearing a coastal belt, except for a few large cities, of all inhabitants, to deny the pirates supplies and bases, but it would have been wiser to have reactivated the navy.

The weakness of the court under child emperors and regents enabled the Mongols to recover some strength and to resume raids on the frontier. Later Ming efforts to check these incursions were on the whole inadequate and sometimes disastrous. It became necessary to station the main army along the Great Wall, manning its garrison cities. The Great Wall itself, which was not part of the Song dominions, and which the Mongols had no interest in maintaining, was in a grave state of decay. The Ming made a thorough job of restoration and it is really the Ming Wall, on the same alignment as the original, that can be seen today.

In the later Ming period a new menace slowly began to take

Two views, dating from the Qing dynasty, of the city of Nanking. The city, which began to be developed in the 13th century, became an important political and economic center and was, under various names, the capital of several southern dynasties. During the Tang period, it was for long the home of the famous poet Li Bo who wrote the celebrated poem *Climbing the Terrace of the Phoenix*, which alludes to a place southwest of the city. In 1368, the founder of the Ming dynasty, having won final victory over the Mongols, made it his capital, and gave it the name Ying tian fu. The population then was only about 173,000 and in order to augment it, the emperor ordered 20,000 wealthy families to go and live there. It was his son, Yung Lo, who decided to move the capital to Peking in the North and who gave to the city its present name (in Chinese, Nan Jing) which means "capital of the south."

THE ENVIRONMENT
AND THE USE OF SPACE

A formal and essential element of the Chinese method of organizing living space is the horizontal development of successive unities, complete in themselves, which go to make up the structure as a whole. In the brick model of a Han house (illustrated above), this can already be seen; in this case it is a dwelling on two floors (the superstructure is of wood and the roofs gently sloping and jutting out). This principle of building becomes even more evident in large-scale dwellings like the one for which the plan is shown below. This was the residence of an imperial official in Xinning, in the province of Hunan, dating from the 18th century. In passing, we may note that, architecturally speaking, the innovations over the centuries are basically unimportant so that this plan may be considered as a perennial archetype of Chinese domestic architecture. The traditional house of a wealthy family was a microcosm protected by walls and, generally speaking, with only one main doorway or gate to the outside. Rich families lived in the same dwelling for four, five or even six generations. Parents and grandparents occupied the central buildings facing south while their children would have their apartments in the pavilions at the sides and servants lodged in the annexes. In the Peking region, houses with an internal courtyard were very popular. Behind the main gateway which had double doors covered with red lacquer, was the "wall of the spirits," a defense against the entrance of malign spirits who, it was believed, could only move in straight lines. From here, one moved on to the first courtyard onto which gave the public rooms. The second and (where one existed) third courtyards were reserved solely for the apartments of members of the family and were surrounded by galleries. The garden was usually found at the back of the building. Its construction (for in Chinese, the phrase is "to construct a garden") followed certain stringent rules. The Chinese garden was never a mere servile imitation of nature but was seen as a work of fantasy and imagination and is therefore valued above all for its power of suggestion. The ideal was to create a flawless nature, a sort of quintessence or poetic version of nature. It never consisted of a space which could be seen at a single glance from a given point; rather, it was a series of settings, more or less isolated from one another, which succeeded each other as

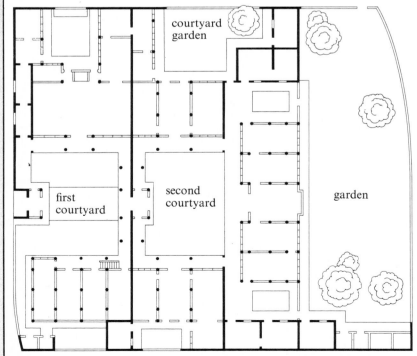

The furnishings of the interiors of these dwellings are revealing evidence of the Chinese culture and way of life. It may be noted that the Chinese were the only people in Asia to use the chair lifted on legs off the floor (bottom center, we see some Chinese chairs of the Ming dynasty: a low table of lacquered wood; a divan and a clothes stand, also of wood and inlaid with mother-of-pearl). It is not known exactly when the chair was introduced into China but certainly during the Han period the Chinese were still sitting on the floor, either on mats or carpets; the chair makes its appearance in art only at the beginning of the 8th century. Probably, it was a novelty imported from Byzantium and in earliest days was used as the seat of honour so that it was considered a symbol of social standing. However, the use of chairs and therefore of tables on raised legs soon became common to all levels of society. The fact that during the Tang dynasty the chair was called the "barbarian bed" explains how, when it was first introduced, the seat was considered an alternative to the traditional Chinese bed. In ancient times, in fact, the bed consisted of a raised platform on which, apart from sleeping, one could talk to friends, guests and members of the family. The two illustrations on this page (center, a painting on silk of the 4th century, and bottom right, a contemporary illustration) both show this social function of the bed.

parts of a homogenous whole and which had to be discovered bit by bit, with a sense of growing wonder and surprise. The garden is therefore seen as a kind of spiritual itinerary (see above, one of the pavilions of the Yuan dynasty's summer palace of Yuanming, near Peking, destroyed in 1860, shown in a picture of the Qing period). It is a kind of aesthetic voyage of discovery, an emotional progression similar to that which is experienced unrolling a painted scroll. It has a temporal dimension, as all Chinese art does, in which space is seen as a fundamental of development.

shape. Southern Manchuria, as far north as Shenyang (Mukden), was a Chinese-settled province. Beyone that the Manchu tribes who inhabited the present provinces of Jilin and Heilongjiang were under Ming suzerainty. These tribes, descendants of the Nuchen from whom sprang the Jin dynasty in Northern China in Song times, once they came under Chinese influence, made rapid progress and acquired a mixed culture, largely Chinese, but retaining many Nuchen-Manchu customs.

With the decline of the Ming empire in the 16th century, suzerainty to China became less acceptable to the Manchus. In 1610, Nurhachu, who had outsmarted his Manchu rivals, proclaimed himself emperor, named his dynasty Qing (The Pure) and renounced allegiance to China. The Ming could not counter this move, and before long Nurhachu, a skillful general and able organizer, had invaded the Chinese province of Liaoning, to the south of his kingdom. For 30 years the new Manchu kingdom flourished in the far north, and for much of this time it was at war with Ming China. Meanwhile, Chinese customs and culture took firm root among the Manchus who, after they conquered Liaoning, came to rule over a numerous Chinese population. When they eventually invaded China, they were no longer a barbarous people, and could pose as exponents of Chinese Confucian civilization.

Few, if any, personalities of the character or capability of the early Ming emperors were to be found in their successors. These monarchs are better remembered by their reign titles which bestowed names to the superb porcelain made in their period. The empire was in effect run by the civil service, with the advantages of continuity that the system provided, and with the drawbacks attached to the rigid orthodox Confucian training and education of the officials themselves. They were an élite, owing their position and careers entirely to proficiency in the very stiff, very literary, and very unpractical syllabus of the public civil service examinations.

The emperor had inherited from his Mongol predecessors a greater absolute authority than Song or Tang monarchs. Following the Mongol devastation, the old one-time aristocratic families, still influential and territorially powerful even in the Song civil service, had fled to the far South. When the Ming came to power they were replaced by a very much more numerous gentry who did not have the same local influence, and hence authority. They were much more dependent on imperial favour, they accepted this enhanced imperial power, which had seemed well justified under the founder Hung Wu, and his son Yung Lo. In the later Ming it gave an opening to eunuch influence shielded by the great authority now vested in the throne.

Early in the 16th century, in the reign of emperor Zheng De (1505–20), eunuch influence grew rapidly. Not since the Han dynasty, 13 centuries earlier, had the eunuchs been so powerful. The unified empire, and the control exercised in the name of the emperor, allowed the eunuchs to sell appointments to the highest bidder, and to demand in return annual payments for continuing court favour. In order to meet these demands, provincial officials resorted to increased taxation and exploita-

Four different types of ship from the Ming period. It was at this time that sailing first became important – especially under the emperor Yong Lo – owing to the expansion of trade. China would export her wares to Southeast Asia and import, in return, raw materials. The Ming fleet, consisting of huge ships, was directly responsible to the court, not to the army and was commanded by the emperor's eunuchs. When the

tion of the people. In 1510, when the eunuch Liu Jin fell from favour, it was found that he had amassed a fortune of 251,583,600 ounces of silver, not to speak of other wealth in jewellery and property. He, like many of his fellows, came of a poor family: this vast wealth had been acquired by corrupt practices during his service in the palace. Eunuchs obviously had no descendants, but they had the collateral members of their family, nephews and brothers, to profit from their speculations.

These abuses brought about armed rebellion, which if not yet on a scale to menace the dynasty, was a drain on its resources and a further cause of decline. There was some recovery under the two long reigns of Jia Jing (1520–66) and Wan Li (1572–1620), not because these two emperors were notably more competent than those they had succeeded, but by the very fact of long continuity and the ability of some able ministers whom they trusted.

But the reign of Wan Li was the last period of real tranquility under the Ming. His successors were short-lived and inexperienced; the frontier troubles with the Manchu kingdom grew more dangerous; and the effects of the long war against Japan (1592–98) to decide the fate of Korea had exhausted the treasury. Korea had been invaded by Hideyoshi, who ruled Japan in the name of the secluded emperor. Somewhat ill-informed about what he was setting out to do, Hideyoshi intended to conquer China. Korea appealed to her Ming suzerain, and emperor Wan Li responded by sending large armies to oppose the Japanese. They won few battles, but Hideyoshi did not succeed in fully conquering Korea, let alone invading China, and when he died the Japanese evacuated the peninsula. Wan Li could claim victory, but the price paid was high.

In recent years the tomb, intact and unrobbed, of Wan Li has been opened and its treasures displayed in a museum in the courtyard of the tomb temple. Words fail to describe the nature of this fabulous treasure trove which includes great quantities of silver and gold ingots which, having no artistic merit as such, are not on display. The exquisite examples of Ming porcelain, the rich embroideries and jewelry which adorned the skeletons of the emperor and his two empresses, bear witness to the enormous wealth which the court could lay claim to, all extorted from an empire which was then in its last stages of prosperity, having just engaged in a long and costly war. Our own age may have the privilege of viewing these priceless works of art, but no such advantage accrued to emperor Wan Li's subjects. The fact that such treasure was buried with Wan Li when it could have been used to help the war in Korea, goes some way to explain the downfall of the Ming dynasty.

Within 25 years of the death of Wan Li, the Ming dynasty had disappeared, not as the direct result of the incessant wars with the Manchus on the frontier, but overthrown by internal rebellion. The élite forces of the army were stationed on the frontier, along the line of the Great Wall, close to the coast, the easiest and most probable route for a Manchu invasion. Thus the rebel leader who had conquered the province of Henan in 1640 was able to sweep northwest through Shaanxi and Shanxi

imperial fleet diminished in importance, the coasts of China were ravished by hordes of pirates, either Chinese or Japanese, who posed a very serious threat to both commerce and communications.

Pages 288–289
A painting from the end of the 15th century showing a naval battle between Japanese pirates and the imperial fleet.

provinces and descend on Peking. The city, which the eunuchs were supposed to defend, was betrayed by them. The last Ming emperor took his own life by hanging himself from a tree (still to be seen) in the palace grounds. The rebel leader proclaimed himself emperor of a new dynasty, the Shun. The general commanding the great army of the frontier, Wu Sangui, refused to acknowledge the usurper, and instead invited the Manchus to enter China having offered the throne to their young king. Thus, in 1644, the Manchus began their rule in China, with Chinese aid and at Chinese invitation. Wu then attacked and defeated the rebel army; the Manchu army entered Peking, and the Qing dynasty was founded.

The Ming dynasty had ruled for two and three-quarter centuries, a long period which in Western terms covers the late Middle Ages and extends beyond the Renaissance. In a short summary it is not possible to cover all the events and changing situations over such a long stretch of time. However, the main characteristics of the dynasty can be assessed.

The Ming, from their origin as rebels against an alien and hated foreign regime, were more nationalist and also more suspicious of foreign contact than previous great Chinese dynasties. The memory of the Mongols did not fade easily. To restore the "rule of Song and Tang" was the avowed aim of the dynasty's founder. In so far as this meant the restoration of institutions created by those dynasties, including a civil service open to all who could pass its difficult entrance examination, and, in early years, the maintenance of a navy, they succeeded. Confucianism as interpreted by Zhu Xi was the established orthodoxy on which the education of the young and the syllabus of the public examinations were based.

Within this framework philosophy revived and has left us some celebrated writers. But at a deeper level it cannot be said that Ming government or administration was a close parallel to that of the Song. Under the Ming much of the humane restraint which had marked Song rule was not in evidence. The penalty of loss of court favour was more likely to be death than exile to a minor magistracy in the distant provinces. The practice of permanent exiling for lesser offenders was widespread; many families in the far southwest of Yunnan are the descendants of these exiles. The throne was more powerful, its authority more easily abused.

The Ming were also conservative; feeling that the Mongol invasion had dealt a harsh blow to all aspects of Chinese culture, which was true, they distrusted foreign influences, believed that the national Chinese culture was not only superior but the only true civilization, and had little curiosity about the world of "Outer Barbarians." The Ming never adopted the policy of absolute seclusion, later followed in Japan, Korea, and Burma, but they certainly did not extend a warm welcome to foreign visitors, or even embassies. After the cessation of the maritime expeditions to Southeast Asia and Africa, there is little evidence of court interest in foreign countries.

But it would be false to treat the Ming dynasty as a period of stagnation, as has sometimes been the case. In art and literature there were striking new forms and original developments. In

A jade vase from the Ming dynasty with floral decoration in relief on the sides. Jade was always regarded as the most precious stone by the Chinese who believed that it was taken from the rainbow by the god of storms and tempests and that it was endowed with magic and curative properties.

Opposite: the side panels of a lacquered wooden box from the Ming period. The technique of lacquer, one of the most ancient of Chinese traditional crafts, reached new heights under the Ming dynasty. The refinement of the decoration may be seen in this illustration: it was generally applied either to a smooth, painted surface or to a relief and then inlaid with gold or mother-of-pearl.

MERCHANTS AND CITY LIFE

The traditional Chinese city, walled and composed of quarters which are themselves surrounded by walls and between which there is no communication, was a place of restriction. Chinese cities did not begin like European mediaeval towns by the efforts of individuals who wished to escape from the despotism of feudal lords. In this huge, agricultural empire, conditions and requirements were different and the towns were founded on purpose to be the centers of administration. Thus they were strictly controlled by economic and judicial authorities.

Under the Tang and, in particular, the Song dynasties, a free and cultivated way of life flourished in the cities: the walled quarters were knocked down and instead there grew up areas of entertainment which became the new centers of social life with tea-houses, small restaurants specializing in various types of cuisine, wine shops, theaters, puppet shows, ballad singers and itinerant acrobats. The cities grew, harbouring a thousand forbidden skills, a thousand activities which seem to denote the dominance of a bourgeoisie. The towns which Marco Polo saw and described were rich, lively places,

dissipated perhaps but human. However, it must be remembered that he lived in China during a strange period, that of the Mongolian domination, when there was an unprecedented expansion of the urban population and when commerce with other countries flourished, thanks to the *pax mongolica* which guaranteed the safety of the great caravan routes across Central Asia. At that point, the embryo of an independent merchant class came into being.

However, its development was arrested; the Chinese were never able to form their own merchant class: their merchants remained merchants and did not turn into capitalists and entrepreneurs. Nonetheless, Marco Polo's wonder at the life and vitality of the Chinese empire was not excessive: during the 13th century, the West lagged behind China which was at a moment of great economic expansion, thanks to the development of this urban middle class – however transitory the phenomenon. It was composed of landowners and rich merchants and their requirements provoked a demand for goods of all kinds, particularly luxuries. Thus, it was not mere chance which led to the development of porcelain production, architecture, interior design and textiles from the 11th to the 13th century.

The black and white illustrations on these pages show details of everyday life in Kaifeng, Hangzhou and Yangzhou. These towns were linked by a

network of canals which were busier during this period than ever before or since. Kaifeng, also called Dong Jing (capital of the East), was the magnificent capital city of the Northern Song dynasty (960–1127). A Song poet, Meng Yuanlao, wrote that in this city ". . . the Imperial Way is 300 meters wide. Along its sides are covered galleries in which the merchants have their stalls. . . . Two canals run parallel to these galleries and in the water grow lotus flowers and water lilies, while on the banks are planted plum trees, peach trees, pear trees and apricot trees: in springtime it seems like an embroidery of beautiful colours." Further evidence of the splendour of Kaifeng during the Song period is the famous painting which measures five meters from side to side (a detail of which is shown on the left) by Zhang Zeduan, now in the Imperial Palace in Peking. It shows, in minute detail, the everyday life of the city, both at work and at play.

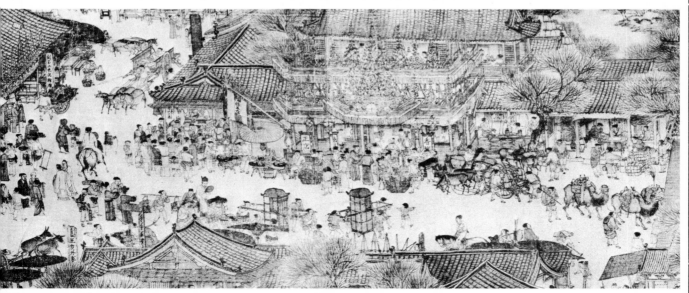

technology the Ming period is not one of inaction. The suspension bridges across great rivers in Yunnan, a province which owes almost all its surviving cultural monuments to the Ming, are astonishing feats of engineering in very difficult topography. The use of waterpower for the mills and the development of canals parallel the first aspects of the industrial revolution in Europe in the 18th century; in China these innovations occured 300 to 400 years earlier.

Architecture in China, as the materials used are rather perishable, does not easily survive for long periods. There is little beyond a few pagodas built of stone or brick, which date from the Tang period, and even Song buildings are rare. Thus the Ming is the first age of which we have important and numerous buildings still standing and in use. There is also some reason to believe that Ming architecture incorporated features which were either uncommon or only experimental in the earlier period. The Ming palaces in Peking, the "Forbidden City," and the temples at the Ming imperial tombs nearby, use the beautiful yellow ceramic tiles for the roofs, with sometimes green tiles on temples. The evidence of archaeological work on the sites of Tang, Song or earlier palaces seems to confirm that ceramic coloured tiles were either not used at all in those ages, or only to a very limited extent. It is significant that the present market area called Liu Li Zhang, in Peking, is known to have been the site of the tile works where the Ming palace tiles were made. The Ming palaces are superb structures: in their proportion, in the restraint of the decoration, and the simplicity of the roof line. In some contrast to this "Northern Style," as it is known in China, the "Southern Style" has much more accentuated curves and upward tilting of the roofs and eaves, and more elaborate decoration on the roof line. As this was the style dominating in Canton and other southern cities known to early European visitors, it is the style commonly reproduced in *chinoiserie*, but it is not the finest example of Chinese architecture.

The painting of the Ming period was often treated as "imitative" by early European connoisseurs. In the sense that the Song tradition continued to inspire the Ming painting this is true, but it is not correct to dismiss it as of secondary importance. Indeed, without the surviving Ming work, which is relatively plentiful, we should only have a scanty knowledge of

Below and opposite: two examples of Ming painting. Painting, like all the other arts, enjoyed a period of great achievement under this dynasty. The taste of the Ming court harked back to an earlier period – that of the Northern and Southern Song and the favourite motifs were again landscapes, flowers and birds. The painting on silk (opposite) is very characteristic of this school: it shows a detail from a work by Lu Ji, painter at the court of Xiaozong between 1477 and 1505. Now in the National Museum, Tokyo.

Pages 296–297 A group of clay statuettes, found in a tomb of the Ming period, which represents the imperial cavalry.

Song painting, based on a small number of genuine pictures. The Ming reproduced Song pictures and also followed the same schools in their own original work. There were some interesting innovations; towards the end of the dynasty a school arose which was far more "impressionist," even abstract, than any previous style in China. Not highly regarded at the time, it is now eagerly sought after.

It is true that Ming painting tended to elaborate the rather subtle conventions of the pictorial art. This has been called "Literary Painting." The pine tree clinging to the face of a cliff, the small figure of a scholar contemplating the sheer magnificence of a mountain, and many other symbolic motifs represent, respectively, the steadfast champion of principle and morality in adverse circumstances, i.e. the Confucian scholar-official, and the relative insignificance of man in the face of nature, an idea with Taoist origins.

Painting was certainly under strong classical or traditional influences, although technique and inspiration were of high quality. Yet this art is known in large measure by Ming copies of earlier work, and therefore does not convey the sense of originality and distinctiveness of the Ming period. Porcelain on the other hand, although developing rapidly under the Song, became perhaps the art with which the Ming are most generally associated. The invention and perfection, first of blue and white, then of the polychrome wares, and the continued refinement of the whole art, both technically in the potting and artistically in the decoration and use of colour, marks the Ming as the great age of Chinese porcelain. It may be that if we had more surviving Song pieces this judgment could be challenged, but it remains a fact that the Ming introduced the use of colour, elaborate design, and reveal increasing technical mastery of the material.

There is no doubt that in literature the Ming, while continuing the Song tradition of Confucian scholarship, made two important innovations, the one favoured with the highest official patronage, the other under the strong disapproval of authority. It was during the reign of emperor Yung Lo (1402–25) that Chinese scholars compiled the first encyclopaedia which in part survives to this time and has been the base on which later publications were founded. It is an immense work, a full compendium of knowledge as recorded in the dynastic histories and in numerous other books, on every subject; but much has been lost. The use and meaning of every work in Chinese literature, when it was first recorded, and in what work, is only a part of the material covered by Yung Lo's encyclopaedia and its later successors. It is thus a key to the mass of disparate facts recorded in the Chinese historical record; other dictionaries, of quotations, place-names, and all kinds of useful tools for research have been drawn from this inexhaustible source. The tradition of lexicography thus started under the early Ming became a continuing feature of later Chinese literature down to the modern age.

The literary innovation disapproved of under the Ming was the birth and rapid development of the novel. It has already been noted that under the Mongol dynasty the Chinese drama took shape and developed, using, in all probability, the synopses of

The red lacquered lid of a round box dating from the Ming period. During the rule of this dynasty, the art of lacquer-working developed considerably and began to use a greater variety of themes than during the preceding Yuan period. Added to the traditional flowers, there were birds, imaginary animals and other motifs reminiscent of an earlier iconography, like the contorted dragon with clutching talons which adorns this box. This return to the past was typical of artists of the Ming period and it may be said that they redeemed a certain lack of imagination with a high level of technical virtuosity. The carving of wood surfaces became especially refined during this period and the shapes of objects were ever more elaborate so that during the Qing period which followed, detailed work, particularly the art of relief carving, reached hitherto unknown heights.

folk tales which storytellers had compiled. The Ming novelists clearly and openly base their work on this source, even preserving the phraseology used by the storyteller when he concluded his episode, and presumably passed the hat round: "Honourable Official, if you wish to know what happened after this, please let the next instalment explain."

The novels fell into two categories, those based on well-known historical events and on popular legends and myths of Buddhist origin: such are the *Romance of the Three Kingdoms* and other historical novels. The legend of the Buddhist pilgrims to India is the base of another famous novel. The other category consists of tales of domestic family life, not associated with any historical event or legendary figures. *Jin Ping Mei*, a title composed of the personal names of the three heroines, is the earliest of these, and is an unabashed erotic story of the life and debauches of a young man of wealth. It has been suggested that it is a concealed satire upon the life of some well-known, perhaps even imperial, personage of the time. It was written in the 16th century, and the authorship has been assigned to a known scholar-official who lived between 1526–93, and was at one time minister of justice. This, if true, makes it somewhat more likely that *Jin Ping Mei* is a satirical criticism of some grandee, or monarch.

The possibility that novels might be thus critical or subversive, as some certainly are, was one major reason for official disapproval. The second was that they were, for the first time in Chinese literature, written in the colloquial, spoken language of the time, not in classical Chinese, as all official and Confucian literature was, down to modern times. Children, schoolboys and other partly-educated people could thus read and enjoy these stories, another cause for disapproval. They were constantly prohibited; readers were severely punished by schoolmasters and parents; yet every literate Chinese had read them; they were well known in verbal form to thousands who could not read, and they are the first examples of a new style, often of very high quality, which has become the inspiration of modern Chinese literature. So much for the efficacy of official prohibitions.

The Ming novels, and their successors in the early years of the Manchu dynasty, give the best possible picture of social life and conditions in the last 400 years. Many of them are expressly critical of the existing regime, presented as some fictional, previous dnasty. Such is *Shui Hu Zhuan* (*Story of the Waters and Lakes*), a tale, not unlike the Robin Hood saga, of unjustly treated men who form an invincible band of outlaws to put right wrongs, punish corrupt and oppressive officials, and engage in guerrilla warfare with the cowardly soldiery of a declining dynasty. Mao Zedong tells how he read and reread this book, and found its revolutionary flavour and exposition of guerrilla tactics much to his taste.

Today the Ming novels are valued both as the first examples and models for writing colloquial Chinese speech and dialogue in a literary form, and for the social ideas which they reveal to have been stirring beneath the bland surface of Confucian orthodoxy. The Ming novels had successors in the early part of

Gateway with five arches at the entrance to the valley of the Ming, about 50 kilometers from Peking. This place, where all the kings of the Ming dynasty except one are buried with their wives and concubines, was chosen as a burial ground by Yung Lo, the founder of Peking, on the advice of the court diviners. The tombs are scattered all around the valley, not in chronological order, as each emperor chose the spot he liked best. The "Way of the Spirits," which is seven kilometers long, runs from a white marble portico past all the tombs and it was along this that the bodies of the emperors were carried for burial (a view of it appears opposite, top left). Along the sides of this road stand the famous stone statues, some of which appear opposite. These are placed symmetrically along its course and represent either animals such as lions, unicorns, camels, elephants and horses, or else court personalities such as generals and highly placed officials. The probable function of these statues was to protect the defunct emperors from evil spirits. Of the 13 tombs, special mention should be made of Yung Lo's, which contains the funeral biers of the emperor and his wife, and of Wan Li's, the only one which is still open to visitors.

Statuette of the Ming period in blue and white porcelain. Under the Mongols, cobalt oxide had been imported into China from Persia and there had followed development in the art of painting blue decoration on porcelain. However, it was under the Ming dynasty that this blue and white china achieved lasting fame. During this period, the technique was developed of painting the white porcelain with cobalt oxide and then glazing before being fired at an extremely high temperature.

Opposite: quadrangular vase made from a mould in the second half of the 16th century. As well as the aforementioned blue and white decoration, this period saw the development of the "five colours" style which used other mineral pigments as well as cobalt and which was then covered by the purest white enamel. The vase, has a mark on the bottom facilitating dating.

the next dynasty, the Qing, and one of the greatest belongs to this period. The *Dream in the Red Chamber* is a novel about the life of a great official family on the verge of decline. The hero is a boy of about 14, the heroines, girls a year or so younger. This in itself is a revolutionary feature; children, in China, were to be seen, but not heard. The tragic love between the boy and the girls, against the background of their conservative-minded elders, the matriarch, and the rather pompous father, uncles and aunts, self-seeking cousins and hangers-on, is a devastatingly true, but critical depiction of the life of a great "extended family," such as was the norm for the upper governing class down to the end of the empire.

The *Dream in the Red Chamber* is now seen as a masterpiece of literature, the paragon of the new style written in the contemporary spoken language. It continues to excite great interest, and indeed controversy. Is it, after all, an example of "decadent" prerevolutionary "feudal" manners and customs, undesirable literature for a liberated democratic readership; or is it a subtle and almost prophetic description and exposé of the evil aspects of the old society, and a powerful protest against the way they worked. Opinions differ, and politics becomes an aspect of the dispute.

Early in the 16th century the first Portuguese navigators and merchants arrived in the South Chinese port of Canton. They were at first welcomed and treated in the same way as were the long-established Arab and Southeast Asian traders. But even as an embassy from the viceroy of Goa was being received in Peking, news came that the Portuguese had involved themselves in hostility with the governor of Canton, so the Chinese court began to revise its opinions about these visitors from the West. The Arabs, who had every interest in blackening the reputation of their trade rivals and enemies, told the Chinese that the Portuguese were not to be trusted; they would seek through trade the opportunity to seize some city and make it their base. They had successfully followed this policy in India (Goa), in Ceylon at Colombo, and in Malaysia at Malacca. Portuguese violence led to them being forbidden to call at Chinese ports (1522). Twenty years later at Ningbo, in the province of Zhejiang, where the conflict at Canton seemed remote, the Portuguese were permitted to trade, and prospered greatly for two years. Then, their indiscipline and arrogance towards the "pagan" Chinese made them very unpopular. They decided to build a fort for their own protection, but as the Chinese saw it, with the intention of seizing the city. They were attacked by Chinese regular troops and all, except for those who took refuge aboard ship, were massacred.

Ming relations with the Western world thus began in an atmosphere of mistrust and violence: it was not until after the traders had created such a bad impression that the missionaries arrived to attempt to give the Chinese a somewhat better image of Western civilization. Saint Francis Xavier, the first missionary to China, died before ever landing in the Chinese empire, on a small island in the Pearl River estuary, near Macao, in 1552. It was not until 1575 that the first missionaries came to Canton, and only at the very end of the century, in 1598, that Matteo

Ricci was permitted to come to Peking, and to reside in the capital. By the end of the dynasty, nearly half a century later, the Portuguese merchants had established themselves in Macao, and the missionaries at the court in Peking. In the last years of the Ming pretenders, after Peking had fallen, many Portuguese mercenaries served in the armies of the fugitive Ming courts (which had found refuge in the south of China), mainly in the artillery, and the empress of the last pretender was actually converted to Christianity. Thus it was in the late Ming period that China first came into closer contact with the Western and European world, both in trading relations and in the beginning of intellectual exchanges between missionary scholars and Confucian officials.

Up to the end of the Ming dynasty the civilization and life of China had been very little influenced by external cultures; Buddhism, introduced from India, had long been assimilated into the Chinese way of life. But the challenge of the West, which was to confront the successors of the Ming, was of a wholly different character and led remorselessly to major transformations.

A Ming vase dating from the 14th–15th century, now in the Freer Gallery, Washington. The decoration is of lotus flowers and aquatic birds outlined between *cloisons* of appliquéd clay; the coloured varnishes would have been applied before the firing of the vase. Because of its decoration and its lively colouring, this must be regarded as one of the best examples of the art of the Ming period when an enlightened system of patronage was in practice at the court.

Opposite: the empress' crown, found in the tomb of Wan Li, the emperor who died in 1620. The tomb furniture is exceedingly rich and includes objects made of gold, silver and jade and also arms. Some of these are exhibited in two recently built showrooms near Wan Li's mausoleum. This elaborate piece of goldsmith's work is made of numerous precious stones set among pearls and some complicated blue enamelled decoration and topped by three dragons in filigree.

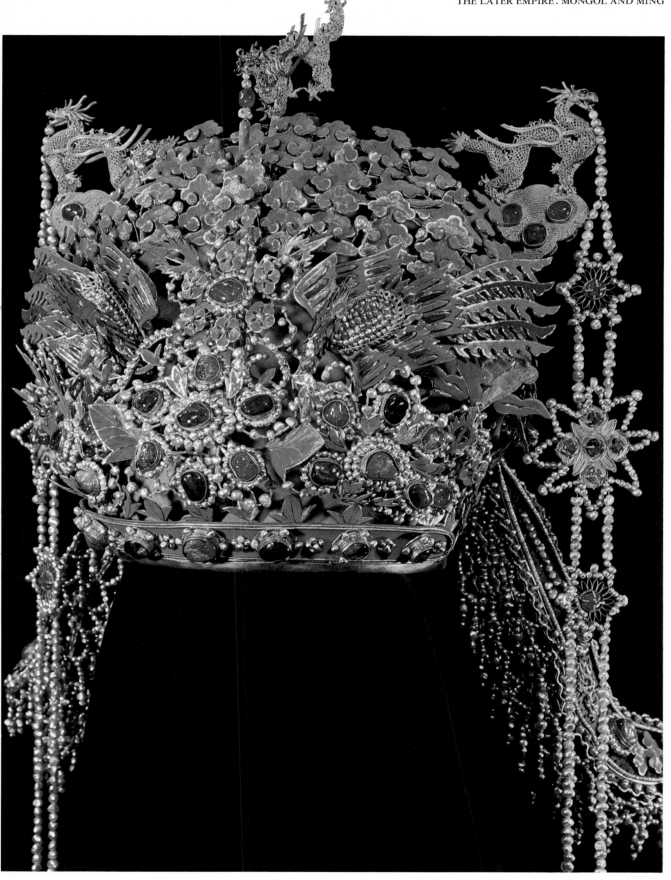

THE LATER EMPIRE:
THE MANCHU OR QING DYNASTY

A landscape by Wang Shimin (1592–1680). After long employment as a government official, Wang Shimin retired to a private life given over to art and study. As well as being a painter and calligrapher, he was a man of letters and composed a good deal of both poetry and prose.

Wang Shimin is known as the greatest of the "Four great Wang," all artists who lived during the Qing period and who had the same name, although not related. Wang Shimin was an especially good painter of landscapes in which, although he made use of the Song and Yuan traditions, he manifests an authentic and original inspiration.

The Qing dynasty established by the Manchu in Peking in 1644 differs from all preceding dynasties in three main aspects. Firstly, the Manchus, although an alien, Nuchen-Tartar people, had for nearly two and a half centuries been under strong Chinese cultural influence and had, since their conquest of Liaoning province, ruled over a Chinese population as numerous as the Manchus themselves. They were not barbarians even though they retained some national customs foreign to the Chinese. Secondly, they entered China not by force, but by invitation, and their assumption of the throne was supported by the most powerful force in North China, the former Ming army. Furthermore when the dynasty fell it was by an arranged abdication, not by a long, desperate struggle for survival as had been the case with the Mongols, the Ming, Song and Tang. The Manchu imperial family survived, and still does: all others perished. Thirdly, the Manchu dynasty was the last imperial dynasty in China, and is unlikely to have a successor. It continued down to the modern age, throughout the all-important centuries during which the ancient isolation of China from Europe was broken down and modern, alien influences of all kinds began to affect the cultural and economic life of the Chinese people.

It is a feature of Chinese history that the period of the highest efficiency and stability of successive imperial dynasties, those of long duration, is between 150 to 200 years at the most. The Han suffered the usurpation of Wang Mang just short of 200 years after the dynasty's foundation; the later Han declined rapidly after 150 years, as did the Tang; and the Song lost North China after little more than 150 years of full control of the empire. The Ming decline, somewhat slower, began within one century of the foundation of the dynasty; and, as it was to prove, the Qing (Manchu) also enjoyed just under 150 years of real stability and prosperity. Chinese historians used to attribute this pattern to the progressive moral decadence of the ruling family; modern historians are more apt to search for economic causes, the accumulation of wealth and land in the hands of a favoured élite, increasing corruption and inefficiency in an overgrown bureaucracy, the excessive concentration of power in the hands of the emperor.

The Qing dynasty exhibits a slight variation on this pattern of rise, prosperity and decline. In 1644, the Manchu ruler was a boy and the state was governed by a regency; his father, an able warrior, had died a year earlier when his son was only 11 years old. When the boy reached manhood he was certainly not cast in the warrior mould, but a man of deep religious, even mystical, inclinations. It appears that he abandoned the throne to become a Buddhist monk, although officially he was noted as "deceased." The Ming army under Wu Sangui had certainly been strong enough to hold North China, and had not the dynasty fallen through internal rebellion, there might never have been a Manchu conquest. This is why, especially in the South of China, Wu Sangui, who invited the Manchus to enter China and occupy the throne in Peking, is still execrated as one of the "great traitors" of Chinese history.

For while the Manchus, with the help of Wu Sangui, were able to take over the northern provinces without opposition, they were to find the conquest of the South a very different matter. At first they relied mainly on Wu Sangui and other dissident Chinese leaders to subdue the successive Ming collateral princes who claimed the throne, and who set up their ephemeral courts in various cities of the South. It was Wu Sangui who hunted the last Ming pretender to the death in remote Yunnan province. These leaders who exercised control over vast territories had to be granted the status and title of princes. Meanwhile the Manchu armies remained in the Yangtze valley.

Inevitably, in 1673, Wu Sangui renounced his allegiance to the Qing dynasty and set about driving the Manchus from China and founding a new dynasty himself. He was no doubt encouraged in this course by the death (or disappearance) in 1661 of the first Manchu emperor to reign in China, Shun Zhi. His heir was a boy of eight, so another regency was necessary. All this seemed at best an unpromising future for the Manchu regime; it seemed probable that they would be confined to North China, like their ancestors the Nuchen-Jin dynasty before them. But the young emperor became the man known to history as Kang Xi (1662–1722), who was the true founder of the Qing dynasty and ruler of all China. When Wu Sangui died, dominion over Southern China passed to his son. In 1682, Kang Xi broke the power of the Wu Sangui family and completed the conquest of the South. He had still 40 years on the throne before him, a reign that was to transform the empire.

Kang Xi inherited two valuable instruments of rule: the Manchu army and the Ming civil service. While still beyond the Great Wall his predecessors had organized this force into a most efficient war machine. All adult Manchu males, and after the conquest of Liaoning, every Chinese male of that province, who had been born a Manchu subject, were formed into eight "Banners" pledged to military and political service, forbidden to engage in commerce, or even agriculture (a rule which could not be enforced), and compelled to live on a court stipend. Kang Xi had at his disposal a well-trained army, stationed in strategic cities and provincial capitals throughout the empire, which were often protected by newly erected walled enclosures. Intermarriage between Manchus and Chinese was forbidden. No Manchu could become a court eunuch. But it was not forbidden to learn Chinese; although Manchu had acquired its own script, derived from Sanskrit, Manchu literature was virtually no more than a translation of Chinese literature and history. The Manchu educated class became from the first ardent students of Chinese literature, and before many generations had passed Manchu, if still learned and spoken by the upper-class Manchus, was to all intents and purposes a dead language. The last emperor Pu Yi records in his autobiography that he only knew one word of Manchu.

The Temple of the Good Harvest (*Qi nian dian*) is the main part of the Temple of Heaven (*Tien Tan*). Here, in Peking, every spring, under the Ming and Qing dynasties, were performed the propitiatory rites which, it was hoped, would bring a good harvest. The Temple of Heaven, built in 1420, includes two other buildings: the Imperial Arch of Heaven (*Huang qiong gu*) and the Circular Mound (*Huan qiu tan*). The Temple of the Good Harvest was destroyed in a fire in 1889; the reconstruction which we see today is an exact copy of the original.

Pages 310–311
Some buildings in the Forbidden City, the imperial palace of Peking. This was built between the 15th and 17th centuries and is composed of pavilions arranged symmetrically around huge courtyards in a rectangular area surrounded by walls and a canal. Outside the Forbidden City at one time, still more walls enclosed the Imperial City where the offices of government were to be found.

This acceptance of cultural assimilation while at the same time endeavouring to maintain a separation in ethnic origin, was the deliberate policy of the early Qing emperors. The need to be highly literate in Chinese stemmed from the necessity of continuing to maintain and employ the Ming civil service, recruited by public examinations conducted in Chinese. Without the services of Chinese administrators the small Manchu minority could not govern. The Manchus were determined to avoid the mistakes of previous dynasties founded by invaders of China. They guarded against racial assimilation, which their ancestors, the Jin and others, had not, and they rejected cultural divisiveness, which had made the Mongols hateful to their Chinese subjects. The Manchus remained of pure descent until the fall of the dynasty; at the same time they lost almost all cultural traits of their own, and were in speech and education wholly assimilated to the Chinese. These were, perhaps, not quite the consequences which the emperor Kang Xi had hoped to achieve.

The Manchus took over the Ming civil service and made very few changes in its organization. The examination system remained in force, was indeed strengthened by further tests which those already in official posts had to undergo during their career. The other important change was to divide the candidates geographically, so that candidates from the more populous southern provinces competed at Nanking, the southern capital, and those from the North at Peking. Moreover one half of the available posts was reserved for Manchu candidates. This meant that half the civil service was recruited from, at most, ten million Manchus, while the other half came from 300 million Chinese, the majority of whom lived in the southern half of the empire, and thus could fill only about one-quarter of the posts available. For a Manchu with education it was a relatively easy task to win a place; for a Chinese it was very much harder, and for a southerner, harder still.

The Manchus distrusted the southern Chinese, who had resisted conquest for nearly 40 years after the Manchus took over in Peking. It was in the South that the secret societies arose, all originally the foci of political opposition to Manchu rule. The breach was never healed: the great rebellions, including the final republican movement, all originated in the South and were led by southerners. For the same reasons the Manchus neglected to create a navy; experienced and competent seamen came predominantly from the southern coastal cities; a navy would have to be manned by them, and could easily become a base for sedition and rebellion. The Mongol decline had begun with the disaffection of their Chinese-manned navy; the Manchus were determined to avoid that peril, and chose to have no significant navy at all. This left them later completely open to attack and pressure from the Western maritime nations, but in the 17th century this danger was not yet apparent.

The Manchus were always conscious that they were a small minority in an empire which was at best neutral towards them, but in large part secretly hostile. Yet, to govern, they depended upon the Chinese. Their response was to embrace Chinese culture wholeheartedly, and in its most orthodox Confucian

The halls of the various pavilions which comprise the Forbidden City are today open to the public. Walking around them, we can admire the precious robes and *objets d'art* with which the emperors of the Ming and Qing dynasties loved to surround themselves. Of special interest are the two bronze sculptures representing the phoenix and the tortoise, both of which are symbolic animals in Chinese mythology.

form. Kang Xi and his successors became well-read scholars, and gave full patronage to the Neo-Confucian doctrine of Zhu Xi. As this was now the dominant, almost the only widespread interpretation of Confucianism, they thus gained the approval and the loyalty of the official class which had been educated in it. The Qing developed very conservative attitudes modelled on the outlook of the Confucian scholar-bureaucracy upon which their power relied. Every innovation became suspect; if it had no authority in tradition, it must be regarded as revolutionary, or at best undesirable.

The Neo-Confucian world outlook emphasized the supremacy of Chinese civilization (originally inspired by antipathy to Tartar and Mongol foes), and the Manchus were acutely aware that the accusation of being themselves of such an origin was damaging and dangerous; they sought in every way to conciliate the scholar gentry and to prove themselves "civilized," that is, good Confucians.

In the age of Kang Xi this policy was probably the only one that could have secured their continuing tenure of the throne. Hostility in the South had been deep and lasting. While the Manchu aristocracy was becoming educated in Chinese, the mass of the "Bannermen," as ordinary Manchus were called, was still largely ignorant of the Chinese language in any form. The Qing dynasty faced a continuing dilemma: if they asserted their privileges as conquerors too strongly they would forfeit the goodwill of the Chinese scholar-officials; if they permitted a complete assimilation between Manchus and Chinese, they would lose control, and the far more numerous Chinese would dominate the empire. This problem might be held in check by very able rulers, but it remained unsolved.

The Qing were very fortunate to have a succession of three such rulers: Kang Xi, his son, Yong Zheng, and Qian Long, his grandson, whose combined reigns lasted 134 years. Both Kang Xi and his grandson Qian Long each reigned for 60 years, and the latter then abdicated so that his reign should not exceed that of his grandfather. Under these three emperors the Qing achieved much. Mongolia, home of the traditional foes of China, was conquered and reduced to a confederacy of princes owing allegiance to Peking. The nomad menace was destroyed forever.

Already the disparity between the huge population of China, constantly increasing, and the relatively static population of the pastoral nomads had made the rise of a new Genghis Khan virtually impossible. Kang Xi, who now used the newly modernized cannon (aided in their manufacture by Jesuit missionaries), had no real difficulty in imposing Chinese rule over all of Mongolia and also Chinese Central Asia (Xinjiang). He repulsed a first Russian attempt to enroach in Northern Manchuria, and still claimed both banks of the Amur river as part of the original Manchu kingdom. Suzerainty over Korea, Annam (Vietnam), Burma and, in a rather less formal manner, Thailand, was acknowledged. Tibet was conquered, and a Chinese resident stationed with a small garrison in Lhasa. The last campaign of Qing imperialism undertaken in the second half of the 18th century was the conquest of Nepal, which was then

Below: a view of the eastern cemetery of the Qing dynasty at Zun Hua (Hebei), about 13 kilometers from Peking. Emperors and empresses of the dynasty are all buried here. The tombs were opened to the public after restoration in 1978. They generally consist of a building with an underground section containing spacious halls where religious rites were celebrated.

Opposite: the central hall of the underground tomb of Qian Long and, right, the stone sarcophagus in which the emperor's body was interred.

left as a vassal kingdom. But this totally useless war did much to exhaust the resources of the empire and prepare the way for the troubles which followed the reign of Qian Long.

These expansions brought great prestige to the empire. The early Jesuits who came to the court of Kang Xi were profoundly impressed by the power and glory, and by the scholarship and competence of the emperor. They admired China for many things which contemporary Europe conspicuously lacked: a unified political system covering a vast region; central control which no local lord or prince could defy; freedom of commerce throughout the empire; rule by a class of highly educated men, not by hereditary aristocrats who could hold high office by blood rather than by brains. The Jesuits themselves found favour and in return offered scientific services. Johann Schall von Bell prepared the dynastic calendar until imprisoned on representations of jealous Muslim astronomers. Ferdinand Verbiest was reinstated in control of the almanac, installed a new set of instruments on the observatory, and promulgated a perpetual calendar. Fontaney cured the emperor of fever with quinine. Régis and eight others prepared the first maps of China to be based on astronomical observation, triangulation, and measurement.

The one sad criticism of the learned fathers was that this magnificent empire was not Christian, was in fact seemingly rather indifferent to all religion. The Qing patronized Buddhism to some degree, so long as it was the orthodox kind, but persecuted sects which they suspected of subversion. The court also subsidized the Taoist popular and magical polytheistic religion, because it was popular and might, if disparaged, lead to trouble among the people. The court, to conform with the Confucianism of the educated, continued with the ceremonies of state worship of Heaven, and with the respect, if not actual worship, due to ancestors. The Jesuits found it wise to treat the ancestral ceremonies as respect rather than worship, but this was a view which was soon to be challenged by other religious orders who rejected the Jesuit interpretation. This led to the celebrated "Rites Controversy" which had more significance for the Christian missionaries than for the Qing court. When Kang Xi finally realized that the pope had condemned the Jesuit opinion, and forbidden them to conduct missions, he was highly incensed. That any foreign potentate, religious or secular, should tell him what could and could not be done by foreigners resident in China, was preposterous. He banned all Christian missionary endeavour. But he retained Jesuits in his service as mathematicians and casters of cannon.

The Manchus were, in the 17th century, militarily supreme in East Asia; they did not make the mistake of attacking Japan, which was then isolated from the rest of the world except for very limited trading contacts, by the policy of the Tokugawa shoguns. Trade with Japan was not very great, the Japanese who were no longer allowed to leave the country nor even build ships capable of sea voyages, were no threat to China. On the other hand the Qing court paid little or no attention to what was going on in Southern Asia or anywhere west of China. The attempts by the Dutch to encroach on the declining Portuguese possessions

Opposite: a ceremonial robe belonging to the Manchu emperor Qian Long.

Above and below: his seal made of jade. On the sides is carved a piece of prose in which the emperor himself celebrates his victory in battle. The reign of Qian Long (1735–1795) is remembered as the most glorious of the Qing dynasty, corresponding, as it did, to a long period of peace and prosperity. The emperor, who was interested in both art and literature, tried to ensure that people would remember the glories of his reign; this he did by making collections of works of art and by building lovely palaces in Peking.

in Southeast China, the rise of English power in India, the growing importance of trade between the European countries and China, did not cause any preoccupation at court. The overseas traders were barbarians; they must not have too much contact with the southern Chinese, who were disloyal; so trade, strictly supervised, was confined to the single port of Canton. The Chinese were forbidden to leave the country and settle in Southeast Asia, as they had been doing in increasing numbers for some centuries. All these provisions sprang from the distrust the Manchus felt for their southern Chinese subjects. The effect was to minimize contact with, and therefore knowledge of, European countries and their relative power.

Under Yong Zheng the empire remained internally at peace and strong. The emperor was a capable administrator, and the only important new conquest, that of Mongolia, had been carried out in his father's reign. The Manchu dynasty had an unusual rule of succession: no crown prince was normally appointed. On his deathbed the emperor signed a paper naming the son whom he intended to succeed him; this was then placed in a sealed and locked casket to be opened only in the presence of the senior princes and highest officials after the emperor had died. The objective was to avoid the constant intrigues which accompanied the succession to the throne in previous dynasties, often culminating in murderous plots.

As a system of selection it could not be wholly secure; in spite of every precaution, if the senior princes and highest officials secretly agreed to favour one son they could find means of seeing that his name appeared, or was alleged to appear, in the last testament of the deceased emperor, in place of the one written down originally. There was also the danger that the emperor might die before he could name a successor. A strong tradition, not of course accepted officially in the Qing dynastic history, relates that such an intrigue secured the succession for Yong Zheng, who was not Kang Xi's real choice. If so it may well be that it was still better than the alternative. Yong Zheng was a rather harsh character, but able and conscientious.

His son Qian Long (1736–96) is remembered as the emperor who sustained the power and glory of the Qing for a further 60 years. He was a scholar, a poet, a fine calligrapher, in every way a highly-educated and hard-working emperor. During the first half or more of his long reign, the prosperity and peace of Qing rule remained unchanged and unchallenged. It must be observed that in the end the Qing suffered from the consequences of their earlier successes, rather than from their failings. As the frontier was now peaceful, the nomad danger finally eliminated, there were no more wars to fight; the army therefore became a garrison force, stationed in the large cities. No Manchu might engage in trade, so the officers and soldiers lived in idleness, maintained by the state. Their military efficiency, professionalism and morale could only deteriorate.

As the empire had now been internally at peace since Kang Xi suppressed the Chinese rebels in the South, more than a century before the end of Qian Long's reign, the population had increased rapidly. Land rose in value, and a growing class of landless peasants emerged. No new industries arose to employ

Two examples of painting from the Qing period which show the then current trend for fanciful stylization. Above: the rocky masses are arranged in order to create an

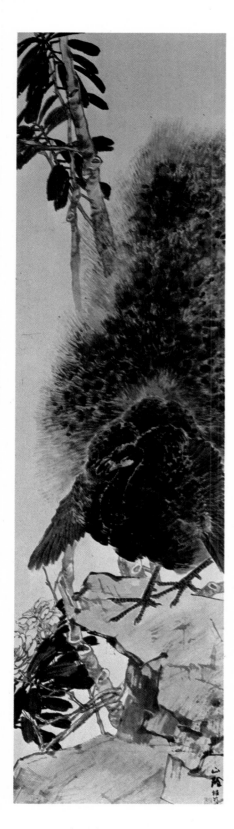

exaggerated vertical effect. Above: a turkey showing off its fine plumage.

an increasing rural population. The court, true to Confucian principles, did not deem it fitting to interfere in economic or commercial matters. Thus, all unseen except to acute observers, behind the splendid facade of Qian Long's later reign, weakness, corruption and decadence had set in. In these final years the empire was racked by the rebellion in the central provinces of the White Lotus sect, a branch of deviant Buddhism. This was not seen for what it was, a danger signal of growing rural discontent in all parts of the empire, but as further proof that only Confucianism could be trusted; all other religions contained the seeds of subversion and must be repressed, or at best held suspect and closely supervised.

At the very close of Qian Long's reign the English government of the day sent an embassy to Peking in an attempt to put relations with China on a regular diplomatic footing, as was the universal practice in Europe. The English hoped to extend their trading rights at Canton, if possible secure the use of other ports, and establish a permanent diplomatic mission in Peking. To Europeans these aspirations might seem by no means excessive on the part of the sea power which at that time dominated the trade routes of the world. The Chinese thought otherwise.

After some difficulties, Lord Macartney was received by the emperor, who had agreed that the ambassador need not perform the *Ketou*, the custom whereby anyone received in royal audience had to prostrate himself before the emperor and strike his forehead on the ground nine times. It was too much for Lord Macartney; he would bow and kneel, he said, as to his own king, but no more. Qian Long, a more enlightened man than his courtiers, had not insisted. However, he did not receive Macartney in the throne hall of the palace, as would have been normal, but at his hunting lodge in Inner Mongolia. To all the English ambassador's requests he returned a blank negative. Trade must be confined to Canton; any trade with foreigners from "beyond the sea" was to their advantage, not China's. "The Celestial Empire produces all commodities in abundance and has no need to import the products of outside barbarians." A permanent diplomatic mission in Peking was unthinkable; no such thing had ever been considered under any past dynasty. Missions from abroad were seen as gestures of homage to the emperor; they would be sent back loaded with gifts of greater value than those they brought, to display the generosity and munificence of the emperor. Lord Macartney and his mission were treated in exactly the same fashion.

But Macartney and his staff of English gentlemen were acute observers, and they had made a long overland journey from Canton to Peking, something the emperor himself had never done. They saw the signs of unrest, the evidence of over-population and poverty, which were not seen by the court. They also observed that the gifts they presented, magnificent clocks, the acme of the precision technology of their age, novel navigational instruments, and some other exhibits of the dawning industrial revolution, excited only cursory attention from the courtiers; they looked upon them as amusing toys, fit for a few moments of play. They displayed no interest whatever in the mechanism, or the scientific theory behind these inventions. Macartney wrote in his report that the Chinese empire was like "a great ship which has been allowed to decay and can never be rebuilt on the same bottom." It was a penetrating observation.

A scandal at the end of Qian Long's reign revealed all too clearly another evil: corruption. The emperor gave, in his last years, his complete confidence to a Manchu of low rank, one He Shen, who had begun his career as a bodyguard. He rose under Qian Long's favour to be the most powerful minister at court. When Qian Long died, the first act of his son and successor was to arrest He Shen and confiscate his wealth; it amounted to the equivalent of 70 million pounds sterling at the 19th century rate of exchange between silver bullion and the pound. This enormous fortune testifies both to the great wealth of the Chinese economy, and the degree of corruption which had infected the civil service and the court itself.

Thus, at the end of the 18th century, after 150 years of power and prosperity, the Qing dynasty was about to enter into its long decline. The immediate successors of Qian Long, Jia Qing (1796–1821) and Dao Guang (1821–51), were not profligate or idle emperors; they were indeed hard working and, especially Dao Guang, austere in private life. But they were limited by an education irrelevant to their problems; they were not men of unusual talents, and they were faced with both old and wholly new difficulties, for which they were unable to find adequate solutions. The aspect of the Chinese monarchy which had made the emperor the sole source of political responsibility and power, might work well enough under a Kang Xi, but was to be disastrous under a man of more modest talent or under a regency exercised by a strong, but ignorant empress.

In 1840 the long simmering discontent of the European, mainly English, merchants at Canton broke into open conflict with the Chinese empire. The immediate cause was the opium trade. This drug, made from poppy seed, was grown in India and imported into China by British traders. It was illegal in China, but the trade was connived at by the imperial officials at Canton and by the British authorities in India and the Far East. Emperor Dao Guang, following the advice of his ministers, decided to enforce the law and prohibit the import and sale of opium. The official he appointed to Canton to carry out this policy was a determined opponent of the trade. He confiscated the stocks held by British merchants and burned them. The resulting quarrel soon led to war, not only about opium, but more legitimately about the vexatious restrictions imposed by Manchu policy on trade and foreign merchants.

The British were easily victorious, largely due to their unchallenged naval supremacy. Canton and Nanking were taken, and the emperor was forced to sue for peace. The Treaty of Nanking, which set up the "Treaty Port System," imposed upon China a heavy indemnity, and the right of foreign traders

The Wall of the Nine Dragons in the Beihai Park in Peking. This was built in 1756 and is 27 meters long and five meters high. The coloured decoration is of enamelled ceramic tiles and represents nine dragons which are playing in the waves.

Porcelain vase of the Qing period. Variety of shape and refinement of technique, married to originality and elegance of design, characterize the porcelain of this period. Occasionally, however, the artist was carried away and produced works which were too ornately decorated to be really pleasing.

Opposite: the Temple of the Ten Thousand Buddhas is part of the complex of buildings which comprise the Summer Palace, outside Peking. This pagoda is built on four floors and is about 50 meters high; it dominates the large artificial lake and the collection of pavilions, bridges and gardens which was planned by the last Manchu emperors and in which the empress Ci Xi took a special interest.

to reside, in their own self-administered concession areas, at a number of designated Treaty Ports which, in addition to Canton, included Shanghai, hitherto a small city of the second administrative grade. The right to station a diplomatic mission in Peking was accepted, but not immediately enforced. Foreign residents were put under the jurisdiction of their own consuls and no longer subject to Chinese law or authority. Missionaries were granted the right to travel in any part of the empire and set up mission stations wherever they chose.

This system, somewhat modified at the expense of Chinese sovereignty, was to endure for exactly a century, until the Japanese invasion of China and the Second World War brought it to a sudden conclusion. At the time, the provisions which were most distasteful to the Qing Court were the claim to have a minister permanently in Peking, and the acknowledgement of equal sovereign status accorded to European nations. The Concessions, the extraterritorial jurisdiction and the customs tariff limitation to five percent, which later generations of Chinese nationalists most resented, were at the time seen as of minor importance: the Manchus were glad to have the troublesome Westerners located outside the cities, and to be free of the bother of trying to grasp the European system of law. The tariff, collected by the newly-formed imperial maritime customs, positively brought in more revenue than the court had formerly received.

But there were other unforeseen and serious consequences of the defeat of the Manchus, particularly in the South. The southern Chinese were in any case disloyal; their hopes were raised by the incompetence shown by the Manchu garrisons of the southern cities, even if they were also capable of bravery. Economic effects, beneficial to the Europeans, were not so to many thousands of Chinese. Internal trade from Canton to the North had been carried by the river system and coolie labour, employing thousands of men. The sea had been too unsafe, due to piracy. Now, abruptly, with the opening of Shanghai, sea-borne trade moved north, Canton lost its unique status as the only port for foreign import and export, and the inland route fell into disuse. Great hardship was experienced by thousands of now unemployed labourers and boatmen. The heavy taxation raised to pay the foreign indemnity fell cruelly upon the poor.

Within ten years the distress and unrest in the South broke out into a formidable rebellion, the Tai Ping rising. The leader was a southerner, a Hakka, and a failed candidate for the civil service. He was also of a mystical temperament, and having made some slight study of a Protestant Christian missionary tract, became, during an illness, subject to visions in which he believed the Christian God had appeared to him and charged him with the task of driving out the Manchus, and bringing the whole Chinese people to Christianity, as he understood it.

This was certainly not the way missionaries, Protestant or Catholic, saw it. The Tai Ping Celestial King, as he styled himself, claimed to be directly inspired by God: he saw himself as the adopted younger brother of Jesus Christ, and if his teaching did include the main doctrines of Christianity, they conformed with no recognized Church; he himself had not been

美仁潘拿捉　　　　　印摘關門雁

THE PEKING OPERA

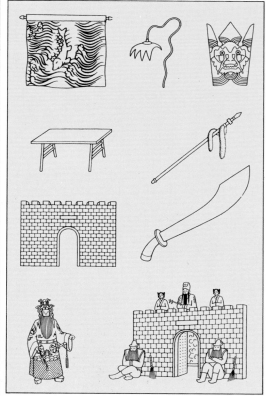

"It developed late but independently," say the Chinese of their theatrical tradition which is a kind of "total spectacle" in which singing, dance, mime, recitation and acrobatics all play a part. Indeed, it was not until the conquest of China by the Mongol Yuan dynasty in the 13th century that the theater began to develop and the two schools were established in the north and south of the country.

By the beginning of the 18th century, various regional styles of theatrical entertainment had developed, all of a "folk" character and all with the common characteristic that they consisted in a "total spectacle." Eventually, one particular form found preference with the public, today called the Peking Opera. It is highly popular and is based on texts which are very often anonymous. These elaborate and reenact old legends and stories from history. Above all, Peking Opera is theater in which the actor is all-important: the stage is empty except for a few very simple props used to express a particular convention (examples of these are shown in the drawings on the left). The attention of the spectators is centered on the facial make-up of the actors, on their rich costumes and on the different headdresses which they wear. All these scenic conventions identify the character which the actor is to play as soon as he appears. The orchestra sits on the stage, ready to follow every gesture of the actor.

In the Peking Opera, there are four main roles (illustrated opposite). From left to right these are: the *chou*, or clown, with fairly simple make-up except for some white around the eyes or nose in the shape of a butterfly and a few other black marks on the face. The *qing*, or painted face, who takes the parts of brave warriors, clever or wicked ministers and judges or governors. His make-up is extremely showy and loud (as we see from the two illustrations of "painted faces," above top). Colours have a

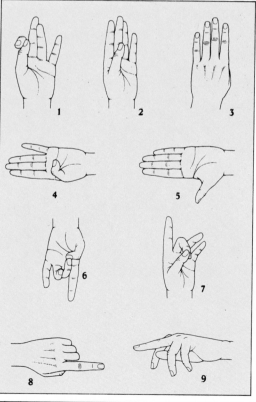

symbolic significance in this form of theater (red, loyalty; black, simplicity; blue, cruelty; white, betrayal; pink, old age). Next comes the *dan* which is a female part subdivided into six role types. Lastly, there is the *sheng*, a male part with various characterizations.

Conventional gestures of the hands are extremely important in this genre and are illustrated on the right: 1. a wish for defense; 2. with this, the *dan* shows uncertainty; 3. thus, the young *sheng* shows embarrassment; 4. the same gesture, seen from the other side of the hand; 5. the *sheng* and *qing* show that there is no hope of escape from a situation; 6. when the *dan* and the young *sheng* want to indicate themselves, they must point their index fingers like this although the *chou* points to his face; 7. one of the 20 ways of pointing the finger in order to point out something; 8. if two characters wish to exclude a third from their conversation, they rest the index finger on the left arm which is usually raised above the shoulder; 9. a variant of the gesture used to express defense.

A view of the palaces of Potala in Lhasa, the capital of Tibet. It was under the Qing dynasty, around the middle of the 18th century, that the Chinese policy of military and diplomatic intervention in Mongolia, Central Asia and Tibet was most successful. In 1751, Tibet became a protectorate of China although it retained a good deal of internal autonomy. By the end of the 18th century, the Chinese empire had reached the farthest reaches of its extent and controlled 11,000,000 sq. kms. of territory.

baptized, nor was his knowledge of the Christian religion in any form complete. But in the context of Chinese popular unrest and southern anti-Manchu feeling, the movement was irresible.

The Tai Ping rebels made themselves master of their native province of Guangxi, then swept north to the Yangtze, and taking city after city, seized Nanking, the southern capital of the empire, where they set up their own capital and proclaimed the Tai Ping dynasty (1853).

There is much evidence that the Tai Ping regime intended to put into effect important social reforms which conformed to their beliefs. There was to be equality between the sexes; fairer land tenure; and they were strongly hostile to the older religions of China, including Confucianism. For these reasons the modern revolutionaries have a soft spot for the Tai Ping rebels. But in practice they never had the opportunity to implement these policies except in the immediate neighbourhood of Nanking itself. The Tai Ping who had been more or less welcome in the southern provinces, apparently expected a similar reception in North China. They sent an expedition north to take Peking; it was too small and composed of southern troops whose dialect was not intelligible in North China. The rebels got to within 130 kilometers of Peking, but gained no local support. The Manchus rallied, and the rebels withdrew to the south.

This retreat marked the turning point in their fortunes. Having failed to grasp that the key to the victory of their cause was the conquest of North China, the Tai Ping were soon forced on the defensive, and before long Qing armies were actually besieging Nanking. The war dragged on for 13 years: much of the Yangtze valley and the southeast was devastated; the war spread up the river to Sichuan, and engulfed Hunan, but inexorably it favoured the imperial forces, notwithstanding that in the meantime the Qing empire had gone to war (1858) with two European powers, England and France, and had had to open up 11 more ports, permit legations at Peking and trade and Christian missions in the interior and legalize the importation of opium.

Ultimately, although defeated by the two foreign powers, the Qing won the Tai Ping war and recaptured Nanking. But the long rebellion had changed the internal political situation drastically. The Manchu "Banner army," the original instrument of Manchu domination, tactically out of date, lacking even artillery, had proved unequal to the task of saving their empire. Instead, the empire's defense was undertaken, and the final victory won, by Chinese armies raised in Hunan and the Yangtze provinces, commanded by the men who raised them, namely Chinese superior officials and gentry from the same region. Their loyalty to the Qing, however, was motivated by Tai Ping hostility to Confucianism and attachment to a foreign creed; this Confucian gentry preferred a Manchu true to their ideals to a Chinese who wished to destroy them. Thus military power, and inevitably civil influence, passed to the new Chinese leadership which dominated the last half century of the Qing dynasty. The Manchus now ruled on Chinese sufferance.

The rivalry between the great Chinese viceroys, as such they became, in the pacified provinces of the Yangtze and the South, and the Manchu court, soon to be controlled by a woman, the empress dowager Ci Xi, became the real field of internal politics for the rest of the dynastic period. The emperor Xian Feng (1851–62) had succeeded his father one year before the outbreak of the Tai Ping rebellion, and had died before it ended. His reign was troubled on all sides; the Tai Ping rebellion seemed at one point likely to drive him from the throne; the armies of Britain and France did drive him from his capital, Peking, in 1860, and he died at his summer hunting palace in Inner Mongolia the next year. He was the last Qing emperor to come to the throne as an adult; but he was accused of living a self-indulgent life (although documents still extant show that he paid much attention to the submissions and advice of his ministers). He died leaving only one son, a child, and not the son of his full empress, but of a concubine from the lesser Manchu nobility, Yehonala, later known to history as the empress dowager Ci Xi. Thus, in the midst of war and rebellion, with the capital in enemy hands, the further danger of a regency in the name of a young boy was added to the troubles of the Qing.

It must be recognized that, grave though the defects of her character were and still more her lack of education, Yehonala acted in this crisis with resolution, courage, and swift decision. The foreign armies had just evacuated Peking (after looting and burning down the Summer Palace), and a counsel of regency had been set up, among whose members were some high Manchu dignitaries who had no love for Yehonala, nor she for them. She contrived, by a trick of protocol (the regents had to accompany the coffin of the late emperor back to Peking, whereas she could travel on ahead), to seize power in the capital and have the members of the regency council immediately put to death for treason. She then became co-regent with the empress, wife of Xian Feng, who being of weak character was soon pushed aside, and for 50 years, until her death, Ci Xi, as she became known, was the effective ruler of China.

She had many of the qualities that make a great ruler, but she also suffered from some severe disadvantages. Firstly, as a woman and regent, she aroused the constant criticism of the Confucian scholars and historians who compared her to the Tang empress Wu. Yehonala was not in fact as able a woman as empress Wu; above all she was educated in only a narrow range of Chinese literature, then considered a sufficient education for women. She was thus from the first virtually entirely ignorant of the Western world, its nations, wealth and power. Nor did she wish to learn. She treated foreigners as "barbarians," a term and way of thought which had already become unrealistic in the time of Qian Long, and were now utterly anachronistic. She thus opposed every sort of innovation which had any connection with foreign ways, inventions, or learning. The leading officials, many of whom had learned to appreciate the use of steamboats in the campaigns along the Yangtze, had a hard time to get court permission for their plans, and ideas about railroad development.

She was a strong character; she dominated her ministers and the senior princes of the dynasty; she put her own candidate, another young child, on the throne when her sickly son died

A crowded street in Canton around the middle of the 18th century. Between the 17th and 19th centuries, the population of China rose very considerably, from 150 million people to about 450 millions (according to an estimate in 1850).

Opposite above: the signing of the Treaty of Nanking (1842) which ended the Opium War between Great Britain and the Chinese empire. As a result of this treaty, five great ports were opened to trade and permission was given for foreigners to live there. Thus China was forced to emerge from its "splendid isolation."

Below: Anglo-French troops attack a Chinese fort (August 1860) in the course of the Second Opium War which was concluded with the Treaty of Tianjin. Advancing to Peking itself, the Western troops destroyed the imperial summer residence and carried off many fine works of art. Victor Hugo wrote: "Governments are sometimes thieves but peoples never! I hope that one day, this booty will be restored to the Chinese."

Pages 330–331
Imperial troops at the conquest of Nanking (1864). From 1854 it had been the capital of the Tai Ping rebels.

before he had come of age. In her last years she not only forced the emperor Guang Xu (whom she had enthroned as a child) into total seclusion, but on the last day of her life (Guang Xu had died the day before) placed yet another child (Pu Yi) on the throne, still hoping to act as regent for years to come.

In one sense her strength and determination kept the dynasty on the throne till her death; in another, her obstinate opposition to reform and innovation doomed the dynasty and the monarchy to extinction. If the Qing, up to and during the Tai Ping rebellion, were still seen by the educated Chinese scholar-class as the protectors of their ideals, their grandchildren were to look upon the Manchus as the principal obstacle to any kind of reform or modernization which could save the Chinese state from destruction.

When Xian Feng died the state of the Chinese economy was no more preindustrial than that of Japan. Resolute reform, led by able men – and they were not lacking in China – could have done just what the Meiji restoration was to do for Japan in this same epoch in transforming a traditional absolute monarchy and high-grade handicraft economy into a modern polity with an advancing modern technological industrial economy. It had happened in Japan; in China it was delayed for more than 50 years, and then became bogged down in political and social revolution which earlier reform would have perhaps avoided. The main reason was the right leadership in Japan, and the wrong, obstructive leadership, in the person of the empress dowager Ci Xi, in China. That the situation was tolerated and accepted, was due largely to the fears which the senior and other members of the imperial family felt, that innovation would open the road to revolution and rebellion; the Manchus clung to Confucian conservatism as their one sure source of support. But the Chinese themselves were soon to call those Confucian values into question.

The record of Ci Xi's regencies is thus one of uniform disaster in foreign relations. After the Anglo-French War of 1858–60, for which she could not be held responsible, there were further defeats. The war with France, in the eighties, led to the loss of suzerainty over Indo-China; war with Japan, in 1895, ended with the loss of Korea and the virtual cession of two ports in southern Manchuria. The court's folly in supporting and countenancing the violently anti-foreign peasant movement, known as the Boxer Rebellion, in 1900, led to an international invasion of North China and the flight of the court to the far western provinces.

Meanwhile the great viceroys of the Yangtze and the South made their own arrangements with the foreign powers and took no part in the defense of the court. Returning to Peking after signing an extraordinary advantageous treaty, the ageing empress was forced to pay reluctant obeisance to the times, but only superficially. When she died in 1908 it was clear that she still saw government and statecraft in terms of palace intrigue and traditional precedents. Her weak and helpless successors barely survived three years before the revolutionary storm broke, and swept away the Qing dynasty.

An all-important fact in the history of modern China was thus

Above: a member of the secret society *Yi he tuan* (of justice and harmony) or *I He chuan* (of the just and harmonious boxer), which explains the Western term "Boxer" used for these people. The Boxers eschewed modern arms and dedicated themselves to defense exercises (fencing and boxing) and the traditional military arts, convinced that they were invulnerable. Since the most ancient times, such secret societies had existed in China, inspired by hatred of the government. Now, added to this, was the Boxers' hatred of "foreign devils" and of those Chinese who had been converted to Christianity. The Boxer rebellion had for years been creeping through the provincial areas of the North and had gained considerable ground there on account of an economic crisis and consequent famines. In 1900, it flared up in Peking and culminated in the siege of the Legations (shown in this popular Chinese print opposite). The Western powers and Japan intervened with an international expeditionary force which put an end to the siege. Thus, the anti-Western party at the imperial court which was supported by the empress herself fell into disrepute. In September 1901, the so-called Boxer Protocol was signed which imposed heavy indemnities upon China but which left her formal sovereignty over her lands.

that, during the last half-century of imperial rule the destiny of China was in the hands of an obstinate, forceful but ignorant woman, representing a weak and declining dynasty which now relied on the support of the most conservative class in China, and was terrified of losing that support by giving countenance to any reform or modernization. Had the Manchus not been alien and of Tartar origin, they would not have been so repugnant to the southern Chinese; but it was precisely in the South that the Chinese people came into closest contact with foreigners and foreign ways, with the burgeoning industrial revolution and with the rising forces of democracy and modern mass industry. The Manchus opposed and feared all these things; therefore the alienated southern Chinese welcomed them as far as they dared, and formed their revolutionary ideals on the model of Western institutions, many of which were very alien to the manners and thinking of the Chinese people as a whole. To be modern meant to be anti-Manchu; and to be anti-Manchu soon came also to be republican.

It would be wrong to think that the Manchus contributed nothing but an inflexible conservatism to the old Chinese culture. They were ardent patrons of letters and art, provided there was no subversion concealed in such work. They continued to support the great task of lexicography which the Ming had begun. Chinese literary and historical criticism in the Qing period broke new ground, for the first time raising doubts about the traditional authorship of some of the classical books, their true date, and the vicissitudes of the oldest texts. Original work was to some degree under the suspicion of being "innovatory" or revolutionary; but reinterpretation of ancient texts and long-held beliefs about the early literature were quite in order. The Manchus had not learned the full technique of modern repression. Handicraft was of a very high quality, until the Tai Ping rebellion brought desolation to many centers, including the great porcelain works in Jiangxi. Silks, jewelry, and ivory carving, work in other media besides porcelain all show very high technical skill and soft refinement. Qing porcelain often deliberately copied Ming models, and in the earlier period is distinguished by the technical mastery of the material, better in the Qing works than in the originals.

During the 19th century, and especially after the Tai Ping rebellion, the first changes in the Chinese outlook on the world in general became apparent. The great viceroys who had suppressed the rebellion could not ignore its lessons. The first of these was that modern armament and steamships were of vital strategic and tactical importance. They therefore persuaded the rather reluctant court to agree to the creation of military arsenals to provide weapons for an improved and modernized army, and to build a navy. They did not perhaps perceive the full consequences of these practical initiatives.

Modern weapons and modern machinery to make them, also modern navigation and naval training, require a knowledge of mathematics and at least some training in science and technology. These arts had to be acquired by the future engineers and naval officers, and they could not be obtained in China at that time. So the young officers and trainees had to be

A caricature of the empress Ci Xi who repressed the "Hundred Days of Reform" (1898) initiated by the emperor Guang Xu (on whose head she is sitting). He dreamed of becoming the "Peter the Great of China" by modernizing the country in the course of a series of reforms suggested to him by a group of young reformers such as Kang Youwei and Liang Qichao. Ci Xi, with the help of general Yuan Shikai and the conservatives at court, succeeded in winning power from Guang Xu who had already ordered various measures of reform which, however, were never put into effect. She then forced him to sign a decree in which he nominated her regent. The young emperor was then imprisoned in a pavilion in the Forbidden City where he remained until his death in 1908. Ci Xi (opposite with some of her ladies-in-waiting) was, however, forced to introduce a few reforms between 1901 and 1908 and in 1906, she sent a delegation to Europe to study the judicial systems of Western states and to work on a constitution for China. However, revolutionary ideas had already gained considerable ground in the country. Ci Xi died in 1908, having dominated the political scene for more than 30 years.

sent abroad, preferably to England, in the case of naval personnel, and to Europe (later America or Japan) for engineers. These young, educated Chinese, drawn from the gentry class – no other source of literates was available – were thus exposed not only to a Western scientific and technical education, but to all the other Western influences which affected their daily lives. They learned English, French or German; they could then read the literature of those languages. It conveyed to them a message rather different to that of their traditional Chinese education.

The ruling powers in China, which now meant, very often, the great viceroys of the post-Tai Ping period, were uneasily aware that the need to send students abroad could have difficult consequences. They devised a policy to guide the nation along the new path. "Eastern learning as the base, Western learning for use:" from the abbreviation of the Chinese words this policy came to be known as *Di Yong* ("Base and Utility"). It meant that whereas moral and ethical teaching, the study of the Chinese classics and history, literature and art, should continue unchanged, as the "base" of education, Western science and technology could be studied for its usefulness in making modern weapons and ships.

The eminent Chinese scholars who thought in this way did not accept that study of Western science and technology must inevitably lead the student to an understanding of the theories behind these techniques and to the philosophic background to such theories. Once the door to the study of the Western European civilization was open it was impossible to stop the mutual intercourse from widening and deepening. There was no longer just the one, unique civilization, that of China.

A young naval officer, Yan Fu, who came from the southern province of Fujian which in Ming times had been the center of Chinese naval activity, realized these facts from his personal experience and high intelligence. He went to England to train as a naval officer, learned to speak and read English, and before long became deeply interested in the social and political systems of the English, his wide reading taking in such writers as John Stuart Mill, Huxley, and others. After his return to China in 1879 he began to translate the works of these and other Western authors into elegant Chinese. This in itself was something unheard of. Other than through translations of the Bible and other works of a religious nature, European literature was virtually unknown to the educated Chinese. Yan Fu was a talented writer, his style appealed to men of taste and learning as the rather crude translations of Christian scriptures did not; these had been made by men more concerned with bringing the Gospel to the Chinese masses than to the notice of scholars. Yan Fu did more than translate, he explained, drawing the necessary conclusions in relation to Chinese problems. Although he remained a relatively obscure naval officer, for 20 years as head of the naval college at Tianjin, his influence in the world of letters and among the ruling class, especially of his own generation, was great.

Yan Fu formulated the fundamental problem facing the Chinese empire and people as "The search for wealth and power." Not personal wealth, but national economic strength, and power in the sense of military as well as economic power, on which the former must be founded, so as to restore to China the preeminent place in the world which, like all Chinese, he saw as hers by right, and which within her own world she had formerly enjoyed. It may be said that this expectation became the real goal of every successive revolutionary regime in the next century, down to the present day. Methods of achieving it were advocated and contested in various ways, but on the real purpose, all were in agreement. Even reactionaries could see that without wealth and power in the national sense, their own hopes were doomed to as much frustration as those of the reformers and revolutionaries. "Base and Utility" might be seen as a means, but it steadily became less respected as the end. To acquire the status of a modern great power it was essential to modernize not only the economic system but also the political and social structure of China. Increasingly the younger generation of educated Chinese despaired of the Manchu court, and turned to revolution as the only prospect open to them. Yan Fu was never of this opinion: he remained a monarchist to his death, but his English education induced him to envisage a constitutional monarchy in China. He distrusted any rapid development of democratic institutions, for which he did not think the Chinese people yet fitted or ready. History was to prove him right.

Yan Fu understood, what many of his successors failed to grasp, that democracy is founded not only on liberty but also on law: he had studied the English legal system; he realized how long and how hard it would be to set up similar institutions in China, where law had a wholly different connotation and record. As is so often the case Yan's criticism of the defects of the existing systems was increasingly heeded by the rising generation: his counsels of caution and restraint were not so popular, and largely disregarded.

Thus the gap between the obscurantism of the court and its most trusted supporters and the mass of the educated Chinese widened rapidly and fatally. In 1898, following the disastrous war with Japan, the young emperor Guang Xu reached his majority: but the empress dowager, nominally in retirement at the Summer Palace, continued to dominate the administration. Guang Xu gave his confidence to young reformers, who urged upon him a wide program of laws to modernize the empire and stave off the collapse of the dynasty. The emperor, who had no foreign education whatever, backed them wholeheartedly; and so it was that the Hundred Days of Reform burst upon an astonished China and a furious conservative civil service.

The new decrees were in fact mild enough, some farseeing and original, but they were, one and all, anathema to the empress dowager and the extreme conservatives. After three months she engineered a *coup d'état* with the backing of the commander of the new army, Yuan Shikai, who by this act betrayed his sovereign. The emperor remained virtually a prisoner till his death in 1908. The reforming ministers either fled or were executed, and China was plunged back into extreme reaction, culminating within two years in the Boxer Rebellion, a violent court-supported anti-foreign movement, which brought about

Pu Yi, the last Chinese emperor, at eight years of age. He was intended to be the successor to Ci Xi and came to the throne in 1908. His father, prince Chun, was made regent. His allegiance was to the faction opposed to general Yuan Shikai, considered in the West to be the strong man of Chinese politics.

the invasion of China by the Western powers, and the imminent collapse of the dynasty. After the death of the empress dowager, in 1908, the dynasty lasted another four years.

It has been argued that Guang Xu's Hundred Days of Reform could have saved the monarchy and averted revolution, just as had the Meiji restoration in Japan 50 years earlier. Had it been possible to put into practice the new policy, this is indeed arguable; but although every reform proposed was at least nominally enacted in the next 20 years, and the contemporary scornful judgment that the innovations, one and all, were impractical and utopian is not at all endorsed today, it must still be questioned whether the profound transformation needed in the Chinese social as well as economic and political system could have been peacefully brought about. It was not a revolution of the accepted type that was inevitable, it was the complete renovation of the whole Chinese civilization, a fundamental need to modify the ideas of the past 2000 years and more to take account of a world entirely changed, vaster, and with a markedly different civilization. It may well be thought that while China, with her bitter experiences, has largely made this adjustment and still retains her own identity, the Western world has yet to take adequate heed of what China is now and will become.

General Yuan Shikai, exiled from the court after the death of Ci Xi, was recalled by the regent Chun in order to make a last defense of the dynasty, now under attack from all sides and obliged to authorize the constitution of provincial assemblies with the aim of electing a national parliament. Yuan agreed to come on condition he was made commander of the empire's armed forces and prime minister. However, behind Chun's back, he was negotiating with the Wuchang rebels (1911) and, in January 1912, he effected the abdication of the Qing dynasty and took the title of president of the Republic.

THE EARLY REPUBLIC

Opposite: foreigners in China at the beginning of the century. Military and economic power on the part of the Western powers and Japan was one of the causes of the decay of the Chinese economy. Nationalism swept across the country, inspiring the masses who suffered badly from the cupidity of foreign traders who fixed the prices of goods which they bought from the peasants.

Above: Qiu Jin, born in 1875 and the first heroine of modern China. She left her family to go and study in Japan, then the aim of all the young Chinese progressives. When she returned to her own country, she dedicated herself to teaching and to organizing a movement in favour of the emancipation of women. She took part in the underground movement whose aim was to bring down the Qing dynasty and free China from Western interference. She was arrested and condemned to death for these activities. The sentence was carried out on 17 July 1907.

On 9 October 1911 a bomb exploded in Hankou, the Treaty Port on the Yangtze, severely damaging a house in the Russian Concession. The imperial police, investigating the outrage, found the house stocked with a variety of weapons and munitions, and they also discovered a list of members of a revolutionary conspiracy. The list contained the names of many officers of the garrison. Next day, these officers, realizing their danger, led a mutiny which at once became a revolution. The army took over the whole of Wuhan, the great urban conglomeration made up of Hankou, Hanyang and Wuchang, proclaimed a republic, and appointed the somewhat reluctant governor, Li Yuanhong, acting president.

The movement started at Wuhan was at once followed by similar revolts, mainly bloodless, throughout the southern provinces. Within a month half of China had gone over to the republic. This collapse of imperial authority was more complete than expected. For several years Sun Yatsen, the republican leader in exile, had attempted to start revolts in the Canton area (he was a native of that city), but had invariably failed to win any significant support. The dynasty had inaugurated reforms since the Boxer Rebellion, and promised more. Western observers of Chinese affairs, although uniformly pessimistic about the future of the Qing dynasty, were equally scornful about the ability of what they called the "Young China" movement to replace the rule of the court in Peking.

In the North the Qing did not face the widespread dislike they engendered in the South. When the revolution broke out at Wuhan the regent called upon Yuan Shikai to resume command of the army and suppress the revolt. Yuan accepted, but on his conditions. He was no friend of the regent who, being a brother of the recently deceased emperor Guang Xu, whom Yuan had betrayed to the empress dowager, had dismissed Yuan when the empress died. But the regent had no recourse but to turn to his personal enemy as his one and last hope.

As the price of his cooperation, Yuan demanded not only the supreme command of the imperial armies but also what amounted to a virtual control of the government. He then attacked the revolutionary forces, and recaptured Hankou and Hanyang. Having established himself as the strong man of the moment, Yuan then turned upon the dynasty, and claiming that no peaceful solution was possible while the Qing dynasty remained in power, induced the now frightened court to agree to abdication on what appeared favourable terms.

On 12 February 1912 the regent issued a decree relinquishing the authority of the throne to a provisional republican government to be formed by Yuan Shikai. The Manchu court had Yuan's assurance that it would not only survive, but be treated with generous respect. The emperor would keep his title, his residence in the Summer Palace – provided the security

situation warranted it – and his court, and would receive generous financial provision towards its upkeep. Compared to the fate of previous imperial families, these terms were indeed humane and unprecedented. They were not in fact ever fully implemented, but they sufficed at the time to bring about a peaceful end to the Chinese monarchy.

It is rather strange that the republican revolutionary party should have accepted the terms so willingly. Sun Yatsen had been in America, raising funds for the revolution, when the revolt at Wuhan broke out. He immediately decided to return to China. He landed at Shanghai on Christmas Day 1911 and went to Nanking, which the rebels had taken on 2 December. He was proclaimed temporary president of the Chinese Republic on 1 January 1912. Yuan, since his recapture of Hankou and Hanyang, had kept in contact with the republicans, and had negotiated with them the impending abdication of the Qing dynasty and his own election as temporary president of the Republic.

It might seem that a conflict between Yuan Shikai and his followers and the real republican revolutionaries of Sun Yatsen was thus inevitable. But probably both sides agreed to the abdication in the hope of achieving victory without war. The danger to be feared was the division of China between North and South, and the opportunity this offered to foreign intervention on one side or the other, with Japan being the most likely beneficiary. The Western powers were convinced, and expressed themselves accordingly, that the Republic should accept Yuan as president, since they saw him as the most capable defender of law and order and protector of their trading interests. Few observers believed the Republic would be more than a temporary expedient; that Yuan would set himself up as the founder of a new dynasty was the widespread expectation of foreign observers.

This of course was exactly what Yuan intended to do, but he set about forming his plan of action with caution and an apparent show of loyalty to the Republic. It had been agreed that the capital should be transferred to Nanking, an idea not welcome to the ministers of the Treaty Powers, who being very comfortably installed in Peking within their defended Legation Quarter, did not want to go south. Yuan arranged a "mutiny" of his own troops, who pillaged and burned down part of the city, not far from the Legation Quarter. He put down the "mutiny" with ostensible severity and then, with the full backing of the diplomatic corps, which had visions of another Boxer Rebellion, declared that he could not leave Peking as it would endanger the peaceful transition of power. The republicans accepted this manoeuvre. A republican delegation had been in Peking on the night of the mutiny, 29 February, to urge Yuan to leave for the new capital at Nanking at once; on 15 February Yuan had been elected president of the Republic, and Sun Yatsen had resigned. Yuan had no real difficulty in persuading the frightened delegates from the South that he must remain in Peking, where in fact he proceeded to organize the new government, mostly made up of his own supporters.

This was still a temporary measure; an election for a

Opposite above: the first republican assembly, held in Shanghai on 21 November 1911. The city was conquered on 3 November by the People's Army.

Below: the scene of a massacre in the course of reprisals taken against the Wuhan rebels on 10 October 1911. This eventually led to the fall of the Qing dynasty and the proclamation of the Republic. After this, the movement spread to the whole of the central south of the country.

Parliament was called, and from August 1912 the election campaign was carried on by the two main parties; the revolutionary republicans, now renamed Guomindang (Kuomintang) or Nationalist Party, and Yuan's followers, whom he named the Republican Party. The election was held in February 1913 and the result was a large majority for the Guomindang. Yuan was faced with the certainty of a new parliamentary government led by his former opponents. The leader of the Guomindang parliamentary group was not Dr. Sun, who does not seem to have sought this position, but Song Jiaoren, an able and cool-headed politician who expected to become prime minister. He and Sun Yatsen were not close: Song came from Hunan province, not from Canton.

On 20 March 1913 Song was shot dead on Shanghai railway station as he prepared to go north to Peking to attend the opening of Parliament. Although hired assassins did the work, no one seriously doubted that Yuan was responsible. He had just secured a large loan of 25 million pounds sterling from the five-power consortium of Great Britain, Japan, France, Germany and Russia, and had not waited for the consent of Parliament before signing the agreement. This irregularity aroused the fury of the Guomindang members.

Sun Yatsen and other leaders of the Guomindang called for armed resistance against Yuan's domination, and in order to forestall such a move, Yuan appointed new military commanders from the North to many southern posts and moved his forces south. The revolt was a failure: Nanking, headquarters of the uprising, was taken and looted by the forces of a notoriously brutal and ignorant general in Yuan's service. Sun Yatsen fled abroad to Japan. Parliament, under the threat of a paid mob of demonstrators, elected Yuan as legitimate full president; having done what he needed to show the Treaty Powers that he was now master of China, Yuan disbanded the Guomindang, in November 1913, and in January 1914 dissolved Parliament itself.

This was the first, the last, and only elected Parliament in Chinese history. It had not distinguished itself, and was mourned by few. One of its few legislative acts had been the financial provision for the salaries of the members themselves. The inaction of Parliament can also be explained by the fact that Yuan's elevation to the presidency had come about through force; although many plans for acts had been produced, none were implemented. For some years ex-members of Parliament moved about the Treaty Ports, Shanghai or Canton, hoping to find support from one or other of the contending power groups, but gradually such "legitimacy" as they could confer seemed less and less significant to those participating in the reality of the power struggle. Yuan Shikai was now a dictator, and was soon to make his move to found a new imperial dynasty.

The Republic had, by the end of 1913, been shown to be a complete failure. It had done nothing to remedy the weakness of China in the international field, not even received recognition by the Treaty Powers (except for USA) until 10 October 1913, by which time it was plainly moribund. The economic problems, the question of land reform, all the essential changes in the social

system which had been ignored by the Manchus, were equally ignored, or at best acknowledged in words but not in deeds, under the new Republic. Only in education was there any real reform; new universities and many schools were opened: to these the younger educated class resorted, both to learn and to teach. The end of the civil service examinations and the importance of political or, soon, military connections for any public career closed the doors to the great mass of the Chinese literate gentry; they found refuge and occupation in the expanding education system.

The mainspring of the first revolution had been anti-Manchu feeling in the South, and to a lesser degree, but no less important, in the western provinces of China, which being then without modern communications of any kind, were less influential in politics. Once the Qing dynasty had abdicated, anti-Manchu feeling rapidly evaporated. Manchus, as such, were not to be seen in the South, and in the North they had long been accepted. There remained no focus for unity in the revolutionary party accept an imprecise commitment to modernization and reform, which were not particularly welcome to large and important sections of Chinese society.

The rural gentry were happy to see the Manchus go; but they had no desire for land reform or social changes. Now that the imperial civil service had been destroyed, and power rested in the hands of men appointed by the military warlord, Yuan Shikai, or his rivals in the South, the best career for the young sons of landlords was no longer the disintegrated civil service (in theory now open to university graduates), but the army. In any case the poorer country gentry could not afford to send their sons to a distant university. In the days of the empire, Confucian scholars able and willing to teach youth the necessary literary skills to compete in the old civil service examinations, had been available in every district. Now their knowledge was of no practical use. The army promised authority, security, and wealth. No one expected it to engage in really dangerous wars, for example against foreign powers, because it lacked the equipment. Everyone knew that an army officer attached to a rising and influential general could soon find himself in a post of command and in a situation where he could acquire wealth, mainly by corruption, but also through favours, nepotism and loyalty to his chief. The ever-swelling armies were to become the career and the stronghold of the rural landed gentry who in imperial times, by virtue of literacy as well as landownership, had been the mainstay of the imperial civil service.

The "higher gentry" as they were sometimes called, the families descended from great officials of the empire, with a long tradition of authority and scholarship behind them, were equally excluded from the new power structure. They had two fields of activity open to them: the diplomatic service – since many of them had a knowledge of foreign languages – and the new universities. The lists of the professorial staff of the greater universities were often filled with the names of families who had been prominent in the imperial civil service, as indeed is still the case. Many of the young followers of Sun Yatsen had the same origin: they were largely men who had studied abroad, in Japan, for the most part, since it was less expensive and closer, or America and Western Europe. They had espoused the revolutionary cause when abroad, and had often remained as exiles in foreign countries. Neither their foreign education nor their long absence overseas fitted them to form a ruling class in China at that time. Most knew very little about the real condition of the Chinese countryside, and their experience included no training for administration. They had grown up as conspirators, and like their leader, they were more skilled at political demonstration and the composition of revolutionary manifestos than at framing workable policies. Once Parliament had been dissolved, they lost their forum and were deprived of their influence.

Throughout the year 1914 Yuan had carefully prepared the way for the consummation of his ambition, the proclamation of the new dynasty. A handpicked political council had replaced Parliament; this was then reinforced by a constitutional council, which began by recommending a long extension of the presidential term of office, with powers which hardly differed in any way from those of a monarch. On the occasion of the winter solstice, December 1914, Yuan sacrificed at the Altar of Heaven in Peking, a rite hitherto only performed by the reigning emperor. By this action Yuan removed all doubts from the minds of the Chinese people as to his intentions. A convention of citizens' representatives was called to pronounce upon the future form of the state, and recommended unanimously that Yuan Shikai ascend the throne as emperor of China. After refusing the throne, as tradition and decency required, Yuan yielded to this "popular" demand, and the proclamation of the new dynasty was fixed for New Year's Day 1915.

But Yuan had miscalculated: the mass of the Chinese people were not yet politically aroused; they offered no coherent opposition although in the South they felt no enthusiasm for their new ruler, and the overseas Chinese communities in Southeast Asia were openly hostile. But the real opposition came from the generals of Yuan's own army. They could accept a life president, and hope that one or other of their number would succeed to similar honour and power; but a new dynasty was a different matter; it appeared to foreclose these avenues of ambition, and furthermore the prospect was that when Yuan, already an old man, died he would be succeeded on the throne by his eldest son, an arrogant and foolish man whose behaviour, even as potential crown prince, aroused the contempt of the people, and augured nothing but folly and ignorance if he came to supreme power. It has also been alleged, probably correctly, that Japan was busy corrupting the generals and inducing them to rebel.

On Christmas Day 1915 the commanding officer in the remote southwestern province of Yunnan denounced Yuan and the new empire, and in January declared his independence of Peking. He was immediately followed in his action by the neighbouring province of Guizhou.

Yuan's plan also had the misfortune to coincide with the outbreak of the First World War. His foreign advisers, British and American, had favoured the establishment of a new dynasty as they had no faith in the republican revolutionaries, nor in Sun Yatsen as a suitable ruler for China. They foresaw that without what they described as a "strong man" in power, chaos would be the most likely consequence of an attempt to rule China by Western democratic practices. But now these advisers were on the same side in a great European conflict, and Japan, although their ally, was left in the Far East with a relatively free hand.

Japan was itself a monarchy, and one in which the throne retained overriding power, but it did not suit the Japanese government to see a new dynasty in China. Above all not one under Yuan Shikai, who had been their opponent in Korea in 1895, and whom they distrusted. They too could see that his heir was unlikely to prove a capable ruler. A weak and distracted China was the opportunity for a strong and expansionist Japan; the war had eliminated Germany's opposition, the Russian revolution was soon to do the same for Japan's old foe; Britain was deeply involved in the struggle, France still fighting off the invader; it was Japan's chance, and Yuan could be an obstacle.

On 18 January 1915 Japan presented the so-called "21 Demands" in secrecy. An ultimatum extracted from the Chinese government (May 8) modified acceptance of the first four groups: 1. Japanese succession to German rights in Shandong; 2. extension to 99 years of the leases in Southern Manchuria with commercial freedom for Japanese there; 3. a half interest in the Han-yeh-p'ing Company which operated iron and steel mills at Hanyang, iron mines at Daye, and a colliery at Pingshan; and 4. a declaration that no part of China's coast should be leased or ceded to any power. The fifth group, calling notably for Japanese advisers in political, financial, and military affairs, and railroad concessions in the Yangtze River Valley (Britain's sphere of interest), was set aside.

Thus the revolt, fired by internal ambitions and sustained by outside support, progressed swiftly. Soon all of the South was up in arms. So when the northern generals urged him to annul his projected empire, Yuan was compelled on 22 March 1916 to abolish the new monarchy and try to reassume his former position as president. This move did not impress the opposition; the war continued, in a desultory fashion, until June 1916, when Yuan died suddenly, "of eating bitterness," as the Chinese put it. The new empire had come to nothing, its creator, now that he had lost the day, regretted by few. In China nothing succeeds like success, and nothing is so swiftly discarded and forgotten as failure. The ancient theory of the "Mandate of Heaven," the authorization claimed by the supreme power to rule on earth, was in practice a sanction for the successful, however success might be achieved, and a condemnation of those who had lost it, no longer to be considered as having any legitimate claim to power.

Yuan had lost the "Mandate of Heaven", but who, if anyone, was now favoured with this divine sanction? The answer was soon all too clear: no one was to be favoured. The reign of Yuan Shikai was the last period for 35 years, till the triumph of the People's Revolutionary Army (the forces of the People's Republic), in 1950, in which China was united under one recognized and established government. This epoch of division

Yuan Shikai at his desk. He succeeded Sun Yatsen as head of the Republic with the agreement both of Sun himself and of the revolutionary republic party (Guomindang). However, he soon betrayed the republican spirit and between November 1913 and January 1914, he dissolved parliament and banned the Guomindang – whose parliamentary leader, Song Jiaoren, he had assassinated.

Yuan Shikai's attempt to become emperor of China and founder of a new dynasty failed in large part because of the opposition of his own generals.

and civil wars can be likened to the normal hiatus between strong dynasties which had marked Chinese history for two millennia; to many who lived through this period, especially foreign observers who knew much less about Chinese history, it seemed to be the prelude to the complete disintegration of the old empire, and its probable partial conquest by some foreign power, most likely Japan.

The "warlord era," as it has often been called, lasted ten years, from the fall and death of Yuan to the establishment of the Nationalist (Guomindang) government in Nanking in 1927. It marked the nadir of modern Chinese history. The nominal government in Peking, recognized by the Treaty Powers, was the puppet of the succession of warlord generals who dominated North China. For much of this period the South had a precarious rival government in Canton, presided over by Sun Yatsen, who also depended on the fickle loyalty of local warlords. The western provinces, under their own warlords, were in effect independent principalities, and would have had the same status in previous times of political confusion; now they made no such claims, acknowledged for purposes of foreign relations the phantom authority of Peking, but conducted their own affairs in total disregard of any other authority.

The objective of the warring generals was wealth: by controlling Peking, the prize, they obtained the surplus revenue derived from the maritime customs and the salt monopoly, both revenues being directed to the payment of foreign debts, and administered by the representatives of foreign powers. The debts had to be honoured, but there remained a large surplus which was at the disposal of whoever controlled the "government" in Peking. The provincial warlords could not touch the customs and salt revenues collected in the provinces they ruled, not even Sun Yatsen's regime in Canton could do so, for fear of foreign armed intervention. They could, and did, control all other revenue, issuing demands for taxes on land for up to 50 years in advance in some instances. They built up huge ill-paid, badly armed and largely useless armies, which by 1925 had attained a total of one and a half million men. These troops lived largely on what they got by looting and pillaging country villages and cities occupied in the civil wars. When a warlord had amassed a huge fortune, he sometimes allowed himself to be defeated by a rival (for a large monetary consideration, naturally), virtually sold his army to the enemy and retired to live in luxury in the foreign Concessions at Tianjin or Shanghai. Southern warlords preferred the British colony of Hong Kong.

Almost all the leading northern warlords proclaimed their intentions at one time or another of reconquering the South and reuniting the country. Some actually attempted to do so, but were usually betrayed by their subordinates, or sold themselves out to a rival. Sun Yatsen equally had hopes of conquering the North and establishing his democratic republic in Peking. He cherished these hopes up to the time of his death in 1925, in Peking, when a turn of the military wheel seemed to offer a chance of peaceful reunification. It was to prove illusory, as had happened so many times in the past. Other events occurred in the same year, which were to spell the end of the warlord era.

Above left: a portrait of Lu Xun (1861–1936), the greatest of modern Chinese writers and, on the right, the frontispiece of his famous novel *The True History of A Q*. Lu Xun was the most impassioned critic of traditional society and its morals which he described as "cannibalistic." Like many other intellectual Chinese of his generation, he spent

some time in Japan studying. Medicine was originally his subject but, as he himself explained, "Studying medicine doesn't get you anywhere. It was necessary to cure the soul of the Chinese people and therefore I gave myself up to literature, convinced that it was the best means of attaining this end." Lu Xun wrote the literature of revolution against the past and coolly examined the spiritual corruption of his compatriots with the avowed aim of rousing them from the lethargy and self-satisfaction which they had acquired in the course of 3000 years. In 1930, he became a Marxist and founded the League of Writers of the Left. The other pictures (wood engravings of the thirties) show the scenes of misery in which the working classes lived, and (above) Shanghai workers on strike, singing the international communist anthem.

The Chinese people had suffered bitterly under this system of misgovernment; the rural areas were infested with bandit gangs, some the size of regiments (often indeed that was what they were, remnants of a defeated army) who swept over the countryside, burning and looting. From these dangers and the hardly less destructive activities of the so-called regular soldiery, the landlords fled to the defended cities or to the foreign Concessions in Shanghai and other Treaty Ports. They left their estates in charge of bailiffs who, to save themselves and some rent for the landlords, made common cause with bandits and soldiers with whom they shared the proceeds from raising rents and squeezing the peasantry. It can be said with hindsight that the misrule of the warlord era sowed the seeds of the true Chinese revolution, the great revolt of the peasants which Mao Zedong was to harness to his communist cause. For this reason modern historians, both Chinese and Western, have found the study of what was for long seen as a dreary and meaningless confusion to be a source of important latent developments.

It was not only the peasantry who suffered; over great areas of China the merchants found it all but impossible to carry on profitable trade; the educated class, now forced to reside in cities where some degree of personal safety prevailed, were frustrated, indeed outraged, by the domination of worthless and for the most part ignorant military rulers, who had no regard whatever for the national welfare and no understanding or care for the fallen status of China in the world at large. They took money, or raised loans, from Japan and any other source they could persuade to lend them funds. In return they bartered away the national resources, railroads, mines, what industry there was.

Among the educated class a silent fury mounted, which at first sought an outlet in demonstrations against the corrupt Peking government, later against the whole system of internal oppression and foreign exploitation. When, in 1919, the Treaty of Versailles ignored China's claims and awarded the former German-leased territory of Qingdao to Japan, rejecting China's right to her own port, the students of Peking University, together with most of the staff, staged a massive demonstration in Peking, which gained popular support and forced the government into refusing to sign the Treaty of Versailles.

This episode is known as the May 4 Movement, and is now honoured as a memorable turning point in Chinese history. In the sense that 4 May 1919 marked the first occasion that the Chinese educated class had openly, and in part successfully, staged a radical protest against their military overlords, it was truly a memorable happening; but it was inspired by prior events which had already deeply influenced the students and the Chinese educated class generally. In January 1915, when Yuan Shikai still ruled, he was called upon by the Japanese to agree to a series of concessions, the so-called "21 Demands" (see page 345), which if accepted in toto would have made China virtually a Japanese dependency. Yuan had tried to get the European powers to intervene and make Japan think again. But the West was at war; Japan had a free hand in the Far East, and neither Britain nor France was willing to antagonize their eastern ally. Not all the Japanese demands were accepted, but those that were

Above: the student demonstration in Peking on 4 May 1919. This date marked the beginning of a new phase in Chinese history. Students and professors made themselves spokesmen for the nation and protested against the signing of the Treaty of Versailles which transferred to Japan the rights and privileges previously exercised by Germany in Shandong. Below, the cover of *Xin Qinnian* (New Youth), a periodical of the new literary movement for the reform of the Chinese language and culture, the pages of which gave voice to all the progressive writers of the time. Apart from its immediate political significance, the May 4 Movement was important because it signified the victory of the antitraditional, anti-Confucian party and of the *bai-hua*, spoken language, over the literary language. The echoes of the October Revolution were being felt in China at this point and, according to Mao, "The stimulus of the Russian revolution and the words of Lenin gave inspiration to the May 4 Movement." Below: Cai Yuanpei, one of the most eminent personalities of the new Chinese culture and rector of the University of Peking at the time of the May 4 Movement when he supported the rebellious students.

had the effect of weakening Yuan's position at a crucial moment in his career, while obviously strengthening that of Japan in China. The menace of Japan thereafter became a major preoccupation among Chinese nationalists.

Between 1920 and 1926 there was war between local warlords. This situation left the national government, which struggled to maintain its envoys abroad, with no real power. Revenues from customs and salt were already pledged and administered for service of foreign loans. Those from railroads and land taxes were absorbed by local armies for which the civilian population felt no concern since they supported no local interests. Since the death of Yuan Shikai there had been no personality, no concrete cause strong enough to direct or to claim the loyalty of all the Chinese.

The Russian revolution, which by 1919 was heading for total victory by the Bolsheviks, as they were then called, also had deep influence on the Chinese educated class. They saw how the most backward, autocratic government in Europe had been overthrown by social revolution of a kind that seemed to offer the one means of defeating their own reactionary opponents backed by foreign powers.

Soon the new Soviet regime, now master of all Russia, was to renounce its "Unequal Treaties" with China and accept the status of diplomatic equality. Here was yet another example. If decadent imperial Russia could go through this transformation, why not China, whose circumstances were so similar, if not identical? The answer seemed plain enough: Marxism was the key to Russia's resurrection, could it not also be the answer to China's problem?

Even before the Chinese communist party was founded in 1921, Marxism had begun to exercise a deep influence on the thinking of the Chinese educated class; the universities were its seedbeds, students its followers, and the professors its exponents. This was something which the warlords were too ignorant to understand, and foreign observers too unaware of Chinese intellectual trends to perceive.

The events of 1925 opened the eyes of both the military warlords and the foreign community. On 30 May of that year students and workers demonstrating in Shanghai against a Japanese textile firm, whose workers were on strike because of their miserable conditions of pay, were fired upon by the International Concession police, a mixed force of Chinese, Sikhs and White Russians, officered by an Englishman. Eleven students were killed, even though the demonstrators were unarmed. The Concession authorities saw this incident as a sad, but inevitable result of disobedience to police orders to disperse, in short, wanton political agitation by foolish youths. The Chinese people saw it, with truly remarkable unanimity, rich and poor, educated and illiterate alike, as a gross affront to their nation and people, an outrage committed by foreigners, all the more heinous since the victims were students, members of the literate former governing class, and respected as such by all Chinese at that period. The result was a mass movement of xenophobia and outraged nationalism which overshadowed even the May 4 Movement in Peking in 1919.

Chen Duxiu (top left) and Li Dazhao (below) were the first to introduce Marxism into China and to organize at the University of Peking, where they both taught, a group for the study of Marxist thought. Li Dazhao found the young Mao Zedong a post as librarian which enabled him to remain in Peking and to extend his experience of Marxism. Li was more interested in the theoretical aspects and Chen in the practical application of revolutionary theory. However, both contributed to the setting up of communist cells in various places and these all sent delegates to Shanghai in July 1921, when the Chinese communist party was founded. In 1927, Li Dazhao was condemned to death by the government of "warlords" in Peking. In 1929, Chen was expelled from the party because he was held responsible for the disastrous policies imposed by the Comintern. He died in 1942, having spent five years, from 1932 to 1937, in a Guomindang prison, convicted of subversive activities.

Peng Pai, shown here with his wife in a photograph taken in 1927, was one of the founders of the communist party and one of the first to spread its ideas amongst the peasants. After the break between the Chinese communist party and the Guomindang, he set up a soviet in Guangdong and began a campaign for the redistribution of land. The soviet was wiped out by the nationalists in 1928 so Peng Pai fled to Shanghai where, however, he was arrested and executed.

A total boycott of British and Japanese businesses was proclaimed and at once enforced by boycott pickets, which seemed to have sprung from nowhere, but which soon became the instrument of the Guomindang (nationalist) party and its ally the infant Chinese communist party. (The communist party was founded in July 1921 at a meeting in Shanghai attended by 12 members from various parts of China; one was Mao Zedong.)

The May 30 Movement spread to all parts of China: missionaries had to abandon their posts and take refuge in the foreign Concessions. In Canton a second bloody incident, when a procession of protesters was fired upon by concealed snipers (their identity was never established), resulted in the boycott spreading to Hong Kong, where it was particularly effective. The port was virtually brought to a standstill, Chinese workers and even domestic servants left their employment, and either retired to Canton or simply stayed at home. The Peking government, dominated by the Manchurian warlord Zhang Zuolin, made feeble protests, but did nothing, meriting the contempt of all Chinese.

The boycott and the activities associated with it gave an immense stimulus to nationalist feeling, not to say rampant xenophobia. The Guomindang suddenly became the patriotic party, no longer derided as ineffectual and utopian, but seen as the standard-bearer of an awakened China. The communist party, which had been admitted to the Guomindang Congress in 1923 on the basis of individual membership and cooperation, now had a certain influence in the nationalist government at Canton. The events of 30 May 1925 had helped to further this development.

China, in the shape of its recognized government, dominated by Zhang Zuolin, derived no benefit from the May 30 Movement; the foreign powers made no concessions, agreed to no modifications of the Unequal Treaties. In this they were to be proved to have acted most unwisely, their attitudes merely reinforcing the power and appeal of the more extreme nationalists. The twin aims of driving the warlords from power and office and freeing the whole country from the shackles of the foreign powers became the driving force of the nationalist movement, the communist party, by its membership of the Guomindang, sharing in the virtually universal public support.

The boycott movement gradually subsided, the missionaries tentatively returned to their missions, the foreigner could again walk the streets of Chinese cities without fear of jeering mobs or personal assault; but the effects in the political field endured and grew stronger. A year later, in the spring of 1926, the Canton nationalist government launched the "Northern Expedition" to overthrow the Peking warlords, reunite China, and then face the Treaty Powers with demands, backed by a vast united people, for full abrogation of the Unequal Treaties. Such was the hope if not quite the general expectation. Some Chinese, even on the left, and almost all foreign residents believed that the Northern Expedition was doomed to failure, and bound to be repulsed and defeated by the armies of the warlords. They were to be proved wrong. The warlords offered little or no resistence to the nationalist advance; Wuhan was taken in October, and the nationalist government transferred there from Canton in December. Only the warlord dominating Shanghai and Nanking now remained in power in South China and the lower Yangtze valley; some of the western warlords remained neutral in the struggle, others gave lip-service allegiance to the new government in Wuhan.

The commander-in-chief of the nationalist armies was Chiang Kaishek (Jiang Jieshe), a native of the Shanghai region, who had risen to high command under Sun Yatsen. As a young man he had studied the military art in Japan, and later Russia, after Sun Yatsen had accepted Soviet aid in reorganizing and supplying the new Chinese army and transforming the Guomindang from a loose democratic party system into a disciplined cell-structured authoritarian party, although not Marxist, on the lines of the Russian communist party.

In December 1926, after occupying the province of Jiangxi and its capital Nanchang, Chiang retired to winter quarters, and not solely for military reasons. The city, close to the south bank of the Yangtze, was within easy reach of Shanghai, and Chiang was concerned to develop the secret contacts which he had formed with Chinese big business, with the magnates and financiers of the greatest industrial and commercial city in China. These men were strongly nationalist in sentiment, despising the uncouth warlords who ruled in China, but also strongly anticommunist. They had ambivalent attitudes towards the Western residents who, in Shanghai, ruled the French Concession and the international Settlement, where the wealthy Chinese lived and carried out their business. They had their reservations, privately expressed, about the alliance of the Guomindang with the communists; they had shown little enthusiasm for the boycott of foreign businesses. However, as they held the moneybags, they could call the tune.

It can hardly now be disputed that during the winter months Chiang came to an understanding, if not a formal undertaking, with big business interests. It was that he would advance and take Chinese Shanghai; the Western nations, alarmed and seeking to delay the panic among their resident countrymen in Shanghai, would send troops to defend the Settlement and Concession. The communists would cause trouble, and to forestall a disastrous foreign war, Chiang would suppress the communists and set up a right-wing Guomindang government. Chiang had already strongly disagreed with the choice of Wuhan as the temporary capital; he wanted it at Nanchang, his own headquarters.

As was to be expected, the advance of the nationalist armies, the collapse of the warlords of South China, and the fall of Wuhan, had deeply disturbed the foreign residents in the Concessions as well as their home governments. China seemed to be slipping into a communist revolution; with memories of May 1925 and its consequences, almost all foreign observers saw the Guomindang as virtually a communist movement. The foreign Concession areas of Shanghai were at once garrisoned with a considerable international force, including Japanese, British and French contingents. Tension rose steadily. In

Sun Yatsen (seated) in 1924 with Chiang Kaishek, then a young nationalist officer just returned from the USSR where he had been studying military techniques with the Red Army. Sun Yatsen died the following year in 1925. Having become commander of the nationalist army, from Canton, where a revolutionary government composed of the communists and the Guomindang nationalists had been set up, Chiang sent an expeditionary force to free the North from the dominion of the "warlords." He aimed to reunite the country and force the foreign powers to annul the unfair treaties which China had so long had to endure. Later, he was to betray the agreement with the communists and became, in fact, one of their fiercest persecutors.

Wuhan it was soon clear that the Guomindang government was dominated by men of the left.

On 3 January 1927 a crowd, led by Liu Shaoqi (one day to be chairman of the Chinese People's Republic, only later to fall foul of the cultural revolution), overran the British Concession at Hankou. The British government, recognizing that nothing in the military sense could be done to restore the Concession, since Hankou, 640 kilometers from the sea, could not be reached in winter by large warships (the level of the Yangtze at that season being too low), sent a member of the Legation staff to negotiate the terms for a return of the Concession to China. This was effected in a businesslike way although at the time there was widespread belief that war between the revolutionary half of China and the European powers was imminent.

At Shanghai affairs came to a crisis in the last days of March 1927. On the 22nd, the communist party, led and directed by Zhou Enlai, rose, and with the backing of the Shanghai workers, seized Chinese Shanghai, expelling the local warlord regime. Two days later the nationalist armies of Chiang captured Nanking, and in the course of disorders that followed, several foreign residents were killed by nationalist troops, and the remainder rescued under cover of a bombardment by British gunboats lying off the city on the Yangtze.

These outrages were attributed by Chiang to communist officers in the nationalist army. Resident British diplomats including the British consular staff knew that they were in fact committed by xenophobic troops commanded by one of Chiang's most trusted commanders, who later rose high in his service. Chiang was at that moment sailing down the Yangtze to Shanghai, where he landed on 26 March to find the Chinese part of the city, not in the hands of his own troops, who had meanwhile arrived, but held by the communist-led militia, a potentially dangerous development as far as he was concerned. The danger of war with the foreign powers, exacerbated by the slayings in Nanking, was acute. At least such was the feeling on both sides. But it was no part of the policy of the European powers, Britain and France, to get involved in what might become a prolonged, exhausting war with revolutionary China. The diplomats and their governments were better informed than the Shanghai foreign residents. They knew of the divisions opening between the right wing of the Guomindang and the communists, and also of the near split between right and left in the nationalist movement itself. They played for time.

They did not have long to wait. On 12 April, Chiang struck at the communist-controlled militia who had seized and now ruled Chinese Shanghai. He massacred hundreds of workers, disarmed or slew those who resisted, and destroyed the communist administration. Zhou Enlai was captured but escaped while awaiting interrogation, which would most surely have been followed by his immediate execution. The communist movement in Shanghai, then its stronghold, was decimated and driven underground. Four days later Chiang proclaimed the establishment of a new nationalist government with Nanking as its permanent capital, thus breaking with the existing government in Wuhan, which he saw as communist-influenced, if not actually communist-controlled. The foreign powers could relax, and the danger of a general war with China passed away.

Meanwhile in Wuhan the left wing of the Guomindang, headed by a new leader, Wang Jingwei, had become suspicious of the communist alliance and suspected the designs of the Soviet Union to promote the communist party to full power. Wang had had a strange career; as a youth he had attempted to assassinate the regent, father of the infant emperor Pu Yi. Imprisoned, rather than executed, a royal clemency rarely shown by their republican opponents, Wang had been freed at the fall of the dynasty. He became the intimate friend and close adviser of Sun Yatsen and when the latter died, had confidently hoped to become his accepted successor. But he was not a soldier, and thus had no military power base. Chiang ousted him from the leadership and Wang, in spite of temporary agreement and insincere reconciliations, never forgave his rival. Since Sun Yatsen's death he had chosen exile in France. He had now returned and in Wuhan obtained the leadership he so much coveted.

He had soon convinced himself that he was challenged not only by Chiang at Nanking, but by the communists. The activity of a man hitherto only known in revolutionary circles, Mao Zedong, gave cause for anxiety. Mao had organized peasant risings, sabotage and support for the advancing nationalist army in his native Hunan province. He was still active there, organizing what came to be known as the Autumn Harvest movement, which was in effect the first attempt at a social revolution directed against the local landlords. These activities caused alarm and resentment among the officers of the Wuhan Guomindang army, who came from the rural landlord class. The threat of a military coup, which would certainly have led to a transfer of allegiance to Chiang's rival government in Nanking, forced Wang and the leaders of the left to break with the communist party. On 15 July 1927 the communist party was expelled from the Guomindang, the Wuhan government and the national revolutionary army. On 8 August, at Nanchang, Chiang's former headquarters, a brigade of the army under the command of a communist officer, Zhu De, mutinied and proclaimed itself the Red Army. This was the beginning of the 22 years of civil guerrilla warfare which ended in the total victory of the Chinese communist party in 1949.

It was now necessary for the Guomindang to heal the split within its own ranks. The warlord Zhang Zuolin still ruled in the North, where the subservient government in Peking continued to be recognized by foreign powers as the government of China. The obstacle to reunion in the nationalist camp lay solely in the rivalry and animosity between Wang and Chiang. Wang refused any accommodation unless Chiang retired from the scene. Chiang, cleverer than his enemy in political manoeuvre, agreed, and soon after married the sister of Sun Yatsen's widow. This matrimonial alliance gave Chiang close contact with one of the wealthiest Shanghai banking families, the Soong. Chiang was now assured of the full backing of the Shanghai financiers, his status established as a defender of the capitalist system and therefore a man eminently suited to head a new nationalist but

Opposite above: workers faithful to the provisional revolutionary government of Shanghai are imprisoned by the troops of Chiang Kaishek whom, in April 1927, they had welcomed as "liberators." Below left: Chiang Kaishek (left) with Wang Jingwei – already a political adversary of Chiang – the new leader of the Guomindang left.

Below right: the bodies of the Shanghai rebels are collected onto wagons. Just a few days previously, on 17 March, when the situation in Shanghai was at breaking point, Chiang Kaishek assured the people that he would cooperate with the communists who had control of all the trade unions and were preparing to organize a strike which would coincide with the entry of Chiang into the city. On the night of 12 April, however, armed bands of men belonging to the local mafia-type red flag and green flag organizations massacred more than 5000 workers, students, communists and left-wing Guomindang members. It was quite clear that their orders had come from Chiang Kaishek himself.

anticommunist government. These credentials sufficed to win him the approval of the European powers, if not of Japan, whose aims and policies were different.

Once Chiang was nominally retired (his undercover command of his armies and the loyalty of their commanders remained intact) Wang was induced to agree to the merging of the two governments, with Nanking as his seat. But Wang soon found himself trapped. A movement to repudiate the agreement sprung up in Wuhan, and to honour his word, Wang himself retired to Canton (his native city) to head a regional regime. The attempt by the communist Red Army to seize Canton in December 1927, for complicity in which Wang was probably wrongly blamed, forced him once more to go into exile in France. On 3 January, Chiang emerged from retirement and assumed supreme command of the revolutionary army, and at the same time became the effective head of the government and leader of the nationalist party.

In April 1928, the Northern Expedition resumed operations (held up during the internecine quarrel of the communists and the Guomindang) against the remaining warlord, Zhang Zuolin, with the aim of completing the reunification of China. The advance of the main army was held up in Shandong province by direct Japanese intervention at Jinan, capital of the province, where Japanese forces drove out the nationalist troops who had captured the city. The nationalist advance was thus halted along the railroad connecting Nanking with the North. But they had an ally. Ever since the revolution of 1911, alone among the warlords, Yan Xishan had remained in power as the military governor of the province of Shanxi, to the west and southwest of Peking. His rule, if authoritarian, had been effective and had resulted in the modernization of communications, industrial advance, and the maintenance of law and order; Shanxi was known as the "Model Province." Secure behind his mountainous provincial borders, Yan Xishan had held aloof from the civil wars of the "warlord era." He now decided to join the rising tide of nationalism; it was his troops in fact that on 8 June 1928 entered Peking.

Zhang Zuolin had not awaited their arrival; he had long since given up hope of being able to defend himself within the Great Wall, but he still expected to be the warlord of Manchuria, his native land, under the patronage of the Japanese. He had left Peking by train, bound for the north. As the train approached Shenyang (ex-Mukden, the old capital of the Manchu kingdom) it crossed the tracks of the Japanese-run South-Manchurian Railroad; a powerful bomb blew the carriage in which Zhang was travelling to pieces, killing the warlord. No one then, or since, had any doubt that the assassination was the work of the Japanese army, who controlled the locality, and who had no further use for a warlord who had lost North China virtually without a fight. He was succeeded by his son Zhang Xueliang who promptly slaughtered all potential rivals, to become the puppet ruler of Manchuria. Thus, being under Japanese domination, Manchuria was the only region which did not acknowledge the authority of the new nationalist government in Nanking.

This was true, up to a point. The communist Red Army had not been eliminated; it had staged attacks on several large cities in the southern provinces: Changsha, Canton and Shantou, operating on orders of the secret party leadership still hiding in Shanghai. There were, however, no eager proletarians awaiting the dawn of the social revolution in these ancient preindustrial cities. The communist army was repulsed, and the cities held or soon retaken by nationalist forces. Defeated and forced into a guerrilla war which was none of their choosing, the various bands and larger formations of the Red Army came together at the mountain stronghold of Jingangshan, on the border between the provinces of Hunan and Jiangxi. Here they met up with Mao Zedong, who had fled to this refuge after failing to take Changsha, followed by a brief capture by the nationalists, from which he escaped by virtue of his strong local Hunan accent, passing himself off as an innocent peasant.

The meeting of Zhu De and Mao Zedong at Jingangshan, one of the inspirational themes of Chinese contemporary art, is celebrated as the nativity of the People's Republic. In this hilly border region the joint leadership of Zhu and Mao established the first "liberated area," a small region which they controlled militarily with an army recruited from the local peasantry, and ruled politically on a communist policy of land reform, protection of the peasantry against landlord oppression, and above all the maintenance of a strict discipline among the troops, and the establishment of a new relationship of confidence and mutual reliance between peasantry and soldiers.

The communists gave the people what they wanted, not a new ideology which they would not understand, but land taken from absentee or oppressive landlords; and security from arbitrary exactions, pillage and violence from bandits or soldiery. On this simple basis of justice and the satisfaction of the peasants' land hunger, the communist regime in Jiangxi grew and organized itself into an unexpectedly formidable force.

Chiang of course was aware that the former mutineers of Nanchang were established in the depths of rural Jiangxi; whether he at first realized their potential menace is unclear; he had in any case his hands full with dissident nationalists in the South, and with his uncertain warlord allies in the North, Feng Yuxiang and Yan Xishan. Thus for three years, until November 1930, Chiang was not able to embark on a serious counterattack to destroy what had become a dangerous threat to his control of the southern provinces. The ragged band of defeated troops who had foregathered at Jingangshan in the spring of 1928 had grown to a force of over 300,000 trained guerrilla fighters; the areas under the control of the communist party in the provinces of Hunan, Jiangxi and Hubei, many of which lay hundreds of kilometers apart had a population nearing 50 million. The main liberated area was on the border between Jiangxi and Hunan, and it was there in the small town of Ruijin, in November 1931, that the Chinese Soviet Republic was proclaimed.

Chiang had launched his first "extermination campaign" in November 1930. It failed; he returned to the attack twice in 1931 with complete lack of success, and indeed with heavy loss, including a number of mass desertions by whole battalions of his

Opposite: Chiang Kaishek with his wife Soong Meiling, the younger sister of Chingling, Sun Yat-sen's wife. For Chiang Kaishek who regarded himself as the rightful, the sole heir of the "father of the Republic," it was an excellent move to ally himself with Sun's family in this way which gave him considerable credibility among the people. However, Chingling opposed the marriage which took place in 1927, denouncing the antidemocratic methods of her brother-in-law. The two sisters reestablished relations during the period of the united front against the Japanese. After 1950, they never again met. They were both very important political personalities even if ideologically far apart and both held responsible positions on opposing sides.

Below, Mao Zedong (left) is seen with Zhu De at the time of the foundation of the first "Red base" in Jingangshan. Zhu De was commander of Chiang Kaishek's forces but on 8 August 1927, with his brigade, he mutinied from the garrison at Nanchang, finally ending up in the hills of Jingangshan with Mao and his Red Army formations. From this meeting of the two leaders dates the birth of the People's Republic of China.

army. The communist guerrilla tactics, expressed in Mao's famous dictum: "When the enemy advance, we retreat, when he retreats, we advance; when he stops, we harass him, when he is tired, we attack him," was wholly unfamiliar to Chiang's army, which had hitherto only fought major engagements with demoralized warlord armies. Many of his conscripts felt no enthusiasm for exterminating peasants like themselves.

The Japanese seizure of Manchuria, in the autumn of 1931, brought this first abortive attempt to destroy the communist movement to a halt. Chiang had other pressing worries to contend with. As a result of their victories, the communists could now organize their forces in the light of the changed situation. The fact that the party continued to be directed by a central political committee which led a precarious clandestine existence in Shanghai, was an obvious anomaly, but the difficulty was that the leadership was urban, with no knowledge of rural realities, and still wedded to the belief that communist revolution could only emerge in the great industrial cities.

The failure of this leadership to direct the military in the field, the defeats in great cities, were factors which, combined with the obvious and striking success of the rural movement led by Mao and Zhu De, finally resulted in the transfer of the central political committee headquarters from Shanghai to Jiangxi. Many quarrels, notable for their obscurity, occurred. Communist party history is far from being fully documented or even divulged; the ascent of Mao, the standpoint and actions of other prominent leaders are often hidden under the decent veils of historical harmony, while others have been reviled or disgraced for actions which were acclaimed at the time and approved.

The Jiangxi Soviet, as it has come to be known, did not in fact have a long life. After the defeats of 1931, and also having had to accept the loss of Manchuria to the Japanese, Chiang planned his next attack with much greater care and with the assistance of a group of German officers, led by General von Seeckt (later to command the German army of occupation in Belgium in the Second World War). New tactics were devised; the communist-controlled area was not to be attacked, but blockaded; it was ringed by a system of blockhouses which gradually advanced. It is nowadays alleged that some of the political leaders from Shanghai, who clung to textbook Marxism, insisted on the use of forms of war other than the guerrilla tactics which Mao and Zhu De had so successfully applied. Whatever the reasons – the shortage of salt caused by the blockade was a major factor – the decision was taken to break out and march to the North. The official explanation, given in July 1934, was that the Chinese Red Army was going to fight the Japanese, still encroaching in Inner Mongolia, whereas the reactionary Chiang insisted on fighting his own countrymen and leaving the enemy a free hand.

The Long March, as this famous episode is called, has affinities with Churchill's remark about Dunkirk: "A retreat is not a victory." But if, from the military point of view, it seemed a disaster for the communist party, with the passage of time it has metamorphosed into the most brilliant political move they had yet made. Had they defended Jiangxi to the last, they might have left behind a great reputation for valour, but the party would

Below: the communist leaders, now turned guerrillas, in a rare photo taken in 1933, in which we see Zhou Enlai (with the beard), Peng Dehuai (second on the left) and Yeh Chien-yi (on the far left). The following year, the communist troops decided to retire before Chiang's nationalist army which had been trying to corner them in Jiangxi. They left the region and, after a 10,000-kilometers march, the famous "Long March," in the course of which they encountered terrible privation and suffered heavy losses, they reached the district of Yenan in the province of Shaanxi.

Opposite: a scene of everyday life in Yenan. In the absence of suitable premises, the communists set up their "factories" in the streets to provide for the needs of Red China. The first administration of the communist government in the liberated zone was set up at Pao An but later moved to Yenan. The communists banned usury, prostitution, opium, infanticide and the sale of small children – all common practices hitherto. Northern Shaanxi and the nearby regions of Gansu and Ningxia were among the poorest in the north of China. Close collaboration between army and peasants was one of the outstanding features of communist life in Yenan.

have been virtually exterminated, and its future put gravely at risk. The escape to the North was an heroic endeavour by any standard of human endurance. In October 1934, 100,000 communist troops accompanied by many civilians, set out from Jiangxi. A year later, less than 30,000 of them arrived at their final destination, near Yenan in Shaanxi. It has been calculated that the Long March which took them through the provinces of West China (Guizhou, Yunnan, Sichuan, Gansu) as well as the eastern mountain areas of Tibet, covered more than 10,000 kilometers. In the Yenan district, remote, poor, and hard to approach, but relatively secure, not easily surrounded, and in touch with the Mongolian steppe, beyond which was the Soviet Union, was a small "liberated area." This was the destination of the Long March. The other factor which marked out Yenan as a valuable base was that it lay to the west of the provinces, Shanxi in particular, through which the Japanese must invade if they were to secure a firm hold on North China. The communists were thus well placed to wage guerrilla war upon the invaders; and in late 1935 everyone in the Far East could see clearly that such an invasion was imminent.

There were other events connected with the Long March which had great importance. Following disputes concerning mistaken tactics, a meeting at the town of Zunyi in Guizhou in January 1935 condemned the Shanghai leadership, of whom little more is heard during the next period. Whether it was on this occasion that Mao was formally elected chairman of the Chinese communist party, the post he held till his death nearly 40 years later, is not quite certain; many records have disappeared, and others have been held back. It was during the Long March that Mao emerged as the undisputed leader of the party, whether he was formally confirmed or not till later is uncertain.

The second major consequence of the Long March was that it spread the news of the communist revolt far and wide through South and West China. The peasants of six or more provinces met the fabulous creatures, saw them march, helped to carry their loads, and were punctiliously paid for their labour. In return they freely gave information about the movement of both the Guomindang and warlord troops. The Red Army may not have stayed long in any district, but it was remembered in many, and with favour by the peasants.

Chiang also reaped some benefit: he did not succeed in destroying the communist party or its army, but he did impose a more substantial authority over the hitherto independent warlords of the western provinces. They had for the most part done no more than immure themselves in strongly defended cities when the communists passed by; Chiang's army, following up (but never intercepting) the Red Army, could take control of territories and provinces where his writ had hardly run before. All China had now heard of the communist revolt, which had been a forbidden topic in the press; it could not be concealed that the Guomindang were facing a challenge, an alternative ideology, and that they had failed to suppress it.

THE WAR WITH JAPAN

During the period 1930 to 1935, while the communists were developing their rural power in Jiangxi and then undertaking the Long March to the northwestern area of Yenan in Shaanxi province, the nationalist government of Chiang in Nanking had had to face other problems, not only from its allies, the warlords, who had joined the nationalist cause, but also, and much more significantly, from Japan.

In 1929, when the new government had barely been set up, the first revolt, at Wuhan broke out, This was led by the generals from Guangxi province who controlled the city and had supported Wang Jingwei when he was in power. Their jealousy of Chiang was the cause of discontent, but they were easily driven back to their native province, where they remained, disgruntled, but no longer in active armed opposition. The next year a revolt in the North appeared much more formidable. Yen Xishan, who had taken Peking from the warlord Zhang Zuolin, aided by Feng Yuxiang, the Christian general, declared independence and invited Wang Jingwei to return from exile to head a new government which would overthrow the dictatorship of Chiang. But although this combination appeared to be formidable, it too, was swiftly destroyed.

Zhang Zuolin's son, Zhang Xueliang, had seized power in Manchuria on his father's assassination, and at the end of 1929 declared his allegiance to Nanking. This act was not to the taste of the Japanese, but at the time it passed without protest. Invited by both sides to join the war in China between Chiang and the northern rebels, Zhang decided to back Chiang, and passed the Great Wall in force on 18 September 1930. His army was much stronger than that of the rebels, and as they were already hard pressed by Chiang's troops from the South, the northern revolt promptly collapsed. Feng Yuxiang fled, ultimately to Russia, where he died in a fire aboard a ship some years later. Yen Xishan took refuge in Dairen, the Japanese port city in South Manchuria, and Wang Jingwei withdrew to France

Nanking reigned supreme, nominally master of all China except the communist region in Jiangxi. It was this situation which had allowed Chiang to turn his full attention to the "extermination campaigns" against the Jiangxi Soviet.

The Japanese were in Manchuria by virtue of treaty rights obtained from China in the last days of the empire, when after defeating the Russians in the war of 1904–5, Japan had taken over the two leased ports of Dairen and Lushun, and obtained the right to station a large force along the line of the South Manchurian Railway which connected these cities (and Korea) with Shenyang and North Manchuria. Russia had obtained similar rights to guard the railroad north from Jilin to her own Siberian frontier, but had renounced these privileges after the revolution. Japan therefore had a powerful army in Manchuria, and the Zhang warlords, father and son, had ruled by their

The Long March lasted from October 1934 until early 1936 (opposite, a contemporary picture celebrates the accomplishment of this epic journey). During pauses along the way, Mao Zedong composed verses to celebrate this epic event, using the language and meters of classical poetry. The brief lyric which follows is an example.

The Long March
The Red Army fears not the trials of the Long March/
And thinks nothing of a thousand mountains and rivers./
The Wuling Ridges spread out like ripples;/
The Wumeng Ranges roll like balls of clay./
Warmly are the cliffs wrapped in clouds and washed by the Gold Sand;/
Chilly are the iron chains lying across/
The width of the Great Ferry./
A thousand acres of snow on the Min Mountains delight/
My troops who have just left them behind.

suffrance. Zhang Xueliang's intervention on behalf of the Nanking government displeased the Japanese army, which at this time was also a powerful political force in Tokyo itself. The Japanese militarists had decided that it was dangerous to allow him to dominate North China as the representative of the Nanking government, and they also had fears that China would become truly united, and emerge, in time, as a strong power. This would frustrate the far-ranging ambitions of the Japanese military and must be prevented by immediate action.

On 18 September 1931 a bomb exploded on the tracks of the South Manchurian railroad, just outside Shenyang. That it was set off by the Japanese was later proved, and no one at the time doubted that it was the work of the Japanese army. But it gave the Japanese the needed excuse for action. They seized the city, and then having disarmed or driven out the troops that Zhang Xueliang had left in Manchuria, rapidly took control of the whole region which comprised the three provinces of Liaoning, Jilin, and Heilongjiang. Zhang Xueliang, who with most of his best troops was at Peking, was obviously not capable of reconquering Manchuria, which the Japanese now set up as an "independent" state with the name of Manchukuo, that is, "Manchuland," arguing that it had never been part of the Chinese empire until the Qing dynasty, themselves Manchu, had conquered China.

This was not wholly true: Liaoning, the most southerly province, had been under the Ming, and before them both the Tang and the Han dynasties, and had had for centuries a purely Chinese population. In fact, the great immigration from North China which had followed the fall of the dynasty and the opening of railroads had brought the Chinese population at this date, 1931, to over 29,000,000 widely spread over all the whole region. Ethnically Manchuria was as Chinese as North China; only a small minority of some 200,000 Manchus remained in the country.

Within a year the Japanese had invited the deposed Qing emperor Pu Yi to become chief executive of the new state. Pu Yi accepted and then, in 1934, was enthroned by the Japanese as emperor of Manchukuo. Protests by the Nanking government to the League of Nations resulted in a Commission of Enquiry being set up which did indeed condemn Japan's illegal aggression but led to no action being taken to implement this condemnation which would clearly have meant war with Japan. The Western powers were not prepared to contemplate such action at a time when the rise of Nazi Germany was reason enough to distract their thoughts from Far Eastern adventures.

In China meantime, Chiang had become the object of increasing, if necessarily muted, criticism. The hope that world-wide diplomatic pressure would force Japan to withdraw from Manchuria gradually faded. Japan moreover was not only unrepentant but still actively aggressive. In January 1932, a Shanghai brawl, in which a Japanese Buddhist monk was killed, gave Japanese troops guarding their section of the International Settlement the excuse to attack and attempt to occupy the neighbouring Chinese suburb of Chabei. The Chinese forces resisted strongly. The Japanese, not expecting such fierce

Portrait of Pu Yi. The child who came to the throne of China when he was only three years old, was installed in 1932 as head of the puppet Japanese government of Manchukuo (the country of the Manchu), which was set up in order to guarantee the "special interests" of the Japanese in the rich province of Manchuria. In 1934, he was declared emperor.

Zhang Xueliang and Chiang Kaishek (right) at Xi'an in 1936. The significance of the Japanese offensive against China was minimized by Chiang Kaishek who felt that the "Red bandits" were his principal enemies so that his attitude to the Japanese was always one of compromise and surrender. In December 1936, he went to Xi'an, capital of the province of Shaanxi, to try to persuade Zhang Xueliang, the commander of the Manchurian army, to mount a full-scale offensive against the communists. Zhang Xueliang, who favoured the communist idea of a united national front against the Japanese, instead arrested Chiang. What happened after this is not quite clear but it seems that Stalin himself intervened to free Chiang Kaishek. What is certain is that there were talks between Chiang Kaishek and Zhou Enlai, at the end of which Chiang was freed. In September 1937, the communists and the Guomindang united against the Japanese who had mounted a large-scale offensive the previous July.

resistance, were repulsed. Meanwhile the confused street fighting spread into the International Settlement's northern quarter of Yangtzepoo. Japanese ships in the river bombarded Chabei, causing vast fires and the loss of thousands of lives. Chinese resistance continued, sustained by the help, moral and material, of thousands of patriotic Chinese from the adjoining areas of the city and the International Settlement.

Chiang Kaishek could not but feel dismayed at this development. He did not want to become involved in a major war with Japan, knowing that he had neither the arms nor the equipment to carry it on with any hope of success. For this reason, having done nothing to stop the Japanese from taking over Manchuria, in 1933 he likewise accepted the Japanese occupation, in the name of Manchukuo, of the province of Jehol or eastern Inner Mongolia, adjoining Manchuria to the west. Having by this action got possession of one of the main approaches to Peking, the Japanese now demanded the demilitarization of a large area of North China. Before long they were insisting on a degree of autonomy for North China which left them in military control of most of the province of Hebei. This systematic nibbling and piecemeal aggression by the Japanese, which continued from 1931 to 1937, greatly damaged the Guomindang's prestige and support. The war against the communists seemed to many Chinese an irrelevance in the face of the menace of Japan. Communist propaganda sought to strengthen this feeling. "Chinese do not fight Chinese," a slogan with strong patriotic appeal, even if then far from true, was soon to be repeated and heard on all sides. The war against the communists was not allowed to be reported either by the Chinese press or foreign journalists. Consequently, defeats or victories were equally only the subject of rumour. The aggressions of Japan were open, obvious, universally reported and occurred in or near centers of population and major cities. Even those Chinese who thought, with Chiang, that the communists were a greater ultimate danger than the Japanese – and these were few – could not rebut the charge that Chiang was neglecting the safety of the nation to pursue a minor vendetta against the communists. The glaring spectacle of Japanese aggression, as contrasted with the obscure and unreported "extermination campaign" against the communists, was a major error in public relations. Chiang, however, firmly believed that he must secure internal peace before resisting external aggression, rejecting the evidence of his own experience, which showed that internal peace could not be secured by "extermination campaigns."

At the end of 1936, rather more than a year since the communists had completed the Long March and were installed in the Yenan redoubt, Chiang decided to conduct another "extermination campaign" to crush them before they could recover strength. Apart from his own troops whom he was transferring from the southeast of China to the northwest, the scene of action, Chiang counted on the support of local Shaanxi troops and the army of Zhang Xueliang, the ex-warlord of Manchuria. Zhang's forces had been sent to the communist front, as the Japanese would not permit them to remain in North

China. It had done little to improve their morale. "Chinese do not fight Chinese" was a slogan which had strong appeal to men who had lost their homeland, not to the communists, but to the alien invader; were they not fighting the wrong enemy? This sense of fellow feeling with the communists, a sentiment also shared by their Shaanxi allies, only added to the growing discontent of the Manchurian troops who were also bored by their continued inaction.

In December, Chiang became aware that preparations for the great "extermination campaign" were faltering; he decided to go to Xi'an, capital of Shaanxi, and headquarters for the forthcoming offensive, to appraise the situation personally and inculcate a greater sense of urgency among his forces. Arrived at Xi'an, he quickly discovered that not only were the troops and lower ranking officers dissatisfied and disheartened, but that the leaders themselves, Zhang Xueliang and his Shaanxi colleague, shared the opinion of their men; both urged Chiang to abandon his campaign and try for a lasting agreement with the communists, so that both armies should be prepared and ready to resist the expected Japanese invasion of all China. For by late 1936 no one any longer doubted that Japan was planning such a move. The disarray of the European powers, their preoccupation with Nazi Germany, the uncertainties of US policy, and the recent purges of the army command in Russia, all these factors seemed to the Japanese army, which now dominated their home government, to make the coming year, 1937, the moment to strike. They also may have feared that either Chiang would defeat the communists and then be forced to resist Japan, or that he would be defeated, and Japan soon faced with a widespread communist-dominated region in North China.

Chiang indignantly rejected any suggestion of overtures to the communist "bandits." He renewed his orders for the speeding up of preparations for the coming offensive; he then retired to Tangshan, a hot-springs resort, once much favoured by the Tang emperors, about 30 kilometers from Xi'an. He proposed to spend Christmas there (Chiang had become a Methodist on his marriage to Soong Meiling). On 12 December, Chiang's personal bodyguards were overpowered by a large force of the now openly mutinous Manchurian army; leading this force was Zhang Xueliang.

Chiang was taken prisoner and held in Tangshan. It was made clear to him that his life depended on his agreeing to call off the war against the communists and cooperate in uniting the whole nation to resist Japan. Chiang was a stubborn man; he refused even to listen. At this point the mutinous generals decided to call in as mediator and negotiator, a man who had risen high in the hierarchy of the communist party – Zhou Enlai. So Chiang had to listen to the arguments and proposals of a man whom he had hunted down, and narrowly missed capturing, nearly ten years earlier, in Shanghai, in 1927.

In Nanking the news of the seizure of the head of the state and commander-in-chief, the Generalissimo as he was popularly called, created the utmost excitement and confusion. It soon became clear that resort to force would not only jeopardize the life of Chiang Kaishek, but would plunge China into a crisis of the utmost gravity and unleash further civil wars; all this in the face of the threatened invasion by the Japanese. There was no man in the Guomindang with the power or prestige to succeed Chiang without a bloody and unending war being waged between rivals.

In the end Zhou Enlai prevailed with Chiang; he was brought to understand that he must agree to the conditions placed before him. He was released on Christmas Day 1936 and returned to Nanking.

Besides bringing the war against the communist to an end, the agreement included the release of political prisoners, and the right of the people to demonstrate against Japanese aggression. It was also agreed that the communist party, now legal, should acknowledge Chiang as the legitimate head of the national government, namely that in Nanking. The communists renamed their area as the "Special Area," of which they regained full control. Their army was renamed the 8th Route Army of the national forces. Under its Chinese title, *Ba Lu Zhun*, it was to become a household name in China in the years to come. The communists had accepted Chiang as national leader for the simple reason that they knew he would now be forced by public opinion and his own prestige to take upon himself the duty of resisting further Japanese invasion.

They knew, as did all observers, that such a war would be followed by severe and destructive defeats, from which only guerrilla warfare could ultimately save China. The Guomindang army was not trained to wage guerrilla war, but to fight it. The Communist forces were experts in this type of warfare and could envisage carrying it on against the Japanese invaders with the backing of the people.

These expectations were soon put to the test. On the 7 July 1937, Japanese forces stationed near Peking came into conflict with Chinese troops. The exact cause of the encounter is obscure and irrelevant. The Japanese were seeking an excuse for action and in this, as previous incidents had shown, were masters of the art. Within a few weeks, negotiations having achieved nothing, the Japanese occupied Peking and Tianjin, driving the Chinese forces westward beyond the Great Wall into the province of Shanxi. Towards mid-August they destroyed any hope of a peaceful solution by launching an attack on Shanghai, using as their base the northern section of the International Settlement, which they were supposedly there to "defend." They bombarded the city and the Settlement, causing heavy casualties. The Chinese resisted fiercely, and it was not until November that, outflanked by the Japanese, who had landed reinforcements in the Yangtze estuary, they were compelled to fall back from Shanghai.

Chinese resistance, which naturally paid no attention to Settlement boundaries, and Japanese misuse of their position in the Settlement to wage aggressive war on China destroyed the status of Shanghai as a neutral refuge for foreign businessmen and residents. Henceforth, until the Western nations were brought into the war with Japan, Shanghai existed as an enclave dominated by the Japanese army.

When, following Pearl Harbor, a state of war existed

Zhou Enlai at the age of 37, photographed at Yenan by the American journalist Edgar Snow. When the new alliance between the communists and the Guomindang against the Japanese was established, Zhou was given the job of mediating between the two suspicious partners and in this way he gained his first experience of diplomacy. In 1940, he joined the Supreme Council for National Defense and during his frequent stays at Chongqing (then Chiang Kaishek's seat of government), his relations with foreign diplomats and journalists were always excellent. It was his idea to invite to Yenan many Western journalists (including Edgar Snow) and they, with their high praise of the communist regime, won credibility for it abroad.

between Japan and the Allied nations, the Japanese simply took control of the whole area, including the French Concession, interned all residents of enemy nationality, and brought the whole Treaty Port system to an abrupt end. In 1942 the Western powers negotiated with their new ally, nationalist China, the abrogation of all the rights, privileges and Concessions which they no longer enjoyed or possessed. It was almost exactly 100 years since the Opium War and the Treaty of Nanking under which the system had been set up.

Compared to China, the Japanese possessed overwhelming military supremacy. The Chinese had no navy capable of the slightest challenge to Japan's mastery of the seas. The air force, small but gallant, was virtually wiped out in the first weeks of war. Chiang's forces had to make do with subquality weapons, very few tanks, little heavy artillery, and limited reserves of ammunition. Most of the few munitions factories which China possessed were in coastal cities which were soon in Japanese hands. On 13 December 1937, the Japanese army entered Nanking, from which the Chinese government had withdrawn up the Yangtze to Wuhan, and covered themselves with ignominy and dishonour by sacking the city, killing and violating thousands of civilians and women. The Japanese claimed in excuse that their troops were enraged by news of a massacre of Japanese residents at the city of Tungzhou, near Peking. There had been a massacre, carried out by mutinous Chinese troops who had been recruited as a puppet army by the Japanese to terrorize the population. In those days before the Second World War, such atrocities made a deep impression on world opinion, the dulling of humanity's conscience by the horrendous events of later years had yet to come.

The Japanese, having taken Nanking, decided to link up the armies advancing south from Peking and Tianjin with their forces which had occupied the lower Yangtze. They succeeded in this, but did not have everything their own way. South of the important railroad junction of Xuzhou, where the line to the west of China crosses that to the north, the Chinese inflicted a severe defeat on the Japanese in a surprise attack. Although the victors had soon to retreat to the west, this victory, the regular nationalist army's only success in the field, did much to boost Chinese morale. It proved the Japanese were not invincible.

The Chinese covered their retreat to the west and blocked the Japanese advance southwards by cutting the dykes of the mighty Yellow River east of Kaifeng. Large parts of the provinces of Henan and Anhui were submerged under a vast flood, while the river took a new course, flowing into the sea south of the Shandong peninsula, hundreds of kilometers south of the old one. It was as if, geography permitting, the Rhone had been diverted from the vicinity of Marseilles to reach the sea at Bordeaux.

It was not until the late 1950s, under the People's Republic, that the river was diverted to its old course, and the devastated regions painstakingly restored to cultivation and ruined villages and towns rebuilt.

Nevertheless the Japanese continued to advance, by sea, along the Yangtze, and in North China by means of the

Opposite above left: soldiers of the Red Army along a stretch of the Great Wall near Peking. The city fell into the hands of the Japanese on 28 July 1937, and by the following year nearly all the towns and cities of the north and center of China had fallen to the enemy.
Right: a Japanese road block in Tianjin.

Below: Japanese soldiers in a village threaten boys whom they probably suspect of being couriers of the partisan army. After the formation of the united front by communists and nationalists (1937), the areas controlled by the communists experienced severe difficulties, particularly during the period 1941–2, when the Japanese attacks were concentrated especially against them, and in most of northern China the Nippon High Command's order of the "three alls" was being carried out: kill all, burn all, destroy all.

railroads. By the end of 1938 they held both banks of the Yangtze, from the gorges to the sea. They had occupied all the major sea ports, all the main cities and were in possession of the railroad network between North China and the Yangtze. But they had not penetrated far into the mountainous western half of China, which was largely without any communications other than the old caravan roads. The gorges of the Yangtze presented an impassable barrier which the Japanese never tried to force. Protected by this rampart, the Guomindang government set up its seat in Chongqing (Chungking), on the banks of the Yangtze, where it remained until the end of the Pacific war in 1945. In the North the Japanese occupied most of Shanxi province, and the eastern half of Henan, but did not reach the mountainous western part of the province. Beyond these borders, especially in western Shanxi, they were confronted with the 8th Route Army, that is, the communist army based at Yenan in the next province westward, Shaanxi. The interior of South China was also at this time not occupied by the Japanese army.

The Japanese had reckoned on a swift Chinese surrender after the fall of Nanking. When this did not happen, they hoped that once Wuhan had fallen, Chiang would realize that victory was unattainable and sue for peace. They were quite wrong. Chiang was well aware that he could not defeat the Japanese army and drive it from China, but he knew that the course on which the Japanese military-dominated government had now set out was certain to bring them into direct conflict with the USA and Great Britain. He also doubted whether his erstwhile friend, Germany, could exercise any restraint upon Japan. The Germans indeed tried to do so, but Japan's idea of the Berlin-Rome-Tokyo alliance did not extend to any interference in her own plans by her Axis partners.

The one political success of the Japanese was the defection from the nationalist government of Wang Jingwei, who had returned to China at the outbreak of war in a gesture of patriotic solidarity, and had been given the position of deputy to Chiang Kaishek. But this reconciliation between the two was to prove no more durable than their former association. Wang listened to the arguments of those who urged a peace with Japan before the communist guerrillas grew too strong, and while there was still time to join what many thought would be the winning side in the coming European war. On 21 December 1938, he fled secretly from Chongqing first to Hanoi, in French Indo-China, but following an attempt on his life, Wang Jingwei came back to Shanghai.

He took up residence within the sanctuary of the International Settlement and opened negotiations with the Japanese. In March 1940, Wang finally committed himself to head a government in Nanking which he claimed to be the legitimate government of China, Chiang and the Chongqing government being treated as "rebels." A treaty signed with Japan made the new Nanking regime the ally of the invader, promised that Japanese troops would be withdrawn from China two years after Chiang had been crushed, but would remain in parts of North China to continue the war against the communist guerrilla armies. Wang acknowledged and recognized

Above: Lin Biao giving a lesson in the open in Yenan. In 1936, Lin Biao ran the political and military anti-Japanese University of Yenan. However, when Chiang Kaishek finally agreed to the united anti-Japanese front, Lin Biao took up command of the united army and led it to a decisive victory.

Below: a photo of Mao Zedong and Zhou Enlai at Yenan during the period of "redressing the balance" begun in 1942. The aim of this campaign was to correct the style of work of the party's cadres and to criticize any too dogmatic expressions of party dogma. In January 1935, Zhou Enlai was at a party conference in Zunyi, in Guizhou, and in the course of the conference he took Mao's part and thus began the firm alliance of these two revolutionary figures. In spite of clear and inevitable differences between them (which never, however, entered the public domain), they were completely complementary: Mao intransigent and theoretical and Zhou moderate and practical. Their partnership has indeed been adjudged one of the factors which led to the success of the revolution. After the takeover of power, particularly during the years of the cultural revolution, the difficult task of Zhou Enlai was to hold together the complex structure of government and in this he succeeded.

Manchukuo and the autonomous administration established by the Japanese in Inner Mongolia.

It was all the purest sham. Militarily, Wang's government was wholly dependent on Japan. Politically it could not take measures of which the Japanese army disapproved, while internationally, after the outbreak of the Pacific war it was recognized only by Germany and her Axis allies. The puppet Nanking government had no jurisdiction over North China, where the Japanese maintained a provisional government in Peking, staffed by discredited old politicians, longtime pensioners of the Japanese army. The reality was that in North China the Japanese were now faced with an active and spreading guerrilla resistance, led, armed and trained by the Chinese communist party in Yenan. The war might have become one of stalemate in the territories to the east of the Yangtze gorges; it had flared into violent action in the plains and the mountains of North China, seriously menacing Japanese plans.

By the time the Japanese invasion started, the Yenan communists, as has been already stated, had officially recognized the supremacy of the Nanking government, and their forces, the renamed 8th Route Army, were already in the field. The communists moved into the province of Shanxi just in time to oppose the Japanese advance into that province from the north. With no answer to Japanese air power, the 8th Route Army reverted to more familiar fighting methods – guerrilla warfare – and withdrew into the wild and difficult mountain country lying between the provinces of Shanxi and Hebei. Part of the army withdrew to similar country in west Shanxi, along the eastern bank of the Yellow River, thus protecting their base at Yenan. These dispositions placed the communist forces on the flank of the Japanese, both in Shanxi and, more important, in Hebei. The Peking-Wuhan railroad which runs south to the Yellow River and beyond along the base of the Taihang mountains, which divide Shanxi from Hebei, was the line along which the Japanese advanced to invade the central provinces. It was a *sine qua non* of Japanese strategy to take and hold all the cities along this line and keep the railroad open. The activity of the communist guerrillas was largely directed to cutting it, and causing maximum disruption of the Japanese lines of communication.

In the mountainous region between Shanxi and Hebei, the communists also organized a liberated zone from which they soon controlled the northern mountains of the two provinces, along which the Great Wall ran and through which opened the passes connecting the Inner Mongolian steppe and the North China plain. From these strongholds, from which the Japanese never succeeded in dislodging them, the communist guerrillas infiltrated into the densely populated plain of Hebei, a continual source of danger to Japanese communications with the south.

The struggle, which continued for eight years until the Japanese surrender, was as much political as military. The Japanese wished to exploit the resources of Hebei to maintain their forces in China; to do so they needed the peaceful submission of the population, and even some measure of collaboration. For years the Chinese peasantry and country townsmen of Hebei had suffered from the oppression of warlords and, at best, indifference of the Guomindang officials who, in their turn, had been ousted by hirelings of the Japanese. These people were basically apolitical, wishing a plague on both houses. The Japanese had therefore an apparently easy task to pacify and rule this apathetic population. But the Japanese had their own traditions of government, which at that period were those of a tightly controlled police state. Subjects must obey the letter of whatever law was laid down from above; disobedience was severely punished. The military had overriding powers, the police were there to enforce them. This was not the kind of government, good or bad, to which the Chinese had ever been accustomed. To them the law was a remote, official prerogative to be avoided at all costs, and if it was inevitably enforced, there were usually ways and means: bribery, nepotism or other forms of favouritism, to evade its worst consequences. The military had for centuries been a despised and feared class of licensed ruffians, not, in times of peace, conspicuous, for they were few. The Chinese were accustomed to easy-going ways; taxes had to be paid, if it was impossible to evade them; the landlord with his armed bullies was a more dreaded menace than any official, and only the combination of these two was really effective in obtaining the obedience and submission of a populace who still cherished the Confucian doctrine which gave the oppressed the right to rebel. The Japanese seem to have understood very little about the Chinese mentality. Those Japanese who knew something of the Chinese way of thinking, long-serving consular officials in China, had no influence in the councils of the ruling military command.

At first, the communist guerrillas were viewed with suspicion. They were not natives of the province; their speech was unfamiliar; there had been no active communist movement in North China except among the students of the universities in the great cities, people quite remote from the countryfolk. The communists tried to rouse the peasantry to a sense of patriotism and resistance, but at first with only modest success. They need hardly have worried; the Japanese did their work for them.

Heavy taxes were imposed; police control was ubiquitous, and while the Japanese concentrated on guarding the cities and their lines of communications, they entrusted the control of the countryside to a specially raised Chinese militia. This force, recruited from disbanded soldiers or other out-of-work, ne'er-do-well, floating elements of the population, and low in morale, reacted towards the people with the utmost brutality.

When the peasants refused to pay new taxes, or caused trouble of any kind, the Japanese, or the puppet forces, came to the village, fined the peasants ruinous sums of money, or burned down their houses. Soon there were thousands of deprived peasants roaming the countryside. These were ready-made recruits for the communist guerrillas. Applying Mao's maxims for guerrilla war, the 8th Route Army was soon making thousands of converts, and converting them either into regular members of the guerrilla army or into a secret militia which, while remaining ostensibly peasants, provided the communist forces with information, shelter, food, and supplies.

Chinese troops on the march during the war against Japan. Even though the communists and nationalists were fighting together against the common enemy, it was really the guerrilla tactics which the communists had adopted in order to escape Chiang Kaishek's "extermination campaigns" which held up the advance of the much stronger and better equipped Japanese army.

The history of the guerrilla war in North and Central China is long and complex; it suffices here to say that the communists gradually gained control, first by winning the support of the people, which soon was almost absolute, and then by extending the "liberated areas" at the expense of the "grey areas," that is those areas where the communists were not in complete control and where they carried out guerrilla warfare. By the end of the war the Japanese forces held little more than the cities and the railroads.

In March 1945, towards the end of the war, it was estimated that of the 914 Chinese counties (*xian*) which were in the Japanese-occupied zone, 678 were under effective communist control. In July, there were 19 liberated areas which between them had more than 100 million inhabitants. The communist forces had grown to 328,000 in the North, with a further 150,000 in the Central provinces; and even in the South, which at first had not seen much active communist resistance, there were now 27,000 guerrillas operating, that is to say, only 3,000 short of the total of the Communist forces which at the end of the Long March had arrived ten years earlier in Yenan.

It was this immense expansion of their forces and of the popular support which it represented, that changed the whole prospect for the communist party in China. Without the Japanese invasion, their struggle for power, or even for survival, might have taken many more years and a different course before it won through. The assumption of leadership in the real resistance to the invader was the basis of the vast background of support, or at least, tolerance which the party won and developed when, finally, the war came to an end. The guerrilla war against Japan was the true foundation of the Chinese People's Republic.

Meanwhile the alliance between the Guomindang and the communist party, enshrined in the agreement of Xi'an, had worn thin, in fact to all intents and purposes had ceased to operate. At first, the growth of the communist guerrilla war did not greatly alarm the Chongqing regime; it was thought most unlikely that the communist forces could be a match for the Japanese army; the concept of liberated and grey areas had not been foreseen, much less understood, by professional soldiers such as Chiang and his commanders who had been taught to look upon guerrillas as bandits.

Chiang simply waited for the inevitable clash between Japan and the USA. But early in 1941, before Pearl Harbor, an event occurred which gravely increased the distrust and deepened the rift between the two parties. The communist party had raised a new guerrilla army operating in the southern provinces, at that time mainly in the mountainous territory of that part of the province of Anhui which lies south of the Yangtze. There is some uncertainty whether the creation of this force, the New 4th Army, had ever been specifically authorized by the national high command, or whether it was created as a natural consequence of the presence of communist nuclei in a region neither completely occupied by the Japanese nor effectively defended by the regular nationalist army. In any case Chiang ordered that the new army should evacuate southern Anhui, cross the Yangtze (in itself a

An armoured car at the head of a Japanese convoy of motor lorries, reequipped with special wheels enabling them to be run on railroad track in the advance towards Canton (March 1941).

hazardous operation when the river was patrolled by Japanese warships) and engage in operations to the north of the Yangtze valley. In other words, Chiang wanted no communist competition for the allegiance of a province very close to Nanking, his former capital. He wanted the New 4th Army far away, in less favourable territory, where their influence on the population might be less, and the dangers of Japanese opposition greater.

The new force obeyed this order, or at least was halfway to doing so when, assembled on the banks of the Yangtze, with part of the army already across, the troops were treacherously attacked by Guomindang forces, who destroyed the army headquarters, killing all the staff officers. Nevertheless a large part of the army escaped across the river and thenceforward operated in the Dabie Shan mountains, between Hubei and Henan provinces. This outrage created a great stir; it was reported abroad and brought severe criticism of the Chongqing government, which was now highly sensitive, above all to American reproof. Chiang had to issue a "face saving" declaration condemning the officers in charge of the attack on the New 4th Army, declaring that it was due to misinterpreted orders, etc., etc. No one believed a word of it, but in China such statements are considered more an apology for wrongdoing than an attempt to make excuses. The Chinese communist party decided, wisely, to accept these explanations, at least officially. It was no coincidence that the communist supply routes now had to pass through territory controlled by the Guomindang, since Japan had occupied all the seaports of China. Up till the fall of Burma early in 1942 these supplies reached China, in short measure, and to a limited extent, solely by way of the "Burma Road," a modern motor road, still unsealed, which had been constructed from Chongqing through Guizhou to Yunnan and Burma in the decade before the war began. The distance was more than 1000 kilometers, and almost the entire route passes over high mountain ranges and crosses mighty rivers. Everything, especially everything needed by an army at war, had to come into China by this road, after passing through Burma from the oceans. It was an inadequate supply line, but it was the only one, except from the far northwest, the western end of Mongolia, and beyond that Soviet Siberia. In the earlier years of the war the Soviets did send considerable quantities of needed supplies and weapons to China by this route, and not only, or even mainly, to the communist forces. The sinuosities of relations between the Chinese communists and their Soviet Russian comrades are complex and still often obscure; that they were rarely clear-cut and straightforward can now be observed.

Chiang may have had to deny any responsibility for the attack on the New 4th Army, but before long he found a more effective way of hampering the expansion of the communist guerrilla war. He deployed many of his best troops in strategic positions south of Yenan and southern Shanxi, from which they could blockade the communist-controlled former occupied zones or newly liberated areas, and prevent supplies getting through. Even medicines and sanitary equipment contributed by the general public in America and Britain never reached Yenan. This policy of breaking the spirit, if not the actual word, of the Xi'an

Chinese peasants armed with spears in support of the Red front. The popular support which the communists first won for themselves during the Long March and kept throughout the war with Japan was the basis upon which it was afterwards possible to found the People's Republic.

agreement was sternly criticized in the West, and convinced the communists that Chiang was still their dedicated enemy. Which was true; the Generalissimo was quoted as saying, "The Japanese are a disease of the skin, the communists are a disease of the heart." Mao Zedong and his colleagues had no more belief in the possibility of really working in harmony with Chiang than had the Generalissimo himself. The war dragged slowly to its end; the Japanese, now suffering severe hindrance in their sea communications with the countries they had conquered in Southeast Asia, due to the dominance of the US navy, sought to open a land route by driving down through South China to the Indo-Chinese border, linking up the half finished railroads of this region and thus securing a safe line of communications with Malaya and beyond. Their attempts to take Changsha from the north were twice beaten back – the only real success which the Guomindang won in South China – but ultimately they took the city. They made efforts to drive inland from Canton to destroy the air bases which the US had set up in Jiangxi and Guizhou provinces. The Japanese occupied Guilin, capital of Jiangxi, but they did not get much farther into the mountainous region of Southwest China, and they never had the time to organize the land route to Southeast Asia, nor build the necessary railroad.

In the North, the continuing expansion of communist power and control had now forced the limited Japanese forces onto the defensive. Gone was the hope of pacifying Hebei; gone, too, any prospect of driving the communists out of these provinces. The Japanese hung on to the big cities, trying to keep the railroads running, and constantly confronted with mounting difficulties. The leaders of the commune of the small city of Xuxian, some 20 kilometers north of the large city of Baoding, on the Peking-Wuhan railroad, recalled in 1958, that in the years of the "War of Resistance" as they called it their city and district, in which they had been the local guerrilla leaders, had been "liberated 22 times." That is, on 22 occasions the Japanese had driven into the district, killing, burning and looting and then withdrawn. On each occasion the communists were back next day.

Neither the communists nor the Guomindang government ever expected that Japan would sue for peace, much less surrender, until such time as the Allied forces had landed in Japan and fought their way to Tokyo. To mount such an invasion, control of the northern half of the Chinese coast was essential. The only suitable port as a base for such a landing was Shanghai. Therefore the Americans according to communist-Guomindang thinking would land at or near Shanghai, take the city and then advance north across the Yangtze to Tianjin. In other words the great American army would move into the war zone where the communist forces operated, and the Guomindang would be left with the easy task of reoccupying the Yangtze valley and the South, where an isolated Japanese army could not long hold out. The Guomindang would be back in Nanking, having suffered only small losses and gained much glory. The communists on the other hand would be in the thick of a hard-fought campaign, in which the Americans would expect them to participate to the full, and the Japanese would

Above: the famous occasion on which Mao and Chiang drank each other's health to celebrate the victory against Japan. Between 12 August and 10 October 1945 a delegation headed by Mao Zedong and Zhou Enlai met with Chiang Kaishek at Chongqing in order to discuss the possibility of communist participation in the government. However, the talks broke down when the Guomindang insisted upon the dissolution of all communist armed forces.

Below: US general George G. Marshall with Mao Zedong and Zhou Enlai in Yenan. His attempt at mediation between the communists and the Guomindang was unsuccessful. The presence of Soviet troops in Manchuria had given the communists several advantages and they were also in possession of a good part of the armaments which the Japanese had abandoned in China. In summer 1946, however, Chiang Kaishek decided that the moment had arrived for the extermination of the communists. Thus began the civil war.

make even more determined efforts to exterminate the danger behind their lines.

What would have happened if this scenario had been played out in real life is one of the great "Ifs" of history. What did happen was that in August 1945 the atomic bomb was dropped on Hiroshima. The Japanese emperor and his advisors, if not the hardliners of the military dominated cabinet, realized that all was over. Within days, obeying the order of the emperor, broadcast by radio, the Japanese forces everywhere laid down their arms and surrendered to the respective Allied commands.

Overnight the whole Chinese political and military situation was transformed. For Chiang, it was the realization of a lifetime's hopes; America had won the war for him, and he would now enjoy the fruits of that victory. Unfortunately for him there was a twist to this situation. The communists had not been caught in the pincers of a great military confrontation as they would have been had history taken a different turn, on the contrary they were now relieved of any pressure or danger; they surrounded the Japanese-held cities, and were soon claiming to be the "Allied commanders" to whom the Japanese garrisons should surrender.

He had one supreme advantage, however, and he at once used it. When the Pacific war suddenly made China the ally of the USA and Great Britain, Chiang had been nominated as commander-in-chief of the China war area, as was natural and inevitable. He had in fact sent troops to Burma to assist, unavailingly as it happened, in its defense when the Japanese invaded. He now asserted his right as commander-in-chief, China area, to order the US Air Force in China to transport his troops to the cities of North China held by the Japanese, and he ordered the Japanese commanders to surrender to no one before his troops arrived. These orders were obeyed.

These events were the root and real cause of the civil war which was to follow and end with the victory of the communist party. In Chongqing, political manouevres to form some kind of coalition government and unite the two regions, now so clearly defined as communist- and non-communist-ruled, all failed on the mutual distrust felt between both parties. Under the protection of the American embassy, Mao Zedong visited Chongqing and conferred with Chiang Kaishek. To no purpose.

Meanwhile, in the North the situation rapidly deteriorated. The Japanese were sent home; the Guomindang occupied the cities, and at once found themselves in an exactly similar situation to the Japanese garrisons they had replaced. The communist forces, in complete control of the country areas, allowed no railroad communication to the cities, claiming that they, by right of victory, should have occupied these cities. When the Japanese surrendered, their Chinese puppet troops had immediately sought service with the Guomindang, fearing their reception at the hands of the communists. The Guomindang commanders accepted these men as a useful auxiliary force and by doing so at once forfeited any support that might have been forthcoming from the peasantry of North China. The specter of civil war loomed ominously closer. No one wanted it, everyone feared it, and no one could prevent it.

THE LAST CIVIL WAR

Opposite: a popular poster honouring the young guerrilla fighter, Liu Hulan, a heroine of the civil war who acted as a courier between the various groups of partisans in her district. This young woman has become a figure of folklore in China and she is often held up as an example to young people.

Above: another poster showing the monument to Liu Hulan with Mao's words: "Great in life but glorious in death."

The Japanese surrender was at first welcomed on a wave of national euphoria. The war was over; let it not be followed by a civil war. That was the overwhelming feeling of the vast mass of the Chinese people. For a brief period it seemed that they might have their wish.

On 10 October 1945, the anniversary of the 1911 revolution, and then celebrated as China's national day, an agreement was signed in Chongqing between the Guomindang government and the communist party. It guaranteed the legality of all parties; the release of political prisoners; the disbanding of the secret police; and the convening of a people's consultative conference to consider the form of a future constitution. Both sides pledged themselves to prevent the outbreak of civil war. It was the American transportation of Chiang's forces to the North which destroyed whatever slight hope there may have been that this agreement could solve China's crisis.

Seeing the way things were going the US government sent General George Marshall, who many years earlier had served in China as commander of the Legation guards at Tianjin, to mediate between the two parties, with the idea of forming a coalition government. He did succeed, after protracted sessions with Zhou Enlai in Nanking, in negotiating a truce, signed in January 1946. The truce was at its weakest in one vital area: Manchuria. When it was only a matter of time before the Japanese surrendered, the Russians had invaded "Manchukuo," meeting with almost no opposition from the Japanese. The Japanese army was disarmed and the emperor Pu Yi deported to Siberia (he was subsequently handed over to the Chinese communist regime in 1950, "re-educated" for nine years, and then set free, to become a minor official in the department of agriculture in Peking).

The Russians, now masters of Manchuria, proceeded to dismantle its industries and ship whole plants and machinery to Siberia. They agreed to withdraw from the country by December 1945, but at the request of the Nanking government, they delayed their evacuation until May 1946. Chiang needed time to get his own forces into the country and to occupy the major cities before they fell into communist hands.

The moment the Japanese in Manchuria surrendered to the Russians, large contingents of the communist regular forces started moving from the neighbouring province of Hebei into the Manchurian countryside where within a short time they had recruited a large following among the peasants and evolved the familiar pattern for protracted guerrilla war – but not against the Russians. The Russians withdrew, handing over the cities of southern Manchuria, as far north as Jilin, to the nationalist troops who were flown in to occupy them. But the most northerly province of Heilongjiang, bordering on Siberia, was never occupied by Guomindang troops, although some

Guomindang officials were flown into Harbin. When the Russians went, the whole province was taken over by the communists.

It may well be that the Russians expected, and hoped, that the communist party and its army would now be transferred to this remote but safe base, abandoning the "liberated areas" within the Great Wall. Then the Russians could have created a new, smaller, but secure "Manchukuo" for the communists in Heilongjiang, which Chiang would have had to accept. The Chinese communist party would be reduced to the position of a small satellite state such as the Russians were at this very time setting up in Eastern Europe. It did not happen because Mao and the communist leadership made no move, then or later, to transfer to Heilongjiang: instead they actively prepared for an all-out civil war in China itself. Chiang gave the signal: on 17 June 1946, he ordered the communist army to withdraw from a large number of liberated areas, stretching from Manchuria down to the Yangtze. Perhaps he hoped they would in fact retire into Heilongjiang. As they did not move, he ordered his forces to attack the communist liberated areas in Central China, a direct threat to communications between the Yangtze valley and the North. The last civil war had begun.

"When the enemy advance, we retire; when he stops, we harrass him; when he retires, we attack him." The famous maxims of Mao for waging guerrilla war in the mountains of Jiangxi 16 years earlier were now put into effect on a vast scale, covering the whole of China. Chiang's armies were allowed what seemed spectacular successes. They advanced into Central China; they even took Yenan in March 1947. They occupied the cities of South Manchuria, and Jehol and Kalgan in Inner Mongolia. Chiang had disregarded the advice of the American general Wedemeyer, not to attempt the occupation of Manchuria until he had consolidated his power in China itself. Chiang was convinced that if he left Manchuria alone, it would be seized by the communists and then be too strong to conquer.

But while the Guomindang armies were achieving their spectacular successes, the Communist forces had been biding their time and now emerged to harry the nationalist armies, strung out along stretched lines of communication from the Yangtze to Southern Manchuria. By the end of the summer the whole of North China and also Manchuria were in the grip of guerrilla war.

The communist forces cut the railroads along which Chiang's armies had advanced; they did not merely occupy the important nodal points or blow up part of the track. In Manchuria particularly, they tore up the rails, then heated them red-hot on fires made from the wooden sleepers, twisted the long rails into corkscrew shapes, and carried them off to be stored away. The stripped roadbed was then often ploughed up. To bring a railroad which had suffered this treatment back to working order was impossible under the existing conditions. In a few months the Guomindang forces had lost almost all they had seemed to have won. The railroads to the North, through Shandong, Henan and Hebei, were either blotted out, cut or only usable on short stretches, and even then were unsafe.

The Red armada crosses the Yangtze on "junks of fortune" under heavy fire from the artillery of Chiang Kaishek, in the middle of April 1949. This was during the last phase of the civil war. Soon after, the communists occupied Nanking and, in May, Shanghai. On 1 October 1949, the People's Republic of China was proclaimed in Peking. The attempt at the beginning of the year by Li Zongren and the other nationalist leaders to form a government with the communists had failed, mainly because of Chiang Kaishek's

The bold advances into Shaanxi, to Yenan, and into Shandong had to be abandoned. In Manchuria, by the end of 1947, the nationalist armies were confined to the major cities. By the middle of 1948 the communist forces, now renamed the People's Liberation Army, numbered 2,800,000 men, nearly three times their strength of a year before. They were well armed with weapons taken from Japanese dumps in the Manchurian countryside and those captured from the defeated nationalists. Chiang's forces meantime had shrunk from 4,000,000 to 3,600,000.

The dwindling manpower of their armed forces was only one source of headache for the Guomindang; there were others even more worrying such as the ebbing away of public support, the low morale of troops and officials, and, not least, raging inflation. Officials had now to be paid, when they were paid, that is, with sacks of flour: so were university professors. Money fell in value by the month, then from day to day and finally by the hour; purchasers in shops were asked to wait while the assistant ran out to learn the latest rate. In August 1948, Chiang introduced a new currency, the gold *yuan* at four to the US dollar, and compelled the populace, under threat of summary execution if they did not comply, to exchange their savings of silver or gold and also their old currency into the new medium. By the end of the year the *yuan* was valued – if one may use the term – at four million to the US dollar.

Inflation eroded wages and destroyed wealth, but nepotism and corruption made matters worse. The economy was controlled by the "Four Families," the Chiang, Soong, Kung and Chen, the last counting the much hated Chen Lifu, head of the secret police, among its members. It was seen that between them they were making huge profits out of the exchange rate, passing through the banks which were alone permitted to handle foreign funds, and which were in effect owned by the Four Families. They had declared all Japanese property confiscate to the Chinese state. In this was included all the property which the Japanese had seized from Chinese owners, who now received no compensation for their losses. The Four Families sold off the "enemy property" at enormous profit having paid nothing at all for it.

The Chinese lived in a world in which every day brought new tales of corruption, nepotism, favouritism and oppression by the regime in power. They were also being made aware, through increasingly verifiable rumours, that the communists, in their ever-growing liberated areas, were not prone to these failings. Even men of property began to feel that they might well be better off under the communists than under the Guomindang. It was this canker at the heart of the Nanking government which truly caused its fall.

After the Japanese War was over most educated Chinese had two major fears; the first, that it would be followed by civil war, which in turn might mean either red revolution, destructive, cruel and ruthless; or extreme right-wing reaction, which would be nearly as bad, meaning oppression, secret police, informers, suspicion and the general spread of fear and loss of confidence. These people pinned their hopes on conciliation, an agreement

absolute refusal to leave the political scene.

to divide, or to disagree, on a coalition, on any alternative to civil war – and they were disappointed. The dreaded civil war came; but, by the end of 1947, it was already clear that what everyone had feared would be a long drawn-out undecisive struggle was going to be before long a clear-cut victory, and, with increasing certainty, the victory of the seemingly weaker side. The communist armies had no air force; Chiang had a new one equipped with American aircraft; the communists had no artillery other than what they could capture; Chiang's army was being lavishly rearmed by the USA; the communists had no navy; the Guomindang had already received several warships from America, who ruled the seas, and thus enabled Chiang to transport his army by sea when the railroads were closed to him. Taking these facts into consideration most foreign observers believed that Chiang must win, even if not so quickly as he had hoped. But they were quite wrong: seen from Shanghai or even Peking (less credulous) was one thing; seen from the countryside or the small city it was quite another. The low morale of even the best of Chiang's troops was evident; the corruption of the system was all too apparent, the incompetence of the officers clearly manifest, and the virtually total lack of popular support quite unconcealed. The Chinese who saw and knew these things came to the big cities with forebodings and warnings; few foreign observers came into contact with such people who had a widespread audience in the mass of the city people.

Consequently, late in 1946, while the American military advisers were mainly inclined to count heads and weapons, the Chinese people were beginning to think that Chiang had lost the "Mandate of Heaven," and was therefore doomed. By mid-summer 1947, there was much to make them sure. A sudden communist counterstroke shattered the Guomindang forces in Central China and led to the establishment of a large communist army in a new base in the Dabashan mountains which divide the world of rice to the south from the corn growing areas to the north, and also the Yangtze province of Hubei from the Yellow River province of Henan. The communists were now in a position to raid and to cut the second great railroad from south to north, the Peking–Wuhan railway. The Guomindang now held two detached large regions of China: the Yangtze valley and all the area to the south (except for small liberated area enclaves) and the major cities of Hebei, Jehol and South Manchuria, which were more or less surrounded by a communist-held countryside, and could only communicate with the southern area by air or by sea.

Chiang decided that his hopes of winning the war now turned, first, on the complete pacification of Manchuria, and then in trapping the communist forces in North China in a pincer between his northern armies and those based on the Yangtze valley. But by spring 1948 it was the communists who made the first decisive move. In April 1948, the People's Liberation Army overran Henan province, thus ending Guomindang rule in the Yellow River valley; and they had succeeded in cutting the Peking–Wuhan railroad. In September they took the city of Jinan, capital of Shandong province. The fact that this was the first major city which the communists not only captured but held

Above: in Shanghai, 1948, in the middle of the civil war, citizens demonstrate against the high cost of living, including raging inflation.

Opposite: between 1937 and 1949, China was hit by inflation of gigantic proportions. In the table (above), we can see how the value of 100 yuan decreased during this period: it could buy a pair of oxen in 1937 and by 1949, only a sheet of paper!
Below: a crowd gathers at the entrance to a Shanghai bank which had promised ten grams of silver in return for 30 kilos of paper money.

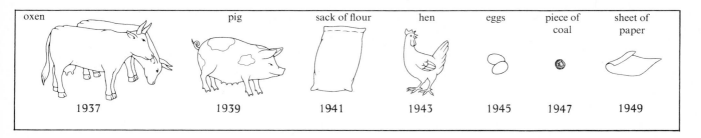

oxen	pig	sack of flour	hen	eggs	piece of coal	sheet of paper
1937	1939	1941	1943	1945	1947	1949

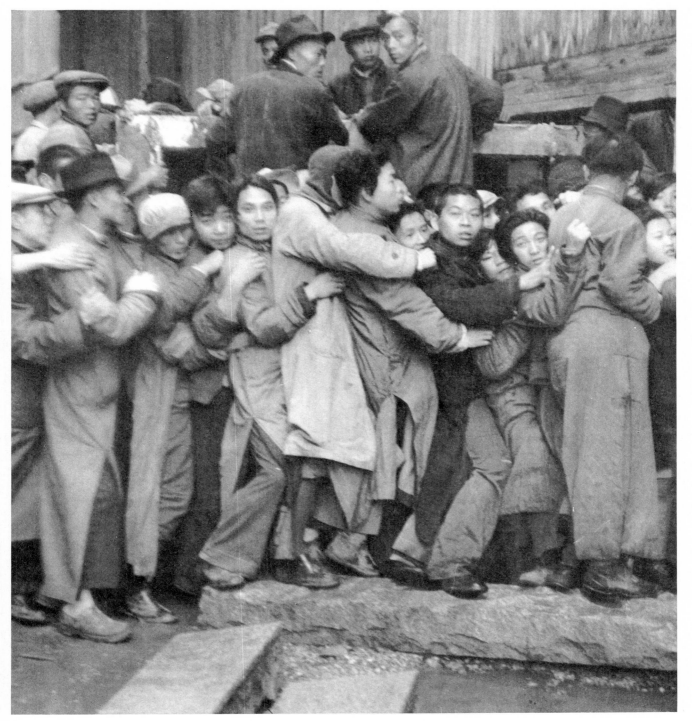

on to, reinforced their confidence that Chiang was no longer in a position to offer counter-retaliatory action.

It was during the summer of 1948 that awareness of the crisis, both military and political, spread widely. In Peking there was an almost open subversive plot, embracing elements of the army, political wings of the Guomindang, old anti-Nationalist adversaries of Chiang and even the supporters of the former Qing dynasty, which was aimed at forcing Chiang to retire so that some more flexible politician might yet be able to negotiate a settlement which would save the country from outright red revolution. It failed, and Chiang hastened to garrison the city with a man whom he had not previously trusted, a northern general who had risen to prominence in opposition to the Japanese in Inner Mongolia. Fu zoyi did not love Chiang, nor did Chiang like him, but the hope was that a northerner could rally support to defend the northern capital.

It was also known in Peking that summer that the communist party had held a very important meeting at what was now its temporary capital, the railroad junction town of Shijiajuang, some 320 kilometers south of Peking. It is believed that on this occasion Stalin, through Chinese leaders who had recently been in Moscow, urged the party not to give up the tactics of guerrilla war and pass to a major offensive, for which, it was said, the communist forces were not yet ready. Stalin's real aim was to decrease the risk of American intervention on a massive scale in favour of a desperate Chiang Kaishek. This advice was turned down by the Chinese communist party; either the party did not fear that the USA would intervene (rightly as it turned out) or did not care one way or the other. The communist leaders were determined to pass to an all-out offensive and try to win the war swiftly, before American opinion could be alerted and mobilized to intervene.

Chiang moved his best troops by sea to the coast of South Manchuria, where they landed and moved towards Shenyang, capital of Liaoning province. Chiang had concentrated about half a million men for the defense of this great city, a vital rail junction and air base, without which he could neither hold nor hope to reconquer the lost countryside of Manchuria. Early in September, Chiang's army was opposed near Jinzhou, in South Manchuria, not far from the Great Wall, by a formidable communist force, commanded by Lin Biao (in later years to be accused and disgraced for having plotted against Mao). Lin Biao was a brilliant general, a veteran of the original communist Red Army which had mutinied at Nanchang in 1927, of the Jiangxi wars and the Long March.

In a battle which Western military critics have described as tactically as accomplished as any of Napoleon's great victories, in 72 hours Lin Biao's troops totally defeated the Guomindang's army of élite troops (American-trained and armed, veterans of the Burma campaign against the Japanese), and destroyed it as a fighting force. Then turning on Shenyang, from which the great garrison had lumbered forth to support its hoped-for deliverers, he also destroyed this force. On 31 October Shenyang was captured and more than a quarter of a million prisoners taken. Changchun to the north, the old capital of Japanese

Above: soldiers from Chiang's nationalist forces give themselves up to the communist army. The fall of Shenyang, vitally important as a supply center, reduced the possibility of further resistance on the part of the nationalists.

Below: an assault by communist troops near the Great Wall in the closing stages of the civil war.

Manchukuo, was the next to fall. Like Shenyang, its defenders had been supplied by air through the summer. This operation could not have continued in the bitter Manchurian winter; capitulation was inevitable. The communists had destroyed the Guomindang in Manchuria, and the flower of Chiang's army. So little did they now fear any recovery of morale among the defeated soldiery of Chiang, that the Communists turned their hordes of prisoners loose, disarmed, to stream home across China, spreading wherever they went the evidence of their own defeat and the magnanimity of their conquerors. It was a superb exercise in public relations, and it paid off handsomely.

Manchuria was lost; inflation had got completely out of hand: the gold *yuan* had fallen to one-millionth of its value since it was introduced in the previous August, three months before the fall of Shengyang. Public confidence in the survival of the Nanking regime was ebbing fast. Yet cool heads in Washington knew that in 1948 there was no possibility of reenlisting a huge American army to wage an unpredictable war in China, which could well involve the Soviet Union. Chiang, however, did not believe the Americans would desert him: he had always counted on America to defeat Japan in the end; so he now counted on America to save him from the communists. The USA did indeed send him all the weaponry his troops could use. When it became clear, late in October 1948, that the communist armies, leaving only a holding force before Peking, were shifting the main body of their troops south through Shandong to strike at Nanking, Chiang could only mobilize what was left of his armies for a desperate defense of the heartland of his regime.

The country south of Shandong, the province of Anhui, is neither mountain nor open plain: a land of low hills and marshy lowlands, with rivers which have unstable and variable courses. So different from the flat plain of North China, and the mountain and valley country of South and West China, this region, where both rice and wheat are grown, and where one culture merges into another, has been since early Chinese history a cockpit of war. It is through here that the northern conqueror must pass to reach the South, and the southern aspirant for power must advance to overthrow his northern foe. Here, from time immemorial, rival armies have fought to decide the destiny of China; and it was here, that these two rival armies met in an encounter which was to decide the fate of modern China.

The battle of Huai Hai takes its name from the Huai river which meanders across the country to the marshy coast. At Xuzhou, the Long Hai railroad, which runs westwards from the coast to Henan, crosses the Peking–Nanking railroad, connecting the North and South. Xuzhou was therefore of great strategic importance.

The battle of Huai Hai, so little noticed at the time in the West, was by any standard one of the world's greatest military encounters. About 600,000 men were engaged on each side, more than a million combatants in all. The communists had as yet no aircraft; the Guomindang forces had adequate air cover and also a preponderance in artillery, although not the absolute superiority they had at the beginning of the civil war. The communist victories at Shenyang and Changchun had provided rich military spoils.

Chiang lost the battle, and it was above all the inflexible tactics which he imposed upon his generals that contributed to his defeat. Unsure of their morale, and consequently sceptical of their ability to take risks, he ordered that any commander abandoning his position would be executed. Even if surrounded, units must fight to the death. One result was that commanders hesitated to come to the help of hard-pressed comrades since they might be condemned for giving up their own positions. The communist forces on the other hand, primarily trained in guerrilla warfare, were above all flexible; they could outmarch their opponents with ease, were ready to change objectives, advance or withdraw in accordance with the tactical situation of the moment. These advantages were shown to outweigh their inferior artillery power and lack of aircraft.

The Guomindang army fought from static positions until, unit by unit, it was surrounded by the swift-moving communist troops. When further resistance was plainly hopeless, the Guomindang forces surrendered, in companies, battalions and finally whole divisions. The field commander in chief, surrounded and cut off from his army and its supreme commander, Chiang Kaishek, laid down his arms. The Guomindang army had virtually ceased to exist; more than two-thirds of its losses consisted of prisoners.

The battle of Huai Hai decided the war. On 31 January 1949, Peking capitulated to the army of Lin Biao, now in command in the North. No Guomindang forces remained in the field between the Russian frontier on the Amur and the remnants of the defeated army from Xuzhou, now withdrawn across the Yangtze for the defense of Nanking. Chiang thought it wise at this moment to go on leave, handing over the conduct of the government to the vice-president, Li Zongren, a former Guangxi general who had always mistrusted his leader, and, covertly or openly, had opposed Chiang's dominant position. Perhaps for that reason he was, at this critical moment, more acceptable to the politicians and remaining influential generals in Nanking. The one hope of the Guomindang was some sort of compromise with the now superior power of the communist party. Some hoped for a division of China into North and South, remembering some historical examples, but choosing to forget their consequences. The partition of historic united countries into communist and anticommunist moieties was at that time not uncommon: there was East and West Germany; North and South Korea, and very soon, North and South Vietnam – almost already a reality. If this proposal was ever put forward seriously, it is certain that the communist leadership would have rejected it outright. On the other hand an accommodation which fell short of partition, or implied a reformed Guomindang subordinate to the communist party, was seen as having some merits.

Having advanced as far as the north bank of the Yangtze, the People's Liberation Army halted (it was the end of December), and for the next three months there was (except for the continuing siege of Peking) a pause in the war. Negotiations

The troops of the People's Army of Liberation enter the towns and cities which have been abandoned by the Guomindang forces. Tianjin was liberated on 15 January 1949, Peking (opposite above) on 31 January, Nanking on 29 April and Shanghai on 27 May (photograph below). In March of the same year, with victory for him and for his party virtually assured, Mao Zedong said: "Victory throughout the country is only the first step in a long march of 10,000 *li*." Chiang Kaishek, the other nationalist leaders and the part of the army which had remained faithful to him, found refuge on the island of Taiwan, declaring that it was the real, true republic of China. It was recognized as such by the United States and some European and South American countries. On the other hand the Soviet Union, the Eastern bloc countries, India, Pakistan and, in 1950, Great Britain, recognized the Peking government.

were opened, mediators from both sides passed to and fro.

The nationalist leaders realized quite clearly that the time had come for Chiang to disappear from the political scene. One possibility was exile. The generals and politicians most closely associated with him would also have to go. Once the figures most obnoxious to the communists would have left the scene, the Nanking government would still have a bargaining point to set against communist demands: Nanking was the legitimate recognized government of China, holder of a permanent seat at the United Nations Security Council, the only regime recognized by the nations of the world, including Soviet Russia, whose ambassador remained accredited to the Guomindang government even after it had been driven from Nanking. This meant that if the existing government could somehow be incorporated into a new government formed by a coalition between communists and nationalists, there could be no question as to its international recognition. What would emerge would simply be a reconstructed government accepted by the whole world. This was the temptation held out to the communist party; it was a real offer, as events were to prove. If Nanking was overthrown by force, there was no obligation on any foreign power to recognize a regime which had used that force to gain its objective.

The resulting negotiations were secret; that is to say, that while everyone knew they were taking place, no communiques were issued by either side, none of the issues at stake were disclosed, no public debate on the merits of this or that proposition was permitted. Therefore it is still far from certain just what was offered, or rejected. What is certain is that Chiang Kaishek soon realized that he was to be allowed no part in any bargaining.

He did not intend to make any such sacrifice. As in his sham retirement in 1927, he still retained the loyalty and the control of the major units of the army and the secret police. The communists made very sweeping demands: the Guomindang army would have to be disbanded or reorganized under communist command; the state system would be entirely overhauled and changed to suit the policies of the communist party. Moreover Chiang and other "war criminals" were to be brought to popular justice. It is quite likely that Li Zongren could not have delivered such terms even if he had accepted them. But he was not given the chance. Chiang took no risk; his secret police acted swiftly, Li Zongren was compelled to resign and leave Nanking, negotiations were broken off, and the war was resumed.

The communist armies therefore crossed the Yangtze in mid-April, and without great difficulty took Nanking. Shanghai was taken a month later, in May. Chiang still held Canton in the South and Chongqing in the far West, but neither of these cities were now likely to be safe refuges for a demoralized army and a host of disaffected politicians. Resistance of a kind continued, first, from Canton, then from Chongqing (cut off except by air) but it tended to melt away with the approach of the communist forces.

By the end of 1949, the Chinese communist party and its

armed forces, the People's Liberation Army, controlled the entire mainland of China, from Siberia to the Indo-China border. The nationalists still held two large islands, Taiwan, which had been restored to China under the Japanese surrender terms, and Hainan, off the coast of Guangdong province in the far South. Hainan was taken without difficulty early in 1950, but before that year was out events were to occur which made the capture of Taiwan by the communists impossible.

Meanwhile, on 1 October 1949 the People's Republic of China was proclaimed in Peking, which became once more the capital of China. The hope of a continuing recognized government had had to be abandoned: there were no negotiations, only submission was required. The dissident Guomindang politicians, who for some years had maintained open opposition to Chiang from the safety of the British Colony of Hong Kong, and the Democratic League, a liberal political party supported by intellectuals, which Chiang had banned (assassinating some of its leaders) after the Japanese surrender, now returned to Peking and were given a very minor role in the new government.

The Guomindang government, after Nanking fell, had moved to the island of Taiwan, followed by the bulk of the army. More than 1,000,000 people in all took refuge in Taiwan. There too, before long, with the fall of the last nationalist strongholds in western China, Chiang Kaishek resumed his post as head of the government, which he still claimed was the legitimate government of all China. The Republic of China, with its temporary capital at Taibei, ruled the island of Taiwan and a few small off-shore islands along the cost of the mainland province of Fujian. That is still the situation today. For, before the year 1950 was out, the outbreak of the Korean war induced President Truman to place Taiwan virtually under direct American protection, guarded by the US Air Force and the Seventh Fleet of the US Navy. This made any Chinese communist invasion of Taiwan impossible. The People's Liberation Army had no air force, no landing craft, and there was as yet no People's Liberation Navy. The Guomindang army on Taiwan was strong enough to put down any uprising among the native, disarmed Taiwanese Chinese.

The nationalist regime was thus able to find at last a safe refuge, under the protection of the USA, and with massive economic and financial aid, to build up over the years a prosperous and expanding economy, while retaining political power virtually exclusively in the hands of the old Guomindang leadership, backed up by an army of exiled mainland troops commanded by exiled mainland officers. There now existed "Two Chinas."

This is a situation which both sides hate and deplore, and which runs counter to the long tradition of the Chinese people and state. For many years it could be directly attributed to American intervention in what was still the Chinese civil war; more recently America has recognized the government at Peking, and ceased to accept Taibei as the government of a "Republic of China" though accepting it as a local regime. Neither Peking nor Taibei regard this as a viable policy: there have been many reports of secret or semisecret contacts

It is 1 October 1949. Mao Zedong, from the parapets of Tien An Men, the Gate of Heavenly Peace of the ancient Imperial Palace in Peking, proclaims the birth of the new régime. Chiang Kaishek, who had moved the seat of the national government from Nanking to Canton, soon left there to take refuge on the island of Taiwan under American protection. In his inaugural speech, Mao said: "Today, our China enters into the family of nations who love peace and freedom.... It will never again be despised! Let us work with all our strength to create a new life of peace and prosperity, to give the best possible living conditions to all the Chinese...."

Opposite: poster celebrating the constitution of the People's Republic of China.

between the two rival regimes, especially since the deaths of their respective leaders and old enemies, Mao Zedong in Peking and Chiang Kaishek in Taibei. Reunion may one day come about, and the new trend in China since the death of Mao may facilitate a settlement. It has not yet had that effect.

Russia, the communist states of Eastern Europe, and some of the new independent states of Asia: India, Pakistan and others, recognized the People's Republic of China as soon as it was proclaimed or very soon after. It was recognized by Great Britain in January 1950, but owing to disagreements about a consulate still maintained in Taiwan and other minor matters, the establishment of full diplomatic relations was delayed for many years, although relations on a *chargé d'affaires* level were immediately instituted. The USA, after some hesitation, refused recognition, and was followed in this attitude by the republics of South America and by some of the Western European states. Within a year or so the diplomatic world was split between nations who recognized Peking, and those which recognized Taibei. So it was to remain for more than 20 years, with few changes.

Mao Zedong had openly acknowledged that in respect of the "Cold War" quarrel, China "leans to one side," that is, supported Russia and other communist countries. He had, not long after the surrender of Peking, gone to Moscow, his first ever journey outside China, and concluded a treaty with the Soviet Union, which many thought very subservient to Russian policy. The USSR was given the right to use Dairen as a naval base, jointly with China; the former Russian railroad in North Manchuria was to be jointly managed, and there was to be mixed Soviet-Chinese enterprises to exploit the minerals of Xinjiang (Chinese Turkestan), a vast province of the far West in which Russian influence had long been important. The terms on which these enterprises operated were exceedingly favourable to the Soviet partner. The main purpose of the treaty was, apart from Russian help in restoring the devastated industries of Manchuria (which Russia had herself despoiled), to guard against any aggression by Japan "or any country allied to Japan." That was a devious way of just saying the USA.

It was certainly a widespread belief in China, held both by communists and noncommunists, that America would never tolerate a communist government of all China, and that hostile intervention was to be expected. There can be little doubt that Mao felt that he must yield to Russia for the time being at any rate, while China was still weak, so as to win Russian protection against a menacing and powerful USA.

It was clear that the communists disliked and feared America, and that the treaty they had concluded with the Soviet Union was founded on that fear. The Cold War atmosphere was deepening every month.

The USA extended full recognition, as that of the legitimate Republic of China, to Chiang's government in Taibei. The lines so drawn remained in force for many years, and were to be deepened and strengthened by the events of June 1950: the invasion of South Korea by the forces – Russian-trained and equipped – of the North Korean regime, set up by the Soviets

Opposite: Zhou Enlai in Moscow, signing the treaty of friendship and alliance with the Soviet Union on 14 February 1950. Stalin is standing behind him. Relations between the two communist parties began to sour in February 1956 (20th congress of the communist party of the USSR) but the ideological break between the Chinese and Soviet parties came at the beginning of the sixties, when the Chinese accused the Russians of revisionism. The Soviet Union withdrew its technicians and stopped all technical aid to China.

Below: Chinese troops crossing the Yalu river at the beginning of the Korean War (1950–53), shortly after the foundation of the People's Republic. China was dragged into this conflict by the conditions of the Cold War and was forced to supply men and equipment at a moment when all her energies should have been concentrated on the internal reconstruction of the country. At the end of the war, however, China was well paid for her part in it by regaining full control of Manchuria which had been previously divided with the USSR.

after the Japanese surrender, and communist in every respect.

The significance of the Korean war for the new regime in China was never fully realized by many Western observers. Firstly, and perhaps most importantly, was the fear that US intervention in support of the South Korean regime, set up under American sponsorship, would mean an invasion of Manchuria, and then of China itself. There is no doubt that very many Chinese of the educated class believed this would happen; the communists and their supporters feared it, and those who were anticommunist more or less looked forward to it. Secondly, the Chinese saw that, although they had not been consulted beforehand, the Soviet had put China in a dangerous position, and before long would expect China to render assistance to the North Koreans which Russia dared not openly give, for fear of a clash between American and Russian troops and the start of a new world war. So China was forced to act with strength, to secure the fidelity and confidence of her own people, and to assist Russia to extract herself from a dangerous collision course with the USA.

At first, it had seemed that the North Korean invaders would sweep all before them. Seoul, the capital, was taken, and the North Koreans drove on south until only the major port of Pusan remained in the hands of the South Koreans. Then, having obtained the support of the United Nations, at a meeting of the UN Security Council from which the Russians most ill-advisedly absented themselves, an United Nations army (at this stage almost completely composed of American forces) landed on the west coast of Korea, cut off the invaders from their base, and forced them into a rapid and costly retreat. Seoul was recaptured and the American forces, now strengthened with some contingents from Britain, Australia and other countries, advanced to the 38th Parallel, the cease-fire line at the time of the Japanese surrender. At this point Zhou Enlai, now minister of foreign affairs in the new Chinese government, issued a warning, by way of the Indian ambassador to China, that if the United Nations army crossed into North Korea, "China cannot stand idly by." This explicit notice of China's historic interest in the country which had been for centuries under her suzerainty and was now a direct neighbour, went quite unheeded by the Western powers. Communist China, had no right to speak of China's interests nor take account of threats to her own territory.

These threats, as would now be generally admitted, were real. General MacArthur, the commander of the United Nations army, was well known as a fanatical anticommunist. The General Assembly of the United Nations had given him authority to enter and subdue North Korea, and he proceeded to do so. No one in China believed that his forces would stop at the Yalu river, which forms the frontier. Twice in the past China had been invaded from North Korea. Even if the enemy did not actually invade, a hostile government established on China's frontier, close to the Manchurian industrial area, would be a standing menace. The Russians too did not wish to see their North Korean protegé destroyed, which would cause them great loss of face throughout Asia. But they also did not want to run the risk of confronting American troops in battle.

So Chinese "volunteers," which, as everyone knew, were units of the People's Liberation Army, poured across the Yalu at the end of October 1950. Their tactics and ability to move through the roadless mountainous regions confounded the more conventional American forces, constrained to use roads for their mechanized transport. The Chinese drove the United Nations army out of North Korea, back beyond the 38th Parallel. This victory was the first ever won by Chinese troops against a Western army. It was hailed, not only in China itself, with delirious delight and pride. Chinese in Hong Kong, living under British rule, and who in many cases had fled Shanghai rather than await communist rule, gave victory parties in their homes. The Chinese press in Hong Kong carried posters, in Chinese only, which read, "Glorious victory of the People's Liberation Army."

The United Nations army rallied in South Korea and when in early 1951, the Chinese in their turn opened an offensive to drive the Americans and their allies out of South Korea, they were repulsed and pushed back until both armies came to a standstill on a slightly more topographically realistic line than the 38th Parallel of latitude, but much on the same alignment. There, for two years, the war stagnated.

General MacArthur wanted to use his overwhelming air power directly against China itself; the European allies of the USA were appalled at this idea; they foresaw Russian intervention, and the real risk of a general war, which would soon involve the use of atomic bombs. It was agreed that there should be no reprisal against Chinese territory, and that the objective of conquering North Korea should be abandoned. This was not at all to the taste of General MacArthur, and such was his open opposition that president Truman deprived him of his command in April 1951. Even then no settlement appeared in sight. Indian mediation finally helped to secure a cease-fire along the actual battle line, a situation which exists to the present day, with a 20-mile demilitarized zone separating the armies of North and South Korea and no political solution in sight.

The consequences of the war were for China far reaching and complex. On the one hand the defeat of the Americans at the Yalu, and the fighting record of the Chinese forces in the subsequent period, had done much to boost the morale of both the government and people and to increase the regime's prestige. No longer could it be said that China must bow to the superior force of the West; for the first time for more than a century the Chinese felt truly independent. This new-found confidence was to be a major stimulant to the Chinese communist party in its home policies; it also showed itself in a reluctance to trade or traffic with the West except on Chinese terms. On the other hand China, condemned for aggression by the United Nations, had now no hope of recognition by that body, which still counted among its members the representative of her enemy, the nationalist government in Taiwan. The continuing hostility of the USA was taken for granted. "All harm short of war," could now be called the policy of the USA towards communist China.

The European countries and their former colonies such as Australia, New Zealand, and Canada were less committed.

A Chinese city in the early fifties. The work of reconstruction and reeducation to be undertaken by the communist party after its accession to power was immense. However, it was helped by the almost total support of the people who were tired of civil war and of the corruption and abuses practiced by the Guomindang. Moreover, the anti-communist campaign of denigration and terrorization carried out by Chiang Kaishek had been proven by the facts and by the witness of those who had known life in the "Red base" areas to be ill-founded and unjust.

Firstly, their real interest in China was trade, and barring the delivery of "strategic materials" this trade continued. America imposed upon her citizens a complete embargo on trade with China. The vast number of the Chinese people had little knowledge and scant interest in foreign countries, remote, beyond the seas, and alien. The disapproval, even the hostility, of these countries meant little or nothing to them. Peking could live with foreign condemnation, especially as it had only limited effects on trade. The people now trusted their government to defend them, and that was compensation enough for the deprivation of strategic materials.

In respect of Russia too the Chinese had benefitted from the Korean war. It had not been under Chinese pressure that the North Koreans had invaded South Korea. But China had to be called upon to pull Russian chestnuts out of a fire which was not of her kindling. Chinese troops had thrown back the Americans, saved North Korea, and it was the Chinese who had finally negotiated the cease-fire. Some 800,000 battle-hardened troops, withdrawn from Korea after the cease-fire, were now concentrated in the Manchurian provinces. There could in these circumstances be no question as to who controlled Manchuria. Within a year the Russians had renounced their participation in the administration of the railroads, given up their rights in the naval port of Lushun (Port Arthur) and the commercial city of Dairen. Manchuria, for the first time in history, was now as much a part of China as any other of its regions. On the other hand China remained dependent on Russia in many respects, especially as regards armaments. Until China had her own arms factories, the Soviet Union was the only source of supply. By 1954, Russia and Eastern Europe accounted for four-fifths of China's foreign trade, Western and Asian countries a mere one-fifth.

Internally, the consequences of the war were to give the government the confidence to proceed with a more overtly communist policy in land reform, commerce and industry, and to embark on a program of vast social change. Inflation, which had continued at a diminishing rate after the liberation (as the communist victory has ever since been termed) was halted completely early in 1953, when a new currency, the *yuan*, was introduced, and has subsequently become one of the most stable in the world. Production, both agricultural and industrial, rose in spite of the war to a level comparable to that of 1937, the last year of peace in China's recent history.

In 1949, when the communist victory in the long civil war was finally assured, the Chinese people as a whole, and the urban population in particular, had little idea of what they might now expect from the new masters of their country. The Guomindang had taught them to expect a bloody and violent tyranny. Rumours filtering through from the liberated areas: the regions already under communist control, suggested on the contrary a rule of efficiency, moderation and justice. As it turned out, there were no rivers of blood but instead, unexpectedly, torrents of words.

The communist party, once in power, set out to convert the Chinese people to its own ideology and to win their cooperation

Above: a demonstration in which peasants burn the deeds of land-ownership. In the course of the civil war – more exactly between May 1946 and December 1947 – the communists gave new force to the struggle for agrarian reform and social reorganization in the country areas. The involvement of the peasant masses in what was truly a struggle of the people was one of the main causes of the communist party's success.

Opposite: a view of the port of Shanghai (in a photo of the fifties) with dense rows of sampans, the large, flat-bottomed craft used for the transport of goods and also as dwelling places. Shanghai was the only Chinese city which could be said to have "Western" characteristics by reason of the many foreigners who lived there and the close commercial links which it had with overseas countries. It was also the only Chinese city which had a considerable industrial development and therefore an urban proletariat and a politically aware intellectual élite.

in the immense task of modernizing China. Experience in the rural regions where they had so long flourished had taught them that persuasion was preferable to force. "The People are the sea; we are the fish." This saying of Mao Zedong accurately expressed the guiding policy of the party. Fish need the sea to swim in and to survive; if the sea is poisoned, they cannot live. So the sea, the Chinese people, must be made into a suitable environment for the communist fish. Force would be needed against "feudal remnants," as the supporters of the Guomindang were called. But the mass of the people must be persuaded to realize that what the communists offered was in their interest, and that they had the duty to support whatever measures were necessary to this end.

So an immense program of instruction was set in motion. Every citizen had to attend meetings organized by the communist cadres in his profession, place of work, or the street in which he lived, which took up hours of his time, often being held at night. Words, words: the Chinese people had not only to listen, but to question, to participate, to suggest, to show themselves ready to comprehend and cooperate. The people were thankful for the prompt restoration of order, the work of salvage and reconstruction which everywhere began to open up communications, bringing back life to half-derelict cities and towns, and for the efforts made to improve food supplies and to revive industry. If anyone had misgivings, it was incumbent upon him or her to undertake instruction in the wholly new outlook and code of moral behaviour now imposed. On the other hand, the people could see and marvel that there was little or no persecution of those who had worked for the enemy including officials of the late Guomindang regime.

The former police force, now renamed the Public Safety Service, was left intact, except for the higher ranks. Not so the secret police and sections of the previous administration which had been actively engaged in anticommunist activities. The numerous ex-soldiers of the Guomindang armies were simply returned to their villages. The development of truly communist, or socialist, policy, had yet to come. The Chinese communists do not describe their regime as "communist"; they claim that real communism has yet to be achieved, and that only when the economy is sufficiently developed. As of now, the middle objective is called socialism.

But before even that stage could begin to be implemented there was a vast task of simple salvage to be undertaken. The railroads were destroyed; the rivers innavigable; the cities filthy and in a state of great disrepair; industry virtually closed down; and in the years since the end of the war with Japan, the ports had been used almost solely for importing foreign food, coal, and other prime necessities.

It was finally expected that in the winter of 1949 Shanghai's population would starve or freeze to death. The enemies of the communist regime confidently predicted this would happen, hoping it would bring down the new regime. They were to be disappointed. By a prodigious effort the railroads were rebuilt, largely by the army. They were mainly used to transport coal from the North to Shanghai and other Yangtze cities. From

fertile Sichuan, nearly 2000 kilometers up the Yangtze, rice was shipped in boats which used the currents of the mighty river. The great city port did not starve, neither did it freeze.

This first year of the communist regime saw an almost incredible transformation in the life of the people, compared to the miseries of recent years. There were no wars anywhere within the borders of China; soon too banditry would be eliminated; travel was once more possible and safe, even comfortable. The cities were cleaned up, and corruption brought to an end.

But there was another side to the story. Land reform, the destruction of the existing land tenure system, was very dear to the hearts of the peasants, and it was for this more than anything else that they had supported the communists, fought for them, and suffered at the hands of the Japanese and the Guomindang. They could not now be denied.

Throughout China, landlords were brought before "People's Courts," which in practice were mass gatherings of villagers, before whom the landlords had to answer for their conduct. They could be denounced for real or imagined cruelties, injustices, oppression, rack-renting, or simply neglect and indifference to the sufferings of their tenants. No reliable statistics of the consequences of these trials exist. Many landlords were executed, but many more were condemned to terms of prison, loss of property and civil rights. There are also many authenticated cases where the accused landlord was either acquitted by general agreement, or judged guilty of only minor faults. It can be argued that although this system was rough justice, the only real alternative would have been a vast *Jacquerie*, the indiscriminate slaughter of hated landlords and probably of their families also.

It did not happen like this. Landlords who were allowed to go free, or those who had served their terms of imprisonment were stripped of all land in excess of the common share. All the peasants, those who already had land and those who had none, had equal shares in the freehold distribution of land, judged according to type of soil, area and fertility. Although the old landlord could retain this same proportion of his former possessions, as a member of a suspect class he was deprived of the right to vote in the local elections, or to hold any office.

This was the first stage of land reform; it satisfied the land hunger and the demand for social justice which animated the mass of the peasantry; and it broke the economic and political power of the class which had provided the officers and officials of the late Guomindang regime. But it did not solve the economic problem of agriculture in an overcrowded rural environment.

This division of land into tiny freehold plots was in itself, as the communists fully appreciated, almost retrograde. Such holdings could not guarantee a livelihood for a family, especially in times of drought. Drought is a recurrent and serious menace in the whole of North China and in some southern areas also. Concurrently with the division of land and the setting up of freehold ownerships, went the drive to create a system of cooperative planning for agriculture.

The purpose of the new policy was to persuade, not force, the peasants to see the advantages of a rationalized system of more

Top: peasants read the proclamation announcing agrarian reform; the law was actually passed on 30 June 1950. All land not cultivated by the proprietor himself was confiscated without reimbursement. Many proprietors, particularly the great landowners, had to appear before tribunals of the people, accused of injustice and of practicing abuses. This rather rudimentary system did manage to avoid worse excesses such as the summary execution of all landowners and their families which was being called for by the rabble.

Above: peasants enrolling in the new agricultural cooperatives. This was the first step towards the collectivization of farming. After this, there followed the "advanced cooperatives" leading eventually to the communes.

Two popular posters which celebrate respectively the birth of the cooperatives (below) and of the communes (bottom). Certainly, the advent of the communes solved the perennial Chinese problems of hunger and oppression and has largely eliminated the specter of famine resulting from drought or flooding which so often threatened the country in the past. It remains to be seen whether the changes which they have brought about in social life will be permanent and whether the commune leaders, who are elected by everyone from a social group of one-time "poor peasants," do not form a new class of privileged peasantry.

collective agriculture, and move them steadily towards the acceptance of a fully collective system. Every farmer knew well enough from his own experience, that a small plot could not keep the family alive or out of debt if the season was bad. So when the cadres came to the villages, or the local party members, recent heroic guerrilla fighters, began to tell the people that cooperation was the only way to solve their problems, they were listened to. The peasants had confidence in the men who had led them in war, had helped to bring the landlords down, and were now spelling out the risks the individual farmer ran.

The first step was to organize rational planting of an identical crop on all adjoining land tenures. In this way a large area could be harvested, weeded, and defended from pests by the joint work of all the landowners together. This first phase was so clearly beneficial to all that it was soon possible to persuade the peasants to go farther along the cooperative road. Rural cooperatives were soon being set up everywhere. Individual owners retained the title to their land, but planting was decided on a village scale and work was shared out among the co-partners. Marketing was undertaken by the cooperative management. Some of these ideas were not essentially either socialist or communist; but they were only the first step.

It was in the middle fifties, that the most important change in China's land tenure system was introduced; it came about by persuasion, not by force. Cooperatives were now promoted to what was called the "higher stage" of cooperative farming. This meant that while the landowners of small plots retained in theory full title to their land, the boundaries between farms and fields were ploughed out (providing extensive areas of extra land for cultivation) and the whole area of the cooperative treated as one large farm. Individual owners had a share of the income proportionate to the size of the land they worked.

With some refinements, this has remained the basic system of land reform in China even under the commune system. True private ownership of agricultural land no longer exists in China. The cooperative or the commune (a combination of several cooperatives) owns all the land. Former owners and workers alike have a share and are entitled to an income based on "work points" allotted according to the nature of the tasks performed, the time taken, and similar factors. The commune system was introduced in 1958, a few years after the establishment of the higher-stage cooperatives, but it was really only a large-scale extension of the previous system although it had wider social implications.

There is now no doubt that both the commune and cooperative systems, even in the early formative stage, when in the early sixties China was afflicted by the worst drought for more than a 100 years, saved millions from death through famine. There is also little doubt that the drought of 1960 showed up the weaknesses as well as the strengths of the new system. The original communes were too big to be farmed as a single integrated unit. The didactic instructions on what and how to plant, which came from central ministries in Peking, were often inapplicable, or even harmful, in differing environments. Local knowledge and experience are not to be disregarded without risk, and local cooperation is won by enlisting local talent rather than by instructions from far-off central government. The party needed to return to its first principles and early practices; the lesson was learned.

Today, the commune, with its system of work brigades, is the accepted and established norm of land tenure in China. It is furthermore a system that works. As productivity has increased so has the independent spirit of those who manage and govern the communes, leaders elected by their fellows though admittedly from a restricted franchise: no former member of the old landlord class can really hope for commune office, even if he is once more allowed to vote. The new élite are the former poor peasants.

The communist party divided the rural population into four categories: landlords, who were deprived of all but the small common share of the village land; rich peasants, who owned farms large enough to support their own families, sometimes employed hired labour, and might even have a few tenants; peasants who owned a farm too small to sustain a family and who therefore sought other work or farmed extra land as tenants. Finally there were the "poor peasants," those with either a tiny plot of their own, who in fact had to live by working for others, or the truly landless who were wholly dependent on work for wages and owned no land at all.

It is these last, or rather their sons, and soon their grandsons, who have literally inherited the earth. They are the élite in the new communes, members of the party and its cadres, the elected managers and directors of the commune and the work brigades. They are in fact, if not in theory, the ruling rural class.

It may be asked how long does someone remain a "poor peasant" who has never known poverty since he was a small child – or may well have never experienced it – and how do his sons and their descendants come to be similarly classed if they were born after the new system of land tenure had given everyone an equal and secure right to a livelihood and a share in the profits of the commune, irrespective of the social origin of one's fathers. These questions have not been answered, but it may be observed that "poor peasant" is in some danger of becoming a title, and an hereditary one at that, carrying as of old, in all parts of the world, an implied or real right to rule in rural areas.

The Chinese communist party, rural in its guerrilla development, scored its greatest and perhaps also its easiest triumphs in the countryside. The communists won over the peasants, they have kept their confidence, and most certainly have enormously improved their standard of living. The cities were different; the gap between urban and rural living conditions was great and even more extreme differences existed between the lives of the poor and the rich in the great cities than in the villages, no matter how oppressive the landlords may have been.

Shanghai, the type of the great, new city, as opposed to Peking, the supreme example of the ancient traditional Chinese city, both exhibited in different ways the problem of the cities for a communist regime which had so far only had the experience of ruling rural areas. Peking had more than 100,000 university

The Red Army was renamed in 1937 the 8th Route Army and then later the People's Army of Liberation. Its principles of discipline have guaranteed that relations between its soldiers and the civil population have always remained excellent. The illustrations on these pages come from a fairly widely read Chinese manifesto which shows very clearly the "Eight points of discipline" expected of a soldier. These include: return all the things you have been lent; be honest in all your dealings with the peasants; pay for anything you have damaged; make sure that all latrines are well away from houses. These rules constitute the code of the Red soldier and have even been set to music in a song which is still current.

students, drawn in the main from the rich or moderately wealthy educated classes. These young people were nonetheless fired with radical enthusiasm, disgusted with the inefficiency, corruption and oppression of the Guomindang and eager to welcome the communist regime. They were easily persuaded to enroll in the party and undergo its rigorous training. Peking, however, had no industry to speak of, in other words no industrial proletariat as such.

Shanghai was the only really developed industrial city in China, it was also the greatest port, with the major concentration of foreign business, commerce and residents. Mainly consisting of the former International Settlement and French Concession, with a fringe of new factories and slums beyond them, the city was modern, built in either Western style architecture or a hybrid Chinese-European style called by the Chinese *yang lou* ("foreign two-story"). Shanghai, more than any other city in China, had been influenced by Western ideas in its life-style and its manners. If it was intrinsically "Chinese" to the foreign residents, since the vast majority of the population was Chinese, it also seemed foreign, or at least "modern" to the Chinese themselves. Shanghai had another characteristic; it was the stronghold of financiers, commercial magnates and a nucleus of industrialists; its well-to-do Chinese were the nearest to a capitalist class of entrepreneurs to be found in China. It was also the stronghold of the Chinese left. Here, alone in China, trade unions had struggled to survive and operate; here the numerous intellectuals of the left had found, in prewar days, a precarious refuge from the persecution of the Guomindang; here it was that the clandestine communist party had for many years, before the flight to Jiangxi, had its headquarters. Shanghai was both the last bastion of the old way of life in China, and the principal source of urban revolutionary power.

The communist party, taking over this strange city, had two problems to consider: how to deal with the foreigners and their control of business and commerce; and what to do with their Chinese counterparts, who might be nationalist in sentiment, but could not be expected to be communist in their sympathies. Much foreign business, especially of the professional type, collapsed at once as the practitioners left for their respective homelands. But big business remained, as did industry.

The policy was to divert these activities along lines which the new government favoured. Import licences controlled the entry of raw materials and foreign goods. If a foreign firm wished to reduce its activity, it was compelled to pay large and generous compensation to dismissed workers. For many firms the conditions proved quite unprofitable, and they closed down, after having to pay out large sums in this way. The shipping lines were able to continue, since they were based on Hong Kong, and they could shed their Shanghai subsidiary activity without ruin. Steadily the number of resident foreigners diminished, and the foreign businesses disappeared. Today only the shipping lines are still active. At the time of the "Liberation" China still depended on foreign shipping for imports and exports, Chinese shipping, or what was left of it after war and revolution, being wholly coastal.

Students in the library of Peking University. The Chinese capital has 25 institutes of higher education as well as the two universities of Qinghua and Peking which are particularly well-known. Following the advent of the People's Republic, scientific and technical subjects became especially popular while the humanities had to adapt themselves to the requirements of communist doctrine. An exception to this is archaeology which has no associated problems of interpretation and which has always been – as it still is – a major area of study.

A much bigger problem, however, was presented by the Chinese bourgeoisie. They were a large class in Shanghai, ranging from wealthy businessmen and financiers to small shopkeepers, architects, engineers and members of the professions generally. Many of these latter left at once for Hong Kong, as did a considerable number of smaller merchants and craftsmen who catered mainly for foreign customers or specialized in Western styles of clothing and living. The industrialists, mainly in the textile business, and the majority of the shopkeepers remained. They were designated as "national bourgeoisie" and provided they accepted the new regime and its many regulations, they were left in peace.

Soon a law was enforced by which industry and commerce became "state-private cooperative," which meant that the former owner managed the business and received a five percent return on profits, the state being responsible for marketing and deciding which goods should be produced. This system continued for many years; gradually the numbers of the "national bourgeoisie" grew less. Sons were unwilling to follow their fathers; they disliked the stigma attaching to the names capitalist and bourgeois. They prefered to train as engineers or in some other skilled profession in which their "class origin" was less obvious.

But in the beginning the communist regime found it necessary to undertake a propaganda campaign against the customs and manners of the bourgeoisie which they regarded as vicious or reprehensible, such as corruption, tax evasion, and the rigging of markets. Tribunals to judge these offences, and a thorough-going system of espionage, delation and denunciation, were instituted. Many hundreds of businessmen were heavily fined, some so persecuted that they preferred to take their own lives, and the bourgeoisie as a whole began to fear that they were about to share the fate of the landlords. This was not, however, the party's intention; the aim was to instill submission, to cow, not to exterminate or eliminate. After 1952 the campaign against the bourgeoisie and its less savoury aspects ceased.

The ending of this campaign also coincided with the start of China's first five-year plan, the objective of which was simply to start an industrial revolution in China which would free the country from its dependence on foreign production in the building of a modern society.

Inevitably, another area of major concern for the new regime was education. Under the Guomindang the universities had suffered continuing inquisition and persecution, not to speak of the severe financial hardship caused by ever-rising inflation. They had therefore become centers of disaffection, and the great mass of students and staff welcomed the downfall of the Guomindang. They were soon to find out that even under the new regime, life had its problems. Scientists were welcomed and every assistance given them in their work; but the humanities presented an altogether different problem. The teaching of sociology for instance had now to conform to Marxist thinking: those who disagreed with this view were permitted to emigrate. History must now be rewritten to emphasize the leadership of the people and expose the vices and oppression of the old ruling class. Economics of course must be strictly on Marxist lines. Chinese classical studies had to take a less prominent place in the curriculum.

Archaeology on the other hand still holds a favourite place; in part, this is due to three factors. First, many of the leading archaeologists were strong supporters of the communist cause; secondly, China possesses, beneath her ancient soil, a potentially unparalleled wealth of archaeological treasure, as excavation has amply revealed in recent years; and thirdly, the subject itself is a "safe" one.

In extending popular education, the communists faced a truly appalling task, nothing less than the elimination of illiteracy which affected 80 percent of the population, being much higher in rural areas than in urban centers. The introduction of basic education, that is teaching people to read a limited number of Chinese ideographs, and producing a popular literature written within these limits had been pioneered many years previously, after the First World War, when it was discovered that the Chinese Labour Corps, which served in France, was made up of men who were illiterate and therefore unable to keep in touch with their relatives in China. Succeeding governments had given some help towards solving the problem, until finally this simplified system was adopted for all primary education.

The communists took over this program, and have achieved striking results. Before the liberation it had made most impact in the cities, but the program really took off when the new regime decided to take it to the villages. Illiteracy may not yet have been eradicated, but the vast majority of Chinese children, and many thousands of adults also, having taken the basic courses, can read and write.

The poverty of the peasants had hitherto discouraged doctors from trying to make a living in rural areas. They preferred to find their patients in the cities. The communist regime must be given the credit for being the first government in China to set up an effective health service. It started with the setting up of village clinics; later came the so-called "barefoot doctors," with a basic training in hygiene and medicine.

The acceptance of the new regime by the educated class had been a welcome development to the communists; but the domination of party members in so many institutions had a hampering effect which many scientists and other academics found objectionable. In 1957, Mao took note of this and introduced a new policy, called the "Hundred Flowers" – from a classical saying, "Let the hundred flowers of art bloom, let the hundred schools (of philosophy) flourish." Criticism of existing practices was invited; and the press was soon publishing shoals of complaining letters about this, that and the other. Before long the new liberty ran to licence – or so many leading communists thought. It had been hoped that criticism would be wholly constructive, about how things were done, not about why they were done. But before long there appeared almost open attacks upon some of the main policies and ideology of communism itself. This was going too far; the policy was abruptly reversed. The "Hundred Flowers" had wilted, but they did leave some traces; Western academic journals for example, previously

A poster extolling the virtues of "The Hundred Flowers," the movement launched in 1956 inviting criticism from the people of Communist-run China. "Over-frankness" could lead to one being labelled right-wing.

banned, and then made available to scholars under the new policy, were not put back on the banned list when the new liberty was repressed.

It is now known, from the many revelations which came to light during the cultural revolution, that during the 1950s, after the Korean war, there were several matters upon which the communist leadership was not agreed. The first stirring of the dispute with Russia which was to grow into an open and outright quarrel, can be traced to the aftermath of the Korean war. Stalin was now dead, and with him went the only figure in the communist world to whom Mao had to defer.

Mao had become, at least in Chinese eyes, the unquestioned leader in the communist world. Khruschev was never given the standing that Stalin had enjoyed, and the rather crude behaviour of the new Russian leader was offensive to Chinese taste. Mao Zedong never got on well with him, and before long they had, as yet secretly, quarrelled. The problem of the continuing existence of a nationalist government, recognised by America, in Taiwan lay at the root of the trouble. In 1959, Khruschev made his visit to the USA, where he was entertained by President Eisenhower. In China, Eisenhower was seen as the head of the enemy country which had consistently opposed the Chinese communist party and government. To the Chinese communists the visit to America, and even more the behaviour of Khruschev when he visited Peking on his return journey, appeared as the conduct of an untrustworthy ally, who was evading his obligations.

There were other causes for offence. In 1958, the communist party had launched two important internal policies; one was the "Great Leap Forward," designed to set the modernization and industrialization of the economy on the path to "overtaking Great Britain in 15 years"; the other was the setting up of the communes as the final solution of land reform. Both programs were seen as important milestones on the road to true communism. This claim was repugnant to the Russians; they did not relish the suggestion that China could progress towards the common goal faster than they could; and they did not like the commune idea at all. It was a system in sharp contrast to their own collective farm agriculture, being managed by elected peasant members, not run by state officials from a remote central government.

In 1958 the chill in the air was perceptible. During that summer the Chinese had engaged in a violent bombardment of the island fortress of Quemoy, lying close to the coast of Fujian province, held since the civil war by Chiang Kaishek's forces. The USA supplied the nationalist air force with modern weapons, the Russians refused similar weapons to China. Thus Quemoy was held, and the Chinese had to limit themselves to a token bombardment at sporadic intervals.

Finally, there was the question of Tibet. The Chinese empire had exercised suzerainty over that country since the 17th century. In the revolution of 1911, the western two-thirds of the country were freed from Chinese rule (which had only recently been underlined with the presence of a Chinese army) and for the next 40 years Tibet, under the Dalai Lama, its reincarnated god-king, was beyond the reach of the successive governments in

The Dalai Lama, religious and political head of Tibet, left his country to take refuge in India in 1959 after an attempt – one of many – on the part of the Buddhist priests to rouse the people against the communist régime had failed. Tibet has been an autonomous region of China since 1951, when it was conquered by the People's Army of Liberation.

China. But in 1951, following a revolt of Tibetan tribesmen in the Chinese eastern part if Tibet, supported by tribesmen from the western zone, the People's Liberation Army moved in and accomplished in a few months what the Guomindang had never been able to do, the total conquest of the country. Suzerainty, communist-style, was restored.

In 1959 sporadic risings, inspired by the Buddhist monks, led to a new revolt against Chinese suzerainty. This time the People's Liberation Army did a more thorough job and the Dalai Dama fled to India. But echoes of the conflict continued to reverberate. In the late 19th century, the Chinese laid claim to a larger tract of territory north of Kashmir. Backed up by the British, anxious to keep the Russians out, they built a road across this wilderness, linking Tibet with the Chinese province of Xinjiang. The Chinese now claimed that the frontier between Tibet and India should be stabilized on the MacMahon Line, as had been agreed with the British. The Indian government, however, saw things differently and in late 1962 troops were sent in to dislodge the Chinese from a number of positions they had occupied. The Indian troops met with stiff resistance, and being poorly equipped for warfare in such high altitudes in winter, were disastrously defeated. The Chinese army advanced to the foot of the Himalayas, at the edge of the plain of Assam; it seemed they might be making for Calcutta. But they made an unilateral decision to withdraw along the crests of the MacMahon Line, at the same time liberating their numerous Indian prisoners.

The consequences of this border war were to reinforce further the antagonism between China and India and to exacerbate the dispute with Russia, for the Soviet Union, far from showing fraternal solidarity with communist China, denounced her action as "aggression" which in the strict sense of the word it was not. The Chinese were soon to explode their first nuclear device, and so join the ranks of the nuclear powers. The contrast between China's weakness under the Guomindang (a persistent malady in fact since the end of the 18th century) and her emergence as the major military power in Asia was a natural source of pride to the Chinese people and a disturbing factor for any potential aggressor.

In 1954 the Geneva Conference was called with a view to ending the war in Korea and Indo-China. One of the delegates was Zhou Enlai. It was the first time that the new government of China had been represented at an international conference; it marked a step forward in the acceptance of the Chinese revolution as an accomplished fact.

Conflicts on matters of internal and external policy which came to the surface in 1959, can be seen today as the precursors of the greater disagreements which were apparent during the subsequent cultural revolution. In December 1959, Mao resigned from the position of president of the government, retaining the much more important post of chairman of the communist party. It was said at the time that he wanted more leisure to devote to the study of political theory, but later it was said that he was forced to resign by critics of the "Great Leap Forward" and the commune system.

China exploded its first atomic bomb on 16 October 1964. From that moment, the People's Republic became one of the nuclear powers. From the time of the first five-year plan for the development of industry, in 1953, tremendous progress has been made. Within four years Chinese factories were producing locomotives, tractors, lorries and cargo ships. Industrial development has greatly transformed towns and cities in the north and center of the country where raw materials are to be found and communications easier. In the south, even though there are rich deposits of coal and other minerals needed for industry, the mountainous nature of the territory means that development is costly and dependent, for the most part, on the construction of new railroads.

In August 1959, the minister for defense, Peng Dehuai, a veteran of the Jiangxi wars and the Long March, was dismissed and arrested because of his open opposition to the dispute with the Soviet Union and his criticism of the commune system. Since the members of the politburo who voted against Peng included men who were subsequently criticized and disgraced for their alleged opposition to Mao's policy, there is no certainty as to the real alignment of the politburo membership on this occasion. What does emerge is that whatever the true source of the disagreement, none of those remaining in high office questioned the policy towards Russia. This seems to have been the aspect of Peng's protests which lacked general support, and perhaps affords the reason why his fellow members were ready to oppose him.

To what extent Mao lost overriding influence, or whether his resignation was simply a tactical retreat, cannot now be determined. Subsequent events would seem to confirm the view that he remained very much in power in the years before the cultural revolution, and that it was in fact his critics who lacked the influence to prevail. Now that many of those critics are once more at the head of affairs, it is all the more difficult to discover what were the real facts of political discord in the late 1950s and early 1960s. During the cultural revolution many documents were published apparently confirming the existence of political plots against Mao, attributed to the same men who once more lead China. Whether these revelations are false or true has not been clarified.

During the years 1962–64, a movement, inspired by Mao Zedong, was launched in China, called "Socialist education." The declared purpose was to bring about a better understanding, and greater enthusiasm for socialism among the younger generation. It was a clever move. The party hierarchs, who, as is now claimed, had combined to reduce Mao's power, could hardly object to "socialist education," so obviously in harmony with the purpose and policies of the regime. But at the same time the new movement was teaching the young to question the establishment, to show disapproval of the bourgeois habits of the intellectuals and of the alleged predilection among some of the leadership for comfortable and even luxurious living. The movement was, as is now clear, a preliminary step towards the cultural revolution.

Other moves followed. Lin Biao, the minister for defense, a hero of the civil war and the war against Japan, who was very close to Mao at this time, introduced reforms in the army of a distinctly proletararian character. Military ranks were abolished; henceforward officers were only to be distinguished from private soldiers by the designation of their command: "Comrade Wang, commanding the 8th Regiment," a cumbersome way of saying "colonel," which must have led to some abbreviations. At the same time Lin introduced – at first for the education of young recruits, but soon as a manual for all ranks – his "Little Red Book," a compilation of quotations from Mao Zedong's writings which emphasized passages urging discipline, strict obedience to Mao and his thinking, good conduct towards the people, and other unexceptional virtues. It was a kind of

Mao Zedong with Lin Biao at his side. The latter was officially designated Mao's successor and his "most faithful companion in arms" at the time of the cultural revolution. Lin Biao, who had been a friend of Mao from the years of Jiangxi and the Long March, was distinguished above all for his strategic skill in the battles against Chiang's army during the civil war. He was minister of defense during the cultural revolution and, in 1966, organized the "red guards" in support of Mao.

simplified version of the teaching of the socialist education movement. It was to become the sacred text of the cultural revolution.

Even if the party hierarchs in charge of the actual conduct of government, like Liu Shaoqi, the head of state (chairman of the national government), and such men as Deng Xiaoping, a close supporter of Lin, realized what Mao had in mind, they did not react, or at that time could not have done so.

The first shot in the cultural revolution was fired early in 1966 when a group of writers in Shanghai attacked and denounced the author Wu Han for a recent play he had produced, called *The Dismissal of Hai Rui*. It is entirely characteristic of China and Chinese culture that a highly political act was wrapped up in a severe literary criticism of a play dealing with an event which happened in the 16th century during the reign of the Ming. Hai Rui was a minister of the Ming court who advocated policies which would have relieved the sufferings of the poor. He was dismissed as the result of the intrigues of other reactionary ministers and courtiers. All pretty routine stuff, one might think; but no. *The Dismissal of Hai Rui* was read as a criticism of Mao himself (in the role of the Ming emperor) and Hai Rui, the fallen minister, meant Peng Dehuai, the dismissed veteran general, who had opposed the quarrel with Soviet Russia and doubted the wisdom of the "Great Leap Forward" and the concept of the communes. The courtiers could easily be equated with the hierarchs of the party. Wu Han was denounced, stripped of his office and deprived of his job. The play was banned. But the implications were clear enough: Wu Han had been a close friend of Peng Zhen, the mayor of Peking, and of Deng Xiaoping, then secretary general of the Chinese communist party. The hunt was up.

The "Great Proletarian Cultural Revolution," as it was officially styled, needs a word of explanation as to the words themselves. The Chinese words *wen hua* do not exactly mean culture in the sense of art, literature, and poetry, etc., but have a wider meaning such as when we use the word "culture" to signify "civilization." The new movement was thus intended to be a revolution of the entire civilization of China, and not only its artistic manifestations. At the time, the summer of 1966, when the movement seemed suddenly to erupt out of nothing, with no apparent background, it was variously interpreted, both by the Chinese and by foreign observers. Some saw it as nothing more than a power struggle between an aging Mao and younger aspirant leaders, and noting the influence and significance of Lin Biao's role, concluded that it was a movement staged by him to lead to the eventual take-over by the army when Mao died. The possibility that Lin Biao was inspired by such ambitions to support Mao with all the resources of the army is far from improbable. And it is a fact that the first great event of the cultural revolution was the mass creation of the "red guards," made up mainly of high school students, often under 16 years of age, rather than university undergraduates. More than 1,000,000 red guards were transported to Peking in August 1966, where they were inspected by Mao and Lin Biao; before long they were being used as an instrument of political pressure

From left to right: Yao Wenyuan, Wen Hungwen, Jiang Qing (Mao's widow) and Zhang Chunqiao. All of these took the political limelight during the cultural revolution, that is, between 1966 and 1968. They were later to be known as "The Gang of Four" and in 1981 were sentenced to terms of life imprisonment.

Opposite: soldiers of the People's Army of Liberation, each with a copy of the "little red book" containing the sayings of Mao Zedong. These mottoes were collected by Lin Biao, then minister of defense, and distributed first among the army then among the general public.

on the party hierarchy. The whole operation: the maintenance, feeding, accommodation (in tents in the main streets of Peking) and the ancillary problems of sanitation and health of so many young people, could not have been managed by any institution other than the army, especially since it was clearly an "anti-party" move. Also the fact that the Chinese army could carry out such a major logistic operation so smoothly, gave cause for thought among Western military observers.

Now that he had the red guards at his command, and in the capital too, Mao proceeded with his plans. "Bourgeois elements," which meant academics, artists, actors, musicians, the whole intellectual spectrum in fact, were persecuted, harried, their books seized and sometimes burned, and they themselves driven from their jobs and their institutions closed down. The entire educational system stopped functioning for six months at least while it was "reorganized," that is to say, proletarianized. Examinations were abolished; students from educated families were at a disadvantage against the children of more or less illiterate peasants. It is hardly surprising that academic and educational standards in the next few years fell to abysmal levels.

Yet this attack on the bourgeoisie, a weak, defenseless and small class, was mere by-play; the real attack was directed at the leading members of the party. Liu Shaoqi was denounced, together with his wife (she for luxurious living); huge marches of red guards shouting abuse and denunciation streamed past his official residence, which, however, with only two policemen guarding it, was never invaded. Soon he was forced to resign, then stripped of his functions, and later driven out of the party and detained until his death. Peng Zhen, the major of Peking, Deng Xiaoping, secretary of the communist party, and several ministers and senior generals (who happened to be in Lin Biao's bad books) were dismissed. Some were paraded in the streets of Peking with dunces' caps on their heads. Every device, short of physical violence, was used to humiliate the men who only weeks before had been leaders of the party and the chief officers of the state. Zhou Enlai alone was the major exception.

It now became clear that the removal of these leaders, who had on various occasions disagreed with Mao, was only the first step. The next move was to be the reconstruction of every aspect of society to conform with the aims of the cultural revolution. The power struggle seemed to have been won by Mao and his supporters; the campaign for the transformation of society now must begin.

In retrospect it is evident that these objectives were too over-reaching, indeed idealistic, and thus rather uncharacteristic of Mao's original line of thought, which as he had once put it, involved the "necessity of taking into account the facts we see before us." It is today accepted that Mao was deeply influenced by his wife Jiang Qing and her group, subsequently held up to opprobrium as the "Gang of Four." There is at least the strong likelihood that after the initial stress of launching the cultural revolution, Mao had begun to succumb to weariness and the progress of his illness, Parkinson's Disease, which ten years later caused his death. At the time, his own approval of the policies of

Life under the cultural revolution. Opposite above left: Jiang Qing, flanked by Lin Biao, speaks to the students of Peking University. Right: a demonstration in support of "The Thought of Mao Zedong," organized by students of the Institute of Foreign Commerce in Peking. Below: a scene common enough during the years of the cultural revolution: citizens accused of "revisionism" are paraded through the city streets.

The cultural revolution, together with the organization of the "red guards" in city schools, is a rather complex phenomenon which very probably had its origins in a clash of ideas at the top. However, it was also, at least in part, a spontaneous movement of the masses – first students and then, in a later phase, workers. In 1968, it finally became necessary to call in the army to restore law and order which in many regions of China had broken down into a state of virtual civil war. The rise to power of Lin Biao, and with him the army, was really a result of this chaotic situation. However, he did not manage to restore calm and so, in September 1971, after some involvement in an attempted *coup d'état*, he disappeared from the political scene accused of the most heinous crimes.

A poster celebrating the downfall of "The Gang of Four." In the bottom right-hand corner, we see a caricature of these "ultra-radicals" in the form of a four-headed serpent being crushed by a pickaxe representing the people.

the committee running the cultural revolution, of which the "Gang of Four" were the most prominent members, appeared complete. "It is right to rebel," and "Bombard the headquarters," his famous exhortations to the young red guards, even if not to be taken quite literally, cannot exonerate Mao from encouraging the exuberance, and soon the violence, of the young.

In order to maintain their enthusiasm, the red guards, and indeed the entire population, were urged to be on the lookout for counterrevolutionaries who were scheming to destroy the cultural revolution. Since the leaders of the party and the army who disapproved of the movement had already been hounded from power, and were now referred to contemptuously as "a small clique of revisionists taking the capitalist road," they could clearly not be considered active counterrevolutionaries any longer. Who then were these hidden enemies?

Before long the young red guards began to look for them among themselves. Jiang Qing had already proclaimed the somewhat novel doctrine that it was not what the majority approved which pointed the way for party followers, but what was sanctioned by those members who were truly motivated by Mao's thought, even if they were the minority.

Thus, very soon, the cultural revolution became a factional struggle inside the party. Quarrels escalated into violence. Arms taken from police and army barracks were used in bloody affrays, and at least one very serious crisis threatened when the military at Wuhan chose to support a faction which Peking subsequently decided was in the wrong. Zhou Enlai had to go to Wuhan, and only his infinite skill as a mediator and negotiator saved China from a new civil war. Although it went unsaid at the time, Zhou Enlai was in constant demand preventing these excesses and saving the country from the worst effects of the cultural revolution. When the red guards invaded and occupied the ministry of foreign affairs, destroying confidential files ("What's so secret about secrets?" asked a young red guard), he protected the foreign minister, accused of "revisionism." When the red guards threatened to extend their activities to Xinjiang, the far-western province rich in uranium deposits, where China has her plants for nuclear and space research, manned by scientists, originally trained in America, and certainly no ardent followers of the cultural revolution, Zhou is said to have remarked, "Xinjiang is too important to national interests to be involved in disorders." At least the nuclear physicists were allowed to carry on without the intervention of the red guards.

What amounted to a virtual admission that the cultural revolution had its negative aspects would, from the lips of anyone else, have been rank "revisionism" and worse. But Zhou always bore a charmed political life. He was indispensable; he kept the essential work and activity of government going, as prime minister he made that his duty and his burdensome task. The collection of taxes, the running of the day-to-day administration continued; some activities were impaired, but foreign trade, for example, continued without no greater disruption than was caused by failures in the communications system, and foreign merchants came and went as before. Zhou

A new leader emerges – Hua Guofeng (above, his portrait is carried in triumph alongside Mao's). One month after Mao's death, he ordered the arrest of the four leaders of the "Left" who were tainted with the excesses of the cultural revolution.

Top: a demonstration directed against "The Gang of Four" and the policies of the cultural revolution.

had never been prominent as an ideologist. He was a communist, and a dedicated one, but he did not frame theories nor disagree with the party line. He carried on with the work, and no one did it better. The full story of the relations between Zhou and Mao during the cultural revolution has yet to be told. When Zhou died, six months before Mao, the sorrow of the nation was significantly expressed most deeply in ways that were no part of the official commemorations.

Throughout the whole of 1967, the factional strife grew, with swings now to the left, now to the right, which must have confused still more the by now disorientated and disunited red guards. Things could not go on like this. Mao himself is said to have bitterly reproved the leaders of red guard factions in Peking for betraying his hopes. Since the party was in complete disarray, the only force able to restore order was the army, and it was now called upon to do so. No doubt this was what Lin Biao was waiting for, or so it is now alleged. The army had to take the situation in hand. In 1968 the red guards were disbanded; many thousands were sent to remote provinces (other than their own) "to teach the peasants the new way of life and society." As in fact the peasants of the communes had reacted very unfavourably to red guard attempts to stir things up in the communes, sending them off with little ceremony, it was highly unlikely that they would listen to such "teaching" from exiled red guards. There is no evidence that they did.

The end of the red guards, who had served their turn and then proved to be a nuisance and a danger, sums up the failure of the cultural revolution. What should have been the most promising material for the construction of the new Chinese society, the young, had proved, when given a taste of power, all too prone to adopt the vices and manners of the older generations. The cultural revolution continued, in the sense that education remained in the hands of the fanatics of the left who refused any return to normal methods of teaching or the readmission of those of whom they disapproved; art and literature remained under the numbing control of Jiang Qing and those who thought as she did.

In April 1969, the 9th Party Congress of the Chinese communist party was held in Peking. It declared that the cultural revolution had been brought to a triumphant conclusion. History has not confirmed that opinion. Lin Biao was named as Mao's "closest comrade in arms," which was taken to imply his recognition as heir apparent. The appointment of Lin Biao seemed to confirm that the cultural revolution had been inspired and used by him as the ladder to supreme power.

In August and September 1969, the second session of the central committee of the Chinese communist party met at Lushan in Sichuan province to resolve a very important question: the nomination of a new head of the state, vacant since the fall of Liu Shaoqi. Lin Biao had hoped for direct nomination as heir at the previous congress, but had met with opposition; he was given honorific titles which did not confer any real power. At Lushan, he tried again, this time adopting a new line. He and his close supporters suggested that there should be a presidency with full powers, and who could be chosen other than Mao

Zedong, a "rare genius." It was also necessary to choose a vice-president, who would automatically succeed in case of the death of the president. Lin Baio's proposal came to grief on an unexpected rock in the person of Mao Zedong himself. He dismissed the idea of "rare genius," nor did he like the office of president, which he regarded as reactionary. In typical Mao style, he made reference to "one who gives kicks under the table, while concealing his feet." Many of those present knew or at least guessed, that the object of this snide remark was Lin Biao.

A year passed, during which it became clearer that Lin's influence was definitely in decline. Then in September 1970 a crisis blew up. All aircraft were grounded. Lin Biao disappeared from public view along with the senior commanders of the army, air force and navy. No explanation was given for nearly nine months. Then bit by bit, it came out. The story was that Lin Biao had plotted to assassinate Mao Zedong; the plot had been discovered, Lin and his fellow conspirators had fled to Russia in a Viscount aircraft, which had crashed in Mongolia, killing all on board. In fact Lin was with his family at the seaside, far from Peking when they were supposed to have fled.

The story has many strange aspects and inconsistencies, but no further clarification has ever been made. Lin Biao remains as great a villain for Mao's present successors as he was during the last six years of Mao's life, when the Gang of Four ruled.

Zhou Enlai died early in 1976, and Mao himself in the following September. Within a month, Mao's widow, Jiang Qing and her supporters were arrested. In 1980 the "Gang of Four" were brought to trial before a people's court in Peking. Jiang Qing was condemned to death, a sentence later commuted to life imprisonment.

Hua Guofeng whom Mao had raised up, and to whom he is said to have bequeathed his succession, was elected chairman of the Chinese communist party, doubling that post with the prime ministership. Deng Xiaoping has returned to favour, with power seemingly at least equal to that of the chairman. Liu Shaoqi has been posthumously rehabilitated with many others.

Government policy has taken a course almost the exact opposite of the cultural revolution, now openly decried as a vile tyranny. Modernization, industrialization, and the acquisition of technological skills are the objectives set by the new regime. In 1977 the program of the "Four Modernizations," agriculture, industry, scientific research, defense, was launched. Education, including examinations, has been restored to a state of normality. Arts and literature are freed from the bonds imposed by Jiang Qing. China has taken her seat at the United Nations and improved her relations with the USA (sparked off by President Nixon's visit). Now in the throes of an industrial revolution of daunting magnitude, China sees her increasing trade with the West as helping to make good the gaps in her technology. She remains as distrustful of Soviet Russia as ever.

It may be that the Chinese revolution has concluded, the elimination of the Gang of Four having been the necessary "whiff of grapeshot," without, however, calling for a Napoleon. What is certain is that this ancient nation is still as vigorous and creative as at anytime in its long history.

Deng Xiaoping, who in April 1976 was condemned as "right-wing," returns to the political limelight. In 1977 he was reinstated and given back all his former powers, since when he has been responsible for the program of accelerated technical development.

Opposite: painting in oil, celebrating China's "new age" of modernization, a program of development to be carried to completion by the end of the century. Introduced in January 1977, this plan for economic self-sufficiency is known as the "four plans for modernization" (agriculture, industry, scientific research and defense). China's present leaders seem determined to utilize to the full the vast resources, human and material, which will permit the country to liberate itself from its past of backwardness and poverty and ensure a better quality of life for its teeming millions.

善行無轍迹

Perfect activity leaves
no track behind it.

THE EYE OF THE WEST

Pliny talked of the Silks and of the *sericae vestae* which cost millions of sesterces in the Roman empire. Then there were Marco Polo, Odorico da Pordenone, the Portuguese merchants, and the Jesuits with Matteo Ricci. It all adds up to a compendium of knowledge – exiguous and in the final analysis prejudiced – concerning the whole course of Chinese history up to the end of the last dynasty. With wonder went respect – at least for the power and grandeur of what was China. On these pages we can see some illustrations from Western books on China in the age of the Enlightenment. There followed the period of colonization. China, however, always succeeded in preserving her sovereignty. The earliest photographs coincide with this colonial period and with the crisis which Chinese society faced when it came into contact with the West. History does not, unfortunately, allow to a people the right to choose what images of themselves should be presented abroad. Documents (and old photographs are documents) can, however, make us think, and only thinking will lead to comprehension and sympathy. The fact remains that the meeting between China, emerging from her "splendid isolation," and the West, one of the high moments of history, was a very painful and difficult affair. The pictures on these pages give some indication of the historical drama which was being played out.

Mandarino di Turon con uno Schiavo che porta la Pipa

Pages 416–417
A Chinese family of good standing. Around 1875. (Photographer unknown.)

On the left: Manchu ladies, c. 1875. (Photographer unknown.)

Below: itinerant craftsmen in Jiujiang in the province of Jiangxi. Date c. 1868. From the left: a seller of soups; fortuneteller predicting a woman's future; a barber and a turner about their respective vocations. (Photo by John Thomson.)

Opposite left: three distinguished old men of Canton in summer clothes. Circa 1861. Right: paddy-fields and tea plantations on the hills of Jiangxi in the southeast of China. 1902. (Photographer unknown.)

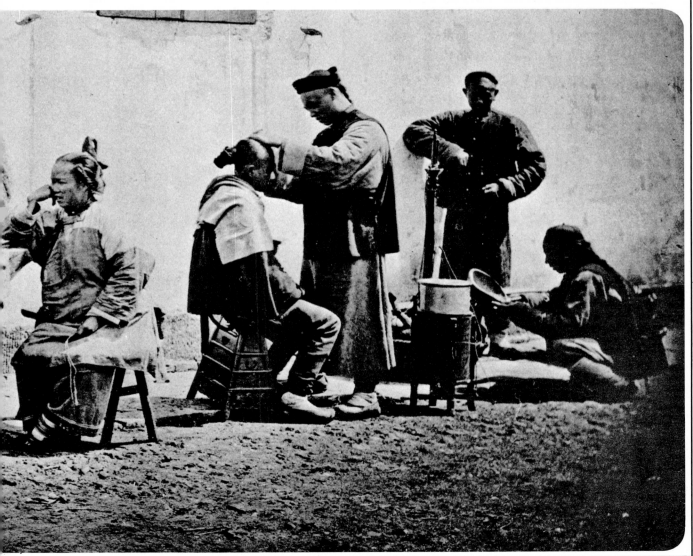

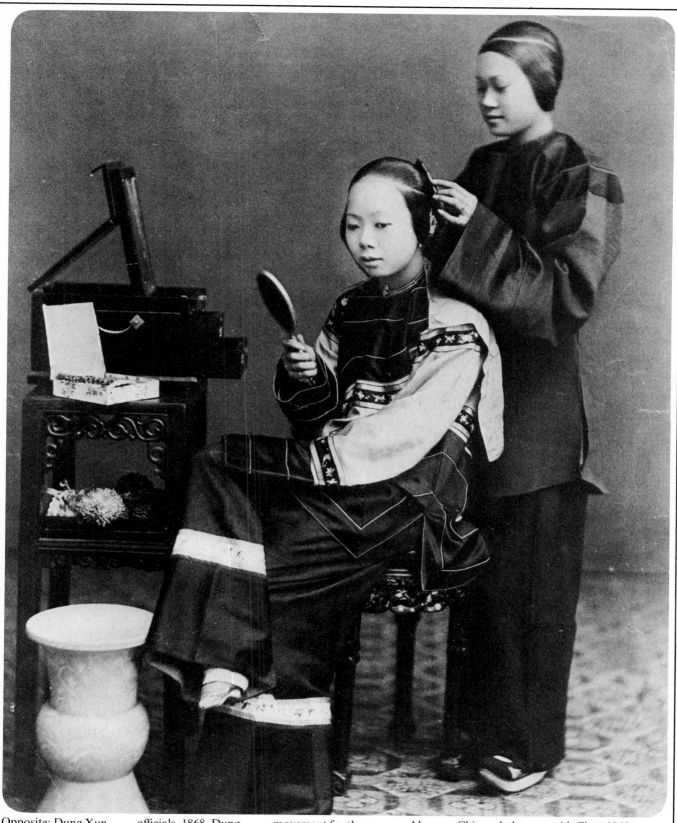

Opposite: Dung Xun, in the middle, with two high-ranking Chinese officials. 1868. Dung Xun was one of the leaders of the movement for the modernization of China. Above: a Chinese lady of quality having her hair arranged by a maid. Circa 1868. (Photos by John Thomson.)

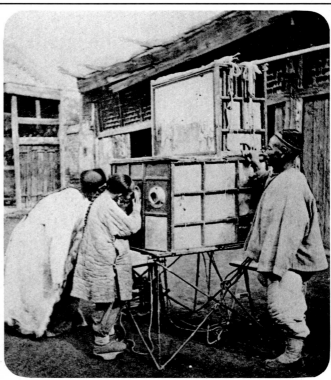

Opposite above left: an itinerant chiropodist at work. Right: with just a few *fen*, one can peer at the marvels of the exotic West.
Below: Gatling gun in the arsenal at Nanking. (All three photographs are by John Thomson.)

Right: the wife and daughter of a Western diplomat about to go on an outing with their "man-horse." Circa 1875. (Photographer unknown.) After the Treaty of Peking (1860), Westerners were permitted to live in various Chinese cities and not just the "open ports."
Below: opium smokers. Circa 1880. (George Eastman House.)

Above left: a watchman in charge of one of the gateways of Peking. Circa 1868. Below left: a thief condemned to the pillory. Circa 1868. (Both photographs by John Thomson.) The writing describes the tribunal which condemned him and the crime he has committed. Below: Chinese pirates beheaded in Hong Kong, 1897. The men standing are British government officials.

Above: a public execution. Circa 1860. Death by decapitation was considered one of the least severe forms of capital punishment as the victim suffered for so short a time. Right: the inhabitants of a village in Gansu crowd outside the house of the photographer Joseph F. Rock in order to listen to his phonograph. April 1925. (Photo by Joseph F. Rock.)

Opposite above: the northern corner of the walls of Peking, October 1860. (Photo by Felice A. Beato.)
Below left: a Canton street with its signs advertising shops and teahouses. Circa 1868. (Photo by John Thomson.)

Right: a Peking *hutung* or alleyway, around 1860. (Photographer unknown.)
Below: view of a country town in the South, on the banks of the river Huai. Circa 1887. (Photo by Thomas Childe.)

為學日益

Learning consists in adding to one's stock day by day.

SCIENCE AND TECHNOLOGY

by COLIN A. RONAN

TAOIST ROOTS

The history of science and technology is an essential ingredient in the development of human culture. Though much work has been done in tracing its Western side back through the ages to its cradle in Mediterranean antiquity, little has been done until recently to study the contribution from Asia and, particularly, from China, one of its two oldest civilizations. The genius of the Chinese people is so often represented as primarily artistic and agricultural, that the achievements of their science and technology often tends to be overlooked.

What the Chinese contributed to science and technology in ancient and mediaeval times was immense, but its character changed after the arrival in Peking of Jesuit missionaries in 1601. The Jesuits brought with them the new mathematically-based experimental science of the scientific revolution – science which is international in its appeal and universal in its scope. Once this had come to China, indigenous Chinese science fused into this new science and has developed as a part of it ever since.

Before the coming of the Jesuits, Chinese science was based on observations and experience; theory was always in a comparatively undeveloped state. Yet they managed to gain an insight into the natural world and anticipated many scientific and technical discoveries of the Greeks; they also managed to keep abreast of the Arabs who had all Greek knowledge at their disposal.

In the West people thought of substance as the touchstone of reality, but the Chinese saw the world in terms of relationships. They saw all things as fitting into a grand scheme where everything was related to everything else, where the universe and man formed one vast organism.

Such a view was particularly echoed by the Taoists, whose unique amalgam of philosophy and religion, magic and primitive or proto-science was the world's only form of mysticism that was not antiscientific. Indeed, the scientific side of Taoism has been largely overlooked, for although the movement was religious and poetic, with democratic and political aspects, it was also strongly magical and scientific.

While the Confucians were concerned with the active management of human society, the Taoists concentrated on a receptive attitude. They wished to make true observations of the world, untrammelled by preconceived theories and unattended by any need to consider social consequences. They looked for a rational explanation for every facet of nature, even those, such as natural disasters, which usually generated terror rather than any other emotion; in contemplation everything, terrible or otherwise, would be seen in its proper perspective.

Practical experience was also valued by the Taoists. The craftsman, they realized, might often be more knowledgeable than the supposedly learned man. They were not averse to doing practical things themselves; to using their hands. They could and would experiment. Yet such an attitude was anathema to the Confucian scholar, to whom manual effort was considered undignified. The Taoists realized too that it was not necessary to have full theoretical understanding before any technological advance could be made; they knew that in the light of practical experience the technologist will often manage to do the right thing for the wrong theoretical reasons.

The primitive scientific teaching was the first aspect of Taoism to die out when its ideas were later discussed and commented on. It petered out because such ideas aroused little interest in the world of bureaucrats who, by the time of the 3rd and 4th centuries, were encouraging a revision of Taoism. As a result of this reassessment mixed Taoist-Confucian schools arose where mundane matters were avoided, but since they attracted the best minds of the day, it was inevitable that some dissatisfaction should be felt against Establishment opinions. One exponent of this movement was the poet Xi Kang who scandalized the Confucians by his skill as a metal worker.

However, from the late 2nd century to the 6th the experimental techniques of the Taoists seem to have flourished, for that period showed a great cultivation of alchemy, and the beautiful literary style of the 6th-century alchemical treatise *Bao Pu Zi* (Book of the Master of Preservation of Solidarity) recommended it to Confucian scholars. Moreover there was also some recurrence of Taoist thought under the Tang, but the Taoists had now to contend with the new school of Neo-Confucianism, which flourished particularly in the Song period (5th century). This form of Confucianism did not reject a study of the natural world and, in considering that morality arose out of nature, emphasized the idea of nature as an organism and came close to a world concept of evolutionary materialism. It was a philosophy that was essentially scientific in quality and was accompanied by a hitherto unparalleled flowering of pure and applied science.

Two very early schools of thought in China which tried to work out a basis of scientific logic were the Mohists – named after the sage Mo Ti – and the Logicians. The former experimented in optics, seem to have had a feeling for geometry and came close to a theory of science. The latter were never very clearly differentiated from the Mohists, or the Taoists for that matter. Both schools died out during the first unification of the empire in the 3rd century B.C.

As with all early civilizations the Chinese had their superstitions, and there were plenty of ways of divining the future. Some of these magical methods, however, led to investigations which had a scientific outcome, as we shall see for example in the case of the magnetic compass. They also generated a reaction, a sceptical tradition which, although always present in Chinese thought, flowered in the Han when its most illustrious figure, Wang Chong, wrote his *Lun Heng* (Discourses Weighed in the Balance), a book which was full of rationalism and took a very critical look at things. At a time when most of his contemporaries still believed in spiritual beings, legends about supernatural births, and even intercourse with dragons, Wang Chong fought such ideas with sound

Detail from a silk scroll of the 17th century, now in the British Museum, London, showing two philosophers engaged in studying the symbols of Yin and Yang. These are the two elements which at once explain and bring together the bipolarity typical of Chinese thought – man-woman; dark-light; earth-sea – each of which contains within itself elements of the other and is therefore always subject to mutation. The frequently recurring symbolism of Yin and Yang has a special place in art. It is often represented by the sign seen in the scroll above: a circle divided into two halves, one light (the Yin, which contains a black spot representing the embryo of the Yang) and one dark (the Yang, containing the embryo of the Yin); these unite in a spiral in the middle of the circle.

scientific arguments. His work led in later centuries to humanistic studies, textual criticism and archaeology.

There were a number of fundamental concepts in Chinese science worked out from the earliest times by Chinese naturalists. These were the idea of the Five Elements, the theory of the Two Basic Forces and the use of an elaborate structure of symbolism as exemplified in the *Yi-jing* (The Book of Changes).

The Five Element theory underwent various changes and modifications, arriving at a stabilized state in Han times. The five elements were water, fire, wood, metal and earth, but it must be emphasized that these were not what we should call elements today; rather they were five sorts of fundamental process. The theory was an attempt to classify the basic properties of material things, evident when these materials underwent change. There were some similarities as well as differences between the Chinese views and those of the Greeks with their four elements, but they seem to have arisen independently.

By the Han, Enumeration Orders had been established. These were expressions of how the Five Elements came into being, and the ways they could react with one another. For instance, in the "Mutual Conquest Order," metal conquers wood because it can cut and carve it; fire conquers metal because it can melt it; and so on, right the way round the cycle, with earth conquering water, and wood conquering earth. Such Enumeration Orders embody principles concerning the rate of change, the principles of Control and Masking. The principle of Control was derived from the Mutual Conquest Order, for a given process of conquest is said to be controlled by that element which, in its turn, conquers the conquering element. For example, metal conquers wood, but fire (which conquers metal) controls the process. The Masking principle was derived from two of the Enumeration Orders and refers to the masking of a change by some other process which creates more of the material than is being destroyed. Thus wood conquers earth, but fire masks the process since fire will destroy wood and create earth (ash) again. The principles of Control and Masking bring in a quantitative, measurable aspect to the process.

The two forces, Yin and Yang, need little description here. The philosophical use of the terms began in the 4th century B.C., and is connected with dark and light: Yin evoked the idea of rain, cold and femaleness, whereas Yang evoked warmth, sunshine, maleness and brightness. They went together, one or the other in domination, operating in wave-like succession.

The philosophical use of Yin and Yang appears in the *Yi-jing*, Book of Changes. This contains a series of 64 symbolic figures of six lines each (broken or unbroken), associated alternately with Yin and Yang which, however, never become separated, although only one is manifest at a time, almost as if we were dealing with dominant and recessive factors in genetics. Like the interaction of the Five Elements they lead to paths of thought which have only in recent times been seen to be valid in examining nature.

The Book of Changes is really a repository of concepts associated with one another through the Five Elements and the

PMATTHEVS RICCIVS MACERATENSIS QVI PRIMVS E SOCIETAE IESV EVANGELIVM IN SINAS INVEXIT OBIIT ANNO SALVTIS 1610 ÆTATIS 60

A portrait by Emmanuel Pereira of Matteo Ricci painted in 1610, a few months before he died. The original painting is now in the Istituto Storico della Compagnia di Gesú, Rome. Matteo Ricci (or Li Ma-tou in Chinese) went to China towards the end of the 16th century as head of a Jesuit mission. However, it was only in 1601, after a two-year wait, that he was allowed to offer his gifts and expound his theology before the celestial throne of the Tang emperor who then gave him permission to live in Peking. It was the Jesuits who introduced the experimental method into China based on mathematics and this was to be of the first importance for several of the disciplines of Chinese science which had previously been based on an organic conception of the universe.

two basic forces Yin and Yang, and ideas of similarity (e.g. like attracts like) and contagion (a relationship between things which have once been in contact). The 64 six-line patterns were significant for extracting a comprehensive symbolism which contained all the basic principles of natural phenomena. Thus it was a giant specialized filing system; a way of achieving peace through the contemplation of nature by way of a vast system of classification. But whereas the Five Elements and Yin and Yang concepts were useful for the development of scientific thought, the Book of Changes seems to have been a handicap because it was a method of pigeonholing novelty.

In the West we are used to thinking and speaking about the laws of nature; the Chinese had no such concept. In the West between the 2nd and 17th centuries the two ideas of natural law, binding all people, and laws of nature controlling all nonhuman affairs, became completely separated in people's minds. In China things took a different turn. There was the arbitrary law of the lawgiver, quite independent of what morality might say, but they also recognized a second law, a sense of rightness, based on ancient custom and usage, which included all such things as filial piety which were felt to be morally right. The latter was the law of right behaviour, which should be taught by magistrates rather than enforced, moral exhortation being superior to legal compulsion. To the Chinese, then, laws arose out of justice and justice arose out of the common people, and must correspond

with what they felt to be right. Law could not exist without ethical sanction.

One can see that the idea of the lawgiver's law could have been applied to the natural world, to give laws of nature, but this was never done. Probably the Chinese lack of a belief in a celestial lawgiver had something to do with this. They did not believe nature was commanded by Heaven to see that things followed their regular course. Such would be the case for a law of compulsion; their concept was rather one in which things were not forced into obedience; they behaved in the way they were observed to do so because of a natural order. Indeed, the natural order of things, the organism of the natural world, precluded a government by a law of compulsion.

The Chinese world-view depended on a harmony, a co-operative effort on a universal scale, because everything was a part of a vast cosmic hierarchy. There was no law of nature to be obeyed, but a pattern of nature into which things fitted and played their part. This view did not bring the Chinese to the universal science of modern man, but it did allow them to make some great achievements in natural science and technology, as the following pages will show.

Ladies engaged in the preparation of silk, detail from a painting attributed to the last Northern Song emperor, Hui Zong (1082–1135), and now in the Boston Museum of Fine Arts. As early as the Zhou period (11th century B.C.) there is evidence of the cultivation of silkworms in the shape of some fragments of the precious weave believed to date from around 1500 B.C. The first descriptions of Chinese spinning mechanisms date from the 11th century (although it is probable that these refer to much older contrivances) while in Europe, the earliest illustration of a loom is 14th century.

"THE LAND OF THE SERES"

The illustrations on these pages are taken from a manual of the 13th century which was further elaborated in the 17th. They show the various stages in the breeding of silkworms, the treatment of the cocoons and weaving.

Legend has it that it was Xiling, consort of the Yellow Emperor, who had the idea of weaving together the fine threads, which were already used for stringing musical instruments, in order to make precious cloth.

It seems that Chinese silks were exported to India from the 4th or 3rd century B.C. and that from the name of the Qin dynasty was derived the Indian word "China" used to denote the country from which the precious cloth was brought. When silk first came to Rome, around the 1st century, it was called *sericum* or cloth made of "ser." Very probably, "ser" was the nearest phonetic approximation that foreigners could

for "gold" and the character which means "its price is equivalent to that of gold." However, the economic and political confusion which reigned during the 3rd and 4th centuries from one end of the Silk Road to the other (the decline and fall of the Roman empire and the end of the Han dynasty with consequent shattering of the fragile Chinese unity) meant that travel by land had become just as perilous as travel by sea.

manage to the Chinese word for silk (*ssu*). Silk became one of China's main exports from the beginning of the 2nd century, and in Rome it was considered to be as valuable as gold. That silk was worth its weight in gold may simply be a saying but it is interesting to note that in a Chinese etymological dictionary of the 1st century, the character *jin*, which is used to describe decorated silk of the highest quality, is composed of the root

In ancient times, only members of the royal family and court were allowed to wear silk: yellow was the colour reserved to the emperor, his chief wife and his heir. The other wives had to wear violet-coloured silk, as did the highest ranking officials, while those of the second and third ranks wore red silk. However, by the 7th century, China was producing so much silk that everyone was allowed to wear it. From the 10th century, weavers began to experiment, adding gold or coloured strands to their looms to create patterns and designs. These portrayed mythological beasts, dragons, stylized leaves and flowers and symbolic figures. Silk was exported ready-woven or wrapped onto skeins. It was forbidden, on pain of death, to reveal the secret of silkworms or to let the cocoons out of the country. If legend attributes to one woman the merit of having invented silk-weaving, it attributes to another the misdeed of taking the secret out of China. In the 5th century, a Chinese princess who went to be married to the king of Khotan, one of the oasis kingdoms along the Silk Road, hid some silkworms' eggs in her hairdo. Thus Khotan began to produce and to export silk. The two monks who took the secret to Byzantium in 550 appear not to have come from China proper, but from Khotan.

The Persians, who controlled both the Indian Ocean and the land-bound routes, were the middlemen of commercial traffic between China and abroad. It is difficult to relate values to today's prices but we may note that in the year 301, a pound weight of silk cost the equivalent of $60, but by the 6th century, during the reign of the emperor Justinian, a pound of best quality silk cost up to $1000.

The Byzantine empire exercised a strict control over silk which was woven and cut out in workshops run by the state. Notwithstanding the high profits to be made from this monopoly, the cost of the raw silk was always excessively high. However, even as late as the 6th century, the West had no idea of how silk was produced. One day, around 550, two monks presented themselves at Justinian's court, claiming to have lived for years in the "Land of the Seres" and to know how to produce silk. In their hollow bamboo staffs they had brought with them the eggs of the silkworm. The secret was a secret no longer but the fact that the West could now make its own silk did not mean that trade with China was at an end, for Chinese silk was always of the highest quality.

MEDICINE

Much in Chinese medicine has yet to be explained in modern terms, but even now it is clear that it was always in an advanced state for its time. Certainly the first Chinese doctors were connected with the deepest roots of Taoism and with the early shamans, the priestly spirit-possessed healers and magicians of North Asian tribes, but by Confucian times (6th century B.C.) physicians were already differentiated from the wandering medical practitioners; by mediaeval times scholars had joined the ranks of medical men and the standing of the profession had risen.

We are fortunate in knowing something of very early Chinese medicine for, in the 6th century B.C., a discussion between a prince of Jin and his physician was recorded. From this we learn that the physician divided diseases into six classes, derived from an excess of one or other fundamental and almost meteorological "exhalations" or qi – an excess of rain caused one disease, of twilight another disease, and so on – showing us that it appears that Chinese medicine grew up independently from the doctrine of the Five Elements which became accepted in every branch of Chinese science and technology. Later, the first four causes were classified together under "fever," leaving one implying psychological illness, with cardiac disease for the sixth.

As early as the 5th and 4th centuries B.C. there were four important characteristic ways in which a physician would diagnose an illness. These consisted of noting the patient's general physical state including colour and cleanliness of the tongue, listening to the heart and breathing and noting the smell of the breath, consideration of the patient's medical history, and a general examination by feel and pulse. Not surprisingly, this has been termed a valid and valuable precursor of contemporary clinical practice. And as early as the time of Confucius acupuncture was already practiced as well as general radiant heat (moxa), and also available were counterirritants, medicated plasters, aqueous and alcoholic decoctions of drugs, as well as massage and gymnastics; all this before the time of the famous Greek physician Hippocrates.

The Chinese Nei Jing (Manual of Corporeal [Medicine]) was their equivalent of the Greek corpus of work attributed to Hippocrates. It had reached the state in which we now have it by the 1st century B.C.; written in dialogue form it systematizes the clinical experience and physiological and pathological ideas of the physicians of the preceding five or six centuries, and shows the original sixfold "meteorological" system developed into a more sophisticated sixfold series.

As might be expected in a society developing a bureaucratic feudalism, prevention of illness was considered of even more importance than its control when it arose, and in spite of fringe activities like the use of charms and prayers of invocation to deities, particularly among the poorer strata of society, and exorcism, Chinese medicine was thoroughly rational. And with their elaborate civil service, entered by the educated gentry only if they passed qualifying examinations, it was not long before such examinations were established in those sciences, including

Drawing of a human figure showing the lines of points suitable for acupuncture relative to the upper right-hand part of the body. These points on the surface of the skin, each of which is linked to one of the vital organs, are joined by a network of imaginary lines, called "meridians," around which circulates positive and negative energy. Once again, we find the influence of Yin and Yang. The point of acupuncture is to attain a state of equilibrium by the correct dispersion or invigoration of this energy by means of the subcutaneous insertion of very fine needles in the appropriate parts of the body. Acupuncture is a very ancient practice which has been in use among the Chinese people for many thousands of years. It exists alongside official medicine, a science all of its own, and can often put the finishing touches to a cure instigated by allopathic medicine. Research is now being carried out into the scientific basis of acupuncture.

Opposite: an illustration from a Tibetan "Treatise on Medicine." It shows the fertilization of the human egg, the growth of the embryo and the development of the foetus up until birth. The text dates from the 8th century, the author combining the principles of Han medicine with traditional Tibetan lore. Although it is certainly weighed down by feudal and religious superstition, this text contains precise information relating to anatomy, the nervous system and the circulatory system.

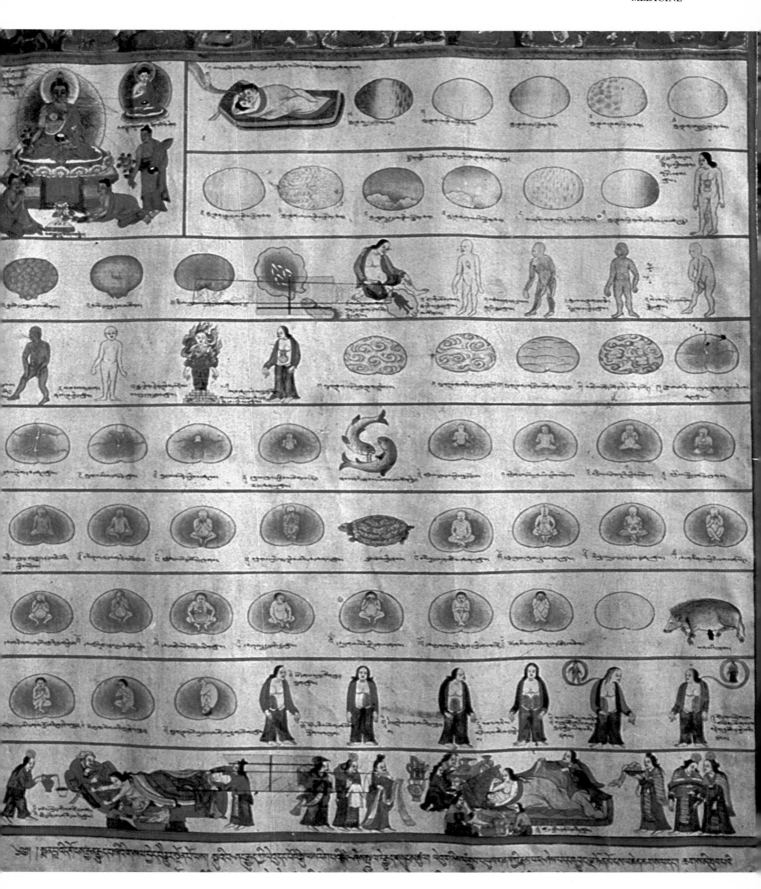

medicine, considered necessary by the state. General educational qualifications were considered necessary in addition to medical knowledge, and by the 5th century there were regius professorships and lectureships in medicine. By the 7th century, under the Tang, an Imperial Medical College was established. This method of qualification spread to the Arab world in the 10th century, and to the West a century later.

The idea of hospitals first arose in China in the time of the Han, before the arrival of Buddhism, but afterwards religious motives led to the establishment of a number of institutions for the care of the sick, not only by the Buddhists but also by the Taoists. However, when Confucianism had regained strength towards the end of the Tang dynasty and especially later during the Song dynasties (10th to 13th century), the government took over more and more of the once religious foundations, and did so throughout the entire country.

Another medical aspect of Chinese bureaucracy was the establishment of quarantine regulations. For example, in the 4th century, during a disastrous epidemic, the Jin emperor applied what were known even then as the "old rules," which prohibited officials whose families had three or more cases of illness from attending court for a 100 days. Lepers were also isolated, and although it is uncertain when such isolation began, we do know that by the 6th century leper colonies had been set up for both men and women.

Reference has already been made to the Chinese use of minerals and herbal remedies; indeed one of the glories of Chinese alchemy was its application in the making of medicines. One of the advantages which bureaucracy brought was its encouragement of the systematization and collation of facts about drugs and the promotion of the publication of the pharmaceutical natural histories. There were also books of standard prescriptions; indeed, in 723 the *Guang Ji Fang* (General Formulary of Prescriptions) was composed by the emperor Xuan Zong himself with his assistants, and sent out to all medical schools, while some of its prescriptions were actually written up on notice boards at crossroads so that ordinary people could take full advantage of them. There were also official regulations of the number of practitioners of medicine in each provincial city, the number depending on the number of families residing there. The bureaucracy too seems to have carried systematization to a still higher degree when, in the 7th century, it arranged for the publication of a large treatise, *Qiao shi Zhu Bing Yuan Hou Lin* (Mr. Qiao's Systematic Treatise on Diseases and their Aetiology), giving a systematic classification of pathological states but omitting any therapy for them.

Ancient Chinese medicine was closely linked with the beliefs of those who may be broadly termed Taoists. Believing that man's life should be led in conformity with nature, they became intimately concerned with preventive medicine and with hygiene, and they also brought to Chinese medicine its very real interest in psychomatic illness. The idea of preventing illness occurs repeatedly in medical texts from the Zhou to the Tang period, the leading idea being that the right systematic course of therapy in the appropriate season prevents the occurrence of

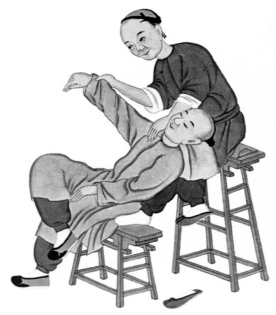

Above: a 19th-century print showing the treatment of an ill person (Wellcome Museum of Medical Science, London). In traditional Chinese medicine, diagnosis was made on the basis of a careful examination of the pulse beat. The human body was likened to a stringed instrument and harmonies and discords could both be discerned by listening to the pulse through which flowed the life-giving substances.

Below: a jade figurine used in ancient times by women in order to point out to their doctors (in front of whom they were not allowed to undress) where they suffered pain (History of Medicine Department, University of Kansas, Kansas City). Many such figurines are known, made of more or less precious stone but usually of jade or ivory.

diseases in the following season. Coupled with this was the administration's system of public hygiene and protection against pests – for example smoke or dust from the winter aster (*Pyrethrum seticuspe*) was used against insects, while there were vermin exterminators, those whose job was to bury corpses of people or animals found on the public highways, and so on. In such ways as these public health as well as medical care is seen to have been a very real concern in ancient and mediaeval China.

MATHEMATICS AND GEOMETRY

Mathematics is the cornerstone of modern science so it is perhaps appropriate that some remarks about it should come first in any description of early Chinese science and technology, especially as it displays some interesting aspects when compared with developments in other civilizations.

Our earliest knowledge of Chinese mathematics comes from oracle bones. These were the shoulder blades of mammals or shells of turtles, which were used for divination by piercing with a heated sharp-pointed bronze instrument, followed by a study of the ensuing cracks. Afterwards questions and answers were inscribed on the bones and it is these inscriptions which have come down to us; they date from the Shang period (about 1520 to 1030 B.C.), were discovered in the Anyang area in Henan province in the early years of this century, and provide an important source of information on early Chinese culture.

The oracle bones show that the Chinese had a simple way of writing numbers as early as the 14th century B.C., and as time went on these developed into the form of "counting rod" characters. The system was based on the use of a counting board, one on which small rods were placed in appropriate positions to represent numbers and then moved about as the numbers changed during the operations of addition, subtraction, multiplication and division. How early counting rods were used in China is uncertain. However, if the Chinese character *suan*, meaning calculation, is indeed an ancient pictograph of counting rods – and there is reason to think it is – then the counting board and the numerals may well go back to the first millennium B.C.

There is no doubt whatsoever that the counting rod system of writing numerals had become stabilized by the 3rd century. By this time there was also a well-defined system of place value incorporated in the numerals: thus where we use 1 for one, and 21 for twenty-one, the Chinese used | and = |, the tens being written horizontally (=) and the units vertically, thus:

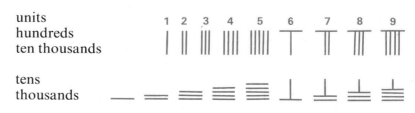

The number 34567 would therefore be written |||≡|||| ⊥ 丌

Before the 8th century, whenever there was a need for what we would write as a zero, the Chinese left a blank space, as they did on the counting board. All calculations therefore used only nine signs, until sometime after the 8th century when a circular written zero appeared. The precise date of its introduction into China is uncertain, but there is strong evidence to show that it was used on inscriptions in both Cambodia and Sumatra as early as A.D. 683, and it seems to have originated in Indo-China at the interface of Hindu and Chinese cultures during the 7th century.

In common with other civilizations, the Chinese were fascinated by numbers and by what appeared to be mystical relationships between them. Essential differences between odd numbers and even numbers were recognized very early, and in China, as in Greece, they were associated with the two sexes, while the Chinese also shared the widespread belief that odd numbers were lucky and even ones unlucky. Yet in spite of this the Chinese seem, all through their history, to have had a preference for concrete numbers rather than just for numbers as such. Here, as elsewhere, they showed a strong practical sense.

One aspect of number symbolism which the Chinese developed was the magic square: a collection of numbers arranged within a square and which, when added in any direction, always gave the same answer. A Chinese legend of the 5th century B.C. is concerned with what is essentially a magic square, although in spite of references in the 2nd and 3rd centuries it was not until the 13th that these numbers became a real part of Chinese mathematical thinking.

In China the basic arithmetical processes: addition, subtraction, multiplication and division, were well known, multiplication being looked on as an abridgement of addition, and carried out in a way similar to our modern method and unlike that generally used in Europe in earlier times. Counting boards and rod numerals made multiplication tables an early natural development, and such tables have been found on bamboo tablets dating from 100 B.C. They were, however, written in words: the so-called Pythagorean type where the numbers are arranged in two coordinates, rather like tables of distances between towns in a motoring handbook, did not appear in China until the 8th century.

The square of a number, obtained by multiplying a number by itself, was known, as was the reverse process, finding the root.

Above: detail from a painting on silk from a Tang screen showing a lady playing *Wei qi* or Chinese chequers. This is a very ancient game: its rules were quoted by the philosopher Mengzi in the 4th century B.C. in a well-known allegory. For 2000 years, *Wei qi* (which was also known in Japan under the name *Go*) was considered one of the "four sublime pastimes" in China together with playing the lute, painting and calligraphy. Nowadays, young Chinese are encouraged to play this complicated game which, it is thought, improves intelligence, decisiveness, will power and perspicacity.

Below: an abacus, the most widely-used calculating device since ancient times and used even today in China for sophisticated mathematical workings such as finding the square root.

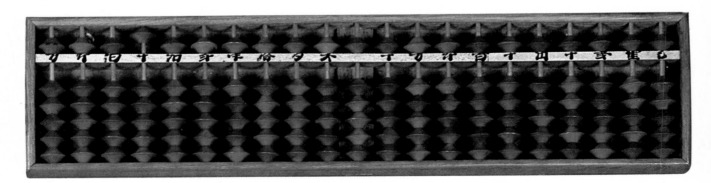

Arabic mathematicians conceived the square of a number as growing out of its root, and our word root is derived from this. On the other hand Latin authors thought of the root of a number as the side of a square and this more geometrical picture was also taken by the Chinese, who became adept at taking roots and thereby laid some sound foundations for the mathematicians of the Song period who, two centuries later, found how to use them in solving algebraic equations.

As far as computation was concerned the Chinese used various aids, of which counting rods and the abacus were the most important. Counting rods were originally thin bamboo sticks about 15 centimeters long which could conveniently be held in a bundle in the hand. Their advantage over writing was that they could readily be removed from the counting board when the numbers they represented were no longer required. Great facility and speed in using the rods could be achieved, and in Tang times they were popular with administrators and engineers. After the 17th-century invention in Europe by John Napier of "Napier's bones" (inscribed rods used for multiplication), the Chinese adopted this variation, using it for extracting square and cube roots. But these numbered rods were soon replaced by other devices such as the slide rule.

The more famous abacus, with its flattened balls sliding on wires fixed to a wooden frame, is also capable of great speed in use. It appears to be a development of an earlier system of balls on wires lying over a simple graduated board, used in China probably during the 2nd century and well known by the 6th. Whether, though, it is earlier than the European use of pebbles on carved slabs is uncertain.

In many early civilizations there was a tendency among mathematicians to avoid fractions, but the Chinese do not seem to have been worried by them. From the 3rd century B.C. they also used a decimal system derived from their standardized measurements of length. This helped them not only to write fractions in a convenient way but also to experience no difficulties when they came upon surds (numbers like $\sqrt{2}$ which cannot be expressed as fractions), although these worried the Greeks who had no decimal system. Decimals also allowed the Chinese to write down very large numbers in a convenient way, using powers of ten such that (in modern notation) 1000 is 10^3, 10,000 is 10^4, and so on. The Chinese also had no difficulty in conceiving negative numbers as early as the 2nd century B.C., whereas these did not appear in Indian mathematics until 500 years later, and were unknown in Europe until the 16th century.

The Chinese never developed anything like the geometry of the Greeks with its axioms, theorems and proofs. Admittedly, in the 4th century B.C., the Mohists, who were contemporaries of Euclid, gave some attention to the subject, drawing up a system of definitions, but this had little if any effect on later Chinese mathematics. Yet in spite of this the Chinese knew of the relationship between the sides of right-angled triangles and devised their own proof of the theorem, different from that derived by Pythagoras. Moreover, they also computed the most accurate value in early times for π (the ratio of the circumference of a circle to its diameter), a value of 3·14159 26 being found in the 5th century, which compares well with the modern value of 3·14159 26536. Yet in Europe such accuracy was not reached for almost another 1200 years.

It is to the Chinese that credit must also be given for having founded coordinate geometry. This method of specifying the positions of points, lines and curves with respect to a grid simply by numbers appeared in China by the 3rd century, derived probably from activities in map-making and tabulating data. In Europe such a geometry did not become fully developed and superior to the Chinese until 14 centuries later.

Chinese mathematical thinking was essentially algebraic – it was associated with numbers and numerical relationships – in contrast with ancient Greece where the approach was geometric, concerned with relationships between shapes. All the same, the Chinese did not use algebraic symbols but wrote out their algebra in words, although a host of single-syllable ideograms were devised for indicating mathematical operations such as multiplication and division, etc. and for referring to general mathematical quantities rather than specific numbers. Moreover, the counting board became laid out so that the specific quantities – unknowns, powers, and so on – always lay in certain predetermined positions.

This use of places on the counting board for certain types of quantity gave rise to a tendency to think in patterns. In the Song period (10th to 13th century) – the high point in the history of Chinese algebra – it led to the development of the matrix or square divided up into compartments to receive the terms of an equation. Since several matrix boards could be used at the same time, this was a remarkable achievement, yet in spite of it no general theory of equations was ever developed by the Chinese.

The Song algebraists were adept at solving equations, and to help them do so they derived what we should now call a binomial theorem. This is a theorem which gives the coefficients for a "binomial" or mathematical expression with two terms, e.g. $(x+1)$, raised to different powers. The coefficents progress in a specific way, as can be seen if we write:

Binomial	Power	Coefficients
$(x+1) = x+1$	1	$1+1$
$(x+1)^2 = x^2 + 2x + 1$	2	$1+2+1$
$(x+1)^3 = x^3 + 3x^2 + 3x + 1$	3	$1+3+3+1$
etc.	etc.	etc.

The pattern formed by the coefficents in the right-hand column is triangular in shape, and this allows a pattern of coefficients to be drawn up without working out each stage by multiplying out the binomial (left-hand column). The realization of this came to the Song algebraists not later than the 12th century, and was used in the solutions of equations involving cubes and higher powers. In Europe the triangular pattern of coefficients is called "Pascal's Triangle" ever since Blaise Pascal published it in the middle of the 17th century, some 500 years after it was in regular use in China; it seems rather likely that China is where it originated.

After the fall of the Song dynasty Chinese algebra progressed

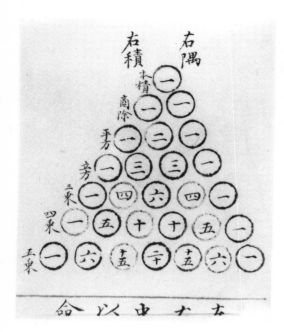

The oldest existing representation of "Pascal's Triangle" in China, from the manuscript *Yung Lo Da Dian* (Great Encyclopaedia of the Yung Lo reign period) of A.D. 1407. The text accompanying the diagram states that the Triangle was made use of by Jia Xian about A.D. 1100.

no further but, even so, its achievements were already notable. Not only did the Chinese fathom out for themselves Pascal's triangle and coordinate geometry, and use a matrix system for solving equations, but they also tackled the question of indeterminate equations (where there are more unknowns than equations to solve them), they devised a method of "finite differences" to determine constants in formulae for celestial motions, and used a Rule of False Position for solving equations. And of course Chinese mathematics as a whole had other advances to add to these. The use of negative numbers, a decimal system, a method for writing large numbers, the extraction of square and cube roots, determination of proportions using a Rule of Three and the writing of fractions in vertical columns are examples. Moreover, although they were not geometrically-minded, the Chinese dealt also with problems like determining the areas of circles and the volumes of solid figures.

The Chinese seemed to have received little from the mathematicians of Egypt or Mesopotamia; they did import the use of the zero sign but even this came from a mutual culture area with India. Chinese mathematics, then, was an indigenous development, which could more than hold its own with the achievements of any other Pre-Renaissance civilization and which exerted an influence far outside its cultural boundaries.

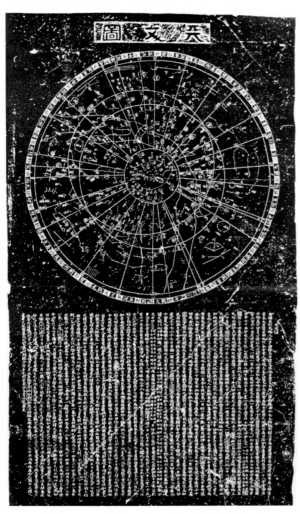

ASTRONOMY

The Chinese may be said to have had a "cosmic religion"; they thought of the universe as a whole, uniting man and nature with the heavens, a view which in the period of the Song (5th century) led to the great conception of the cosmos as an organism. Astronomy was therefore significant to them. It also had another aspect for, as an agricultural people, a seasonal calendar was of prime importance to them and in fact one was compiled by the emperor and his government, which all who owed allegiance to the emperor had to accept. Yet such a calendar is based not only on the seasons but on the aspects of the heavens which herald them, so once again astronomy was of importance, but now linked with governmental edicts. Thus it came about that in China astronomy was closely linked with the emperor – the Son of Heaven – and his court; astronomers were part of the official government service and accommodated within the walls of the imperial palace.

The belief that the heavens responded to the conduct of the emperor and his court, so that failures in administration would be displayed in celestial events, made it necessary for the heavens to be observed regularly and any unusual events recorded. Such records go back to about 1300 B.C. and form the longest unbroken series available in the records of any civilization.

These records are now being found invaluable to modern research. This is because for cyclic phenomena, like eclipses of the sun and moon and the appearance of comets, early records are of great importance and the meticulously kept old Chinese records present unique evidence. Moreover, the Chinese had no preconceived ideas to hamper them, whereas in the West the belief in the changelessness of the heavens prevented observations being either made or recorded. Thus sunspots, which are a guide to solar activity, had been recorded since 28 B.C. in China but in the West not until the 17th century, and the observation of a nova or a supernova – when a star suddenly appears in the sky where one has not been visible before – was neglected in the West until the 16th century. Novae and supernovae are caused when a star expels a vast mass of hot glowing gas, and it is important to know of past recurrences. The Chinese "guest star" of 1054, the gaseous remnants of whose exploding envelope we now call the Crab Nebula, is a prime example; it went unrecorded in the West. The earliest Chinese recording of such a phenomenon goes back to 1300 B.C.

Every civilization has divided the skies into areas of manageable proportions so that the positions of the stars may be charted and the movements of sun, moon and planets traced. In the West, from ancient times until the closing decades of the 16th century, positions were given using coordinates known as celestial latitude and longitude. These coordinates are not aligned with terrestrial latitude and longitude: celestial longitude is measured along the ecliptic, the apparent path of the sun's annual movement round the sky, and celestial latitude is measured upwards and downwards from the ecliptic to the pole of the ecliptic (a point 90° away). The Chinese, however, used coordinates which are the analogues of terrestrial latitudes and

Above: a star chart dating from 1274. In China, astronomy was not practiced merely by isolated observers of the heavens but from time immemorial was a function of the astronomers of the civil service. Observation, research and charting were therefore the work of a group rather than of an individual working alone.

Opposite: Adam Schall, the German Jesuit missionary, is here portrayed in mandarin dress in an engraving now in the Biblioteca Marciana, Venice. Schall was president of the imperial academy of astronomy of Peking and wrote various treatises on astronomy and mathematics (in Chinese) as well as taking responsibility for the reform and compilation of the new Chinese calendar.

P. Adam Schall Germanus I. Ordinis Mandarinus

449

longitude. We now call these coordinates right ascension, which is measured eastwards along the celestial equator (the celestial equivalent of the terrestrial equator), and north polar distance, which is measured from the north or south celestial pole to the celestial equator.

Interestingly enough these Chinese coordinates are the ones which Western European astronomers adopted at the end of the 16th century (although the Westerners measured "vertical" distances from equator to poles, instead of from poles to equator). The reason for the change of coordinates in the West is not completely clear but the reason why the Chinese adopted this system was the attention they devoted to the celestial pole.

The Chinese concern with the pole was connected with their picture of the microcosm, man, and the macrocosm, the universe. The celestial pole, about which the stars all appeared to revolve, corresponded to the emperor on earth, about whom revolved the vast bureaucracy of the state. The circumpolar stars – those close enough to the pole to be always above the horizon – were considered most significant, and those in the appropriate positions were used as key stars to define the limits of their 28 equatorial constellations or "lunar mansions," or "lodges," known as *xiu*. Some of the key stars were very dim. Thus the Chinese system was very different from that in the West, which still has 12 zodiacal constellations, lying along the zodiac, which is a band about 9° wide and centered on the ecliptic. Their division into degrees was also different from that in the West, because there are 365¼ Chinese degrees in a circle, not 360 as we use. The choice of 28 *xiu* was connected with the time taken for the moon to make a complete circuit of the stars (27·322 days).

The Chinese carefully charted and catalogued the stars. From as early as the 4th century B.C. three catalogues were drawn up by three different astronomers, catalogues which remained in use for the next 1000 years, though in the 4th century the three were combined into one in a star map, as was done again a century later when they were charted in three different colours to correspond with the three original catalogues. There is a long tradition of Chinese celestial cataloguing and map-making and the early catalogues were extensive, the earliest containing no less than 1464 stars. They were therefore larger than their Western counterparts, most of which were later than the Chinese.

It is not then perhaps surprising that with their meticulous cataloguing and charting the Chinese were the first to realize that the stars are not really fixed in space but have individual motions of their own. This they discovered early in the 8th century; it was not known in the West until a 1000 years later.

Star maps were constructed at least as early as the 3rd century and probably even earlier (in Han times). Although no maps have survived from these times, it is known from Han carvings and reliefs that star groups were represented by dots or circles connected by lines, a convention which spread later to the Arabs and thence to the West, and is still in use today. There is, however, a manuscript map dating from the year 940 from Dunhuang in Gansu province; this is almost certainly the oldest star chart from any civilization still in existence except for those

Below: the observatory at Peking in an engraving from a work by the Flemish Jesuit missionary Ferdinand Verbiest *Astronomica europea sub imperatore tartaro-sinico Cam-Hy appelato ...*, published in 1687. From the top center, proceeding in an anti-clockwise direction, the instruments shown are: a sextant, quadrant, an azimuth, ecliptic armillary sphere, a celestial globe and an equatorial armillary sphere.

Opposite: an early drawing of the Chinese telescope taken from a treatise on astronomy which was published in China in 1626.

stylized carvings and fresco paintings of antiquity. This map has two particular points of interest: it is painted in three colours: white, black and yellow, to correspond with the three ancient schools of cataloguing of almost 1400 years earlier, and the charts contain two projections or methods of delineating the "curved" surface of the sky on a flat sheet. The circumpolar stars are shown in a polar projection in which the stars are drawn within a circular area on the chart, and the rest are on what we should today call a Mercator projection, where parallels of declination (equivalent to parallels of terrestrial longitude) are straight lines, with the right ascensions (equivalent to terrestrial longitudes) equally spaced. The chart thus anticipates Mercator's projection, which was devised in the West in 1569, by more than 600 years.

Calendars and calendar periods

The preparation of calendars always presented problems to early civilizations because religious festivals were based on a lunar calendar, which came first, while the seasons depend upon the apparent position of the sun and demand a solar or annual calendar. The problems arose because the lunar cycle and solar cycle are incompatible; the period between new moon and new moon is $29\frac{1}{2}$ days and the solar cycle takes $365\frac{1}{4}$ days. In very early times, from the 13th century B.C., the Chinese had a 60-day count, and from the 1st century B.C. this was extended to number the years in cycles. As early as Shang times the length of the year was known to be $365\frac{1}{4}$ days, but it was not until the 11th century that months of 30 and 31 days were introduced. A seven-day week was also used but this was a comparatively late import from Central Asia; the characteristic Chinese period was a week of ten days. The Chinese themselves had originally divided the 12 months of the year into 24 fortnightly periods, a very ancient method of computation.

To reconcile the incompatible lunar and solar periods, calendar makers of all civilizations have concerned themselves with long cyclic periods or "resonances" during which the motions of the sun and moon come approximately into agreement. Probably the best known example of this is what is known in the West as the "Metonic cycle," a period of 19 years ($=6939\frac{3}{4}$ days approximately) which comes close to 235 lunar months measured from new moon to new moon ($=6932\frac{1}{2}$ days). In China this period was known as the *jang*. A still longer period of four times this length, the *bu*, was also known: it gives a period of 27,759 days, which is very close to 941 lunar months ($=27,759\frac{1}{2}$ days). Other resonances were recognized; these included sexagenary cycles and a duodenary cycle.

The sexagenary cycle is very old, and its count in 60s was made up of 12 characters which, combined alternately with a set of ten characters, gave 60 combinations. The 22 characters are common on oracle bones; in the time of Shang they were used strictly as a day count and only in the 1st century B.C. were they used for years as well. Their origin may have been Babylonian (since that nation counted in 60s). It was useful because six cycles made approximately one year and also broke down into six ten-day periods or approximately two lunar months.

The duodenary cycle of 12 brings us to Chinese studies of the apparent motions of the planets. The planets, as is well known, appear generally to move eastwards among the stars, now and again stopping in their tracks and then for a short time moving back westwards (retrograde motion). The time taken for a planet to complete one complete circuit of the stars (and including all retrograde as well as forward motion) is known as its "synodic" period, and by the end of the 1st century the Chinese had reliable figures for all the five planets then known. In the West such information was also derived from observation, but it came a little later, in the 2nd century. Jupiter attracted Chinese attention very early on because its synodic period is almost 12 years, and this seemed to fit in some way with the 12 characters of the sexagenary cycle and approximately with the number of lunar months in the year.

Ideas of the universe

The Chinese never worked out a theory of planetary motion: they were content to observe the planets' movements and calculate positions, but they had ideas about the nature of the universe as a whole. There was much speculation about this during the period of the late Warring States and early and late Han dynasties, and three views seem to have predominated. The first and oldest of these seems to have been the *Kai Tien* or "Hemispherical Dome" theory. In this the heavens were thought of as an inverted bowl with the earth itself conceived of rather like a second inverted bowl, square in shape, beneath it. The two were separated at the "rims" by an ocean, and the distance of the heavens above the earth was taken as 80,000 *li* (about 46,000 kilometers). The constellation we call the Great Bear was in the center of the heavens, which were round and rotated. The sun and moon had motions of their own and the rising and setting of celestial bodies were illusions, because no such body could pass underneath the earth. This theory has something in common with Babylonian ideas which also favoured a double bowl explanation, though the Chinese emphasis on a round heaven and a square earth was their own.

The second theory was held by the *Hun Tien* school, which favoured a celestial sphere for the heavens. This was a view which also commended itself to the Greeks, and at about the same time (4th century B.C.) as it was adopted in China. This theory was also linked with the idea of a spherically shaped earth at the center of the celestial sphere. The theory was well described late in the 1st century by Jang Heng who conceived of the earth as floating on water – a view which later fell into disuse – but who also looked beyond the sphere itself to an infinite universe.

The third theory, the *Xuan Yeh* or Infinite Empty Space concept, is comparatively late, and in spite of the mention of infinite space by Jang Heng, it is usually associated with his younger contemporary Qi Meng. This view held that the heavens were "empty and void of substance ... having no bounds," with the sun, moon and stars floating freely in this empty space. The sun, moon and five planets have their "advances and recessions [which] are not the same. It is because

Top: drawing of an armillary sphere with graduated hoops for the measurement of the positions of the heavenly bodies.

Above: Guo Shou-Jing's equatorial torquetum, the measuring circles of which pivoted about an axis parallel to the earth's polar axis.

they are not rooted [to any basis] or tied together that their movements can vary so much."

This is a very enlightened view, and with its celestial bodies separated by considerable distances and floating freely in an infinite universe, far more advanced than any theory produced by the ancient Greeks, with their closed spherical universe of spheres each one nesting inside another, which restricted European thinking for so long. It was a view which pervaded Chinese thinking, and which later, with the *Hun Tien* view of a spherical universe, which was so useful when it came to measuring the positions of celestial bodies, formed the background to all Chinese astronomy.

The *Xuan Yeh* theory posed the question of how the celestial bodies floated, and running through astronomical thinking was the concept of a "hard wind" which supported them, probably a Taoist idea which may well go back to the earliest use of bellows in metallurgy when powerful jets of air were generated. And if this worked to support the sun, moon, and planets was it also the way the earth was supported? And if it were, perhaps this meant that the earth moved also? Some Chinese thought that it did, first imagining that it oscillated rather than rotated.

Instruments

In common with many other civilizations the first astronomical instrument that the Chinese developed was the gnomon, a simple vertical pole planted in the ground. Since in midsummer the noonday sun is at its highest, and at its lowest at midwinter, the length of the noonday shadow allowed these dates to be determined. The gnomon could also be used to observe the apparent rotation of the night sky. By the 2nd century a special jade measuring ruler or "gnomon shadow template" was in use to obtain standardization in the measurements of shadow length. The gnomon led to the development of sundials, both permanent and portable. In the 10th to 13th century some very large gnomons and other shadow measuring instruments were constructed in China and in the Arabic countries. The idea behind this was that the larger the instrument the less would be the significance of errors in the marking of their scales, and some 80 kilometers southeast of Luoyang there still stands a Chinese example of this kind, Chou Kung's tower for the measurement of the sun's shadow which had a gnomon 12 meters in length.

In Europe reliance was placed on sundials until the arrival there of the mechanical clock in the 14th century, but the Chinese interested themselves in the clepsydra or water clock which they brought to its highest state of perfection. The clepsydra was in use in Babylonia and Egypt very early on and falls into two main types; the inflow in which water flows into a vessel to record the passing of time, and the outflow where time is obtained by noting how much water has flowed out of a vessel which began full of water. The clepsydra may have been known in China as early as the 7th century B.C.; by the beginning of Han times the inflow type was favoured and means were soon devised to ensure that the inflow vessel received an even flow of water irrespective of the head of water in the original reservoir. Some Chinese clepsydrae incorporated a steelyard balance (a balance

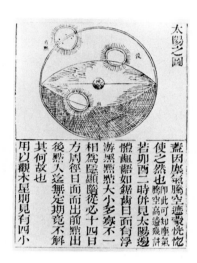

Above: a drawing showing the different heights of the sun in relation to the horizon at various times. It is taken from a manual of astronomy of the Ming period.

It seems certain that the use in China of armillary spheres, the basic instrument of astronomical measurement, was known from the time of the Han dynasty, around 100–130, that is shortly before Ptolemy. However, even as early as the 1st century B.C., there is evidence of a nearly completed armillary sphere while by 1088, the great sphere of Kaifeng, worked by clockwork, had been built.

453

with unequal arms) to indicate time by weighing the water which had flowed in, or the mercury in the case of small portable timekeepers.

For observing the stars the Chinese used long empty "sighting tubes," as the Babylonians had done before them: for the dim stars such as many of those which determined the beginning of the *xiu* these were useful since they cut out extraneous light. In ancient times the Chinese also made use of a serrated jade template derived from the jade disc known as a *pi*: this allowed the celestial pole to be determined as well as the directions of winter and summer solstice and the positions of some circumpolar stars.

But the most important of all the Chinese instruments was the armillary sphere (sphere of rings) which was essentially a framework depicting the celestial sphere with its circles, such as the meridians and the celestial equator. Fitted with a small sighting tube it could be used for determining the positions of celestial bodies. The simplest models were already available in the 4th century B.C. and by the 1st century some at least seem to have been water-driven to follow the apparent motion of the stars across the sky. Later, in the 8th century with the invention in China of the clock escapement, which is the basis of all mechanical timekeeping, they could compare the motions of celestial bodies on a mechanically driven sphere with those they observed, and so immediately note any discrepancies, a vital factor in all Chinese official astronomy.

With such clock-driven astronomical equipment the Chinese anticipated the West by some 1100 years. Again, the Chinese concern with the celestial pole, and coordinates measured with reference to it and to the celestial equator, led Gou Shou-Jing in the 13th century to construct an equatorial torquetum or observing instrument, the measuring circles of which were pivoted about an axis which lay parallel to the earth's polar axis, so that not only could the equatorial type of celestial coordinates be read very easily but also the apparent rotation of the stars could be followed by one rotation only, not two as was required with the ordinary armillary sphere. Such a method of equatorially mounting instruments was not adopted until some five centuries later in the West.

Reconstruction of a mural showing a calendar illustrated with figures of spirits and imaginary beasts, from the period of the Warring States. The preparation of the calendar, essential for the regulation of agriculture through the course of the seasons, has always been considered one of the most essential functions of the Chinese government and, as such, had excited an almost religious awe. It was the emperor's privilege to issue the calendar, with all due solemnity, while the court held a monopoly upon its publication and sale.

METEOROLOGY

In early civilizations there was often little differentiation between weather lore and events in the heavens. Rain came from the heavens, where the stars were. Only gradually was it appreciated that the weather was something which originated in the air above the earth and not in the heavens: Aristotle in ancient Greece made this clear, and it was understood also by the Chinese. Coloured by his scheme of the universe, Aristotle classified some astronomical phenomena as meteorological, while the Chinese, because of their belief that the heavens and the weather displayed divine reprimands for failures on the part of their rulers, observed and kept meticulous records of meteorological phenomena. As a result, for a long time the Chinese were in advance of the West not only in the records they kept but also in many of the techniques of measurement they used.

The oracle bones show that some very early weather prediction took place but, by and large, it was in the recording of the weather that the Chinese excelled. From as early as 1216 B.C., rainfall, wind direction and snowfall were recorded for every ten-day period, while records were kept for the more severe conditions of floods and droughts, whirlwinds and waterspouts, for longer intervals.

The need to monitor weather conditions was vital to a country like China, where there was a vast canal transport system and where flooding could have the most disastrous consequences if early steps were not taken to try to do something about it. In consequence the Chinese used rain gauges which, by 1247 at the latest, were to be found in every provincial and district capital, which was supposed to report its results back to the central government. Snow gauges were also used in China at the same time; these consisted of bamboo cages set up in highlands and beside mountain passes. Such gauges were unknown in the West, rain gauges not appearing in Europe until after the first quarter of the 17th century.

Wind direction was noted, using kites, although there are some indications that it was in China that the weathercock, possibly the earliest of all pointer-reading devices, was first used. There is evidence that the Chinese also attempted during the Han dynasty to construct an anemometer for measuring wind speed and it is just possible that it may have had hemispherical cups similar to those which are used in modern instruments. Records were also kept of temperature and humidity, and of thunderstorms.

The Chinese attempted to explain the events they recorded, and although some of their ideas were superseded in the days of post-Renaissance science, it is clear that they realized the existence of a circulation of water from land to air and back by precipitation. They also observed rainbows and were able by the 11th century to explain the cause, thus anticipating the Arabs by 200 years, and made detailed studies of mock suns – systems of rings and reflected images around the sun – describing them some 2000 years before they appeared in the literature of the West.

A mobile meteorological station in Tibet for collecting data regarding the direction of the wind. As long ago as the Han period, there is evidence of the construction of an early anemometer which was very close to a modern instrument in its use of hemispheres. Rotating weathercocks, the earliest indicators of direction, were first used in ancient China. The earliest records of natural phenomena and also the first logical attempts to predict drought and floods began to be made around 1216 B.C.

455

The tides

Until modern times more interest in the tides was shown in China than anywhere else. Perhaps this is not surprising in view of the fact that Chinese tides have a considerable range: for instance, at the mouth of the Yangtze the difference at a spring tide between high and low water is 3·5 meters, while its tidal bore has a range of six meters.

The Chinese drew up systematic tide tables and seem, by the 2nd century B.C., to have thought that there was a link between the tides and the moon. A similar suggestion was made about the same time in Greece. Three centuries later, though, the Chinese had established the moon's influence which, of course, fitted in well with their concept that the heavens and earth reacted with each other. Then, in the 11th century, thanks to their systematic records, they recognized that at various places where there were delays between theoretical high and low tide and its actual arrival, these were due to the shoreline and other local causes. In this they were again more enlightened than the West before the Renaissance.

EARTH SCIENCES

Geology as we know it is a science whose foundations lie no farther back than the 17th century, yet a study of the earth, its crust and the formation of its features has a far longer history. And though a full study of the earth sciences in China has yet to be made, it is already clear that the Chinese made some notable achievements in this field.

Early on the Chinese showed a clear appreciation of geological features. Paintings and book illustrations show a recognition of exposed strata and with such accuracy that collections of these illustrations provide a whole textbook of descriptive geology. Admittedly the aim of such illustrations was artistic rather than scientific, but the Taoist ethic of keeping close to nature ensured that what was shown should be the real world. Indeed, this was taken so seriously that for many centuries painters had available guidebooks, which included a host of geological structures, and often some descriptive phrases such as "mountain wrinkles," or "outline mountain ranges like a pile of cut-off wheel-rims."

Geological questions such as the origin of mountains, the uplifting of strata, the effects of erosion and the deposition of sediments are all referred to frequently in Chinese literature. In the West the appearance of seashells on high ground was always taken as evidence of the Flood, but in mediaeval China there was an appreciation of the fact that these could be due instead to the uplifting of land that had once been submerged. Indeed the Taoists had a peculiar technical term, *sang tien*, meaning "mulberry grove," for such land, derived perhaps from a place-name or the name of a star constellation. Possibly some stimulation to consider vast geological changes came from the arrival in China during the 1st century of the Buddhist idea of periodical cataclysmic upheavals, but if so, the Chinese certainly treated it all in a wholly realistic fashion.

This appreciation of the changing geological scene meant that the Chinese were able to recognize fossils at an early date and long before their nature was understood either in the Islamic countries or in Europe. Fossil plants seem to have been recognized first, petrified pine trees being described probably as early as the 3rd century. But fossil animals were also known, although there was some confusion about what the species were. Thus the fossils of brachiopods, with their resemblance to bivalve molluscs such as mussels, were known as "stone swallows," and, on occasions when frost and then sun attacked high rocks which contained them so that the pieces splintered off and fell to the ground, there were accounts of how these swallows were seen to fly. Yet a true explanation was provided by the 12th century.

Stone fishes were recognized by the 6th century and by the 12th there were detailed descriptions of the strata in which they were found. It is indeed clear that from as early as about the 1st century the Chinese defined and recognized fossil material, and did so with more precision and comprehension than was ever done in the pre-Renaissance West. Certainly some earlier Greek writers had mentioned the land and the sea being once mixed up to explain the appearance of shells and animal remains on high ground, but this was not followed up, so that later it was seen as an interesting comment but no more than that.

There is no doubt that from the 2nd to 15th century it was China where the earth sciences developed most; in their knowledge of the earth the Chinese were far in advance of the West. The situation was similar to that in map-making where, after an initial impetus in the Old World, there was a hiatus in Western countries but continual progress in China. In the making of maps and charts this situation continued until Arabic developments in the 9th century, the Chinese inventing the rectangular grid as a basis for plotting features, and also the world's first relief maps. The Chinese held their superiority in the earth sciences until the 17th century.

China possesses some natural seepages of petroleum which were long recognized, the products sometimes being put to good use as in the 2nd century when petroleum grease from at least one local seepage was used for lubricating cart axles. Some excellent descriptions survive of such seepages. A 2nd-century reference to one in the mountains south of Yanshou says it gave a fatty "sticky liquid"; in 1070 the polymath Shengua wrote of samples he had taken which burned with a thick smoke. The deposit from this could, he claimed, be used to make an ink superior to that from pinewood resin which was in such demand that its continual use would, he feared, lead to deforestation – a remarkably prescient observation for the 11th century.

Mineralogy

We can say that the study of the minerals to be found in the earth's crust predates geology because the listing of stones, metals and minerals goes back far into antiquity, although the modern science of mineralogy only began in the 18th century.

All civilizations seem to have been interested in minerals and their formation and it may well be that Babylonia and Egypt

Vegetable and animal fossils found recently in Shandong, in the region where, 15 million years ago, during the Miocene epoch, there was a large lacustrine basin which was eventually filled up by the eruption of a volcano. This area is extremely interesting to palaeontologists by reason of the huge variety of specimens which it contains, all marvellously well preserved, some of which indicate the existence of animals unknown elsewhere.

were the common source of the similar ideas which the Greeks and Chinese were discussing at about the same time. Both thought of minerals growing in the earth due to some presence – an emanation of one kind or another – but the Chinese broke new ground when they suggested that minerals underwent slow chemical change while still buried. They also had the idea that metals and minerals changed into one another, but in this we now know they were mistaken.

The Chinese first classified materials into stones and rocks on the one hand, and metals and alloys on the other, with a separate classification for jade. Naturally enough colour played an important part in classifying minerals, which were widely used in preparing medical remedies, in contrast to the West where minerals were excluded from medicine until the 16th century.

Various minerals were familiar to the Chinese and used by them. They knew of fuller's earth, of coal and of alum, which was used to fix dyes and in tanning, sizing paper, glassmaking, fireproofing wood and in medicine as an astringent to stop bleeding. Ammonium chloride (sal ammoniac) was important chemically and in medicine, in which after the 10th century another mineral, borax, also had a place. Asbestos too was known and used for its fire-resistant qualities, although it was sometimes thought to have animal connections – hence the stories of the salamander and the phoenix – because fibres were thought to be only of animal or vegetable origin. Because of its beauty jade held a special place, and a technology for working what is a very hard mineral was developed early on; Neolithic jade tools have been recovered, while by the 13th century B.C. the Shang people were carving it. The chief invention for working jade was the rotary disc knife, the earliest use of which is uncertain. There is a 12th-century reference to it, but as craftsmen tend to keep their techniques secret, its use probably goes back well before this.

In China from very early times an association was recognized between rocks, minerals and plants. By the 4th century B.C. the Chinese were aware that the presence or absence of different plants was a clue to the presence of minerals and metallic ores in a given area, and that the condition of the plants themselves also provided additional clues. By the 15th century the Chinese were also claiming that metals could be extracted from specific plants, an assertion which modern research has confirmed because it has been found that some plants do indeed take up metal if it is present beneath them. Thus the mediaeval Chinese were the forerunners of what is now a vast and rapidly growing body of scientific theory and practice which goes under the name of geo-botanical prospecting.

Seismology

China may have no volcanoes but it is one of the world's great areas of seismic disturbance. Records of earthquakes are numerous and were kept from early times, the earliest, which is still extant, dating back to 780 B.C., when the courses of three rivers were interrupted. From this time constant records were kept up to 1644, by which time there had been no less than 908 recorded shocks, which provide the longest and most complete recordings we have for any part of the earth's surface. Some of the shocks were severe, one in February 1556 killing more than 800,000 people in the provinces of Shaanxi, Shanxi and Henan. Yet in spite of such activity no great progress was made in ancient or mediaeval China towards a theory of earthquakes, which in Europe too was only formulated after the Renaissance.

But if the Chinese did not develop the theoretical side they certainly produced the ancestor of all seismographs or earthquake recorders. This was the invention of the astronomer, geographer and mathematician Zhang Heng (78–139). The basic information about Zhang's instrument appeared in a reference to him in a 5th-century history, and although it is fairly explicit there is still some doubt about certain details. Nevertheless the general arrangement is certain and there is no doubt either about how it worked or about its success.

The seismograph took the form of a large bronze wine jar, two meters in diameter, and surmounted by a domed cover. Around the outside of the jar were eight dragon heads, each having a moveable lower jaw which held a bronze ball. Eight bronze toads were placed on the floor round the jar, each facing a dragon head. When a distant earthquake shock was felt, the appropriate dragon's mouth would open to release its ball, which would then fall into the mouth of the toad below it. The instrument thus recorded not only the arrival of an earthquake shock but also the direction from which it came, for there was a device inside the jar which locked the mechanism after one ball had been released so that no second ball could be dropped, thus obviating any possibility of confusion.

The mechanism consisted essentially of a very heavy pendulum – still the basis of many modern seismographs – which on swinging moved various levers that both released the ball and locked the release mechanism against further action. Zhang Heng's seismograph was a great achievement; it was sensitive enough to record shocks too slight to be detected even by observers in its vicinity and preceded the first European seismography by almost 1600 years.

The world's first working seismograph, constructed by Zhang Heng in about the year 130 during the last years of the Han dynasty. Inside a large bronze jar with a diameter of about two meters, hung a pendulum which, when it registered movements of the earth (even though they were at a great distance), activated a series of levers. They in their turn make a bronze ball fall from the mouth of a dragon placed on the perimeter of the jar directly into the mouth of a bronze toad sitting underneath. This instrument not only made possible the recording of earthquakes but could even establish the direction from which they came.

Zhang Heng, who was one of the greatest mathematicians and astronomers of his age, also designed the earliest armillary spheres and was the first to apply driving power to the rotation of astronomical instruments.

PHYSICS

Physics is a study in which traditional Chinese culture has never been strong, although there is no lack of material in Chinese literature on physical subjects. And it is interesting to see that Chinese physical thinking was dominated not by any atomic ideas but by wave concepts. Recognition of the wavelike succession of Yin and Yang, each continually waxing and waning, recurs throughout Chinese texts from as early as the 4th century B.C., and was an outlook which fitted in well with the general Chinese idea of the universe as a whole, where everything reacted with everything else.

It was the Mohist school of thought which concerned itself most with the basic problems in physics. They were concerned with establishing standards of measurement and adopting units which were neither too great nor too small. Indeed decimalized measurement was adopted very early on. Some foot rules of the 6th century B.C. already show decimal divisions and three centuries later this was adopted more widely. Later, in the 8th century, a true metric system was adopted based on astronomical measurement – namely, the distance involved in a change of a unit of terrestrial latitude.

The Mohists also discussed the balance of forces in weighing and in pulleys and pulley blocks, and understood the theory of equilibrium – the latter, it seems, about half a century before it was expressed in the West. They also discussed problems of tension and fracture. On the other hand there seems to have been no theoretical ferment in China on the subject of the center of gravity as there was in the West, but some trial-and-error methods were followed, notably in the suspension of the L-shaped pieces of stone used as chimes and in the "Advisory Vessels" – hydrostatic "trick" vessels, which altered their position depending on the amount of water they contained. The technicians of the Han period seem also to have been familiar with the "Archimedes principle" (the displacement of a specific amount of water by a solid body of particular weight), as well as the principles of buoyancy.

Little was done in China on the physics of moving bodies, although the Mohists did briefly discuss the question and seemed to have some insight into relative motion. Heat was studied, the successive boiling phases of liquids discovered, and there was a careful classification of different kinds of flame and of combustion, including that of the human body, which shows some understanding of what today we should call metabolic rate and heat output. However, the Chinese never came to any theory of heat, but neither did the West until well after the scientific revolution.

The study of light
Research into optics by the Arabs exceeded anything ever attempted by the Chinese, although the Mohists did carry out experiments with mirrors and sources of light. The Mohist propositions on optics are to be found in a rather fragmentary text of the 4th century B.C. which nevertheless shows that they knew light travels in straight lines, and were aware of the use of

Above: a picture showing the god Fu Hsi, holding a set-square, and his wife Nu Kua, holding a compass. The two are linked together by the tails of serpents. Representations of this type, imbued with the spirit of Taoism, reiterate the idea which is at the basis of Chinese scientific thought: it is not individual, cellular theories which are important; the logic upon which things depend is a force which binds together, the force of Yin and Yang, the principles which complement each other as the elements complement each other and which interact in order to form an organic universe.

Opposite: "The chariot looking towards the south," a device invented probably in the 3rd century by the physicist and engineer Ma Chun. A figure mounted upon a carriage looks always towards the south whatever the direction the chariot moves in. This was probably used as a simple type of gear mechanism.

the pinhole and of the concept of the focal point – the point of intersection of the rays on one side of a pinhole when light enters from the other to give an inverted image, characteristic for example of the camera obscura.

The Mohists also studied mirrors, both flat and curved. They were aware of multiple reflections from combinations of flat mirrors, and of lateral inversion (where left and right are interchanged in a mirror image). As far as curved mirrors were concerned, they experimented with both concave and convex surfaces, were aware of real and inverted images and could, it seems, differentiate between the focal point of a concave mirror and its center of curvature.

Burning mirrors were used in ancient China as in other early civilizations, and predate the Mohists, the earliest mention being in the 6th century B.C. However, the Chinese also had another type of mirror, a "magic mirror," which had two surfaces of unequal curvature. A design was cut in the back of the mirror so that the front reflecting surface varied in thickness and curvature at the point where the design lay. When one looked at the mirror two images were seen, one (the pattern) appearing to come from the back. Such mirrors were constructed in the 5th century and, because of their mystery at the time, became treasured possessions.

Burning glasses were also used in China, for as early as the first millennium B.C. there was an indigenous Chinese glass industry, derived from ancient Mesopotamia, while later the Mohists discussed refraction as seen when a partly submerged object appears bent. It is also possible that later still, in the Tang period, some kind of magic lantern was devised and that a variety of zoetrope – an ancestor of the cinema – was also invented in China. But the claim sometimes made that spectacles were invented in China seems to be based on a corrupt text and to be without foundation.

The concept of sound

Whereas the ancient Greeks analyzed sound, the Chinese were concerned with relationships. Moreover, in China there were two distinct currents, one the literary tradition of scholars, and the other an oral tradition of craftsmen, expert in acoustics and music. Chinese acoustics was primarily "pneumatic" and concerned with the behaviour of *qi*, something which could be channelled or piped yet was not solely a movement of air: their conception was indeed halfway between what we should now call a rarified gas and radiant energy.

Very sensitive to the timbre of sounds, the Chinese changed their conception of sound itself over the years. In an early stage sounds were thought to bode good or ill, but later changes in timbre and pitch came to be appreciated and they grouped instruments according to the way the sound was generated; by the 4th century B.C. they had recognized sound as a vibration. Indeed it was in China that vibrating single-reed instruments were first developed; their *sheng* or mouth organ goes back far into the Zhou epoch and is the ancestor of the harmonica group of instruments like the harmonium and the accordion.

It was also in the 4th century B.C. that sound became also

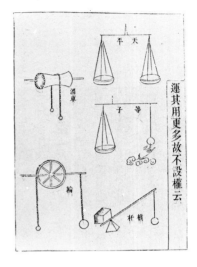

Drawings from a manual of the Ming period showing the principle of balances, levers and the pulley.

Chinese mathematics were algebraic rather than geometric and this influenced the development of other sciences, particularly physics, mathematics and engineering. Scientific thought developed without a basis in Euclidean geometry (which was the starting point of the Western scientific revolution), the elements of which were only introduced into the country under the Mongolian Yuan dynasty (13th to 14th century) and widely taught by the Jesuits in the 17th century.

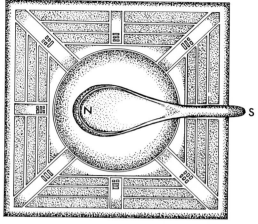

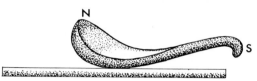

The first example of a magnetic compass, made of a divining table divided into sections, called a *shi* (which made its first appearance around the 3rd century B.C.) and a lodestone in the shape of the Dipper or Plough (sections of the Great Bear constellation) or of the Chinese spoon.

From the 1st century, we learn from written evidence of the existence of a "spoon which controls the south," regardless of the position in which it was placed. It appears that in China they used the concept of magnetic direction to indicate the south rather than the north. This fits in with Chinese cosmic symbolism which sees the emperor as the Pole Star, sitting on his throne which must perforce be in the north, so that he is facing south. It is clear that the Chinese understood magnetic direction well before the West had any understanding of polarity.

classified by pitch and there was a pentatonic (five-note) scale. However, the notes were not conceived from high to low, as in the West, but arranged either side of a chief note; an analogy of a court with its attendant officials. The notes of this scale were named at the latest by 300 B.C. There was also a heptatonic (seven-note) scale and, later still, a 12-note series was recognized, being derived from developments in bell-making.

A mathematical appreciation of the notes of a scale, and the measurement of pitch produced by vibrating strings and columns of air, led to some valuable achievements in musical intonation (the fixing of the pitches of the notes in a scale). And in 1584, the Manchu prince Ju Cai-Yu, who was a mathematician and a musicologist, derived mathematically an "equal temperament" method of tuning, thus giving equal intervals between every note of a scale. This was identical to that used in Europe a little later and it is certainly possible that the European discovery of equal temperament was not independent.

The magnetic compass

The most important of all Chinese work in physics was the discovery of the magnetic compass. Its beginnings lie in the use of special boards for divination. These *shih* or divining boards, which probably go back to the 3rd century B.C., consisted of two layers; an upper disc corresponding to heaven and which rotated on a pivot, and a lower square which corresponded to earth. The stars of the northern circumpolar constellation of the Dipper (or Plough) were marked on the upper disc. Both had the 24 cardinal points or azimuth directions marked around them, and they seem to have been used for finding direction. For divination symbolic pieces were thrown on to these boards, and among the pieces was a spoon symbolizing the Dipper (Plough). This spoon had a flat surface underneath the bowl so that it could rotate, and at some time, certainly by the 1st century, it seems to have replaced the rotating circular "heaven plate."

In common with other civilizations the Chinese knew of the magnetic properties of lodestone and this "magic" power seems to have led in the 1st or 2nd century B.C. to the construction of some of the symbolic pieces from lodestone and then later to making the "Dipper" spoon out of this material too. Once this had been done, the directional property of the lodestone was apparent and so the "south-pointing spoon" was discovered. With its flat surface underneath the bowl, there was of course much friction between the spoon and the board beneath it, and to avoid this the practice grew up of placing a piece of lodestone inside a pointed piece of wood, which could be floated, or balanced on an upward projecting pin.

Later, between the 1st and 6th century, it was discovered that the south-seeking property of the spoon could be transferred to small pieces or needles of iron which could also be made to float on water. Then, sometime before the 11th century, the Chinese also found that an iron needle could be magnetized by being cooled from red heat while held in a north-south direction. The advent of the magnetic needle brought a degree of precision in reading direction that was impossible with the south-pointing spoon and in the Tang epoch (8th or 9th century) this led to the discovery of magnetic diclination (the fact that magnetic north and south do not coincide with geographical north and south).

The magnetic compass was used first by the Chinese for divination in the siting of civil engineering works, but by the late 11th century it was certainly being used for navigation, a century before its use in Europe. However, it is highly likely that the navigational use of the magnetic compass in China goes back to the 10th century, that is 300 years before it came to Europe.

CHEMISTRY

Chemistry is another branch of science which is of comparatively recent origin, beginning in the West in the 17th century and reaching China a century later. Yet in China, as in other countries, there had always been what can be called a proto-chemistry, which ran side by side with the more mystical study of alchemy. To both studies the early Chinese made many contributions which filtered westwards along the trade routes to the Arabs and from them to Europe. Indeed, although the words "elixir" and "chemistry" are usually taken to be Arab in origin, it now seems that they really derive from China.

Developed from techniques originally used in cooking, Chinese alchemy was a particularly Taoist interest. This was to some extent because the Taoists were never shy of doing manual tasks, whereas the Confucians felt they lowered the status of the philosopher, and alchemy is nothing if not an experimental study. Its purpose, though, was partly mystical as well as practical, and knowledge was advanced in the laboratory not only by experimental work but also by prayer and incantation.

But early science often ran side by side with magic, and the Taoist adepts were only following a general trend. Their main goal was to find a means of physical immortality; they were fascinated by youth and were sure that some means could be found to prevent ageing. To this end, they devoted much time to the preparation of the body by special practices which included gymnastics and breathing exercises. They were of course unsuccessful in their quest but it led them to many chemical discoveries on the way. One of these was how to forestall the bodily decay of the dead, which they achieved by sealing tombs so that they were airtight, thus setting up anaerobic conditions inside them. In 1972 a tomb of this kind was excavated in Henan province and the body of a woman recovered. Although she had died in about 186 B.C., over 2000 years before, the condition of the corpse was like that of a person who had died only a week or so previously. Yet this relatively perfect preservation was achieved without embalming, mummification or tanning.

The Chinese attitude to the earth and to the universe, considering it as an organism, also lay behind much Taoist alchemical research, and led to a belief in underlying relationships between the Five Elements, the planets and various mineral substances. Again, the continually changing balance of Yin and Yang led them to consider cyclic fluctuations and brought them close to appreciating wave motion, so important in modern science and where, as soon as a maximum state of any

Two illustrations from a manual of the martial arts dating from the Ming dynasty. It contains numerous drawings showing the use of weapons of war which were known in China and also of armaments defined as "mysterious," which were known to exist in other countries. These include the arquebus which was introduced to China from the Islamic countries.

It was the Chinese who invented "fire lances" (pointed spears inserted into bamboo canes and then fired from them) at the beginning of the 12th century. From this were eventually derived the gun with a barrel and the cannon. The first writings on the subject of the preparation and use of explosive missiles and on the construction of such arms dates from the end of the Tang dynasty (9th century).

varying quantity is reached, the process of going over to its opposite necessarily follows. This inherent change and instability gave rise to what has been called the "first law of Chinese chemistry and physics."

Theoretical ideas marched parallel with developments in laboratory equipment, some of it quite sophisticated. The ordinary oven was improved and became more specialized, developing into stoves and furnaces designed in such a way as to give the alchemist considerable precision control over temperature. Special reaction vessels were invented, often of a type which could be completely sealed, made of metal and sometimes bound with wire to withstand the very high pressures developed inside them. Bamboo tubing was used to connect one piece of equipment with another, and though there were no thermometers, the Chinese appreciated the need for temperature stabilization and made much use of water baths and other means to keep an even heat. They also understood the need to weigh materials carefully and steelyard balances were widely used, as were sundials and water clocks to ensure accurate timing for different processes.

A particularly important piece of alchemical – and chemical – equipment developed in China was the still. It seems to have come into existence independently of the Hellenistic still invented in the West, and certainly was different in design. It was derived from a Chinese Neolithic cauldron which stood on three hollow legs and which evolved into a double steaming vessel, the upper compartment of which was separated from the lower by a grating. Later this had a basin of cooling water placed on top so that the distilled liquid dripped off into a cup placed on the grating. Used in China certainly as early as the Tang period (7th century), it is this East-Asian type of still which, in modern times, has become the molecular still of the 20th-century chemist.

The discovery of gunpowder

In preparing elixirs some concentrated and pure solutions were often required and in the 2nd century B.C. this led to the preparation of "frozen-out wine," a very concentrated form of alcohol obtained by a process in which all the water is frozen out first. By the time of the Tang the Chinese alchemists had learned how to distil their alcohol, a technique which needs a still with a cooling system and which, because of the different design of the Hellenistic still, Western alchemists did not have for another four or five centuries until the East-Asian design became known to them.

Other preparations deriving from Chinese alchemical research were minerals like the arsenic sulphides for medicinal use, known long before they were used in the West; industrially the Chinese also became expert in the extraction of copper. They also amassed considerable knowledge of the alkaline metals, which they were able to separate out. Saltpetre (potassium nitrate), acted upon by frozen-out vinegar (60 percent acetic acid), provided them with many insoluble organic substances, and by experimenting with it in combination with both sulphur, which had been mined for centuries, and charcoal, which was

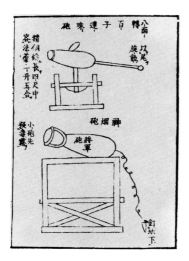

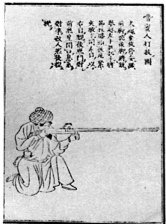

ASCETICISM AND CARE OF THE BODY

In every civilization, exercise and care of the body depend upon education and attitude and are therefore part of that civilization's culture. In China and the East in general, the Hellenic idea of athleticism, which only leads to the development of the body, does not prevail. Instead, there is the idea of asceticism which propounds the simultaneous and harmonious development of both mind and body. For Chinese doctors, as for all other ancient forms of medicine which could offer little hope of successful treatment, prevention was better than cure. Chinese medicine is based on the idea of a "correct physiological mean" which corresponds

to a "correct moral mean." Illness would be avoided if you preserved this state of equilibrium and took heed of certain advice (concerning bathing, massage, gymnastics, breathing exercises and diet). If, in spite of preventory measures, you succumbed to illness, traditional medicine would come to your aid in the form of medicines or treatment techniques such as acupuncture (which is still in use in China today and enjoying a particular vogue in the West). Less well known is another technique based on the same principles as acupuncture, that of moxibustion. This consists in the application of heat, supplied by burning dry leaves of artemisia, shaped into a cone, to the part of the body being treated (see left).

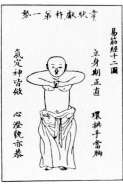

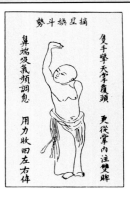

Breathing exercises in a treatise from the Qing dynasty. Buddhism introduced into China the idea of physical exercises helping to lead to bodily perfection. These were commonly used during the Tang period.

1   2   3   4   5

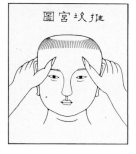

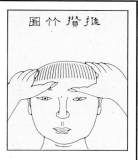

The gymnastic exercises invented by Hua To (141–208) are still practiced in China today and are known as the game of "the five animals. These are: 1. the tiger (head bent, fists held tight, breath held); 2. the bear (the body gently inclined, feet steady, muscles controlled and circulation therefore stimulated); 3. the stag (breathing stopped, the head turned round like a stag looking at its tail); 4. the monkey (imitating the monkey who wants to shin up a tree – this aids transpiration); 5. the bird (adopting the position of an animal attempting to fly with arms outstretched and breathing carefully controlled). The game of the five animals is based on principles expounded in the *Nei Jing*, which constitutes the canon of Chinese medicine and which dates from the 5th century B.C. The system of gymnastics which is most popular in modern China is called "extended pugilism" (some of the positions of which are shown at the bottom of these pages). It is also known as ghost-boxing and is partly inspired, like the game of the five animals, by the natural positions taken up by animals. It is in fact a series of exercises which are meant to lead to self-fulfillment and to guarantee long life. Its movements are generally circular and the raised arms, like the moving legs, describe innumerable circles which are all linked to one another. The trunk of the body and the loins constitute the center of gravity from which movements start which gradually involve the whole body. One therapeutic practice which has been widely used in China since the most ancient times is that of massage. The illustrations above show massage with the thumbs which have been dipped in sesame oil and extract of aromatic plants. Left: an augural illustration of children in a fantastic show of acrobatic exercises.

widely available, they formed a new substance with explosive reactions. This was gunpowder. First used militarily in the 10th century, it was widely adopted in China during the next 200 years and reached the Islamic countries in the 13th century, whence it spread to Europe a century later.

Chinese alchemy and early chemistry showed its practitioners that chemical reactions could provide not just mixtures but totally new chemical entities; it led them to the tabulation of different categories of substances, so presaging modern chemical affinity theory, and the Chinese care in weighing and measuring brought them to an understanding of combining weights and proportions, a vital aspect of modern chemical science.

AGRICULTURE AND THE BIOLOGICAL SCIENCES

We turn now to a very brief consideration of agriculture in China and the Chinese achievements in the biological sciences of botany and zoology. Much work remains to be done on their contribution to these subjects but nevertheless something can be said to give an indication of the very real advances they made.

In China there are two main fertile areas; each is close to one of the two great rivers: the Yellow River in the north and the Yangtze some 600 kilometers farther south. In the northern and northwestern area there is fertile loess soil, formed from the dust blown long ago from the Gobi desert, while the lower northern area is mainly silt carried down by the waters of the Yellow River. With good manuring this allows intensive cultivation of crops which do not need artificial irrigation, such as wheat, millet, barley, beans and hemp.

Climatic conditions are different farther south and west where, even though these areas are centered on the Yangtze, irrigation is required. Here we find mainly rice, and in winter when the rice fields become dry, there is a second crop of wheat, beans and rape seed or barley. This area also bears subsidiary crops of mulberry trees and cotton. Not all the crops were indigenous: wheat and barley had been introduced in late Neolithic times from Western Asia, and cotton came from India from the 6th to the 8th century; in the 11th century, special strains of rice from Champa in Indo-China were brought in to encourage double cropping, and five centuries later Chinese farmers had bred a type which would ripen in 60 days or less. Later still, in the 16th century, the sweet potato, maize, peanuts and tobacco came from America, and 100 years after this the common potato made its appearance.

The Chinese have continually had to face the problem of providing enough food for a growing population, and from at least Han times cultivation was far more intensive than anything known in the West. Indeed it has been claimed that the Chinese practiced market gardening rather than farming, and certainly they sowed their crops so that plants could be weeded easily and given individual attention. In South China during the 1st or 2nd century the practice grew up of planting in seed beds and then transplanting later, while the irrigation pools for the rice fields supported water chestnuts, beans and cucumbers, and duck

Several drawings from an agricultural manual of the Ming period showing work in the paddy-fields (above); ploughing the fields (opposite); and two typical agricultural tools (below): the harrow, used to break up the clods of earth, and the roller used for firming up the ground. China's economy has always been based on agriculture and on the necessity, even in ancient times, of providing for a continually growing population. Thus as long ago as the Han period, intensive farming was introduced. As well as this, technical innovations were continually being made in order to ensure a good crop; these included devices for irrigation, the practice of fertilization, the construction of waterworks to overcome the problems of erosion and of the silting up of the rivers and consequent flooding; and finally the organization of waterways and overland routes for the transportation of produce. The success of these operations was to lead, over the centuries, to the predominance of certain areas, the so-called "key economic areas," which were to be decisive in the political and social history of China.

were raised there. In addition mulberry trees for breeding silkworms were grown on the banks of the irrigation channels, and these also gave shade to the water buffalo whose tramping about firmed up the ground.

In the West crop rotation had been practiced by the Romans, who left the ground fallow in alternate years, but in most parts of China from Han times onwards fallowing was only carried out as a last resort. However, the Chinese knew that some crops, like legumes, enriched the soil whereas some others, such as wheat, weakened it, and although the first literary references to a true crop rotation come from the 6th century, it is very probable that the practice goes back earlier than this. The Chinese also made good use of fertilizers; animal and human manure being used from a very early date, while around the Yangtze mud dredged up from the canals was regularly spread over the ground.

Some additional land was reclaimed for agriculture from the 9th century to well into the 13th. In Song times terracing was practiced, and other forms of reclamation adopted; some lakes were drained and turned into fields with earth walls to keep out the water – rather in the manner of the later poldered fields of the Dutch – and bamboo rafts covered with water weed and earth were another way of increasing the areas which could be cultivated. All this of course helped affect the economic balance which moved from North to South as the Yangtze area became a center of migration with its two crops a year.

Up to the time of the Tang dynasty (9th century) the Chinese developed a number of characteristic agricultural implements. After this time there was little change, mainly because there was no demand for anything larger or more elaborate; the implements were all admirably suited to the kind of farming the Chinese carried out, for their farms were smaller rather than larger. They had a seed-drill plough, a range of harrows and rollers and they fitted hoes to a framework so that they could be pulled between the rows of crops. The one notable change which came later was the rotary winnowing-fan which arrived in the 13th century, but remained unknown in Europe until the 18th. Indeed Europe did not have agricultural implements until much later than China because the larger-scale Western farming demanded much bigger machinery and this was not possible with early technology. Which explains for instance why the West had to wait so long for an effective seed-drill plough.

Botany

The modern science of botany did not begin until the 17th century: in earlier times botany was purely descriptive but to this the Chinese made some notable contributions. In the West, little descriptive botany was done after the Greeks until the Renaissance, but in China there was no such hiatus and botany developed continuously from at least the 3rd century B.C. to modern times.

China had a number of advantages for botanists. There is a wide variety of plants for study because the country supports almost every kind of terrain from coniferous forests in the North to deciduous forests, woodlands, grassland, scrubland, semi-desert and even desert. To this must be added the bureaucratic machinery of state, which considered the correct use of land to be of singular importance and thus encouraged the beginnings of geobotany to provide it with a correct knowledge of plants and the different environments in which they flourished. This also stimulated the Chinese to examine soils carefully from probably as early as the 7th century B.C., whereas in the West, there was no such study at all until modern times. The pressing need for producing more food also meant that there was the stimulation of trying to grow crops outside their normal areas.

Another not unimportant factor in the development of botany in China was the nature of the Chinese language itself. The earliest pictographs were ideally suited for representing trunks, stems, leaves and fruit, so a botanical language was there at the start, and new characters could readily be added when required, since there was no fixed archaic language, as there was for instance in the West, to be used for botanical nomenclature. As early as the 3rd century B.C. we therefore find that besides everyday names for plants there was a technical two-term description, and this proved useful for developing a classification of "natural families." Indeed the Chinese possess a vast botanical literature which contains a succession of dictionaries and encyclopaedias that have helped keep their botanical nomenclature and terminology stable.

The most important class of botanical literature was, however, the series of pharmaceutical natural histories known as *Ben Zao* which started up in the 2nd century B.C. In these Chinese scholars collected together the continually increasing knowledge of plants, animals and minerals, and though the West later developed a similar kind of collection in its herbals and bestiaries, the Chinese works differed in containing much less material of a fabulous kind. When wood-block illustrations were developed in China during the 13th century the plants could be illustrated and the Chinese drew them with accuracy so that they could readily be recognized; this did not happen in the West for another 300 years.

Of all these Chinese pharmaceutical natural histories the most astonishing is the vast compilation made in 1583 by Li Shizhen. Not only did he present his facts critically, he also gave his own choice of name for a plant as well as the other names in use, thus foreshadowing the international nomenclature system we use today.

In mediaeval times many monographs and shorter publications also appeared, each concerned with specific species or genera, and it was in the 14th century that the "esculentist movement" arose. This was a movement which lasted until the 17th century and which concerned itself with measures to be taken in case of famine by indicating wild plants which could be used as emergency foods; thus it was a forerunner of present-day efforts to widen the sources of mankind's food supply.

Lastly, no mention of Chinese botany, however brief, can overlook the contribution it made to the range of ornamental plants such as the peony, rose and chrysanthemum, all of which appeared first in Chinese gardens and were later imported into Europe: indeed it has even been said that most of our garden plants are of Chinese origin.

A popular illustration showing a girl collecting medicinal herbs with a reaping hook. The study of botany in China developed considerably from the 3rd century B.C. and works dealing with botany and vegetable cures were written regularly from then onwards. The Chinese were particularly good at drawing plants and flowers with great precision.

Opposite: illustrations from an encyclopaedia of botany (*San-ts'ai t'u-hui*) from the Ming period (1610). From left to right: lotus flower, pine branch with cones, narcissus, peony, leafy branch of bamboo, day lily, autumn chrysanthemum, bamboo cane, and orchid leaves.

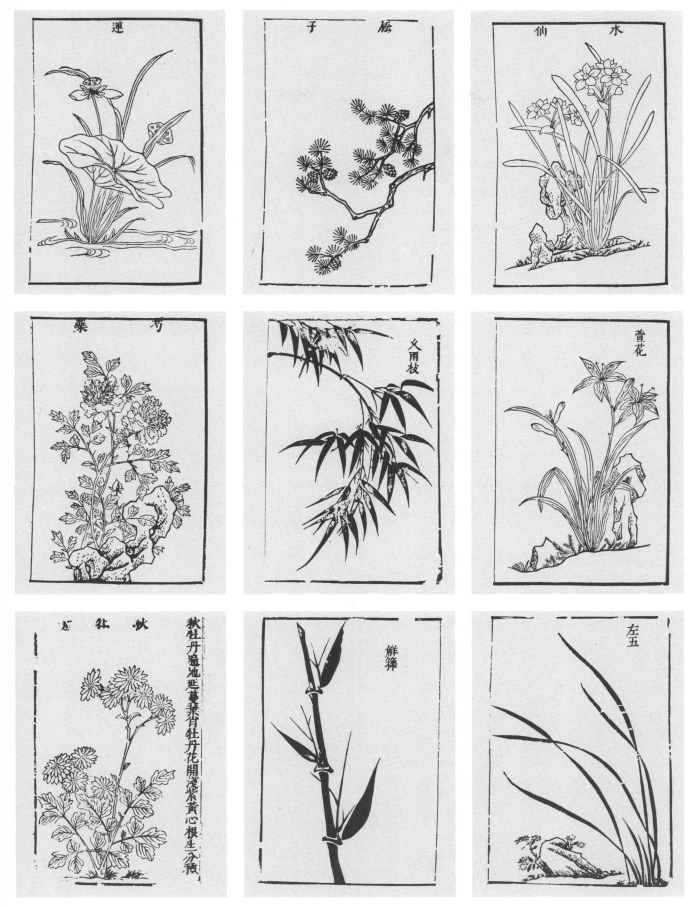

Zoology

At present there is no book in a Western language on Chinese zoology which, like Chinese botany, was a part of natural history and was concerned too with animals or animal products which might be used in medicine. Nevertheless in both ancient and mediaeval China there are various accounts of animals and their behaviour which deserve to be better known.

Chinese zoological literature is extensive and works date from almost every period; these include the encyclopaedias which appeared from the 4th century B.C. onwards as well as the pharmaceutical natural histories. From Tang times there were also monographs on particular species, though fewer than those on botany. All the same, Chinese zoologists had much to write about for the country had many interesting animals. In very early times, when the climate was warmer, these included the elephant and the rhinoceros. Yet there is still a wide variety of wildlife including a rare species of deer (Père David's deer), the gibbon monkey, the panda bear, the giant salamander and the Yangtze dolphin. As well there are a number of animal varieties which the Chinese selectively bred: among these are the water buffalo, the Mongolian pony, the Pekinese dog and a host of different kinds of goldfish.

A peculiar Chinese specialization was the domestication and breeding of insects. The best-known case is that of the silkworm, the domestication of which began in Shang times and was of course the basis for the large Chinese silk industry. But the silkworm was only one of a number of domesticated insects. There was for instance the scale insect (*Ericerus sinensis*) which flourished on a kind of ash tree (*Fraxinus*) and was cultivated in Sichuan province for the scales of white wax with which its body is covered and which is also secreted by the female. This was used for candles and also medicinally. Then there was another scale insect, the lac, and insects similar to the cochineal – that is of the Coccidae family – all of which were bred for their colouring substances which could be used in dyeing.

Besides insects with a commercial use, we find that the Chinese also bred crickets for sport. Kept in cages until released to fight with other crickets, they played a similar role to the birds bred in the West for cockfighting. In company with the people of other nations, the Chinese also kept bees from the very earliest times, but they used their honey largely as an ingredient in medicines, as its presence in apothecaries' shops even today bears witness.

Perhaps one of the most surprising aspects of the Chinese use of insects is the oldest known case of biological plant protection. In the 3rd century it was recorded that it was the habit of farmers who cultivated citrus trees to buy bags of ants which they hung on the trees as a protection from spiders, beetles and other pests. The species of ant used has been identified as *Oecophylla smaragdina* because this practice still continues and indeed modern Chinese science is very active in the field of plant protection by biological methods.

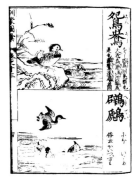

Top: drawings of aquatic animals from a book written in 1666. Above: two pages of the *Pen-ts'ao p'in-huei tsing-yao*, a treatise dealing with botany and pharmacy compiled and illustrated by Liou Wen-t'ai around 1505. On the left-hand page may be seen the lepidopterus insect *Attacus cynthius*, the larvae hatching out on the leaves of the ailanthus (or tree of the gods). It was used as a remedy for heart disease, ailments of the abdomen and also as a cure for impotence. The right-hand page shows a tiger; according to popular belief, the tiger's bones were thought to be an antidote against fear, palpitations and respiratory diseases. Even today, "tiger's wine" and "tiger's balm" are used as medicaments.

Opposite: deep-drilling mechanism used for the extraction of brackish water from the subsoil. Archaeological and documentary evidence confirm that as early as the Han dynasty (2nd to 1st century B.C.), use was being made of subsoil resources. These were recovered by means of systems which, although basically simple, contained the fundamental techniques which eventually led to modern advances in the field. A rod, consisting in many cases of a long bamboo pole with a sharp and very heavy end, and later containing an additional "hammerhead," was pushed into the earth with a battering motion by a group of men or draught animals pulling up the cutting head and then letting it drop back.

THE SALT INDUSTRY AND DEEP BOREHOLE DRILLING

Salt (sodium chloride) is essential for health, and in China the preparation of salt for human consumption is very ancient, going back at least 3000 years. Powdered salt is mentioned as early as the 7th century B.C., so it is clear that the salt industry in China is of great antiquity. In China sources of common salt – so-called to distinguish it from other chemical salts – are sea salt, which accounts for some 76 percent of production, deep deposits of brine (16·5 percent), salt from salt lakes (5·4 percent), rock salt, which is salt in its mineral form (1 percent), and salt as a by-product from the mining of gypsum (0·4 percent). Vast deep deposits of brine occur in western China, and its extraction from the 2nd century B.C. onwards made the people of the Han dynasty the first to devise and master the techniques of deep borehole drilling, techniques which have been extended and developed in the West in modern times.

The Chinese were also the first people to make use of natural gas, which arose as a by-product of the drilling.

Because of its importance, salt production was linked with political power in China from a very early date. For instance the salt resources of Sichuan were partly responsible for its recurring independence whenever widespread political disturbances occurred in China, while in the 2nd century B.C. and then on later occasions, central government nationalized the salt industry because it was always a useful source of revenue.

Since salt obtained from seawater formed more than three-quarters of China's total production, we might expect to find that there was a variety of methods used for extracting it. The most primitive was to sprinkle seawater on to a wood fire and then, after the fire had gone out, separate the salt from the ashes. Another simple method was just to dry seaweed in the sun and then to extract the salt by immersing the seaweed in boiling water. But slightly more elaborate methods were used as well when it came to extracting the salt left by the tide. Where the shore was only submerged by shallow water at high tide and the brine retained when the tide ebbed, evaporation in the sun was enough to permit salt to be swept up and then taken for refining. If on the other hand the foreshore was submerged by deep water at high tide, a different method had to be used. Deep pits were dug at low tide and covered with reed mats on which a layer of sand was then placed. When the tide came up the seawater would drip through the sand and the matting, which acted as filters, and then at low tide the brine in the pits was taken up in buckets and poured out to evaporate in the sun. Lastly, a special technique was used when the areas concerned only received salt spray from the sea. Such land, which was of course above the high-tide mark, was scattered with the ashes of reeds, rice and wheat stalks. The formation of dew would then draw up a brine into the ashes and the resulting brackish mixture would then be collected.

Once the brine had been obtained it had to be refined and the simplest way to do this was to leave it in the sun to evaporate. Drying in this way was slow but it enabled the calcium sulphate which is present in seawater brine to be reduced by anaerobic bacteria to calcium sulphide, which appears as a black "slush" underneath the salt. This slush could then be separated from the salt. Because of the Chinese dislike of wasting anything, the calcium sulphide was not thrown away but was used medicinally as an emetic, as a protection against insect bites, or as a medicine for ringworm and scabies, and also for treating the sores of animals.

If drying in the sun could not be done, then the brine was passed through filters made of reed matting, and then poured into large iron pans where it was boiled. While the brine was heating, millet chaff and soap-bean pods were added: these not only assisted the salt to precipitate but also combined with the calcium sulphate present as an impurity. When the brine was of low concentration a biological method of purification could be adopted by using the "cleaver worm," a small crustacean which removed impurities by digesting them. The concentration of the resulting brine was in all cases monitored by floating lotus seed pods in it: this was a simple and useful indication not only for refining but also in assessing the salt tax that was payable.

Where rock salt, which is crystalline, was being refined, flat bowl-shaped pans were used and the brine evaporated. To assist in removing any calcium sulphate a suspension of soybeans was mixed into the brine and, at the appropriate moment during evaporation, some salt was added to act as a nucleus for crystallization.

Deep borehole drilling

To tap the underground salt resources in Sichuan some means had to be found to extract the brine. The Chinese adopted the method of sinking boreholes, a method which was also in use in the West in ancient times. However, the Western boreholes never reached a depth greater than about 180 meters, whereas in China deep borehole drilling was developed from the 1st century B.C. onwards, and this allowed them to make many borings at twice this depth. Later, improvements in technique made it possible for the majority of borings to reach depths of 850 meters and, on some occasions, this was extended to 1200 meters.

Deep borehole drilling is essentially a controlled method of chipping away a narrow cylinder of rock below ground. What is remarkable about the Chinese techniques is that they were so effective and astonishingly advanced for their time. For instance, they always used a very heavy bit, weighing some 180 kg, until in the 17th, or possibly the 16th, century, they devised the crucial development of the "jar." This was a drilling bit made in two parts, linked together by a tube. At the bottom of the tube was that section of the bit which carried the actual cutting head, and above it was the second section in the form of a solid metal cylinder. When the jar was drawn up the two sections separated, and then, as it fell, the cutting head hit the rock first and almost immediately received a second blow from the solid cylinder. Such a jarring movement was effective in cutting and at the same time in releasing the cutting end from the rock.

Spoil was withdrawn from the hole by bamboo buckets each

Drawings showing (above) various stages in the production of salt and (below) the weighing, counting and transportation of the same product. In China, most salt is made from seawater but considerable quantities are also obtained from underground wells of brackish water, from salt lakes and from layers of rock salt.

Like the iron industry, the salt industry was under state control from the time of the Han dynasty. Among the methods used for the extraction of salt, the most ancient consisted in sprinkling seawater on a wood fire and, when it was extinguished, recovering the salt from the ashes, or else allowing the seawater to evaporate in the sun. Another method was to pour brackish water, filtered through rush matting, into huge iron cauldrons and then to boil it.

fitted with a valve, and special tools were available for removing broken bits or other debris. The borehole itself was lined as drilling progressed. The actual drilling was carried out from a drilling platform where two to six men stood on a long hardwood lever. One end of the lever was connected to the bit by way of a cable which ran up to a pulley at the top of the drilling derrick, which was some 55 meters high, and then down to the bit itself. The drill dropped on to the rock when the men jumped off the other end of the wooden lever.

The cable was another crucial Chinese invention. It was made of strips of bamboo skin pressed into long pliable bands which were joined by strong hemp covered with rawhide. It was immensely flexible but at the same time nonelastic and vastly superior to the rod or pole used in Europe. Indeed, it caused a sensation when it reached the West in 1823.

The brine from boreholes was often carried away by pipelines, made of bamboo with the joints between sections being sealed with tung oil, lime and canvas. These pipes went overland, being supported on trestles where necessary, and pumps were inserted in the lines wherever needed. The boreholes also gave artesian water and natural gas, and from the 2nd century the gas was used systematically for heating the basins in which the brine was evaporated.

THE TECHNOLOGY OF IRON AND STEEL

In the Old World some 2500 years elapsed between the first working of iron and the first appearance of cast iron, but in China iron could be melted and cast almost as soon as it was discovered. This is an astonishing contrast, but to appreciate what is involved it may be as well to recall some basic facts about iron itself, a metal whose properties depend not only on small quantities of metallic and nonmetallic substances alloyed with it, but also on the succession of treatments which it receives.

When iron ore is heated in a blast furnace the metal melts, loses oxygen and becomes what is called "cast iron." It is hard and brittle and cannot be welded, nor is it malleable; it is suitable only for use where it is not likely to receive shocks or impact. Cast iron contains a relatively large amount of carbon – between 1·5 percent and 4·5 percent – but if it is purified so that the carbon content is reduced to only some 0·06 percent, and the carbon together with the sulphur and phosphorus originally present pass away as slag, this purer product is known as "wrought iron." It is tough, fibrous and malleable, and can be used for wire, nails, horseshoes and agricultural implements. In mediaeval times and later, cast iron was always known in China as "raw iron" and wrought iron as "ripe iron."

The main thing about steel is that its carbon content is between that of cast and wrought iron: in low carbon steels it ranges from 0·1 percent to 0·9 percent and in a high carbon steel it can be as much as 1·8 percent. The higher the carbon content, the harder the steel: this is ideal for a cutting edge, although the rest of a blade needs to be ductile and have a good appearance. These associated properties depend not only on the steel but also on its treatment. Hardening by plunging hot steel into a cool liquid – quenching – was a very early discovery. Annealing or slow cooling makes it more ductile, while raising it to a moderate heat and then cooling – tempering – provides a steel with a combination of hardness and ductility.

The passage from one form of iron to another has been achieved in a number of ways. Reduction of carbon from cast iron may be done by puddling (stirring) the molten metal, while the problem of introducing more carbon into wrought iron was solved in ancient times by "cementation," that is, by packing soft bars of iron with charcoal and heating for a considerable time. This process gave a "blister" steel – steel with a hard outside casing – and was the oldest steelmaking process in the West, but in modern times, when it became possible to generate greater heat, specific amounts of carbon were added; later still suitable proportions of cast iron and wrought iron were melted together, and today direct conversion from cast iron to steel is achieved by the Bessemer process, blowing a blast of air through the white hot metal to oxidize the carbon before a specific additional amount of carbon is added.

In Roman times cast iron appears only to have been made accidentally, perhaps from overheated furnaces, while the Greek furnaces were essentially "bloomeries" in which ore was heated with charcoal; here only some of the slag was melted, resulting in a pasty "bloom" which needed long hammering on an anvil to

Opposite: the hammering of iron which is first heated in a furnace.

Below: a team of ironworkers, led by a chargehand and supervized by soldiers with spears. Both illustrations are taken from a manual of the Ming period.

The Chinese came relatively late to a knowledge of the use of iron (around the 6th century B.C.). However, almost as soon as they discovered the mineral, they developed techniques for smelting and working it. Archaeological evidence shows that cast iron was widely used from the 4th to 3rd century B.C. This evidence takes the form of agricultural tools, cooking utensils, knives and iron swords which replaced in the course of these centuries objects made of wood and stone.

free the remaining slag embedded in it. Ancient and mediaeval wrought iron doubtless had a variable carbon content.

Chinese techniques

In China the Iron Age did not begin until the 6th century B.C., some seven centuries later than in the West. The earliest Chinese products may have been blooms like those of the Western part of the ancient world, but cast iron had made its appearance at the latest by the 4th century B.C., when it was used for agricultural implements, for weapons and for pots as well as iron moulds for making castings. This means that from very early the Chinese were able to generate sufficient heat to liquefy the metal completely, and to have done so some 17 centuries before it could be achieved as a matter of course in the West.

There seem to have been a number of factors which helped the Chinese to achieve this result. In the first place it appears that their blast furnaces either used an ore rich in phosphorus or had a phosphorus-rich material added, since in either case melting would occur at a somewhat lower temperature. The second is that clays which could resist high temperatures were available, and this meant that suitable blast furnaces could be built; they were small but efficient. The clays also allowed crucibles to be made and these were used in the processing in some parts of the country. Coal could be piled round them, and so provide another way of heating sufficient to give a true cast iron.

Besides these there were technological innovations which helped the smelters. The double-acting single-cylinder piston bellows, which we shall meet again in discussing Chinese mechanical engineering, were important because they gave a continuous blast of air, and later water power was applied to the blowing either with these piston bellows or with a larger hinged type of bellows which came in about the 1st century, or a little before. The use two centuries later of iron nozzles on the pipes of the larger bellows brought yet another increase in efficient blowing. Thus ancient and mediaeval China had an abundance of cast iron; a totally different situation from the civilizations of the Western World.

The most important factor about Chinese steelmaking was the quantity of cast iron that was available. To begin with they may well have used cementation but it is clear that they soon moved over to using a blast of air with which to reduce the carbon in a process which came to be called "the hundred refinings," and which was in operation by the 2nd century B.C. About 1800 years later, in the 17th century, both the Chinese and Japanese devised techniques of using air blasts to produce something very similar to cast steel, thus preempting Bessemer's process by a couple of centuries.

However, from the 5th century onwards the Chinese had another method of making steel, which is now known as the "cofusion" process. Here the desired carbon content was obtained by putting billets of wrought iron into a bath of molten cast iron. Theoretically this remarkable method was the ancestor of a number of 19th-century Western techniques including the Siemens-Martin open-hearth process.

It has long been known that fine weapons can be produced by

welding together hard and soft steels so that the result is a good cutting edge on a truly flexible and resilient blade. The Chinese were using a technique for this by the 3rd century and it was transmitted to the Japanese 400 years later. Yet it does not seem to have been necessarily a Chinese invention, for it was used by some Western countries too and may well therefore have had its origin in Central Asia, perhaps in the 2nd century, from where it then spread eastwards and westwards.

However, some of the Chinese steel blades show a veining, sometimes described as "fish gut" effects, or as a "coiling snake" or "pine tree" design. Such veining can appear on blades made by cofusion or by welding, or from the "wootz" crucible steel of India, that is to say from a high carbon-content steel. Throughout the Middle Ages the high quality wootz steel from Hyderabad was the principal source of material for the famous "Damascene blades" of the Muslims, and it now seems clear that this steel was also imported into China in the 6th century, although home-produced steel was the chief Chinese source.

As soon as cast iron became available in Europe, in the late 14th century, the various ways of using it became known within the next 200 years. This surely is too short a time for the techniques and proper furnaces required to have been invented independently and one must therefore conclude that it was from China that the information originally spread.

MECHANICAL ENGINEERING

Astronomers in ancient and mediaeval China, as we have seen, were part of the governmental civil service, and so also to some extent were artisans and engineers, although on a lower plane. Nearly every dynasty had its elaborate imperial workshops and arsenals and, at some periods in Chinese history, trades which possessed the most advanced techniques were "nationalized," as happened in the later Han period to the salt and iron industries.

There was also a tendency for technicians to gather around the figure of some prominent official who encouraged them as his personal followers. And whenever a particularly large or unusually complex piece of machinery was constructed this seems to have been done in the imperial workshops or under the close supervision of important bureaucratic officials. Yet not all manufactures or handicrafts were carried out under state control; most were produced independently by and for the common people, and carried out on a small scale.

The mechanical engineering developed in traditional China was still in the "eotechnic" phase; that is, engineering construction was mainly from the basic naturally occurring materials, stone, wood and bamboo with a little bronze or iron. Yet if materials were somewhat restricted this did not affect the inventiveness or ingenuity of the Chinese, to whom the West owes a real debt for a host of inventions.

The Chinese themselves made good use of every one of their inventions, and until the scientific revolution in Europe in the 16th and 17th centuries were generally far ahead of the West. Once the new scientific movement emerged it spread outwards

Opposite: a drawing from the Qing dynasty showing the working of a blast furnace in which the ferrous ore is heated and cast in order to obtain wrought iron. The heights which the Chinese achieved in the art of bronze-making, of which they were the unequalled masters, shows their ability and expertise in the field of smelting and casting. They were also the first to make use in iron-working of bellows powered by water.

Above: a drawing from the Ming period showing a driving belt worked by a crank for the excavation and transport of minerals.

over the world and now, in the 20th century, its advanced technology in such fields as transport, communications, nuclear physics and electronics is at last beginning to repay its indebtedness to the East.

The variety of Chinese invention as displayed in the field of mechanical engineering was enormous. Certainly the Chinese were unaware of the screw or of the crankshaft or even of a force pump for liquids (although they had a very efficient force pump for air), but their own developments brought new techniques and ideas to the West in plenty, as the table below shows, even though delays in transmission were often considerable. Let us see some of these Chinese achievements in more detail.

TRANSMISSION OF MECHANICAL TECHNIQUES FROM CHINA TO THE WEST BEFORE THE 18TH CENTURY

Mechanical technique	Approximate lag in centuries
Cardan suspension	10–14
Clockwork escapement	6
Crossbow (as an individual arm)	14
Draw-loom	4
Edge-runner mill	12
Edge-runner mill with application of water power	16
Efficient harness for draught animals:	
Breast strap (postilion)	8
Collar	4
Helicopter top (spun by cord)	11
Kite	19
Metallurgical blowing engines, water power	11
Piston bellows	20
Rotary fan and rotary winnowing machine	16
Sailing carriage	11
Silk-handling machinery (a form of flyer for laying thread evenly on reels appears in the 11th century, and water power is applied to textile mills in the 14th)	3–13
Square-pallet chain pump	15
Wagon-mill	12
Wheelbarrow	10
Zoetrope (moved by ascending hot-air current)	12

TRANSMISSION OF MECHANICAL TECHNIQUES FROM THE WEST TO CHINA BEFORE THE 18TH CENTURY

Crankshaft	3
Force pump for liquids	18
Screw	14

Based on a table in volume IV, part 1, of Dr. Joseph Needham's *Science and Civilisation in China*, Cambridge University Press, Cambridge, 1965.

The wheel and some other basic mechanical inventions
The wheel is one of man's earliest and most fundamental inventions, and archaeological evidence shows that it seems to have been known first in the Mesopotamian area. In company with early civilizations farther west, the Chinese adopted the solid wheel but, by the 4th century B.C., this had given way to elegantly constructed spoked wheels with separate hubs and rims; these were all rigorously tested before use.

But the main development in China was the design of wheels

not in one plane but shaped as a flat cone: a technique usually known as "dishing." In China the wheelwrights achieved this by fixing the spokes not only radially outwards from the hub but also at an angle to the axle so that the rim would lie farther from the side of the vehicle than the hub. Dishing in this way gave the wheels greater strength against the sideways thrusts which carts suffered when carrying heavy loads over uneven or rutted ground. Dished wheels do not appear in European illustrations until the 15th century, by which time the Chinese wheelwright had been using the method for at least 1800 years.

The wheel is not only a device for carrying a vehicle along, it is also a means of transmitting rotation; of carrying rotary motion from one place to another. This can be achieved either by using a belt drive, which we shall return to in a moment, or by gearing. A gear is, in essence, a wheel with projections on it (the teeth of the gear), and in its simplest form consists of a wheel with one or more projections on its rim which engage with a rod or lever, or even projections on another wheel. If the wheel operates a lever which is weighted at one end then we have a triphammer, and though there seems to be no evidence of this device in Europe before the 12th century, the triphammer was widespread in ancient China for hulling rice, and by Han times was driven by water power.

Ropes, cords and chains wrapped round wheels and axles were known from early antiquity, being familiar to both Babylonians and Egyptians. The grooved wheel or pulley was also an ancient invention; it was well known in China in Han times, as were cranes and other lifting tackle like the windlass, though there is evidence which indicates they were far older than this. A minor invention based on the windlass is the reel of a fishing rod. Pictures of such fishing rods in China go back to the 13th century, but literary sources take us back to the 3rd or 4th century. The invention therefore may well be Chinese.

Gearing was developed in the West in Hellenistic times, probably about the 3rd century B.C., and it seems likely that this happened in China in the Qin and first Han times, in other words at about the same time. Certainly toothed wheels were much used in the second Han dynasty, in the period of the Three Kingdoms period and the Qin, and it was during Han times (about 100 B.C.) that the Chinese developed a ratchet and pawl, so vital when one wants a wheel which will turn in one direction

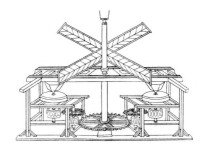

Two drawings from an agricultural manual of the 16th century showing the technical principle underlying the use and application of the cogwheel.

The rotary movement determined by the principal source of energy (above, wind; below, water) is transmitted by pairs of cogwheels which, in their turn, set in motion a more or less complex series of gears designed to give a constant and uniform motion.

but not in the other. Then, in the 1st century, in the second Han dynasty, they began to make gears with the teeth in a chevron pattern on the rim; these were definitely the forerunner of the helical gears which the West devised 19 centuries later.

Another Chinese innovation, this time from the 3rd century B.C., the period of the Warring States, was that of roller bearings, which allowed axles to rotate with a minimum of friction. Thus from very early they were well set for the development of all kinds of rotating machinery, of which silk-reeling machines are a typical and important example.

Silk-reeling machinery

The manufacture of silk in China is certainly very old; silk remnants have been found which go back before 1500 B.C. The organized breeding of silkworms seems, however, to be a later development which did not occur until the Zhou period (11th century B.C.) or a little earlier. Then the whole art of sericulture was developed, and this concerned not only silkworm breeding but also the processing of the thread. The silkworm moth (*Bombyx*) weaves a cocoon which contains between 600 meters and one kilometer of silk and, with so long a continuous fibre, some form of thread-reeling machine would have been a necessity.

The silk-reeling or winding machines which were developed by the Chinese are important mechanically. The earliest descriptions come from the 11th century, but there is every reason to believe that they relate to equipment from far earlier times. Certainly, it is possible to reconstruct completely the classical Chinese silk-reeling machine from a text of about 1090.

The mechanical interest of the machine is that it takes the individual fibres from cocoons in a heated bath and after passing them through guiding eyes and over rollers, reels them using a "flyer" to cause the fibres to oscillate from side to side so that they are reeled evenly on the take-up spool. The whole machine is treadle-operated, a crank arm being used to turn the reciprocating motion of the treadle into a rotary motion for reeling and for operating the flyer. Power is transmitted by a belt-drive.

The origins of wheels for spinning thread, silk or otherwise, are obscure. In Europe they did not appear until very late, the oldest datable drawing being of the 14th century. Chinese

On this page and opposite below: different types of animal-drawn carts used as the principal means of transporting agricultural products. Below: draught animals attached to carts with a collar harness connected to the shafts by means of traces. Compared to the harness in use in the West which wound round the throat and underbelly of the animal, the Chinese collar harness was a most useful innovation since it allowed the animal (horse, donkey or mule) greater freedom and therefore the ability to work at full capacity. Below left: illustration of a Chinese wheelbarrow being drawn with animal assistance. This was a more efficient barrow than the wheelbarrow of the West because its wheel was in the center and so the load was balanced, enabling greater loads to be carried than would otherwise have been the case.

multiple-spindle spinning machines were certainly earlier than this, and a drawing by Leonardo da Vinci in the 15th century of a cord-making machine is almost an exact copy of a Chinese machine. The presence of sometimes three and sometimes five spindles makes it seem likely that the Chinese machines of this period were a mature development of an earlier, simpler design. Spinning would, after all, have been carried out in the earliest times when the cocoons of "wild" silkworms were used, for the Chinese always avoided wasting anything, and we know that waste cocoons were used for making yarn for a rough silk fabric. What is more, there is a tradition of making yarn from short lengths of silk fibre from wild cocoons, so this may be the real origin of all spinning wheels.

A precursor of the Western spinning wheel may have been the quilling wheel which was used for winding yarn on to the bobbins of weavers' shuttles. This had a driving wheel and a small pulley, both mounted on a framework and connected by an endless belt. The earliest Western pictures seem to be from the 13th century, and once again we find that the earliest Chinese illustrations predate these by a century. However, texts and reliefs dating from the 1st century B.C. to the third century indicate that the quilling wheel was in use very much earlier, brought about almost certainly by the need for dealing with the long continuous fibres of the silkworm.

Mills

In milling and grinding the Chinese made some valuable and original contributions. They developed the longitudinal edge-runner mill, a mill in which the grinding stone is held vertically and runs in a groove or channel. It was favoured extensively by metallurgists and by pharmacists and is still in use in China, although but little known in Europe. This kind of mill is ancient; it was certainly devised during Han times and possibly as early as the period of the Warring States, and appears in a number of variations with either one grinding stone or two mounted close together, or in some cases, with the two stones mounted at the opposite ends of a beam which is pivoted at its center. In this latter case the grindstones run in a circular channel, and it may be that mills of this kind stimulated the invention of the

An ancient type of handloom still used today for weaving silk, and (below) drawings from a manual of sericulture of the 16th century showing the various stages in the production of silk. From the left: the drawing and winding of the thread using a reel, followed by the process of weaving.

In China, known from earliest times as "The Land of Silk," the breeding of silkworms and the organized production of this precious material have been of major importance: it probably began in the early days of the Han dynasty and certainly not later than the 3rd century B.C. A painter of the Song dynasty (1270) shows a type of spinning jenny worked by a driving belt, an essential element in the changeover from the use of the rotary motor to the longitudinal motor. Documents of the 13th century testify to the use of textile machines powered by water, one of the earliest forms of energy.

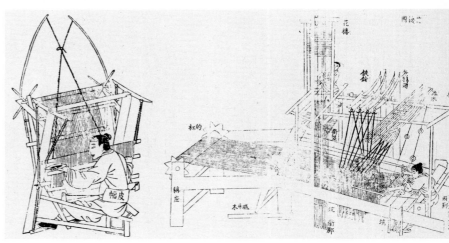

differential gear which was used in that singular Chinese invention, the "south-pointing carriage." Here, using a geared drive from one or other of the two road wheels, a figure mounted on a large gear, able to mesh with one or other gears from the drive, always kept pointing southwards, irrespective of the direction in which the carriage travelled.

Another Chinese contribution was what in the West were called either "camp mills" or "field mills." These were mills which were driven either by gearing or by a chain or rope drive from the wheels of the vehicle on which they were mounted. Such travelling mills are usually assumed to have been invented in the West during the 16th century, yet they were in use in China more than a millennium before this. In the 4th century in North China "pounding carts" were used, hulling rice with tilt-hammers or grinding wheat with millstones, both being driven from the cartwheels as the vehicle was on the move; thus the Chinese invention predates that of Western Europe by 1300 years.

The wheelbarrow and horse harness

The wheelbarrow has been a familiar sight in the West since the 12th or 13th century. It is poorly adapted for carrying heavy weights because, with a single wheel at the front, the load is distributed between the wheel and the handles, and a great strain is put on the person using it when the load is heavy. The Chinese wheelbarrow on the other hand can readily carry six adults and is incomparably more efficient, even though invented at least nine centuries before the Western model.

The convenience and effectiveness of the Chinese wheelbarrow lies in the fact that its single wheel is placed centrally so that the barrow balances about it. So effective is this design that it could be used with an animal drawing it and sometimes barrows were fitted with a sail so that they could be borne along by the force of the wind. The date at which sails were first fitted to wheelbarrows in China is unknown, although descriptions by European visitors in the 16th century make it evident that it was an accustomed use by this time. Such wind-propelled barrows were in recent use in Henan and coastal provinces such as Shandong.

A Chinese invention of the greatest importance was an efficient harness for horses. In the West there were severe limits on the load which a horse could pull because of the restrictive nature of the harness. This was designed so that it fitted round a horse's throat and girth, and any heavy load caused the throat strap to press on the animal's windpipe. This type of harness was also used by the Chinese but it was not long before they made fundamental changes. By ancient and mediaeval times they had a breast-strap harness with the shafts of the vehicle pulling at a point level with the breast strap. Fully developed by Han times, this change may go back well into the 3rd century B.C.; it brought a considerable increase in efficiency.

The Chinese in Central Asia also developed an idea of their own, the horse collar. It seems to have been adapted from the padded saddle used on Bactrian camels, and was fitted to the horse either with a framework attached to the shafts of the vehicle or with the shafts attached directly to the collar itself. This may have been invented as early as the Han, though it did not come into general use in China until the 5th century. Both developments took a long time to filter through to the West, which did not have them until at least 500 years later.

Bellows, fans and other inventions

The ability to use efficient means to ensure that furnaces had a good draught of air was vital in metallurgy, and one of the crucial Chinese inventions in this field was the double-acting piston bellows. The bellows consisted of a long rectangular chamber in which a piston moved. On the forward stroke it pushed the air ahead of it through an aperture and thence out of the pump by way of an exit valve. In making the forward stroke, the piston also drew in air from behind it through another valve. On the backward stroke the piston pushed the air behind it out through an aperture and the exit valve, at the same time drawing in air through a valve into that part of the chamber it had just exhausted. The result of this is that at each stroke of the piston, whether it is moving forwards or backwards, there is a constant blast of air. This was simple, effective and remarkable considering that its invention may well have been as early as the 4th century B.C. It was in use all over China for metallurgy, though the West had no equivalent until the 17th century, more than two millennia later.

A second early Chinese invention concerned with a controllable air current was a winnowing machine with a rotary fan. This was an efficient way of removing chaff from grain and the Chinese developed two types of machine. The first, invented before the Han dynasty, used a treadle-operated fan with four or six blades in an open framework, and in the second, which is of Han date, the fan was driven by a handle and crank. The unhusked grain was put into a hopper and the grain itself dropped through a sieve, the fan blowing away the chaff. The latter type was, and still is, to be found in use in Europe, although it did not reach the West until the 18th century.

The Chinese had a considerable knowledge of the wind as well as the creation and control of draughts of air. Examples of this can be seen in their kites, which were used not only as toys but also for military purposes such as signalling, and even for leaflet raids by cutting the controlling string when they floated over the desired area. Kites may have appeared in China as early as the 4th century B.C., but they did not reach the West until the 16th century.

The helicopter is another Chinese invention, for helicopter tops, with rotating blades set spinning by a cord and known as "bamboo dragonflies," appeared in China as early as the 4th century. Both the kite and the helicopter reached the West at around the time when new ideas were being formulated and the scientific revolution was taking place, and both were to play a part in the beginning of Western aeronautics.

The Chinese were also the inventors of a gimbals mounting, which is often called the Cardan Suspension, because it was first described in the West in the 16th century by the mathematician Jerome Cardan who, however, laid no claim to the invention.

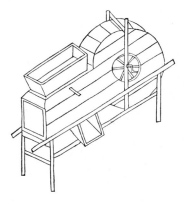

Example of a rotating winnower worked by a crank, from a 14th-century drawing. This was used for sifting the impurities out of cereals. A type of pedal sieve was known in China at a time which probably predates the Han dynasty but one worked by a handle or crank was in use by the 1st century B.C. as we know from excavations of Han tombs.

Below and on the opposite page: two different applications of the paddle wheel in irrigation: worked by water power (below) and by hand (opposite above). The chain pump, worked by paddles, became essential to agricultural life, especially in the paddy-fields, where it was necessary to channel water in order to extend the cultivable land.

Cardan's description was of a chair in which an emperor could sit upright even if his bearers tilted its supports, and he also pointed out that it had been used as a way of suspending oil lamps. Indeed, the Arabs had suspended lamps in this way, so that however the mounting might swing, the lamp remained upright, but the invention was not theirs. The gimbals mounting had its origin in China, where it was well known by the year 180, being used for bedwarmers and unspillable incense burners, and presumably came to the West through Iran.

An important machine which was characteristically Chinese was the square-pallet chain pump. Used for raising water, it made use of an endless chain of flat plates or pallets which drew the water up as they passed through a trough or "flume." Found all over the country by the 2nd century, it may well have been known as far back as the 4th century B.C. It did not become well known in the West until the 18th century.

The origin of mechanical clockwork

Of all scientific machines the clock is the oldest and the most important. For a long time its origins were obscure, because this complex mechanism appeared in the West in the early 14th century, doing so quite suddenly and with, it seemed, no ancestry of any kind. We now know, however, that its origins lay in China. The direct ancestor of Western mechanical clocks was the astronomical clock tower of Su Song built in 1090 at Kaifeng in Henan, then the capital of the empire.

The clockwork was a giant water wheel with small scoops or buckets, which were fed one at a time from a constant-level reservoir. As soon as one scoop was filled the wheel was released to rotate just far enough to allow the next scoop to move into place to be filled. This regular intermittent motion, allowing the wheel to escape one tooth at a time (escapement), is the heart of mechanical timekeeping. Yet at the time of Su Song's clock tower it was not new, for the principle of the escapement is to be found in some clock-driven astronomical instruments in the 8th

Reconstruction, by John Christiansen, of the astronomical clock tower built between 1088 and 1092 by Su Song, in the imperial palace of Kaifeng. It is thought to be the first mechanical clock in history, with an escapement mechanism based on the transmission of energy obtained from a huge water wheel. However, this escapement mechanism, which was fundamental to the contemporary development of mechanics, is referred to as early as the 8th century in documents which speak of hydro-mechanical clocks. In this drawing, we observe (right bottom) the great wheel worked by water (force of propulsion) while on the left can be seen the apparatus used to tell the time – figures moving in circles being used to show the hour. Immediately above is a celestial globe and (on top) an armillary sphere, both made to rotate by means of clockwork.

century. Thus the essence of mechanical timekeeping was reached in China some 600 years before any device incorporating it appeared in the West.

CIVIL ENGINEERING

No ancient civilization accomplished more in civil engineering, both in scale and techniques, than China, although this is not always appreciated. Here we can only sketch Chinese achievements in this field.

Roads
The two chief road-building civilizations of antiquity were the Roman and the Chinese. Roman roads, which have been likened to walls laid horizontally, had one main defect; they could not allow for any expansion or contraction due to the weather or to faulty drainage. In the West roads which are thin and display elasticity only appeared in mediaeval times, but in China roads of this kind had long been known. They were made of tamped rubble and gravel giving what has been termed a kind of "water-bound macadam."

Chinese bureaucracy early systematized the capacities of roads (and of canals) and as soon as the empire was first unified under the first Qin emperor Shi Huang Di a gauge of chariot wheels and other standardizations were made. Indeed Shi's roads were specified by the number of vehicles which could ride abreast, graded from one-width up to nine-width. Main highways seem to have been 15 meters wide and to have had trees planted along them at 9-meter intervals, and the inner lanes were reserved for the emperor and authorized members of the ruling house.

As early as the 3rd century B.C. there were some 6800 kilometers of highway in China and a century later this had risen to more than 32,000 kilometers. By the 3rd century the total Chinese road system was between 55 percent and 75 percent of the Roman; the lower Chinese figures being partly due to the large waterway transport system which China had developed.

Once the Chinese road system had been engineered, it was welded into a great social institution by deploying a whole army of messengers, coachmen and "stationmasters" along it. In principle there was a "post office" with clerk every five kilometers, a cantonal office every 15 kilometers and every 25 kilometers a post station, the short distances enabling signals by flag, drum, fire or smoke to be transmitted. In Tang times this post system had a force of some 21,500 officers, managed by 100 officials in the capital. Couriers managed between them to cover 190 kilometers in 24 hours, although sometimes this was exceeded.

Walls and buildings
The most ancient method of walling in China, both for houses and for unroofed walls, was tamped earth, built up layer by layer in wooden shuttering which resembled that used today for holding concrete while it sets. Rubble was used as a foundation

for walls and bamboo stems were placed between each layer to hasten the drying-out. Bricks were also used in building, at first being made of sun-dried mud, but baked bricks were used during the period of the Warring States and the Han dynasty, when Chinese craftsmen were the first to master the art of making large hollow terra-cotta ornamental bricks.

All the earliest cities in China were walled; the cores of these walls being earth or rubble which, in later times, became dressed with brick or stone. But the most remarkable of all Chinese fortifications is of course the Great Wall, which extended for well over 3000 kilometers – almost one-tenth of the earth's circumference and the one manmade structure visible to astronauts in orbit round the earth. In addition, the Wall has a number of loops which themselves extend a distance of almost 2900 kilometers, and in its prime it possessed a total of some 15,000 watchtowers. This immense structure, constructed during the Qin dynasty (3rd century B.C.), was an extension and linking up of a number of separate walls built in the period of the Warring States.

Chinese architecture embodies the great Chinese principle that man cannot be thought of apart from nature, and so always strove to achieve integrated organic planning, in its buildings and their location, and in the layout of towns and cities. This led to the production of a formal layout within a general walled compound. Another characteristic is that except in thatched cottages the house always stands on a raised platform, and there is a lavish use of colour and a great emphasis on the roof.

The sweeping curves of Chinese roofs are not only aesthetic: their shape derives from their construction. In the West builders restricted themselves to straight and rigid sloping principal rafters but in China the most important element in roof construction was the longitudinal purlin which supported the main rafters making it possible for the roof to be arranged to any profile. These purlins were supported by a framework independent of the walls which were never load-bearing. The Chinese design of curved roof admits the maximum amount of slanting winter sunshine but only the minimum of high summer sunlight; it also reduces lateral wind pressure because of its low height and steep pitch. At least as early as the 10th century cast-iron pillars were sometimes used as roof supports.

The pagoda, a familiar feature of the Chinese landscape, is half foreign in origin, having been derived from Indian Buddhism. This prevented it from being sited within city walls where it might compete with the drum towers and gate towers of cosmic-imperial authority. Nevertheless many pagodas are based on a typical Chinese style of small square one-story building, and one remarkable Chinese development in some of them was the use of bronze for the construction material and, by the 11th century, of iron.

Bridges

Chinese bridges, like the buildings, have a beauty all their own, besides being of great utility in a country with many rivers and a vast system of artificial waterways. The first bridges were beams set across trestles but their spans were limited to some six meters.

Opposite: a suspension bridge made of bamboo in Zhupu in the province of Sichuan and (below) the famous Zhaozhou (Chaochow) Bridge in the province of Hebei. The latter is the first ogival arch bridge of any civilization and was built in 610 by the engineer Li Chun. It is still standing today. It is entirely built of stone but makes use of iron plates to link together the huge blocks which bear the weight of the structure. Suspension bridges made of bamboo have been built ever since ancient times for crossing rivers or gorges. Documents from the Sui period (7th century) provide evidence of the existence of suspension bridges made of iron cables, proof, if any were needed, of the high quality of Chinese ironworking.

However, during the Song dynasty unique giant beam bridges were constructed, especially in Fujian province, with lengths in excess of 120 meters and spans up to 21 meters, achieved by using huge stone masses weighing up to 200 tonnes each.

The Chinese also built many cantilever bridges in timber as early as the 4th and 5th centuries, possibly deriving the technique from the Han practice of constructing pavilions over lakes using cantilever-like brackets. Arched bridges too were a notable feature of Chinese bridge-building and besides their beauty a characteristic factor in their construction was the Chinese invention of built-in shear walls running through the structure to resist deformation and allowing an elegant design with the minimum quantity of material. Chinese engineers also invented a completely circular structure where the arch above water had a corresponding inverted arch deep underneath. However, the greatest aesthetic, engineering and economic development came when, in the 7th century, the Chinese designers abandoned semicircular arches and used a flatter design.

The other Chinese innovation was the suspension bridge. Using, at first, bamboo cables for supporting the roadway, they devised a way of taking the inner core of the bamboo and weaving round it plaited strips taken from the outer silica-containing layers. These cables resisted wear over long periods and had a tensile strength more than three times that of hemp. Such bridges were first constructed in the 3rd century B.C. Iron chain suspension bridges followed later; possibly, it seems, in Han times in view of their advanced iron and steel technology, but certainly such bridges were being constructed by the 6th century. In Europe they did not appear until the 18th century.

Canals and waterways
China has an abundance of waterways and canals, for the Chinese have been outstanding among the nations of the world in their control and use of water; with one-fifth of the world's population their irrigated land is one-third of the world total. Water control was needed because of the country's climate, with dry winters and very wet summers, and the need for irrigation. Of the four main rivers in China, the Yellow River's flooding was the most difficult to control and there were two approaches – the use of strong high dykes and of low dykes set well apart – and both had their advantages and disadvantages. The struggle to control the river was a long one, and for the large projects involved a vast labour force was required, but this the Chinese were well able to organize.

Irrigation projects began very early, at least by the 8th century B.C., and by the 5th century the Yellow River was being tackled and the first irrigation reservoir constructed. In the 3rd century BC there was the building of the Zheng guo Canal irrigation system, some 150 kilometers long, which is still in use today, and later in the same century the complex (Guanxien) system in Sichuan which prevented flooding as well as providing irrigation over an area of 8000 square kilometers.

Water transport was vital in China, not only for military and civil use but particularly for the bureaucratic administration,

The Red Flag Canal in Henan, completed during the seventies, which is cut along the sides of the Taihang mountains, and is more than 1500 kilometers long. This is one of the great works of irrigation carried out in the province which have led, in just a few years, to its becoming the largest producer of grain in the country.

since taxes were paid in grain which had to be shipped to the capital. Such a waterway, designed primarily for transport rather than irrigation, was the "Magic Transport Canal" of the 2nd century B.C. Connected with the Li River it had a total length of some 32 kilometers.

But the most gigantic of the Chinese waterway schemes was the construction, during the Sui dynasty, in the 6th century, of the Grand Canal. This linked up many smaller canals constructed in earlier centuries but even so it entailed a vast amount of work. Its total length was almost 1700 kilometers and it rose to 42 meters above sea level. Its successful completion was an astonishing feat, connecting as it did two of the world's largest rivers, the Yangtze and the Yellow River, the latter one of the most changeable rivers in the world.

In building their canals the Chinese needed locks and double slipways, and these they had early in their history. It was they too who invented the "pound lock" between two levels, into which water pours under strict control. The gates to such locks in China moved vertically, being made of logs or baulks of timber, and it is clear that the invention came in the 10th century, some 400 years before such locks appeared in Europe.

SHIPBUILDING AND NAVIGATION

China's extensive coastline, which stretches for some 5000 kilometers, and its two extensive waterways, the Yellow and Yangtze Rivers, have acted as a stimulus to shipbuilding from ancient times. A large artificial canal system, used for transport as well as for irrigation, has also encouraged the building of river craft. Indeed early travellers from the West and the countries of the Near East always remarked on the abundance of shipping they found, and in the 17th century one chronicler went so far as to write that he could well believe the claim that there were more vessels in China than in all the rest of the world. But the stimulation for the Chinese to build craft for their waterways was due not only to the extent of those waterways, but also to the presence of a naturally occurring material eminently suited to shipbuilding, the giant bamboo (*Dendrocalamus giganteus*), which can grow to a height of 24 meters and reach a diameter of 30 centimeters.

The suitability of bamboo for building vessels is still appreciated even in modern China where for instance the bamboo rafts of the Ya River in Sichuan move up and down the 160 kilometers of intractable waterway between Yazhou and Jiading. These rafts must be some of the shallowest draught cargo-carriers in the world, for even with a load of seven tonnes their depth below the waterline is often as little as 7·5 centimeters, and never exceeds 15 centimeters. Consequently they can navigate waters which are impassable to heavier vessels.

But of course bamboo was not restricted to building rafts; it was used in masts and in sails for all types of shipping. Moreover its characteristic nature – short sections separated by septa which look like rings on the outside – played its part in Chinese boat design. The junk is an example of this. Traditionally a development of the raft, the Chinese junk has a flat or only slightly curved bottom and no keel, and its sides, made of planking, curve upwards; indeed its shape is very like a hollow cylinder split in half and bent up at each end. Its stern is square-ended and it has neither stem nor sternpost, while one of its most unusual features is that it possesses no internal skeleton of ribs, but has solid partitions instead. These partitions or bulkheads give the boat immense strength and they also confer another great advantage, for they divide up the boat into a number of watertight compartments.

This Chinese invention of watertight compartments was noticed and reported on by Marco Polo (1254–1324), but little attention seems to have been paid in the West to what he wrote in this respect. Only late in the 18th century was reference made to the Chinese method, which was soon adopted in British naval shipbuilding, almost five centuries after Marco Polo's report. After this, British naval architecture did not stop at watertight compartments but also adopted another Chinese idea, that of free-flooding compartments.

In some types of Chinese craft the foremost, and sometimes also the sternmost, compartment had been made free-flooding. This was achieved by the simple expedient of drilling holes in the planking. The method was used on the salt boats which shoot the rapids down from Culiuqing in Sichuan, on the gondola-shaped boats of Poyang Lake, and many seagoing junks. The Sichuanese boatmen claimed that this reduced the boat's resistance to water to a minimum, and certainly it must cushion the shocks of water pounding on the vessel when it pitches in the rapids.

Chinese sailors also claimed that the free-flooding compartment stopped junks flying up into the wind. Clearly then this invention, which was introduced at least as early as the 5th century, had advantages from the seamen's point of view, but it also had an additional use. Fishing boats with a free-flooding compartment could bring their catch to port and market in live condition. Yet it took 1200 years before it was used in the West.

If the bamboo raft could navigate waters too shallow for an ordinary boat, another Chinese invention to enable shipping to use narrow channels, even though these had become silted up, was the articulated junk, used on the Grand Canal. It was a very long narrow barge, with a shallow draught, built in two separate parts which were pivoted with respect to each other, but could be separated when desired. Coupling and uncoupling was simple, and the vessel was fitted with a collapsible mast and leeboards to prevent lateral movement. When a silted-up area was reached the barges were separated so they could each negotiate the shallow winding channels, whereas a longer heavier vessel would be forced to wait for a rising water level, and the two halves could bank alongside one another.

This type of articulated vessel was also used for naval purposes, for a 17th-century illustration shows it in use for minelaying, the forward portion being filled with explosives and left beside the target with a time fuse, while the aft portion silently withdrew. The invention may not be very old and perhaps dates only from the late 16th century, but the principle

of articulation which it enshrines was one which became very important in the railroad age, as exemplified by trains of carriages and especially in the articulated locomotive.

Propulsion

Wind power was the chief means of propelling the Chinese freshwater junk and all their ocean-going vessels. It was a form of propulsion that was universally used in ancient times, and the types of sail that were used varied enormously. This wide variety was a result of man's desire not only to sail with a favourable breeze, blowing in the direction in which he wanted to travel, but also to be able to sail directly in the face of the wind. This last he was never able to do by sails alone, though he came close to it after the practical experience of nearly 3000 years.

Different nations seem to have favoured different types of sail. The Polynesians for instance preferred a triangular-shaped sail with one curved edge, while Arab seamen used the "lateen" sail, another triangular-shaped sail but with straight edges and sometimes with an extra curved edge making it a trapezium with one curved side. The Chinese adopted the "lugsail" or ear-shaped sail, which was a development of the ancient square sail, and the canted sail (a square or rectangular sail canted or tilted over at an angle). The lugsail kept the lower boom or supporting bar, or the lower edge, horizontal, but the upper supporting bar, the "yard," was canted. The fore or leading edge of the sail was shorter than the others.

The Chinese used bamboo for their yards and their booms, and because it was so light in relation to its strength, it allowed them to use thinner pieces to brace their huge lugsails at various places in between. This had many advantages. In the first place bracing allowed bamboo matting to be used for sails and, secondly, it prevented the sails from tearing or blowing away: indeed a Chinese sail may have half its area full of holes, and still draw well.

A third benefit which bamboo bracing brought the seamen was that it allowed sails to be furled with great ease, for as soon as the sail is lowered, it naturally collapses into a number of pleats. It seems never to have jammed, and it obviated the need ever to send men up aloft in bad weather, as was the case with canvas sails. Lastly, this way of mounting a sail made it possible for the Chinese to sail very nearly into the wind, a point that we shall come to again later.

The efficiency and easy handling of the Chinese lugsail, rigged as described, is well attested by European mariners who have handled it. Nothing, it has been said, can surpass the handiness of the rig, and no vessel is more suited or better adapted to its purpose than the Chinese junk, which uses sails of this kind. Clearly, the Chinese lugsail is one of the foremost achievements in man's use of wind power. Yet we know little of its origin, though there is evidence to support the idea that it arose from the plaiting together of successive palm branches, the central stem providing a naturally built-in batten.

The lugsail is not the only type used in Chinese ships. The ancient square sail has persisted on the upper Yangtze, but it is stiffened by ropes sewn in, these being aligned vertically, not

Drawings of ships with the characteristically Chinese sails which are lowered like a Venetian blind, each part folding down on the next; this is because they are ribbed with bamboo (opposite above) and the sails actually made of bamboo matting (above). The use of such sails, which have always been thought of as typically Chinese right up to the present day, gave Chinese sailors some considerable advantages. They were able to take in the sails without having to roll them up and this gave the ship greater possibility of manoeuvre, being able to adapt more quickly and easily to weather conditions; nor was it necessary to send men up the rigging to furl the sails in adverse weather conditions. Besides, this type of sail could withstand damage better than the conventional type used in the West. Because of

this, the Chinese were most efficient sailors. It seems they did everything short of designing a ship which could sail against the wind!

Opposite below: terra-cotta model of a ship found in a Han tomb of the 1st century in the eastern suburbs of Canton.

Below: a reconstruction of a model rowing boat. The original Han model, which is about 53 cms. long, shows a flat-bottomed ship with cabins covered with matting and, especially interesting, the earliest example of a vertical rudder which revolved on an axis in the stern of the boat. This meant that the rudder could easily be turned in any direction.

horizontally. When these sails are furled, they are rolled in. Square tall narrow sails of cloth are used on the Qiantang River. A spritsail – a sail that is very nearly square but has a tilted upper edge, with a boom running diagonally across it and fixed to the mast at its lower end – is also to be found in China. This type of sail was used in Europe but the Chinese version differs in being stiffened horizontally, though it has no battens.

A form of ship propulsion invented by the Chinese towards the end of the 5th century or a little earlier was the paddle wheel, known in China as the "water-wheel boat." It was manpowered and driven by a treadmill. The water-wheel boat seems primarily to have been used for military purposes, and an early (5th century) account of a battle describes how the enemy were afraid when they saw boats apparently moving on their own, boats which were probably driven by paddle wheels since the enemy would have been familiar with propulsion by sails and oars.

Certainly there is evidence for experiments with paddle-wheel propulsion after this date, but it was early in the 12th century, at the beginning of the Southern Song dynasty, that the treadmill paddle-wheel ships really became important. After the forced transfer of the capital from Kaifeng to the South in 1126, a Chinese navy was established, based on southern expertise. A highly developed paddle-wheel ship was one of the outcomes. These were large vessels, 60–90 meters long, which could carry 700–800 men and might have 20 or more eight-bladed paddle wheels. Yet it took a long time for the paddle wheel to reach Europe: the earliest knowledge of it seems to be at least some 800 years later, while no practical use appears to have been made of it until almost the middle of the 16th century.

Steering and seamanship

We must return now to the sail and to the problem of sailing into the wind. With the large square sails of the West, the best a mariner could do with his ship was to "wear about"; this meant that he had first to turn sideways to the wind, then turn again so that the wind was behind him, with the ship going the opposite way. Next he turned so that the ship moved sideways once more, but this time in the opposite direction. In other words, the mariner had to make his ship perform a series of loops, but the distance moved forward into the wind for each loop was small, and the whole procedure was tedious and time-consuming.

It was a necessary manoeuvre too for a ship with lateen type sails. With the rig of the Chinese lugsails all this could be avoided and "fore-and-aft" sailing carried out. Here the ship moved in a zigzag course, first tacking to one side of the wind and then to the other. How close to the wind a ship could sail in this way depended on the rig of the sails and here the Chinese appear to have had the advantage.

Fore-and-aft sailing as well as any other manoeuvre at sea, even wearing about, means that a ship has to be steered. With a paddle-wheel method of propulsion this presents no difficulties; to steer, the paddles on one side of the ship can be driven hard and those on the opposite side moved slowly, or kept stationary, or even rotated in an opposite direction. But with a sailing ship there is no such method at the disposal of a mariner, and the

Below: in this drawing, an attempt is made to reconstruct the probable appearance of a boat with 23 paddle wheels (11 along each side and one at the stern). This was invented by the naval architect Gao Xuan and others around 1130. Ships with paddle wheels set in motion by a horizontal cylinder begin to appear in documents of the 5th and 6th centuries where it is stated that they were used as battleships on lakes and rivers. Later, in the 12th century, a propulsion mechanism with a greater number of wheels was introduced in the construction of warships which turned out to be of decisive importance during battles for control of the Yangtze.

Opposite: a junk with sails stitched to horizontal rods, very common in Chinese waters even today. These are the development of the traditional Chinese raft and have a flat bottom with no keel and a square transom in the stern. Like the rafts, the junk is characterized by a low draught which means that it can sail even with a heavy load in very shallow waters which are unaccessible to other types of boats.

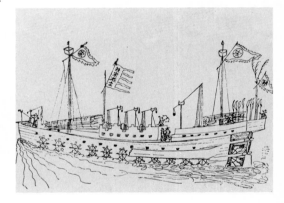

most widely used and ancient method of steering was to use an oar or a paddle held at an angle over the rear or after part of the ship where a large steering oar had its greatest effect.

When a ship is under way something more than a steering oar is required and it is here that the Chinese scored a singular success. The alternative to the steering oar is a rudder and what the Chinese did was to devise the central axial rudder – a rudder which lay in the center of the stern and was pivoted on an axis so that it could be turned in either direction. Such a rudder was discovered early in China; there are literary references to it in the 5th and 6th centuries, but its date has been pushed back earlier than this. Pottery models of ships with axial rudders have been found in tombs of the second Han dynasty, and from these it is clearly evident that the invention had taken place at least by the 1st century – 11 centuries before such rudders were used in the West.

Having invented the central axial rudder, the Chinese also made some changes in it. One was the balanced rudder, where part of the rudder blade is in front of the axis on which it pivots, and part behind. This was current in China at least as early as the 11th century but was still regarded in Europe as new at the end of the 18th. The other was the fenestrated rudder – a rudder with holes – which was not adopted in Europe until the beginning of the present century in the era of the iron and steel ship.

THE ABSENCE OF A UNIVERSAL SCIENCE

We have now sketched, very briefly, something of the achievements of Chinese science and technology. There remains of course the question why, with so great a talent, the Chinese never developed a universal science such as arose in the West at the time of the scientific revolution.

The advent of modern science at the time of the scientific revolution appeared in those branches of science which were readily amenable to mathematical description. Such mathematization did not enter into Chinese science. Moreover the Western concept of laws of nature played its part too because these laws governed specific behaviour under all conditions. As we saw at the beginning it was a different attitude from that which looked on the cosmos as a vast cooperative exercise, an organism in harmony with itself. The latter is an outlook which is now coming to play a valid part in science, but in the first place something more mathematically precise was required for a new view to be formulated.

It is clear, though, that there were many other factors involved – intellectual, philosophical, theological – if modern science was to be born. And it must be remembered that China did not have a military feudalism like Europe but a feudalism that was bureaucratic. Military feudalism gave birth to capitalism, but bureaucratic feudalism could never do this. In the early beginnings of modern science the capitalist spirit of personal enterprise was a vital stimulating force, though whether such an environment is still necessary is another matter. Nevertheless it seems that differences in the structure of government and society between East and West may have been a vital factor.

WRITERS, ARTISTS, SCIENTISTS

Names in bold are Pinyin, those in roman Wade-Giles

Bai Juyi (Pai Chü-i). Bai Juyi (772–846) sat the imperial examinations when he was still extremely young, and secured his first post in the imperial library. In his early years he produced works of scholarship which won him fame in court circles. He inveighed strongly against the corrupt usages of the time, and was exiled from the capital on this account, passing several years without any official post. He was subsequently rehabilitated and made governor of Henan. Unlike the other great Tang poets, Bai laid stress on the social and educative function of poetry (it is said that he used to read his verses to an old illiterate woman, and that if she could not understand any expression he would change it without further ado). He carefully avoided erudition in his style, drawing his inspiration from the themes of everyday life. He also wrote long historical ballads, the only ones of their kind in Tang poetry.

Ban Gu (Pan Ku) (32–92). Ban Gu's fame is linked to that of the historical work *Han Shu* (The Han Annals), the collective efforts of the Ban family. It was begun by Ban Gu's father, Ban Biao, and the last part was finished by his sister, Ban Jiao. *The Han Annals* are China's first dynastic history, and the work was taken as model by all later dynastic historians. Its 120 chapters treat all the events which took place during the period of the Han dynasty, from 206 B.C. to A.D. 9 in minute detail. Ban Gu also wrote poetry, including the famous poem called *The Two Capitals* in praise of the beauty of Changan and Luoyang.

Bi Sheng (Pi Sheng). According to Shen Gua, author of a famous collection of essays on the history of science and technology, published in 1086, Bi Sheng (c. 1012–68) was the inventor of movable print, which he began to put to use around 1040. As with many other inventions, the actual authorship of this discovery is uncertain, but it is certainly true that in this field China was four centuries ahead of Europe. The name of Bi Sheng is linked with this major development, although information on his life is scanty and worthless. The invention of printing with movable type led in the Far East to considerable developments in the production of the written word and the diffusion of knowledge, as it did later with greater effect and more revolutionary consequences in the West.

Cao Xueqin (Ts'ao Hsüeh-ch'in). Cao Xueqin was born in Nanking around 1720 into a family of Chinese civil servants in the employ of the Manchu Qing dynasty, and died in Peking in 1763. His name is inextricably linked with the fame of the novel *The Dream of the Red Chamber*, written after his family's financial ruin. His childhood and youth were spent in wealth and luxury in Nanking, followed by the poverty of his Peking days. He wrote the novel between 1752 and 1762; it is probably autobiographical, with the protagonist representing the author himself. At Cao's death only the first 80 chapters were completed, and Gao E, a writer from Peking, completed the work in a further 40 chapters which he based on Cao's notes. In *The Dream of the Red Chamber* the splendour and decadence of a large, wealthy Chinese family and the impossible love of the hero and his cousin are described with great delicacy and penetration. *The Dream of the Red Chamber* is at once "decadent" and "revolutionary," a contradictory and often ambiguous work which is nevertheless imbued with truth. Considered one of the masterpieces of world literature, it has recently been subjected to harsh criticism in China, since it has been one of the "formative" works for the Chinese educated classes ever since it appeared, a state of affairs which some groups wish to reverse.

Du Fu (Tu Fu). Du Fu lived between 712 and 770. He failed the imperial examinations, only gaining a modest post at the age of 42 in honour of his poetic ability. He was disgraced after the revolt of An Lushan, and was forced to leave the capital and seek any kind of employment in the provinces. The subjects of his poetry were influenced by these unhappy events. At first he celebrated the joy of wine and the beauties of nature, in common with all the poets of his time, but later he began to write bitter criticism of the horrors of war and the misery of the people. His poetry is elaborate and scholarly, though never shackled by meter, of which he was a dexterous master. He was insufficiently recognized by his contemporaries, but was both admired and imitated by the poets of the 10th and 11th centuries.

Gu Kaizhi (Ku K'ai-chih). A painter of the Sei dynasty who lived between 334 and 406. Without rival in the art of portrait painting, somewhat eccentric, he was also a writer, poet, and temple painter. His fame is chiefly linked with the scroll entitled *Admonitions of the Instructress to the Palace Ladies*, preserved in the British Museum. This contains nine scenes with inscriptions inculcating moral values such as the nobility of sacrifice, political honesty, humility in glory, the sense of duty, and so forth. The female figures are drawn with unusual nobility and beauty, and with a warmth and life which enable us to say that Gu was the initiator of a style of pictorial description which developed from brief accounts into more elaborate and richer compositions. Another of his famous works is the *Nymph of the Lo River* preserved in the Freer Gallery of Art, Washington. This is clearly a later copy, but it is of considerable importance because it contains the first examples of landscape painting, a genre which was to be perfected in subsequent ages, and to become one of the lasting glories of Chinese civilization.

Gu Yanwu (Ku Yen-wu). Gu Yanwu (1613–82) was a philosopher and scholar and is considered the father of the critical study of the classical texts of the Confucian school. Thanks to his patient research, works which had fallen into oblivion were republished, and critical editions brought out of ancient works which had been reworked or cut in later ages. He was also interested in archaeological studies, but always refused to take part in the imperial examinations held by the foreign Qing dynasty, calling himself a patriot and a supporter of the deposed Ming. He wrote a vast outline of the historical geography of China, taken from over a thousand sources, and a famous *Treatise on Ethnic, Political and Economic Geography* which is a mine of information on China at the end of the Ming period, and most of which was collected at firsthand during the course of his long study tours throughout the country. His most famous work, still read today, is his *Annals of Everyday Wisdom*, a kind of miscellany of notes and short essays on economic, administrative, religious, and social problems.

Guan Hanqing (Kuan Han-ch'ing). Guan, who lived from 1125 to 1205, is considered the father of Chinese theater, and the chief exponent of the so-called northern style of theater, which differs sharply from the southern in having a limited number of acts, four at the most, with an optional prologue, while any work in the southern style has an indefinite number of acts, varying between 20 and 40. We have very little information on Guan Hanqing's life. We know only that he began his official career under the Jin, but retired with the advent of the Mongol Yuan dynasty. Sixty dramas are attributed to him, of which only 17 have come down to us, among which are: *The Injustice suffered by Dou E* and *The History of the Old Barrel Organ*.

Guo Moruo (Kuo Mo-jo). Guo Moruo (1892–1977) was a historian, poet, scholar and scientist, qualifying in medicine at the Japanese university of Kyushu, and one of the outstanding figures in contemporary Chinese culture. A man of radical politics, he became a Marxist around 1924, but only joined the Chinese communist party in 1958. He was accused of revisionism in 1966 during the cultural revolution, but agreed to public self-criticism, and was nominated a member of the revolutionary committee of the Academy of Sciences. He used his undisputed intellectual prestige to support the "Gang of Four," but in October 1976, after Mao's death, he became one of the first to make violent accusations against the "wicked" policies which had governed China in the ten years between 1966 and 1976. In the course of his long life he held some of the highest offices, such as president of the National Committee for Culture and Education, and president of the National Association of Writers and Artists.

Han Gan (Han Kan). Han Gan was the most famous painter of imperial horses in the Tang court. The precise date of his birth is not known, but he was active between 720 and 760. According to legend he worked while he was a boy as apprentice to a wine merchant who numbered among his customers the great painter and poet Wang Wei. The latter, one day noticing the youth drawing skilfully with a stick on the sand, took him as his pupil. Subsequently Han Gan abandoned the traditional models and devoted himself exclusively to painting horses. It is said that when the emperor rebuked him for deviating from the accepted canons, he replied, "Your Majesty, your servant does have masters, Your Majesty's horses." One of his most famous paintings depicts a tied-up horse pawing the ground in an attempt to get free. It is called the *Night Shining White Steed*, and is in a private collection in London.

Han Yu (Han Yu). Han Yu was a philosopher and writer who lived between 773 and 819 and who advocated reform in prose and a return to the style of the Han period, simpler and closer to the spoken language. The style adopted by Han Yu and his followers is known as *gu wen*, ancient style, but in fact his style was completely novel. In his philosophy he was a strenuous opponent of Buddhism and Taoism. A work which has remained famous in history was his *Memorial on the Buddha's Bone*, a protest to the emperor in which he ridiculed and censured the superstitious cult accorded in a certain temple to a bone which was said to be a relic of the Buddha.

Hong Sheng (Hung Sheng). Hong Sheng (1645–1704) was the author of one of the most famous dramas in the Chinese theatrical repertory, *The Pavilion of Long Life*. It follows the rules of a style of theatrical writing which developed around the second part of the Ming period, and to which several famous writers contributed, in which the style was highly refined, and intended to be read rather than performed. *The Pavilion of Long Life* recounts the unhappy love of the Tang emperor Xuanzong for the beautiful Yang Guei Fei. Hong Sheng was relieved of all his duties and exiled to a distant province by the emperor Kangxi, of the foreign Manchu dynasty, who considered the nationalistic spirit of the work an attack on his authority. Hong Sheng wrote eight other plays which have not come down to us, and an anthology of poetry. *The Pavilion of Long Life* is considered one of the masterpieces of Chinese literature of all time and enjoyed great popularity in spite of its initial censorship.

Hu Shi (Hu Shih). Hu Shi (1891–1962) won a scholarship to study in the United States, financed out of the Boxer indemnity funds. He studied at Cornell University, and then at Columbia, where he was a pupil of John Dewey. Returning home, he obtained a post in the University of Peking, where he taught until 1937. He is considered the chief exponent of pragmatism in China, and made a decisive contribution to the struggle for the adoption of the spoken language *bai-hua*, launching the first decisive appeal for the "literary revolution" from the pages of the review *New Youth*, to which many other intellectuals and students of Marxist tendencies, including Mao Zedong himself, contributed. Hu Shi was an iconoclast and a critic of the traditional system, but never became a Marxist, opposing at the same time the policies and ideology of the Guomindang. In 1937 he moved to the United States of America, and in 1948 he was asked to return home and stand as a candidate for the presidency of the Republic. He refused, partly as a result of the events, which were rapidly bringing the communists to power. In 1958 he left the United States to settle in Taiwan, where the nationalist government of Chiang Kaishek nominated him president of the Academia Sinica. In China he was so hated by the communist party that in 1954 a special committee was set up for the study and criticism of Hu Shi's ideology. Among his other works he wrote a monumental *History of Chinese Philosophy*.

Hua Do (Hua To). Hua Do lived between 136 and 208, and was the first great surgeon and pioneer of anaesthetic techniques. He probably also experimented with operations in trepanation. He treated the tyrant Cao Cao, who tried to retain his services as court doctor; Hua Do refused, and was thrown into prison on Cao Cao's orders and killed. According to legend, Hua Do wanted to leave his writings on medicine to the jailer, but the latter refused for fear of incurring the tyrant's wrath. All the texts attributed to Hua Do are thus later compilations made by his disciples. It is, however, known for certain that Hua Do used Indian hemp in anaesthesia, and was the first to recognize the advantages of hydrotherapy, massage, and gymnastics. A treatise on physical education using positions inspired by the animal kingdom and known as "The Game of the Animals" is attributed to him.

Kong fu zi (Confucius). According to tradition, Confucius, the latinized form of Kong fu zi, lived between 551 and 479 B.C. The first accurate biography is found in *The Han Annals*, the first dynastic history of China written in 86 B.C. This relates how he was born in poverty in the state of Lu (present-day Shandong), and became a civil servant, reaching an elevated position. When he was forced into exile as a result of political intrigue, he wandered from state to state for some ten years, hoping to convince the sovereigns of the states he visited to put into practice his theory of just and harmonious social relations. The teachings of Confucius have come down to us thanks to his disciples, who diligently compiled them and published them in the *Analects*, a collection of his sayings and maxims. Confucius is also credited with having drawn up the *Classics* (or Canons), although in reality his activity was restricted to interpreting them, since they already constituted the cultural heritage of the past in his day. "I hand down, I do not create," Confucius declared, emphasizing that he did not intend to found an original philosophical system. In this way, although Confucius is the beginning, and hence the founder, of Chinese culture, in the widest sense of the term, his role has been an ambiguous one, and by always appealing to tradition, he mortgaged Chinese thought throughout its history to traditionalism, so that innovations had to be smuggled in under the guise of revivals from the golden age of antiquity in order to win prestige and acceptance.

The practical effects of the teachings of Confucius on society were to lend authority to the hierarchy and place limits on every form of individual freedom by imposing the observance of various rites, although at the same time it did not exclude the possibility of universal betterment, since Confucian doctrine presupposes the original equality of all men, who resemble each other in natural qualities, but differ in acquired habits. The method of transforming a "common man" into a "superior man" is study: thus Confucius passed into history as the "supreme educator," and although Confucianism became ossified in the practice of bureaucratic government, it was always capable of renewing itself by going back to this "democratic" vein.

Kong Shangren (K'ung Shang-jen). Kong Shangren (1648–1718) was a descendant of Confucius, whose family name he bore, and was one of the major dramatists of the Qing period. His fame is linked above all to his work *The Peach-Blossom Fan*, a realistic historical play describing events which took place shortly before the author's birth in the conquest of Nanking by the invading Manchus. The play was mounted for the first time in 1700, and scandalized court circles in the capital, Kong lost his post in the imperial civil service and was exiled to a distant province.

Lao She (Lao She). Lao She (1898–1966) was born in Peking of a Manchu family. He taught Chinese literature in the University of Tianjin, moving to London in 1924, where he was made lecturer in Chinese language at the School of Oriental Studies (now School of Oriental and African Studies). He returned to China in 1930, and after the advent of communism he was elected a deputy to the People's National Assembly. In 1966, during the cultural revolution, he was accused of being a "bourgeois writer" and underwent physical violence from the Red Guards from which he died. In 1978 his memory was rehabilitated, and his books which had disappeared from circulation, were all republished. He was a prolific writer, and was translated in the West from the thirties on; his most famous work is his novel *The Rickshaw Boy*. Lao She tells of the daily lives of the poor in a language full of popular expressions and has a keen eye for the comic side of events, even in tragedy. He also wrote some of the most famous comedies of contemporary theater, among them *The Tea Shop* and *The Ditch of the Dragon's Beard*.

Laozi (Lao Tzu). 604 B.C. has been proposed as an approximate date for Laozi's birth. In his *Historical Records*, Sima Qian says that his personal name was Erh, his nickname Tan, and his family name Li; Laozi means only "Old Master." Laozi was a contemporary of Confucius, and the founder of the most important stream of Chinese philosophy after Confucianism, Taoism. His teaching is laid out in the work called *Dao De Jing* (The Book of the Way and of Virtue). It is mainly the first part which is obscure, in which the *Dao* (*Tao*) is defined: this is the first principle, immutable though changing in appearance, great, detached, and recurrent. The work is divided into three parts, the first elucidating its cosmological conceptions, the second treating of the behaviour of the wise man, and the last, in which the principles on which a good system of government should be based are expounded. For Laozi, the aim of individual existence is spiritual and bodily peace, and this can be obtained through "nonaction," that is to say, through natural and spontaneous action, as simple and innocent as that of a child, rather than through complete inactivity. Thus when we turn to the art of government, the ideal governor is the one who governs the least possible, allowing the people to do what they can without imposing laws and restrictions on them, thus imitating Heaven, which has no care of men. Taoism was attacked by Confucianism, especially for its degenerate superstitions, but remained a living thread in the warp of Chinese culture, opposing the rigid morality of the Confucians with its doctrine of freedom from conventions and hypocrisy.

Li Bai (Li Tai-po). Exceptional for a Chinese man of letters, Li Bai (702–62) never sat the imperial examinations which gave access to the civil service. He was a fervent Taoist, and spent several years in retreat, but in 742 he was invited to the court through the influence of the emperor's sister, who was also a Taoist nun. He was nominated a member of the imperial academy, and for several years he celebrated the beauty of the emperor's favourites, drunkenness, and the joy of living, in a language rich in musical and rhythmic devices. He subsequently

fell from the emperor's favour, and led the life of a vagabond. Legend relates that one night, when he was more than usually drunk, and while he was in a boat on the river, he saw the moon reflected in the water, and was so drawn by its beauty that he leaned out to embrace it, and drowned.

Li Hui (Li Hui). Li Hui, who lived in the 3rd century, between 220 and 280, is one of the outstanding figures in the history of Chinese mathematics. He studied new methods of solving equations, and succeeded in finding the approximate value of 3·14 for π by drawing a regular hexagon in a circle and bisecting it repeatedly until he arrived at a polygon of 96 sides. He was also the author of the valuable commentary on *The Art of Calculation in Nine Chapters* by an unknown author, and the classic text of Chinese mathematics, which dates from about the first century.

Li Shizhen (Li Shih-Chen). Li Shizhen (1518–98) was a doctor and writer, and the author of an immense work on pharmacopoea, the *Bencao gangmu*, which he finished in 1578, after 27 years of research. The book is in 53 volumes, three of which are of illustrations, embracing the three kingdoms of nature: animal, vegetable, and mineral. In it 1893 drugs are described, of which 1704 belong to the vegetable kingdom. The *Bencao gangmu* summarizes all Chinese pharmacological research up to the 16th century, and was reprinted and commented upon many times. In it we find the first mention of a method of vaccination against smallpox based on the same principle which gave birth in the West to the science of immunology.

Li Yu (Li Yü). Li Yu (937–78) was the last emperor of one of the most glorious of China's dynasties, the Tang, and is also held to be one of the finest authors of ballads. Some 40 of his compositions survive, in which he celebrates love and the refined pleasures of life. After he was deposed by the founder of the Song dynasty, Li Yu expressed his sorrow at his sad imprisonment and his regret for the ease of the past in soulful strains. He was accused of plotting against the new ruler, and forced to commit suicide by taking poison.

Liang Kai (Liang K'ai). Liang Kai (c. 1182–1253) was a painter during the last part of the Song period, when artists began to react against academic conformity and the caste ethos of the court painters. He was a disciple of the Ch'an Buddhist sect (better known in the West under its Japanese name of Zen), and renounced all worldly honours to retire to the peace of a monastery. His artistic technique was completely original, and the works attributed to him frequently combine huge backgrounds of landscape or monochrome backgrounds with human figures executed with a few vigorous brushstrokes. His masterpiece is the *Portrait of the Poet Li Bo*, preserved in the National Museum in Tokyo, which evokes the intense vitality of the subject with only a few strokes to convey line, depth, and movement.

Lin Shu (Lin Shu). In the period leading up to the republican revolution, Lin Shu (1852–1924) had had high hopes for reform, both in politics and literature, but after 1915 he became decidedly hostile to the new cultural movements and the radicalism of the student youth, on which he himself had had considerable influence. Without any knowledge of any European language he translated 180 books by European authors, mostly into Chinese. He had the works translated orally by his assistants, and then transcribed them in literary Chinese, replete with literary devices and archaic forms. Among his most famous translations are *La Dame aux Camélias* by Dumas, *David Copperfield* by Dickens, *Ivanhoe* by Scott, and *Uncle Tom's Cabin* by Harriet Beecher Stowe.

Lin Yutang (Lin Yü-t'ang). Lin Yutang (1895–1976) is famous for his essays in English on Chinese culture. He graduated in literature from Harvard, and from 1928 to 1935 he was the English editor in the foreign languages section of the publications of the Academia Sinica. During this period he dedicated himself to projects for romanizing Chinese and studied a system for cataloguing the characters. He was a prolific writer, but did not achieve great success in his own country with his works written in his mother tongue, while the books which he wrote directly in English, such as *My Country and My People* and *Moment in Peking* brought him great fame, especially in the United States. His position towards the classical Confucian tradition was favourable, making him an object of hate to all elements of left-wing Chinese culture. His major achievement as a philologist and linguist was the monumental *Chinese-English Dictionary for Modern Use*, published in Hong Kong in 1972, the fruit of a lifetime of study and research.

Liu Zongyuan (Liu Tsung-yüan). Liu Zongyuan lived between 773 and 820, and along with Han Yu promoted the *gu-wen*, or "ancient" style, a fashionable reaction against the then dominant style of obscure and elaborately balanced prose. He is famous as the Chinese Aesop, and wrote the first allegorical tales in Chinese literature, directing his invective against the corruption of the ruling class and the more absurd and irrational aspects of traditional morality. He also wrote short fantasies which are gathered in a famous collection called *Notes of Lu-Zheng*. Liu is thought to be the finest prose stylist in the whole of Chinese literature, and he was an elegant practitioner of the minor genre known as *hsiao-shuo*, "small talk," in the sense of novella or anecdote (the same term as was later to be used for novel). He was also a poet and calligrapher of note, and a fervent Buddhist. His poems are to be found in the collection of *Three Hundred Tang Poems* compiled in the 18th century under the Qing dynasty.

Lu Xun (Lu Hsün). Lu Xun (1881–1936) is the greatest writer of the Chinese "new literature," and he dominated and influenced the whole culture of modern China. When he was 20 years old he went to Japan to study medicine, but gave it up in the conviction that his compatriots were more in need of someone to shake their spirits out of their centuries-long apathy than of doctors able only to cure their bodies. With this aim in mind, he dedicated himself to literature, and in particular to criticism and satire, diagnosing the country's ills, and laying bare the contradictions and horrors of its tradition and of the Confucian ideology. His first novel, *Diary of a Madman*, appeared in 1918 in the review *New Youth*, marking the birth of the new literature in *bai-hua* (spoken language).

After teaching in various universities, he finally settled in 1927 in Shanghai, where he founded in 1930 the league of left-wing Chinese writers to which belonged most of the intellectuals who were concerned to redefine their role in society. Lu Xun's literary production consists of 16 collections of essays, three anthologies of stories, prose poems and novels. He was also very active as a translator, and it is interesting to note that the number of his translations is greater than that of his original works. In spite of differences with the communists, he was always respected by them, and in 1940 Mao proclaimed him a "giant of the cultural revolution in China." He had enormous influence on the youth and intellectuals of the twenties and thirties, and he has exercised a decisive role in building up a new social and civil conscience.

Ma Jun (Ma Chün). Ma Jun was an engineer of exceptional ability who lived in the 3rd century and invented the chain pump with square paddles which then spread throughout the whole area of Chinese culture. He also devised a swivelling crossbow, as Leonardo da Vinci was later to do, and successfully completed a simple type of differential gear. He also perfected the hand loom and built a puppet theater powered by water, and the famous "south-facing chariot." Our information on his life and personality comes from a work which his friend, the writer Fu Xuan, dedicated to his memory. Fu Xuan describes the complete

inability of a man of genius like Ma Jun to converse with sophisticated scholars of classical formation, and to this lack of communication and inability to make himself understood by the bureaucracy of letters, he attributes the fact that Ma Jun never obtained an important position in the public service and never had the means at his disposal to put many of his inventions into practice.

Mei Lanfang (Mei Lan-fang). Mei Lanfang (1884–1961) was born into a celebrated family of actors, and is considered to have been the greatest interpreter of Peking Opera, specializing in *dan* roles (female characters). He was also famous in Europe and the United States of America, where he had great success in 1920, being enthusiastically welcomed by both public and critics, and being awarded an honorary degree by a university in California. In China he was proclaimed "King of actors" for winning in Shanghai in 1912 270,000 votes from his admirers in an actors' competition.

He was responsible for reintroducing the ancient practice of combining singing and dancing on the stage, abolished about the 10th century. From that period on actors came on stage solely to sing. Mei was the first to sing, dance, and fence on stage, and in this way he brought new life to the Chinese theater, and gained sufficient prestige to establish his own school. He refused to take part in any production during the Japanese invasion, in spite of the insistence of the occupying powers and the collaborationist government, and he let his moustaches grow so that he could not interpret the female roles which were his speciality. After the communist victory, in 1950, he was nominated director of the Chinese Institute for the Theater, and he was elected deputy to the People's National Congress in 1954 and 1958. He left a book of memoirs, *Forty Years of the Stage*, which is one of the most valuable sources for the study of the theater during a troubled period of rapid social change.

Meng Haoran (Meng Hao-jan). Meng was born in 689 and died in 740. He was considered one of the best poets of his day, under the Tang dynasty, the golden age of poetry. He failed the imperial examinations in 737 and retired to live on Lu-men mountain in Hubei. He may have been forced into this decision because some of his ruses had aroused the anger of the emperor Xuanzong, whom he had met at the residence of another great poet and civil servant, and a friend of his, Wang Wei. From this time on, Meng lived only for poetry, and literary critics compare him to Wang Wei, both in style and feeling. His compositions form part of the collection of *Three Hundred Tang Poems* compiled in the 18th century.

Mengzi (Meng Tzu). Mengzi (latinized to Mencius) lived, according to tradition, between 371 and 289 B.C., and represented the idealist stream of Confucianism. His book *Mengzi* (The Book of Mencius) was later included among the classics which formed the basis of Confucian orthodoxy for nearly 1000 years. Mencius' main theory was the original goodness of human nature; every man possesses the four sentiments: compassion, modesty, shame and justice, just as he possesses two arms and two legs. Since man is essentially a political animal, whose existence has meaning and worth only in society, these virtues can only be deployed in social relations. The state is a moral institution, and the sovereign should possess these ethical qualities in supreme measure: if it becomes clear that he does not have them, the people have the right to remove him. This is the theory of the "removal of the mandate of Heaven" which proved so influential in Chinese history by legitimizing violent changes of dynasty through the centuries. Mencius also preached the equal distribution of land, and his book expounds the ancient system of "common land," called the "well system." According to this, every square *li* of land (c. 500 square meters) was to be divided into nine equal squares, which were assigned to eight families who thus obtained an equal measure of land, while all together they cultivated the central field and gave its produce to the state as tax. The arrangement of the nine squares resembles the Chinese character meaning "well." Mencius was very popular from the 9th to the 11th century, especially as his thought had certain features in common with Buddhism.

Mi Fu (Mi Fu). Mi Fu (1051–1107) was an imperial civil servant and a famous painter, a typical example of the gentleman-artist, both versatile and eccentric. He is said to have gone about dressed in the manner of the Tang period, 300 years earlier, and he nearly ruined himself collecting examples of ancient writings. His house was a museum of the works of the artists of the time who were his friends, and of the masters of the past. Mi Fu was one of the most famous exponents of the southern school of landscape painting, but although various works are attributed to him, their authenticity is in doubt. Most of these works are in the "Mi Fu style," but at least they allow us to gain an idea of the master's style. He excelled at painting highly rarefied and poetic landscapes, with mountains swathed in mist, with small pavilions, and occasionally tiny human figures on their flanks.

Mozi (Mo Tzu or Mo Ti). Mozi (Master Mo) lived probably between 479 and 381 B.C. He founded a school of philosophy which had a great following before China was unified under the empire, in the 3rd century, but he failed to make any deep impression on the later history of Chinese thought. Mozi was the first declared opponent of Confucianism, rejecting all its values, including the sanctity of tradition and rites. The *Mozi* (The Book of Master Mo) is our chief source for the study of his thought, which centered around his idea of "universal love." This is in strong contrast to the Confucian ethic, which centered around the complex social system based on the family, and believed in a graduated hierarchy of affection related to the particular bonds uniting different individuals.

Nalan Xingde (Na-lan Hsing-teh). Nalan Xingde (1655–85) was a member of the Manchu race which occupied China in 1644 and a member of the imperial family which founded the Qing dynasty. He was greatly attracted by Chinese culture, absorbing it to such a degree that he may be called the greatest poet of the Chinese language in the whole of the Qing dynasty. He wrote of his grief at the loss of his wife, and his impossible love for another woman, renewing the poetical genre of the ballad which had flourished at the time of the Song dynasty.

Ouyang Xiu (Ou Yang Hsiu). Ouyang Xiu (1007–72) was the foremost prose stylist of the Song period, adopting a clear, simple style of writing in contrast to the balanced, rhythmic style called *pien-wen*. He is celebrated for his compositions in the *fu* genre, part prose, part poetry, which reached its peak during the Han period, and which he modernized and gave new content. His two most famous *fu* are the *Fu of Autumn's Voice* and the *History of the Pavilion of the Old Drunkard*. Ouyang Xiu held important posts in the administration and directed the committee of scholars charged with compiling the *New History of the Five Dynasties*. He was also interested in archaeology, and published the texts of ancient inscriptions on bronze furnished with explanatory notes.

Pei Xiu (P'ei Hsiu). Pei Xiu (224–71) was a statistician and geographer who is considered to have been the father of Chinese cartography. In 267 he was appointed minister of public works, in which post he fixed the principles for correct cartographic representation, emphasizing the importance of "the relations of division," that is to say, that the land to be represented should be drawn on a smaller scale but divided on a fixed system of relations into the squares of a mesh consisting of equidistant parallel horizontal lines, intersected by other parallel vertical lines, also equidistant, and on the same scale as the first lines. This network has nothing to do with the meridians and parallels, but played the same part as the scale on modern maps. The principles laid down by Pei Xiu provided the backbone of Chinese cartography until the encounter with the West.

Pien Qiao (P'ien Ch'iao). Pien Qiao lived in the 5th century B.C., and was the first to recognize medicine as a separate branch of learning, distinct from magic and superstition. He was the author of the classic *Nan Jing* (The Classic of Difficulty), which was a kind of commentary on the most ancient Chinese medical text, the *Nei Jing* (Classic of the Interior) which discusses 81 controversial points in medical science.

Qi Baishi (Ch'i Pai-shih). Qi Baishi (1860–1957) was one of the greatest painters in contemporary China, as well as a poet and calligrapher, in accordance with Chinese artistic tradition. His skill in painting can be seen in his ability to express the essence of his subject in a few brush strokes. His favourite subjects were flowers, fruit, crabs, prawns, mice, which he painted in watercolour with acute observation. He had a jolly disposition and illustrated the lesser aspects of reality in the calligraphic manner known as "ideal painting."

Qu Yuan (Ch'ü Yüan). Qu Yuan lived, according to tradition, between 340 and 280 B.C. He was China's first great poet, and held high positions at the court of the Chu kingdom. He lost favour with the sovereign, however, as a result of obscure machinations on the part of his rivals, and was banished. According to legend, when he heard that the kingdom of Qin was about to make war on his distant homeland, he threw himself in despair into the waters of the River Mi-lo and died. It was the fifth day of the fifth moon, and from that day on, the great festival of the dragons' barques has been dedicated every year in China to the memory of Qu Yuan. His masterpiece is the *Li Sao*, a poem in 374 verses in which he reflects bitterly on the state and the lack of wisdom in ruling monarchs.

Sima Guang (Ssu Ma-kuang). Sima Guang (1019–86) was a politician and famous writer, the leader of the conservative party and the opponent of the reformer Wang Anshi, repealing all the latter's "new laws" in 1085. Like his rival Wang, he composed poetry in the traditional genres, but his fame is chiefly linked with his monumental historical work entitled *A General Mirror To Serve the Government*, in which he describes the history of China from 403 to 959, taking the events in strict chronological order, on the model of the dynastic annals, in years, months, and days. Nonetheless, Sima Guang took account of the developments in the study of history, and his work is based on accurate research into the original sources, and remains one of the masterpieces of world historiography.

Sima Qian (Ssu-ma Ch'ien). Sima Qian lived between 145 and 85 B.C., and is held to have been the founder of Chinese historiography. His general history of China from the origins up to 90 B.C. was the model for all later dynastic histories. His work is called the *Historical Records*, and was the fruit of patient research and compilation of material which his father, Sima Tan, had already begun.

Sima Qian succeeded his father as court astrologer in 98 B.C. He fell into disgrace for having defended a general who had been taken prisoner by the Huns, and was sentenced to castration, a punishment which he suffered consoled by the thought that he would still be able to finish the great work on which he had been working for years. His style is simple and bare; he did not disdain popular expressions, nor did he alter historical truth for philosophical or moral ends.

Sima Xiangru (Ssu-ma Hsiang-ju). Sima Xiangru lived between 179 and 117 B.C. He was the author of a number of *fu* (lyrical compositions in a rhythmic meter) written with an extraordinarily rich vocabulary, which won him the favour of the emperor and admission to the court. His contemporaries acclaimed him as "divine," and praised his *fu*, *The Beautiful Lady* and *Mister Nobody*, as the acme of stylistic perfection. In later ages he was blamed for having contributed to the decadence of the genre by his excessively recherché style.

Su Shi (Su Shih). Su Shi (1036–1101) is generally held to have been the stylistically most perfect and most delightful poet of the Song period. He entered the imperial civil service while still extremely young, but he was a failure as a politician, and alternated between high posts at court and long periods of exile. He is also known by the soubriquet of Su Dong-po, "Su of the eastern slope," because in one of his periods of retirement from public life he had a hut built on the eastern slope of a hill, where he spent his time writing poetry and observing nature together with his refined companion, Zhao Yun. Although Su Shi was not a convinced Taoist, nor indeed a Confucian or Buddhist, he had absorbed the Taoist contemplative love of nature, and his verses reflect this feeling. His most famous composition is called *The Fu of the Purple Rock*.

Su Song (Su Sung). Su Song (1020–1101) was an engineer, mathematician, and astronomer, whose fame is linked with one of the most famous ventures in the measurement of time and in astronomy. In 1090, at Kaifeng, he perfected the astronomical clock, a complex mechanism with an escapement system, gearing, and transmission chains, a celestial globe, and an armillary sphere. This machine is one of the most precise pieces of clockwork ever invented. It was turned mainly by a slow-moving continuous wheel driven by rotating buckets fed by a tank kept at a constant level.

Tang Xianzu (T'ang Hsien-tzu). Tang Xianzu (1550–1616) was one of the most famous dramatists of the Ming period. He first won fame when still extremely young with his *Pavilion of the Peonies*. This is the story of a girl, who falls in love with a boy who appears to her in a dream, and who dies as a result of her impossible love. Three years after her death, the student Liu sees the ghost of an unknown girl in a dream, who invites him to dig up the place where she is buried, beneath the pavilion of the peonies. Liu obeys, and finds her corpse miraculously preserved. With the aid of a wonder-working potion the girl is restored to life, and recognizes Liu as the man whom she saw and fell in love with in her dream. Tang has been called the "Chinese Shakespeare"; the play is a literary masterpiece, and develops through 55 acts. Four other plays of the same author survive, all of which are set in motion by a dream vision of the protagonist, and known in consequence as *Tang's Dreams*.

Tao Yuanming (T'ao Yuan-ming). Tao Yuanming lived between 365 and 427, in a period of war and troubles. He was also known as Tao Qian. He quickly abandoned his career in the civil service and retired to farm and write poetry in freedom. The epitaph which he wrote for himself on his deathbed is to be found in every anthology of Chinese literature, and runs, "He wrote for his own pleasure and to relieve his soul, and so he finished." Apart from his *Funeral Hymn for Himself* written in 427, he is famed for his *Journey to the Spring of the Peach Blossom*, in which he describes an idyllic utopian world.

Wang Chong (Wang Ch'ung). Wang Chong (27–97) was an exponent of the rationalist school of thought which made considerable progress towards the end of the Han dynasty. He was the author of a monumental work called *Lung hen* (Measured Discourses), in which he criticized current superstitions on the basis of arguments drawn from experience and explained various different phenomena as produced solely by natural causes. He was a convinced materialist, denying the possibility of a life after death, holding that just as a fire needs fuel, so the spirit, the senses, and perception cannot exist independently of the body. In his book he discusses problems of physics, biology, and genetics, analyzing them all from a critical and rationalist point of view.

Wang Shimin (Wang Shih-min, 1592–1680). Wang Shimin was a poet, prose writer, painter, and calligrapher, and the greatest of the "four Wangs," four painters of the Qing dynasty period who have entered history in this way because they all shared the same family name, although they were not related. Wang Shimin was not only closely acquainted with the painting of the Song and Yuan periods, but in many of his paintings he was a direct imitator of them. In others, however, the lyrical treatment of his themes derives purely from his personal inspiration. The other Wangs were also eclectics, and this is in fact typical of all Qing art and aesthetics; they did, however, frequently attain a level of originality which is not otherwise to be found in the artists of the last dynasty, in whom the narrative treatment of landscape painting lost all its grandeur, becoming refined, formal, and affected, but devoid of all spiritual or emotional content.

Wang Shizhen (Wang Shih-chen). Wang Shizhen (1526–90) is generally thought to have been the author of the famous Ming dynasty novel, *Jin Ping Mei* (the title of which is made up of three characters which occur in the name of a maid and two of the hero's wives), although the attribution is doubtful. The *Jin Ping Mei* is a realistic novel, which owes its fame, both in China and abroad, chiefly to its erotic character. However, it also provides an extremely detailed picture of manners, drawn by a man well versed in the mind of his contemporaries, and can be numbered among the masterpieces of world literature. According to legend, the author steeped the pages of his manuscript in a powerful poison, and then gave it to his worst enemy, a minister, to read first, certain that the latter would be so absorbed by the story that he would read it without putting it down, and would die at the end through having slowly absorbed the poison by licking his finger to turn the pages.

Wang Wei (Wang Wei). Wang Wei (699–759) was a man of many parts, an excellent musician, a scholar in the science of medicine, a good painter, and poet. He passed the imperial examinations very young, and had a rapid and brilliant career, reaching the top of the civil service in a short space of time. He was forced by the rebel An Lushan to take part in his government, but was treated with clemency by the emperor Xuanzong, who continued to put his trust in Wang after his return to the capital, offering him the post of ministerial vice-counsellor. No original paintings by Wang Wei survive, only a few reproductions from later times. His poems have survived, however, and these praise nature, unaffected by human passions, creating a picturesque effect. It was said of him that "his poems are pictures, and his pictures poems." In spite of the troubled political developments in which he found himself caught up against his will, he devoted a large part of his life to silent meditation on the vastness of the universe, and was profoundly influenced by both Taoism and Buddhism.

Wen Iduo (Wen J-tuo). Wen Iduo (1898–1946) is generally held to be the greatest poet of the new poetry in *bai-hua* (spoken language). At first he devoted himself to creating a new metrical system on the model of Western poetry, but he later rejected this type of "acculturation" and expressed himself freely, giving first place to the content of his verse. His poetry reveals an austere, solitary character, and his burning patriotism is filled with pride and an incredulous melancholy for the shameful state into which China had fallen. He was accused by the left of "not understanding much about politics," but continued to be a harsh critic of the Guomindang regime, and died assassinated by the Brown Shirts of Chiang Kaishek in July, 1946.

Wen Zhenming (Wen Cheng-ming). Wen Zhenming lived between 1470 and 1559 and is considered one of the "four great masters of the Ming dynasty." At first he followed the landscape style of the Song and Yuan dynasties, but in his later years he developed a more personal style, paying attention not only to the grand and obvious beauties of scenery, but also to the more humble details, which he made his main themes, such as rugged rocks, dying trees, the odd clump of orchids, or two solitary tree trunks. In these paintings he was able to portray the essence of the subject without excessive description. His last works are in the Yiyoshi collection in Tokyo.

Wu Daozi (Wu Tao-tzu). Wu Daozi lived some time between 680 and 760, and was undoubtedly the greatest painter of the Tang dynasty. Critics have always given praise to the huge size and variety of his production, most of which was on religious themes. In him the great myths of Mahayana Buddhism found their interpreter, and he was able to translate their transcendental symbolism into a more human pictorial language. It is said that a large part of the decorations of the Buddhist temples of Luoyang and Changan were done by Wu Daozi, but unfortunately only copies of his works have survived, mainly of rock carvings traced onto paper. It is possible to gain an impression of some of the characteristics of his style from these carvings nonetheless, revealing him as a majestic and innovative artist, especially in his treatment of background landscapes.

Wu Jingzi (Wu Ching-tzu). Wu Jingzi (1701–54) was a member of a family of decayed landowners. He failed the imperial examinations on a number of occasions, and lived a life of great privation and frustration. In order to vindicate himself before his colleagues, he wrote a novel called *The Secret History of the Civil Servants*, the harshest of satires on the mandarinate, and a violent denunciation of the alleged democracy of the examination system, which was theoretically open to everyone, but was in practice limited to the rich, with time and money enough to devote themselves to the long and difficult preparation necessary. Wu's corrosive pen draws a picture of general corruption, incompetence and nepotism, and his novel was rigorously censored.

Xuanzang (Hsüan Tsang). Xuanzang was a Buddhist monk who lived during the Tang dynasty period, from 602–64. He was sceptical of the reliability of the Chinese translations of the Indian sacred texts, and in 629 he set out alone on a long voyage across the deserts of Central Asia to procure from India the original manuscript of the metaphysical treatise *Lands of the Masters of Yoga*. He studied with the best teachers in India, and mastered Sanskrit so well that his translation of the *Dao De Jing* of Laozi, commissioned by the king of Kamarupa, was considered perfect. He returned to his own country after 16 years, and with the assistance of other monks, he occupied himself translating the Buddhist classics into Chinese and devoted himself to teaching philosophy. He is remembered for his adventurous journeys, and as a rigorous philologist (it was he who was responsible for introducing strict rules of translation and transcription of alphabetical languages into Chinese), as well as the only man in all Chinese history to understand in depth the whole of the immense heritage of Buddhist philosophy.

Yan Fu (Yen Fu). Yen Fu (1854–1921) was one of the first liberal reformers. He had high hopes for the westernization of China, and the introduction of modern scientific and liberal political institutions. He proclaimed the need to abolish the system of imperial examinations for recruiting civil servants, and was a bitter critic of Confucianism. He had an indirect but profound effect on the development of Chinese thought, being the first translator of Western philosophical works, ranging from *The Wealth of Nations* by Adam Smith to Montesquieu's *Spirit of the Laws*. His Chinese translations of T. H. Huxley's *Evolution and Ethics* and other Western works were accompanied by his own notes, in which he lent his support to the concepts of natural selection and the survival of the fittest, which he had learnt from his readings of Darwin and Spencer, holding that these laws were valid not only for animal species, but for nations as well.

Yan Su (Yen Su). Yan Su lived during the Song period, under the reign of Ren Zong (1023–64), and was famed as a painter, scholar, technician, and engineer. The most interesting of his many works are those treating of the recording of time and the phenomenon of the tides. In spite of his abilities and his natural gift for technical matters, he held administrative posts in provincial cities throughout his life, and the peak of his career was when he was made head of the ministry of ceremonies, without any contact with technical or public works bodies. This detail shows how undervalued and unimportant was the social position of technicians in the bureaucratic society of mediaeval China. This was because all hope of advancement in the public service depended on the support of high-ranking officials and the patronage of those trained in classical humanist culture.

Zhang Chongqing (Chang Chung-Ch'ing). Zhang Chongqing lived from roughly 166 to 230, and was a famous doctor who codified Chinese symptomatology and therapeutics, and was the author of a treatise called *On Fevers Caused by the Cold*. In another famous work, *Prescriptions from the Golden Chest*, he explained in detail the techniques of acupuncture, moxibustion, massage, and respiratory therapy. His prescriptions include febrifuges, diuretics, emetics, sedatives, and stimulants. He has entered history as one of the founders of Chinese medicine.

Zhang Heng (Chang Heng). Zhang Heng (78–139) invented the first known seismograph, and was also the first to apply motive power to turn astronomical instruments. He invented the first armillary spheres and was one of the most famous mathematicians of his time. Zhang Heng's seismograph was set up in 132, and revealed the location of earthquakes, which were thought to be a sign of a disturbance of the natural harmony.

Zhang Qian (Chang Ch'ien). Zhang Qian was minister of the emperor Wu (140–86 B.C.) of the later Han, and in 138 he was sent on a mission to Bactria to seek help against the Huns, who captured him and held him prisoner for more than ten years. He managed to escape, and set out on a long voyage across Ferghana, Indo-Scythia, and Sogdiana, collecting information on various other countries including Parthia, Syria, Chaldea, and India. He returned to China in 126, bringing with him plants and animals unknown in his own country, including the vine, hemp, and the walnut. His mission of exploration opened a new era in the relations of China with the rest of the world, and was followed shortly by the Chinese conquest of the Tarim basin, reached by means of the famous "Silk Road."

Zhao Mengfu (Chao Meng-fu). Zhao was a famous scholar of Buddhism and Taoism, a much admired calligrapher and a landscape artist of renown. He lived from 1254–1322. Although he was descended from the deposed Song imperial dynasty, he made his career in the Mongol Yuan court, reaching the rank of imperial minister. He is credited with a large number of paintings of horses running free and unrestrained. Sometimes Mongol warriors appear on the backs of his horses. One of his most famous works is an ink drawing on paper called *The Sheep and Goat*, in which skin and wool are portrayed with great mastery by means of smudges of ink wash carefully diluted on the brush. His son Zhao Yong was also a famous landscape painter, and like his father he abandoned the delicate style of the Song period, returning to a more austere style in which figures and objects were meticulously represented. Zhao Mengfu and his son may be considered the first representatives of the *wenrenhua* (writers' painting), the art to which complete artists versed in poetry, calligraphy, and painting devoted themselves.

Zhu Xi (Chu Hsi). Zhu Xi lived from 1130 to 1200, and was the founder and chief exponent of the Neo-Confucian school of philosophy which opposed Buddhism and Taoism, yet at the same time feeling the influence of these two schools, as can be seen from the attempt to provide Confucianism with a system of metaphysics. Zhu Xi analyzed the ancient classics with a rigorous philological method, making his versions of them the foundation of Confucian orthodoxy. He was a poet as well as a scholar and philosopher, and author of the historical *Summary of the General Mirror*, in which he took up and interpreted Sima Guang's work in the spirit of Neo-Confucianism.

Zhuangzi (Chuang Tzu). Zhuangzi (or Master Zhuang) was one of the three great figures in Taoist philosophy, along with Laozi and Liezi. Information on the life of Zhuangzi is scanty and dubious, but he probably lived from 369 to 286 B.C. We do know that he wrote the *Zhuangzi*, which consists of a series of short treatises, anecdotes, fables, and apologias, in which real persons, monsters, and talking animals all take their turn in subtle argumentation and in upholding paradoxical theses. In the 8th century, under the Tang, the *Zhuangzi* was raised to the status of a classic, and in some periods it was included in the syllabus of the imperial examinations for selecting candidates for the civil service, in spite of the fact that Confucius himself is mocked by several characters in the text, including some of his best disciples. The *Zhuangzi* is considered one of the liveliest works in Chinese literature on account of its brilliant style and rich vein of fantasy, while some critics have seen in it the origins of the novel.

CHRONOLOGICAL TABLE OF EVENTS

5000 B.C. Beginning of the Chinese Neolithic era, best known through the two cultures of Yangshao, in the western part of the northern Chinese plain, and Longshan in the province of Shandong.

Tradition tells of the age of the five emperors or five sages, cultural heroes whose titles were non-hereditary. The last of them, Yu, who had charge of the waters, was succeeded by his son who was to found the Xia dynasty.

2205–1766 Dates usually ascribed to the reign of the Xia dynasty which numbered 17 kings.

1766 Beginning of the Shang dynasty. Oracle bones. Bronze smelting. Their kingdom included Shaanxi, Henan, part of Shandong, Shanxi and Hebei.

1400–1200 Period in which the ideographic script of the oracle-bone inscriptions first made its appearance.

1122 Usually accepted as marking the end of the Shang dynasty, although 1100 is the more likely date.

1100 Wu, duke of Zhou, won a victory over king Zhouxin of the Shang dynasty, assumed the title of king and began the Zhou dynasty. The kingdom was divided into fiefs which were assigned to relatives of the new king. One of these, given to the Song, had been ruled by the heirs to the Shang dynasty. Kong fu zi (Confucius) claimed to be a descendant of the Song princes.

841 The deposition of a weak king brought in the *Gung He* (Public Harmony) regency. From this point, the recording of Chinese history can be said to begin.

722 The Rong and Di, barbarian tribes, who most probably were nomads, invaded the Zhou kingdom and destroyed its capital at Xi'an. A new capital was founded at Luoyang in the province of Henan. Thus began the period of the Eastern Zhou.

722–481 The Chun Qiu period, so called from the *Annals of Spring and Autumn*, the chronicle of the Lu state, attributed, with reservations, to Confucius.

551–479 The traditionally accepted life span of Confucius.

513 Cast iron is mentioned for the first time.

479–381 Presumed life span of Mozi (Mo Ti), the first to
(approx.) question the doctrine of Confucianism.

453 (or 403) Period of the Warring States: Chinese boundaries
–221 were enlarged with the addition of the states of Chu (in the middle Yangtze valley), Wu (along the lower reaches of the Yangtze) and Yue (on the south-eastern coast).

371–289 Life span of Mengzi (Mencius).

325 The rulers of the larger Chinese states assumed the title of *wang* (king) so that the Zhou king now held sway only over his capital of Luoyang.

3rd century Writing of the *Dao De Jing*, containing the fundamental tenets of Taoism.

234 Death of Han Fei, the leading thinker of the "School of Law."

221 King Zheng (Qin), having destroyed and annexed the other Warring States and thus unified China, assumed the title of *Shi Huang Di*, first emperor, forcing the rest of the empire to adopt the Qin administrative system which had been inspired by the "School of Law." Building of a "Great Wall" to protect the northern boundaries against the incursions of the Xiong Nu.

213 "Burning of the Books."

210–202 Shi Huang Di died while on a voyage off the eastern coast in search of the "islands of the immortals" (210). The Qin dynasty ended (206) in a welter of intrigue, assassination, revolution and civil war. The ultimate victor was Liu Bang, a village headman and founder of the Han dynasty (202).

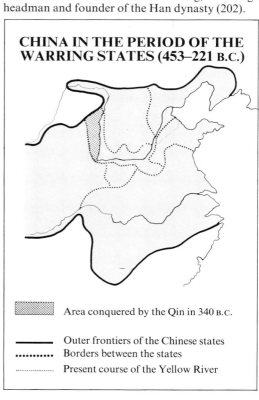

CHINA IN THE PERIOD OF THE WARRING STATES (453–221 B.C.)

Area conquered by the Qin in 340 B.C.

—— Outer frontiers of the Chinese states
·········· Borders between the states
················ Present course of the Yellow River

202 B.C. –A.D. 9	Empire of the Early or Western Han.	9	Wang Mang, head of the "consort family" (for some time, the emperors had only married women of the Wang family), deposed the emperor and mounted the throne.
154	Crushing of the revolt of the "Seven Kingdoms" in the eastern states. Later, in an effort to weaken the powers of local rulers, the system of equal inheritance by all the sons of a reigning family was introduced, a move which led to the consolidation of centralized government.	9–23	Xin dynasty – which began and ended with the reign of Wang Mang.

202 B.C.
–A.D. 9   Empire of the Early or Western Han.

154   Crushing of the revolt of the "Seven Kingdoms" in the eastern states. Later, in an effort to weaken the powers of local rulers, the system of equal inheritance by all the sons of a reigning family was introduced, a move which led to the consolidation of centralized government.

141–87   Reign of the emperor Wu, marking the first major Chinese expansion since Shi Huang Di, the first Qin emperor. Wu conquered the kingdom of Nan Yue (the region of Canton and North Vietnam) in 111, the kingdom of Yue (Fujian) in 110, and Northern Korea in 108. After the visit of Wu's minister Zhang Qian to Central Asia (139–126) had shown possibilities in the way of trade with the West and of new alliances against the barbarian nomads, offensives were renewed against the Xiong Nu (124–121) which assured communications, along the caravan route through Kashgar, with India, Persia and the frontiers of the Roman world. On the advice of the merchant Song Hung-yang important economic measures were put into practice: a state monopoly for the coining of money; state control of the iron industry; and the setting up of provincial granaries in order to stabilize the price of grain. Confucianism permeated both public and private life.

28   Scientific notation of sunspots.

A.D. 2   First recorded census of Chinese population: 57,671,400 (or 12,366,470 families).

9   Wang Mang, head of the "consort family" (for some time, the emperors had only married women of the Wang family), deposed the emperor and mounted the throne.

9–23   Xin dynasty – which began and ended with the reign of Wang Mang.

23–25   Popular uprisings and rebellions by the Han nobility (now reduced to the ranks of private citizens) against the new dynasty (23). The Han dynasty was restored by Liu Xiu, belonging to a collateral branch, who transferred the capital from Changan to Luoyang.

25–220   Empire of the Late or Eastern Han.

65   First evidence of a Buddhist community, at Pengcheng, Jiangsu.

73   General Ban Chao sent to reestablish Chinese control in Central Asia, which had been allowed to lapse under Wang Mang: in 30 years of campaigning, he advanced to the shores of the Caspian Sea.

126–144   In a drive to cut the power of the consort families, the emperor Han Shun Di installed a government of eunuchs who proved highly susceptible to corruption.

139   Death of Zhang Heng, astronomer, mathematician, poet, and inventor of the first seismograph.

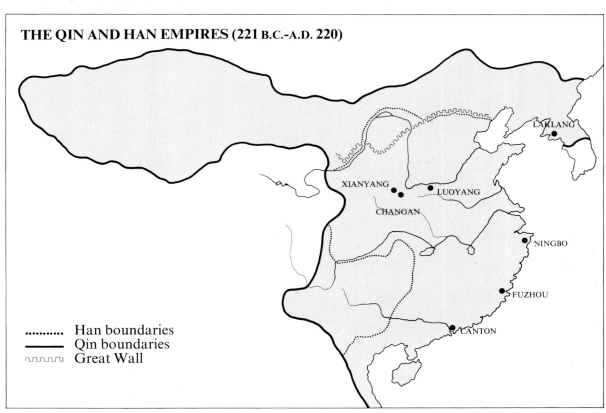

THE QIN AND HAN EMPIRES (221 B.C.–A.D. 220)

LAKLANG

XIANYANG   LUOYANG

CHANGAN

NINGBO

FUZHOU

CANTON

·········· Han boundaries
—— Qin boundaries
ᴨᴨᴨᴨ Great Wall

147	Arrival at Luoyang of the Parthian monk An Shigao, the first translator of Indian Buddhist texts into Chinese.
167–168	On the death of the emperor Han Huan Di, who was succeeded by the 12-year-old heir Han Ling Di (167), the empress mother, acting as regent, tried to further the cause of the men of letters at court, in opposition to the powerful eunuchs. They were accused of plotting against the throne by the eunuchs and a purge followed.
184	Misgovernment in the provinces led to the rebellion of the "Yellow Turbans," led by Zhang Zhue. The forces used to quell the rebellion proved themselves to be ungovernable.
189–220	The death of the emperor Ling Di, who died without direct heirs, brought general disruption throughout China. The eunuchs were massacred and Luoyang sacked. The ensuing civil war ended with China divided into three kingdoms and the downfall of the Han dynasty.
220–265	Period of the Three Kingdoms: the Wei (220–65), the Shu Han (221–63) and the Wu kingdom (222–80).
3rd century	Visit by a Roman embassy to Nanking, capital of the Southern Wu kingdom.
265	Sima Qian dethroned the Wei king and founded the Jin (Zin) dynasty. Since, in 263, Wei had absorbed Shu Han, Sima had only to conquer Wu, which he did in 280, to reunify China once again.
265–316	Period of the Western Jin (Zin) dynasty (at Luoyang). Internal power struggles, the restlessness of the barbarian mercenaries, the sack of Luoyang (311), the general state of anarchy and conditions of growing misery, all encouraged considerable migration of the population to the South. The Western Jin dynasty succumbed eventually to the incursions of the Chinese-influenced barbarians from the north, to be reconstituted under Sima Rui in Nanking.
304–439	Period of the Sixteen Kingdoms of the Five Barbarians (in northern China).
317–589	Periods of the Southern dynasties (in Nanking): Eastern Jin (Zin) 317–420; Song 420–79; Qi 479–502; Liang 502–57; Chen 557–89.
386	Foundation of Northern Wei dynasty by the Toba Tartars.
412	Arrival in Shandong of the Chinese Buddhist monk Faxian after visits to India, Ceylon and Sumatra.
439–534	The Northern Wei empire (empire of the Toba or Tabgatch, one of the three Xianbei tribes) which united northern China. (The period 440–589 is known to Chinese historians as the Nan Bei period, or the period of the Northern and Southern empires: in the North, the Wei and their successors,

the "Chinesified" barbarians, in the South, the various dynasties which succeeded each other in Nanking.)

534–557	Empire of the Eastern Wei (deriving from the breakup of the Northern Wei empire).
535–556	Empire of the Western Wei, based in Changan, following the breakup of the Northern Wei empire.
556–581	Empire of the Northern Zhou (which followed that of the Western Wei).
557–577	Empire of the Northern Qi (which succeeded that of the Eastern Wei and in turn overthrown by the Northern Zhou).
581–617	Period of the Sui empire. The overthrow of the Zhou dynasty by general Yang Jian (in Changan, 581) and the subsequent conquest of southern China (entry into Nanking, 589) ended the period of division which had started in the 3rd century, with the setting up of the Three Kingdoms.
604–618	Reign of the emperor Yang Di, the second and last of the Sui rulers and, according to folklore, the prototype of the "wicked emperor."

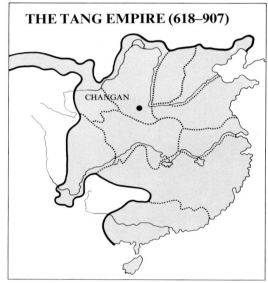

THE TANG EMPIRE (618–907)

CHANGAN

618	General Li Yuan (later to become emperor Gao Zu), in charge of the northern defenses against the nomads of the Shanxi, incited to rebellion by his son Li Shi-min (the future emperor Tai Zong), took over Changan and founded the new Tang dynasty.
618–907	Tang dynasty.
626–649	Reign of the emperor Tai Zong; his reign marked the beginning of a great expansion of Chinese power. The problem of the Turks, who had emerged as the new power in the steppes, was resolved, thus opening the routes through Central Asia (630). The oases of Transoxiana passed under

505

Chinese rule which was also extended beyond the Pamir river to Samarkand, Bukhara and Tashkent. A Chinese expeditionary force intervened as far away as the kingdom of Magadha, in India, in order to secure a succession favourable to Chinese interests (648). Later, Manchuria (660) and Korea were to come under Chinese domination. In the 7th century under the Tang, China ruled Asia from Korea to Iran, from the valley of the Ili to Vietnam.

629–645   Visit to India by the Chinese Buddhist monk Xuanzan.

643   Embassy from Byzantium arrives in Changan.

654–705   Reign of the empress Wu: Wu Zhao was the concubine of both the emperor Tai Zong and Gao Zong (649–83) and became particularly influential from 654. She became empress in 655 and reigned after the death of Gao Zong (683). In 684, she dethroned the legitimate emperor, put to death hundreds of nobles and various members of the royal family and usurped the imperial title (690) which she bore until 705 when the emperor Zetian ascended the throne. She remains the only woman to have been empress in her own right throughout the course of Chinese history. Among her instruments of power were the government service examinations, systematically organized in 669, and the Buddhist clergy who exercised great political and economic influence under her patronage.

712–756   Reign of the emperor Xuan Zong (Ming Huang): considered the high point of the Tang Dynasty. Xuan Zong was a strong supporter of the arts, poetry and literature, founding the Academy of Letters in 725 and establishing schools in every prefecture and district in the empire in 728. He is also credited with being the patron under whom Chinese drama first flourished.

751   The Arabs rout a Chinese army at Alma Ata on the river Talas.

755–763   A rebellion by the commander of the army of the northern frontier, An Lushan, who occupied Luoyang and Changan. The emperor Su Zong recaptured the capital with the help of Tibetans and Uighurs. But the empire's northern defense system had collapsed and local commanders took over power in the provinces.

9th century   In this century the Buddhist Sutra, found at Dunhuang, was written, the first example of a book with wood engravings.

868–884   Rebellion of Huang Chao. Having put himself at the head of the garrison stationed on the frontier between the kingdom of Nanzhao (Yunnan) and Annam, then a Chinese province, Huang Chao sacked southern China and after 13 years of raiding, took Changan (880), forcing the court to flee. After this rebellion, the last years of the Tang dynasty were lived out amid chaos and anarchy.

907   Zhu Quanzhong founded the Liang dynasty in Kaifeng. Thus opened another period of division for China (the Five Dynasties and the Ten Kingdoms).

907–960   The Five Dynasties and the Ten Kingdoms: in Kaifeng, a number of dynasties followed in very quick succession: the Later Liang (907–23); the Later Tang (923–36); the Later Jin (936–46); the Later Han (947–50) and the Later Zhou (951–60). In the meantime, the rest of the empire was divided into the Ten Kingdoms which were almost exactly the same as the military zones organized by the Tang dynasty.

946–1125   Empire of the Liao (Kitan) in the northwestern corner of China. The Kitans were Chinese-influenced Tartars who had driven out the Turks from the northeastern regions and extended their territories within the Great Wall. One of the capitals of the Kitan was to be Peking, for the first time seat of a dynasty.

960   Zhao Guang-yin (later the emperor Song Tai Zu), one of the generals of the Zhou dynasty, was proclaimed emperor in Kaifeng. He extended his power to the southern states using peaceful methods.

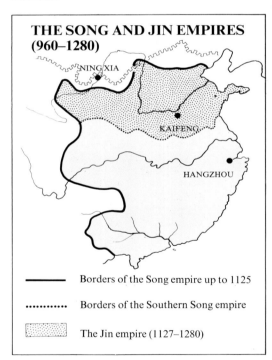

THE SONG AND JIN EMPIRES (960–1280)

NING XIA
KAIFENG
HANGZHOU

——— Borders of the Song empire up to 1125

········· Borders of the Southern Song empire

▧ The Jin empire (1127–1280)

960–1126   Empire of the Northern Song (in Kaifeng). This was a period of welcome unity after the fragmentation which had followed the breakup of the Tang dynasty. The only states which were outside Chinese sovereignty at this point were the Liao empire (Hebei and Shanxi), and the Xia empire in northwestern Mongolia, Vietnam and Korea.

990 (approx.) First mention of the compass in a Chinese text.

1017–1073	Life span of the philosopher Zhou Tunyi.	1275–1291	Marco Polo in the service of Kublai Khan, one of the many foreign officials employed at the Mongol court.
1038–1227	Empire of the Western Xia (Tartars) in north-western China.	1276	Hangzhou, capital of the Southern Song empire, falls to the Mongols.

1017–1073 Life span of the philosopher Zhou Tunyi.

1038–1227 Empire of the Western Xia (Tartars) in north-western China.

1041–1048 First experiments in typesetting with movable characters.

1067–1085 Conservatives and "Innovators": the "innovator" Wang Anshi was called to the government (1067). He brought in new laws: fiscal, administrative and military. He was later ousted from government (1076) and afterwards superseded by the man who had previously opposed him, the historian Sima Guang, who repealed the new laws in 1085.

1100–1126 Reign of Hui Zong, the last of the Northern Song emperors, a patron of the arts and a considerable painter himself. Following the invasion of the Jin and the fall of Kaifeng, he died a prisoner.

1115–1234 Empire of the Jin in northeastern China. In 1126 the Jin conquered northern China, and the Song had to retire to the South.

1116 A Chinese text describes the liquid compass and cites the value of the magnetic declination.

1126 Following the Jin invasion, the Song retired to the South under the rule of an emperor from a collateral branch of the family. The Jin penetrated as far as Hangzhou.

1127–1279 Empire of the Southern Song (at Hangzhou).

1130–1200 Life span of Zhu Xi, the founder of Neo-Confucianism.

1131 General Yo Fei, commanding the Song army, forced the Jin forces back across the Yangtze. However, he was the victim of a plot by prime minister Cai Jing while preparing for the conquest of the North. The frontier eventually stabilized at the northern watershed of the Yangtze valley.

1210 Genghis Khan began the assault on China with his invasion of the Jin empire (northern China). Fall of Peking.

1224 Genghis Khan attacked the Xia empire. Huge migrations of the population southwards before the Mongol advance.

1235 The Mongols attacked the Song empire in the South.

1263 The Mongol emperor Kublai Khan ascends the throne. The new emperor transferred the capital from Karakorum to Peking, which was rebuilt.

1271–1368 Yuan dynasty: the Mongols absorbed the empires of the Xia (1227) and the Jin (1234) and adopted the dynastic name of the Yuan (1271). From 1276 to 1279 they occupied the southern empire of the Song and thus controlled the whole of China.

1275–1291 Marco Polo in the service of Kublai Khan, one of the many foreign officials employed at the Mongol court.

1276 Hangzhou, capital of the Southern Song empire, falls to the Mongols.

1279 The last Song emperor perishes in the destruction of the Song fleet off the coast of southern China.

1281 A vain attempt by the Mongols to invade Japan: the "divine wind" (*kamikaze*) destroyed the joint Chinese and Korean fleets.

1300 (approx.) The death of Wang Shifu, a Peking playwright and author of *Xixiangji*.

1348–1368 Togan Timour, the last of the Yuan dynasty, progressively lost control of the empire which was torn asunder for 20 years by anti-Mongol rebellions.

1356 Zhu Yuanzhang (later the emperor Ming Hung Wu), founder of the Ming dynasty, occupies Nanking which he makes his capital.

1368–1644 Period of the Ming empire.

1369 The Ming armies take Karakorum, the one-time capital of Genghis Khan.

15th century The Ming emperors repair, reconstruct and extend the Great Wall.

1402–1424 Reign of the emperor Yung Lo. The first Chinese encyclopaedia is compiled.

1405–1433 The emperor Yung Lo instigated a series of maritime expeditions, commanded by Zheng He, a Muslim from the Yunnan, using huge, specially constructed ships to reach Southeast Asia and the Indian Ocean, the Red Sea and East Africa.

1421 The capital of China moved from Nanking to Peking.

1505–1520 Reign of the emperor Zheng De. The influence of the eunuchs was at its height: massive corruption everywhere in the provincial administrations.

1514 The Portuguese land in Guangdong.

1522 Following violence and rivalry with Arab merchants, Portuguese merchants were forbidden to put into port in China. Also, the Ming were beginning to use cannons acquired from the Portuguese.

16th century The *Jin Ping Mei*, a romance of possible satiric and critical intent, was written. The Ming period saw the birth and rapid development of the novel in China.

1552 Francesco Saverio, the first Christian missionary to be sent to China, died on an island in the estuary of the Pearl River without ever having set foot in the empire.

1575	The first Christian missionaries reach Canton.
1592–1598	War against Japan on behalf of China's vassal state, Korea.
1598	Father Matteo Ricci obtained permission to enter Peking where he lived until his death in 1610.
1610	Nurhachu, chief of the Manchu, proclaimed himself emperor (Qing dynasty) and independent from the rest of China.
1627	The beginning of the great army and peasant insurrections marking the end of the Ming dynasty.
1636	In Peking, the Jesuit missionary Adam Schall directs the production of artillery pieces made of cast iron.
1644	The rebel Li Zicheng takes Peking. The last Ming emperor hung himself in the garden of the imperial palace. Wu Sangui, the commander of the northern frontier army refused to recognize the usurper and offered the throne to the Manchu emperor. Wu Sangui's campaign against the Ming forces in the South was a major factor in the consolidation of Manchu power (Ming-Qing period).
1644–1911	Period of the Qing (Manchu) empire. The Manchu, a minority people, became the dominant force in China, adopted the language and the culture of the Chinese but maintained a rigid racial separation.

THE MANCHU EMPIRE
(1644–1911)

1661–1722	Reign of the emperor Kang Xi. Kang Xi put down Wu Sangui's revolt and repulsed an attempt by the Russians to invade northern Manchuria, imposed Chinese rule over Mongolia and Central Asia (Xinjiang) and conquered Tibet. During this period Chinese sovereignty was extended to Korea, Annam, Burma and Thailand.
1673	Wu Sangui's rebellion and the secession of the southern provinces. The South was only reconquered after the death of Wu Sangui in 1678.
1685–1686	The Qing armies lay siege to the Russian fortress of Albazin.

1689	Treaty of Nerchinsk between the Russian and Chinese empires.
1697	The Qing occupy Outer Mongolia.
1705–1706	The first attempt by the Qing dynasty to occupy Lhasa, Tibet.
1723–1735	Reign of the emperor Yong Zheng.
1736–1796	Reign of the emperor Qian Long.
1751	Qing empire definitely established its rule in Tibet.
1758–1759	An uprising by the inhabitants of the Tarim Basin in Sinkiang, prelude to Chinese conquest of the area.
1762	A census puts China's population at 200,000,000.
1763	Death of Cao Xueqin who left his romance *The Dream of the Red Chamber* unfinished.
1774	Revolt of the "White Lotus" sect. Similar rebellions, which were a symptom of the economic and social unease in the empire since the growing population had increased the value of land and created a class of landless peasants, were frequent occurrences towards the end of Qian Long's reign.
1791–1792	Military expedition sent to Nepal: this last act of military expansionism on the part of the Qing dynasty exhausted the resources of the state.
1793	An embassy from England, led by Lord Macartney, arrives in Peking.
1796	Abdication of Qian Long who, having ruled for 60 years, did not wish to have a longer reign than that of his great ancestor, Kang Xi.
1799	The emperor Jia Qing, upon the death of his father Qian Long, arrested the powerful minister He Shan and confiscated the riches he had acquired in a long career – a sum equal to 70 million guineas in the 19th century. This very serious scandal revealed the depth of corruption of the administration.
1830	A census shows China's population (394,780,000) has nearly doubled in under 70 years.
1840	Opening of the Opium War between England and China.
1842	The Treaty of Nanking ended the first Sino-British war, with Hong Kong being ceded to the British and the opening to foreign trade of the ports of Canton, Shanghai, Amoy, Fuzhou and Ningpo. China was forced to grant extraterritorial jurisdiction and other concessions to foreign countries which were to last for over a century.
1850	Rebellion of the Tai Ping whose leader thought he was Jesus' younger adoptive brother and that he was also inspired by God.

1853	The Taiping, having taken possession of Guangxi province, marched northwards and took over Nanking which they called the Heavenly City.
1858	By the treaty of Aigun, territories east of the Ussuri river are ceded to the Russians.
1858–1860	Anglo-French war against China.
1860	English and French troops sack Peking.
1861	Death of the emperor Xian Feng in a hunting reserve in Mongolia where he had withdrawn in order to avoid the Anglo-French attack on Peking. His concubine Yehonala (later the empress Ci Xi) returned to the capital, assumed power and put to death all the members of the council of regency. She reigned until her death in 1908.
1864	The Tai Ping rebellion ended with the siege and capture of Nanking by the imperial forces and the suicide of the rebel leader.
1868	China's first steamships.
1872	First Chinese students sent to study in the West.
1879	Yan Fu, a marine official, returned to China after a period of study in Great Britàin and began to translate into Chinese Western works on politics and sociology.
1883–1885	The Franco-Chinese War, at the end of which China ceded her sovereignty over Indo-China.
1898	The "Hundred Days of Reform." The reformers' aims which would have led to the modernization of the processes of state were backed up by the emperor Guang Xu but provoked a severe response from the empress mother Ci Xi who arranged a *coup d'état* with the help of Yuan Shikai, commander of the new, modernized army. The reformist leader Tan Sitong was executed.
1894–1895	The Sino-Japanese war. Ended by the treaty of Shimonoseki which ceded to Japan Formosa (Taiwan) and the Pescadores.
1900–1901	The Boxer Rebellion. A siege of foreign embassies in Peking led to intervention by an international expeditionary force.
1911	Outbreak of the Chinese revolution. What began as a mutiny on the part of the garrison of Hankou soon spread. The army proclaimed the republic. The regent appealed once more to Yuan Shikai who assumed full civil and military powers.
1912	Sun Yatsen proclaimed president of the united provinces of China (1 January). Abdication of the Qing dynasty. Sun Yatsen's renunciation of the presidency in favour of Yuan Shikai.
1913	At the parliamentary elections, the revolutionary republican party or Guomindang (Kuomintang) won an easy victory over the followers of Yuan

	Shikai, who, however, having control of the army, had himself reelected with full powers. Shortly after, he dissolved parliament.
1914–1916	Yuan Shikai attempted to install a new dynasty but the revolt of the army in the South and the pressure exercised by his generals in the North induced him to resign. He died in June 1916.
1916–1927	The "era of the warlords." During this time China was ruled by the generals and military governors of the provinces.
1919	The May 4 Movement: a movement of protest, initially started by the staff and students of the University of Peking against the terms of the treaty of Versailles which ceded to Japan concessions formerly held by the Germans, ignoring Chinese claims.
1921	Chinese communist party founded in Shanghai.
1925	The death in March of Sun Yatsen. The May 30 Movement in Shanghai; the international police put down a demonstration by students and workers thus initiating a huge movement of boycott and discrimination against foreigners.
1926	The nationalist government in Canton starts the "march northwards" with the aim of overthrowing the warlords. Chiang Kaishek led the nationalist forces. He took Wuhan and transferred the seat of government there.
1927	Communist uprising in Shanghai, led by Zhou Enlai (22 March). The nationalist army took Nanking. Chiang Kaishek arrived in Shanghai to wreak vengeance on the newly-installed communist administration and proclaim a new nationalist government with its capital in Nanking, thus breaking all ties with the government of Wuhan. On 8 August, an army brigade commanded by Zhu Di mutinied at Nanchang and proclaimed itself the "Red Army."
1928	Yan Xishan, the warlord of Shanxi province, joined with the nationalists and took Peking. The Red Army, after being repulsed in various attacks on southern cities regrouped in Jingangshan. Zhu Di and Mao Zedong met at Jingangshan, setting up the first "red base."
1931	The "red base," comprising the provinces of Jiangxi and Hunan was proclaimed the "Chinese Soviet Republic" (Ruijin, November). The Japanese, already in Manchuria, under the treaty rights of the Russian-Japanese war of 1904-05, now occupied the whole region, giving it the new name of Manchukuo, and appointing as head of state the deposed Chinese emperor Pu Yi.
1933	The Japanese occupied, in the name of Manchukuo, the Chinese province of Jehol (Inner Western Mongolia).
1934	Pu Yi proclaimed emperor of Manchukuo, satellite state of Japan.

1934–1935 The Long March. Under pressure from the "extermination campaigns" organized by Chiang Kaishek, 100,000 communists set off from Jiangxi province (October 1934), led by Mao Zedong and Zhu De. At the end of their 10,000-kilometer march, 30,000 communists arrived in Yenan in the province of Shaanxi. Emergence of Mao Zedong as leader of the communists.

1936 The "Xi'an Incident." Chiang Kaishek went to Xi'an to direct his campaign of extermination against the communists but was held in the spa resort of Tangshan by his supposed colleague, general Zhang Xueliang, and forced to sign a document, drawn up by Zhou Enlai, in which he agreed to join forces with the communists in order to defend the country from the Japanese.

1937 On 7 July, with "the incident of the Marco Polo Bridge" as pretext, the Japanese launched a major offensive and occupied Peking, Tianjin, Shanghai and Nanking. The Sino-Japanese war and the occupation by Japan of very extensive areas of Chinese territory ended with the surrender of Japan at the end of the Second World War.

1938 In order to stop the advance of the Japanese troops, the Chinese opened dykes in the Yellow River which as a result changed its course, flowing south into the Shandong peninsula. The Japanese occupied Hankou and Canton while Chiang Kaishek's government was forced to retire to Chongqing.

1940 Wang Qingwei set up a Japanese-controlled government of China in Nanking.

1942 The Western powers negotiated terms with the government of China abrogating all rights and privileges gained at the time of the Opium War.

1945 Agreement reached at Chongqing between the communist party of China and the Guomindang government of Chiang Kaishek (10 October).

1946 Summer sees the beginning of the struggle between the Guomindang and the communist forces. At first, the Guomindang have the upper hand.

1948 The battle of Huai Hai towards the end of the year, sees the victory of the communist forces and the end of nationalist hopes on the mainland of China.

1949 On 1 October the People's Republic is proclaimed in Peking. The nationalist government flees to Taiwan.

1950 After a visit to Moscow by Mao Zedong, his first outside China, a treaty is signed between the USSR and China. China intervenes in the Korean war: Chinese "volunteers" cross the Yalu River into North Korea.

1951 Chinese occupy Tibet, reestablishing the control over the country which they lost in 1911.

1953 China's first five-year plan for the industrialization of the country.

1955–1956 Introduction of farming cooperatives.

1957 The policy of "A Hundred Flowers."

1958 Beginning of the "Great Leap Forward," with the aim of extending the system of communes throughout the country.

1960 The Soviet Union withdraws its technical advisers and ceases all economic aid to China.

1962 The Sino-Indian War on the Himalayan border.

1965 At 73 years of age, Mao swims the Yangtze at Wuhan.

1966 The beginning of the "Great Proletarian Cultural Revolution." Gathering of 1,000,000 Red Guards in Peking. Among the disgraced leaders are Liu Shaoqi, Deng Xiaoping and Peng Jen.

1968 The army assumed control. Thousands of Red Guards dispersed to the distant provinces.

1969 The 9th party conference of the Chinese communist party declared the cultural revolution triumphantly at an end and acclaimed Lin Biao "Mao's closest comrade in arms." Soviet-Chinese incidents along the river Ussuri frontier.

1970 Lin Biao disappeared from political life (September). After a few months, it was announced that he had died in an air disaster over Mongolia while fleeing after the discovery of a plot to kill Mao.

1971 The People's Republic of China joins the United Nations (October) and obtains a seat on the Security Council, formerly held by the Republic of Nationalist China (Taiwan).

1972 Visit to China by Richard Nixon, president of the United States.

1976 Death of Zhou Enlai, followed in September by the death of Mao Zedong. Hua Guofeng, already prime minister, elected president of the Chinese communist party. Arrest of Mao's widow, Jiang Qing and of her followers. Opening of the campaign against the "Gang of Four."

1977 The return to power of Deng Xiaoping who becomes prime minister (July).

1979 Halfway through February, Chinese troops invaded North Vietnam but withdrew after a few weeks.

1980 The posthumous rehabilitation of Liu Shaoqi. In October, Hua Guofeng resigned as prime minister but remained chairman of the communist party. Zhao Zyiang succeeded to the vacant post.

BIBLIOGRAPHY

The following is not an exhaustive bibliography but rather a guide to the history, culture and geography of China. It must be remembered that the main sources are in Chinese and therefore that the works here cited are only a part of the vast corpus available to the specialists. We have only listed relatively recent works since these are easily obtainable from bookshops and libraries.

Academy of Traditional Chinese Medicine, *Outline of Chinese Acupuncture*, Peking 1975

Ackerman, P., *Ritual Bronzes of Ancient China*, New York 1945

Balazs, E., *La Bureaucratie céleste. Recherches sur l'économie et la société de la Chine traditionelle*, Paris 1968

Bermann, G., *La salud mental en China*, Buenos Aires 1970

Bertuccioli, G., *La letteratura cinese*, Florence 1968

Biggerstaff, K., *The Earliest Modern Government Schools in China*, Ithaca, N.Y. 1961

Borsa, G., *La Nascita del Mondo Moderno in Asia Orientale*, Milan 1977

Borsa, G., *L'Estremo Oriente fra due mondi*, Bari 1961

Bowie, R. R. and Fairbank, J. K., *Communist China, 1955–59: Policy Documents with Analysis*, Cambridge, Mass. 1962

Boyd, A., *Chinese Architecture and Town Planning 1500 BC–1911 AD*, Chicago 1962

Buchanan, K., *The Transformation of the Chinese Earth: Aspects of the Evolution of the Chinese Earth from the Earliest Times to Mao Tse-tung*, London 1970

Cahill, J., *Chinese Painting*, Paris and Geneva 1964

Carrère d'Encausse, H. and Schram, S. R., *Le Marxisme et l'Asie 1853-1964*, Paris 1965

Carter, T. F., *The invention of printing in China and its spread westward*, New York 1955

Chammers, J., *Peasant Nationalism and Communist Power*, Stanford 1962

Chang, Chung-li, *The Chinese Gentry; studies on their role in XIXth century Chinese society*, Seattle 1955

Chang, Hsin-Pao *Commissioner Lin and the Opium War*, Cambridge 1964

Chang, J. K., *Industrial Development in Pre-Communist China*, Chicago 1969

Chang, Kwang-Chih, *The Archaeology of Ancient China*, New Haven 1968

Ch'ên, J., *Mao and the Chinese Revolution*, London 1965

Ch'ên, J., *Yuan Shih-k'ai 1859–1916: Brutus assumes the purple*, Stanford 1961

Ch'ên, K. K. S., *Buddhism in China: A Historical Survey*, Princeton 1964

Ch'êng, Te-K'un, *Prehistoric China: vol 1, Archaeology in China*, Cambridge 1959

Chesneaux, J., *L'Asie orientale aux XIX et XX siècles*, Paris 1966

Chesneaux, J., *La Cina contemporanea, storia documentaria dal 1895 ai nostri giorni*, Bari 1975

Chesneaux, J., *Le mouvement ouvrier chinois de 1919 à 1927*, Paris 1962

Chesneaux, J. and Bastid, M., *De la guerre franco-chinoise à la fondation du parti communiste chinois, 1885–1921*, Paris 1969

Chesneaux, J. and Bastid, M., *Des guerres de l'opium à la guerre franco-chinoise, 1840–1885*, Paris 1969

Chi, Chao-ting, *Key Economic Areas in Chinese History as Revealed in the Development of Public Works for Water Control*, London 1936

Chien, Yuan, *Western and Central Asians in China under the Mongols*, Los Angeles 1966

Chow, Tse-tung, *The May Fourth Movement: Intellectual Revolution in Modern China*, Cambridge, Mass. 1960

Ch'ü, T'ung-tsu, *Law and Society in Traditional China*, Paris and The Hague 1961

Ch'ü, T'ung-tsu, *Local Government in China under the Ch'ing*, Cambridge, Mass. 1962

Clubb, O. E., *20th Century China*, New York 1964

Cohen, P. A., *China and Christianity: Missionary Movement and the Growth of Chinese Antiforeignism, 1860–1870*, Cambridge 1963

Collotti Pischel, E., *Le origine ideologiche della rivoluzione cinese*, Turin 1959

Collotti Pischel, E. (ed.), *Storia dell'Asia*, Florence 1980

Corna Pellegrini, G. (ed.), *Geografia sociale e economica della Cina*, Milan 1973

Corradini, P., *La Cina*, Turin 1969

Creel, H. G., *Confucius: The Man and the Myth*, New York 1949

Creel, H. G., *The Birth of China: A Study of the Formative Period of Chinese Civilization*, New York 1954

Cressey, G. B., *Land of the 500 Million: A Geography of China*, New York 1955

Davis, F. L., *Primitive Revolutionaries of China: A Study of Secret Societies, 1840–1911*, London 1969

Deleyne, J., *Chinese Economy*, Paris 1971

Dewall, M. Von, *Pferd und Wagen im frühen China*, Bonn 1964

Dumont, R., *Révolution dans la campagne chinoise*, Paris 1957

Eberhard, W., *History of China*, Berne 1948

Edkins, J., *Chinese Buddhism: a volume of sketches, historical, descriptive, and critical*, New York 1968

Fairbank, J. K. (ed.), *Chinese Thought and Institutions*, Chicago 1957

Fairbank, J. K. and Reichauer, E. O., *East Asia: The Great Tradition*, Boston 1970

Fairbank, J. K., Reichauer, E. O and Craig, A. M., *East Asia: The Modern Transformation*, Boston 1965

Fei, Hsiao-t'ung, *Peasant Life in China: A Field Study of Country Life in the Yangtze Valley*, London 1939

Fêng, Yu-lan, *A Short History of Chinese Philosophy*, Princeton 1948

Feuerwerker, A., *China's Early Industrialization: Sheng Hsuan-huai (1844–1916) and Mandarin Enterprise*, Cambridge, Mass. 1959

FitzGerald, C. P., *China: A Short Cultural History*, London and New York 1965

Franke, H. and Trauzettel, R., *Das chinesische Kaiserreich in Fischer Weltgeschichte, vol. XIX*, Frankfurt 1968

Franke, W., *Chinas Kulturelle Revolution, die Bewegung vom 4. Mai 1919*, Princeton 1967

Franz, M., *The Taiping Rebellion*, Seattle 1966

Gabinelli, C. and Gibelli, M. C., *Città e territorio in Cina*, Bari 1967

Gasster, M., *Chinese Intellectuals and the Revolution of 1911: The Birth of Modern Chinese Radicalism*, Washington 1959

Gernet, J., *La Chine ancienne*, Paris 1964

Gernet, J., *La vie quotidienne en Chine à la veille de l'invasion mongole*, Paris 1959

Gernet, J., *Le Monde Chinois*, Paris 1972

Gernet, J., *Les aspects économiques du Buddhisme dans la société chinoise du V au X siècle*, Saigon 1956

Giuganino, A., *La pittura cinese*, Rome 1960

Gourou, P., *La Terre et l'Homme en Extrême Orient*, Paris 1947

Granet, M., *La pensée chinoise*, Paris 1934

Granet, M., *La Religion des Chinois*, Paris 1951

Grimm, T., *Erziehung und Politik im konfuzianischen China der Ming-Zeit*, Wiesbaden 1960

Guillermaz, J., *Histoire du parti communiste chinois 1921–1949*, Paris 1968

Guillermaz, J., *Le parti communiste chinois au pouvoir 1949–1972*, Paris 1972

Gumilev, L. N., *Khunnu*, Moscow 1960

Haldane, C., *The Last Great Empress of China*, London 1965

Hermann, A., *An Historical Atlas of China* (new edition by Norton S. Ginsburg and with a prefatory essay by Paul Wheatley), Chicago 1966

Hinton, W., *Fanshen: A Documentary of Revolution in a Chinese Village*, New York 1967

Ho, Kan-chih, *A History of the Modern Chinese Revolution*, Peking and Edinburgh 1959

Ho, Ping-ti, *Studies on the Population of China 1368–1953*, Cambridge, Mass. 1959

Hsia, Chin–tsing, *A History of Modern Chinese Fiction 1917–1957*, New Haven and Toronto 1961

Hsiao, Kung-chüan, *Rural China: Imperial Control in the 19th Century*, Seattle 1961

Hsüen, Chün-tu, *Huang Hsing and the Chinese Revolution*, Stanford 1961

Hsu, I. C. Y., *China's Entrance into the Family of Nations: The Diplomatic Phase, 1856–1880*, Cambridge, Mass. 1960

Hucker, C. O. (ed.), *Chinese Government in Ming Times: 7 Studies by Tilemann Grimm and others*, New York 1969

Isaacs, H., *The Tragedy of the Chinese Revolution*, London 1958

Jansen, M. B., *The Japanese and Sun Yat-sen*, Cambridge, Mass. 1954

Johnson, C. A., *Peasant Nationalism and Communist Power: The Emergence of Revolutionary China, 1937–1945*, Stanford 1962

Kaltenmark, M., *Lao-tseu et le taoïsme*, Paris 1965

King, F. H. H., *Money and Monetary Policy in China, 1845–1895*, Cambridge 1965

Kracke, E. A., *Civil Service in Early Sung China, 960–1067, with particular emphasis on the development of controlled sponsorship to foster administrative responsibility*, Cambridge, Mass. 1953

Kratochvil, P., *The Chinese Language Today*, London 1968

Lach, D. F., *Asia in the Making of Europe: vol. 1: The Century of Discovery*, Chicago 1965

Lattimore, O., *Studies in Asian Frontier History*, London 1962

Levenson, J. R., *Modern China and its Confucian Past: vol. 1: The Problem of Intellectual Continuity*, New York 1964

Li Chi, *The Beginnings of Chinese Civilization: Three Lectures Illustrated with Finds at Anyang*, Seattle 1957

Li, C. M., *Economic Development of Communist China, 1949–1958*, London 1960

Lifton, R. J., *Thought Reform and the Psychology of Totalism: A Study of Brainwashing in China*, New York 1961

Liu, James Tzü-chien, *Reform in Sung China*, Cambridge, Mass. 1959

Liu Wu-Chi, *An Introduction to Chinese Literature*, London 1966

Loewe, M., *Everyday Life in Early Imperial China during the Han Period 202 BC – AD 220*, London 1968

MacFarquhar, R. (ed.), *The Hundred Flowers Campaign and the Chinese Intellectuals*, New York 1960

Macleavy, H., *The Modern History of China*, London 1961

Mänchen-Helfen, O., *The World of the Huns: Studies in their History and Culture*, Berkeley 1973

Margoulies, G., *La langue et l'écriture chinoises*, Paris 1957

Marsh, R. M., *The Mandarins: The Circulation of Elites in China, 1600–1900*, Glencoe, Ontario 1961

Masataka, B., *China and the West 1858–1860: The Origin of the Tsungli Yamen*, Cambridge 1964

Masi, E., *Breve storia della Cina contemporanea*, Bari 1979

Maspero, H., *Le taoïsme et les religions chinoises*, Paris 1971

Meisner, M., *Li Ta-chao and the Origins of Chinese Marxism*, Cambridge, Mass. 1967

Melis, G., *Cina di Mao 1949-1969*, 1971

Melis, Salvini, Sormani and Weber, *La Cina dopo Mao*, Bari 1980

Mikami, Y., *The Development of Mathematics in China and Japan*, New York 1961

Mingione, E., *L'uso del territorio in Cina*, Milan 1977

Mizuno, S. and Nakashiro, T., *Yün-kang, the Buddhist Cave-Temples of the Vth Century in North China*, 16 vols, Kyoto 1951–56

Mu, Fu-sheng, *The Wilting of the Hundred Flowers: The Chinese Intelligentsia under Mao*, New York 1962

Needham, J., *Clerks and Craftsmen in China and the West: Lectures and Addresses on the History of Science and Technology*, Cambridge 1970

Needham, J., *Science and Civilisation in China*, Cambridge 1954

Needham, J., *The Grand Titration, Science and Society in East and West*, London 1969

Nivison, D. S. and Wright A. F. (eds.), *Confucianism in Action*, Stanford 1959

North, R. C., *Chinese Communism*, Stanford 1966

North, R. C., *Moscow and Chinese Communists*, Stanford 1963

Parsons, J. B., *The Peasant Rebellions of the Late Ming Dynasty*, Tucson, Arizona 1970

Pelliot, P., *Les débuts de l'imprimérie en Chine*, Paris 1953

Perkins, D. H., *Market Control and Planning in Communist China*, Cambridge, Mass. 1966

Petech, L., *Profilo Storico della Civiltà Cinese*, Turin 1971

Pirazzoli, M., and T'serstevens, *Chine, Architecture Universelle*, Fribourg 1970

Pisu, R., *Le cause della rivoluzione cinese*, Milan 1977

Powell, R. L., *The Rise of Chinese Military Power 1895–1912*, Princeton 1955

Prusek, J., *Chinese History and Literature*, Prague 1970

Pulleyblank, E. G., *The Background of the Rebellion of An Lushan*, New York 1975

Purcell, V. W. W. S., *The Boxer Uprising: A Background Study*, Cambridge 1963

Reclus, J., *La révolte des T'ai-p'ing (1851–1864)*, Paris 1972

Ronan, C. A., *The Shorter Science and Civilisation in China (an abridgement of Joseph Needham's original text)*, Cambridge 1978

Sabattini, M., *I movimenti politici della Cina*, Rome 1972

Salvini, G., *L'economia della Cina 1949–1978*, Milan 1978

Sarzi Amade, E., *Le due vie dell'economia cinese*, Milan 1972

Schiffrin, H. Z., *Sun Yat-sen and the Origins of the Chinese Revolution*, Berkeley 1970

Schram, S. R., *Mao Tse-tung: A Biography*, New York 1967

Schurmann, H. F., *Ideology and Organization in Communist China*, Berkeley 1966

Schurmann, H. F. and Schnell, O. (eds.), *The China Reader*: vol 1, *Imperial China: The Decline of the Last Dynasty and the Origins of Modern China, the 18th and 19th Centuries*; vol II, *Republican China: Nationalism, War, and the Rise of Communism 1911–1949*; vol III, *Communist China: Revolutionary Reconstruction and International Confrontation, 1949 to the Present*, New York 1967

Schwartz, B., *Chinese Communism and the Rise of Mao*, Cambridge 1951

Schwartz, B., *In Search of Wealth and Power: Yen Fu and the West*, Cambridge, Mass. 1964

Science for the People, Inc., *China: Science Walks on Two Legs*,

New York 1974

Selden, M., *The Yenan Way in Revolutionary China*, Cambridge, Mass. 1971

Shih, V.Y.C., *The Taiping Ideology: Its Sources, Interpretations and Influences*, Seattle 1967

Siren, O., *Chinese Paintings*, New York 1956–58

Snow, E., *Red Star over China*, New York 1961

Snow, E., *The Other Side of the River*, New York and London 1963

Sofri, G., *Il mondo di produzione asiatico. Storia di una controversia marxista*, Turin 1969

Sprenkel, S. Van Der, *Legal Institutions in Manchu China (A Sociological Analysis)*, London 1962

Sullivan, M., *The Birth of Landscape Painting in China*, Berkeley 1962

Sung, Lien, *Yüan Shih*, Chapters 93 and 94, translated as *Economic Structure of the Yüan Dynasty* by H. F. Schurmann (ed.), Cambridge, Mass. 1956

Sung, Ying-hsing, *T'ien-kung k'ai-wu*, translated as *Chinese Technology in the XVIIth Century* by E. T. Z. Sun and S. C. Sun, London 1966

T'an, Ch'un-lin, *Chinese Political Thought in the Twentieth Century*, New York 1971

T'an, Ch'un-lin, *The Boxer Catastrophe*, New York 1955

T'ang Leang-li, *The Inner History of the Chinese Revolution*, London 1930

Tawney, R. H., *Land and Labour in China*, London 1932

Teng, Ssu-yü and Fairbank, J. K., *China's Response to the West: A Documentary Survey 1839–1923*, Cambridge, Mass. 1954

Tsien, R. H., *Land and Labour in China*. London 1932

Tsien Tche-hao, *La republique populaire de Chine: droit constitutionnel et institutions*, Paris 1970

Vecchiotti, I., *Che cosa è la filosofia cinese*, Rome 1973

Wakeman, F., *The Fall of Imperial China*, New York 1975

Waley, A., *The Opium War through Chinese Eyes*, London 1958

Watson, W., *Archaeology in China*, London 1960

Watson, W., *China: Before the Han Dynasty*, London and New York 1961

Welch, H., *The Parting of the Way: Lao Tzu and the Taoist Movement*, Boston 1957

Welch, H., *The Practice of Chinese Buddhism, 1900–1950*, Cambridge, Mass. 1966

Whiting, A. S., *China crosses the Yalu: the decision to enter the Korean War*, New York 1960

Willetts, W., *Chinese Art*, London 1958

Wilson, R. G., *The Long March 1935: The Epic of Chinese Communism's Survival*, New York 1971

Witke, R., *Comrade Chiang Ch'ing*, Boston, Mass. 1977

Wittfogel, K. A., *Oriental Despotism. A Comparative Study of Total Power*, New Haven 1957

Wright, A. F., *Buddhism in Chinese History*, Stanford 1959

Wright, A. F. (ed.), *The Confucian Persuasian*, Stanford 1960

Zagoria, D. S., *The Sino-Soviet Conflict 1956–1961*, Princeton 1962

Zürcher, E., *The Buddhist Conquest of China: The Spread and Adaptation of Buddhism in Early Medieval China*, Leiden 1959

Reviews and Periodicals

Acta Astronomica Sinica, Peking

Archives of the Chinese Art Society of America, New York

Ars Orientalis, Washington

Asian Survey, Berkeley

Beijing Daxue Xuebao (University Journal), Peking

Beijing Review, Peking

Bulletin de l'Ecole Française d' Extrême Orient

Bulletin of Concerned Asian Scholars, Hong Kong

Bulletin of the School of Oriental and African Studies, London

China Quarterly, London

China Reconstructs, Peking

Chinese Literature, Peking

Cina, Roma

Current Scene, Hong Kong

Documentation Française, La Paris

Documentazione sui Paesi dell'Est, Milan

Eastern Horizon, Hong Kong

Far Eastern Economic Review, The Hong Kong

Harvard Journal of Asiatic Studies, Cambridge, Mass.

Journal Asiatique, Paris

Journal of Oriental Studies, Hong Kong

Kaogu (Archaeology), Peking

Li shi Yanjiu (Historical Studies), Peking

Mondo Cinese, Milan

Narody Azii i Afriki, Moscow

Problemy Vostokovedenija, Moscow

Project, Paris

Scientia Sinica, Peking

Acta Physiologica Sinica, Shanghai

T'oung Pao, Leiden

Vento dell 'Est, Milan

Zhexue Yanjui (Philosophical Studies), Peking

Zhongguo Huihua yu Shafa (Chinese painting and Calligraphy), Peking

518

PICTURE SOURCES

Yoshinori Aboshi: 194. Enzo Angelucci: 77, 90. AP Wirephoto: 407b. Benteli Verlag, Berne: 260, 261 (photo Kodansha). Biblioteca Nazionale, Rome, 472b. Bibliothèque Nationale, Paris: 251bl, 284–285, 340b, 414–415a, 426–427 (photo Thomas Childe), 438–439. Boston Museum of Fine Arts, Boston: 83b, 163 (photo Kodansha), 193 (photo Kodansha), 207, 430–431 (photo Kodansha), 436–437. British Museum, London: 162 (photo Kodansha), 164 (photo Kodansha), 204b, 212–213 (photo Kodansha), 236–237, 270 (photo Kodansha), 285 (photo Kodansha), 292–293, 434. By permission of the Syndics of Cambridge University Library, Cambridge: 447. Camera Press: 402, 405. Lorenzo Camusso: 98–99, 105, 124, 125. Chao-ying Fang Collection: 230–231. Chen Li Ren: 65ar. China News Service: 28–29, 40–41, 80–81, 85, 170, 176b, 198, 230, 268, 271, 314, 315, 388–389. China Publishing Co.: 352. Giancarlo Costa: 432, 444b, 449, 461. C.R.A.: 334, 351. Culver Pictures: 355bl, 358–359. Daily Herald: 367l, 372. Daitokuji: 256 (photo Kodansha). Eastfoto: 342–343, 384–385, 407al. Elaine Ellman Collection, New York: 421 (photo John Thomson). Essex Institute, Salem, Mass.: 419al. Freer Gallery of Art, Washington: 227, 236a, 272–273a, 304 (photo Kodansha). Fujii Yurinkan: 296–297, 316 (photo Naomi Maki). Hirotoshi Fukuda: 169ar (photo Kodansha). George Eastman House: 423b. Mauro Galligani: 25, 29, 42. Gulbenkian Museum, University of Durham, Durham: 255. Guozi Shudian, Peking: 4, 9, 12, 17, 20–21, 24, 26a, 27, 32, 34–35, 38, 39, 46–47, 65bl, 285b, 441, 455, 456, 457, 461, 485b, 486, 487, 488–489. Haksutsuru Fine Art Museum, Hyōgo Prefecture: 259bl. Harvard University (The Arnold Arboretum), Cambridge, Mass.: 425b (photo Joseph F. Rock). John Hillelson Agency: 424bl, 424br (photo John Thomson). Hillelson-Kahn Collection, London: 426a (photo Felice A. Beato). Historiographical Institute, Tokyo: 288–289 (photo Kodansha). Motoaki Horaishi: 409b (photo Kodansha). India Office Library and Records, London: 415br. Dara Janekovic: 65br. Japan Press Service: 48, 323, 476–477b. Keystone Press Agency: 367r, 380. M. Kitano: 226. Konchiin: 257 (photo Mainichi Newspapers). Kyoto National Museum, Kyoto City: 243 (photo Kodansha). Library of Congress, Washington: 240–241, 419ar (photo Underwood and Underwood), 424–425, 427. Giorgio Lotti: 28, 33, 37. Magnum: 59 (photo K. S. Karol), 365 (photo Edgar Snow, Nym Wales), 381 (photo Henri Cartier-Bresson), 392 (photo Henri Cartier-Bresson). Masaaki Matsumoto: 291. Matsuyama Art Center, Matsuyama: 145, 149l, 152a, 154, 155a, 155bl, 259r. The Metropolitan Museum of Art, New York: 158 (Munsey

Bequest/photo Kodansha), 173 (by kind permission of the Cultural Relics Bureau, Peking/photo Seth Joël), 210 (photo Kodansha), 257 (photo Kodansha). Shiro Minamimura: 65al, 176a, 177, 178, 181, 183, 199ac, 229. Minneapolis Institute of Arts, Minneapolis: 157 (photo Kodansha). Torao Miyagawa: 215. Mondadori Archives: 66, 67, 94, 95, 107, 216, 251, 333, 335, 340a, 345, 355bl, 357bl, 361, 362, 368, 368–369, 371, 372–373, 376, 377, 379, 382, 384, 386, 390–391, 401, 402, 440, 470, 482. Musée Cernuschi, Paris: 156, 192, 209 (photo Kodansha), 223 (photo Kodansha). Musée Guimet, Paris: 83a. Museum of the Imperial Palace, Peking: 82, 228–229b, 230–2331b, 251c, 272–273b, 276, 290, 294, 305, 312, 313, 318, 319 (photo Cultural Relics Publishing House, Kodansha). Museum of New Mexico, Santa Fé: 418. Museum and Art Gallery, City Hall, Hong Kong: 414–415b. Museum Rietberg, Zurich: 159. Ryoichi Nakashima: 182a, 186b, 195a, 199ar, 301. National Gallery of Art, Washington: 322 (photo Kodansha). National Palace Museum, Taibei: 97ar. New York Public Library (Stuart Collection/photo John Thomson), New York: 418–419, 420, 422al, 422ar, 422b, 424a (photo John Thomson). Nihon Keizai Shinbun Inc.: 168. Osaka Municipal Museum of Fine Arts, Osaka City: 208 (photo Heibonsha Ltd.). Östasiatiska Museet, Stockholm: 165 (photo Kodansha). Peabody Museum of Salem, Salem, Mass.: 426b (photo John Thomson). People's Art Publishers of China: 26b, 52a, 87, 89, 92, 116, 130, 131, 135, 137, 144r, 280–281, 300, 312a, 313ar (photo Kodansha). David Percival Foundation of Chinese Art, London: 258br (photo Kodansha). Princeton, Private Collection: 140–141 (photo Kodansha). Francesco Radino: 30, 31, 43, 51, 52b, 54, 70–71, 84, 86, 91, 106–107, 108, 110, 111–112, 117, 118–119, 121, 123, 398–399. Radio Times Hulton Picture Library: 336, 337, 342, 356. Ringart Collection: 363. Roger-Viollet, Paris: 329b. Royal Collection, Stockholm: 165. Royal Ontario Museum, Toronto: 284, 298–299. Kazuteru Saionji: 144l, 147b, 246, 247. Sakamoto Photographic Institute: 302. Seikado Bunko: 258–259 (photo Asahi Shinbun Publishing Company), 301 (photo Chou Da Sheng), 493 (photo Chou Da Sheng). Sekai Bunka Photo: 309. Takeshi Sekino: 147a, 151a, 152b, 169a, 169b. Senoku Hakukokan: 156 (photo Asaki Shinbun Publishing Company). Shi Jia Fu: 326–327. Masao Shimizu: 155br, 187b, 199al, 199c, 262, 263, 277br. The St. Louis Art Museum, St. Louis: 149r (photo Kodansha). Tokyo National Museum, Tokyo City: 143, 166, 264–265, 275, 295, 303 (photo Kodansha). The Toyo Bunko: 283, 329a. Paul Thomson: 340a. Time-Life Picture Agency: 367b. Topkapi Palace Museum, Istanbul: 277a (photo Kodansha). K. P. and S. B. Tritton: 452. The University Museum, Philadelphia: 231 (photo Kodansha). U.S.I.S.: 388a. Victoria and Albert Museum, London: 201 (photo Kodansha). Visnews: 355a. Wellcome Museum of Medical Science, London: 442a. Wen Wu: 150. William Hayes Fogg Art Museum, Harvard University, Cambridge, Mass.: 153 (photo Kodansha). William Rockhill Nelson Gallery of Art and Atkins Museum of Fine Art, Kansas City: 161, 224–225 (photo Kodansha). Daniel Wolf Collection, New York: 338, 416–417, 423a.

In addition we would like to thank Kodansha Ltd., Tokyo, for obtaining the following illustrations on our behalf: 28–29, 40–41, 48, 65al, 65ar, 80–81, 85, 144l, 145, 147a, 147b, 149l, 151a, 152a, 152b, 154, 155a, 155bl, 155br, 156, 159, 168, 169al, 169ar, 169b, 170, 176a, 176b, 177, 178, 181, 182a, 183, 186b, 187b, 194, 195a, 198, 199al, 199ar, 199ac, 199c, 208, 215, 226, 229, 230, 246, 267, 257, 258–259, 259r, 259bl, 262, 263, 268, 271, 277br, 283, 291, 296–297, 301, 302, 309, 314, 316, 323, 326–327, 329a, 388–389, 476–477, 493.

Illustrations have also been taken from the following publications:
Antiquities of New China, Cultural Relics Publishing House, 1963
Archaeological Academic Review, Kao Gu Publishing House
Art by Lu Xun, People's Art Publishers of China
Astronomica europaea sub imperatore tartaro-sinico Cám-Hý appellato (F. Verbiest), Bencard at Dillingen, 1687
Bronze and Jade Ware of Yin and Shou, Nihon Keizai Shinbun Inc., 1959
China Review, China Pictorials Publishing House
Chinese Folk Designs, Dover Publications, New York, 1949
Cultural Relics, Cultural Relics Publishing House
Cultural Relics excavated during the Cultural Revolution, Cultural Relics Publishing House, 1972
Cultural Relics of New China, Foreign Languages Publishing House, 1972
Cultural Relics of Xin Jiang, Cultural Relics Publishing House, 1975
Da Wen Kou, Cultural Relics Publishing House, 1962
Glorious Thirty Years, Liberation Army Pictorial Publishing House, 1957
Jiang Shan Ru Ci Duo Jiao, People's Publishing House of Shanghai, 1976
Kao Gu, Kao Gu Publishing House
Keiryo, Literature Department of Kyoto University, 1953–54
Liaozhai Zhiya (Pu Sangling), 12th century
Mao: Réalités d'une Légende, Robert Laffont S.A. et Groupe Express S.A., Paris, 1976

Mural Paintings of Han Tang, Cultural Relics Publishing House, 1974
People's Pictorial Review, People's Pictorial Publishing House
Pictorial Reference Book of Oriental History, The Toyo Bunko, 1925
Report on Excavation of Paintings and Stone Tombs of Yu Man, Cultural Relics Publishing House, 1953
San-ts'ai t'u hui, c. 1610
Science and Civilisation in China (J. Needham), vol. III, Cambridge 1959
Selected Drawings and Statues of Si Chuan, Han Period, Qun Lian Publishing House, 1955
Selected Drawings by Workmen, People's Art Publishers of Tianjin, 1975
Selected Stone-Drawings of Si Chuan and Statues of the Han Period, Cultural Relics Publishing House, 1957
Shu Ching T'u suo
Viaggio nell'interno della Cina e nella Tartaria (Lord Macartney), vol. III, Venice 1779.
Xiao Dun, History and Language Institute of the Central Academic Institute, 1959

The drawings, diagrams and maps are based on graphic material from the following works: Keith Buchanan, *The Transformation of the Chinese Earth*, London 1970 (by kind permission of Professor Keith Buchanan and Messrs. G. Bell and Sons Ltd.); William Willetts, *Chinese Art*, London 1958; Helmut Brinkler, *Bronzen aus den alten China*, Zurich 1979; Jacques Gernet, *Le Monde chinois*, Paris 1972; *Trésors de Chine et de Haute Asie*, Paris 1979; A. F. P. Hulsewé, *China im Altertum*, Propyläen-Weltgeschichte, vol. II, Frankfurt-Berlin, drawings by Uli Huber; Various authors, *Le civiltà dell 'Oriente*, 4 vols., Rome 1958–62; Henri Maspero, *Le Taoïsme et les religions chinoises*, Paris 1971; M. Pirazzoli and T'serstevens, *Chine*, Fribourg 1970; Academy of Traditional Chinese Medicine, *An Outline of Chinese Acupuncture*, Peking 1975.

The Chinese quotations which introduce the five chapters of the book are taken from the 3rd-century *Dao De Jing* and are accompanied by their English translation, *The Way and Its Power*, translated by Arther Waley, London 1934.

The Publisher wishes to thank Mr L. Carrington Goodrich and Aperture Inc., New York; Robert Laffont S.A. and Groupe Express S.A., Paris; Rand McNally and Co., Chicago (for the map of China on pages 10–11); Mr Nicholas Lee (for the photograph of Colin A. Ronan on the jacket). Thanks are also due to Francesca Ronan, Susan Blair and Marinella Chiorino for their collaboration.